Lecture Notes of the Institute for Computer Sciences, Social Informatics and Telecommunications Engineering 84

T0074259

Natarajan Meghanathan   Nabendu Chaki
Dhinaharan Nagamalai (Eds.)

Advances in Computer Science and Information Technology

Networks and Communications

Second International Conference, CCSIT 2012
Bangalore, India, January 2-4, 2012
Proceedings, Part I

 Springer

Volume Editors

Natarajan Meghanathan
Jackson State University, Jackson, MS, USA
E-mail: nmeghanathan@jsums.edu

Nabendu Chaki
University of Calcutta, Calcutta, India
E-mail: nabendu@ieee.org

Dhinaharan Nagamalai
Wireilla Net Solutions PTY Ltd., Melbourne, VIC, Australia
E-mail: dhinthia@yahoo.com

ISSN 1867-8211   e-ISSN 1867-822X
ISBN 978-3-642-27298-1   e-ISBN 978-3-642-27299-8
DOI 10.1007/978-3-642-27299-8
Springer Heidelberg Dordrecht London New York

Library of Congress Control Number: 2011943315

CR Subject Classification (1998): H.4, C.2, I.2, H.3, D.2, I.4, H.5

Typesetting: Camera-ready by author, data conversion by Scientific Publishing Services, Chennai, India

Printed on acid-free paper

Springer is part of Springer Science+Business Media (www.springer.com)

Preface

The Second International Conference on Computer Science and Information Technology (CCSIT-2012) was held in Bangalore, India, during January 2–4, 2012. CCSIT attracted many local and international delegates, presenting a balanced mixture of intellect from the East and from the West. The goal of this conference series is to bring together researchers and practitioners from academia and industry to focus on understanding computer science and information technology and to establish new collaborations in these areas. Authors are invited to contribute to the conference by submitting articles that illustrate research results, projects, survey work and industrial experiences describing significant advances in all areas of computer science and information technology.

The CCSIT-2012 Committees rigorously invited submissions for many months from researchers, scientists, engineers, students and practitioners related to the relevant themes and tracks of the conference. This effort guaranteed submissions from an unparalleled number of internationally recognized top-level researchers. All the submissions underwent a strenuous peer-review process which comprised expert reviewers. These reviewers were selected from a talented pool of Technical Committee members and external reviewers on the basis of their expertise. The papers were then reviewed based on their contributions, technical content, originality and clarity. The entire process, which includes the submission, review and acceptance processes, was done electronically. All these efforts undertaken by the Organizing and Technical Committees led to an exciting, rich and high-quality technical conference program, which featured high-impact presentations for all attendees to enjoy, appreciate and expand their expertise in the latest developments in computer network and communications research. In closing, CCSIT-2012 brought together researchers, scientists, engineers, students and practitioners to exchange and share their experiences, new ideas and research results in all aspects of the main workshop themes and tracks, and to discuss the practical challenges encountered and the solutions adopted. We would like to thank the General and Program Chairs, organization staff, the members of the Technical Program Committees and external reviewers for their excellent and tireless work. We sincerely wish that all attendees benefited scientifically from the conference and wish them every success in their research.

It is the humble wish of the conference organizers that the professional dialogue among the researchers, scientists, engineers, students and educators continues beyond the event and that the friendships and collaborations forged will linger and prosper for many years to come.

January 2012

Natarajan Meghanathan
Nabendu Chaki
Dhinaharan Nagamalai

Organization

General Chairs

David C. Wyld   Southeastern Louisiana University, USA
Natarajan Meghanathan   Jackson State University, USA

General Co-chairs

Jae Kwang Lee   Hannam University, South Korea
Michal Wozniak   Wroclaw University of Technology, Poland

Steering Committee

Abdul Kadhir Ozcan   The American University, Cyprus
Brajesh Kumar Kaushik   Indian Institute of Technology - Roorkee, India
Dhinaharan Nagamalai   Wireilla Net Solutions Pty Ltd., Australia
Eric Renault   Institut Telecom-Telecom SudParis, France
John Karamitsos   University of the Aegean, Samos, Greece
Kamalrulnizam Abu Bakar   Universiti Teknologi Malaysia, Malaysia
Khoa N. Le   University of Western Sydney, Australia
Nabendu Chaki   University of Calcutta, India

Program Committee

A.P. Sathish Kumar   PSG Institute of Advanced Studies, India
Abdul Aziz   University of Central Punjab, Pakistan
Abdul Kadir Ozcan   The American University, Cyprus
Andreas Riener Johannes   Kepler University Linz, Austria
Andy Seddon   Asia Pacific Institute of Information
     Technology, Malaysia
Armendariz-Inigo   Universidad Publica de Navarra, Spain
Atilla Elci   Eastern Mediterranean University, Cyprus
B. Srinivasan   Monash University, Australia
Balasubramanian K.   Lefke European University, Cyprus
Boo-Hyung Lee   KongJu National University, South Korea
Brajesh Kumar Kaushik   Indian Institute of Technology, India
Charalampos Z. Patrikakis   National Technical University of Athens,
     Greece
Chih-Lin Hu   National Central University, Taiwan
Chin-Chih Chang   Chung Hua University, Taiwan
Cho Han Jin   Far East University, South Korea
Cynthia Dhinakaran   Hannam University, South Korea

Danda B. Rawat	Old Dominion University, USA
Debasis Giri Haldia	Institute of Technology, India
Dhinaharan Nagamalai	Wireilla Net Solutions Pty Ltd., Australia
Dimitris Kotzinos	Technical Educational Institution of Serres, Greece
Dong Seong Kim	Duke University, USA
Emmanuel	Bouix iKlax Media, France
Eric Renault	Institut Telecom - Telecom SudParis, France
Farhat Anwar	International Islamic University, Malaysia
Firkhan Ali Bin Hamid Ali	Universiti Tun Hussein Onn Malaysia, Malaysia
Ford Lumban Gaol	University of Indonesia
H.V. Ramakrishnan	MGR University, India
Ho Dac Tu	Waseda University, Japan
Hoang, Huu Hanh	Hue University, Vietnam
Hwangjun Song	Pohang University of Science and Technology, South Korea
Jacques Demerjian	Communication & Systems, Homeland Security
Jae Kwang Lee	Hannam University, South Korea
Jan Zizka	SoNet/DI, FBE, Mendel University in Brno, Czech Republic
Jeong-Hyun Park	Electronics Telecommunication Research Institute, Korea
Jivesh Govil	Cisco Systems Inc. - CA, USA
Johann Groschdl	University of Bristol, UK
John Karamitsos	University of the Aegean, Samos, Greece
Johnson Kuruvila	Dalhousie University, Halifax, Canada
Jose Enrique Armendariz-Inigo	Universidad Publica de Navarra, Spain
Jungwook	Song Konkuk University, South Korea
K.P. Thooyamani	Bharath University, India
Kamaljit I. Lakhtaria	Atmiya Institute of Technology and Science, India
Khamish Malhotra	University of Glamorgan, UK
Khoa N. Le	University of Western Sydney, Australia
Krzysztof Walkowiak	Wroclaw University of Technology, Poland
Kshetrimayum	Indian Institute of Technology-Guwahati, India
Lopes Domingos	University of Lisbon, Portugal
Lu Yan	University of Hertfordshire, UK
Luis Veiga	Technical University of Lisbon, Portugal
Marco Roccetti	University of Bologna, Italy
Michael Peterson	University of Hawaii at Hilo, USA
Michal Wozniak	Wroclaw University of Technology, Poland
Mohsen Sharifi	Iran University of Science and Technology, Iran
Muhsin Abbas	University of Babylon, Iraq
Murugan D.	Manonmaniam Sundaranar University, India
N. Krishnan	Manonmaniam Sundaranar University, India

Nabendu Chaki	University of Calcutta, India
Natarajan Meghanathan	Jackson State University, USA
Nicolas Sklavos	Technological Educational Institute of Patras, Greece
Phan Cong Vinh	London South Bank University, UK
Ponpit Wongthongtham	Curtin University of Technology, Australia
Rajendra Akerkar	Technomathematics Research Foundation, India
Rajesh Kumar P.	The Best International, Australia
Ramayah Thurasamy	Universiti Sains Malaysia, Malaysia
Rituparna Chaki	West Bengal University of Technology, India
S. Hariharan	B.S. Abdur Rahman University, India
Sagarmay Deb	Central Queensland University, Australia
Sajid Hussain	Fisk University, USA
Salah S.	Al-Majeed University of Essex, UK
Sanguthevar Rajasekaran	University of Connecticut, USA
Sarmistha Neogyv	Jadavpur University, India
Sattar B. Sadkhan	University of Babylon, Iraq
Sergio Ilarri	University of Zaragoza, Spain
Serguei A. Mokhov	Concordia University, Canada
Shivan Haran	Arkansas State University, USA
Somitra Sanadhya	IIT-Delhi, India
Sriman Narayana Iyengar	VIT University, India
SunYoung Han	Konkuk University, South Korea
Susana Sargento	University of Aveiro, Portugal
Syed Rahman	University of Hawaii-Hilo, USA
Syed Rizvi	University of Bridgeport, USA
Velmurugan Ayyadurai	Center for Communication Systems, UK
Vishal Sharma	Metanoia Inc., USA
Wei Jie	University of Manchester, UK
Yan Luo	University of Massachusetts Lowell, USA
Yannick Le	Moullec Aalborg University, Denmark
Yao-Nan Lien	National Chengchi University, Taiwan
Yeong Deok Kim	Woosong University, South Korea
Yuh-Shyan Chen	National Taipei University, Taiwan
Yung-Fa Huang	Chaoyang University of Technology, Taiwan

External Reviewers

Amit Choudhary	Maharaja Surajmal Institute, India
Abhishek samanta	Jadavpur University, Kolkata, India
Anjan K.	MSRIT, India
Ankit	BITS, Pilani, India
Aravind P.A.	Amrita School of Engineering India
Ashutosh Dubey	NRI Institute of Science and Technology, Bhopal, India

Ashutosh Gupta   MJP Rohilkhand University, Bareilly, India
Babak Khosravifar   Concordia University, Canada
Balaji Sriramulu
Balakannan S.P.   Chonbuk National University, Jeonju, Korea
Bhupendra Suman   IIT Roorkee, India
Cauvery Giri   RVCE, India
Chandra Mohan   Bapatla Engineering College, India
Debdatta Kandar   Sikkim Manipal University, India
Doreswamyh Hosahalli   Mangalore University, India
P. Sheik Abdul Khader   B.S. Abdur Rahman University, India
Durga Toshniwal   Indian Institute of Techniology, India
Gopalakrishnan Kaliaperumal   Anna University, India
Govardhan A.   JNTUH College of Engineering, India
Hameem Shanavas   Vivekananda Institute of Technolgy, India
Hari Chavan   National Institute of Technology, Jamshedpur,
                                 India
Kaushik Chakraborty   Jadavpur University, India
Kota Sunitha   G. Narayanamma Institute of Technology and
                                 Science, Hyderabad, India
Lavanya   Blekinge Institute of Technology, Sweden
Mahalinga V. Mandi   Dr. Ambedkar Institute of Technology,
                                 Bangalore, Karnataka, India
Mohammad Mehdi Farhangia   Universiti Teknologi Malaysia (UTM),
                                 Malaysia
Murty Ch.A.S.   JNTU, Hyderabad, India
Mydhili Nair   M.S. Ramaiah Institute of Technology, India
Naga Prasad Bandaru   P.V.P. Siddartha Institute of Technology, India
Nagamanjula Prasad   Padmasri Institute of Technology, India
Nagaraj Aitha   I.T. Kamala Institute of Technology and
                                 Science, India
Nana Patil   NIT Surat, Gujrat, India
Omar Almomani   Universiti Utara Malaysia, Malaysia
Osman B. Ghazali   Universiti Utara Malaysia, Malaysia
Padmalochan Bera   Indian Institute of Technology, Kharagpur,
                                 India
Pappa Rajan   Anna University, India
Parth Lakhiya
Pradeepini Gera   Jawaharlal Nehru Technological University,
                                 India
R.M. Suresh   Mysore University, India
Rabindranath Bera   Sikkim Manipal Institute of Technology, India
Rajashree Biradar   Ballari Institute of Technology and
                                 Management, India
Rajesh Kumar Krishnan   Bannari Amman Institute of Technology, India
Ramin Karimi   University Technology Malaysia

Reena Dadhich	Govt. Engineering College Ajmer, India
Reshmi Maulik	University of Calcutta, India
Rituparna Chaki	West Bengal University of Technology, India
S. Bhaskaran	SASTRA University, India
Saleena Ameen	B.S. Abdur Rahman University, India
Salini P.	Pondichery Engineering College, India
Sami Ouali	ENSI, Manouba, Tunisia
Samodar Reddy	India School of Mines, India
Sanjay Singh	Manipal Institute of Technology, India
Sara Najafzadeh	University Technology Malaysia
Sarada Prasad Dakua	IIT-Bombay, India
S.C. Sharma	IIT - Roorkee, India
Seetha Maddala	CBIT, Hyderabad, India
Selvakumar Ramachandran	Blekinge Institute of Technology, Sweden
Shriram Vasudevan	VIT University, India
Soumyabrata Saha	Guru Tegh Bahadur Institute of Technology, India
Srinivasulu Pamidi	V.R. Siddhartha Engineering College Vijayawada, India
Subhabrata Mukherjee	Jadavpur University, India
Subir Sarkar	Jadavpur University, India
Suhaidi B. Hassan	
Sunil Singh	Bharati Vidyapeeth's College of Engineering, India
Suparna DasGupta	
Swarup Mitra	Jadavpur University, Kolkata, India
Tsung Teng Chen	National Taipei University, Taiwan
Valli Kumari Vatsavayi	AU College of Engineering, India
Yedehalli Kumara Swamy	Dayanand Sagar College of Engineering, India

Technically Sponsored by

Software Engineering & Security Community (SESC)
Networks & Communications Community (NCC)
Internet Computing Community (ICC)
Computer Science & Information Technology Community (CSITC)

Organized By

ACADEMY & INDUSTRY RESEARCH COLLABORATION CENTER (AIRCC)
www.airccse.org

Table of Contents – Part I

Networks and Communications

Wireless and Mobile Networks

Network Security

Table of Contents – Part II

Advances in Computer Science and Engineering

Table of Contents – Part III

Advances in Computer Science and Information Technology

Ad Hoc and Ubiquitous Computing

Adaptive Quorum Based MAC Protocol in Non Uniform Node Distribution of Wireless Sensor Networks

L. Sherly Puspha Annabel[1] and K. Murugan[2]

[1] St. Joseph's College of Engineering, Chennai – 600119, India
[2] Anna University Chennai – 600025, India
shirley_lawrence_2000@yahoo.com, murugan@annauniv.edu

Abstract. The lifetime of a sensor network depends mainly on the sensor node's battery power. Therefore it is necessary to use sensor node battery power very efficiently. Most of the existing powers saving protocols have been designed in such a way that the sensor nodes are put into sleep state when there is no transmission. These protocols fail to adjust dynamically a sensor node's sleep duration based on its traffic load. This periodic and regular sleep and awake method of these protocols cause high latency and high energy consumption. A host must be allowed to sleep longer if it is not involved in data transmission frequently. Thus, to efficiently manage a host's energy, we need not only have a power saving mechanism but also a scheme to guarantee data transmission. In this paper we propose an Adaptive Quorum Based MAC Protocol (AQMAC) that enables sensor nodes to sleep under light loads in non uniform node distribution thereby decreasing the latency and increasing the throughput. We also used q-Switch Routing coupled with the non uniform node distribution strategy that switches the data flow among its corresponding next-hop forwarding nodes in order to balance energy dissipation among them and to reduce the transmission latency.

Keywords: Power Saving Protocol, MAC, Non Uniform Node Distribution, Quorum, Energy Hole Problem.

1 Introduction

Wireless Sensor Network (WSNs) is widely used in a variety of applications like health care, object tracking, battlefield surveillance, environmental monitoring, industrial automation etc. Sensor nodes are often operated by batteries and have limited processing and memory resources. Thus, it is important to design energy-efficient protocols for WSNs

In wireless sensor networks, Medium Access Control plays a key role in determining utilization of channels, delays in networks and energy consumption. Sensor nodes are able to sense, collect and transmit data to other sensor nodes within their transmission range. Most of the energy in sensor nodes is wasted in idle listening as nodes wait for other node to send data and also because nodes can transmit data only to nodes that are not in sleep mode. These constraints make the node to wake up

N. Meghanathan et al. (Eds.): CCSIT 2012, Part I, LNICST 84, pp. 1–9, 2012.
© Institute for Computer Sciences, Social Informatics and Telecommunications Engineering 2012

often to check if the other node is awake and also ready for transmission. Several MAC protocols have been proposed to reduce the time a sensor node spends in idle listening by maintaining a schedule that indicates when a sensor should be awake for data transmission. However these MAC protocols suffer from long latency and fail to adapt to node's traffic load. The main aim of this paper is to efficiently put the nodes in sleep state and dynamically adjust the nodes sleep duration based on its traffic load and thus prolong the node's lifetime and increase the throughput.

The proposed protocol in this paper is a synchronous MAC protocol which is based on quorum based wake-up scheme in non uniform node distribution [5] of wireless sensor networks. The wake-up frequency of a sensor node is determined according to each node's traffic load. A node is allowed to sleep longer if less traffic is involved. Since latency is also an important issue, we have also used q-Switch Routing [5] technique with non uniform node distribution strategy. This identifies q or (q-1) relay candidates for the source node to send the data to the sink. The rest of this paper is organized as follows. Related works are presented in Section 2. Preliminaries are described in Section 3. Section 4 describes the details of the proposed protocol. Section 5 presents the simulation results.

2   Related Work

Many MAC Protocols like SMAC [9], TMAC [10] PMAC [7] and QMAC [4] were introduced to conserve energy. SMAC puts the sensor nodes to sleep periodically if the sensor nodes are not involved in data communication and hence avoids idle listening. By keeping the duty cycle low SMAC reduces sensor node's power consumption. This fixed duty cycle in SMAC may result in long transmission delay. SMAC fails to adjust the duty cycle based on the traffic load of each sensor node.

TMAC is an extension of SMAC and follows adaptive duty cycle. A sensor node will go to listen state and will not come to sleep state until there is no activity for a time T_A. By minimizing the amount of time spent in idle listening, TMAC saves considerable amount of energy which may cause early sleeping problem wherein potential receivers may go to sleep too early. This problem reduces the number of hops a data can travel in a time frame which will further cause long transmission latency.

PMAC is another MAC protocol wherein sensor nodes exchange patterns to get information about the activity in its neighbourhood. Based on these patterns, when there is no traffic in the network a sensor node can put itself into a long sleep for several time frames. If there is any activity in the neighbourhood, a node will know this through the patterns and will wake up when required.The disadvantage here is two sensor nodes will not be able to meet if they do not correctly receive the other's pattern. This results in idle listening and long transmission delay.

The QMAC protocol achieves power saving by increasing the amount of sleep intervals. For an n × n grid, each host is awake for $(2n-1)/n^2$ intervals. The quorum size that is fixed for all nodes in the same corona remains the same throughout its lifetime. Thus during extreme traffic conditions the network suffers due to latency in transmission.

3   Preliminaries

We made the following assumptions in this paper.

- All the nodes are static after deployment and have the same transmission range.
- Each sensor node has a unique ID and sends the data to the sink node placed at the center.
- All the nodes are deployed non uniformly i.e. the number of nodes around the sink is more, and more the distance from the sink, the number of nodes deployed is lesser.
- The circular area is divided into R adjacent coronas i.e. the ith corona is denoted as C_i. The width of each corona is 1 unit length.
- Sink node can communicate directly with the nodes in the corona nearer to the sink C_1.

3.1   Non Uniform Node Distribution

Nodes that are closer to the sink not only transmit data sensed by them but also transmit the data that are sent by the nodes in outer coronas [3]. Therefore the nodes in the inner corona that are nearer to the sink deplete their energy much faster than the nodes in the outer corona that are farther from the sink which will lead to energy hole problem [5]. An efficient way to overcome this problem is by adding more and more nodes to these heavy traffic areas i.e. in the inner most corona. The node density in the innermost corona C_1 will be high. Since the width of each corona is 1 unit length, data can be transmitted from the source node in the outer most corona to the next inner corona via one hop and to the sink via i hop. The nodes in the outermost corona C_R needs to forward only the data generated by them. The numbers of inner corona's nodes are increased in geometric progression with a common ratio of q [5].

4   Adaptive Quorum Based MAC Protocol (AQMAC)

In non-uniform node distribution, the sensor nodes that are closer to the sink are heavily loaded. A protocol has to be designed in such a way that they not only be capable of adjusting each sensor node's listen/sleep frequency according to their traffic loads but also guarantee sensor nodes to meet each other. QMAC allows the nodes to meet each other using quorum [8]. It makes use of fixed quorum size and fails to adjust the quorum size based on the traffic load of each sensor node which will lead to latency in transmission. In order to reduce the energy consumption further we present our Adaptive Quorum Based MAC protocol (AQMAC) that achieve power conservation and guarantee that any two hosts will wake up concurrently during the same time intervals through the use of adaptive quorum size based on its traffic load [4] and [6].

4.1   Quorum Concept

The quorum concept ensures intersecting time intervals for any two nodes [8]. If the quorum size is large for both the nodes then fewer intersecting time frames are obtained whereas for smaller quorum size more intersecting time frames are achieved. To handle heavy traffic the quorum size is reduced and during light traffic quorum size can be increased. Because grid based quorums are used, any two nodes can wake up and meet each other at some time frame. In a grid-based quorum, one row and one column are picked in an n × n grid. For an n × n, each host is awake for $(2n-1)/n^2$ intervals. Figure 1 show an example of quorum interval selections, where the first row and first column is selected by host A and the second row and second column is selected by host B [2] and [4]. Host A will wake up at time intervals 0, 1, and 2 while host B will wake up at time intervals 1, 2, and 3. Host A and B will have the intersecting time intervals 1 and 2 during which the data will be transmitted.

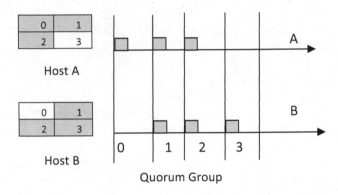

Fig. 1. Host A and Host B meet each other interval at 1 and 2 in a fixed quorum of size 2

In the QMAC protocol, all hosts in a corona share the same grid size of n × n [4]. When there is heavy traffic the quorum size is reduced so that the number of wake up time intervals will be increased and can send the data during the wake up time intervals. During light traffic quorum size can be increased so that the number of wake up time intervals can be reduced. On the other hand, the amount of conserved energy can be reduced with a small grid size [2]. In order to achieve better performance, it is necessary to dynamically adjust the grid size for each individual host since they have different traffic loads and different performance requirements.

Two hosts with different grid size will intersect with each other. For example, in Figure 2 host A has a 3 × 3 grid and its quorum intervals are 1, 4, 6, 7 and 8. Host B has a 4 × 4 grid and its quorum intervals are 2, 6, 8, 9, 10, 11 and 14. Host A wakes up more frequently than host B, but they have intersections during host B's quorum group. Host A and Host B will have the intersecting time intervals 6,8 and 10 during which the data will be transmitted. This adaptive quorum will increase the intersecting time intervals. Based on the defined traffic load limits, the quorum size will be chosen dynamically by each sensor node.

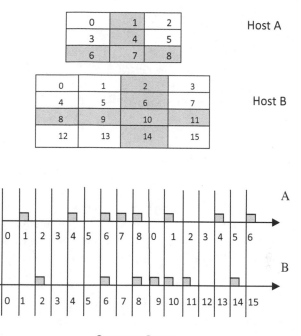

Fig. 2. Host A with grid size 3x3 and Host B with grid size 4x4 meet each other

The idea behind AQMAC is to increase a sensor node's grid size, in order to prolong its sleep duration when its traffic is light, and to decrease its grid size, making it wake up more frequently, when its traffic load is heavier [6]. In AQMAC, the grid size is selected according to its traffic load, TL_i. Four grid sizes can be selected based on the three traffic limits, limit1, limit2, and limit3. We assume the network environment to be overloaded when each host's traffic load was more than 10 kbps. Therefore we set grid size to 1×1 when its traffic load exceeds 10 kbps. Hence we assume limit1 = 10 kbps. When the traffic load decreases, a sensor node's wake up frequency should also be reduced, accordingly. The limit2 and limit3 are defined as being proportional to the wake up frequency, when compared to a 1×1 grid. In an $n \times n$ grid, we picked $2n-1$ among n^2 time intervals as the quorum intervals. That is, a sensor node with a grid size of $n \times n$ woke up at the fraction of $(2n-1)/n^2$, compared to a node with a grid size of one. When a host's packet arrival rate is reduced to $(2n-1)/n^2$, when compared to being overloaded, we should also increase its grid size to $n \times n$, this implies

limit2 = 10 $*(2n-1)/n^2$ where n = 2 then limit2 = 7.5 Kbps
limit3 = 10 $*(2n-1)/n^2$ where n = 3 then limit3 = 5.5 Kbps
limit4 = when TLi < 5.5 kbps

Therefore the following four grid sizes are selected based on the conditions

1×1 grid size is selected if ($TL_i \geq 10$Kbps)
2×2 grid size is selected if (10 Kbps > TL_i ≥ 7.5 Kbps)
3×3 grid size is selected if (7.5 Kbps > TL_i ≥ 5.5 Kbps)
4×4 grid size is selected if (5.5 Kbps > TL_i)

4.2   Latency Reduction Using q-Switch Routing

In order to reduce the latency further in AQMAC we used q-Switch routing [5] in AQMAC which will be termed as AQMAC-LR (Latency Reduction). The sensor nodes will be deployed from the outer most corona to the inner most corona in such a way that the number of nodes in the coronas increases with the geometric progression with a common ratio of q. Each sensor node in corona C_R can communicate directly with (q-1) different nodes in C_{R-1}. Each sensor nodes in C_{i+1} can communicate directly with q different nodes in C_i, where $1 \leq i \leq R-2$. Therefore either (q-1) or q nodes will be deployed in the reachable area in the next inner corona for each node in C_i. The process can be repeated until deployment in C_1 is finished. In network initialization phase the sensor nodes find their relay nodes and record their ID numbers. When the initialization phase gets finished there are N_R q-ary trees formed. Among all the relay nodes, the node with highest energy will be considered as relay node. The node in outer corona treated as source node. It chooses a relay node among its q or q-1 relay nodes, and forwards data of its own to the selected relay node or child node. The selected relay node sends its own data and those from the upstream node or so-called parent node. This process will be repeated until the data arrive at a node in corona C_1 from where the data will be delivered to the sink.

5   Simulation Results

We implemented the proposed protocol using NS2 simulator [1]. We also implemented PMAC, QMAC, and QMAC-LR (Latency Reduction) which uses

Table 1. Simulation Parameters

Parameter	Value
Number of nodes	28
Common ratio of geometric progression	3
Number of nodes in outer most corona	1
Total number of corona	4
Transmission range of a sensor node	25m
Width of each corona	25m
Transmit energy of each node	60mW
Receive energy of each node	45mW
Idle energy of each node	45mW
Sleep energy of each node	0W

q-Switch Routing on QMAC for comparison purposes. 2 nodes are deployed in C_2 and 6 nodes are deployed in C_3 and 18 nodes are deployed in C_4 based on the geometric progression whose value is 3. Each node has an initial energy of 50J. Packet size was set to 128 bytes and hosts were supplied with different constant bit rate traffic, between 1 and 24 packets per second to simulate light loads and heavy loads. Below we have made observations from three different aspects.

5.1   Impact of Alive Nodes

Figure 3 explains the fraction of live sensor nodes of different MAC protocols. The outer corona has large amount of live sensor nodes in C_4 since the node in outer corona have light traffic load whereas the number of live nodes in corona C_1, C_2 and C_3 are quite low since the nodes in inner coronas have heavy traffic. Since more number of nodes are deployed in the corona C_1 near the sink the proposed protocol AQMAC and AQMAC-LR retains maximum remaining energy compared to that of PMAC, QMAC, and QMAC-LR.

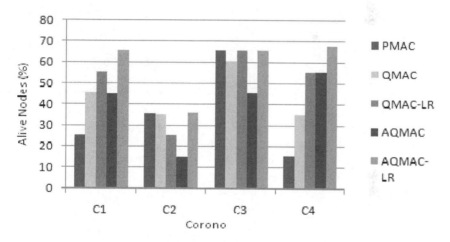

Fig. 3. Fraction of live sensor nodes of different MAC Protocols

5.2   Impact of Successful Transmission Ratio

The successful transmission ratio represents the ratio of the number of the number of data packets sent by the source node to the number of packets received by the sink node. Here the successful transmission ratio of protocols like PMAC and QMAC is low since more energy is depleted than AQMAC and AQMAC-LR protocols. QMAC's lowest transmission ratio implies most of the nodes in C_1 have exhausted their energy and thus packets are not allowed deliver the data to the sink successfully. Figure 4 explains the differences among PMAC, QMAC, QMAC-LR, AQMAC and AQMAC-LR. Compared to PMAC and QMAC we observe that the AQMAC-LR shows high successful transmission ratio.

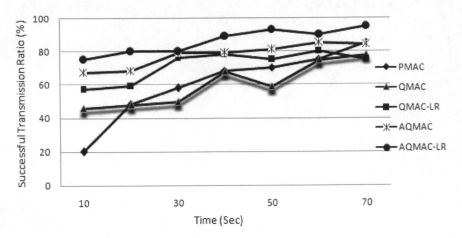

Fig. 4. Successful Transmission Ratio of different MAC Protocols

5.3   Impact of Latency

Latency represents the delay between the moment a data packet is sent by the data source and the moment the sink receives the data packet. Figure 5 explains that AQMAC has lower latency compared to PMAC. Initially PMAC has lower latency because nodes in PMAC remain awake at every time frame. QMAC-LR is the latency reduction that is done on QMAC using q-Switch Routing. With multiple next-hop candidates capable of achieving the relay job, sensor nodes running AQMAC-LR have lot of chances to meet one of their next-hop group members and transmit their data whenever they want. Thus they have a lower delay when compared with nodes running AQMAC. As time increases, all the protocols produce a longer delay because of the pending packets that has to be delivered.

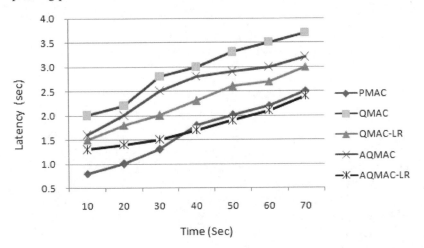

Fig. 5. Latency of different MAC Protocols

6   Conclusion

Energy conservation is essential in wireless sensor networks. Deployment of more number of nodes near the sink reduces considerable amount of energy conservation. Based on their distance from the sink the sensor nodes have different loads. Hence we applied the concept called quorum to make the sensor nodes to adjust their sleep and awake time dynamically based on their traffic loads. In this paper we have proposed a new energy-conserving MAC protocol that applies the concept of adaptive quorum to enable the sensor nodes to adjust their sleep durations based on their traffic load in non uniform node distribution of sensor networks. To reduce the transmission delay we have also used q-switch routing by enabling a group of next-hop nodes to accomplish the relaying job. Simulations proved that our AQMAC and AQMAC-LR is an improved MAC protocol in terms of energy efficiency and throughput for non uniform node distribution in sensor networks. In these protocols it is very hard to determine fixed traffic limits to change the quorum sizes. In future, issues such as each node's pending packets, transmission delay should also be taken into consideration for finding the quorum sizes.

References

1. The Network Simulator - ns-2 (2005), http://www.isi.edu/nsnam/ns/
2. Lai, S., Ravindran, B., Cho, H.: Heterogenous Quorum-Based Wake-up Scheduling in Wireless Sensor Networks. IEEE Transactions on Computers 59, 1562–1573 (2011)
3. Wu, Y., Li, X.-Y., Liu, Y.: Energy-Efficient Wake-Up Scheduling for Data Collection and Aggregation. IEEE Transactions on Parallel and Distributed Systems 21, 275–287 (2010)
4. Chao, C.M., Lee, Y.W.: Quorum-Based Energy-Saving MAC Protocol Design for Wireless Sensor Networks. IEEE Trans. on Vehicular Technology 59(2), 813–822 (2010)
5. Wu, X., Chen, G., Das, S.K.: Avoiding energy holes in wireless sensor networks with non uniform node distribution. IEEE Trans. on Parallel Distrib. Syst. 19(5), 710–720 (2008)
6. Chao, C.M., Sheu, J.P., Chou, I.C.: An adaptive quorum-based energy conserving protocol for IEEE 802.11 ad hoc networks. IEEE Trans. on Mobile Computing 5(5), 560–570 (2006)
7. Zheng, T., Radhakrishnan, S., Sarangan, V.: PMAC: An adaptive energy-efficient MAC protocol for wireless sensor networks. In: Proc. IEEE Int. Parallel Distrib. Process. Symp., Denver, CO, pp. 65–72 (2005)
8. Harada, T., Yamashita, M.: Traversal Merge Operation: A Nondominated coterie Construction Method for Distributed Mutual Exclusion. IEEE Transactions on Parallel and Distributed Systems 16, 183–192 (2005)
9. Heidemann, W., Ye, J., Estrin, D.: Medium access control with coordinated adaptive sleep for wireless sensor networks. IEEE/ACM Trans. on Networking 12(3), 493–506 (2004)
10. Dam, T.V., Langendoen, K.: An adaptive energy-efficient MAC protocol for wireless sensor networks. In: Proc. ACM SenSys, Los Angeles, CA, pp. 171–180 (November 2003)

Mobile Agent in InVANET – Traffic Management

V. Arun[1] and K.L. Shunmuganathan[2]

[1] Sathyabama University, Chennai, India
[2] Department of CSE, RMK College of Engineering, Chennai, India
arunvragavan@gmail.com, kls_nathan@yahoo.com

Abstract. Intelligent vehicular ad hoc networks (InVANETs) provide an effective communication between vehicles with dynamic mobility. This paper enhances the traffic management system using mobile agents called as Intellect Mobile Agent (IMA). IMA is used to identify the traffic in the path from source to destination and provides an effective way to transport through less traffic scenario. IMA designed with an algorithm which calculates the amount of traffic as a parameter and finds a least path to reach the destination. The vehicle sends the IMA with the destination node which traces the traffic path. IMA identifies the path with least traffic using probability calculation and directs the vehicle to reach the destination.

Keywords: Traffic management, mobile agent in InVANETs, Intellect Mobile Agent.

1   Introduction

Traffic on roads is concentrated in signal area due to heavy flow of vehicles. The traffic can be reduced by directing the vehicles to the destination through least traffic area. InVANETs technology provides an efficient way to implement Intellect Mobile Agent (IMA). IMA is an mobile agent which helps vehicle to get traffic less short path. Roadside Equipment (RE) is placed in the signal which calculates the number of vehicles and communicates with IMA. RE senses the number of nodes in the signal area and intimate to the IMA.

1.1   Notations Used

IMA- Intellect Mobile Agent
RE- Road side Equipment
TF – Traffic Flag
ILRE- Identify Linking RE Mobile Agent

2   Category

A group of area is grouped as category which holds the group of RE. Normally, category represents a city with few RE. The RE holds the data about neighbor RE and shortest route to reach any RE in the category.

N. Meghanathan et al. (Eds.): CCSIT 2012, Part I, LNICST 84, pp. 10–20, 2012.
© Institute for Computer Sciences, Social Informatics and Telecommunications Engineering 2012

3   Road Side Equipment

RE informs the road side warnings to the vehicles in the road. It should be implemented in the signal area where vehicles gather for the pass. RE should be designed
with a database that holds the shortest route for various area RE within the category.
Category refers to a collection of RE in a place. When the IMA reaches the RE, it will
get updated. RE should capable of holding the shortest path to various areas, checks
for traffic in the scanning area, raising the flag TF when there is traffic and updates
the IMA.

In figure 1, the inner circle represents RE and the outer circle represents the area of
calculating the traffic area. RE scans the number of vehicles in the region of traffic.
Vehicles are represented as nodes in the network.

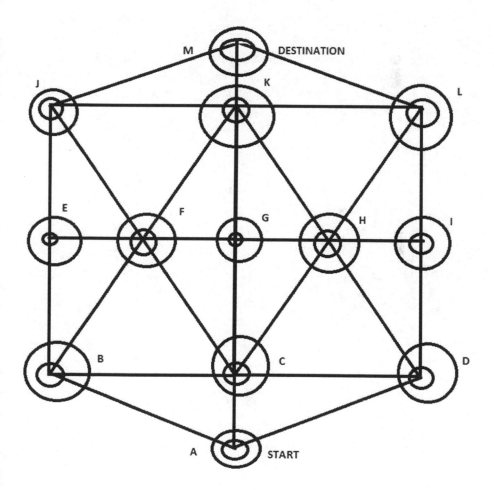

Fig. 1. Category for IMA

3.1   Algorithm

```
Begin
Variable TF = false
Variable Crictical_pt
If Number of nodes>0
Crictical_pt =  Area of coverage / (Average vehicle area*
Number of nodes)
Else
Crictical_pt= Area of coverage
If critical_pt < threshold_value
TF=true
End
```

RE raises the TF by calculating the above algorithm. The critical_pt is a value that represents the concentration of traffic in the area. It depends on the area covered by the RE, the average space occupied by the vehicle depending upon the type and number of nodes (vehicles).

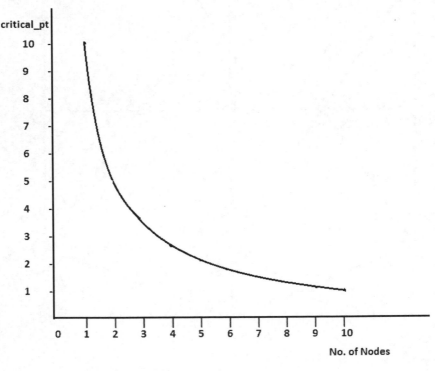

Fig. 2. Graph between critical poin and no. of nodes

Figure 1 describes a category with various RE. If the unit value is considered for average vehicle area and 10 m^3 as area of coverage, the graph between critical_pt and number of vehicles will be as follows.

The figure 2 shows the relation between the critical_pt values that decides to raise the TF.

RE calls the algorithm when an IMA strikes it and remains the state of TF for next collision. The database of RE should contain the shortest path to reach destination and the RE connected to it with distance.

4   Intellect Mobile Agent

IMA is a mobile agent that is generated in the starting point from the RE. IMA initially reads the shortest route to reach destination from the RE in Starting point [1]. IMA migrates to the next RE listed in the shortest path. When it reaches the next RE, it checks for the TF. If the flag is not raised, the process is continued[4]. Else the IMA clone itself and migrate to the neighbor RE. The process is continued and if IMA reaches the destination, it returns back to the starting RE. IMA holds the data about destination path with short distance and traffic free. RE instructs to the vehicle about the path and directs it to reach the destination. IMA is designed effectively using Agent Communication Language (ACL) which is a descriptive KQML-like language for agent communication[2].

4.1   Algorithm

```
Begin
Var
Drop=false
        Clone=false
        Clone_value=0
        Short_path= shortest path from start to destination
        Neighbor_re = next  RE in short_path
        Distance=0
        Previous_re= Current RE
        Sh_distance= distance to reach destination (short-
        path)
repeat
Previous_re= Current RE
Move to Neighbor_re
Distance= distance of neighbor RE
```

```
if RE == destination
return to Starting RE
if TF = true
if cloned==true
Drop the IMA
break
return to Previous_re
Clone IMA
Clone Value= number of neighbor RE -1
Neighbor_re = one of neighbor not cloned for
Else
Neighbor_re= next RE in shortest path
If Distance > 2* sh_distance
Informs to user
Until RE==destination
End
```

4.2   Illustration

Consider a scenario in which a vehicle prepare to start from A to reach M. Vehicle communicate to the RE in the A. RE holds the shortest path to reach the destination M. Since the RE is not a dynamic node, the shortest path will not be alerted regularly. So, it holds the shortest path for various destinations in a category.

Let the database of RE in A holds data as follows:

Table 1. Neighbor node

Neighbor Node
B
C
D

Table 2. Database of RE to serve IMA

Destination	Shortest path	Distance (m)
B	B	1500
C	C	150
D	D	1640
E	B-E	2200
F	C-G-F	1100
G	C-G	900
H	C-G-H	1200
I	D-I	2100
J	B-E-J	2700
K	C-G-K	1900
L	D-I-J	2780
M	C-G-K-M	3120

The Re in the A starts sending the IMA with following initializations for the algorithm.

> Drop=false
> Clone=false
> Clone_value=0
> Short_path= C-G-K-M
> Neighbor_re = C
> Distance=0
> Sh_distance= 3120

Let the TF is raised in B,I,F,K which is indicated by a cross in the diagram.

In figure 3 arrow represents the flow of IMA through RE. Stroked arrow shows that the IMA is dropped due to the raise of TF.

A vehicle start at a point A and it communicate with the RE which creates the IMA with initializations to reach destination M . The IMA moves to the next RE as in the Neighbor_re value such as to C. IMA checks for the TF, since TF is not raised because of no traffic at C. So IMA updates the distance parameter and migrates to the next RE at G. Same process is done at G. It migrates to K which is TF raised RE. When IMA identifies that TF flag is raised, it returns to the previous_re value to G. Here IMA is cloned for number of neighbor RE -1 and migrates to all RE nodes. The original node is send to K to make a check for TF flag. If the TF flag is raised, then the IMA is return back. Since it is already cloned, it is dropped. The IMA which migrates to the node H may update the distance parameter. Likewise the IMA reaches the destination node M with calculated path and distance. If the path is higher than twice of the shortest path, it informs the user about it. User wishes to drop IMA.

Consider if the node F and J is not raised with TF flag. The IMA cloned at G also migrate through F-J and reach the destination M. But the updated distance may be higher than the IMA through H-L-M. Both IMA reaches the user and user decides the path.

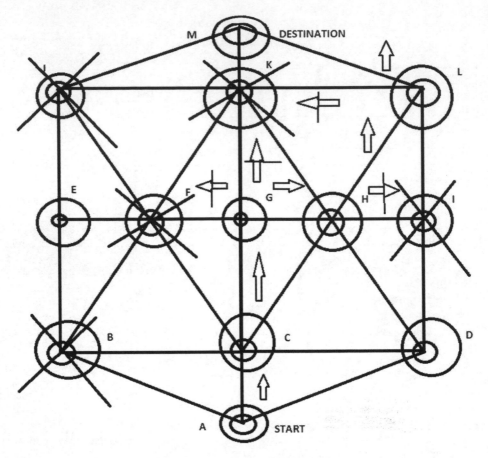

Fig. 3. Category with TF raised RE

The process of identifying the path is updated whenever the vehicle reaches the RE and the RE is initialized as starting RE. This is because of constant change in the traffic flow[3].

4.3   Linker RE

When a user need to travel to a long distance beyond a category, linking RE plays vital role to connect various categories. The RE which connects the two categories is known as linking RE. The database of Linking RE holds the category that connects and shortest path that connects other categories. When a user requests the shortest traffic path to reach the destination which is in another category, there is a need of one mechanism to identify the linking RE to reach the destination. A mobile agent is required for this task and is called as Identify Linking RE Mobile Agent (ILRE). ILRE calculates the linking RE which has the least short path to reach destination and returns the sub destination in each category [5].

The database of each RE contains the location RE and the category region that covers it. The user should choose the region manually when the destination is not in the category.

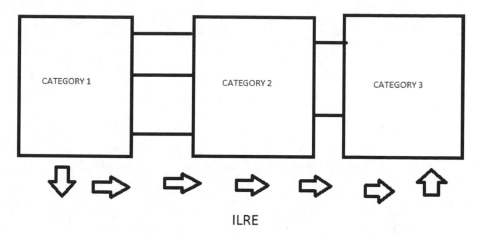

Fig. 4. Flow of ILRE through categories

The figure 4 describes the ILRE through the categories and arrow indicates the flow.

4.4   Role of ILRE

- Identifies the shortest path.
- Detects the Linking RE between categories which links the required category.
- Direct the IMA to reach the linked RE as the destination.
- When it reaches the Linking RE, destination of the IMA changes to the next Linking RE or destination RE (if it reaches the same category).

Algorithm

```
Begin

Var

Dest= destination RE

Clone_value= no. of linking RE in category

Status = false

Dest_Cat= The category that has destination RE

Clone LRE to clone_value

Get shortest path to Linking RE
```

```
Move to Linking RE
Read status
If status=true
Inform user
Else
Drop
Clone IMA
Repeat
IMA destination=Linking RE
Move along IMA
Store IMA path
Alter IMA destination
If category= dest_cat
IMA destination=destination RE
Else
IMA destination= linking RE
Until category =dest_cat
Inform path to User
End
```

Illustration

The ILRE clone itself to the number of linking RE in a category. Each ILRE reaches the Linking RE and checks for the way to reach the destination RE. If the Linking RE pays way to reach the category to reach destination, it access the shortest path to reach and reports to the user else the ILRE is dropped [6].

The returned ILRE creates an IMA to reach the linking RE by assigning the destination of the IMA as linking RE. Using IMA algorithm, the shortest path to reach the Linking RE is achieved. ILRE now alters the destination of the IMA and stores the shortest path identified by the IMA. The process continues until the destination is reached. When the Mobile Agents are in destination category, ILRE sets the destination RE as the destination of the IMA. The entire path stored is informed to the user and when each RE is reached, IMA updates the path since traffic is dynamically altered. Figure 5 explains the detail migration path of Mobile Agents.

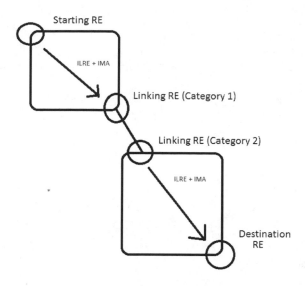

Fig. 5. Migration of ILRE + IMA

5   Conclusion and Future Work

- Flows of vehicles are reduced and direct them in such a way to reduce the traffic [7].
- The user may reach the destination in short time.
- Extends the use by uniting the small cities as category.
- Computational load.

The category plays a vital role to unite various cities together and provide many ways for the mobile agent to travel around. Computational load is more to calculate mobile agent to define next category. Future work involves in minimizing the computational load and enhances the interaction with the user. To enhance the implementation that should have interaction with user in a way to suggest the path with accident parameters to determine the path to destination.

References

[1] Tonguz, O., Wisitpongphan, N., Bai, F., Mudalige, P., Sadekar, V.: Broadcasting in VANET. In: Mobile Networking for Vehicular Environments (2007)
[2] Lange, D.B., Aridor, Y.: Agent Design Patterns Elements of Agent Application Design. In: Proceedings of Autonomous Agents. ACM Press (1998)
[3] Rogers, A., Jennings, N.R., Corkill, D.D.: Agent Technologies for Sensor Networks (2009)

[4] Osborne, M.A., et al.: Towards Real-Time Information Processing of Sensor Network Data Using Computationally Efficient Multi-Output Gaussian Processes. IEEE Press (2008)

[5] Rehák, M., Pechoucek, M., Grill, M., Stiborek, J.: Adaptive Multiagent Sys-tem for Network Traffic Monitoring (2009)

[6] Movaghar, S.R.: Universal vehicular ad-hoc network design: The case for dynamic addressing and relative positioning system

[7] Prakash, A., Tripathi, R.: Vehicular ad hoc networks toward Intelligent Transport Systems

The Design of Observers for Nonlinear Control Systems around Equilibria

Sundarapandian Vaidyanathan

R & D Centre, Vel Tech Dr. RR & Dr. SR Technical University
Avadi-Alamathi Road, Avadi, Chennai-600 062, India
sundarvtu@gmail.com
http://www.vel-tech.org/

Abstract. This paper investigates the local observer design for nonlinear control systems with real parametric uncertainty around equilibria. In this paper, new results are derived for a general class of nonlinear systems with real parametric uncertainty. In this paper, it is first shown that equilibrium-state detectability is a necessary condition for the existence of local asymptotic observers for any nonlinear system and using this result, it is shown that for the classical case, when the state equilibrium does not change with the real parametric uncertainty, and when the plant output is purely a function of the state, there is no local asymptotic observer for the plant. Next, it is shown that in sharp contrast to this case, for the general case of problems where we allow the state equilibrium to change with the real parametric uncertainty, there generically exist local exponential observers even when the plant output is purely a function of the state. In this paper, a characterization and construction procedure for local exponential observers for a general class of nonlinear systems with real parametric uncertainty has also been derived under some stability assumptions. It is also shown that for the general class of nonlinear systems considered, the existence of local exponential observers in the presence of inputs implies, and is implied by the existence of local exponential observers in the absence of inputs.

Keywords: Nonlinear observers, exponential observers, real parametric uncertainty, nonlinear control systems.

1 Introduction

The design of observers is an important problem in the control literature because state estimators are needed for system monitoring and for the implementation of state feedback control laws designed for control systems.

For linear control systems, the observer design problem was introduced and fully solved by Luenberger [1]. For nonlinear control systems, the observer design problem was introduced by Thau [2]. During the past three decades, a large research effort has been devoted to the construction of observers for nonlinear control systems ([2]-[16]).

This paper investigates the nonlinear observer design problem for a general class of nonlinear systems with real parametric uncertainty. In this paper, we consider a general class of nonlinear systems described by

N. Meghanathan et al. (Eds.): CCSIT 2012, Part I, LNICST 84, pp. 21–30, 2012.

$$\dot{x} = f(x, \lambda) + g(x, \lambda)u$$
$$y = h(x, \lambda) \tag{1}$$

where $x \in \mathbb{R}^n$ is the state, $\lambda \in \mathbb{R}^l$ is the real parametric uncertainty, $u \in \mathbb{R}^m$ the input and $y \in \mathbb{R}^p$ the output. We assume that the state x is defined in an open neighbourhood of an isolated state equilibrium $\bar{x}$ in $\mathbb{R}^n$ and the input u belongs to a class $\mathcal{U}$ of admissible input functions.

In Sections 2 and 3, we assume that $\mathcal{U}$ consists of all locally $\mathcal{C}^1$ functions u with $u(0) = 0$.

In Section 4, we assume that $\mathcal{U}$ consists of all inputs of the form

$$u = r(\omega) \tag{2}$$

where ω is the state of a *neutrally stable* exosystem given by

$$\dot{\omega} = s(\omega) \tag{3}$$

We also assume that the parametric uncertainty λ takes values in an open neighbourhood G of the origin of $\mathbb{R}^l$. We set $Y = h(X, G)$. We also assume that

$$f(\bar{x}, 0) = 0, \ g(\bar{x}, 0) = 0 \ \text{and} \ h(\bar{x}, 0) = 0$$

In this paper, it is first shown that *equilibrium-state detectability* is a necessary condition for the existence of local asymptotic observers for the nonlinear system (1). Using this condition, we establish that for the classical case of problems when the state equilibrium does not change with the real parametric uncertainty, there does not exist any local asymptotic observer for the nonlinear plant. Next, we show that in sharp contrast to this case, for the general case of problems where we allow the state equilibrium to change with the real parametric uncertainty, there typically exist local exponential observers even when the plant output is purely a function of the state.

In this paper, we also derive necessary and sufficient conditions for local exponential observers and using this, we deduce a simple construction procedure for the design of exponential observers for the nonlinear plants with exogenous inputs. In this context, we also derive a new result which states that under some stability assumptions on the plant, the existence of local exponential observers for the nonlinear plant (1) in the presence of inputs implies and is implied by the existence of local exponential observers for the plant (1) in the absence of inputs. Thus, this new result simplifies the nonlinear observer design problem significantly.

2   Basic Definitions

In this paper, we study the nonlinear observer design problem for the nonlinear plant (1). Since λ is a real parametric uncertainty, it may not be available for measurement. Thus, we may consider λ as an additional state variable and estimate λ as well.

Thus, we consider the plant (1) in an extended form as

$$\dot{x} = f(x, \lambda) + g(x, \lambda)u$$
$$\dot{\lambda} = 0$$
$$y = h(x, \lambda) \tag{4}$$

In this paper, we derive new results for local asymptotic observers and exponential observers for the nonlinear plant (4) with real parametric uncertainty around the equilibria $(x, \lambda) = (\bar{x}, 0) \in \mathbb{R}^n \times \mathbb{R}^l$.

Definition 1. *[16] Consider the nonlinear system* (candidate observer) *defined by*

$$\begin{aligned}
\dot{z} &= \phi(z, \mu, y, u) \\
\dot{\mu} &= \psi(z, \mu, y, u)
\end{aligned} \tag{5}$$

where the state z of the candidate observer (5) is defined locally (say, in the neighbourhood X of $\bar{x}$ of $\mathbb{R}^n$) and the state μ of the candidate observer (5) is defined locally (say, in the neighbourhood G of the origin of $\mathbb{R}^l$). We assume that ϕ and ψ are locally $\mathcal{C}^1$ mappings such that

$$\phi(\bar{x}, 0, 0, 0) = 0 \quad and \quad \psi(\bar{x}, 0, 0, 0) = 0$$

We say that the candidate observer (5) is a **local asymptotic** *(resp.* **local exponential***) observer for the plant (4) if the following conditions are satisfied:*

(O1) If $(x(0), \lambda(0)) = (z(0), \mu(0))$, then $(x(t), \lambda(t)) = (z(t), \mu(t))$ for all $t \geq 0$ and for all $u \in \mathcal{U}$.

(O2) There exists a neighbourhood V of the origin of $\mathbb{R}^n \times \mathbb{R}^l$ such that for all values of $(z(0), \mu(0)) - (x(0), \lambda(0))$ in V, the measurement error $(z(t) - x(t), \mu(t) - \lambda(t))$ decays to zero asymptotically (resp. exponentially) as $t \to \infty$. □

We define the estimation error by

$$e \triangleq \begin{bmatrix} e_1 \\ e_2 \end{bmatrix} = \begin{bmatrix} z \\ \mu \end{bmatrix} - \begin{bmatrix} x \\ \lambda \end{bmatrix} \tag{6}$$

Then the error satisfies the differential equation

$$\begin{aligned}
\dot{e}_1 &= \phi(x + e_1, \lambda + e_2, y, u) - f(x, \lambda) - g(x, \lambda)u \\
\dot{e}_2 &= \psi(x + e_1, \lambda + e_2, y, u)
\end{aligned}$$

We consider the composite system

$$\begin{aligned}
\dot{x} &= f(x, \lambda) + g(x, \lambda)u \\
\dot{\lambda} &= 0 \\
\dot{e}_1 &= \phi(x + e_1, \lambda + e_2, y, u) - f(x, \lambda) - g(x, \lambda)u \\
\dot{e}_2 &= \psi(x + e_1, \lambda + e_2, y, u)
\end{aligned} \tag{7}$$

Next, we state a simple lemma which provides a geometric characterization of the condition (O1) in Definition 1.

Lemma 1. *([16]) The following statements are equivalent.*

(a) The condition (O1) in Definition 1 holds for the composite system (4)-(5).

(b) For all $x \in X, \lambda \in G$ and for all $u \in \mathcal{U}$, we have

$$\phi(x, h(x, \lambda), u) = f(x, \lambda) + g(x, \lambda)u \ \text{ and } \ \phi(x, h(x, \lambda), u) = 0$$

(c) The submanifold defined via $e = 0$ is invariant under the flow of the composite system (7).   □

Lemma 2. ([16]) Consider the plant (4) and the candidate observer (5). Then the condition (O1) of Definition 1 holds if and only if ϕ and ψ have the following form:

$$\phi(z, \mu, y, u) = f(z, \mu) + g(z, \mu)u + \alpha(z, \mu, y, u)$$
$$\psi(z, \mu, y, u) = \beta(z, \mu, y, u)$$

where α and β are locally $\mathcal{C}^1$ mappings with

$$\alpha(\bar{x}, 0, 0, 0) = 0 \ \text{ and } \ \beta(\bar{x}, 0, 0, 0) = 0$$

and also such that

$$\alpha(x, \lambda, h(x, \lambda), u) = 0 \ \text{ and } \ \beta(x, \lambda, h(x, \lambda), u) = 0 \qquad □$$

3 A Necessary Condition for Local Asymptotic Observers for Nonlinear Systems

In this section, we shall show that if the plant (4) has a local exponential observer of the form (5), then the plant (4) must be *equilibrium detectable, i.e.* if $(x(t), \lambda(t))$ is the solution of the system (4) with small initial condition $(x(0), \lambda(0)) = (x_0, \lambda_0)$ near the equilibrium $(\bar{x}, 0)$ satisfying $y(t) = h(x(t), \lambda(t) \equiv 0$, then $(x(t), \lambda(t))$ must converge to $(\bar{x}, 0)$ asymptotically as $t \to \infty$.

Since $\lambda(t) \equiv \lambda_0$, the equilibrium-state detectability requirement is equivalent to requiring that the solution $(x(t), \lambda(t))$ yielding zero-output for the plant (4) must be such that $x(t) \to \bar{x}$ asymptotically as $t \to \infty$ and $\lambda_0 = 0$.

Theorem 1. *A necessary condition for the existence of a local exponential observer for the plant (4) is that the plant (4) is equilibrium-state detectable, i.e. any solution trajectory $(x(t), \lambda(t))$ of (4) with small initial condition (x_0, λ_0) near the equilibrium $(\bar{x}, 0)$ satisfying*

$$y(t) = h(x(t), \lambda(t)) \equiv 0$$

must be such that $x(t) \to \bar{x}$ asymptotically as $t \to \infty$ and $\lambda_0 = 0$.

Proof. This is a simple consequence of Lemma 2 for local asymptotic observers.

In classical bifurcation theory, a standard assumption is that there is a trivial solution from which the bifurcation is to occur ([17], p149). Thus, in the classical bifurcation case, the control plant (4) is often assumed to satisfy

$$f(\bar{x}, \lambda) = 0 \ \text{ and } \ g(\bar{x}, \lambda) = 0 \tag{8}$$

Next, as a consequence of Theorem 1, we establish the following result.

Theorem 2. *Suppose that the plant (4) satisfies the assumption (8) so that $x = \bar{x}$ is an equilibrium for all values of the parameter λ and also that the output function y is purely a function of x, i.e. it has the form $y = \gamma(x)$. Then there is no local asymptotic observer for the plant (4).*

Proof. We show that the plant (4) is not equilibrium-state detectable. Suppose that we take $x(0) = \bar{x}$ and $\lambda(0) = \lambda_0$, where $\lambda_0 \neq 0$ is any small initial condition. Then we have $x(t) \equiv \bar{x}$ for all t and it follows that

$$y(t) = h(x(t), \lambda(t)) = \gamma(x(t)) = \gamma(\bar{x}) = 0$$

However, $\lambda(t) = \lambda_0 \neq 0$. This shows that the plant (4) is not equilibrium-state detectable. From the necessary condition given in Theorem 1, it is then immediate that there is no local asymptotic observer for the plant (4). □

4   Observer Design for Nonlinear Systems around Equilibria

In this section, we suppose that the class $\mathcal{U}$ consists of inputs u of the form

$$u = r(\omega), \tag{9}$$

where ω satisfies the autonomous system (*exosystem*)

$$\dot{\omega} = s(\omega) \quad \text{with} \quad s(0) = 0 \tag{10}$$

The state ω of the exosystem (10) lies in an open neighbourhood W of the origin of $\mathbb{R}^q$. One can view the equations (9) and (10) as an *input generator*. We assume that the exosystem dynamics (10) is *neutrally stable* at $\omega = 0$. Basically, this requirement means that the exosystem (10) is Lyapunov stable in both forward and backward time at $\omega = 0$.

In this section, we first derive a basic theorem that completely characterizes the existence of local exponential observers of the form (5) for nonlinear plants of the form (4). We note that this result holds for both classical and general cases of systems with real parametric uncertainty.

Using (9) and (10), the plant (4) can be expressed as

$$\begin{aligned}
\dot{x} &= f(x, \lambda) + g(x, \lambda)r(\omega) \\
\dot{\lambda} &= 0 \\
\dot{\omega} &= s(\omega) \\
y &= h(x, \lambda)
\end{aligned} \tag{11}$$

Also, the composite system (7) can be written as

$$\begin{aligned}
\dot{x} &= f(x, \lambda) + g(x, \lambda)r(\omega) \\
\dot{\lambda} &= 0 \\
\dot{\omega} &= s(\omega) \\
\dot{e}_1 &= \phi(x + e_1, \lambda + e_2, h(x, \lambda), r(\omega)) - f(x, \lambda) - g(x, \lambda)r(\omega) \\
\dot{e}_2 &= \psi(x + e_1, \lambda + e_2, h(x, \lambda), r(\omega))
\end{aligned} \tag{12}$$

Theorem 3. *Suppose that the plant dynamics in (11) is Lyapunov stable at the equilibrium* $(x, \lambda, \omega) = (\bar{x}, 0, 0)$. *Then the candidate observer (5) is a local exponential observer for the plant (11) if and only if*

(a) *The submanifold defined via* $e = 0$ *is invariant under the flow of the composite system (12).*

(b) *The dynamics*

$$\dot{e}_1 = \phi(e_1, e_2, 0, 0)$$
$$\dot{e}_2 = \psi(e_1, e_2, 0, 0) \tag{13}$$

is locally exponentially stable at $e = 0$.

Proof. The necessity follows immediately from the Definition 1 for local exponential observers and Lemma 1. The sufficiency can be established using Lyapunov stability theory as in [16]. ☐

As an application of Theorem 3, we establish the following result which states that when the plant dynamics in (11) is Lyapunov stable at $(x, \lambda, \omega) = (\bar{x}, 0, 0)$, the existence of a local exponential observer for the plant (11) in the presence of inputs implies and is implied by the existence of a local exponential observer for the plant (11) in the absence of inputs.

For the purpose of stating this result, we note that the unforced plant corresponding to $\omega = 0$ is given by

$$\dot{x} = f(x, \lambda)$$
$$\dot{\lambda} = 0 \tag{14}$$
$$y = h(x, \lambda)$$

Theorem 4. *Suppose that the plant dynamics in (11) is Lyapunov stable at* $(x, \lambda, \omega) = (\bar{x}, 0, 0)$. *If the system*

$$\dot{z} = \phi(z, \mu, y, u)$$
$$\dot{\mu} = \psi(z, \mu, y, u)$$

is a local exponential observer for the full plant (11), then the system defined by

$$\dot{z} = \phi(z, \mu, y, 0)$$
$$\dot{\mu} = \psi(z, \mu, y, 0)$$

is a local exponential observer for the unforced plant (14). Conversely, if the system

$$\dot{z} = \eta(z, \mu, y)$$
$$\dot{\mu} = \sigma(z, \mu, y)$$

is a local exponential observer for the unforced plant (14) near $(x, \lambda) = (\bar{x}, 0)$, *then the system defined by*

$$\begin{bmatrix} \dot{z} \\ \dot{\mu} \end{bmatrix} = \begin{bmatrix} \phi(z, \mu, y, u) \\ \psi(z, \mu, y, u) \end{bmatrix} \overset{\Delta}{=\!=} \begin{bmatrix} \eta(z, \mu, y) \\ \sigma(z, \mu, y) \end{bmatrix} + \begin{bmatrix} g(z, \mu)u \\ 0 \end{bmatrix}$$

is a local exponential observer for the full plant (11) near $(x, \lambda, \omega) = (\bar{x}, 0, 0)$.

Proof. The first part of this theorem is straightforward. The second part of the theorem follows by verifying the conditions (a) and (b) given in Theorem 3.   □

Let (C^*, A^*) denote the linearization pair for the unforced plant (14), *i.e.*

$$C^* = [C \quad Z] \text{ and } A^* = \begin{bmatrix} A & P \\ 0 & 0 \end{bmatrix}$$

where

$$C = \frac{\partial h}{\partial x}(\bar{x}, 0), \quad Z = \frac{\partial h}{\partial \lambda}(\bar{x}, 0), \quad A = \frac{\partial f}{\partial x}(\bar{x}, 0), \quad P = \frac{\partial f}{\partial \lambda}(\bar{x}, 0),$$

In view of the reduction procedure outlined in Theorem 4, we first derive some important results on the exponential observer design for the unforced plant (14). First, we state the following necessary condition for the local exponential observers that can be established in [16].

Theorem 5. *If the unforced plant (14) has a local exponential observer near the equilibrium $(x, \lambda) = (\bar{x}, 0)$, then the pair (C^*, A^*) is detectable.*   □

Corollary 1. *If the full plant (11) has a local exponential observer near the equilibrium $(x, \lambda, \omega) = (\bar{x}, 0, 0)$, then the pair (C^*, A^*) is detectable.*

Proof. The assertion follows immediately from Theorems 4 and 5.   □

Using the necessary condition given in Theorem 5, we establish the following result, which gives a simple necessary condition for the existence of local exponential observers for the unforced plant (14).

Theorem 6. *If the unforced plant (14) has a local exponential observer near the equilibrium $(x, \lambda) = (\bar{x}, 0)$, then the pair (C, A) is detectable and*

$$rank \begin{bmatrix} Z \\ P \end{bmatrix} = l = dim(\lambda)$$

Proof. Suppose that the unforced plant (14) has a local exponential observer near the equilibrium $(x, \lambda) = (\bar{x}, 0)$. Then by Theorem 5, the pair (C^*, A^*) is detectable. Note that by PBH rank test [19], a necessary and sufficient condition for (C^*, A^*) to be detectable is that

$$rank \begin{bmatrix} C^* \\ \xi I - A^* \end{bmatrix} = n + l \tag{15}$$

for all complex numbers ξ in the closed right-half plane (RHP), *i.e.* in the region, where $Re(\xi) \geq 0$.

We note that

$$\begin{bmatrix} C^* \\ \xi I - A^* \end{bmatrix} = \begin{bmatrix} C & Z \\ \xi I - A & -P \\ 0 & \xi I \end{bmatrix}$$

Thus, it is immediate that (15) holds for all complex numbers ξ in the closed RHP only if

$$\begin{bmatrix} C \\ \xi I - A \end{bmatrix} = n$$

for all complex numbers ξ in the closed RHP and

$$\text{rank} \begin{bmatrix} Z \\ P \end{bmatrix} = l.$$

In view of the PBH rank test for detectable [19], the above necessary condition is the same as requiring that (C, A) is detectable and

$$\text{rank} \begin{bmatrix} Z \\ P \end{bmatrix} = l.$$

This completes the proof.   □

Corollary 2. *If the full plant (11) has a local exponential observer near the equilibrium* $(x, \lambda, \omega) = (\bar{x}, 0, 0)$, *then the pair* (C, A) *is detectable and*

$$\text{rank} \begin{bmatrix} Z \\ P \end{bmatrix} = l = dim(\lambda)$$

Proof. This is a simple consequence of Theorems 4 and 6.   □

Next, we show that the necessary condition given in Theorem 5 is also sufficient for the existence of a local exponential observer for the unforced plant (14) when the unforced plant dynamics in (14) is Lyapunov stable.

Theorem 7. *Suppose that the plant dynamics in (14) is Lyapunov stable at* $(\bar{x}, 0)$ *and suppose also that the matrix* $A^\star - K^\star C^\star$ *is Hurwitz for some matrix* $K^\star$. *Then the system defined by*

$$\begin{bmatrix} \dot{z} \\ \dot{\mu} \end{bmatrix} = \begin{bmatrix} f(z, \mu) \\ 0 \end{bmatrix} + K^\star [y - h(z, \mu)] \tag{16}$$

is a local exponential observer for the unforced plant (14) near $(x, \lambda) = (\bar{x}, 0)$.

Proof. It is easy to check that the candidate observer (16) satisfies the conditions (a) and (b) of Theorem 3.

When $(C^\star, A^\star)$ is detectable, by the reduction procedure outlined in Theorem 4, we can use the local exponential observer (16) constructed for the unforced plant (14) to construct a local exponential observer for the full plant (11).

Theorem 8. *Suppose that the plant dynamics in (11) is Lyapunov stable at* $(\bar{x}, 0, 0)$ *and suppose also that the matrix* $A^\star - K^\star C^\star$ *is Hurwitz for some matrix* $K^\star$. *Then the system defined by*

$$\begin{bmatrix} \dot{z} \\ \dot{\mu} \end{bmatrix} = \begin{bmatrix} f(z, \mu) + g(z, \mu)u \\ 0 \end{bmatrix} + K^\star [y - h(z, \mu)] \tag{17}$$

is a local exponential observer for the full plant (11) near the equilibrium $(\bar{x}, 0, 0)$.

Proof. The assertion is a simple consequence of the reduction procedure outlined in Theorems 4 and 7 . □

Corollary 3. *Suppose that the plant dynamics in (11) is Lyapunov stable at $(\bar{x}, 0, 0)$ and that the output function y is purely a function of x, i.e. it has the form $y = \gamma(x)$. Assume that equilibrium $x = \bar{x}$ of the plant dynamics of x in (11) changes with the real parametric uncertainty λ. In this case, the system linearization pair $(C^\star, A^\star)$ has the form*

$$C^\star = [C \quad 0] \ \ and \ \ A^\star = \begin{bmatrix} A & P \\ 0 & 0 \end{bmatrix}.$$

If the pair $(C^\star, A^\star)$ is detectable, then the full plant (11) has a local exponential observer given by Eq. (17), where $K^\star$ is any matrix such that $A^\star - K^\star C^\star$ is Hurwitz. □

Remark 1. It is a well-known result in Control Systems that the system linearization pair $(C^\star, A^\star)$ is generically observable [20]. Thus, from Corollary 3, there generically exist local exponential observers of the form (17) for the full plant (11) under the following conditions:

(a) The plant dynamics in (11) is Lyapunov stable at $(x, \lambda, \omega) = (\bar{x}, 0, 0)$.
(b) The equilibrium $x = \bar{x}$ of the plant dynamics in x changes with the real parametric uncertainty.
(c) The output function y is purely a function of x, *i.e.* it has the form $y = \gamma(x)$. □

5   Conclusions

In this paper, we showed that *equilibrium-state detectability* is a necessary condition for the existence of local asymptotic observers for any nonlinear system. Using this result, we established that for the classical case, when the equilibrium does not change with the parametric uncertainty and when the plant output is purely a function of the state, there is no local asymptotic observer for the plant. We also showed that in sharp contrast to this case, for the general case of problems where we allow the state equilibrium to change with the parametric uncertainty, there typically exist local exponential observers even when the plant output is purely a function of the state. Next, we derived a procedure for local exponential observers for a general class of nonlinear systems with real parametric uncertainty under some stability assumptions and showed that the existence of local exponential observers in the presence of inputs implies, and is implied by the existence of local exponential observers in the absence of inputs.

References

1. Luenberger, D.: Observing the state of a linear system. IEEE Trans. Military Electronics 8, 74–80 (1964)
2. Thau, F.E.: Observing the states of nonlinear dynamical systems. Internat. J. Control 18, 471–479 (1973)
3. Kou, S.R., Elliott, D.L., Tarn, T.J.: Exponential observers for nonlinear dynamical systems. Inform. Control 29, 204–216 (1975)

4. Krener, A.J., Isidori, A.: Linearization by output injection and nonlinear observers. Systems & Control Letters 3, 47–52 (1983)
5. Bestle, D., Zeitz, M.: Canonical form observer design for nonlinear time-variable systems. Internat. J. Control 38, 419–431 (1983)
6. Krener, A.J., Respondek, W.: Nonlinear observers with linearizable error dynamics. SIAM J. Control & Optimiz. 23, 197–216 (1985)
7. Xia, X.H., Gao, W.B.: Nonlinear observer design by canonical form. Internat. J. Control 47, 1081–1100 (1988)
8. Xia, X.H., Gao, W.B.: On exponential observers for nonlinear systems. Systems & Control Letters 11, 319–325 (1988)
9. Gauthier, J.P., Hammouri, H., Othman, S.: A simple observer for nonlinear systems - Applications to bioreactors. IEEE Trans. Automatic Control 37, 875–880 (1992)
10. Tsinias, J.: Observer design for nonlinear systems. Systems & Control Lett. 13, 135–142 (1989)
11. Tsinias, J.: Further results on the observer design problem. Systems & Control Lett. 14, 411–418 (1990)
12. Phelps, A.R.: On constructing nonlinear observers. SIAM J. Control Optimiz. 29, 516–534 (1991)
13. Gauthier, J.P., Kupka, I.A.K.: Observability and observers for nonlinear systems. SIAM J. Control Optimiz. 32, 975–994 (1994)
14. Krener, A.J., Kang, W.: Locally convergent nonlinear systems. SIAM J. Control Optimiz. 42, 155–177 (2003)
15. Sundarapandian, V.: Observers for nonlinear systems (D.Sc. Dissertation). Washington University, St. Louis (1996)
16. Sundarapandian, V.: Local observer design for nonlinear systems. Math. Computer Modelling 35, 25–36 (2002)
17. Guckenheimer, J., Holmes, P.: Nonlinear oscillations, Dynamical Systems and Bifurcations of Vector Fields. Springer, New York (1983)
18. Isidori, A.: Nonlinear Control Systems. Sprigner, New York (1989)
19. Rugh, W.J.: Linear System Theory. Prentice, New Jersey (1996)
20. Wonham, W.M.: Linear Multivariable Control. Springer, Berlin (1974)

A Node Stability Index-Based Connected Dominating Set Algorithm for Mobile Ad Hoc Networks

Natarajan Meghanathan

Jackson State University
Jackson, MS 39217, USA
nmeghanathan@jsums.edu

Abstract. We propose a Node Stability Index (NSI)-based algorithm to determine stable connected dominating sets (CDS) for Mobile Ad hoc Networks (MANETs). The NSI of a node is defined as the sum of the predicted Link Expiration Times (LETs) of the links with its neighbor nodes. The NSI-CDS algorithm prefers to include (to the CDS) covered nodes that have the largest NSI value, computed based on the sum of the LETs of the uncovered neighbors. The NSI-CDS has been observed to have significantly longer lifetime than the maximum density-based CDS (MaxD-CDS) and the ID-based CDS (ID-CDS). The tradeoff is a modest increase in the CDS Node Size which however contributes significantly to the robustness of the CDS as well as to a lower hop count per path, especially in high-density networks.

Keywords: Stability, Connected Dominating Sets (CDS), Link Expiration Time, Mobile Ad hoc Networks, Maximum Density CDS, ID-CDS.

1 Introduction

A Mobile Ad hoc Network (MANET) is a resource-constrained dynamically changing network of arbitrarily moving wireless nodes that operate under limited battery charge, transmission range and bandwidth. By virtue of all these resource constraints, MANET routes are often multi-hop in nature and change with time depending on node mobility and availability. MANET routing protocols are preferred to be on-demand in nature to optimize resource usage [1][2]. The MANET on-demand routing protocols typically employ a global broadcast request-reply cycle, called flooding, to discover the paths (for unicasting) as well as trees and meshes (for multicasting) [3]. With flooding, a source node initiates the broadcast of the Route Request (RREQ) packets and these packets are forwarded exactly once by every other node to their neighbor nodes. However, with flooding, the network incurs lot of control overhead in requiring each node to broadcast (even though it is done only once) the RREQ message to the neighborhood. The redundancy of retransmissions is such that every node in the network gets a copy of the broadcast message from each of its neighbors.

Recent studies in the literature (e.g. [4][5][6]) have demonstrated that a connected dominating set (CDS) of the underlying network can be used as a backbone to broadcast a message from one node to all the other nodes in the network. A CDS of a

N. Meghanathan et al. (Eds.): CCSIT 2012, Part I, LNICST 84, pp. 31–40, 2012.
© Institute for Computer Sciences, Social Informatics and Telecommunications Engineering 2012

network graph is defined as the subset of the nodes in the network such that every node in the network is either in the CDS or is a neighbor of a node in the CDS. The message to be broadcast (such as a RREQ message) is forwarded only by the nodes that are part of the CDS and the non-CDS nodes (i.e., nodes that are not in the CDS) merely receive the message from one or more neighboring CDS nodes that cover their non-CDS neighbors. The efficiency of broadcasting using a CDS lies in minimizing the number of redundant retransmissions and this depends on the number of nodes that are part of the CDS (referred to as CDS Node Size). The CDS with the minimum number of nodes is referred to as a Minimum Connected Dominating Set (MCDS). Determining the MCDS for a network graph is an NP-complete problem [7]. Several heuristics have been proposed to closely approximate the optimal solution in polynomial time. The Maximum Density-based CDS (MaxD-CDS) algorithm [8] studied in this paper is one such heuristic to minimize the CDS Node Size and is based on the strategy of preferring to include nodes that have the maximum number of uncovered neighbors as part of the CDS.

In this paper, we show that aiming for the minimum number of nodes for the CDS in MANETs may not be a good strategy from a stability point of view. For a CDS to exist at any time instant, two conditions must hold: (i) The nodes that are part of the CDS must stay connected – i.e. reachable from one another directly or through one or more intermediate CDS nodes and (ii) Each non-CDS node should have at least one CDS node as a neighbor node. In the case of a MCDS, like the MaxD-CDS studied in this paper, the CDS nodes are far away from each other as we have to cover the non-CDS nodes spanning over the entire network with minimum number of CDS nodes. Thus, there are fewer links among these MCDS nodes and these links are also vulnerable to break at any time as the physical distance between the two constituent end MCDS nodes of a link is likely to be quite close to the transmission range of the nodes. With mobility, two CDS nodes that share such a vulnerable link between them could move away from the transmission range of each other at any time. Similarly, the probability of a non-CDS node not having any of its neighbor nodes to be a MCDS node is also high as there are only few nodes that are part of the MCDS. Thus, a MCDS has to be frequently reconfigured due to failure in maintaining the above two conditions for its existence. Hence, even though broadcasting through a MCDS may sound a promising idea to minimize the number of redundant retransmissions, the cost of frequently determining such a MCDS may overweigh the benefit obtained by actually getting to use the MCDS.

It is essential to ensure that a CDS is stable enough to avoid the overhead of frequent reconfigurations. This forms the objective of our work in this paper. To determine a stable CDS, we explore the idea of using the predicted link expiration time (LET) [9] of the Flow-Oriented Routing Protocol (FORP) [10] that has been observed (in [11][12]) to yield routes that are even twice the lifetime of the routes determined by the minimum-hop Dynamic Source Routing (DSR) protocol [13]. We introduce a term called the Node Stability Index (NSI) that is defined as the sum of the LETs of the links connected to the node. From a CDS-point of view, the NSI of a node is defined as the sum of the LETs of the links with its uncovered neighbors (i.e., nodes that are not yet covered by a CDS node). We propose an algorithm based on this notion of NSI, hereafter referred to as the NSI-CDS, and it is based on the idea of preferring to include nodes that have the largest NSI as part of the CDS. The algorithm starts with including the node with the largest NSI to the CDS and adding all of its neighbor nodes to the covered node list. The NSI-values of each node in the network is updated as the sum of the LETs of the links with its uncovered neighbor nodes. During subsequent iterations of the algorithm, we pick a covered node that has the largest NSI value (of course, only if the NSI value is greater than zero), add it to the CDS and include all of its uncovered neighbor nodes to the list of covered nodes. The above procedure is repeated until all the nodes are covered.

The rest of the paper is organized as follows: Section 2 explains the design of the NSI-CDS algorithm. Section 3 presents the simulation environment, the simulation results featuring the NSI-CDS, MaxD-CDS and the ID-CDS and interprets them with respect to metrics such as CDS Lifetime, CDS Node Size, CDS Edge Size and Hop Count per Path. Section 4 concludes the paper.

2   Node Stability Index Connected Dominating Set Algorithm

The objective of the proposed Node Stability Index (NSI)-based CDS construction algorithm is to determine a long-living CDS without any substantial increase in the number of nodes constituting the CDS. We adopt the unit-disk graph model [17] according to which there exists a link between two nodes i and j if and only if the distance between the two nodes is less than or equal to the fixed transmission range. The network is homogeneous in nature and that all nodes operate with an identical and fixed transmission range, denoted as R in equation (1). The set of neighbors of a node i, $Neighbors(i)$, consists of those nodes that are within in the transmission range of node j. The predicted link expiration time (LET) of a link $i - j$ between two nodes i and j, currently at (X_i, Y_i) and (X_j, Y_j), and moving with velocities v_i and v_j in directions θ_i and θ_j (with respect to the positive X-axis) is computed using the formula proposed in [9]:

$$LET(i, j) = \frac{-(ab + cd) + \sqrt{(a^2 + c^2)R^2 - (ad - bc)^2}}{a^2 + c^2} \tag{1}$$

where $a = v_i*\cos\theta_i - v_j*\cos\theta_j$; $b = X_i - X_j$; $c = v_i*\sin\theta_i - v_j*\sin\theta_j$; $d = Y_i - Y_j$

At any moment, every node maintains a LET-table comprising of the estimates of the LET values to each of its neighbor nodes based on the latest beacons received from the neighbor node. Nodes periodically exchange beacons in the neighborhood. The beacon message broadcast by a node includes the current location of the node, the velocity at which the node is moving and the direction of movement of the node (denoted as the angle subscribed with respect to the positive X-axis). A node obtains its location information through the Global Positioning Scheme (GPS) [14] or any other relevant location service schemes (e.g. [15]). The Node Stability Index (NSI) of a node i during the working of the NSI-CDS algorithm is defined as the sum of the LET of the links with the neighbor nodes j that are not yet covered by a CDS node. The NSI of a node i is represented formally as:

$$NSI(i) = \sum_{\substack{j \in Neighbors(i) \\ j \notin Covered-Nodes-List}} LET(i, j) \tag{2}$$

The key data structures maintained and used in the NSI-CDS algorithm are as follows: (i) *CDS-Nodes-List*: This list includes all the nodes that are part of the CDS; (ii) *Covered-Nodes-List*: This list includes all the nodes that are either part of the CDS or is at least a neighbor node of a node in the CDS and (iii) *Priority-Queue*: This list includes all the nodes that are in the *Covered-Nodes-List* (but not in the *CDS-Nodes-List*) and are considered the candidate nodes for the next node to be selected for inclusion in the *CDS-Nodes-List*.

The NSI-CDS algorithm (pseudo code in Figure 1) works as follows: For every iteration, the algorithm selects one node from the *Priority-Queue* (the node is also in the *Covered-Nodes-List*) and adds it to the *CDS-Nodes-List*. The criterion to select a covered node from the *Priority-Queue* and include it in the *CDS-Nodes-List* is to give preference for the covered node with the maximum value of the Node Stability Index (NSI). As defined before, the NSI of a node is the sum of the Link Expiration Times (LETs) of the links with the uncovered neighbors of the node (i.e., the neighbor nodes that are not yet in the *Covered-Nodes-List*). Before the first iteration, since none of the nodes are in the *Covered-Nodes-List*, the NSI of a node is simply the sum of the LETs of the links with all of its neighbor nodes. The node with the maximum of such NSI value is the first node to be added to the *Covered-Nodes-List*, *Priority-Queue* and eventually to the *CDS-Nodes-List*. All the uncovered neighbors of the newly included node to the *CDS-Nodes-List* are now included in the *Covered-Nodes-List* as well as in the *Priority-Queue*. After every iteration, the NSI values of the nodes in the network and the *Priority-Queue* are recomputed based on the updated *Covered-Nodes-List*. Nodes whose NSI value is zero are removed from the *Priority-Queue*. The above procedure is repeated until there is at least one node that is not yet in the *Covered-Nodes-List*; if the underlying network is connected, the *Priority-Queue* will remain non-empty until all nodes are added to the *Covered-Nodes-List* and the algorithm finally returns the *CDS-Nodes-List*. If the *Priority-Queue* gets empty and there is at least one node to be added to the *Covered-Nodes-List*, then it implies the underlying network is disconnected and the algorithm returns NULL.

Input: Snapshot of the Network Graph $G = (V, E)$, where V is the set of vertices and E is the set of edges

Auxiliary Variables and Functions:
CDS-Nodes-List, Covered-Nodes-List, Priority-Queue, startNode
Dequeue(*Priority-Queue*) – Extracts, from the queue, the node with the maximum *NSI* (> 0) – in case of a tie, a node is randomly chosen and extracted from the queue.
Neighbors(s) – List of neighbors of node s in graph G

Output: *CDS-Nodes-List* // contains the nodes that are part of the NSI-based CDS
         NULL // if the underlying network graph is disconnected

Initialization: *CDS-Nodes-List* = Φ; *Covered-Nodes-List* = Φ; *Priority-Queue* = Φ;
$\forall i \in V, \ NSI(i) = \sum_{j \in Neighbors(i)} LET(i, j)$

Fig. 1. Pseudo Code for the NSI-CDS Algorithm

Begin Construction of NSI-CDS
      startNode = the node $u \in V$ with the largest NSI value
      Priority-Queue = {*startNode*}; *Covered-Nodes-List* = {*startNode*}

      while (|*Covered-Nodes-List*| < |*V*| and *Priority-Queue* ≠ Φ) **do**
          node *s* = Dequeue(*Priority-Queue*)
                    where $s \in$ *Covered-Nodes-List* and $s \notin$ *CDS-Nodes-List*
          CDS-Nodes-List = *CDS-Nodes-List* U {*s*}
          $\forall v \in$ *Neighbors*(*s*),
              if $v \notin$ *Covered-Nodes-List* **then**
                  Covered-Nodes-List = *Covered-Nodes-List* U {*v*}
                  Priority-Queue = *Priority-Queue* U {*v*}
              end if

        $\forall u \in V$, $NSI(u) = \{ \sum LET(u,v) \mid v \in$ *Neighbors*(*u*)
                                    AND $v \notin$ *Covered-Nodes-List*}
        $\forall u \in$ *Priority-Queue*,
            if $(NSI(u) = 0)$ **then**
                remove node *u* from *Priority-Queue*
            end if

        if (|*Covered-Nodes-List*| < |*V*| and *Priority-Queue* = Φ) **then**
            return NULL // the network is disconnected and there is no CDS
        end if

      end while

    return *CDS-Nodes-List*

End Construction of NSI-CDS

Fig. 1. (*Continued*)

There can be at most O(|*V*|) iterations and O(|*E*|) edges have to be explored spread across all of these iterations. The dequeue operation during the beginning of each iteration takes O(|*V*|) time if the *Priority-Queue* has been implemented as an array and O(log|*V*|) time if implemented as a binary heap. After the inclusion of a node to the *CDS-Nodes-List* and its neighbor nodes to the *Covered-Nodes-List*, it takes O(|*V*|+|*E*|) time to re-compute the NSI values of all the nodes by exploring their incident edges and this is the most time-consuming step (compared to the dequeue operation) in each iteration. Thus, the overall-time complexity of the NSI-CDS algorithm can be represented as O(|*V*|*(|*V*| + |*E*|)). The MaxD-CDS and the ID-CDS algorithms also incur the same run-time complexity as the number of uncovered neighbors of a node has to be updated during each of the iterations.

3   Simulations

The performance of the NSI-CDS is compared with that of the Maximum Density-based CDS (MaxD-CDS) and the ID-based CDS (ID-CDS). The MaxD-CDS algorithm prefers to include into the CDS, a covered node with the maximum number of uncovered neighbors. The ID-CDS algorithm prefers to include into the CDS, a covered node with the largest node ID. To be fair to all the nodes in the network, every time a new ID-CDS is constructed, we randomly distribute the IDs of the nodes in the network. All of the simulations (including the implementation of the three CDS algorithms) are conducted in a discrete-event simulator developed in Java.

For a fixed network area (1000m x 1000m) and transmission range per node (250m), we conduct simulations with 50 nodes and 100 nodes representing networks of low density and high density respectively. The mobility model used in our simulations is the Random Waypoint model [16] with the velocity randomly chosen from the range $[0, \ldots, v_{max}]$ each time a node changes its direction. The value of v_{max} is varied by conducting simulations with 5 m/s, 25 m/s and 50 m/s representing scenarios of low, moderate and high mobility respectively.

The simulation strategy for each of the CDS algorithms is as follows: We obtain a centralized view of the network topology by generating mobility trace files for a simulation time of 1000 seconds for each combination of network density (50 and 100 nodes) and node mobility (v_{max} = 5, 25 and 50 m/s). We sample the network topology for every 0.25 seconds. If a CDS does not exist for a particular time instant, we run the CDS algorithm on the network topology snapshot at that time instant and tend to use that CDS during the subsequent time instants as long as the CDS exists (we check for existence of a CDS using the strategy described in the next paragraph). The above procedure is repeated for the entire simulation time of 1000 seconds.

In the simulations for each CDS algorithm, we use a CDS as long as it exists. We consider a CDS to 'exist' for a particular time instant if it is connected (i.e. the CDS nodes are reachable from one another directly or through multi-hop paths) and covered all nodes in the network (i.e. every non-CDS node has at least one CDS node as a neighbor node). If a CDS is determined to be not connected or not covering all the nodes in the network at a particular time instant, we determine a new CDS by running the CDS construction algorithm on a network graph snapshot corresponding to that time instant. The connectivity amongst the CDS nodes at a particular time instant is determined by running the Breadth-First-Search (BFS) algorithm [7] on a CDS-induced network sub graph involving only the nodes that are part of the CDS and the set of edges that may exist between any two CDS nodes at that time instant.

To measure the hop count per path, we run the BFS algorithm on a CDS-induced sub graph for 15 source-destination (s-d) pairs – the role of the source or destination could be assigned to any node in the network. The CDS-induced sub graph for a particular time instant comprises of all the nodes in the network and edges that may exist between any two CDS nodes and between a CDS node and a non-CDS node. Two non-CDS nodes have to communicate through one or more CDS nodes as intermediate nodes, even if the two non-CDS nodes are direct neighbors. However, two CDS nodes can communicate directly if they are neighbors of each other.

Each data point in Figures 2 through 5 is an average computed over 10 mobility trace files generated for every combination of network density and node mobility values considered in the simulations. The following are the performance metrics measured in our simulations: (i) *CDS Lifetime*: We keep track of the duration of existence of each of the CDS used for the entire simulation time and compute the average value of the CDS lifetime, considering all the mobility profiles for the particular simulation condition. (ii) *CDS Node Size*: This is a time-averaged value of the number of nodes that are part of the CDS used for every time instant (i.e., the duration of the usage of the CDS is taken into consideration) over the entire simulation. (iii) *CDS Edge Size*: This is a time-averaged value of the number of edges that exist between any two CDS nodes for every time instant over the entire simulation. (iv) *Hop Count per s-d Path*: This is a time-averaged value for the number of edges (hops) in the paths determined for every *s-d* pair on CDS-induced sub graphs, considered over the entire simulation time and all the *s-d* pairs.

3.1   CDS Node Size and CDS Edge Size

The NSI-CDS includes more nodes (refer Figure 2) compared to the MaxD-CDS. The MaxD-CDS algorithm has only one objective – to cover all the nodes in the network with the minimum number of CDS nodes and hence nodes having a larger number of uncovered neighbors are preferred for inclusion to the CDS. However, such a greedy strategy is bound to have a negative effect on the CDS lifetime because it would be difficult to cover all the nodes in the network with fewer CDS nodes and also expect the CDS nodes to be connected among themselves with fewer edges that exist between these nodes. On the other hand, the NSI-CDS algorithm primarily aims to determine a stable CDS that will exist for a longer time and minimizing the CDS Node Size is only a secondary objective embedded with the primary objective of maximizing the CDS Lifetime. Thus, the number of nodes forming part of the NSI-CDS is bound to be larger than the number of nodes that are part of the MaxD-CDS. We observe that the NSI-CDS Node Size is about 45% and 75% more than the MaxD-CDS Node Size for low density and high density networks respectively. The Node Size for the ID-CDS is about the same as that of the NSI-CDS; with the NSI-CDS incurring slightly larger number of nodes (at most 3% in low-density networks and 10% in high-density networks) than the ID-CDS.

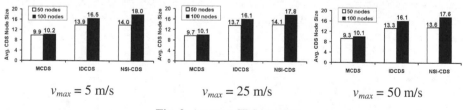

$v_{max} = 5$ m/s $v_{max} = 25$ m/s $v_{max} = 50$ m/s

Fig. 2. Average CDS Node Size

The larger the CDS Node Size - the larger will be the CDS Edge Size and more stable and robust will be the CDS to link failures. Since the MaxD-CDS has the lowest CDS Node Size, it also has the lowest CDS Edge Size and vice-versa for the NSI-CDS. In its pursuit to form a CDS with the least number of nodes, the MaxD-CDS algorithm chooses CDS nodes that are far away from each other such that each

CDS node individually covers as many uncovered neighbor nodes as possible. As a result, the CDS nodes are more likely to be away from each other; thus, the number of edges that are part of the CDS spanning the entire network is very low. The ID-CDS and NSI-CDS algorithms are relatively insensitive to the # of edges added to the CDS.

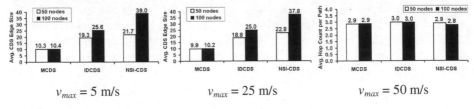

$v_{max} = 5$ m/s $v_{max} = 25$ m/s $v_{max} = 50$ m/s

Fig. 3. Average CDS Edge Size

3.2   CDS Lifetime

The lifetime of a NSI-CDS is significantly longer compared to that of a MaxD-CDS and an ID-CDS. For a given scenario of node mobility and network density, the sum of the lifetimes of an ID-CDS and MaxD-CDS is still less than the lifetime incurred by NSI-CDS. The stability of the NSI-CDS can also be attributed to the relatively larger CDS Edge Size that accompanies the modest increase in the CDS Node Size. Thus, even though we can say that there is a tradeoff between the CDS Lifetime vs. the CDS Node Size and Edge Size, this tradeoff is more favorable towards the NSI-CDS and it significantly gains in the Lifetime metric with a very modest increase in the Node Size. On the other hand, in pursuit of minimizing the number of nodes that are part of the CDS, the MaxD-CDS is quite unstable, especially as the node mobility and/or the network density increases. NSI-CDS is more scalable with respect to the increase in network density and node mobility. The modest increase in the Node Size (at most by 30%) at larger network density helps NSI-CDS to incur a significant gain in the Lifetime. On the other hand, in the case of MaxD-CDS, with very few additional nodes (at most 7% more nodes) to cover about 100% more nodes in the network, as we double the node density, the MaxD-CDS turns out to be quite unstable and has very low lifetime. Even the ID-CDS based approach performs significantly better than the MaxD-CDS approach in high-density networks. The lifetime per ID-CDS is about twice the lifetime per MaxD-CDS for most of the simulation conditions.

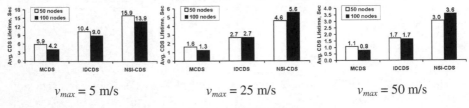

$v_{max} = 5$ m/s $v_{max} = 25$ m/s $v_{max} = 50$ m/s

Fig. 4. Average CDS Lifetime

3.3   Hop Count per Path

The three CDS algorithms almost incur the same hop count per path for low-density networks. However, with increase in the network density to 100 nodes, the NSI-CDS incurs a relatively slightly lower hop count (about 7-10% lower) compared to the MaxD-CDS and ID-CDS. This could be attributed to the presence of a larger number of nodes and edges as part of the NSI-CDS-induced sub graph that enables the discovery of paths that have fewer hops between the source (s) and destination (d) nodes. With fewer node and edges, the MaxD-CDS incurs more hops per s-d path. The ID-CDS incurs even slightly more hops per s-d path. The MaxD-CDS nodes could be relatively more heavily used compared to the other two CDS algorithms, because only very few nodes are part of the MaxD-CDS and all communication has to go through these CDS nodes. This could lead to premature failure of critical nodes, mainly nodes lying in the center of the network, leading to reduction in network connectivity, especially in low-density networks. With the NSI-CDS, as multiple nodes are part of the CDS, the packet forwarding load can be distributed across several nodes and this could enhance the fairness of node usage as well as incur relatively lower end-to-end delay per data packet.

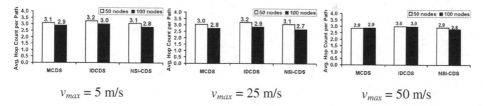

$$v_{max} = 5 \text{ m/s} \qquad\qquad v_{max} = 25 \text{ m/s} \qquad\qquad v_{max} = 50 \text{ m/s}$$

Fig. 5. Average Hop Count per Source-Destination Path using the CDS Nodes

4   Conclusions

We have proposed a Node Stability Index (NSI)-based algorithm to determine stable connected dominating sets for mobile ad hoc networks and it is based on the notion of the predicted link expiration times (LETs). The NSI-CDS algorithm has the same run-time complexity as the other standard algorithms based on maximum density (MaxD-CDS) or node ID (ID-CDS). The MaxD-CDS and ID-CDS have been observed to be very unstable in the presence of node mobility. We do observe a tradeoff between the CDS Lifetime vs. the CDS Node Size. However, the tradeoff is more favorable towards the NSI-CDS. The NSI-CDS is 2.5 to 3.5 times more stable than the MaxD-CDS and 1.5 to 2.0 times stable than the ID-based CDS; this gain in the CDS Lifetime is achieved by including at most 25-45% and 3-10% more CDS nodes than MaxD-CDS and ID-CDS respectively. The relatively moderate larger number of constituent nodes and edges make the NSI-CDS more robust to node mobility and link failures as well as contribute to a lower hop count per path, especially in high-density networks.

References

1. Broch, J., Maltz, D.A., Johnson, D.B., Hu, Y.C., Jetcheva, J.: A Performance Comparison of Multi-hop Wireless Ad hoc Network Routing Protocols. In: International Conference on Mobile Computing and Networking, pp. 85–97. ACM, Dallas (1998)
2. Johansson, P., Larson, T., Hedman, N., Mielczarek, B., DegerMark, M.: Scenario-based Performance Analysis of Routing Protocols for Mobile Ad hoc Networks. In: International Conference on Mobile Computing and Networking, pp. 195–206. ACM, Seattle (1999)
3. Siva Ram Murthy, C., Manoj, B.S.: Ad Hoc Wireless Networks: Architectures and Protocols, 1st edn. Prentice Hall (2004)
4. Sakai, K., Sun, M.-T., Ku, W.-S., Okada, H.: Maintaining CDS in Mobile Ad Hoc Networks. In: Li, Y., Huynh, D.T., Das, S.K., Du, D.-Z. (eds.) WASA 2008. LNCS, vol. 5258, pp. 141–153. Springer, Heidelberg (2008)
5. Sheu, P.-R., Tsai, H.-Y., Lee, Y.-P., Cheng, J.Y.: On Calculating Stable Connected Dominating Sets Based on Link Stability for Mobile Ad hoc Networks. Tamkang Journal of Science and Engineering 12(4), 417–428 (2009)
6. Bao, L., Garcia-Luna-Aceves, J.J.: Stable Energy-aware Topology Management in Ad hoc Networks. Ad hoc Networks 8(3), 313–327 (2010)
7. Cormen, T.H., Leiserson, C.E., Rivest, R.L., Stein, C.: Introduction to Algorithms, 3rd edn. MIT Press (2009)
8. Meghanathan, N.: An Algorithm to Determine the Sequence of Stable Connected Dominating Sets in Mobile Ad hoc Networks. In: The 2nd Advanced International Conference on Telecommunications. IARIA, Guadeloupe (2006)
9. Su, W., Lee, S.-J., Gerla, M.: Mobility Prediction and Routing in Ad hoc Wireless Networks. International Journal of Network Management 11(1), 3–30 (2001)
10. Su, W., Gerla, M.: IPv6 Flow Handoff in Ad hoc Wireless Networks using Mobility Prediction. In: Global Telecommunications Conference, vol. 1a, pp. 271–275. IEEE, Rio de Janeireo (1999)
11. Meghanathan, N.: Exploring the Stability-Energy Consumption-Delay-Network Lifetime Tradeoff of Mobile Ad hoc Network Routing Protocols. Journal of Networks 3(2), 17–28 (2008)
12. Meghanathan, N.: Path Stability based Ranking of Mobile Ad hoc Network Routing Protocols. ISAST Transactions Journal on Communications and Networking 1(1), 66–73 (2007)
13. Johnson, D.B., Maltz, D.A., Broch, J.: Ad hoc Networking. Addison-Wesley (2001)
14. Hofmann-Wellenhof, B., Lichtenegger, H., Collins, J.: Global Positioning System: Theory and Practice, 5th edn. Springer, Heidelberg (2004)
15. Keiss, W., Fuessler, H., Widmer, J.: Hierarchical Location Service for Mobile Ad hoc Networks. ACM Mobile Computing and Communications Review 8(4), 47–58 (2004)
16. Bettstetter, C., Hartenstein, H., Perez-Costa, X.: Stochastic Properties of the Random-Way Point Mobility Model. Wireless Networks 10(5), 555–567 (2004)
17. Kuhn, F., Moscibroda, T., Wattenhofer, R.: Unit Disk Graph Approximation. In: Workshop on the Foundations of Mobile Computing, pp. 17–23. ACM, Philadelphia (2004)

Energy Efficient Dynamic Routing Protocol for Wireless Sensor Networks

Md Golam Murshed and Alastair R. Allen

Department of Engineering, University of Aberdeen
King's College, Fraser Noble Building,
Aberdeen, United Kingdom, AB24 3UE
{mg.murshed,a.allen}@abdn.ac.uk

Abstract. One of the most significant challenges for Wireless Sensor Networks (WSN) is long-lived sensor nodes and minimization in overall power consumption, As the nodes spend substantial energy in sending and receiving data, a robust and power-aware routing protocol can maximize the network lifetime. In this paper, a cluster based dynamic and energy efficient routing scheme with optimal transmission range (DEOR) for wireless sensor networks is proposed in order to maximize the network lifetime. In this protocol, nodes are classified in different ranks depending on the nature of their power consumption in terms of both direct communication to the Base Station and optimal transmission range. Each node maintains a routing table to choose the next hop node to relay the data and after successful transmission it updates that routing table. Computer simulation of this dynamic routing protocol has been done and a better outcome has been observed compared to one of the multihop routing strategies.

Keywords: Wireless Sensor Network, Energy Hole Problem, Optimal Transmission Range, Routing Table.

1   Introduction

Wireless Sensor Network (WSN) is a rising and enabling technology for low-cost and unattended monitoring of a wide range of application areas like environment, industry, health and space. The recent advances in micro-electro-mechanical systems and integrated digital electronics have promoted wireless communication, sensing and processing combined together in a tiny device, called a sensor node or mote. These sensor nodes are low-powered, economically cheap, and multifunctional, that can monitor and respond to changes in target parameters of the environment in which they were deployed.

A typical WSN consists of a number of sensor nodes that communicate with each other via wireless channels to perform a common task, and sensed data are gathered in a previously assigned sink node or gateway called the Base Station (BS). Usually, the

N. Meghanathan et al. (Eds.): CCSIT 2012, Part I, LNICST 84, pp. 41–52, 2012.
© Institute for Computer Sciences, Social Informatics and Telecommunications Engineering 2012

BS is a more powerful device than the deployed sensor nodes and plays a vital role administering the whole network, such as decision making, routing table updating etc. In WSN, collected data from a remote sensor node can either be sent to BS directly or by using other intermediary nodes. From a group of node, some times a node is selected as Clusterhead (CH) to gather local data from others and then pass it to other node or BS.

WSN has some unique features such as limited power and bandwidth, stringent memory capacity and small scale processing ability etc. These features have caused many challenges to WSN that demanded energy efficiency in all levels of network implementation, ensuring quality of service. Effective and proper use of the energy resources of sensor nodes and maximizing the network lifetime are important design parameters for the network topology and routing protocol [1]. Therefore, in this paper we address the topic of energy efficient data routing protocol in a homogeneous WSN consisting of a large number of static sensor nodes deployed randomly in a 2D field and a static sink or Base Station used to collect data from sensor nodes.

Most sensor nodes are equipped with limited energy reserves. For instance, Mica2 of Crossbow sensor board uses a 1.5 Amp-Hour (Ah) 3 Volt battery [2]. On the other hand, sensors are unattended and in most cases it is not feasible to change the power supply. In terms of power consumption, the most power consuming task is data transmission. Approximately 80% of power consumed in each sensor node is used for data transmission [3]. Because of the nature of node distribution, the traffic load is not evenly distributed over the network [4]. The CHs that are closer to the BS relay more traffic than the other nodes and have a tendency to die first, creating a gap around the BS. As a consequence, the rest of the nodes in the network become unavailable to the BS and the whole network become useless. These CHs are called 'hot spot' and the problem has been identified as the hot spot problem or self-induced black hole effect.

We address the problems mentioned above, and propose a cluster based dynamic and energy efficient routing scheme with optimal transmission range (DEOR) that ensures quality of service and balanced energy consumption among different areas of the network. In our proposed scheme, we try to confine each node's transmission range to achieve optimal power consumption, and based on that, we divide the network into several energy bands and classify accordingly. The CHs of one energy band will dynamically select the next CH of an adjacent band depending on the cost function calculated based on certain parameters. We performed computer simulations of the proposed scheme and present the result of the simulations to prove the effectiveness and compare it with a greedy algorithm based routing protocol. The numerical results show that our proposed scheme offers attractive energy efficiency.

2   Related Works

Energy efficient routing in sensor networks is a challenging problem because of its resource constraints and the nature of operation. Many proposals have been made so far addressing these problems.

LEACH [5] is a well known hierarchical cluster-based routing protocol where cluster formation is dynamic and clusterheads are chosen based on probabilistic value. The key features of LEACH are: (i) dynamic formation of clusters and CH based on localized coordination and control, (ii) data aggregation to reduce size of data, (iii) one hop communication to the sink or Base Station. Single hop routing adopted by LEACH is not practical in many applications where the sensor field is large. Moreover, since the nodes situated far away from the BS consume comparatively more energy, the network size shrinks as time passes.

PEGASIS[6]   forms a chain of nodes to transmit data to BS. It uses a greedy algorithm to select the member node of the chain and each node sends and receives from neighbour nodes and only one node is selected from that chain to transmit data to BS. In each round, a randomly chosen sensor node acts as CH and transmits data to BS. When a sensor fails or dies because of low battery power, the chain is reconstructed using the same greedy algorithm. This protocol tried to overcome the shortcomings of LEACH but it can not minimize the number of hops which eventually incurs extra energy.

The concept of LEACH has been extended in HEED [7] by using residual energy and node density in a cluster. In the paper [8], the authors propose a cluster based protocol, Even Energy Dissipation Protocol (EEDP), for data gathering from CH. It tries to balance the energy consumption of all the CHs of the entire network instead of CH rotation inside the cluster. In this protocol, multiple chains composed of CH are formed and sensor data are passed to the base station using those chains. The algorithms OFFIS and 2L-OFFIS [9], have considered some parameters such as distance, remaining battery power, link usage to select the next hop node in multihop routing. Using a Fuzzy Inference System, the next hop node is selected among some candidate nodes and this selection procedure constitutes the optimized route from source to sink. This protocol also suffers from the hot spot problem.

The paper is organized as follows. Section 3 provides the energy model of a sensor node and the overall power consumption trends of the sensor networks describing the energy hole problem. In section 4, the solution to the energy hole problem and the description of our proposed protocol is presented. Section 5 presents the results of the simulation program of our proposed protocol. The protocol has been compared with PEGASIS and better outcome has been gained. In Section 6, the conclusions of this paper are drawn.

3   Problem Formulation

We notice that overall energy consumption in various locations in a WSN is different irrespective of the deployment strategy. If the network follows the direct communication method, nodes far away from BS drain out more energy than the nearer ones. This section presents the mathematical explanation of the contradictory phenomena of WSN where we first present the energy model and then the mathematical model.

3.1   Energy Model

The energy consumed by a sensor node is used in three ways- transmitting, receiving and processing. We use the same energy model mentioned in LEACH [5]. If the data rate is b bits/second, to transmit a data packet of b bits over a distance d, the corresponding power consumption for transmission and receiving are as follows;

$$P_{Tx} = \beta_1 b + \beta_2 d^\alpha b, P_{Rx} = \beta_1 b$$

Here, $\beta_1 = 50$ nJ/bit is the amount of energy dissipated by the radio to run the transmitter or receiver circuitry and $\beta_2 = 100$ pJ/bit/m^2 is the transmit amplifier power. α is the path exponent that indicates the rate at which the path loss increases with distance. Typically we consider α takes the values 2, 3 or 4 in wireless communications which actually depends on the environment. Therefore, it is understandable that while transmitting, the radio circuitry consumes more power than receiving data.

To transmit a message from one node to another node within transmission range R is the total of energy spent to send and to receive. Then we can express the total energy, E_{n2n}, to send b bit data as

$$E_{n2n} = b\left(2\beta_1 + \beta_2 d^\alpha\right)$$

Our energy model only considers the power for transmitting and receiving, excluding power for processing and sensing tasks which are negligible and depend on computational hardware architecture and processing complexity.

3.2   The Energy Hole Problem

The imbalanced traffic distribution in WSN creates a bottleneck problem which is referred to as the Energy Hole Problem [10], which degrades the performance and the lifetime of the WSN. In[4] and [10] the authors explained the nature of the energy hole problem with the help of simulation and mathematical analysis. According to [10], the per node traffic load near the BS is

$$Load_{innermost\_band} = \frac{M^2}{\pi} b$$

and the per node energy consumption rate (ECR) is

$$ECR_{innermost\_band} = \alpha_1 b + \gamma_1 (\frac{M^2}{\pi} - 1) b + (\beta_1 + \beta_2 d^k) \frac{M^2}{\pi} b$$

Here the authors assumed that the sensor field is divided into M concentric bands and γ_1 is the energy dissipated by the radio when receiving data.

Following the same model in [10], if we divide the sensing field into M concentric bands, we can calculate the probable difference in the number of sensor nodes in each band. The area differences between the bands are

$$\pi 3r^2, \pi 5r^2, \pi 7r^2, \dots.$$

if we assume the radius of the bands are increased by r. If the node density is δ and if it is uniform throughout the network we can say that the number of nodes in each band increases as the radius of the network increases. Therefore, the total initial energy in each band, $B_x, x \in [1.M]$, has a significant impact on the lifetime of the network and we can say that

$$E_{init}(B_1) < E_{init}(B_2) < E_{init}(B_3) < .. < E_{init}(B_{M-1}) < E_{init}(B_M)$$

On the other hand, nodes in the inner bands are relaying more data than the other nodes in the outer bands. So these two phenomena of WSN are responsible to create energy hole or hot spot problem.

4   Description of DEOR Protocol

In this section, we first define some assumptions, and then we describe the band formation across the network, cost function calculation and dynamic route selection, as well as the role of Base Station (BS).

4.1   Assumptions

In this work, we assume a sensor network where n static but identical sensor nodes are deployed randomly and uniformly in the 2D circular sensing field. Once deployed, this network must work unattended and all its resources are non-renewable. All nodes have the same initial energy and same resources to carry on their sensing, computing and communication activities with the same maximum transmission range. We assume that the transceiver is equipped with omni directional antennas and data can be sent to every node around it within transmission range. The BS is static and could either be placed at the centre or just outside the sensing field. The nodes in the network are location aware and able to communicate with at least one neighbour node. We implement our routing protocol in a multi-hop WSN that is data from any part of the network can be sent to BS via multi-hop. Furthermore, each node is assigned a unique ID and a database of these IDs is kept in BS. The nodes are able to compute their residual energy, buffer size, and channel quality (based on Signal to Noise Ratio) with neighbour nodes. Additionally, we assume that there is an ideal MAC layer protocol implemented in the node protocol stack so that there is no collision and retransmission. Therefore, our technique basically works on network layer of the protocol stack.

4.2   Power Optimal Transmission Range

A wireless link is a broadcast mechanism, and increasing the power to transmit a data packet results in interference with other nodes in the network and draining the battery of the node. Therefore, it is necessary to use the optimum energy to transmit data packets to the next neighbour node so that it does not consume maximum power. A node can reach to another node using its maximum capability with the expense of shorter life-time while shorter transmission rang demands more hops. However, power consumption also increases with the number of hops as well. The strength of transmitting power used by a node determines the bit rate of a wireless link [1]. The bit error rate can be reduced if the transmitting power is increased up to a predefined level to restrain the noise interference. So we need tradeoffs choosing suitable transmission range for data communication. Many researches has been done so far to distinguish the optimal transmission range to prolong the node lifetime and it can be summarized that selecting an appropriate transmission range which is energy efficient is heavily dependant on the application and the environment of the network.

At this stage we refer to two research works [11] and [12] which tried to figure out the maximum and minimum limits of node transmission range and also the generalized optimal transmission range for a particular route. In [11] the authors formulated a routing scheme with optimal power management in terms of transmission range. In this work, end-to-end frame error rate from source node to destination node is defined which acts as the base to formulate a power-cost equation at any error rate.

In [12], the authors tried to specify the boundaries of optimal transmission range based on the data rate generated by the sender nodes. According to the authors, the boundary of the transmission range R can be defined as

$$R_{min} = \max\left[\sqrt{\frac{2.E_{elec}}{\varepsilon_{amp}}}, 2.R_s\right], R_{max} = \min\left[R_{MAX}, \frac{L}{\sqrt{\alpha\pi}}\right]$$

where R_{MAX}, R_s, E_{elec}, ε_{amp}, α, and L stand for the physically maximum transmission range of a sensor node, sensing range of a node, energy to run the transmitter or receiver circuitry, transmit amplifier power, the ratio of average Voronoi cell size to the area size of the neighbour nodes and length of a square shaped sensing field respectively.

For calculating the optimal transmission range that makes the minimum power consumption in topology management, the total data rate (λ) of the network must be bound. If $\overline{P}$ is the total power dissipated by all nodes during the lifetime, the conditions that make the optimal transmission range in the boundary as previous equations are given by

$$\frac{\partial}{\partial R}\overline{P}(R_{min}, \lambda) < 0, \frac{\partial}{\partial R}\overline{P}(R_{max}, \lambda) > 0$$

Therefore, it is possible to preset an optimal transmission range for routing scheme which is adjustable based on the environment and the sensor network application. In our routing protocol, we propose to use optimal transmission range, denoted as R_{mn_cst}, for the link i that dissipates minimum power to exceed SNR threshold of ψ. A high level of power used for transmission can acquire better link quality and high SNR but that drains the battery of the node very quickly. Hence the nodes must use an optimal transmission for hop to hop data transmission.

4.3   Band Classification among Nodes

We propose to divide the sensing field into different circular regions or bands, B_i. These bands are formed based on the node-to-Base Station distance which makes the basis of power consumption. As we are assuming the sensing field as a circle of radius r_{BS} and BS is situated at the centre, theoretically we can partition the whole sensing field with radius, r_{BS}, into M different but adjacent bands. But in a real life scenario, this partition might not work ideally because of attenuating factors present in the environment. Therefore, we propose this band classification among nodes to be launched by the BS. The BS has the information about the sensing place of interest and hence the sensor field radius. Thus, it theoretically divides the field into some adjacent bands and assigns the width of each band.

In section 3.2, we found that the area differences among the bands (and hence among the circles) is increased continuously if the radius of each concentric circle is increased by r. If we wish to keep the area of each band equal, we must have to reorganise and control the width of each band. Let us assume, we have M circles $C_i, i \in [1, M]$ with radius $r_j, j \in [1, M]$ and area $A_{C_i}, i \in [1, M]$. We also assume that the sensor field is divided into M adjacent bands $B_x, x \in [1, M]$ with width $w_y, y \in [1,5]$ and area $A_{B_x}, x \in [1, M]$. Since we want $A_{B_1} = A_{B_2} = ... = A_{B_M}$, we need to choose different widths of different bands based on r_1. Now we get

$$A_{B_1} = A_{C_1} = \pi r_1^2, A_{B_2} = A_{C_2} - A_{C_1}, ...A_{B_M} = A_{C_M} - A_{C_{M-1}}$$

and it is possible to derive the width of each band based on r_1. Thus we finally obtain

$$w_1 = r_1, w_2 = (\sqrt{2} - 1)r_1, w_3 = (\sqrt{3} - \sqrt{2})r_1, w_4 = (2 - \sqrt{3})r_1, w_5 = (\sqrt{5} - 2)r_1, ...$$
and so on.

The whole sensor field can be depicted as figure1.

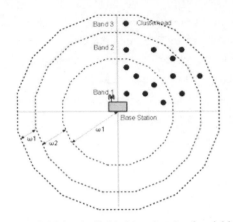

Fig. 1. A sensor field that is divided into bands of variable width

Before the band formation takes place, the BS has prior information about the sensing field size and nodes' capabilities such as radio range, processing ability, initial battery power and energy dissipation due to data transmission in ideal conditions. Consequently the BS decides the number of bands and their widths for a specific WSN application in that particular geographic location with the resources available. At the time of deployment, the threshold value of SNR, ψ, is defined with all the nodes individually so that nodes can communicate with their neighbour nodes with undistorted data.

4.4   Routing Table

Each CH maintains a routing table containing data about neighbour nodes of adjacent band closer to the BS. The routing table contains *node_id*, *cluster_head*, *neighbour_distance($d_{i,j}$)*, BS_distance($d_{j,BS}$), *hop_support(h)*,and *residual_energy(e_j)* as the fields which represent node id, clusterhead indicator, distance with neighbour node, distance with BS, number of nodes from previous band are being hosted, residual energy of a CH of the next downstream band respectively.

In each round of data transmission, the sender, i, uses the cost function mentioned below to determine the best neighbour CH, j, to send the data:

$$C_{i,j} = W_1.d_{i,j} + W_2.d_{j,BS} + W_3.h_j + W_4.e_j$$

Here, W is the weight which is adaptive and dependent on network application. These weights can be changed dynamically by the BS if situation demands. Before relaying the data, the sender CH always executes its cost function and the record of a node that provides the lowest cost from that database is chosen as best candidate. Hence, the next hop of the route is determined. After every z rounds, all CH nodes that form a route chain to BS include their residual energy, load condition (to upgrade *hop_support*) with the data packets so that BS gets information about all the CHs and it can update all the clusterhead nodes by broadcasting the message. The routing algorithm for z rounds is given below;

Algorithm. Routing Decision Making

Require: The updated data in the routing table about the CH of next downstream band and the weight value for W_1, W_2, W_3, W_4

i: The sender node
j: The candidate neighbour node
z: The number of operational round defined by BS
k: The number of record in the table

$d_{i,j}$: The distance between node i and j.

$d_{j,BS}$: The distance between BS and node j.

h_j : The number of hosted CH in the previous round

e_j : The residual energy of the candidate neighbour CH

$C_{i,j}$: The cost for a route

next_hop: NULL
max_cost: 0
for (1 to z)
    if(*next_hop*== NULL)
        for(1 to k) calculate $C_{i,j} = W_1.d_{i,j} + W_2.d_{j,BS} + W_3.h_j + W_4.e_j$;

           if($C_{i,j} \geq max\_cost$) $max\_cost= C_{i,j}$; **end if**
        end for
    end if
        next_hop=i; send(data to node i)
end for
next_hop= NULL; read(received UPDATE message); update(routing table)

For instance, in figure 2, CH1 and CH2 are making decision about the next hops. CH1 can send data to three CHs of the next band which are CH3, CH4, and CH5. But the cost function prefers CH4 as the next hop and it is sending data to CH4. Similarly, CH3 is the best next hop node for CH2 to relay the data.

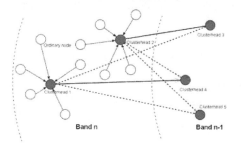

Fig. 2. Routing decision making in the network

5   Simulation Results

The proposed scheme has been tested in a simulator written in C++ and programmed for this proposed scheme. We compared the proposed scheme with another routing scheme called PEGASIS [6] where each CH relays the data to the nearest neighbour. In simulation result reveals that if the number of hop to BS is decreased, significant energy efficiency can be gained.

5.1   Node Placement and Initialization

In the simulation, 100 nodes are considered in an area of 100×75 square units. We use Cartesian coordinates to locate the sensors. These sensor nodes represent the CHs of the actual network field. The BS is located at origin (0, 0). Initially, in our simulation, we assume a simple model according to [5] where the radio dissipates $E_{elec} = 50$nJ/bit to run the transmitter or receiver circuitry and $\varepsilon_{amp} = 100$pJ/bit/m^2.

5.2   Power Consumption Comparison

Total energy consumed to send a data packet of size 32bit has been calculated in this simulation for both the PEGASIS and DEOR. We run the simulation for all 100 nodes individually to send data to BS. The result for one-round data transmission from every node is shown in figure 3.

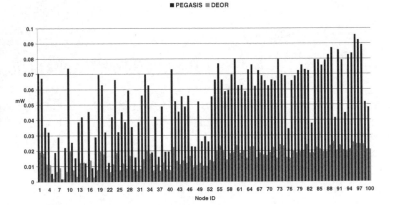
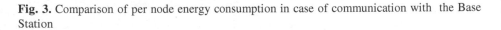

Fig. 3. Comparison of per node energy consumption in case of communication with the Base Station

From the figure 3 it can be inferred that the average energy gain is 30% and in some cases more than 50% gain is achieved.

5.3   Route Selection

In PEGASIS, the next neighbour node is chosen using Greedy Algorithm. In that case, the closest neighbour node of the sender node is chosen every time for that particular chain. But in our proposed routing, the next neighbour node is chosen with the help of a routing table that chooses the best candidate for the next hop based on cost function. The proposed routing scheme reduces the number of hop needed to reach to BS. Selected routes from nodes 1, 75, 89 and 100 for PEGASIS and DEOR are given in figures 4 and 5 respectively.

From figure 4 and 5 it is quite clear that our proposed protocol takes less hops and uses the shortest route to send data to base station. Moreover, our protocol chooses different CH nodes for different routes near the BS that eliminates the hot spot problem.

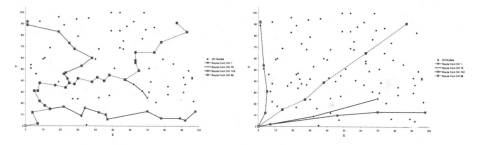

Fig. 4. Example routes selected by PEGASIS   **Fig. 5.** Example routes selected by DEOR

6   Conclusion

In this paper, we proposed a dynamic routing protocol with optimal transmission range for wireless sensor networks that minimizes the number of hops and hence consumes less energy compared to a multihop routing protocol of its kind. This strategy achieves an even distribution of energy consumption based on its dynamic decision for selecting next relay node. Moreover, this technique is aware of the location of the next relay node and also able to prioritize the network demand depending on the application.

This protocol proposes a concentric model of bands, where the centre is base station, in order to classify the energy consumption of different nodes in different areas of the sensor field. Our simulation result shows that network life time is maximized if we adopt DEOR protocol. Our next target is to propose a rotation scheme with nodes in different bands to get a more healthy balance among the nodes.

References

[1] Rappaport, T.S.: Wireless Communications Principles and Practice, 2nd edn. Prentice Hall (2001)
[2] Crossbow. IMOTE2 data sheet (2007a),
     http://www.xbow.com/Products/Product_pdf_files/Wirelesspdf/
     Imote2Datasheet.pdf

[3] Kimura N., Jolly, V., Latifi, S.: Energy restrained data dissemination in WSN. International Journal of Distributed Networks, 251–256 (2006)

[4] Noori, M., Ardakani, M.: Characterizing the Traffic Distribution in Linear Wireless Sensor Networks. IEEE Communications Letters 12(8) (2008)

[5] Heinzelman, W.B., Chandrakasan, A.P., Balakrishnan, H.: An application-specific protocol architecture for wireless microsensor networks. IEEE Transactions on Wireless Communications 1(4), 660–670 (2002)

[6] Lindsay, S., Raghavendra, C.S.: PEGASIS: Power-Efficient Gathering in Sensor Information Systems. In: Proceedings of IEEE Aerospace Conference, Big Sky, MT, vol. 3, pp. 1125–1130 (March 2002)

[7] Younis, O., Fahmy, S.: HEED: A hybrid, Energy-efficient, Distributed clustering approach for Ad-Hoc networks. IEEE Transactions on Mobile Computing 3(4), 366–369 (2004)

[8] Mandala, D., Du, X., Dai, F., You, C.: Load balance and energy efficient data gathering in WSN. Wireless Communication And Mobile Computing 8, 645–659 (2008)

[9] Azim, M.A., Kibria, M.R., Jamalipur, A.: An optimized forwarding protocol for lifetime extension of WSN. Wireless Communications and Mobile Computing 9(1), 103–115 (2008)

[10] Li, J., Mohapatra, P.: An analytical model for the energy hole problem in many-to-one sensor networks. In: Proceedings of IEEE 62nd Vehicular Technology Conference, pp. 2721–2725 (2005)

[11] Lu, Y., Sheu, T.: An efficient routing scheme with optimal power control in wireless multi-hop sensor networks. Computer Communications 30(14-15), 2735–2743 (2007)

[12] Shin, J., Chin, M., Kim, C.: Optimal transmission range for topology management in wireless sensor network. In: Proceedings of International Conference on Information Networking, Germany, pp. 177–185 (2006)

[13] Song, C., Liu, M., Cao, J., Zheng, Y., Gong, H., Chen, G.: Maximizing network lifetime based on transmission range adjustment in wireless sensor networks. Computer Communications 32(11), 1316–1325 (2009)

Generalized Projective Synchronization of Hyperchaotic Lü and Hyperchaotic Cai Systems via Active Control

Sarasu Pakiriswamy[1] and Sundarapandian Vaidyanathan[2]

[1] Dept. of Computer Science and Engineering, Vel Tech Dr. RR & Dr. SR Technical University
Avadi-Alamathi Road, Avadi, Chennai-600 062, India
sarasujivat@gmail.com

[2] Research and Development Centre, Vel Tech Dr. RR & Dr. SR Technical University
Avadi-Alamathi Road, Avadi, Chennai-600 062, India
sundarvtu@gmail.com

Abstract. This paper investigates the problem of designing active feedback controllers for achieving generalized projective synchronization (GPS) of identical hyperchaotic Lü systems (Chen *et al.* 2006) and non-identical hyperchaotic Cai system (Wang and Cai, 2009) and hyperchaotic Lü system. The synchronization results (GPS) derived in this paper have been established using Lyapunov stability theory. Since the Lyapunov exponents are not required for these calculations, the active feedback control method is very effective and convenient for achieving the general projective synchronization (GPS) of hyperchaotic Lü and hyperchaotic Cai systems. Numerical simulations are shown to demonstrate the effectiveness of the synchronization results derived in this paper.

Keywords: Active control, hyperchaos, generalized projective synchronization, hyperchaotic Lü system, hyperchaotic Cai system.

1   Introduction

Chaotic systems are nonlinear dynamical systems, which are highly sensitive to initial conditions. The sensitive nature of chaotic systems is commonly called as the *butterfly effect* [1].

Hyperchaotic system is usually defined as a chaotic system with more than one positive Lyapunov exponent. Since hyperchaotic system has the characteristics of high capacity, high security and high efficiency, it has the potential of broad applications in nonlinear circuits, secure communications, lasers, neural networks, biological systems, and so on. Thus, the studies on hyperchaotic systems, *viz.* control, synchronization and circuit implementation are very challenging works in the chaos literature.

In most of the chaos synchronization approaches, the *master-slave* or *drive-response* formalism is used. If a particular chaotic system is called the *master* or *drive system* and another chaotic system is called the *slave* or *response system*, then the idea of synchronization is to use the output of the master system to control the slave system so that the output of the slave system tracks the output of the master system asymptotically.

The seminal work by Pecora and Carroll ([3], 1990) is followed by a variety of impressive approaches for chaos synchronization such as the sampled-data feedback

N. Meghanathan et al. (Eds.): CCSIT 2012, Part I, LNICST 84, pp. 53–62, 2012.

synchronization method [4], OGY method [5], time-delay feedback method [6], back-stepping method [7], active control method ([8]-[9]), adaptive control method [10], sliding control method [11], etc.

In generalized projective synchronization [12], the chaotic systems can synchronize up to a constant scaling matrix. Complete synchronization [13], anti-synchronization [14], hybrid synchronization [15], projective synchronization [16] and generalized synchronization [17] are special cases of generalized projective synchronization. The generalized projective synchronization (GPS) has applications in secure communications.

This paper deals with the problem of designing active feedback controllers for the generalized projective synchronization (GPS) of identical hyperchaotic Lü systems (Chen *et al.* [18], 2006) and non-identical hyperchaotic Cai system (Wang and Cai, [19], 2009) and hyperchaotic Lü system (2006).

This paper is organized as follows. In Section 2, we provide a description of the hyperchaotic systems studied in this paper. In Section 3, we derive results for the GPS between identical hyperchaotic Lü systems (2006). In Section 4, we derive results for the GPS between non-identical hyperchaotic Cai system (2009) and hyperchaotic Lü system (2006). In Section 5, we summarize the main results obtained in this paper.

2   Systems Description

The hyperchaotic Lü system ([18], 2006) is described by the dynamics

$$
\begin{aligned}
\dot{x}_1 &= a(x_2 - x_1) + x_4 \\
\dot{x}_2 &= -x_1 x_3 + c x_2 \\
\dot{x}_3 &= x_1 x_2 - b x_3 \\
\dot{x}_4 &= x_1 x_3 + d x_4
\end{aligned}
\tag{1}
$$

where x_1, x_2, x_3, x_4 are the *state* variables and a, b, c, d are constant, positive parameters of the system.

The system (1) is hyperchaotic when the system parameter values are chosen as $a = 36$, $b = 3$, $c = 20$ and $d = 1.3$.

Figure 1 depicts the state orbits of the hyperchaotic Lü system (1).

The hyperchaotic Cai system ([19], 2009) is described by the dynamics

$$
\begin{aligned}
\dot{x}_1 &= p(x_2 - x_1) \\
\dot{x}_2 &= q x_1 + r x_2 - x_1 x_3 + x_4 \\
\dot{x}_3 &= x_2^2 - s x_3 \\
\dot{x}_4 &= -\epsilon x_1
\end{aligned}
\tag{2}
$$

where x_1, x_2, x_3, x_4 are the *state* variables and p, q, r, s, ϵ are constant, positive parameters of the system.

The system (2) is hyperchaotic when the system parameter values are chosen as $p = 27.5$, $q = 3$, $r = 19.3$, $s = 2.9$ and $\epsilon = 3.3$.

Figure 2 depicts the state orbits of the hyperchaotic Cai system (2).

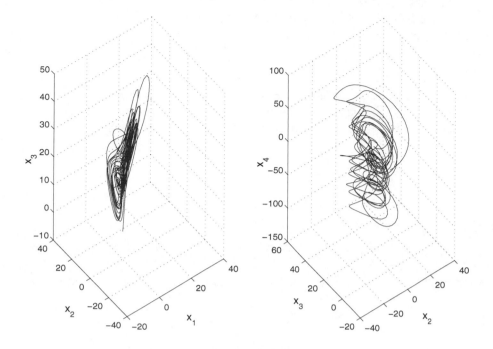

Fig. 1. State Orbits of the hyperchaotic Lü System

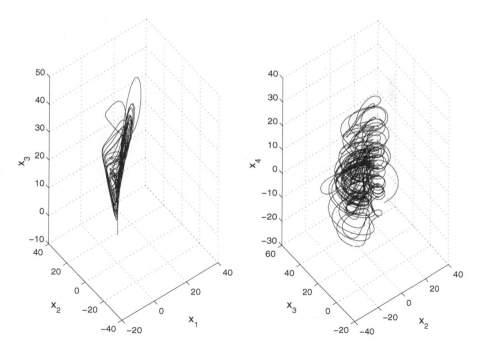

Fig. 2. State Orbits of the hyperchaotic Cai System

3 Generalized Projective Synchronization of Identical Hyperchaotic Lü Systems

3.1 Main Results

In this section, we discuss the design of active controller for achieving generalized projective synchronization (GPS) of identical hyperchaotic Lü systems ([18], 2006).

Thus, the master system is described by the hyperchaotic Lü dynamics

$$
\begin{aligned}
\dot{x}_1 &= a(x_2 - x_1) + x_4 \\
\dot{x}_2 &= -x_1 x_3 + c x_2 \\
\dot{x}_3 &= x_1 x_2 - b x_3 \\
\dot{x}_4 &= x_1 x_3 + d x_4
\end{aligned}
\tag{3}
$$

where x_1, x_2, x_3, x_4 are the *state* variables and a, b, c, d are constant, positive parameters of the system.

Also, the slave system is described by the controlled hyperchaotic Lü dynamics

$$
\begin{aligned}
\dot{y}_1 &= a(y_2 - y_1) + y_4 + u_1 \\
\dot{y}_2 &= -y_1 y_3 + c y_2 + u_2 \\
\dot{y}_3 &= y_1 y_2 - b y_3 + u_3 \\
\dot{y}_4 &= y_1 y_3 + d y_4 + u_4
\end{aligned}
\tag{4}
$$

where y_1, y_2, y_3, y_4 are the *state* variables and u_1, u_2, u_3, u_4 are the active controls.

For the GPS of (3) and (4), the synchronization errors are defined as

$$
e_i = y_i - \alpha_i x_i, \quad (i = 1, 2, 3, 4)
\tag{5}
$$

where the scales $\alpha_1, \alpha_2, \alpha_3, \alpha_4$ are real numbers.

A simple calculation yields the error dynamics

$$
\begin{aligned}
\dot{e}_1 &= a(y_2 - y_1) + y_4 - \alpha_1 [a(x_2 - x_1) + x_4] + u_1 \\
\dot{e}_2 &= -y_1 y_3 + c y_2 - \alpha_2 [-x_1 x_3 + c x_2] + u_2 \\
\dot{e}_3 &= y_1 y_2 - b y_3 - \alpha_3 [x_1 x_2 - b x_3] + u_3 \\
\dot{e}_4 &= y_1 y_3 + d y_4 - \alpha_4 [x_1 x_3 + d x_4] + u_4
\end{aligned}
\tag{6}
$$

We consider the active nonlinear controller defined by

$$
\begin{aligned}
u_1 &= -a(y_2 - y_1) - y_4 + \alpha_1 [a(x_2 - x_1) + x_4] - k_1 e_1 \\
u_2 &= y_1 y_3 - c y_2 + \alpha_2 [-x_1 x_3 + c x_2] - k_2 e_2 \\
u_3 &= -y_1 y_2 + b y_3 + \alpha_3 [x_1 x_2 - b x_3] - k_3 e_3 \\
u_4 &= -y_1 y_3 - d y_4 + \alpha_4 [x_1 x_3 + d x_4] - k_4 e_4
\end{aligned}
\tag{7}
$$

where the gains k_1, k_2, k_3, k_4 are positive constants.

Substitution of (7) into (6) yields the closed-loop error dynamics

$$\begin{aligned}
\dot{e}_1 &= -k_1 e_1 \\
\dot{e}_2 &= -k_2 e_2 \\
\dot{e}_3 &= -k_3 e_3 \\
\dot{e}_4 &= -k_4 e_4
\end{aligned} \tag{8}$$

We consider the quadratic Lyapunov function defined by

$$V(e) = \frac{1}{2} e^T e = \frac{1}{2} \left(e_1^2 + e_2^2 + e_3^2 + e_4^2 \right) \tag{9}$$

which is positive definite on $\mathbb{R}^4$.

Differentiating (9) along the trajectories of the system (8), we get

$$\dot{V}(e) = -k_1 e_1^2 - k_2 e_2^2 - k_3 e_3^2 - k_4 e_4^2 \tag{10}$$

which is a negative definite function on $\mathbb{R}^4$, since k_1, k_2, k_3, k_4 are positive constants.

Thus, by Lyapunov stability theory [20], the error dynamics (8) is globally exponentially stable. Hence, we obtain the following result.

Theorem 1. *The active feedback controller (7) achieves global chaos generalized projective synchronization (GPS) between the identical hyperchaotic Lü systems (3) and (4).* ∎

3.2 Numerical Results

For the numerical simulations, the fourth order Runge-Kutta method is used to solve the two systems of differential equations (3) and (4) with the active controller (7).

The parameters of the identical hyperchaotic Lü systems are chosen as

$$a = 36, \quad b = 3, \quad c = 20, \quad d = 1.3$$

The initial values for the master system (3) are taken as

$$x_1(0) = 24, \quad x_2(0) = 8, \quad x_3(0) = 10, \quad x_4(0) = 12$$

The initial values for the slave system (4) are taken as

$$y_1(0) = 15, \quad y_2(0) = 12, \quad y_3(0) = 4, \quad y_4(0) = 20$$

The GPS scales α_i are taken as

$$\alpha_1 = 4.58, \quad \alpha_2 = 3.49, \quad \alpha_3 = -7.21, \quad \alpha_4 = -5.34$$

We take the state feedback gains as $k_1 = 4$, $k_2 = 4$, $k_3 = 4$ and $k_4 = 4$.

Figure 3 shows the time response of the error states e_1, e_2, e_3, e_4 of the error dynamical system (6) when the active nonlinear controller (7) is deployed. From this figure, it is clear that all the error states decay to zero exponentially in 1.5 sec and thus, generalized projective synchronization is achieved between the identical hyperchaotic Lü systems (3) and (4).

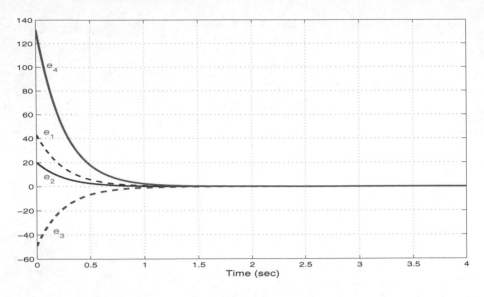

Fig. 3. Time Responses of the Error States of (6)

4 Generalized Projective Synchronization of Non-identical Hyperchaotic Lü and Hyperchaotic Cai Systems

4.1 Main Results

In this section, we derive results for the generalized projective synchronization (GPS) of non-identical hyperchaotic systems, *viz.* hyperchaotic Cai system ([19], 2009) and hyperchaotic Lü system ([18], 2006).

Thus, the master system is described by the hyperchaotic Cai dynamics

$$
\begin{aligned}
\dot{x}_1 &= p(x_2 - x_1) \\
\dot{x}_2 &= qx_1 + rx_2 - x_1x_3 + x_4 \\
\dot{x}_3 &= x_2^2 - sx_3 \\
\dot{x}_4 &= -\epsilon x_1
\end{aligned}
\tag{11}
$$

where x_1, x_2, x_3, x_4 are the *state* variables and p, q, r, s, ϵ are constant, positive parameters of the system.

Also, the slave system is described by the controlled hyperchaotic Lü dynamics

$$
\begin{aligned}
\dot{y}_1 &= a(y_2 - y_1) + y_4 + u_1 \\
\dot{y}_2 &= -y_1y_3 + cy_2 + u_2 \\
\dot{y}_3 &= y_1y_2 - by_3 + u_3 \\
\dot{y}_4 &= y_1y_3 + dy_4 + u_4
\end{aligned}
\tag{12}
$$

where y_1, y_2, y_3, y_4 are the *state* variables, a, b, c, d are constant, positive parameters of the system and u_1, u_2, u_3, u_4 are the active controls.

For the GPS of (11) and (12), the synchronization errors are defined as

$$e_i = y_i - \alpha_i x_i, \quad (i = 1, 2, 3, 4) \tag{13}$$

where the scales $\alpha_1, \alpha_2, \alpha_3, \alpha_4$ are real numbers.

A simple calculation yields the error dynamics

$$
\begin{aligned}
\dot{e}_1 &= a(y_2 - y_1) + y_4 - \alpha_1 \left[p(x_2 - x_1) \right] + u_1 \\
\dot{e}_2 &= -y_1 y_3 + c y_2 - \alpha_2 \left[q x_1 + r x_2 - x_1 x_3 + x_4 \right] + u_2 \\
\dot{e}_3 &= y_1 y_2 - b y_3 - \alpha_3 \left[x_2^2 - s x_3 \right] + u_3 \\
\dot{e}_4 &= -f y_2 - \alpha_4 \left[-\epsilon x_1 \right] + u_4
\end{aligned}
\tag{14}
$$

We consider the active nonlinear controller defined by

$$
\begin{aligned}
u_1 &= -a(y_2 - y_1) - y_4 + \alpha_1 \left[p(x_2 - x_1) \right] - k_1 e_1 \\
u_2 &= y_1 y_3 - c y_2 + \alpha_2 \left[q x_1 + r x_2 - x_1 x_3 + x_4 \right] - k_2 e_2 \\
u_3 &= -y_1 y_2 + b y_3 + \alpha_3 \left[x_2^2 - s x_3 \right] - k_3 e_3 \\
u_4 &= f y_2 + \alpha_4 \left[-\epsilon x_1 \right] - k_4 e_4
\end{aligned}
\tag{15}
$$

where the gains k_1, k_2, k_3, k_4 are positive constants.

Substitution of (15) into (14) yields the closed-loop error dynamics

$$
\begin{aligned}
\dot{e}_1 &= -k_1 e_1 \\
\dot{e}_2 &= -k_2 e_2 \\
\dot{e}_3 &= -k_3 e_3 \\
\dot{e}_4 &= -k_4 e_4
\end{aligned}
\tag{16}
$$

We consider the quadratic Lyapunov function defined by

$$V(e) = \frac{1}{2} e^T e = \frac{1}{2} \left(e_1^2 + e_2^2 + e_3^2 + e_4^2 \right) \tag{17}$$

which is positive definite on $\mathbb{R}^4$.

Differentiating (17) along the trajectories of the system (16), we get

$$\dot{V}(e) = -k_1 e_1^2 - k_2 e_2^2 - k_3 e_3^2 - k_4 e_4^2 \tag{18}$$

which is a negative definite function on $\mathbb{R}^4$, since k_1, k_2, k_3, k_4 are positive constants.

Thus, by Lyapunov stability theory [20], the error dynamics (16) is globally exponentially stable. Hence, we obtain the following result.

Theorem 2. *The active feedback controller (15) achieves global chaos generalized projective synchronization (GPS) between the non-identical hyperchaotic Cai system (11) and the hyperchaotic Lü system (12).* ∎

4.2 Numerical Results

For the numerical simulations, the fourth order Runge-Kutta method is used to solve
the two systems of differential equations (11) and (12) with the active controller (15).
  The parameters of the hyperchaotic Cai system (11) are taken as

$$p = 27.5, \quad q = 3, \quad r = 19.3, \quad s = 2.9, \quad \epsilon = 3.3$$

The parameters of the hyperchaotic Lü system (12) are taken as

$$a = 36, \quad b = 3, \quad c = 20, \quad d = 1.3$$

The initial values for the master system (11) are taken as

$$x_1(0) = 11, \; x_2(0) = 24, \; x_3(0) = 18, \; x_4(0) = 15$$

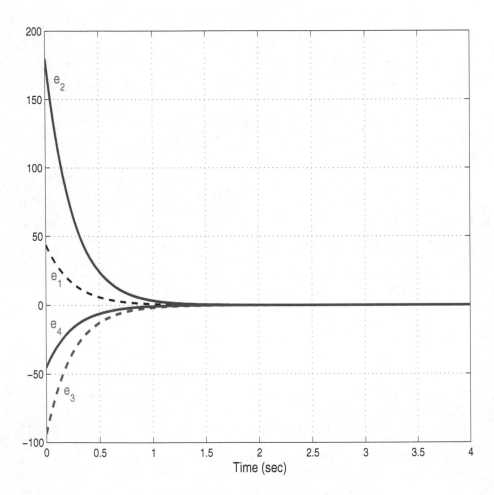

Fig. 4. Time Responses of the Error States of (14)

The initial values for the slave system (12) are taken as

$$y_1(0) = 20, \ y_2(0) = 16, \ y_3(0) = 5, \ y_4(0) = 7$$

The GPS scales α_i are taken as

$$\alpha_1 = -2.15, \quad \alpha_2 = -6.83, \quad \alpha_3 = 5.49, \quad \alpha_4 = 3.48$$

We take the state feedback gains as $k_1 = 4$, $k_2 = 4$, $k_3 = 4$ and $k_4 = 4$.

Figure 4 shows the time response of the error states e_1, e_2, e_3, e_4 of the error dynamical system (14) when the active nonlinear controller (15) is deployed.

From this figure, it is clear that all the error states decay to zero exponentially in 1.7 sec and thus, generalized projective synchronization is achieved between the non-identical hyperchaotic Cai system (11) and hyperchaotic Lü system (12).

5 Conclusions

In this paper, we derived active control laws for achieving generalized projective synchronization (GPS) of the following hyperchaotic systems:

(A) Identical hyperchaotic Lü systems (2006)
(B) Non-identical hyperchaotic Cai system (2009) and hyperchaotic Lü system.

The synchronization results (GPS) derived in this paper for the hyperchaotic Lü and hyperchaotic Cai systems [(A) and (B)] have been proved using Lyapunov stability theory. Since Lyapunov exponents are not required for these calculations, the proposed active control method is very effective and suitable for achieving GPS of the hyperchaotic systems addressed in this paper. Numerical simulations are shown to demonstrate the effectiveness of the synchronization results (GPS) derived in this paper.

References

1. Alligood, K.T., Sauer, T., Yorke, J.A.: An Introduction to Dynamical Systems. Springer, New York (1997)
2. Liao, T.L., Tsai, S.H.: Adaptive synchronization of chaotic systems and its application to secure communications. Chaos, Solitons and Fractals 11, 1387–1396 (2000)
3. Pecora, L.M., Carroll, T.L.: Synchronization in chaotic systems. Phys. Rev. Lett. 64, 821–824 (1990)
4. Yang, T., Chua, L.O.: Control of chaos using sampled-data feedback control. Internat. J. Bifurcat. Chaos 9, 215–219 (1999)
5. Ott, E., Grebogi, C., Yorke, J.A.: Controlling chaos. Phys. Rev. Lett. 64, 1196–1199 (1990)
6. Park, J.H., Kwon, O.M.: A novel criterion for delayed feedback control of time-delay chaotic systems. Chaos, Solit. Fract. 17, 709–716 (2003)
7. Yu, Y.G., Zhang, S.C.: Adaptive backstepping synchronization of uncertain chaotic systems. Chaos, Solit. Fract. 27, 1369–1375 (2006)
8. Ho, M.C., Hung, Y.C.: Synchronization of two different chaotic systems using generalized active control. Physics Letters A 301, 424–428 (2002)

9. Sundarapandian, V.: Global chaos synchronization of Liu-Su-Liu and Li chaotic systems by active nonlinear control. CIIT International Journal of Digital Signal Processing 3(4), 171–175 (2011)
10. Chen, S.H., Lü, J.: Synchronization of an uncertain unified system via adaptive control. Chaos, Solitons and Fractals 14, 643–647 (2002)
11. Konishi, K., Hirai, M., Kokame, H.: Sliding mode control for a class of chaotic systems. Phys. Lett. A. 245, 511–517 (1998)
12. Zhou, P., Kuang, F., Cheng, Y.M.: Generalized projective synchronization for fractional order chaotic systems. Chinese Journal of Physics 48(1), 49–56 (2010)
13. Sundarapandian, V.: Global chaos synchronization of Shimizu-Morioka and Liu-Chen chaotic systems by active nonlinear control. Internat. J. Advances in Science and Technology 2(4), 11–20 (2011)
14. Sundarapandian, V.: Anti-synchronization of Lorenz and T chaotic systems by active nonlinear control. Internat. J. Computer Information Systems 2(4), 6–10 (2011)
15. Sundarapandian, V.: Hybrid synchronization of hyperchaotic Rössler and hyperchaotic Lorenz systems by active control. Internat. J. Advances in Science and Technology 2(4), 1–10 (2011)
16. Mainieri, R., Rehacek, J.: Projective synchronization in three-dimensioned chaotic systems. Phys. Rev. Lett. 82, 3042–3045 (1999)
17. Wang, Y.W., Guan, Z.H.: Generalized synchronization of continuous chaotic systems. Chaos, Solit. Fract. 27, 97–101 (2006)
18. Chen, A., Lu, J., Lü, J., Yu, S.: Generating hyperchaotic Lü attractor via state feedback control. Physica A 364, 103–110 (2006)
19. Wang, H., Cai, G.: Controlling hyperchaos in a novel hyperchaotic system. J. Information & Computing Science 4(4), 251–258 (2009)
20. Hahn, W.: The Stability of Motion. Springer, New York (1967)

Energy Efficient Stable Connected Dominating Set Construction in Mobile Ad Hoc Networks

R. Ramalakshmi and S. Radhakrishnan

Department of Computer Science Engineering, Kalasalingam University, India
{rama,srk}@klu.ac.in

Abstract. One of the important issues in ad hoc wireless network is to construct virtual backbone for efficient broadcasting. A Multi Point Relay (MPR) is a set of 1-hop neighbours to cover all 2-hop neighbours of a node. It is a promising approach for broadcasting in ad hoc networks. A Connected Dominating Set (CDS) based virtual backbone has been used where only the nodes in the set relay messages. A node in the CDS consumes more energy and the energy depletes quickly than other nodes. Although previous CDS construction algorithms achieve good results in terms of the size of the CDS, a minimum size CDS does not necessarily guarantee the optimal network performance from an energy efficient point of view. In this paper, we propose a distributed algorithm for energy efficient stable MPR based CDS construction to extend the lifetime of ad hoc wireless networks by considering energy and velocity of nodes. The simulation results show that our algorithm can save a significant amount of energy and increases the lifetime up to 25% than previous works.

Keywords: Connected Dominating Set, Multi Point Relay, Ad Hoc Networks, Energy Efficient.

1 Introduction

Wireless ad hoc networks are self configuring network and they can be deployed for many applications such as automated battlefield, search and rescue and disaster relief. Mobile ad hoc network (MANET) consists of wireless nodes that communicate with each other without any infrastructure. A communication session is achieved either through a single hop radio transmission if he communication parties are within the transmission range, or through relaying by intermediate nodes otherwise. Two important features of an ad hoc network are its dynamic topology and resource limitation. Every node in mobile ad hoc networks can move in any direction at any time and any speed. A temporary infrastructure or a virtual backbone can be formed to provide communication. This virtual backbone may be broken due to the node movement. The resource constraints include battery capacity, bandwidth, and CPU speed, etc. These two features make routing decision very challenging.

A network can be modeled as a Unit Disk Graphs (UDG) where two nodes are connected if they are within each other's transmission range. To support various network functions some wireless nodes are selected to form a virtual backbone. It is

N. Meghanathan et al. (Eds.): CCSIT 2012, Part I, LNICST 84, pp. 63–72, 2012.
© Institute for Computer Sciences, Social Informatics and Telecommunications Engineering 2012

proved that multipoint relaying (MPR) is an efficient stated for on-the-fly broadcasting in Mobile Ad Hoc Networks. The relaying nodes which are selected by the source node are responsible for flooding a receiving packet. A connected dominating set (CDS) consists of all the relay nodes. There are many algorithms based on MPR to reduce the size of the CDS [1, 2, 11, 12, 13, 14], where nodes are chosen based on its ID or degree. The CDS selection has to consider other information such as energy, bandwidth and mobility in order to provide suitable links for some specific applications. In this paper, we propose an approach to generate quality connected dominating set based on MPR by considering the energy and link velocity factors. None of the existing works considered the energy of nodes and their mobility together for the CDS construction.

1.1   Problem Definitions

The connected dominating set or virtual backbone is proposed to facilitate routing, broadcasting and establishing a dynamic infrastructure. Minimizing the CDS produces a simpler abstracted topology of the MANET and allows for using shorter routes between any pair of hosts. A wireless network is usually modeled as a unit disk graph $G = (V, E)$ where V is the set of nodes and E is the set of links in the network. Each node has uniform transmission range R. Each node in V is associated with coordination in 2-D Euclidean space. A wireless link $(u,v) \in E$ if and only if the Euclidean distance between nodes u and v is smaller than transmission range R.

Connected Dominating Set

Let the closed neighbors of a node x is N[x]. A subset $S \subseteq V$ is called a dominating set (DS) of G if $S \cup N[v] = V$ where $N[v] = S_{u \in s} N[u]$. The subset S is called Connected Dominating Set if the graph G', induced by S is connected i.e, G'[S] is connected.

Multipoint Relay

For a given a graph $G=(V,E)$ and a node $v \in V$, let $N(v)$ and $N_2(v)$ represent the set of 1-hop and 2-hop neighbors of v, respectively. MPR asks for a minimum sized subset S of $N(v)$ such that every node in $N_2(v)$ is within the coverage of at least one node in S.

The rest of the paper is organized as follows: Section 2 describes the works related to CDS construction; Section 3 describes the energy efficient stable connected dominating set construction algorithm. We describe our simulation environment and the performance metrics in Section 4. Section 5 concludes the paper.

2   Related Works

There are many work on MPR based CDS construction for efficient broadcasting in Manet. Adjih et al [12] proposed a source independent MPR called the MPR-CDS. The algorithm starts by having every node v calculate its source dependent MPR. After that every node v decides whether it belongs to the MPR-CDS or not according to the following simple rules:

- Rule 1: Node u ∈ MPR-CDS iff v has the smallest ID in tis 1-hop neighborhood.
- Rule 2: Node v ∈ MPR-CDS iff v ∈ w's MPR where w's ID is the smallest in v's 1-hop neighborhood.

In [1] Wu, has noticed that in many occasions nodes added by rule-1 of MPR-CDS algorithms are useless. Moreover the algorithm used to calculate the source dependent MPR does not benefit from Rule-2 of the MPR-CDS algorithm. In [1] Wu modified Rule 1 as follows:

- **EMPR:** node v ∈ MPR-CDS iff v has the smallest ID in its 1-hop neighborhood and v has at least two unconnected neighbors.

Moreover, Wu modified the MPR calculation algorithm in [12] by having every node v start by adding all its free neighbors to its MPR set. A node u is a free neighbor of node v iff $u \in N(v)$ and v is not the smallest ID neighbor of u.

Chen et al [11] observed that the node degree is more related to the size of a CDS than the node ID and three improvements are proposed. They replaced the EMPR rule with two rules based on degree called DEMPR.

- Rule 1: node v ∈ MPR-CDS if v has the largest node degree among all its one-hop neighbors and v has two unconnected neighbors.
- Rule 2: node v ∈ MPR-CDS if v has been selected as an MPR and its selector has the largest node degree among its one-hop neighbors.

Badis et al [13], proposed heuristic referred to as the QoS based MPR-1(QMPR-1) follows the same steps as the original MPR heuristic but it modifies the tie breaking procedure. Instead of a maximum node degree, a node with high bandwidth is chosen when multiple choices exist.

There are few works on energy efficient CDS construction. In [6] Kim extended the Mac-layer timer based connected dominating set protocol by considering energy level at each node to construct energy aware CDS. In [7] Ruiyun Yu proposed an energy efficient dominating tree construction (EEDTC) algorithm with two phases, marking phases followed by connection phase. In the marking phase, a Maximal Independent Set (MIS) is constructed and connectors are added to make it as CDS. In [14], Wu proposed a method to calculate power aware connected dominating set. They used degree and residual energy level of nodes to reduce the CDS size to prolong the lifespan of the nodes in the CDS.

Only few works are done in stable connected dominating set construction. In [15], Change proposed Dynamic Power-aware and Stability-aware Multipoint relays which avoid selecting the border nodes as the forwarding nodes. They used power adaptive broadcasting by reducing the transmission range of mobile nodes to save energy. In [4], Meganathan proposed an algorithm to determine stable connected dominating set based on node velocities. His algorithm prefers slow moving nodes with lower velocity rather than the usual approach of preferring nodes with a larger number of uncovered neighbours. They compared their method with another work which is based on node degree.

Although previous CDS construction algorithms achieve good results in terms of the size of the CDS, a minimum size CDS does not necessarily guarantee the optimal network performance from an energy efficient point of view. This motivated us to construct an energy efficient stable connected dominating set prolong the network lifetime.

3   Energy Efficient Stable Connected Dominating Set Construction Algorithm (EES-CDS)

3.1   Notations and Assumptions

We assume that every node in the network has same transmission range R. Two nodes are connected if the Euclidean distance between the nodes is less than R. We used the notations for our algorithm as in Table 1.

Table 1. Notations

$N(u)$	Open neighbour set of node u
$N[u]$	Closed neighbour set of node u $N[u] = N(u) \cup \{u\}$
$N_2(u)$	2-hop neighbour set of node u
Erg_x	remaining residual energy at node x
Vel_x	Velocity of node x
$MPR(u)$	MPR set of node u
Deg_u	No of uncovered 2-hop neighbours of u

3.2   EES-CDS Algorithm

Our algorithm for energy efficient stable connected dominating set construction (EES-CDS) consists of two phases: Neighbour Discovery Phase and CDS Formation Phase. During the Neighbour Discovery Phase, there is an initial exchange of messages via which a node u, made aware of its $N_2(u)$. In the CDS Formation Phase, a node u locally selects a set MPR(u) of its $N(u)$ as its multipoint relays by using simple greedy algorithm and pruning rules are applied to reduced the connected dominating set size. In [1], Wu proposed a simple decentralized algorithm for the formation of connected dominating set in ad hoc networks. This algorithm is based on marking process. In [14], Dai proposed two rules for power aware CDS construction using node degree and residual energy level of nodes.

In this work, we have modified the rules proposed by [14] with energy level and velocity to prolong the stability and to reduce the size of a connected dominating set generated from the marking process. Let the graph induced by CDS be G'.

Rule 1: Consider two marked vertices v and u in G'. The marker of v is changed to gray if one of the following conditions holds:

i) $N[v] \subseteq N[u]$ in G and $Erg_v < Erg_u$

ii) $N[v] \subseteq N[u]$ in G and $Vel_v > Vel_u$ when $Erg_v = Erg_u$

iii) $N[v] \subseteq N[u]$ in G and $Deg_v < Deg_u$ when $Erg_v = Erg_u$ and $Vel_v = Vel_u$

The above rule indicate that when the closed neighbour set of v is covered by that of u, vertex v can be removed from G' if the energy level of v is smaller than u. Velocity is used to break a tie when energy levels of u and v are same. Degree is used to break the tie if both energy levels and velocity of u and v are same. Node ID can be used to break the tie, in case all the values are same.

Rule 2: Assume that u and w are two marked neighbours of marked vertex v in G'. The marker of v can be changed to Gray if one of the following conditions holds:

1. $N(v) \subseteq N(u) \cup N(w)$, but $N(u) \not\subseteq N(v) \cup N(w)$ and $N(w) \not\subseteq N(u) \cup N(v)$ in G

2. $N(v) \subseteq N(u) \cup N(w)$ and $N(u) \subseteq N(v) \cup N(w)$, but $N(w) \not\subseteq N(u) \cup N(v)$ in G and one of the following conditions holds:

    a. $Erg_v < Erg_u$ or
    b. $Erg_v = Erg_u$ and $Vel_v > Vel_u$ or
    c. $Erg_v = Erg_u$ and $Vel_v = Vel_u$ and $Deg_v < Deg_u$

3. $N(v) \subseteq N(u) \cup N(w)$ and $N(u) \subseteq N(v) \cup N(w)$, but $N(w) \subseteq N(u) \cup N(v)$ in G and one of the following conditions holds:

    a. $Erg_v < Erg_u$ and $Erg_v < Erg_w$ or
    b. $Erg_v = Erg_u < Erg_w$ and $Vel_v > Vel_u$ or $Deg_v < Deg_u$ when $Vel_v = Vel_u$
    c. $Erg_v = Erg_u = Erg_w$ then

        i. $Vel_v > Vel_u$ and $Vel_v > Vel_w$ or
        ii. $Vel_v = Vel_u > Vel_w$ and $Deg_v < deg_u$ or
        iii. $Vel_v = Vel_u = Vel_w$ and $Deg_v = min\{Deg_v, Deg_u, Deg_v\}$

The above rule indicates that when v is covered by u and w; the conditions are

1) if neither u or w is covered by the other two among u, v and w then v is unmarked.

2) if neighbour set of v is covered by u, w and neighbour set of u is covered by v, w but neighbours of w are not covered by u, v then v is unmarked if the energy level of v is smaller than u. Velocity is used to break the tie if energy levels are same. Degree is used to break the tie if both energy and velocity values are same.

3) If neighbour set of v, u and w are covered by the other two among u, v and w then node v is unmarked with conditions: energy level of v is less than v and w; the energy level of v is same as u but smaller than w, velocity value is used for unmarking. If velocity values are same then degree of v is used to break the tie.

The procedure for the energy efficient CDS construction algorithm is given in Table 2.

Table 2. Algorithm for Energy Efficient Stable CDS Construction

Algorithm: EES-CDS
>   Input: An undirected graph G(V, E)
>   Output: EES-CDS

- **Neighbour Discovery phase**
  Nodes periodically exchange *hello* messages for neighbour discovery. Every node sends and receives *hello* messages but does not forward them. A *hello* message generated by a node u contains its ID, Energy (Erg$_u$), Velocity (Vel$_u$) and list of neighbours N(u). This one hop neighbourhood exchange enables every node *u* to obtain its two hop neighbourhood information.
- **CDS Formation Phase**
  1. MPR Selection
     > i.   Initially all nodes are in White colour
     > ii.   Every node *v* assigns its N(*v*) to MPR(*v*) if it has two unconnected neighbours.
     > iii. Marks all the nodes in MPR(*v*) to Black Colour
     > iv.   Marks all the neighbours of MPR(*v*) to Gray Colour
  2. Apply Proposed Rule 1 and Rule 2 to construct minimum size CDS.

It is clear that node *u* only has to wait for the information about its two hop neighbours. The set of all MPR is a connected dominating set of the entire network. The node terminates the construction phase by communicating its final decision to all its neighbours Figure.

4   Simulation Results and Analysis

4.1   Simulation Environment

In this section, the simulation results are reported and analyzed. We implemented our algorithm EES-CDS in ns-2.34. To evaluate the performance of our algorithm, we also implemented the approach proposed by Wu in [1] and Meganathan in [4]. To generate a network, *n* nodes are randomly placed in a 1000m x 1000m region. Each node has uniform transmission range 250m and is associated with an initial energy values from 1J to 15J. In our simulations, the number of nodes *n* has been assigned the values 50, 100, 150, 200, 250. This allows us to test our algorithm from sparse to dense networks. Any two nodes distance less than the transmission range are considered neighbours. Each node moves randomly in this area with a speed in the range [0..V$_{max}$] and a pause time of 10s. The values of V$_{max}$ are 5, 10 and 25m/s. Each simulation is conducted for 600s and it is repeated 10 times. The parameters used in our simulation are listed in Table 3.

Table 3. Simulation Parameters

Network Area	1000m
Number of Nodes	50..250
Transmission Range	250m
Mobility Speed	5m/s, 10m/s, 25m/s
Initial Energy	1J..15J.
Energy for transmission	1.4W
Energy for Receiving	1.0W
Idle energy	0.013W
Pause time	10s
Simulation Time	600s
Propagation Model	Two-ray Ground
MAC	IEEE 802.11
Antenna	Omni Antenna
Mobility Model	Random Way Point

We implemented this algorithm by using three messages: The first message is for exchanging the list of neighbours, the second is used by a node u to communicate to a neighbour v for which u is the MPR selector and the final one is used by a node to make every neighbour aware of its final decision.

4.2   Result Analysis

We measured the performance of our work in terms of

- Average CDS Size
  It describes the no of nodes included in the CDS to act as broadcast relay nodes. Figure 1 (a-c) shows the average no of nodes included in the CDS with different mobility values 5m/s, 15m./s and 25m/s. The results show that CDS generated by our algorithm is larger than Wu[1] and less than Meganathan [4]. In [1], Wu used node degree for selection and Meganathan in [4] selected nodes with only lower velocity. The average size of the CDS increases with network density.

- CDS Stability
  The simulation stops when the energy level of at least one node becomes 0. Figure 2 (d-f) shows the comparison of our work with Wu [1] and Meganathan [4] in terms of lifetime. Our work outperforms well than the other two works because nodes in the CDS generated by our algorithm has high energy level and minimum velocity. The CDS stability is high when the node velocity is low. In [4], priority is given to slow moving nodes but they don't consider the energy level of the nodes.

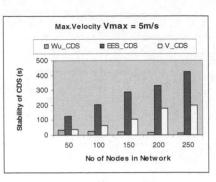

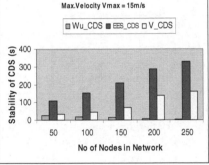

Fig (a)   Fig (d)

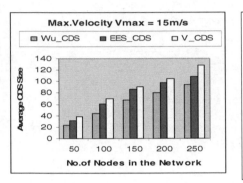

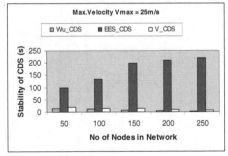

Fig (b)   Fig (e)

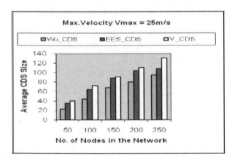

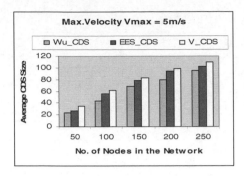

Fig (c)   Fig (f)

Fig. 1. (a-c) Average CDS Size with Velocity V_{max}= 5, 15, 25m/s

Fig. 2. (d-f) Stability of CDS with Velocity V_{max}= 5, 15, 25m/s

5   Conclusion and Future Work

In this paper, an algorithm for power efficient stable connected dominiating set construction is proposed. We have proposed two rules to reduce size of the connected dominating and to prolong the life span of the nodes. Our algorithm is based on resiudual energy level, velocity and degree to construct the connected dominating set so that the life of the backbone can be stable. The results from the siumation show that our work outperforms in terms of stablity and it increases the lifetime by 25% to 30%. We plan to perform energy efficient broadcasting through the generated CDS as our future work.

Acknowledgement. The authors would like to thank the Project Coordinator and Project Directos of TIFAC-CORE in Network Engineering, Kalasalingam University for providing the infrastructure facilities in Open Source Techhnolgy Laboratory and also thank Kalasalingam Anadam Ammal Charities for providing financial support for this work.

References

[1] Wu, J., Lou, W.: Extended Mutlipoint Relays to Determine Connected Dominating Sets in MANETs. IEEE Transaction on Compuers 55, 334–347 (2006)

[2] Wu, J.: An Enhanced Approach to Determine a Small Forward Node Set Based on Multipoint Relay. In: Proc. IEEE Semi-Ann. Vehicular Tech. Conf. (2003)

[3] Meganathan, N., Farago, A.: On the Stability of Paths, Steiner Trees and Connected Dominating Sets in Mobile Ad Hoc Networks. Ad hoc Netoworks 6, 744–769 (2008)

[4] Maganathan, N.: Use of Minimum Node Velocity Based Stable Connected Dominating Sets for Mobile Ad hoc Networks. IJCA special issues on "Mobile" Ad-Hoc Networks, 89–96 (2010)

[5] Dai, F., Wu, J.: An Extended Localized algorithms for Connected Dominating Set Formation in Ad Hoc Wireless Networks. IEEE Trans. Parallel and Distributed Systems 15 (2004)

[6] Kim, B., et al.: Energy-Aware Connected Dominating Set Construction in Mobile Ad Hoc Networks. Auburn University Technical Report, CSSE05-07 (2005)

[7] Yu, R., Wang, X., Das, S.K.: EEDTC: Energy-Efficient Dominating tree Construction in Multi-hop Wireless Networks. Pervasive and Mobile Computing 5, 318–333 (2009)

[8] Funke, S., Kesselman, A., Meyer, U., Segal, M.: A simple improved distributed algorithm for minimum Connected dominating set in unit disk graphs. ACM Transactions on Sensor Networks 2, 444–453 (2006)

[9] Wan, P., Alzoubi, K K.M., Frieder, O.: Distributed construction of connected dominating set in wireless ad hoc networks. In: Proc. 21th Annual Joint Conference of the IEEE InfoCom (2002)

[10] Wu, Y., Wang, F., Thai, M.T., Li, Y.: Constructing k-connected m-dominating sets in wireless sensor networks. In: Proc. Military Communications Conference (2007)

[11] Chen, X., Shen, J.: Reducing Connected Dominating Set Size with Multipoint Relays in Ad Hoc Wireless Networks. In: Proc 7th Int. Sym. Parallel Architectures, Algorithms and Networks, pp. 539–543 (2004)

[12] Adjih, C., Jacquet, P., Viennot, L.: Computing Connected Dominating sets with multipoint relays. Technical Report, INRIA (October 2002)
[13] Badis, H., et al.: Optimal Path Selection in a Link State QoS Routing Protocol. In: Proc. IEEE VTC 2004 Spring (2004)
[14] Wu, J., Dai, F., Gao, M., Stojmenovic, I.: On calculating Power Aware Connected Dominating Sets fro Efficient Routing in Ad Hoc Wireless Networks. Journal of Communication and Networks 4 (2002)
[15] Change, Y., Ting, Y., Wu, S.: Power-Efficient and Path-Stable Broadcasting scheme for Wireless Ad Hoc Networks. In: Int. Conf. Advanced Information Networking and applications Workshops (AINAW 2007) (2007)

Hybrid Synchronization of Arneodo and Rössler Chaotic Systems by Active Nonlinear Control

Sundarapandian Vaidyanathan and Suresh Rasappan

Research and Development Centre, Vel Tech Dr. RR & Dr. SR Technical University
Avadi-Alamathi Road, Avadi, Chennai-600 062, India
sundarvtu@gmail.com
http://www.vel-tech.org/

Abstract. This paper investigates the hybrid chaos synchronization of identical Arneodo systems (1981), identical Rössler systems (1976) and non-identical Arneodo and Rössler systems. In hybrid synchronization of chaotic systems, one part of the systems is synchronized and the other part is anti-synchronized so that complete synchronization (CS) and anti-synchronization (AS) co-exist in the systems. The co-existence of CS and AS is very useful in secure communication and chaotic encryption schemes. Active nonlinear control is the method used for the hybrid synchronization of the chaotic systems addressed in this paper. Since the Lyapunov exponents are not required for these calculations, the active control method is effective and convenient to achieve hybrid synchronization of the two chaotic systems. Numerical simulations are shown to verify the results.

Keywords: Hybrid synchronization, chaos, Arneodo system, Rössler system, active nonlinear control.

1 Introduction

Chaos is very interesting nonlinear phenomenon, exhibiting sensitive dependence on initial conditions. Synchronization of chaos is an important research problem, which has been attracting considerable interest in the chaos literature. Chaos synchronization has been widely explored in a variety of fields including physical systems [1], chemical systems [2], ecological systems [3], secure communications ([4]-[5]), etc.

Since Pecora and Carroll published a seminal paper ([6], 1990) for synchronizing two identical chaotic systems with different conditions, many chaos synchronization methods have been developed extensively over the past few decades ([6]-[20]). Some important methods for the chaos synchronization are the PC method [6], sampled-data feedback synchronization method [7], OGY method [8], time-delay feedback method [9], backstepping method [10], adaptive design method [11], sliding control method [12], etc.

So far, many types of synchronization phenomenon have been presented such as complete synchronization [6], phase synchronization ([3],[13]), generalized synchronization ([5], [14]), anti-synchronization ([15], [16]), projective synchronization [17], generalized projective synchronization ([18], [19]) etc.

Complete synchronization (CS) is characterized by the equality of state variables evolving in time, while anti-synchronization (AS) is characterized by the disappearance

N. Meghanathan et al. (Eds.): CCSIT 2012, Part I, LNICST 84, pp. 73–82, 2012.

of the sum of relevant state variables evolving in time. Projective synchronization (PS) is characterized by the fact the master and slave systems could be synchronized up to a scaling factor, whereas in generalized projective synchronization (GPS), the responses of the synchronized dynamical states synchronize up to a constant scaling matrix α. It is easy to see that the complete synchronization and anti-synchronization are the special cases of the generalized projective synchronization where the scaling matrix $\alpha = I$ and $\alpha = -I$, respectively.

In hybrid synchronization of chaotic systems [19], one part of the systems is synchronized and the other part is anti-synchronized so that complete synchronization (CS) and anti-synchronization (AS) co-exist in the systems. The co-existence of CS and AS is very useful in secure communication and chaotic encryption schemes.

This paper is organized as follows. In Section 2, we discuss the hybrid synchronization between identical Arneodo systems ([21], 1981). In Section 3, we discuss the hybrid synchronization between identical Rössler systems ([22], 1976).In Section 4, we discuss the hybrid synchronization between non-identical Arneodo and Rössler systems. In Section 5, we conclude with the main results obtained in this paper.

2   Hybrid Synchronization of Identical Arneodo Systems

In this section, we consider the hybrid synchronization of identical Arneodo systems ([21], 1981).

Thus, we consider the *master* system as the Arneodo dynamics described by

$$\begin{aligned}
\dot{x}_1 &= x_2 \\
\dot{x}_2 &= x_3 \\
\dot{x}_3 &= mx_1 - sx_2 - x_3 - x_1^2
\end{aligned} \tag{1}$$

where $x_i(i = 1, 2, 3)$ are the *state* variables and s, m are positive constants.

The Arneodo system (1) is chaotic when $s = 3.8$ and $m = 7.5$.

The state orbits of the chaotic Arneodo system are shown in Figure 1.

We consider the controlled Arneodo system as the *slave* system, which is described by the dynamics

$$\begin{aligned}
\dot{y}_1 &= y_2 + u_1 \\
\dot{y}_2 &= y_3 + u_2 \\
\dot{y}_3 &= my_1 - sy_2 - y_3 - y_1^2 + u_3
\end{aligned} \tag{2}$$

where $y_i(i = 1, 2, 3)$ are the *state* variables and $u_i(i = 1, 2, 3)$ are the active controls.

For the hybrid synchronization of the identical Arneodo systems (1) and (2), the *errors* are defined as

$$e_1 = y_1 - x_1, \quad e_2 = y_2 + x_2 \text{ and } e_3 = y_3 - x_3 \tag{3}$$

A simple calculation yields the error dynamics as

$$\begin{aligned}
\dot{e}_1 &= e_2 - 2x_2 + u_1 \\
\dot{e}_2 &= e_3 + 2x_3 + u_2 \\
\dot{e}_3 &= me_1 - se_2 - e_3 + 2sx_2 - y_1^2 + x_1^2 + u_3
\end{aligned} \tag{4}$$

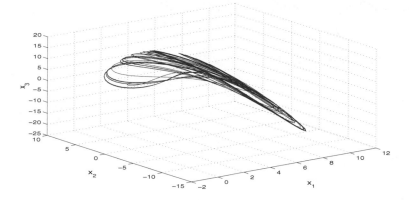

Fig. 1. State Orbits of the Arneodo System (1)

We consider the active nonlinear controller defined by

$$
\begin{aligned}
u_1 &= -e_2 + 2x_2 - k_1 e_1 \\
u_2 &= -e_3 - 2x_3 - k_2 e_2 \\
u_3 &= -me_1 + se_2 - 2sx_2 + y_1^2 - x_1^2
\end{aligned}
\tag{5}
$$

where k_1 and k_2 are positive constants.

Substitution of (5) into (4) yields the linear error dynamics

$$
\dot{e}_1 = -k_1 e_1, \quad \dot{e}_2 = -k_2 e_2, \quad \dot{e}_3 = -e_3
\tag{6}
$$

We consider the quadratic Lyapunov function defined by

$$
V(e) = \frac{1}{2} e^T e = \frac{1}{2} \left(e_1^2 + e_2^2 + e_3^2 \right)
\tag{7}
$$

Differentiating (7) along the trajectories of the system (6), we get

$$
\dot{V}(e) = -k_1 e_1^2 - k_2 e_2^2 - e_3^2
\tag{8}
$$

which is a negative definite function on $\mathbb{R}^3$, since k_1, k_2 are positive constants.

Thus, by Lyapunov stability theory [23], the error dynamics (6) is globally exponentially stable. Hence, we obtain the following result.

Theorem 1. *The identical Arneodo systems (1) and (2) are globally and exponentially hybrid synchronized with the active nonlinear controller (5).*   ■

Numerical Simulations

For the numerical simulations, the fourth order Runge-Kutta method with time-step $h = 10^{-6}$ is used to solve the two systems of differential equations (1) and (2) with the active controller (5).

The parameters of the identical Arneodo systems (1) and (2) are selected as $s = 3.8$ and $m = 7.5$ so that the systems (1) and (2) exhibit chaotic behaviour. Also, we take $k_1 = 2, k_2 = 2$.

The initial values for the master system (1) are taken as

$$x_1(0) = 6, \ x_2(0) = 8, \ x_3(0) = 2$$

and the initial values for the slave system (2) are taken as

$$y_1(0) = 9, \ y_2(0) = 4, \ y_3(0) = 3$$

Figure 2 shows the hybrid synchronization of the Arneodo systems (1) and (2).

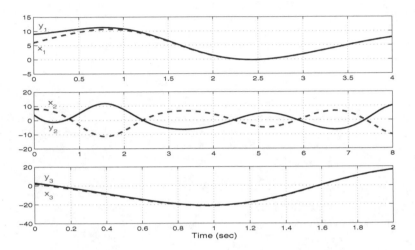

Fig. 2. Hybrid Synchronization of Identical Arneodo Systems

3   Hybrid Synchronization of Identical Rössler Systems

In this section, we discuss the hybrid synchronization of identical Rössler systems. Thus, we consider the Rössler system [22] as the *master* system, which is described by the dynamics

$$\dot{x}_1 = -x_2 - x_3$$
$$\dot{x}_2 = x_1 + ax_2 \qquad\qquad (9)$$
$$\dot{x}_3 = b + (x_1 - c)x_3$$

where $x_i (i = 1, 2, 3)$ are the *state* variables and a, b, c are positive constants.

When $a = 0.2, b = 0.2$ and $c = 5.7$, the Rössler system (9) is chaotic. The state orbits of the Rössler system are shown in Figure 3.

Next, we consider the controlled Rössler dynamics as the *slave* system, which is described by

$$\dot{y}_1 = -y_2 - y_3 + u_1$$
$$\dot{y}_2 = y_1 + ay_2 + u_2 \qquad\qquad (10)$$
$$\dot{y}_3 = b + (y_1 - c)y_3 + u_3$$

where $y_i (i = 1, 2, 3)$ are the *state* variables and $u_i (i = 1, 2, 3)$ are the active controls.

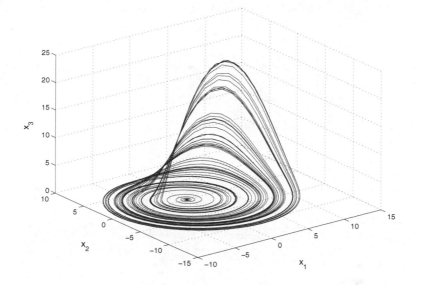

Fig. 3. State Orbits of the Rössler System (9)

For the hybrid synchronization of the identical Rössler systems (9) and (10), the *errors* are defined as

$$e_1 = y_1 - x_1, \quad e_2 = y_2 + x_2 \text{ and } e_3 = y_3 - x_3 \tag{11}$$

A simple calculation yields the error dynamics as

$$\begin{aligned}
\dot{e}_1 &= -e_2 - e_3 + 2x_2 + u_1 \\
\dot{e}_2 &= e_1 + ae_2 + 2x_1 + u_2 \\
\dot{e}_3 &= -ce_3 + y_1y_3 - x_1x_3 + u_3
\end{aligned} \tag{12}$$

We consider the active nonlinear controller defined by

$$\begin{aligned}
u_1 &= e_2 + e_3 - 2x_2 - k_1e_1 \\
u_2 &= -e_1 - ae_2 - 2x_1 - k_2e_2 \\
u_3 &= -y_1y_3 + x_1x_3
\end{aligned} \tag{13}$$

where k_1 and k_2 are positive constants.

Substitution of (13) into (12) yields the linear error dynamics

$$\dot{e}_1 = -k_1e_1, \quad \dot{e}_2 = -k_2e_2, \quad \dot{e}_3 = -ce_3 \tag{14}$$

We consider the quadratic Lyapunov function defined by

$$V(e) = \frac{1}{2}e^T e = \frac{1}{2}\left(e_1^2 + e_2^2 + e_3^2\right) \tag{15}$$

Differentiating (15) along the trajectories of the system (14), we get

$$\dot{V}(e) = -k_1 e_1^2 - k_2 e_2^2 - c e_3^2 \qquad (16)$$

which is a negative definite function on $\mathbb{R}^3$, since k_1, k_2, c are positive constants.

Thus, by Lyapunov stability theory [23], the error dynamics (14) is globally exponentially stable. Hence, we obtain the following result.

Theorem 2. *The identical Rössler systems (9) and (10) are globally and exponentially hybrid synchronized with the active nonlinear controller (13).* ∎

Numerical Simulations
For the numerical simulations, the fourth order Runge-Kutta method with time-step $h = 10^{-6}$ is used to solve the two systems of differential equations (9) and (10) with the active controller (13).

The parameters of the identical Rössler systems (9) and (10) are selected as $a = 0.2, b = 0.2$ and $c = 5.7$ so that the systems (9) and (10) exhibit chaotic behaviour. Also, we take $k_1 = 2, k_2 = 2$.

The initial values for the master system (9) are taken as

$$x_1(0) = 6, \ x_2(0) = 17, \ x_3(0) = 12$$

and the initial values for the slave system (10) are taken as

$$y_1(0) = 1, \ y_2(0) = 10, \ y_3(0) = 2$$

Figure 4 shows the hybrid synchronization of the Rössler systems (9) and (10).

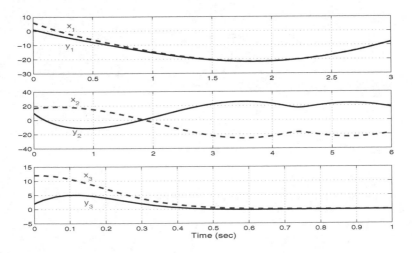

Fig. 4. Hybrid Synchronization of Identical Rössler Systems

4 Hybrid Synchronization of Arneodo and Rössler Systems

In this section, we discuss the hybrid synchronization of non-identical chaotic systems, *viz.* Arneodo and Rössler chaotic systems. Thus, we consider the Arneodo system [21] as the *master* system, which is described by the dynamics

$$
\begin{aligned}
\dot{x}_1 &= x_2 \\
\dot{x}_2 &= x_3 \\
\dot{x}_3 &= mx_1 - sx_2 - x_3 - x_1^2
\end{aligned}
\tag{17}
$$

where x_1, x_2, x_3 are the *state* variables and s, m are positive constants.

Next, we consider the controlled Rössler dynamics [22] as the *slave* system, which is described by

$$
\begin{aligned}
\dot{y}_1 &= -y_2 - y_3 + u_1 \\
\dot{y}_2 &= y_1 + ay_2 + u_2 \\
\dot{y}_3 &= b + (y_1 - c)y_3 + u_3
\end{aligned}
\tag{18}
$$

where y_1, y_2, y_3 are the *state* variables, a, b, c are positive constants and u_1, u_2, u_3 are the active controls.

For the hybrid synchronization of the non-identical systems (17) and (18), the *errors* are defined as

$$
e_1 = y_1 - x_1, \quad e_2 = y_2 + x_2 \quad \text{and} \quad e_3 = y_3 - x_3
\tag{19}
$$

A simple calculation yields the error dynamics as

$$
\begin{aligned}
\dot{e}_1 &= -e_2 - y_3 + u_1 \\
\dot{e}_2 &= e_1 + x_1 + x_3 + ay_2 + u_2 \\
\dot{e}_3 &= b - ce_3 - mx_1 + sx_2 + (1 - c)x_3 + x_1^2 + y_1 y_3 + u_3
\end{aligned}
\tag{20}
$$

We consider the active nonlinear controller defined by

$$
\begin{aligned}
u_1 &= e_2 + y_3 - k_1 e_1 \\
u_2 &= -e_1 - x_1 - x_3 - ay_2 - k_2 e_2 \\
u_3 &= -b + mx_1 - sx_2 - (1 - c)x_3 - x_1^2 - y_1 y_3
\end{aligned}
\tag{21}
$$

where k_1 and k_2 are positive constants.

Substitution of (21) into (20) yields the linear error dynamics

$$
\dot{e}_1 = -k_1 e_1, \quad \dot{e}_2 = -k_2 e_2, \quad \dot{e}_3 = -ce_3
\tag{22}
$$

We consider the quadratic Lyapunov function defined by

$$
V(e) = \frac{1}{2} e^T e = \frac{1}{2} \left(e_1^2 + e_2^2 + e_3^2 \right)
\tag{23}
$$

Differentiating (23) along the trajectories of the system (22), we get

$$
\dot{V}(e) = -k_1 e_1^2 - k_2 e_2^2 - ce_3^2
\tag{24}
$$

which is a negative definite function on $\mathbb{R}^3$, since k_1, k_2, c are positive constants.

Thus, by Lyapunov stability theory [23], the error dynamics (14) is globally exponentially stable. Hence, we obtain the following result.

Theorem 3. *The non-identical Arneodo system (17) and Rössler system (18) are globally and exponentially hybrid synchronized with the active nonlinear controller (21).* ■

Numerical Simulations

For the numerical simulations, the fourth order Runge-Kutta method with time-step $h = 10^{-6}$ is used to solve the two systems of differential equations (17) and (18) with the active controller (21).

The parameters of the Arneodo and Rössler systems are selected so that they are chaotic, *viz.*

$$s = 3.8, \quad m = 7.5, \quad a = 0.2, \quad b = 0.2, \quad c = 5.7$$

The initial values for the master system (17) are taken as

$$x_1(0) = 2, \ x_2(0) = 8, \ x_3(0) = 5$$

and the initial values for the slave system (18) are taken as

$$y_1(0) = 16, \ y_2(0) = 3, \ y_3(0) = 12$$

Figure 5 shows the hybrid synchronization of the non-identical Arneodo system (17) and Rössler system(18).

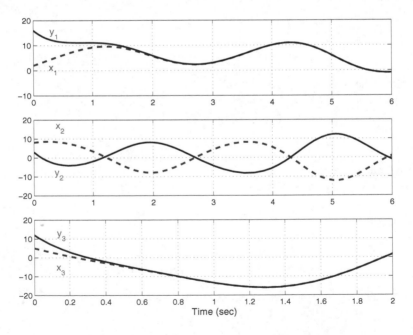

Fig. 5. Hybrid Synchronization of Arneodo and Rössler Systems

5 Conclusions

In this paper, we have used active nonlinear control method so as to achieve hybrid chaos synchronization of the following chaotic systems:

(A) Identical Arneodo chaotic systems (1981)
(B) Identical Rössler chaotic systems (1976)
(C) Non-identical Arneodo and Rössler chaotic systems

Numerical simulations are also shown to verify the proposed active nonlinear controllers to achieve hybrid synchronization of the chaotic systems addressed in this paper. Since Lyapunov exponents are not required for the calculations, the proposed nonlinear control method is effective and convenient to achieve hybrid synchronization of the identical and non-identical Arneodo and Rössler chaotic systems. Numerical simulations are given to illustrate the synchronization results.

References

1. Lakshmanan, M., Murali, K.: Chaos in Nonlinear Oscillators: Controlling and Synchronization. World Scientific, Singapore (1996)
2. Han, S.K., Kerrer, C., Kuramoto, Y.: Dephasing and burstling in coupled neural oscillators. Phys. Rev. Lett. 75, 3190–3193 (1995)
3. Blasius, B., Huppert, A., Stone, L.: Complex dynamics and phase synchronization in spatially extended ecological system. Nature 399, 354–359 (1999)
4. Feki, M.: An adaptive chaos synchronization scheme applied to secure communication. Chaos, Solit. Fract. 18, 141–148 (2003)
5. Murali, K., Lakshmanan, M.: Secure communication using a compound signal from generalized synchronizable chaotic systems. Phys. Rev. Lett. A 241, 303–310 (1998)
6. Pecora, L.M., Carroll, T.L.: Synchronization in chaotic systems. Phys. Rev. Lett. 64, 821–824 (1990)
7. Yang, T., Chua, L.O.: Control of chaos using sampled-data feedback control. Internat. J. Bifurcat. Chaos 9, 215–219 (1999)
8. Ott, E., Grebogi, C., Yorke, J.A.: Controlling chaos. Phys. Rev. Lett. 64, 1196–1199 (1990)
9. Park, J.H., Kwon, O.M.: A novel criterion for delayed feedback control of time-delay chaotic systems. Chaos, Solit. Fract. 17, 709–716 (2003)
10. Yu, Y.G., Zhang, S.C.: Adaptive backstepping synchronization of uncertain chaotic systems. Chaos, Solit. Fract. 27, 1369–1375 (2006)
11. Liao, T.L., Tsai, S.H.: Adaptive synchronization of chaotic systems and its applications to secure communications. Chaos, Solit. Fract. 11, 1387–1396 (2000)
12. Konishi, K., Hirai, M., Kokame, H.: Sliding mode control for a class of chaotic systems. Phys. Lett. A. 245, 511–517 (1998)
13. Ge, Z.M., Chen, C.C.: Phase synchronization of coupled chaotic multiple time scales systems. Chaos, Solit. Fract. 20, 639–647 (2004)
14. Wang, Y.W., Guan, Z.H.: Generalized synchronization of continuous chaotic systems. Chaos, Solit. Fract. 27, 97–101 (2006)
15. Zhang, X., Zhu, H.: Anti-synchronization of two different hyperchaotic systems via active and adaptive control. Inter. J. Nonlinear Science 6, 216–223 (2008)
16. Chiang, T., Lin, J., Liao, T., Yan, J.: Anti-synchronization of uncertain unified chaotic systems with dead-zone nonlinearity. Nonlinear Anal. 68, 2629–2637 (2008)

17. Qiang, J.: Projective synchronization of a new hyperchaotic Lorenz system. Phys. Lett. A 370, 40–45 (2007)
18. Jian-Ping, Y., Chang-Pin, L.: Generalized projective synchronization for the chaotic Lorenz system and the chaotic Chen system. J. Shanghai Univ. 10, 299–304 (2006)
19. Li, R.H., Xu, W., Li, S.: Adaptive generalized projective synchronization in different chaotic systems based on parameter identification. Phys. Lett. A 367, 199–206 (2007)
20. Li, R.-H.: A special full-state hybrid projective synchronization in symmetrical chaotic systems. Applied Math. Comput. 200, 321–329 (2008)
21. Arneodo, A., Coullet, P., Tresser, C.: Possible new strange attractors with spiral structure. Commun. Math. Phys. 79, 573–579 (1981)
22. Rössler, O.E.: An equation for continuous chaos. Phys. Lett. A 57, 397–398 (1976)
23. Hahn, W.: The Stability of Motion. Springer, New York (1967)

Realization of SDR in Partial Reconfigurable FPGA Using Different Types of Modulation Techniques

Neenu Joseph and P. Nirmal Kumar

Department of ECE, Anna University, Chennai
neenuj@gmail.com,
nirmal@annauniv.edu

Abstract. The increase in the consumer demand and the exponential growth for wireless systems, which enables consumer to communicate in any place by means of information, has in turn led to the emergence of many portable wireless communication products. The present research works primarily targets to integrate as much as signal processing applications in a single portable device. Since integration through software applications compromises system speed, integration through hardware will be the better compliment. Software Defined Radio (SDR) Technology yields to achieve this small form factor system while keeping power consumption under the limit. SDR enables soft changeable system functionality, such as receiver demodulation technique. The flexibility of changing the receiver functionality in runtime is usually attained by FPGA. However, using a complete FPGA for reconfiguration of a particular functionality is not an efficient method in terms of power consumption and switching time. We proposed a SDR architecture using a recent advancement in FPGAs, called Partial Reconfiguration (PR). PR helps to change certain portion of FPGA, while the rest keeps functioning. It also reduces the total hardware usage and hence the power. The different demodulation technique and other signal processing application from an external memory unit can be loaded into FPGA PR modules while the other parts of FPGA doing a constant data processing.

Keywords: Partial Reconfiguration in FPGA, Modulation Techniques, Wireless communication.

1   Introduction

SDR is a collection of Hardware and software in which all the radio functions can be implemented using software coding or firmware on a processing system. These software can be alterable according to the applications in communication system. The processing systems include Field Programmable Gate Arrays (FPGA), Digital Signal Processors (DSP), General Purpose Processors (GPP), Programmable System on Chip (SoC) or other Application Specific Programmable Processors. The use of SDR technologies allows new wireless features like Third Generation (3G) and Fourth Generation (4G) capabilities to be added to existing Generation for mobile applications and radio systems without requiring new hardware.

N. Meghanathan et al. (Eds.): CCSIT 2012, Part I, LNICST 84, pp. 83–89, 2012.
© Institute for Computer Sciences, Social Informatics and Telecommunications Engineering 2012

By using SDR Technique a family of Radio products used in communication to be developed in common platform architecture and lot of research work is going on in this area allowing new products will come quickly into market. Since the software to be reused across radio products, the development cost reduces dramatically. This type of wireless communication enables the user to communicate with whomever they need to communicate and in whatever manner according to their wish. For example video call is available in Third generation. Likewise any type of applications can be include using SDR in a single chip. The main advantage SDR engineers is to provide a single radio transceiver capable of playing the roles of cordless telephone, cell phone(GSM and CDMA), wireless fax, wireless e-mail system, pager, wireless videoconferencing unit, wireless Web browser, Global Positioning System unit, and other functions still in the realm of science fiction, operable from any location on the surface of the earth, and perhaps in space as well.

The General block diagram of SDR is shown in Figure 1. The radio frequency signal comes from antenna is down converted to baseband frequency range with the help of transceivers. The analog to digital converter will give the digital data to the processing module. The processing module will be a combination of FPGA and DSP in most cases. FPGA will be reconfigured by DSP according to the incoming signals modulation scheme or depends on the user's interest. Finally the original message signal will be given to a respected sink device.

The SDR is software radio in which all the physical layers are software defined. It effectively uses the area in FPGA.

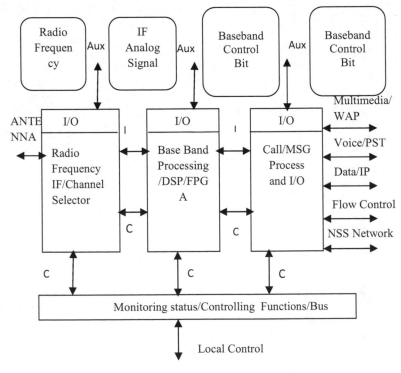

Fig. 1. Basic Diagram of SDR

2   General Implementation

The generalized implementation (block diagram) method of SDR system architecture is shown in figure 2. All software part is done in FPGA. This can be alter according to the applications.

The FPGA shown here is used for the soft reconfiguration and the DSP or any GPPs will do controlling of the FPGA and other data flow tasks. The combination of devices like DSP,FPGA, GPP is used in SDR, due to the advantage and disadvantage of each device.

DSP –   good for software processing, branches but lack in parallelism.
FPGA– gives parallel architecture, high data rates but issues with software routine executions.
GPP– good for managing and controlling memories and peripherals but not optimized for algorithms development.

In most cases DSP is used because the combination of controlling ability and signal processing power.   The different demodulation techniques configuration will be loaded into a memory unit initially. The choice will be given to user to select the required demodulation technique. Once the DSP receives the command to change the receiver demodulation, it reconfigures the FPGA by loading corresponding bit stream

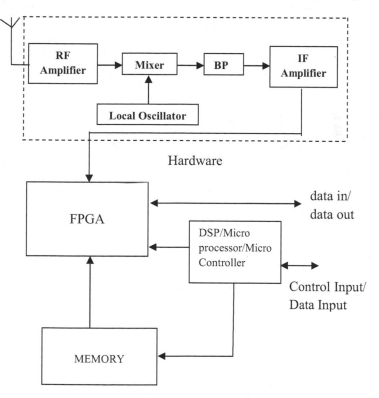

Fig. 2. General Implementation

from memory. Typical FPGA reconfiguration time will be in the order of 100s of milliseconds and this is huge delay when come into real time. Further this delay will increase if DSP running some other default communication task in parallel.

3 Proposed System Architecture

Due to the Rapid development in FPGAs, now we have all the following resources in single FPGA.

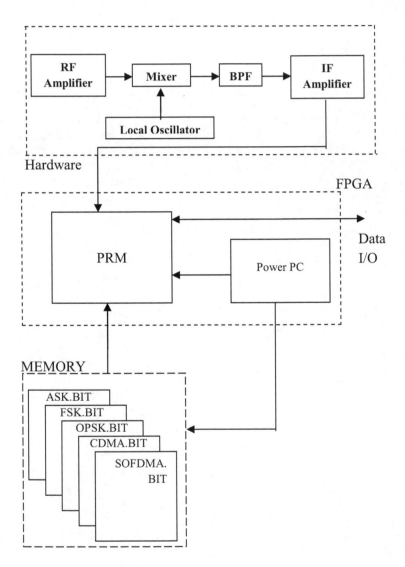

Fig. 3. Proposed system Architecture

Huge amount of Logic blocks: For more parallel logic designs.

DSP Slices: For signal processing algorithm implementation.

PowerPC: Embedded processor can be used as GPP. All these units can operate in parallel.

As shown in the block diagram, we have proposed a SDR architecture with only FPGA due to the availability of massive parallelism and Partial Reconfigurable ability. Since the newer FPGA provides PR modules, it is possible to change of the certain part of FPGA alone and hence we can avoid complete FPGA for reconfiguration. The embedded PowerPC and DSP slices can do a work of a GPP or DSP. Hence it is also not required to use dedicated ASIC for the controlling and signal processing purpose. The proposed architecture embeds everything into a single FPGA which in turn reduces the total resource utilization and hence the power and speed.

Our design mainly concentrates on runtime reconfiguration of demodulation techniques in Partial Reconfiguration blocks of an FPGA and keeping the rest of the baseband process unchanged. The modulation/demodulation techniques will be ASK, FSK, BPSK QPSK SOFDMA and CDMA.

4   Partial Reconfiguration

Xilinx introduced this method of reconfiguration to the market recently. As "Field Programmable Gate Array" name suggests, it gives user the flexibility to reconfigure the hardware on field instead of going through the complete ASIC design process for small modification or updation in the design. The new Partial Reconfiguration capability of recent FPGAs further enhances the flexibility by allowing partial configuration on an operating FPGA using partial bit files.

After a full bit file configures the FPGA, partial bit files can be downloaded to modify reconfigurable regions in the FPGA without compromising the integrity of the applications running on those parts of the device that are not being reconfigured.

As shown in Figure 4, the function implemented in Reconfigurable Block A is modified by downloading one of several partial bit files, A1.bit, A2.bit, A3.bit or

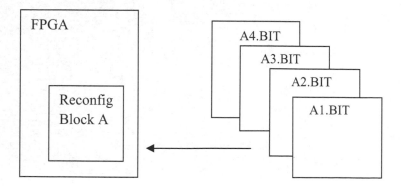

Fig. 4. Partial Reconfiguration in FPGA

A4.bit. The logic in the FPGA design is divided into two different categories, reconfigurable logic and static logic. The reconfigurable block A represents reconfigurable logic and the rest are static logic. The static logic remains functioning and is completely unaffected by the loading of a partial bit file. The reconfigurable logic is replaced by the contents of the partial bit file. There will be a Configuration controller which is part of the static module. This takes care of loading and unloading of dynamic modules. The command to this controller will be given from PowerPC with the reconfiguration data.

5   Conclusion

Realization of SDR in Partial Reconfigurable FPGA using different types of Modulation Techniques Developing using Xilinx FPGA. Due to the Realization is done by using the help of Partial Reconfiguration. The Speed and performance can be improved. The area also can be decreased. The New Xilinx, Vertex Series FPGA provides the provision of Partial Reconfiguration. The power Consumption can be reduced by applying power reduction Techniques in the blocks. In future, more types of modulation techniques can be done in same chip using Partial Reconfiguration with high performance.

This Receiver can be used in Mobile stations, Radio Stations etc. The use of Partial reconfiguration any function can alter at any time without affecting the current operation. The demodulation Techniques in the receiver side is stored in partial Reconfigurable blocks. The physical layers of SDR implemented in the FPGA.

6   Result

The Simulation is done by using Modelsim 6.4a. The Synthesis is done by using Xilinx ISE Software. The Simulation results are shown in the figure 5 and figure 6.

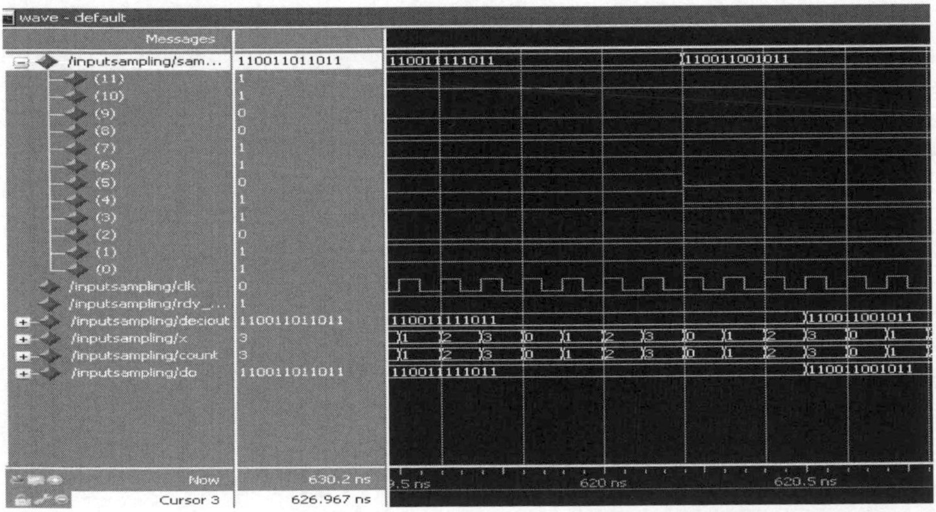

Fig. 5. Input Sampling in SDR

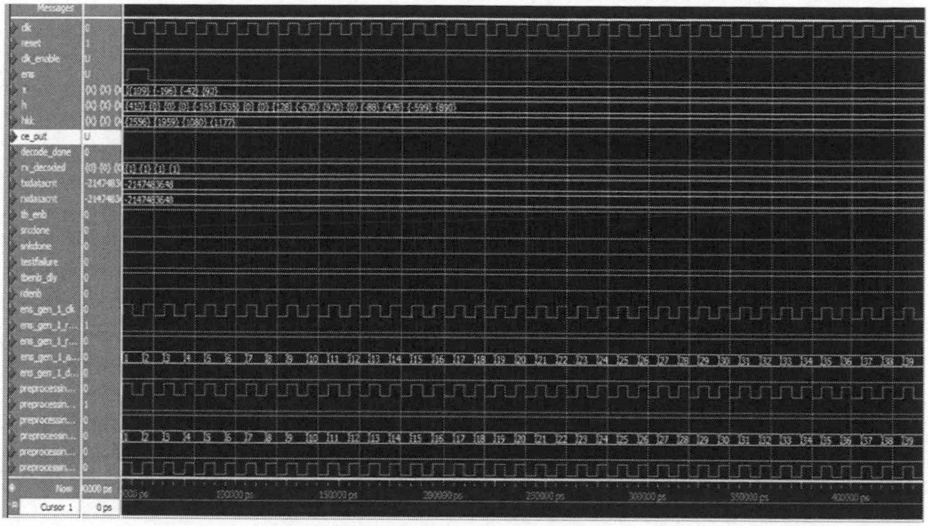

Fig. 6. Simulation Result

References

[1] Bhargav Alluri, V., Robert Health, J., Lhamon, M.: A new Multichannel, coherent Amplitude Modulated, time Division Multiplexed. Software Defined Radio Architecture and Field Programmable Gate Array

[2] Partial Reconfiguration of Virtex FPGAs in ISE 12:- Xilinx

[3] Glossner, J., Inacu, D., Lu, J., Hokenek, E., Moudgill, M.: A Software Defined Communications baseband design. IEEE Communication Mag. 41(1), 120–128 (2003)

[4] Zhigang, L., Wei, L., Yan, Z., Wei, G.: Multi standard SDR base band platform. In: Proc. IEEE Int. Conf. Computer Networks and Mobile Computing, pp. 461–464 (2003)

[5] Yoshida, H., Tsurumi, H., Suzuki, Y.: Broadband RF front-end and software execution procedure in software defined radio. In: Proc. IEEE Veh. Technol. Conference, vol. 4, pp. 2133–2137 (1999)

[6] Rivet, F., Deval, Y., Begueret, J.B., Dallet, D., Belot, D.: A disruptive software-defined radio receiver architecture based on sampled analog signal processing. In: Proc. IEEE Radio Frequency Integr. Circuits (RFIC) Symp., June 3-5, pp. 197–200 (2007)

[7] Abidi, A.A.: The path to the software-defined radio receiver. IEEE J. Solid-State Circ. 42(5), 954–966 (2007)

[8] FPGA Run-Time Reconfiguration: Two Approaches, http://www.Altera.com

[9] A software Defined Radio for the masses, part1: Gerald Youngblood, AC5OG

[10] A software Defined Radio for the masses, part2: Gerald Youngblood, AC5OG

[11] Partial Reconfiguration User Guide:- Xilinx

[12] Mitola, J.: The software radio architecture. IEEE Commun. Mag. 33(5), 26–38 (1995)

[13] SDR IEEE P1900 Standard, http://standards.ieee.org

A Recommender System for Sweaty Sock Syndrome

L. Arockiam, S. Charles, C. Lalitha, and I. Carol

Department of Computer Science, St Joseph's College, Tiruchirappalli

Abstract. Dermatosis disease is also known as Sweaty Sock Syndrome (SSS). Most of the children and young teenagers are affected by SSS. It damages the skin of the children and the young teenagers with red soles on the feet. A new methodology is used to find the stages of Sweaty Sock Syndrome using Multilayer perceptron (MLP) and EM clustering technique. The symptoms and stages of SSS are classified by using predictive modeling. In Multilayer perceptron technique, data objects are classified based on the stages of SSS and find out their efficiency and accuracy. EM Clustering is an unsupervised technique, which is characterized the objects based on the weights. Supervised learning identifies the various symptoms of SSS disease. It categorizes the data such as initial, non severe and severe by using learning by example. Learning by observation method categorizes the data into different clusters, which is grouped as initial, non severe and severe. It helps to know the various stages of dermatosis by using predictive and descriptive modeling. This prediction helps to recommend the patients those who are affected by SSS and provide suggestion to the patients.

Keywords: Multilayer Perceptron (MLP), EM Clustering, Sweaty Sock Syndrome (SSS), Dermatosis.

1 Introduction

The skin is an indicator of a person's health and beauty. The outer pollutants and inner toxins affects the human skin such as scars, stretch marks, hyper pigmentation, under-eye dark circles, redness, dryness, scaly skin, itchy rash, wrinkles, cracked skin etc, so that the skin needs a special care and provides a comprehensive solutions to remain staying youthful, vibrant and clear. This study finds the knowledge by using supervised and unsupervised learning algorithms. To find the efficiency of artificial neural network technique by using the Root mean square error and Mean absolute error. The SSS is a painful dermatitis, which affects the children aged from 5 to 16. It makes the socky skin becomes scaly and cracked. The supervised learning process identifies the patients' objects using Multilayer perceptron, which categorizes as Initial, Severe and Non-Severe [8.9]. The predictive modeling is used to differentiate the case which falls into three categories such as Initial, Severe and Non- Severe stages. Multilayer perception has been employed to predict the knowledge about the disease. Symptoms stage is a class variable used for classification. In descriptive modeling the cluster instances are categorized based on the symptoms of the SSS .Each cluster reveals the identity of the symptoms of SSS [10, 11].

N. Meghanathan et al. (Eds.): CCSIT 2012, Part I, LNICST 84, pp. 90–96, 2012.
© Institute for Computer Sciences, Social Informatics and Telecommunications Engineering 2012

2   Motivation

2.1   Sweaty Sock Syndrome

Sweaty Sock Syndrome causes the plantar skin to appear glazed, fissured and infect the children's hand with similar signs. This disease affects the boys, their age lies between four and eight. The infection of the feet becomes prominent in the toes and sole resulting in shiny and glazed look. It affects the skin becomes flaky and fissures are developed. [3]. Sweaty Sock Syndrome symptoms seen in 'atopic' children, such as atopic eczema, asthma, or hay fever. It creates the irritation, which is immense when the movement of the foot up and down is sweaty. The foot becomes wet due to the usage of synthetic shoes [4].The following symptoms are found such as scars, stretch Marks, under eyed circle, acne, wrinkles, dryness, redness, cracking, and scaling of weight-bearing surface of foot.

2.2   Expectation Maximization (EM) Clustering

This algorithm used to estimate the parameters by employing iterative approach. It classifies the objects into different clusters based on the mean. It assigns each objects into different clusters according to a weight, which represents the probability of membership [1].

2.3   Multi-layer Perceptron

The Multilayer Perceptron is one of the techniques for classification task. It is a network of simple neurons called perceptrons. It implies a single output from various valued inputs forming a combination to input weights and then releasing it through non linear activities [13].

3   SSS Approach

In Phase I, the patient dataset has been collected from dermatologists. The patient dataset contains the symptoms such as redbloodshotEyes, wrinkles, scars, itchrash, crackedheel, dryness and hayfever. The information has been analyzed and used for the experiment. In this dataset, demographic information is gathered from the patients. The result dataset contains the demographic and patient symptoms information is used for analysis.

In Phase II and III, Predictive and Descriptive mining methods are used to find the impact of disease in the urban area. The methods are EM clustering and Multi Layer Perceptron respectively. Each cluster reveals the stages of the SSS disease and designates the cluster as 1) Initial 2) Non -Sever 3) Severe. The Multi Layer Preceptron is assigned to SSS stages of the patients. The six sigmoid nodes are used as inputs, the weights are assigned to each node, and six output layers are classified based on SSS stages. According to the stages based classification, the ten sigmoid nodes are used as input and three output layers are classified based on the stages of SSS. In Phase IV, the association between symptoms and SSS stage are analyzed using interesting measures.

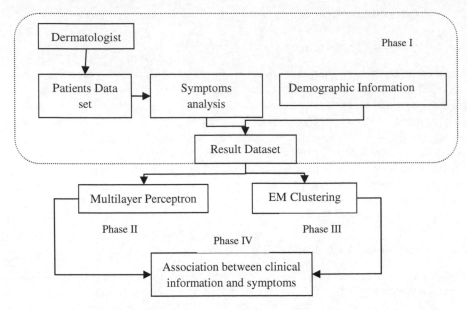

Fig. 1. Sweaty Sock Syndrome Approach

4   Results and Discussions

The dataset containing 300 patients' objects are used to find the association between SSS symptoms and their stages of the patient. The physician's interpretation of clinical data

Table 1. Cluster assignments and Sweaty Sock Syndrome Symptoms

Cluster			Symptoms
C 0	C 1	C2	Stages
80	0	32	Initial
11	0	59	Non- Severe
0	0	118	Severe

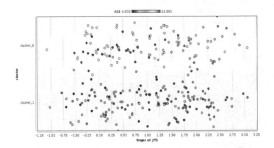

Fig. 2. Clustering of Sweaty Sock Syndrome disease

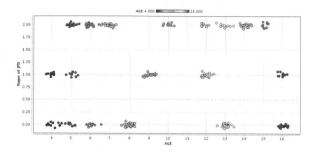

Fig. 3. Classifications of Sweaty Sock Syndrome stages with age

Table 2. Confusion Matrix for Sweaty Sock Syndrome Stages

Experiment	Actual category	Predicted Category		
		Initial	Non severe	Severe
Training Data	Initial	11	0	0
	Non Severe	0	7	0
	Severe	0	0	12
Validation Data	Initial	99	0	0
	Non Severe	0	63	0
	Severe	0	0	108

and clinical images are used in the medical dataset. The knowledge is occurred from mining technique, which is used to find the interesting patterns from the dataset.

Table 1 show that various clusters and corresponding stages are categorized. It reveals that the various stages of the SSS. The patient affected by SSS as initial stage is clustered in C0. C1 cluster contains those who are affected by the SSS as Non-Severe. C2 cluster contains those who are affected by the SSS as Severe. It divulges that there is a misclassification occurs in descriptive modeling.

Table 2 show that the classification of data objects existed in the patient's dataset. In training model, eleven patient objects are categorized as Initial stage, seven objects are categorized as Non-Severe and twelve objects are categorized as Severe. In validation   model, 99 patient objects are categorized as Initial   stage, 63 objects

Table 3. Error rate in SSS dataset

Types of Error	Training set (%)	Testing set (%)	Cross-validation (%)	Test Split (%)
Mean Absolute Error	0.009	0.0055	0.0047	0.0025
Root Mean Squared Error	0.0115	0.0076	0.0062	0.0033
Relative Absolute Error	2.0462	1.2555	1.0848	0.5852
Root Relative Squared Error	2.4468	1.6123	1.3263	0.7002

are categorized as Non-Severe and 108 objects are categorized as Severe. This divulges that there is no misclassification occurs in this modeling. Fig 2 and Fig 3 reveals the classification of Sweaty Sock Syndrome stages.

Table 3 shows that the error rate of the dataset in predictive modeling. It reveals that the various types of errors are measured, which is Mean Absolute Error, Root Mean Square Error, Relative Absolute Error and Root Relative Square Error. The Root Mean Squared Error rate value is low relatively the Root Relative Squared Error value is low. It indicates that the classification model is good. So that it is good enough to classify the SSS stages.

The lift and gain chart is used for calculating the efficiency rate for SSS dataset using MLP. Lift and gain values are used to find the target value based on the order of purity. (Stages of SSS=Initial, severe and nonsevere). The training and validation test yields same percentage of objects. It reveals that shows the accuracy of the model.

The lift shows the value of 2.7 and meets the percent of population as 38 percent. A gain chart reveals that there is an improvement in the model. The figure 4a, 4b and 4c shows the average gain is nearly 2.0001. Only there is a slight variation can occur between training and test data.

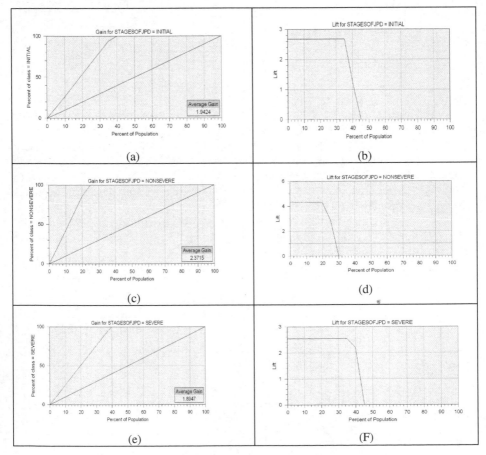

Fig. 4. Lift and Gain chart for SSS

The accuracy measure reveals that the dataset doesn't contain any erroneous data. The sensitivity is the proportion of the patients who are affected by the SSS analysis, which shows that the classification is accurate. The specificity is the proportion of the patients who are not affected by the SSS. Sensitivity and Specificity would be both 1. The sensitivity value shows that the most of them are affected by Initial stage, Non-Severe stage. Some of them are affected in Non-Severe stage in SSS. The prediction can also be viewed as a mapping or function $Y = f(X)$ where X is the input and the output Y is a Nominal value [12]. The mapping or function model shows the association between X and Y. The lift and cosine measure are used to find the correlation. The correlated value of X and Y are 1.789, which is positively correlated, meaning that the X and Y are associated with each other. The cosine value of X and Y are 0.612, meaning that there is a positive correlation between X and Y. Table 4 provides a recommendation for the patients based on symptoms of SSS.

Table 4. Recommendation for SSS

SSS stages	Recommendation
Initial Stage	Reduce friction, Lubricate the dry skin
Non -Sever Stage	Reduce friction, Lubricate the dry skin, Skin cleansers
Sever Stage	Skin cleansers, Have a rest day, Topical steroids, Moisturizer ingredients

5   Conclusion

In this Paper, two popular mining methods are used to predict the patient information. EM clustering technique categorizes the patients' information into three clusters such as cluster 0, 1 and Cluster 2.The Non-Severe stage falls into both clusters 0 and 2. In this categorization, there is a misclassification in the data and reveals that the patient Non–Severe symptoms are related with initial and severe stages. In Multilayer perceptron technique, the three stages are identified as Initial, Severe and Non-Severe stages. It divulges that the there is a perfect classification. Children and teenagers with SSS and atopic dermatitis are excluded. Standard treatment is advised for the children and teenagers. It comprises general advice on foot protection and liberal application of emollients for all the children, and topical corticosteroids for acute flare-ups of erythematous and pruritic feet for short duration to some children. The correlation analysis unveils that the symptoms and stages have strong association. The association between each entity is identified by using classification.

References

[1]   Wu, X., Kumar, V., Ross Quinlan, J., Ghosh, J., Yang, Q., Motoda, H., McLachlan, G.J., Ng, A., Liu, B., Yu, P.S., Zhou, Z.-H., Steinbach, M., Hand, D.J., Steinberg, D.: Top 10 algorithms in data mining. Springer- Verlag London Limited (2008); Knowl. Inf. Syst. 14, 1–37

[2] Park, K.C., Kim, S.H.: Juvenile Plantar Dermatosis: An expression of Atopic Dermatitis. The Scoul Journal of Medicine 3(2), 113–117 (1989)

[3] Brar, K.J., Shenoi, S.D., Balachandran, C., Mehta, V.R.: Clinical Profile of forefeet eczema: A study of 42 cases. Department of skin and STD, Indian J. Dermatol. Venereol. Leprol. 71, 179–181 (2005)

[4] Van Diggelen, M.W., Van Dijk, E., Hausman, R.: The enigma of juvenile plantar dermatosis. Am. J. b Dermatopathol. 8, 336–340 (1986)

[5] Bonnotte, B., Favre, N., Moutet, M., Fromentin, A., Solary, E., Martin, M., Martin, F.: Role of tumor cell apoptosis in tumor antigen migration to the draining lymph nodes. Journal of Immunoly 164(4), February 15 (2000)

[6] Gibbs, N.F.: Juvenile plantar dermatitis. Can sweat cause foot, rash and peeling. Postgrad. Med. 115, 73–75 (2004)

[7] Hintz-Madsen, M., Hansen, L.K., Larsen, J., Drzewiecki, K.: A Probabilistic Neural Network Framework for Detection of Malignant Melanoma. Artificial Neural Networks in Cancer Diagnosis, Prognosis and Patient Management, 141–183 (2001)

[8] Ayers, E., Nugent, R., Dean, N.: A Comparison of Student Skill Knowledge Estimates Educational Data Mining. In: 2nd International Conference on Educational Data Mining, Cordoba, Spain, July 1-3, pp. 1–10 (2009)

[9] Choi, S.C., Rodin, E.Y.: Statistical Methods of Discrimination and Classification. In: Advances in Theory and Applications. Pergoman Press (1986)

[10] Duda, R.O., Hart, P.E., Stork, D.G.: Pattern Classification, 2nd edn. John Wiley & Sons Inc. (2000)

[11] Stasis, A.: Decision Support System for Heart Sound Diagnosis, using digital signal processing algorithms and data mining techniques. PhD Thesis Athens, National Technical University of Athens (2003)

[12] Agrawal, R., Imielinski, T., Swami, A.: Mining association rules between sets of items in large databases. In: Proceedings of the ACM SIGMOD Conference, Washington, DC (1993)

[13] Jervis, B., Yu, S., Saatchi, M., Allen, E.: The Sensitivity of Multilayer Perceptrons for Differentiating Between CNV Waveforms of Schizophrenic, Parkinson's Disease and Huntington's Disease Subjects. In: Ifeachor, E., Rosen, K. (eds.) International Conference on Neural Networks and Expert Systems in Medicine and Healthcare, pp. 275–282 (1994)

[14] Pal, S.K., Mitra, S.: Multilayer Perceptron, Fuzzy sets and Classification. In: IEEE International Conference on Neural Networks, vol. 1(5) (1992)

[15] Gardner, M.W., Dorling, S.R.: Artificial neural networks (the multilayer perceptron)-A review of applications in the atmospheric sciences. Atmospheric Environ. 32, 2627–2636 (1998)

Enhanced AODV Routing Protocol
for Wireless Sensor Network Based on ZigBee

Dilip Kumar Ahirwar, Prashant Verma, and Jitendra Daksh

Department of Electronics and Telecommunication, SVNiT, Sagar, India
{dilipahirwar03,prashantverma80,jitendra.daksh}@gmail.com

Abstract. ZigBee is a very important technology for Wireless Sensor Networks which is targeted at radio-frequency (RF) applications that require a low data rate, long battery life, and secure networking. The Ad hoc On Demand Distance Vector (AODV) routing algorithm is a routing protocol designed for ad hoc mobile networks. It is an on demand algorithm, meaning that it builds routes between nodes only as desired by source nodes. It maintains these routes as long as they are needed by the sources. In this paper we will discuss about the performance of enhanced AODV in wireless sensor networks based on ZigBee.

Keywords: ZigBee, Sensor Networks, AODV, IEEE 802.15.4, Simulation Analysis.

1   Introduction

Recently, a variety of wireless solutions with different parameters in terms of coverage, data rate, network topology, mobility etc. the concepts of wireless sensor networks[1] has been increasing day by day in terms of short range wireless technologies. ZigBee [2] is one of such technology that is being populated. Especially ZigBee using IEEE 802.15.4[3] is very important wireless sensor network technology [4] since it needs supporting of frequent movement.

The scope of this paper is to analyze a set of performance parameters on AODV [5] routing protocol modified named as enhanced AODV because of their simplicity and performances when implemented in ZigBee. The paper concentrates on the performance analysis of AODV for better understanding of protocol efficiency and flexibility. the paper is organized in two sections as follows.Section I describes about the overview of technology and protocols [6], which explains the protocol mechanisms used in the analysis. Section II explains the related work of comparing two protocols. Section III gives the simulation scenario and show results by ns-2[7].

Section I

2   ZigBee Technology

ZigBee is one of wireless network technologies which are widely used from the low power environment. So it was organized very simple structure and offered low price.

N. Meghanathan et al. (Eds.): CCSIT 2012, Part I, LNICST 84, pp. 97–102, 2012.

Physical and MAC(Medium Access Control) layer of ZigBee was used to IEEE 802.15.4 standard. MAC layer was access to wireless channel through CSMAICA mechanism. Application and Network layer had been constituted ZigBee alliance. Application layer is made up APS (Application Support Sublayer), ZDO(ZigBee Device Object) and application framework[7]. Network layer does exchange the information between terminal nodes.

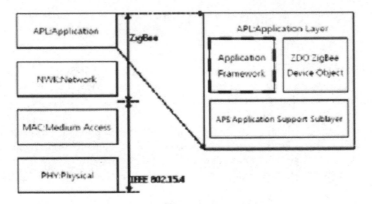

Fig. 1. ZigBee Alliance Structure

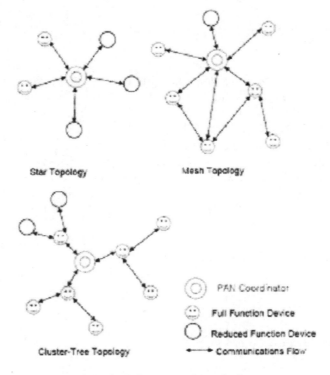

Fig. 2. ZigBee network topologies

Section II

3   Route Discovery of EAODV

AODV (Adhoc on demand distance vector routing) is a kind of route protocol[8], which is based on distance vector algorithm[9]. It only request route when necessary, and do not need nodes maintaining routes that are not in use currently, which means available route only related with notes that are communicating but not AODV.

As an improvement from AODV [3], EAODV Route protocol algorithm inherits many characteristics from its origin, however, they still differs in some aspects. EAODV, similarly, is a kind of on-demand distance vector route protocol and is mainly characterized by the followings: firstly, every node in the network only send route grouping when needing communication but not exchange route information periodically to achieve routes of all other host computers. Secondly, routing tables of nodes only need maintaining the routes between itself and other nodes instead of mastering topology structures of network.

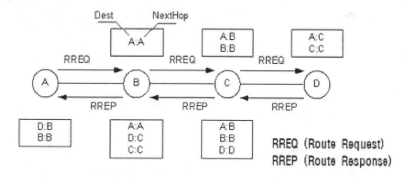

Fig. 3. AODV Route Discovery

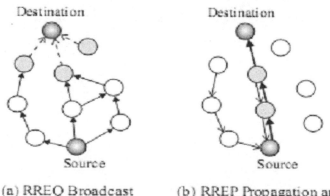

(a) RREQ Broadcast   (b) RREP Propagation and
                            Subsequent Route

Fig. 4. Route Discovery Cycle

There are just two kinds of message control frames in EAODV route protocol, routing request RREQ and Routing response. Similar to AODV, when source node needing to send data does not have an available route to the destination node, a process of route establishment is started. Firstly, a RREQ bag is broadcasted to the network and transmitted to the destination node by intermediate nodes. Secondly, as return, destination node that received the request should unicast a RREP bag to the source node. After the RREP bag is, conversely against the requesting path, transmitted to and received by the source node, a route between the two nodes is established. In the process of transmission of routing requesting bag to the destination, nodes in the network that can receive the request also establish a return path from destination to source. When destination node receives the routing request and return a routing response, nodes in the return odes in the return path establish the forward route.

The whole process of EAODV route establishment is shown as fig.4. Figure (a) shows the process of the establishment of reverse route. Node s wants to communicate with node d, but there is no route between them. Therefore, node s broadcasts a routing request bag to ask all nodes receiving its bag to transmit the request to node d until it reaches the destination node. In this process, a reverse route is established. Figure (b) shows the process of the establishment of forward route. Receiving the routing request bag from node s, node d should return a routing response bag to node s. Return bag is transmitted along the established reverse route to node s. Lastly, the forward route is established.

Section III

4   The Simulation of Route Protocol EAODV

This paper employed simulation tool NS2 to make a function comparison in network throughput between AODV and it's evolve done EAODV. For the quantitative comparison between the two protocols, a uniform simulation surrounding is necessary [10], which means only halt time can be changed in the simulation. Simulation surrounding is a system of 7 mobile nodes, in which topology range is 500m*500m and node's moving speed is 2m/s.

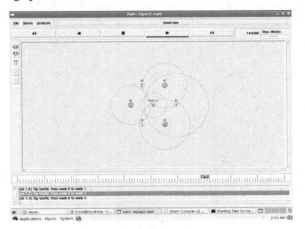

Fig. 5. Simulation Scenario

Table 1. Simulation Parameters

Parameter	Value
Channel Type	Channel/wireless channel
Radio propagation model	Propagation/two ray Ground
Network interface Type	Phy/WirelessPhy
Mac Type	Mac 802_15_4
Interface queue type	Queue/DropTail/Pri Queue
Link layer type	LL
Antenna model	Antenna/OmniAntenna
Max packet in ifq	150
Number of mobile nodes	7
Routing protocol	AODV

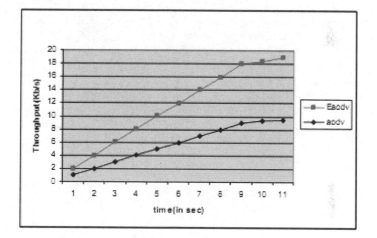

Fig. 6. Graph showing throughput vs. time

5   Conclusion

In this paper, we propose the enhanced AODV routing protocol for optimized path in wireless sensor network based on ZigBee and analyze performance by the simulation program. Enhanced AODV routing protocol is designed for frequency movement. There are many advantages in wireless sensor network, because many sensors are located anywhere and frequency movement be happen. From this simulation results, improved AODV almost shows good performance than original AODV. Especially, it is showed good performance in appointed scenario perfect. However it is not perfect in random scenario. So we will research this situation at future work. If it solve this problem,this is perfect routing protocol for wireless sensor network.

This paper makes an improvement on AODV routearithmetic and the simulation. Since its arithmetic of on-demand searching method, EAODV can rest the sensor nodes in the most time, which prolong the lives of nodes. Characters, such as simple, easy to adding new nodes and little protocol load, dominate that EAODV is very suitable in some unusual application of wireless sensor network.

References

1. Callaway Jr., E.H.: Wireless Sensor Networks: Architectures and Protocols, 352 pages. CRC Press (August 2003) ISBN 0-8493-1823-8
2. ZigBee Document 053474r13, ZigBee Specification (December 2006)
3. IEEE Publications are available from the Institute of Electrical and Electronics Engineers, 445 Hoes Lane, P.O. Box 1331, Piscataway, NJ 08855-1331, USA
4. Al-Karaki, J.N., Kamal, A. E.: Routing Techniques in Wireless Sensor Networks: A Survey. IEEE Wireless Communication, 6–27 (December 2004)
5. FC3561.AdHoc On-Demand Distance Vector (AODV) Routing. IETF (2003)
6. Fall, K., Varadhan, K.: The ns Manual (formerly ns Notes and Documentation) (2001)
7. Perkins, C.E., Royer, E.M.: Ad hoc On-Demand Distance Vector Routing. In: Proceedings of the 2nd IEEE Workshop on Mobile Computing Systems and Applications, New Orleans, LA, pp. 90–100 (February 1999)
8. Akkaya, K., Younis, M.: A Survey on Routing Protocols for Wireless Sensor Networks. Department of Computer Science and Electrical Engineering University of Maryland, Baltimore County
9. Zhang, Y., Zhang, H.-X., Liu, L.-K., Guo, H.: A Modified Algorithm for Reducing the Overhead and Delay of AODV in Adhoc Networks. Video Engineering, 165–168 (2005)
10. Xu, L.M., Pang, B., Zhao, Y.: NS and Network Simulation. Postal and Telecommunications House Publishers, Beijing (2003)\

Sliding Mode Controller Design for the Global Chaos Synchronization of Coullet Systems

Sundarapandian Vaidyanathan[1] and Sivaperumal Sampath[2]

[1] R & D Centre, Vel Tech Dr. RR & Dr. SR Technical University
Avadi-Alamathi Road, Avadi, Chennai-600 062, India
sundarvtu@gmail.com
[2] Institute of Technology, CMJ University
Shillong, Meghalaya-793 003 India
sivaperumals@gmail.com

Abstract. In this paper, new results based on the sliding mode control are derived for the global chaos synchronization of identical Coullet chaotic systems (1981). The stability results for the sliding mode control based synchronization schemes derived in this paper are established using Lyapunov stability theory. Since the Lyapunov exponents are not required for these calculations, the sliding mode control method is very effective and convenient to achieve global chaos synchronization of the identical Coullet chaotic systems. Numerical simulations are shown to illustrate the effectiveness of the sliding mode control results derived in this paper for the identical Coullet chaotic systems.

Keywords: Sliding mode control, global chaos synchronization, chaos, Coullet system.

1 Introduction

Chaotic systems are dynamical systems that are highly sensitive to initial conditions. This sensitivity is popularly known as the *butterfly effect* [1]. Since the pioneering work by Pecora and Carroll ([2], 1990), chaos synchronization problem has been studied extensively in the literature. Chaos theory has been applied to a variety of fields including physical systems [3], chemical systems [4], ecological systems [5], secure communications ([6]-[8]) etc.

In the last two decades, various control schemes have been developed and successfully applied for the chaos synchronization such as PC method [2], OGY method [9], active control ([10]-[12]), adaptive control ([13]-[15]), time-delay feedback method [16], backstepping design method ([17]-[18]), sampled-data feedback synchronization method ([19]-[20]) etc.

In most of the chaos synchronization approaches, the master-slave or drive-response formalism is used. If a particular chaotic system is called the master or drive system and another chaotic system is called the slave or response system, then the goal of the global chaos synchronization is to use the output of the master system to control the slave system so that the states of the slave system track the states of the master system asymptotically. In other words, global chaos synchronization is achieved when

N. Meghanathan et al. (Eds.): CCSIT 2012, Part I, LNICST 84, pp. 103–110, 2012.

the difference of the states of master and slave systems converge to zero asymptotically with time.

In this paper, we derive new results based on the sliding mode control ([21]-[23]) for the global chaos synchronization of identical Coullet systems ([24], 1981). The stability results for the sliding mode control based synchronization schemes derived in this paper are established using Lyapunov stability theory [25]. In robust control systems, sliding mode control is often adopted due to its inherent advantages of easy realization, fast response and good transient performance as well as its insensitivity to parameter uncertainties and external disturbances.

This paper has been organized as follows. In Section 2, we describe the problem statement and our methodology using sliding mode control. In Section 3, we discuss the global chaos synchronization of identical Coullet systems ([24], 1981). In Section 4, we summarize the main results obtained in this paper.

2   Problem Statement and Our Methodology Using Sliding Mode Control

In this section, we detail the problem statement for global chaos synchronization of identical chaos systems and our methodology using sliding mode control (SMC) and Lyapunov stability theory.

Consider the chaotic system described by

$$\dot{x} = Ax + f(x) \tag{1}$$

where $x \in \mathbb{R}^n$ is the state of the system, A is the $n \times n$ matrix of the system parameters and $f : \mathbb{R}^n \to \mathbb{R}^n$ is the nonlinear part of the system. We consider the system (1) as the *master* or *drive* system.

As the *slave* or *response* system, we consider the following chaotic system described by the dynamics

$$\dot{y} = Ay + f(y) + u \tag{2}$$

where $y \in \mathbb{R}^n$ is the state of the system and $u \in \mathbb{R}^m$ is the controller of the slave system.

If we define the *synchronization error* e as

$$e = y - x, \tag{3}$$

then the error dynamics is obtained as

$$\dot{e} = Ae + \eta(x, y) + u, \quad \text{where } \eta(x, y) = f(y) - f(x) \tag{4}$$

The objective of the global chaos synchronization problem is to find a controller u such that

$$\lim_{t \to \infty} \|e(t)\| = 0 \text{ for all initial conditions } e(0) \in \mathbb{R}^n \tag{5}$$

To solve this problem, we first define the control u as

$$u(t) = -\eta(x, y) + Bv(t) \tag{6}$$

where B is a constant gain vector selected such that (A, B) is controllable.

Substituting (6) into (4), the error dynamics simplifies to

$$\dot{e} = Ae + Bv \tag{7}$$

which is a linear time-invariant control system with single input v.

Thus, the original global chaos synchronization problem can be replaced by an equivalent problem of stabilizing the zero solution $e = 0$ of the linear system (7) be a suitable choice of the sliding mode control.

In the sliding mode control, we define the variable

$$s(e) = Ce = c_1 e_1 + c_2 e_2 + \cdots + c_n e_n \tag{8}$$

where $C = \begin{bmatrix} c_1 & c_2 & \cdots & c_n \end{bmatrix}$ is a constant vector to be determined.

In the sliding mode control, we constrain the motion of the system (7) to the sliding manifold defined by

$$S = \{x \in \mathbb{R}^n \mid s(e) = 0\} = \{x \in \mathbb{R}^n \mid c_1 e_1 + c_2 e_2 + \cdots + c_n e_n = 0\}$$

which is required to be invariant under the flow of the error dynamics (7).

When in sliding manifold S, the system (7) satisfies the following conditions:

$$s(e) = 0 \tag{9}$$

which is the defining equation for the manifold S and

$$\dot{s}(e) = 0 \tag{10}$$

which is the necessary condition for the state trajectory $e(t)$ of the system (7) to stay on the sliding manifold S.

Using (7) and (8), the equation (10) can be rewritten as

$$\dot{s}(e) = C\,[Ae + Bv] = 0 \tag{11}$$

Solving (11), we obtain the equivalent control law given by

$$v_{eq}(t) = -(CB)^{-1}CAe(t) \tag{12}$$

where C is chosen such that $CB \neq 0$.

Substituting (12) into the error dynamics (7), we get the closed-loop dynamics as

$$\dot{e} = [I - B(CB)^{-1}C]Ae \tag{13}$$

where C is chosen such that the system matrix $[I - B(CB)^{-1}C]A$ is Hurwitz.

Then the controlled system (13) is globally asymptotically stable.

To design the sliding mode controller for the linear time-invariant system (7), we use the constant plus proportional rate reaching law

$$\dot{s} = -q\,\text{sgn}(s) - ks \tag{14}$$

where $\text{sgn}(\cdot)$ denotes the sign function and the gains $q > 0, k > 0$ are determined such that the sliding condition is satisfied and sliding motion will occur.

From equations (11) and (14), we obtain the control $v(t)$ as

$$v(t) = -(CB)^{-1}[C(kI + A)e + q\,\text{sgn}(s)] \tag{15}$$

Theorem 1. *The master system (1) and the slave system (2) are globally and asymptotically synchronized for all initial conditions $x(0), y(0) \in \mathbb{R}^n$ by the feedback control law*

$$u(t) = -\eta(x, y) + Bv(t) \tag{16}$$

where $v(t)$ is defined by (15) and B is a column vector such that (A, B) is controllable. Also, the sliding mode gains k, q are positive.

Proof. First, we note that substituting (16) and (15) into the error dynamics (7), we obtain the closed-loop dynamics as

$$\dot{e} = Ae - B(CB)^{-1}[C(kI + A)e + q\,\text{sgn}(s)] \tag{17}$$

To prove that the error dynamics (17) is globally asymptotically stable, we consider the candidate Lyapunov function defined by the equation

$$V(e) = \frac{1}{2}s^2(e) \tag{18}$$

which is a positive definite function on $\mathbb{R}^n$.

Differentiating V along the trajectories of (17) or the equivalent dynamics (14), we obtain

$$\dot{V}(e) = s(e)\dot{s}(e) = -ks^2 - q\,\text{sgn}(s) \tag{19}$$

which is a negative definite function on $\mathbb{R}^n$.

Thus, by Lyapunov stability theory [25], it is immediate that the error dynamics (17) is globally asymptotically stable for all initial conditions $e(0) \in \mathbb{R}^n$.

This completes the proof.   ∎

3   Global Chaos Synchronization of Identical Coullet Systems

3.1   Main Results

In this section, we apply the sliding mode control results obtained in Section 2 for the global chaos synchronization of identical Coullet systems ([24], 1981).

Thus, the master system is described by the Coullet dynamics

$$\begin{aligned}
\dot{x}_1 &= x_2 \\
\dot{x}_2 &= x_3 \\
\dot{x}_3 &= ax_1 - bx_2 - cx_3 - x_1^3
\end{aligned} \tag{20}$$

where x_1, x_2, x_3 are the states of the system and $a > 0, b > 0, c > 0$ are parameters of the system.

The slave system is also described by the Coullet dynamics

$$\dot{y}_1 = y_2 + u_1$$
$$\dot{y}_2 = y_3 + u_2 \qquad (21)$$
$$\dot{y}_3 = ay_1 - by_2 - cy_3 - y_1^3 + u_3$$

where y_1, y_2, y_3 are the states of the system and u_1, u_2, u_3 are the controllers to be designed.

The Coullet systems (20) and (21) are chaotic when $a = 5.5, b = 3.5$ and $c = 1.0$. The chaotic portrait of the Coullet system is illustrated in Figure 1.

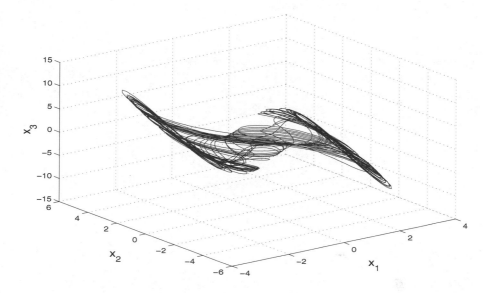

Fig. 1. Chaotic Portrait of the Coullet System

The chaos synchronization error e is defined by

$$e_i = y_i - x_i, \quad (i = 1, 2, 3) \qquad (22)$$

The error dynamics is easily obtained as

$$\dot{e}_1 = e_2 + u_1$$
$$\dot{e}_2 = e_3 + u_2 \qquad (23)$$
$$\dot{e}_3 = ae_1 - be_2 - ce_3 - y_1^3 + x_1^3 + u_3$$

We can write the error dynamics (23) in the matrix notation as

$$\dot{e} = Ae + \eta(x, y) + u \qquad (24)$$

where the associated matrices are

$$A = \begin{bmatrix} 0 & 1 & 0 \\ 0 & 0 & 1 \\ a & -b & -c \end{bmatrix}, \quad \eta(x, y) = \begin{bmatrix} 0 \\ 0 \\ -y_1^3 + x_1^3 \end{bmatrix} \text{ and } u = \begin{bmatrix} u_1 \\ u_2 \\ u_3 \end{bmatrix} \qquad (25)$$

The sliding mode controller design is carried out as detailed in Section 2.

First, we set u as

$$u = -\eta(x, y) + Bv \tag{26}$$

where B is chosen such that (A, B) is controllable. We take B as

$$B = \begin{bmatrix} 0 \\ 1 \\ 1 \end{bmatrix} \tag{27}$$

In the chaotic case, the parameter values are $a = 5.5, b = 3.5$ and $c = 1.0$.

The sliding mode variable is selected as

$$s = Ce = \begin{bmatrix} 10 & 4 & 1 \end{bmatrix} e \tag{28}$$

which makes the sliding mode state equation asymptotically stable.

We choose the sliding mode gains as $k = 1$ and $q = 0.1$. We note that a large value of k can cause chattering and an appropriate value of q is chosen to speed up the time taken to reach the sliding manifold as well as to reduce the system chattering.

From equation (15), we can obtain $v(t)$ as

$$v(t) = -3.1e_1 - 2.1e_2 - 0.8e_3 - 0.02\text{sgn}(s) \tag{29}$$

Thus, the required sliding mode controller is obtained as

$$u(t) = -\eta(x, y) + Bv(t) \tag{30}$$

where $\eta(x, y), B$ and $v(t)$ are defined in equations (25), (27) and (29).

By Theorem 1, we obtain the following result.

Theorem 2. *The identical Coullet systems (20) and (21) are globally and asymptotically synchronized for all initial conditions with the sliding mode controller u defined by (30).* ∎

3.2 Numerical Results

For the numerical simulations, the fourth-order Runge-Kutta method with time-step $h = 10^{-6}$ is used to solve the Coullet systems (20) and (21) with the sliding mode controller u given by (30) using MATLAB.

For the Coullet systems, the parameter values are taken as those which result in the chaotic behaviour of the systems, viz.

$$a = 5.5, \quad b = 3.5 \text{ and } c = 1.0$$

The sliding mode gains are chosen as

$$k = 1 \quad \text{and} \quad q = 0.1$$

The initial values of the master system (20) are taken as

$$x_1(0) = 3, \quad x_2(0) = 2, \quad x_3(0) = 1$$

and the initial values of the slave system (21) are taken as

$$y_1(0) = 1, \quad y_2(0) = 5, \quad y_3(0) = 4$$

Figure 2 depicts the synchronization of the identical Coullet systems (20) and (21).

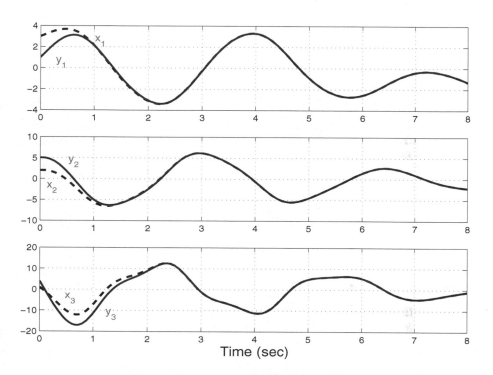

Fig. 2. Synchronization of the Identical Coullet Systems

4 Conclusions

In this paper, we have used sliding mode control (SMC) to achieve global chaos synchronization for the identical Coullet chaotic systems (1981). Our synchronization results for the identical Coullet chaotic systems have been established using Lyapunov stability theory. Since the Lyapunov exponents are not required for these calculations, the sliding mode control method is very effective and convenient to achieve global chaos synchronization for identical Coullet chaotic systems. Numerical simulations are also shown to illustrate the effectiveness of the synchronization results derived in this paper using sliding mode control.

References

1. Alligood, K.T., Sauer, T., Yorke, J.A.: Chaos: An Introduction to Dynamical Systems. Springer, New York (1997)
2. Pecora, L.M., Carroll, T.L.: Synchronization in chaotic systems. Phys. Rev. Lett. 64, 821–824 (1990)
3. Lakshmanan, M., Murali, K.: Chaos in Nonlinear Oscillators: Controlling and Synchronization. World Scientific, Singapore (1996)
4. Han, S.K., Kerrer, C., Kuramoto, Y.: Dephasing and burstling in coupled neural oscillators. Phys. Rev. Lett. 75, 3190–3193 (1995)
5. Blasius, B., Huppert, A., Stone, L.: Complex dynamics and phase synchronization in spatially extended ecological system. Nature 399, 354–359 (1999)
6. Kwok, H.S., Wallace, K., Tang, S., Man, K.F.: Online secure communication system using chaotic map. Internat. J. Bifurcat. Chaos 14, 285–292 (2004)
7. Kocarev, L., Parlitz, U.: General approach for chaos synchronization with applications to communications. Phys. Rev. Lett. 74, 5028–5030 (1995)
8. Murali, K., Lakshmanan, M.: Secure communication using a compound signal using sampled-data feedback. Applied Math. Mech. 11, 1309–1315 (2003)
9. Ott, E., Grebogi, C., Yorke, J.A.: Controlling chaos. Phys. Rev. Lett. 64, 1196–1199 (1990)
10. Ho, M.C., Hung, Y.C.: Synchronization of two different chaotic systems using generalized active network. Phys. Lett. A 301, 421–428 (2002)
11. Huang, L., Feng, R., Wang, M.: Synchronization of chaotic systems via nonlinear control. Phys. Lett. A 320, 271–275 (2004)
12. Chen, H.K.: Global chaos synchronization of new chaotic systems via nonlinear control. Chaos, Solit. Frac. 23, 1245–1251 (2005)
13. Chen, S.H., Lü, J.: Synchronization of an uncertain unified system via adaptive control. Chaos, Solit. Frac. 14, 643–647 (2002)
14. Lu, J., Han, X., Lü, J.: Adaptive feedback synchronization of a unified chaotic system. Phys. Lett. A 329, 327–333 (2004)
15. Samuel, B.: Adaptive synchronization between two different chaotic dynamical systems. Adaptive Commun. Nonlinear Sci. Num. Simul. 12, 976–985 (2007)
16. Park, J.H., Kwon, O.M.: A novel criterion for delayed feedback control of time-delay chaotic systems. Chaos, Solit. Fract. 17, 709–716 (2003)
17. Wu, X., Lü, J.: Parameter identification and backstepping control of uncertain Lü system. Chaos, Solit. Fract. 18, 721–729 (2003)
18. Yu, Y.G., Zhang, S.C.: Adaptive backstepping synchronization of uncertain chaotic systems. Chaos, Solit. Fract. 27, 1369–1375 (2006)
19. Yang, T., Chua, L.O.: Control of chaos using sampled-data feedback control. Internat. J. Bifurcat. Chaos 9, 215–219 (1999)
20. Zhao, J., Lu, J.: Using sampled-data feedback control and linear feedback synchronization in a new hyperchaotic system. Chaos, Solit. Fract. 35, 376–382 (2008)
21. Slotine, J.E., Sastry, S.S.: Tracking control of nonlinear systems using sliding surface with application to robotic manipulators. Internat. J. Control 38, 465–492 (1983)
22. Utkin, V.I.: Sliding mode control design principles and applications to electric drives. IEEE Trans. Industrial Electr. 40, 23–36 (1993)
23. Saravanakumar, R., Vinoth Kumar, K., Ray, K.K.: Sliding mode control of induction motor using simulation approach. Internat. J. Control of Computer Science and Network Security 9, 93–104 (2009)
24. Arneodo, A., Coullet, P., Tresser, C.: Possible new strange attractors with spiral structure. Commun. Math. Phys. 79, 573–579 (1981)
25. Hahn, W.: The Stability of Motion. Springer, New York (1967)

Generalized Projective Synchronization of Double-Scroll Chaotic Systems Using Active Feedback Control

Sundarapandian Vaidyanathan[1] and Sarasu Pakiriswamy[2]

[1] Research and Development Centre, Vel Tech Dr. RR & Dr. SR Technical University
Avadi-Alamathi Road, Avadi, Chennai-600 062, India
sundarvtu@gmail.com
[2] Dept. of Computer Science and Engineering, Vel Tech Dr. RR & Dr. SR Technical University
Avadi-Alamathi Road, Avadi, Chennai-600 062, India
sarasujivat@gmail.com

Abstract. This paper deploys active feedback control method for achieving generalized projective synchronization (GPS) of double-scroll chaotic systems, *viz.* identical Li systems (2009), and non-identical Lü-Chen system (2002) and Li system. The synchronization results (GPS) derived in this paper using active feedback control method have been established using Lyapunov stability theory. Since the Lyapunov exponents are not required for these calculations, the active feedback control method is very effective and suitable for achieving the general projective synchronization (GPS) of double-scroll chaotic systems. Numerical simulations are presented to demonstrate the effectiveness of the synchronization results derived in this paper.

Keywords: Chaos, active control, generalized projective synchronization, Li system, Lü-Chen system.

1 Introduction

Chaotic systems are nonlinear dynamical systems, which are highly sensitive to initial conditions. Chaos is an interesting nonlinear phenomenon and has been rigorously studied in the last two decades. In operation, a chaotic system exhibits an irregular behavior and produces broadband, noise-like signals, thus it is found to be very useful in secure communications [1].

In most of the chaos synchronization approaches, the *master-slave* or *drive-response* formalism is used. If a particular chaotic system is called the *master* or *drive system* and another chaotic system is called the *slave* or *response system*, then the idea of synchronization is to use the output of the master system to control the slave system so that the output of the slave system tracks the output of the master system asymptotically.

Since the seminal work by Pecora and Carroll ([2], 1990), a variety of impressive approaches for chaos synchronization have been used for chaos synchronization such as the PC method [2], sampled-data feedback synchronization method [3], OGY method [4], time-delay feedback method [5], backstepping method [6], active control method [7], adaptive control method [8], sliding control method [9], etc.

In generalized projective synchronization [10], the chaotic systems can synchronize up to a constant scaling matrix. Complete synchronization [11], anti-synchronization

N. Meghanathan et al. (Eds.): CCSIT 2012, Part I, LNICST 84, pp. 111–118, 2012.

[12], hybrid synchronization [13], projective synchronization [14] and generalized synchronization [15] are special cases of generalized projective synchronization. The generalized projective synchronization (GPS) has important applications in secure communications.

This paper addresses the generalized projective synchronization (GPS) of double-scroll chaotic systems, viz. Li system ([16], 2009) and Lü-Chen system ([17], 2002).

This paper is organized as follows. In Section 2, we derive results for the GPS between identical Li systems (2009). In Section 3, we derive results for the GPS between non-identical Lü-Chen system (2002) and Li system (2009). Section 4 summarizes the main results derived in this paper.

2   Generalized Projective Synchronization of Identical Double-Scroll Systems

2.1   Main Results

In this section, we derive results for the generalized projective synchronization (GPS) of identical Li systems ([16], 2009).

Thus, the master system is described by the Li dynamics

$$
\begin{aligned}
\dot{x}_1 &= a(x_2 - x_1) \\
\dot{x}_2 &= x_1 x_3 - x_2 \\
\dot{x}_3 &= b - x_1 x_2 - c x_3
\end{aligned}
\tag{1}
$$

where x_1, x_2, x_3 are the *state* variables and a, b, c are constant, positive parameters of the system.

The Li system (1) is chaotic when $a = 5$, $b = 16$ and $c = 1$. Figure 1 depicts the state orbits of the *double-scroll* attractor given by Li dynamics (1).

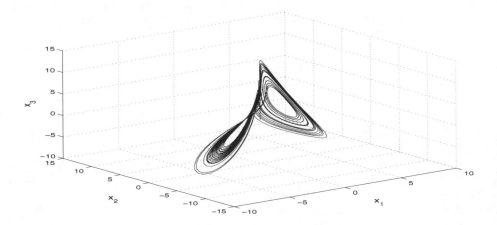

Fig. 1. State Orbits of the Li System

Also, the slave system is described by the controlled Li dynamics

$$\dot{y}_1 = a(y_2 - y_1) + u_1$$
$$\dot{y}_2 = y_1 y_3 - y_2 + u_2 \tag{2}$$
$$\dot{y}_3 = b - y_1 y_2 - c y_3 + u_3$$

where y_1, y_2, y_3 are the *state* variables and u_1, u_2, u_3 are the active controls.

For the GPS of (1) and (2), the synchronization errors are defined as

$$e_1 = y_1 - \alpha_1 x_1$$
$$e_2 = y_2 - \alpha_2 x_2 \tag{3}$$
$$e_3 = y_3 - \alpha_3 x_3$$

where the scales $\alpha_1, \alpha_2, \alpha_3$ are real numbers.

A simple calculation yields the error dynamics

$$\dot{e}_1 = a(y_2 - y_1) - \alpha_1 a(x_2 - x_1) + u_1$$
$$\dot{e}_2 = y_1 y_3 - y_2 - \alpha_2(x_1 x_3 - x_2) + u_2 \tag{4}$$
$$\dot{e}_3 = b - y_1 y_2 - c y_3 - \alpha_3(b - x_1 x_2 - c x_3) + u_3$$

We consider the active nonlinear controller defined by

$$u_1 = -a(y_2 - y_1) + \alpha_1 a(x_2 - x_1) - k_1 e_1$$
$$u_2 = -y_1 y_3 + y_2 + \alpha_2(x_1 x_3 - x_2) - k_2 e_2 \tag{5}$$
$$u_3 = -b + y_1 y_2 + c y_3 + \alpha_3(b - x_1 x_2 - c x_3) - k_3 e_3$$

where the gains k_1, k_2, k_3 are positive constants.

Substitution of (5) into (4) yields the closed-loop error dynamics

$$\dot{e}_1 = -k_1 e_1$$
$$\dot{e}_2 = -k_2 e_2 \tag{6}$$
$$\dot{e}_3 = -k_3 e_3$$

We consider the quadratic Lyapunov function defined by

$$V(e) = \frac{1}{2} e^T e = \frac{1}{2} \left(e_1^2 + e_2^2 + e_3^2 \right) \tag{7}$$

which is positive definite on $\mathbb{R}^3$.

Differentiating (7) along the trajectories of the system (6), we get

$$\dot{V}(e) = -k_1 e_1^2 - k_2 e_2^2 - k_3 e_3^2 \tag{8}$$

which is a negative definite function on $\mathbb{R}^3$, since k_1, k_2, k_3 are positive constants.

Thus, by Lyapunov stability theory [18], the error dynamics (6) is globally exponentially stable. Hence, we obtain the following result.

Theorem 1. *The active feedback controller (5) achieves global chaos generalized projective synchronization (GPS) between the identical Li systems (1) and (2).* ∎

2.2   Numerical Results

For the numerical simulations, the fourth order Runge-Kutta method is used to solve the two systems of differential equations (1) and (2) with the active controller (5).

The parameters of the identical Li systems are selected as $a = 5, \ b = 16, \ c = 1$ so that the systems (1) and (2) exhibit chaotic behaviour.

The initial values for the master system (1) are taken as

$$x_1(0) = 4, \ x_2(0) = 12, \ x_3(0) = 6$$

The initial values for the slave system (2) are taken as

$$y_1(0) = 20, \ y_2(0) = 5, \ y_3(0) = 14$$

The GPS scales α_i are taken as $\alpha_1 = -2.3, \ \alpha_2 = 0.5, \ \alpha_3 = 1.8$.

We take the state feedback gains as $k_1 = 4, \ k_2 = 4$ and $k_3 = 4$.

Figure 2 shows the time response of the error states e_1, e_2, e_3 of the error dynamical system (4) when the active nonlinear controller (5) is deployed. From this figure, it is clear that all the error states decay to zero exponentially in 2 sec and thus, generalized projective synchronization is achieved between the identical Li systems (1) and (2).

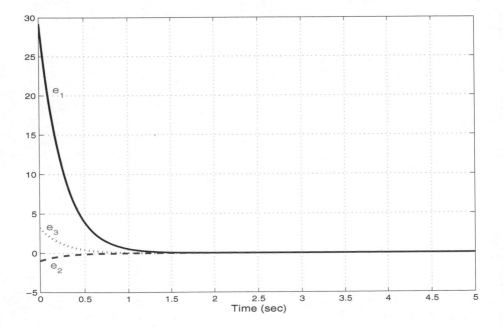

Fig. 2. Time Responses of the Error States of (4)

3 Generalized Projective Synchronization of Non-identical Double-Scroll Systems

3.1 Main Results

In this section, we derive results for the generalized projective synchronization (GPS) of non-identical double-scroll systems, *viz.* Lü-Chen system ([17], 2002) and Li system ([16], 2009).

Thus, the master system is described by the Lü-Chen dynamics

$$\begin{aligned}
\dot{x}_1 &= p(x_2 - x_1) \\
\dot{x}_2 &= -x_1 x_3 + r x_2 \\
\dot{x}_3 &= x_1 x_2 - q x_3
\end{aligned} \tag{9}$$

where x_1, x_2, x_3 are the *state* variables and p, q, r are constant, positive parameters of the system.

The Lü-Chen system (9) is chaotic when $p = 36, q = 3$ and $r = 15$.

Figure 3 depicts the state orbits of the *double-scroll* attractor given by Lü-Chen dynamics (9).

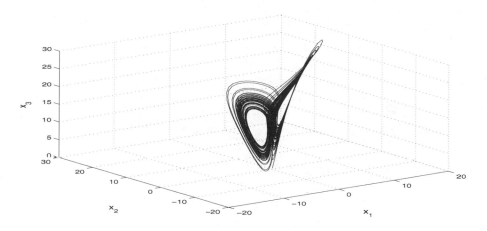

Fig. 3. State Orbits of the Lü-Chen System

Also, the slave system is described by the controlled Li dynamics

$$\begin{aligned}
\dot{y}_1 &= a(y_2 - y_1) + u_1 \\
\dot{y}_2 &= y_1 y_3 - y_2 + u_2 \\
\dot{y}_3 &= b - y_1 y_2 - c y_3 + u_3
\end{aligned} \tag{10}$$

where y_1, y_2, y_3 are the *state* variables and u_1, u_2, u_3 are the active controls.

For the GPS of (9) and (10), the synchronization errors are defined as

$$
\begin{aligned}
e_1 &= y_1 - \alpha_1 x_1 \\
e_2 &= y_2 - \alpha_2 x_2 \\
e_3 &= y_3 - \alpha_3 x_3
\end{aligned}
\tag{11}
$$

where the scales $\alpha_1, \alpha_2, \alpha_3$ are real numbers.

A simple calculation yields the error dynamics

$$
\begin{aligned}
\dot{e}_1 &= a(y_2 - y_1) - \alpha_1 p(x_2 - x_1) + u_1 \\
\dot{e}_2 &= y_1 y_3 - y_2 - \alpha_2(-x_1 x_3 + r x_2) + u_2 \\
\dot{e}_3 &= b - y_1 y_2 - c y_3 - \alpha_3(x_1 x_2 - q x_3)^{\cdot} + u_3
\end{aligned}
\tag{12}
$$

We consider the active nonlinear controller defined by

$$
\begin{aligned}
u_1 &= -a(y_2 - y_1) + \alpha_1 p(x_2 - x_1) - k_1 e_1 \\
u_2 &= -y_1 y_3 + y_2 + \alpha_2(-x_1 x_3 + r x_2) - k_2 e_2 \\
u_3 &= -b + y_1 y_2 + c y_3 + \alpha_3(x_1 x_2 - q x_3) - k_3 e_3
\end{aligned}
\tag{13}
$$

where the gains k_1, k_2, k_3 are positive constants.

Substitution of (13) into (12) yields the closed-loop error dynamics

$$
\begin{aligned}
\dot{e}_1 &= -k_1 e_1 \\
\dot{e}_2 &= -k_2 e_2 \\
\dot{e}_3 &= -k_3 e_3
\end{aligned}
\tag{14}
$$

We consider the quadratic Lyapunov function defined by

$$
V(e) = \frac{1}{2} e^T e = \frac{1}{2} \left(e_1^2 + e_2^2 + e_3^2 \right)
\tag{15}
$$

which is positive definite on $\mathbb{R}^3$.

Differentiating (15) along the trajectories of the system (14), we get

$$
\dot{V}(e) = -k_1 e_1^2 - k_2 e_2^2 - k_3 e_3^2
\tag{16}
$$

which is a negative definite function on $\mathbb{R}^3$, since k_1, k_2, k_3 are positive constants.

Thus, by Lyapunov stability theory [18], the error dynamics (14) is globally exponentially stable. Hence, we obtain the following result.

Theorem 2. *The active feedback controller (13) achieves global chaos generalized projective synchronization (GPS) between the non-identical Lü-Chen system (9) and Li system (10).*   ∎

3.2   Numerical Results

For the numerical simulations, the fourth order Runge-Kutta method is used to solve the two systems of differential equations (9) and (10) with the active controller (13).

The parameters of the Lü-Chen system (9) and Li system (10) are taken as in the chaotic case.

The initial values for the master system (9) are taken as

$$x_1(0) = 14, \ x_2(0) = 7, \ x_3(0) = 4$$

The initial values for the slave system (10) are taken as

$$y_1(0) = 3, \ y_2(0) = 15, \ y_3(0) = 22$$

The GPS scales α_i are taken as $\alpha_1 = 3.8, \ \alpha_2 = -0.3, \ \alpha_3 = -2.7$.

We take the state feedback gains as $k_1 = 4, \ k_2 = 4$ and $k_3 = 4$.

Figure 4 shows the time response of the error states e_1, e_2, e_3 of the error dynamical system (12) when the active nonlinear controller (13) is deployed. From this figure, it is clear that all the error states decay to zero exponentially in 2 sec and thus, generalized projective synchronization is achieved between the non-identical Lü-Chen system (9) and Li system (10).

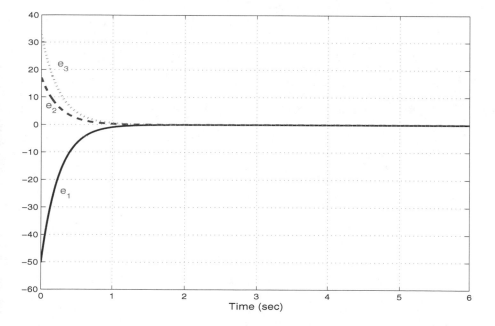

Fig. 4. Time Responses of the Error States of (12)

4 Conclusions

In this paper, active feedback control method has been deployed to achieve generalized projective synchronization (GPS) of double-scroll chaotic attractors, *viz.* identical Li systems (2009), and non-identical double-scroll attractors, *viz.* Lü-Chen system (2002) and Li system (2009). The synchronization results derived in this paper have been proved using Lyapunov stability theory. Since Lyapunov exponents are not required for these calculations, the proposed active control method is very effective and suitable for achieving GPS of the double-scroll chaotic attractors addressed in this paper. Numerical simulations are presented to demonstrate the effectiveness of the synchronization results derived in this paper.

References

1. Liao, T.L., Tsai, S.H.: Adaptive synchronization of chaotic systems and its application to secure communications. Chaos, Solitons and Fractals 11, 1387–1396 (2000)
2. Pecora, L.M., Carroll, T.L.: Synchronization in chaotic systems. Phys. Rev. Lett. 64, 821–824 (1990)
3. Yang, T., Chua, L.O.: Control of chaos using sampled-data feedback control. Internat. J. Bifurcat. Chaos 9, 215–219 (1999)
4. Ott, E., Grebogi, C., Yorke, J.A.: Controlling chaos. Phys. Rev. Lett. 64, 1196–1199 (1990)
5. Park, J.H., Kwon, O.M.: A novel criterion for delayed feedback control of time-delay chaotic systems. Chaos, Solit. Fract. 17, 709–716 (2003)
6. Yu, Y.G., Zhang, S.C.: Adaptive backstepping synchronization of uncertain chaotic systems. Chaos, Solit. Fract. 27, 1369–1375 (2006)
7. Ho, M.C., Hung, Y.C.: Synchronization of two different chaotic systems using generalized active control. Physics Letters A 301, 424–428 (2002)
8. Chen, S.H., Lü, J.: Synchronization of an uncertain unified system via adaptive control. Chaos, Solitons and Fractals 14, 643–647 (2002)
9. Konishi, K., Hirai, M., Kokame, H.: Sliding mode control for a class of chaotic systems. Phys. Lett. A 245, 511–517 (1998)
10. Zhou, P., Kuang, F., Cheng, Y.M.: Generalized projective synchronization for fractional order chaotic systems. Chinese Journal of Physics 48(1), 49–56 (2010)
11. Sundarapandian, V.: Global chaos synchronization of Shimizu-Morioka and Liu-Chen chaotic systems by active nonlinear control. Internat. J. Advances in Science and Technology 2(4), 11–20 (2011)
12. Sundarapandian, V.: Anti-synchronization of Lorenz and T chaotic systems by active nonlinear control. Internat. J. Computer Information Systems 2(4), 6–10 (2011)
13. Sundarapandian, V.: Hybrid synchronization of hyperchaotic Rössler and hyperchaotic Lorenz systems by active control. Internat. J. Advances in Science and Technology 2(4), 1–10 (2011)
14. Mainieri, R., Rehacek, J.: Projective synchronization in three-dimensioned chaotic systems. Phys. Rev. Lett. 82, 3042–3045 (1999)
15. Wang, Y.W., Guan, Z.H.: Generalized synchronization of continuous chaotic systems. Chaos, Solit. Fract. 27, 97–101 (2006)
16. Li, X.F., Chlouveakis, K.E., Xu, D.L.: Nonlinear dynamics and circuit realization of a new chaotic flow: A variant of Lorenz, Chen and Lü. Nonlinear Analysis 10, 2357–2368 (2009)
17. Lü, J., Chen, G.: A new chaotic attractor coined. Internat. J. Bifurcation and Chaos 12(3), 659–661 (2002)
18. Hahn, W.: The Stability of Motion. Springer, New York (1967)

Mobile Ad Hoc Netwoks Security Attacks and Secured Routing Protocols: A Survey

Supriya[1] and Manju Khari[2]

[1] M.Tech (Information Security), Ambedkar Institute of Technology, GGSIPU
supriya.14489@gmail.com
[2] Computer Science Engineering Department, Ambedkar Institute ofTechnology. GGSIPU
manjukhari@yahoo.co.in

Abstract. Ad-hoc networks are the collection of autonomous nodes where all the nodes are configured dynamically without any centralized management system. Mobile Adhoc Networks (MANETs) are self-configuring network of mobile routers connected via a wireless link. However,the feature of decentralization and dynamic configuration of nodes makes MANETs vulnerable to various security attacks,that are otherwise not so common in a wired network. For mitigation of these attacks,several secured routing protocols are being proposed till now. This paper provides the view of overall security breaches present in the Ad-hoc Networks till now and will discuss in brief about the several proposed secure routing protocols.

Keywords: Security breaches, Secured routing protocols, blackhole attacks, constraints.

1   Introduction

Mobile Ad-hoc Networks are the networks comprising of autonomous nodes that utilize multi-hop radio-relaying and work without the support of any infrastructure. There is no centralized mechanism for routing of packets in MANETs. The communication between the nodes is solely on the basis of mutual trust.

In MANETs,the nodes that are available in radio-frequency of each other communicates directly and for communication with other available nodes,intermediate nodes are being used. To provide security to MANETs,a protocol is required which encapsulate a set of all necessary security mechanisms in it.

In order to work in a secure and reliable ad-hoc network environment,some security criterias are necessarily be addressed[1][3]:

Security Attacks in MANETs
Categorisation of attacks in MANETs is as follows[5]:

- **Active Attacks:** An active attack attempts to destroy or modify the data being exchanged in the network,hence disrupting the normal functioning of attacks. Further these attacks are divided into:

N. Meghanathan et al. (Eds.): CCSIT 2012, Part I, LNICST 84, pp. 119–124, 2012.
© Institute for Computer Sciences, Social Informatics and Telecommunications Engineering 2012

- **External attacks:** These are carried out by the outsider nodes i.e. the nodes not belonging to the concerned network.
- **Internal attacks:** These attacks occur because of compromised nodes present inside the network.
- **Passive Attacks:** These attacks do not interfere with the running operations of the network. It just performs the eavesdropping of the data exchanging via the concerned network.

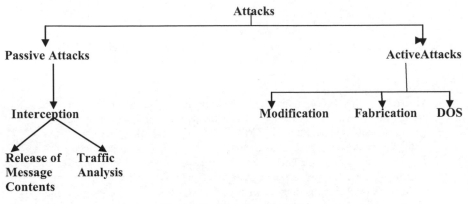

Fig. 1. Classification of Attacks

Broad categorization of some of the preliminary attacks on the basis of their active and passive nature.[7]:

Table 1. Categorisation of Attacks

Attack Name	Passive Attacks	Active Attacks
Impersonation		✓
Eavesdropping	✓	
Masquerading		✓
Denial of Service		✓
Traffic Analysis	✓	
Replay		✓
Message Modification		✓

Several major attacks that are being studied till now in order to provide security to MANETs are as follows[2][3][7]:

- **Routing Attacks:** These attacks are aimed on the routing protocols and are being performed in a manner to disrupt the operation of the network.
  These attacks are further categorized into following:

  - ➢ Routing Table Overflow
  - ➢ Routing Table Poisoning

> ➢ Packet Replication
> ➢ Route Cache Poisoning
> ➢ Rushing Attack

- **Wormhole Attacks:** In wormhole attacks,the malicious nodes pretends to provide the shortest path between the two distant nodes. If the source node opts for this route,then,it gives rise to a loop and the packets sent via this route are either dropped or keep on revolving but don't reach to their legitimate destination.

  Modes of wormhole attacks[9]:

  > ➢ Wormhole Attack using Encapsulation
  > ➢ Wormhole Attack using Out-Of-Band Channel
  > ➢ Wormhole with High Power Transmission
  > ➢ Wormhole using Packet Relay
  > ➢ Wormhole using Protocol Deviations

- **Blackhole Attacks:** In these attacks,the malicious node keep on sending positive replies for the route requests it is getting,inspite of the fact that whether the related routes are available or not.Ultimately,drops all the packets that are routed to its destination via this node.

  Like-Jellyfish Attack

  Blackhole attacks are further categorized into[10]:

  > ➢ Internal Blackhole
  > ➢ External Blackhole

- **Grayhole Attacks:** This attack on MANETs also provides the smallest route to the nodes that are searching for a route to send the packets.But here,malicious nodes drops the packets with some probability.There is no certainty of the fact whether the packet will be surely dropped or will be surely forwarded.

- **Denial of Service Attacks:** In this attack,the main aim of the attacker is to flood the network,so that maximum resources of the network are being consumed at their par like network bandwidth and energy resources etc.

  Several DOS attacks are as follows:

  > ➢ Sleep Deprivation Torture
  > ➢ Jamming Attack
  > ➢ SYN Flooding
  > ➢ Link Spoofing Attack

- **False Information Attacks:** Malicious nodes commutes the wrong information about the legitimate nodes,hence isolating them while themselves remain connected in the network. This type of attacks includes stacking attack.

- **Incomplete Information:** Malicious nodes misleads the communication process in the network by providing incomplete information.
- **Modification:** Packets may be modified or malicious packets may be inserted in the network by the illegitimate node.
- **Fabrication/Masquerading:** A malicious node having bad reputation in the network,register itself as a new node/new user in the network.
- **Sybil Attack:** In this attack,a malicious node impersonate itself as more non-existent nodes,to give a feel of being several malicious nodes conspiring together.
- **Blackmailing:** This attack makes use of false information attack for propagating wrong reputation of a node hence,blackmailing the node alongwith creating DOS attack.
- **Replay Attacks:** It includes replay of previously captured routing traffic by the malicious node.It is done to create errorneous routing information and misleading the network.
- **Selective Misbehaving Attacks:** Node act as malicious for certain traffic and otherwise remains the good node. Hence,behaving in a selective manner.
- **On-off Attacks:** To conceal its identity and preventing itself from being detected, a malicious node keeps on changing its behaviour between good and bad.
- **Conflicting Behaviour Attacks:** Here,the main aim of malicious nodes is to break the trust-relationship among the legitimate nodes of the network which is the basis of communication in MANETs.
- **State Pollution Attacks:** Malicious nodes provide incorrect responses regarding the requested parameters,leading to broadcast of duplication address detection messages repeatedly.This obstructs the entry of new node in the network.
- **Session Hijacking Attacks:** In this attack,malicious nodes makes use of spoofing attack,hijacks the session by spoofing the ip address of victim's system.
- **Location Disclosure Attacks:** Here,malicious node collects the route map and other information regarding the nodes by analyzing and monitoring the traffic. This helps in planting more attacks onto the network.
- **Device Tampering Attacks:** The main cause of this attack is the absence of central administration which makes it easy for mobile nodes to change their identities.
- **Neighbour Attacks:** In this,attacker/malicious mode forwards the packet without recording the id in the packet,hence providing the misleading route,which will ultimately result in disrupted route.
- **Byzantine Attacks:** Here,the malicious nodes work in collusion and carries out the attack that create more disrupting or degrading attacks.They do so by creating routing loops,selective dropping of packets etc.[8]

Secure Routing Protocols for MANETs

Mainly,MANETs works on TCP/IP structure for providing the better communication.

Because of the mobility factor of nodes involved in MANETs,they provide efficient functionality but it is the main reason of attacks performed on these networks,some of which we have been discussed so far. Broad categorization of routing protocols is as follows:

> Routing Information Update Mechanism
> Use of Temporal information for routing
> Routing Topology
> Utilization of specific resources

Designing issues for a secure routing protocol for MANETs

- **Mobility:** Routing protocols for ad-hoc networks must be an efficient mobility management protocol that can effectively manage with the path-break disruption occur due to the dynamic topology of the MANETs.
- **Bandwidth Constriants:** In wireless ad-hoc networks,there is an availability of limited radio band. Therefore,for better services,a routing protocol which can use the bandwidth optimally minimizing all the overheads is well-suited for MANETs.
- **Error-Prone Shares Broadcast Radio Channel:** It is must for a wireless ad-hoc network routing protocol to interact with MAC layer so that it always have an availability of alternative routes to avoid collisions to cater the requirement of dynamic topology of ad-hoc networks.[11]
- **Hidden and Exposed Terminal Problems:** There may be the terminals in the network that are not in the transmission range of the sender but are there in the transmission range of the receiver,which may give rise to collision of packets while communication.This is referred to as the problem of hidden terminals.

  To overcome this,an efficient protocol is required like Medium Access Collision Avoidance for Wireless [12], Floor Acquisition Multiple Access [13], Dual Busy Tone Multiple Access [14].

  There may also be a condition in wireless network(MANETs) where a node is blocked due to transmission of a nearby transmitting node that are transmiting to another node. This problem is referred to as exposed terminal problem.
- **Resource Constraints:** The most important and limited resources that become a constraint for nodes in MANETs are battery life and processing power. Therefore, a routing protocol is required which can manage these resources optimally.

2   Conclusion

In this paper,all types of attacks to which MANETs are vulnerable are being presented. A brief overview of issues required to be considered for designing a secure routing protocols is also presented towards the end of this paper. However,MANETs are still in a premature state and provides a wide scope of research. To utilize the dynamicity and robustness of these networks successfully and reliably,it is required to understand its security needs. This will enable to mitigate the security breaches and making it a more suitable communication medium. The flexibility and scalability of MANETs will make them an ideal platform for communication in near future.

References

[1] Li, W., Joshi, A.: Security Issues in Mobile Ad Hoc Networks-A Survey, Department of Computer Science and Electrical Engineering, University of Maryland, Baltimore County (2007)

[2] Jawandhiya, P.M., Ghonge, M.M., Ali, M.S., Deshpande, J.S.: A Survey of Mobile Ad Hoc Network Attacks. International Journal of Engineering Science and Technology 2(9), 4063–4071 (2010)

[3] Singh, K., Yadav, R.S., Ranvijay: A Review Paper on Ad Hoc Network Security. International Journal of Computer Science and Security 1(1) (2008)

[4] Zhou, L., Haas, Z.J.: Securing Ad-Hoc Networks. IEEE Network Magazine 13(6), 24–30 (1999)

[5] Garg, S.K.: Review of Secured Routing for Wireless Ad Hoc Network. International Journal of Computing and Business Research 2(1) (2011)

[6] Hu, Y., Perrig, A., Johnson, D.B.: Rushing Attacks and Defense inWireless Ad Hoc Network Routing Protocols. In: Procedings of the ACM Workshop o Wireless Security 2003, pp. 30–40 (September 2003)

[7] Cho, J.-H., Swami, A., Chen, I.-R.: A Survey on Trust Management for Mobile Ad Hoc Networks. IEEE Communications Surveys and Tutorials (2011)

[8] Manikandan, K.P., Satyaprasad, R., Rajasekhararao, K.: A Survey on Attacks and Defense Metrics of Routing Mechanism in Mobile Ad Hoc Networks. International Journal of Advanced Computer Science and Applications 2(3) (2011)

[9] Raote, N.S., Hande, K.N.: Approaches towards Mitigating Wormhole Attack in Wireless Ad-Hoc Network. International Journal of Advanced Engineering Sciences and Technologies 2(2), 172–175 (2011)

[10] Biswas, K., Ali, L.: Security Threats in Mobile Ad-Hoc Network. Blekinge Institute of Technology, Sweden (2007)

[11] Fullmer, C.L., Garcia-Luna-Aceves, J.J.: Solutions to Hidden Ternimal Problems in Wireless Networks. In: Proceedings of ACM SIGCOMM, pp. 39–49 (1997)

[12] Bharghavan, V., Demers, A., Shenker, S., Zhang, L.: MACAW: A Media Access Protocol for Wireless LANs. In: Proceedings of ACM SIGCOMM, pp. 212–225 (1994)

[13] Fullmer, C.L., Garcia-Luna-Aceves, J.J.: Floor Acquisition Multiple Access(FAMA) for Packet-Radio Networks. In: Proceedings of ACM SIGCOMM, pp. 262–273 (1995)

[14] Deng, J., Haas, Z.: Dual Busy Tone Multiple Access(DBTMA):A New Medium Access Control for Packet Radio Networks. In: Proceedings of ICUPC, vol. 1, pp. 973–977 (1998)

Privacy and Security in Digital Networks from the Perspective of Modeling and Software Development

Erich Ortner

Darmstadt University of Technology
Department for Development of Application Systems
Hochschulstrasse 1, 64289 Darmstadt, Germany
ortner@winf.tu-darmstadt.de

Abstract. This is a report about cooperation projects with the Common IT-department of the Hessian judicial authority (Gemeinsame IT-Stelle der hessischen Justiz, called GIT in the following) and other Hessian public institutions. In the context of modeling and software development using state-of-the-art schema management technologies, the area of protection and security in digital networks undergoes changes towards more responsibility in dealing with technology, organization and human users. From the perspective of language theory, the available commercial systems such as NetWeaver (SAP), WebSphere (IBM) or SharePoint Server (MS) can be seen as schema-management systems. From the point of view of programming and transaction technology it will be interpreted as servicebase-management systems. Concerning the current protection and security of GIT's application systems two solutions will be presented here, parts of which have already been implemented. Thus, this paper focuses on the standardization of data elements and the standardization of functional elements, which ensure the domain-specific semantic integrity of data and functions in enterprises and administrations. At the end, we will discuss the change we are witnessing among IT experts as well as IT users globally due to language-based technologies such as Semantic Web, Wikis, Google, Facebook, etc., here shown using the example of the Hessian judicial authority. This change is reflected also in education, especially with respect to providing language-based modeling know-how for everybody.

Keywords: Network Security, Schemata Management, Language-Based technology.

1 Introduction

Language-based computer sciences [Ort05] today are intertwined with nearly every field in economy, science, politics and society. This close technological linkage, "ubiquitous computing", more and more frequently raises the question of how much responsibility computing must assume for crises and undesirable

N. Meghanathan et al. (Eds.): CCSIT 2012, Part I, LNICST 84, pp. 125–137, 2012.

developments, as for example in the recent financial crisis. With the description of the current joint project "Protection and security for the digital networks, stationary and mobile IT devices of the Hessian judicial authorities" we aim at clarifying the following:

1. What are today's requirements from the perspective of protection and security in digital networks as well as for end devices used for the development of application systems (with regard to modeling and software development), e.g. [Bur10], and which of these requirements can actually be fulfilled?
2. Which (language-based) schema management systems are available (e.g. [HR01] and [GR02]), and what is their common theoretical basis (e.g. [WOI]) – particularly in the context of a semantic integrity, i.e. concerning the content, of data and functions?
3. Which consequences derive from 1. and 2. for the education of (young) people by IT experts and IT users [Hei10] and additionally for anyone who is confronted with the "ubiquitous" language-based technologies?

We believe that it is possible to reach agreement among the experts in science and practice today that the IT-development of the last 30 years has partly undergone the following transitions:

Science: From hardware-oriented programming to user-oriented and content-oriented modeling.

IT industry: From computer-based (algorithmic) technologies to language-based technologies (which integrate the human intelligence).

User-enterprises: Shift of focus from data to the human being and finally to the processes.

From the perspective of development and operation of "adaptable application systems" based on language-technology the situation grows more acute: In the era of the Internet, protection and security is also a question of using (normal) languages in a disciplined way. A fact which is still not estimated sufficiently but has great potential for the solution in this context is the following principle: "First modeling with linguistic competence (IT), then the execution based on terms (users)". In the following this will be the basis of our reasoning.

2   Protection and Security in Digital Networks – State of the Art

In today's permanent debate about protection and security in digital (and social) networks the following subjects are – sometimes unfortunately in an incompetent and anti-progressive way – being fueled by the global press:

- Cloud Security instead of cybercrime using malware;
- on the Internet, a criminal service society has been established, whose criminal energy could fundamentally endanger states and societies;

- alternatively, some strategy papers (e.g. [Bur10]) rightly and constructively stress that nowadays it is vital to protect the "content" (e.g. externalized knowledge, application software) and no longer to concentrate exclusively on securing access to the systems or their "formal consistency" [Ort05] in enterprises and administrations.

After more than 30 years of research in the field (e.g. since [WO80]), it is a known fact in professional circles that computer science today is more a language-based than computer-based engineering science. Hence, here we look at the perpetual subject "protection and security in IT" – 30 years ago it was decreed to EDV (private economy) and ADV (public sector) – primarily against the background of programming and modeling languages as well as "normal languages" (e.g. users' expert languages) which are used in the development and operation of entire application systems (as opposed to only the software parts). One of the last interviews with Edsger W. Dijkstra (1930-2002), excerpts of which have now been published in Comm. of the ACM, No 8, Vol 53, August 2010, forms an excellent integrated background from the point of view of programming languages and their development as well as software engineering.

Due to the development of various languages, our modern options shift to the content-side of IT-solutions. Naturally, the protection measures of securing the "outer form" or the "containers" for these contents as was central 30 years ago continue to be available.

In Germany, the Federal Data Protection Act and its amendment §6.1, the so-called "ten commandments", regulates the wide range of judicial measures available. It became effective on the first of January 1979. With respect to basic software and software engineering, already prior to the commencement of the Act, since the beginning of the 1970s, a multitude of security concepts and techniques were developed, e.g. identification/authentification, cryptography, access matrix, "system enforced integrity", i.e. data integrity ensured by database management systems. Measured against the "ten commandments", Wedekind described them systematically, and from a methodological and ethical point of view, in Germany also pioneeringly. See [Wed78] and [Wed80].

Looking at this subject again today from the perspectives of adaptive application systems and (data) modeling (e.g. [Ort05]) and schema-based software-development [Pei10], we can base a simple model of states and functions of the information transformation in application systems which also includes the language-based approach, i.e. the users' language usage (see figure 1). Hereby, we use the term "term" [Kue10] mainly as a synonym of the term "type" [Pei10]. Schemas, which can be modeled, represent the universal aspect of things [WOI] and form the intension of "terms" or "types", respectively.

Compared with solutions in the physical world, the central terms of this subject can be defined as follows:

- Reliability is a function-related term. If a car starts without problems every morning, we call this reliable.
- Securing is the act of providing security. Thus, security can be considered to be state-related (see fig. 1): A car may be safe due to its crumple zone.

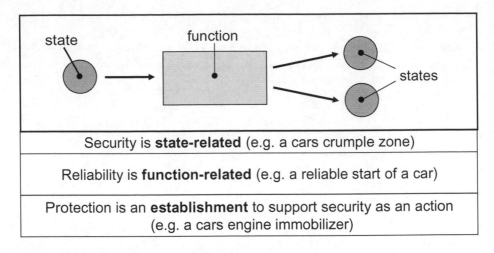

Fig. 1. (Data) states and functions in IT-based information processing

– Protection (or privacy for personal data and rights) is an "establishment"
for preventing the unauthorized and inappropriate usage of something: A
car is protected by its engine immobilizer.

For the protection of content in application systems there are two solutions (establishments): on the one side, data (IT) and externalized knowledge (human beings) and on the other side processing functions (of the IT) and responsible actions (man). Before presenting these in detail, section 3 resumes in short the neutral schema management system architecture, which any application development is based on. As it is this theory which enables managing the above approaches in the first place, namely neutral to changes of content or implementation, as well as appropriate to human beings and IT.

3   Servicebase Management Systems and Neutral Schema Management Technology

In line with IBM's slogan "Let us make the planet a little smarter", this section demonstrates how all application fields in IT, as they were practiced, for example, at GIT, can be merged using a neutral schema management technology (basic systems). The foundations of language theory have been regularly published since the 1980s, last in [WOI] as a "constructive schema-tenet" of language-based computer sciences [Ort05].

The joining of application fields through a common, generic basic technology leads us to the implementation of a neutral architecture of schema management systems even prior to the development of the actual application systems (i.e. the object-language schemas). They serve as language-based basic technologies (i.e. basing on a generic theory of "schema and instances", or basic system models) as they may underlie any development of application systems for (digital) networks as well as IT end-devices, across the operating systems. Figure 2 shows such an architecture of basic systems including in brackets their corresponding primary modeling languages, or their models respectively. In accordance with the inventor of the relational model, Ted Codd, we used the same modeling language for object data (data model) and also for the meta data level (meta model) for database management systems and for the administration of meta data in repositories (meta database management system) [Dat07]. Since their reconstruction these languages are also called rational model-languages in general (fig 2) or in particular rational data models against the background of Lorenzen's ortho-languages and tenet of elementary syntax [Wed81], [Ort82].

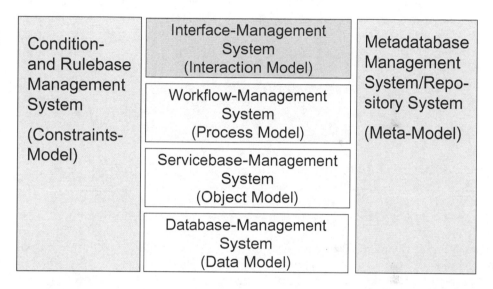

Fig. 2. Language-based basic technologies and rational modeling languages

Servicebase-management systems are based on the object model of programming languages such as Java or Enterprise Java Beans (e.g. [BMH06]) for the development of programs or "service-means". We need to consider that with the development of service-oriented architectures (SOA) the term "services" is often used instead of "service means" (software) when algorithms (software) are addressed, which are to be implemented by the IT (really IT-service-means). Here, Paul G. Huppertz has contributed very useful and precise definition work in recent years [Hup06]. His work and results should be integrated in the system development of the various sciences (e.g. computer sciences and business sciences) with regard to a future global "service science" [MKS10].

For workflow management systems (fig. 2) we take the process model as a basis, as to some extent developed in [Fis10]. For the Interface Management System an interaction model, if applicable based on a markup theory (e.g. [Car72]) and the dialogic logic [Inh03] may be sufficient. And for the "Condition and Rule Base-Management System" (fig. 2) we can use a restraints model such as the

SBVR (Semantics of Business Vocabulary and Business Rules) presented by the OMG (Object Management Group). For joining the levels and the components of language-based basic technology (fig. 2) by programming, several technologies may serve. Here, a comprehensive technology from the field of SOA is the so-called "enterprise service bus" (e.g. [EHH+08]). While for example for connecting the service-means-base management system and the database management system, recently JBoss Community's "Hibernate" (e.g. [BK07]) which uses "object relational mapping" (ORM) has become popular. The architecture shown in figure 2 is characterized by the fact that its components are largely neutral towards each other, but also beyond the application system to be developed. This means in particular that changes made to the objects and applications which are maintained in a schema management system are easy to control and have only a limited effect on the changes in another schema management system. This is about the implementation of "neutrality statements" such as "data neutrality", "process neutrality", "controlling neutrality", "rule neutrality", "methods neutrality" or "user neutrality". The architecture is called "Darmstädter Modell" because it has been developed from Darmstadt [HL05] and because of its step-by-step organization and its long-lived orientation for the research in basic systems (since the 1970ies).

4   Solution 1: Data Element Standardization

From the perspective of the language-based basic technologies this is a field of application for repository systems, as described for example in [Ort05].

From the perspective of the contents to be managed, basing on this, the data integrity described in this section (e.g. [SW85], [RK88], [ORS90]) and the compliance of application functions – through man as well as IT – described in the next section (e.g. [KH93], [Pei10]) are the subject of solution development.

When standardizing data elements, we need to follow the concept [ORS90] that a sufficient (but limited) number of standardized data elements of an enterprise or administration can be assembled in an assessable and controlled way together with every data storage (files, databases) and uses of data (data descriptions in programs and at user interfaces). The content of these data elements must also be standardized (as related to each particular expert field). In principle, by defining standards for data elements we manage the precepts for the possible propositions about the objects of an organization in the context of all reconstructed (modeled), constructive (basic) constraints, the so-called semantic, structural, pragmatic and technical integrity rules [SW85].

Hereby, data elements are defined as follows [ORS90]:

- A data element is the smallest unit for structuring data or information related to users and/or IT.
- A data element must be defined neutrally with regard to its use and generally as to content, i.e. it is not designed for single, current application situations and from an overall perspective of an enterprise, on schema level (universal form and content).

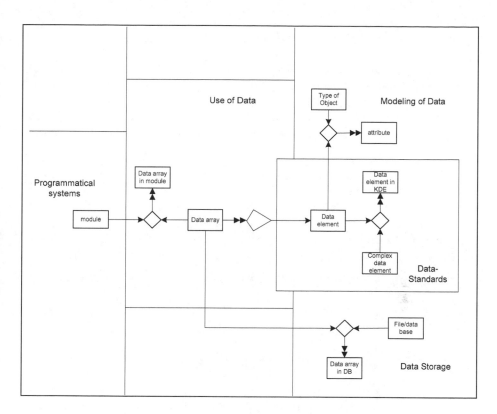

Fig. 3. Repository meta schemas for data element standardization and the management of data element standards

- Its "semantics" (meaning, use, subject-specific content) shape the data element, not only its name nor exclusively its form or syntax nor the structure (grammar) of the (subject-specific) linguistic expression.

Therefore the standardization of data elements is an application, implementation, operational and organizational establishment of "system enforced integrity" (e.g. [GR02]) – with the help of a 3-schema organization for the integrity rules (e.g. [RK88]) – on the data resources side in an enterprise or another organizational unit. Figure 3 shows the meta schema (documentation structure) of a repository system [Ort97] which is able to manage data element standards as well as the documentation of their use in the partial systems or partial results of the development. In addition to the repository system, the solution must comprise a further establishment, namely a centralized organization of all integrity rules of an enterprise and, if applicable, in accordance with the 3-schema approach. This is necessary to truly fulfill the requirement of "system enforced integrity".

The decisive advantages of "system enforced integrity" in the case of data element standardization with a centralized management of the integrity rules in an enterprise can be summarized as follows:

– The interfaces between the developed solutions or components are unified (based on content) and the integration and reusability of data elements is improved.
– The user interfaces are subject-specifically standardized with regard to their semantics and put on a common, subject-specific terminology so that users will be able to intelligently handle IT-solutions.
– Redundancies and the multiple use of data collections in an organization can be controlled, which enables effective and efficient data integrity management.

The third component, no less important for reaching the goal of "system enforced integrity", is the realization of the permanent tasks involved in data element standardization and data element management in enterprises or administrations. In [ORS90] and [Ort97] several organizational rules and job descriptions to this avail are discussed.

5   Solution 2: Standardization of Functional Elements

The introduction to [Ort82] still conceded that in this work a constructive and language-critical foundation of the development of application systems based on Frege's language logic could only succeed with regard to the data resources of an enterprise. Due to research results such as [Pie02] and [Fis08], however, in the meantime this has proved successful theoretically also for performing the (subject-specific) functions in an organization (enterprise, administration, department, etc.) – at any rate from the perspective of computer sciences or the programming languages and language-based modeling. What was practically possible with data element standardization in enterprises (firstly at DATEV) in the 1980s under IBM's database developers' slogan "system enforced integrity" seems to become possible today under the slogan "system enforced compliance" [BHT09], also with regard to the standardization of functional elements, concerning the IT-functions and user functions of an organization in the context of protection and security requirements, it can even be found on the World Wide Web [SHBL06].

Here, the standardization of functional elements intervenes far more in the planning of actions (e.g. work) and in the event management (e.g. business processes) in an organization than data element standardization. Data element standardization quasi standardizes what can be said in an organization. The standardization of functional elements, however, additionally regulates and controls what happens in an organization.

We want to stress once more, that functional element standards represent normalized and standardized possibilities of operations (and actions) with objects on schema level (event schemas). Their instances must be understood as singular operations or actions which are bound to particular places and times, i.e. singular, volatile events. Figure 4 shows the "content" (schema and instances) of a service-base management system, modeled as a prototype for a repository application for the standardization of functional elements in a service company, e.g. a hairdresser, because a practical implementation at the Hessian judicial authority is not yet available. A separate but integrated repository [Ort05] was added. It includes an inventory of all the business rules (regulation) of an enterprise or administration (Condition and Rulebase Management System, figure 2) as well as the management of this inventory using language-based basic technologies [FLOZ10] during the development and operation of the application systems as a further establishment that is organized in accordance with the 3-schemas approach.

EXECUTEwork (Work#,	DESCRPTION,	DIAGRAMM,	WTIME, ...)
001	CUTTINGhair	„interaction schema"	20min
002	GETTINGwater	„action schema"	05min
003	DISPOSEtrash	„action schema"	03min
...	...	...	...

MAKINGconversation(CONV#,	DESCRIPTION,	DIAGRAMM,	WTIME, ...)
ooa	WeatherEvents	„dialogue schema"	05min
oob	VacationEvents	„dialogue schema"	15min
ooc	MAKINGappointment	„dialogue schema"	03min
...	...	...	...

Work#: Number of work element   WTIME: target time for work
CONV#: Number of conversation   WTIME: target time for convers.

Fig. 4. Standardization of functional elements and management using database management systems

The dynamic management of the service delivery, e.g. by preparing the work (specific organizational unit) in an enterprise or administration, could happen as follows due to the relational model on the second linguistic level [Ort05] similar to SQL:

SELECT interaction schema is: CUT_hair
AND dialog schema is:
DISCUSSING_will_Italy_be_world_champion
FROM Service enterprise (or processing-place) is:
Hair salon Dietrich, Constance
WHERE Service provider (hair dresser) is: Fina Origlio
AND Service user (customer) is: Erich Ortner
FOR Date is: Saturday, April 24, 2010, 8:00 am

To entirely establish the task "standardization of functional elements" in an enterprise or an authority, the operational and organizational structure of this function must be included. It would be useful to establish it together with the function "standardization of data elements" as a department or staff position.

Both solutions, the standardization of data elements as described in the previous section, and the standardization of functional elements described in this section, are therefore "establishments" (consisting of man, organization and technology) for protecting the "content" [Bur10] and not solely the "form" (structure, architecture) of unauthorized access to or by the application system that uses IT. As not to be suspected of censorship of the content, we suggest both solutions for systems for a fair, competitive an humane way to lead our professional dependent life and not as a regulation for creative people or the jointly secured "free" life of the citizens of a country. Today, digital networks are ubiquitous all over the world. We ought to keep in mind the difference between the practice of "need-driven" engineering sciences and their systems and the effect of the "free sciences", (e.g. art or those sciences who deal with the free world citizens who are equipped with universal rights and their way of life) and their respective orientation knowledge [Mit01].

6   Outlook

If language-based technologies are to be used efficiently, the future IT users must be assisted at the best from their early youth on [WO04] in their normal language competence. Only IT experts must additionally be trained to deal with programming languages (algorithmics) with regard to developing new applications in an "engineer-like" way (systematically and creatively). Teaching language competence is the responsibility of our general schools with regard to a "world-class education" [Inh08]. IT experts, however, are usually trained at universities and the organization of their studies should be "T-shaped" [Hei10]. Choosing the teaching subjects (e.g. [KL84]) for language education very carefully would be wise in order to prevent producing once again "typographers" (programmers) instead of linguistically competent "authors" (modelers) and enlightened "readers" (users) who are able to develop and use language-based applications in digital and social networks responsibly.

Application development using language-based technologies in digital networks or for end devices today – in times of ubiquitous computing – is to educate users, and actually all of us, from early on to use language in a disciplined, responsible and reflected way. Languages (verbally) include ethics. Here, we ought to work together, so that we can cope, peacefully and with measured prosperity for all, with the huge challenges we are facing, as predicted already about 40 years ago in a report by the Club of Rome (published in 1972), also counting on man's practical reason.

Being "constructive language-critical modelers", often, using constructive logic and rational grammar [Lor87], we can control the language worlds more precisely than the physical world. If we can control the physical world with language artifacts [ZLO10], then we should be able to cope more easily with our real problems on the basis of a constructive logic, ethic and philosophy of science [Lor87] than on a merely algorithmic and analytic (formal) basis [HB34], [HB39], [BK08]. Or, to say it in Paul Lorenzen's words with the intention of saving the world: "In a constructive re-orientation, all sciences serve a peaceful life and modest prosperity."

References

[BHT09]   Burgemeestre, B., Hulstijn, J., Tan, Y.-H.: Rule-based versus Principle-based Regulatory Compliance. In: Proceeding of the 2009 Conference on Legal Knowledge and Information Systems, pp. 37–46. IOS Press, Amsterdam (2009)

[BK07]   Bauer, C., King, G.: Java persistence with Hibernate: Revised edition of Hibernate in action. Manning, Greenwich, Conn. (2007)

[BK08]   Baier, C., Katoen, J.-P.: Principles of model checking. MIT Press, Cambridge (2008)

[BMH06]   Burke, B., Monson-Haefel, R.: Enterprise JavaBeans 3.0, 5th edn. Auflage. O'Reilly Media, Sebastopol (2006)

[Bur10]   Burke, B.E.: Unified Content Security: Securing the Borderless Enterprise, Framigham, MA (2010)

[Car72]   Carl, W.: Bertrand Russell: Die Theory of Descriptions. Ihre logische und erkenntnisteoretische Bedeutung. In: Speck, J. (Hrsg.) Grundprobleme der großen Philosophen, pp. 215–163. Vandenhoeck u. Ruprecht, Göttingen (1972)

[Dat07]   Date, C.J.: Logic and databases: The roots of relational theory. Trafford Publ., Victoria (2007)

[EHH+08]   Engels, G., Hess, A., Humm, B., Juwig, O., Lohmann, M., Richter, J.-P., Voß, M., Willkomm, J.: Quasar enterprise: Anwendungslandschaften serviceorientiert gestalten. dpunkt.Verl., Heidelberg (2008)

[Fis08]   Fischer, M.: Über Sinnhaftigkeit und Bedeutsamkeit der Frege'schen Logik im Software-Engineering: Diplomarbeit, Darmstadt (September 8, 2008)

[Fis10]   Fischer, M.: Eine Logik zur Abbildung arbeitsteiliger komplexer Prozessschemata. In: Ortner, E. (Hrsg.) Konstruktive Informatik, pp. 23–30. Shaker Verlag, Aachen (2010)

[FLOZ10]   Fischer, M., Link, M., Ortner, E., Zeise, N.: Servicebase Management Systems: A Three-Schema-Architecture for Service-Management. In: Fähnrich, K.-P. (Hrsg.) Informatik 2010, Bonn, pp. 730–735. Gesellschaft für Informatik (2010)

[GR02]   Gray, J., Reuter, A.: Transaction processing: Concepts and techniques, 9th edn. Auflage. Morgan Kaufmann, San Francisco (2002)

[HB34]   Hilbert, D., Bernays, P.: Grundlagen der Mathematik I, Berlin (1934)

[HB39]   Hilbert, D., Bernays, P.: Grundlagen der Mathematik II, Berlin (1939)

[Hei10]   Heinemann, E.: Jenseits der Programmierung: Mit T-Shaping erfolgreich in die IT-Karriere starten. Hanser, München (2010)

[HL05]   Haerder, T., Lehner, W. (Hrsg.) Data Management in a Connected World: Essays Dedicated to Hartmut Wedekind on the Occasion of His 70th Birthday. Springer-Verlag GmbH, Heidelberg (2005)

[HR01]   Haerder, T., Rahm, E.: Datenbanksysteme: Konzepte und Techniken der
            Implementierung, 2nd edn. Auflage. Springer, Berlin (2001)
[Hup06]   Huppertz, P.G.: IT-Service - Der Kern des Ganzen. live IT!L, Bad Hom-
            burg (2006)
[Inh03]   Inhetveen, R.: Logik: Eine dialog-orientierte Einführung. Ed. am Guten-
            bergplatz, Leipzig (2003)
[Inh08]   Inhetveen, R.: Abschied von der Bildung. In: Heincmann, E. (Hrsg.) An-
            wendungsinformatik, pp. 235–242. Nomos-Verl.-Ges., Baden (2008)
[KH93]   Knolmayer, G., Herbst, H.: Business Rules. Wirtschaftsinformatik 35(4),
            386–390 (1993)
[KL84]   Kamlah, W., Lorenzen, P.: Logical propaedeutic: Pre-school of reasonable
            discourse. University Press of America, Lanham (1984)
[Kue10]   Kuenne, W.: Die philosophische Logik Gottlob Freges: Ein Kommentar.
            Mit den Texten des Vorworts zu "Grundgesetz der Arithmetik" und der
            "Logischen Untersuchungen I - IV". Klostermann, Frankfurt am Main
            (2010)
[Lor87]   Lorenzen, P.: Lehrbuch der konstruktiven Wissenschaftstheorie. BI-
            Wiss.-Verl., Mannheim (1987)
[Mit01]   Mittelstraß, J.: Wissen und Grenzen: Philosophische Studien. Suhrkamp,
            Frankfurt am Main (2001)
[MKS10]   Maglio, P.P., Kieliszewski, C.A., Spohrer, J.C.: Handbook of Service Sci-
            ence. Springer Science+Business Media LLC, Boston (2010)
[ORS90]   Ortner, E., Rössner, J., Söllner, B.: Entwicklung und Verwaltung stan-
            dardisierter Datenelemente. Informatik Spektrum 13(1), 17–30 (1990)
[Ort82]   Ortner, E.: Aspekte einer Konstruktionssprache für den Datenbank-
            Entwurf. Dissertation, Technische Universität Darmstadt, Darmstadt
            (Mai 1982)
[Ort97]   Ortner, E.: Methodenneutraler Fachentwurf: Zu den Grundlagen einer
            anwendungsorientierten Informatik. Teubner, Stuttgart (1997)
[Ort05]   Ortner, E.: Sprachbasierte Informatik: Wie man mit Wörtern die Cyber-
            Welt bewegt. Edition am Gutenbergplatz, Leipzig (2005)
[Pei10]   Peirce, B.C.: Type Theory Comes of Age. Communications of the
            ACM 53(2), 16–17 (2010)
[Pie02]   Pierce, B.C.: Types and programming languages. MIT Press, Cambridge
            (2002)
[RK88]   Roehrle, J., Kratzer, K.: Verwaltung von Integritätsbedingungen in einem
            Datenwörterbuch. Angewandte Informatik 30(1), 18–26 (1988)
[SHBL06]   Shadbolt, N., Hall, W., Berners-Lee, T.: The Semantic Web Revisited.
            IEEE Intelligent Systems 21(3), 96–101 (2006)
[SW85]   Steinbauer, D., Wedekind, H.: Integritätsaspekte in Datenbanksystemen.
            Informatik Spektrum 8(2), 60–68 (1985)
[Wed78]   Wedekind, H.: Zur Durchführung des § 6,1 BDSG. Datenschutz und
            Datensicherheit (4), 181–185 (1978)
[Wed80]   Wedekind, H.: Erweiterung einer Entwicklungsmethodologie für Daten-
            banksysteme um eine Komponente zum Schutz vor Missbrauch von per-
            sonenbezogenen Daten: Zu einer Methodologie und Teleologie einer Ange-
            wandten Informatik. Angewandte Informatik (7), 255–265 (1980)
[Wed81]   Wedekind, H.: Datenbanksysteme: Eine konstruktive Einführung in die
            Datenverarbeitung in Wirtschaft und Verwaltung, 2. Auflage. B.I.-Wiss.-
            Verl., Mannheim (1981)

[WO80]   Wedekind, H., Ortner, E.: Systematisches Konstruieren von Daten-
           bankanwendungen: Zur Methodologie der Angewandten Informatik. Carl
           Hanser Verlag, München (1980)
[WO04]   Wedekind, H., Ortner, E.: Toward universal literacy: From computer sci-
           ence upward. Communications of the ACM 47(6), 101–104 (2004)
[WOI]   Wedekind, H., Ortner, E., Inhetveen, R.: Informatik als Grundbildung. 6
           Aufsätze: Informatik-Spektrum 27(2) (2004), bis 28(1) (2005)
[ZLO10]   Zeise, N., Link, M., Ortner, E.: Controlling of Dynamic Enterprises by
           Indicators – A Foundational Approach. In: zur Muehlen, M., Su, J. (eds.)
           BPM 2010 Workshops. LNBIP, vol. 66, pp. 521–530. Springer, Heidelberg
           (2011)

A Logical Topology to Find Alternate Routes in WDM Lightwave Network

Santosh Das and Abhijit Makhal

Department of Computer Science
Dream institute of Technology
West Bengal, Kolkata 700104
{das2008.santosh,jontromanab.abhijit}@gmail.com

Abstract. In today's environment, as the need for more bandwidth for intensive networking applications such as data browsing, video conferencing, etc increase, so also does the need for high bandwidth-transport network facilities. Optical WDM networks show great promise in handling such high data volume problems, and it is expected that they will form the backbone of the next generation of high volume light wave networks. Multihop networks show the most promise in that they offer the greatest flexibility of design. This paper describes an approach to modify the routing algorithm for finding out the alternate routes on the occurrence of single node fault in WDM optical network where GEMNET is used as a physical topology and also try to find out the link which carries the maximum number of light paths in the network for randomly generated source-destination pair.

Keywords: Gemnet, optical network, WDM.

1 Introduction

Now a days more bandwidth required for networking applications such as data–browsing , video conferencing etc. are widely used. Optical fiber is used as a communication medium for this type of applications. The technology which is mainly used in optical fiber communication is wavelength division multiplexing(WDM).Optical WDM networks show great promise in handling such high data volume problems, and it is expected that they will form the backbone of the next generation of high volume light wave networks. But in WDM network there is a limitation on the total number of nodes in a column in the network. The limitation is that there is only p^k nodes in any column in the network, where p is the degree of each node in the network and k is the number of column in the network.

But later in GEMNET this limitation is eradicated. GEMNET is a logical topology which is a generalization of the shuffle-exchange connection..In WDM optical network several nodes are communicating via optical fiber . Here several wavelengths of lights are transmitted through a single fiber simultaneously. This provide a great benefit for high volume of data transmission. Another advantage of using GEMNET as a topology is that scalability, that means the addition of new nodes in the network

N. Meghanathan et al. (Eds.): CCSIT 2012, Part I, LNICST 84, pp. 138–145, 2012.

is quiet easy. The flexibility is that there is no restriction of the total number of nodes in the network providing the condition that the total number of nodes are evenly divisible by the total number of columns in the network.

Here we have attempted to modify the routing algorithm for finding out the alternate routes on the occurrence of single node fault in WDM optical network where GEMNET is used as a physical topology and also try to find out the link which carries the maximum number of light paths in the network for randomly generated source- destination pair.

Here the first problem is to find out alternate routes in case of single node fault, to reach the destination from source avoiding the faulty node for randomly generated source- destination pair in WDM optical network.

Another problem is to find out the link which carries maximum number of light paths for randomly generated source destination pair.

2   GEMNET

An attractive approach to interconnect computing equipment(nodes) in a high speed, packet –switched network is to employ a regular interconnection graph. It is desirable that the graph have 1) small nodal degree(for low network cost), 2) simple routing (to allow fast packet processing), 3) small diameter(for short messege delays), and 4) growth capability, viz. the graph should be scalable (so that nodes can be added to it at all times) with a modularity of unity (i.e. it should always be possible to add one node to or delete one node from an existing (regular) graph while maintaining regularity). We examine such a new network structure, called Generalized shuffle-exchange Multihop Network(GEMNET).

GEMNET[1] can serve as a physical, multihop topology for constructing the next generation of lightwave networks using wavelength-division multiplexing(WDM) .Given a low loss optical bandwidth of approximately 30 terabits per second and a peak electronic processing speed of a few gigabits per second, innovative parallelism and concurrency mechanisms are needed to exploit this huge opto-electronic bandwidth mismatch .WDM has emerged as the most promising choice since, unlike other alternatives, it only requires end-user equipment to operate at the bit rate of a WDM channel(peak electronic speed).

Generally a GEMNET has three parameter. They are K,M & P where K represents the number of column ,M represents the number of rows and K*M nodes are arranged in a cylindrical structure and the degree of each node is represented by P. The structure is the generalization of shuffle-exchanged connectivity pattern using directed links.. The generalization allows any number of nodes in a column as opposed to the constraint of P^K nodes in a column.

2.1   Interconnection Pattern of GEMNET

Let N be the number of nodes in the network. If N is evenly divisible by an integer y, there exist a GEMNET with K=y columns.

In the corresponding (K,M,P) GEMNET, the N=K*M nodes are arranged in K columns(K>=1) and M rows (M>=1) with each node having degree P. Node a (a= 0,1,2,…….., N-1) is located at the intersection of column c (c=0,1,2,……., K-1) and row r (r= 0,1,2,…….., M-1), or simply location (c ,r), where c=(a mod K) and r =| a/ K | . The P links emanating out of a node (c, r) is connected to node (c1,r1) , where c1= (c+1) mod K and r1 =((r * P) +i) mod M . and i = 0,1,2,……, P-1).

The largest distance between the two nodes is the diameter of the network. GEMNET's diameter is obtained as follows. Starting at any node, note that each and every node in a particular column can be reached for the first time on the | log $_P$M| th hop. This means that there were one or more nodes not covered in the previously visited column. Due to cylindrical nature of GEMNET[1] , the nodes in this column will be finally covered in an additional K-1   hops. Thus , D = | log$_P$M | + K-1.

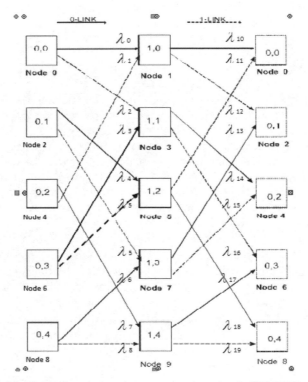

Fig. 1. The interconnection pattern and routing in GEMNET

2.2   The Routing In GEMNET

Let (c_s, r_s) and (c_d , r_d) be the source node and the destination node, respectively.

We define the " column distance " delta as the minimum no of hops required to reach a node in column c_d from a node in column c_s.

c_d represent destination column.

c_s represent source column.

when $c_d> c_s$,then , delta = c_d – c_s because (c_d- c_s) forward hops from any node in column c_s will cover a node in column c_d. When $c_d < c_s$, delta is given by, delta = $(c_d+ k)$ - c_s because, after "sliding "c_d forward by K (i.e. $c_d+ K$), due to wraparound, the situation becomes the same as when $c_d >= c_s$. Thus delta can be generalized as:

delta =$[(K + c_d) – c_s]$ mod K.

The hop distance from source node (c_s, r_s) to destination node (c_d , r_d) is given by the smallest integer h of the form (delta+ jk) , j=0,1,2,... satisfying the following expression ,

$$R = [M + r_d – (r_s . p^h) \bmod M] \bmod M < P^h$$

where R is called the route code , specifies a shortest route from the source node to the destination node when it is expressed as a sequence of h base P digits.

Often, the p^h nodes covered on the h th hop could be greater than the number of nodes in that column. This means that multiple shortest paths may exist to some nodes in that column. Having calculated R, if ($R+ x* M$) < P^h for x = 1,2,3,............., then ($R+x*M$) is also a routing code with path-length h for any x that satisfies this enequality. Thus , if the shortest path from node a to node b is h hops, the number of shortest paths is given by $Y=[(P^h- R)/ M]$.

Hence , for a given N , the number of alternate shortest paths increases as M decreases. The larger the number of shortest paths, the more opportunity there is to route a packet along a less congested path and the greater is the network's ability to route a packet along a minimum length path when a link or node failure occurs.

3   Results

Here we developed an algorithm for finding out alternate shortest paths avoiding the faulty node on the occurrence of single node fault in the WDM optical network.In the next section we have provided a step-by-step approach for the algorithm to avoid the faulty node.

3.1   Survivable Routing of GEMNET in Presence of Single Node Fault

Survivable routing means the method of finding the alternative shortest paths in WDM optical network if there is an occurrence of single node fault. It can be shown that in case of the occurrence of one node fault in the network alternative paths can route the messege to the destination for randomly generated source-destination pair avoiding the faulty node.

The steps are as follows...

1. At first it should be checked wheather the source node is equal or not with the faulty node.The same method should be applied for destination node. If source or destination node is faulty the connection is discarded.
2. Next the number of multiple shortest paths for same hop count for first source-destination pair has to be found out.
3. Next the first path among the multiple shortest paths of same hop count has to be taken and stored in an array of structure called currentpath. Likewise all other paths of same hop count are stored in the currenpath array of structure for first source- destination pair.
4. Then it is assumed that there is no faulty node in that currentpath array of structure.

5. Next it is checked from very first to the last node of the currentpath, wheather , each node is equal or not with the faulty node. If it is equal then there exist a faulty node in the currentpath & the path is faulty.
6. Next that faulty path is discarded and step 5 is followed for the next path of same hop count of that particular source-destination pair.
7. If any path of that hop count is found where there is no faulty node then that is the desired path and that path is accepted. If it is found that there is a faulty node in each path of same hop count of that particular source-destination pair, then the hop count is increased and the same procedure is repeated from step 2 to 6.
8. After getting the right path for first source-destination pair from the randomly generated request set (source-destination pair) , the same steps from 1 to 7 followed as before for next source destination pair and so on for all source destination pair .

In the image 2 the connectivity of each node with the other nodes are shown on the basis of total number of nodes ,no. of columns, and degree of each node

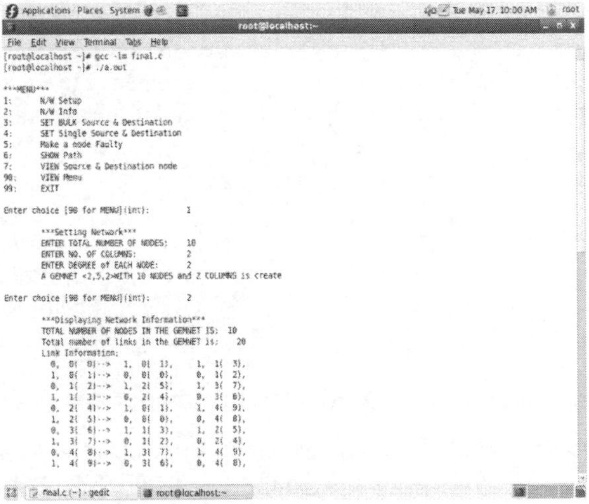

Fig. 2.

In Fig 3 the number of source destination pair,the number of shortest paths between every source –destination and the entire path from source to destination are shown . Starting from a source node it passes through a number of nodes and reach to the destination. Here the total paths are shown and the required number of hops to reach from source to destination are also shown. If there has been multiple shortest path of same hop count is exist then it shows all the paths of same hop count from a source to destination.

If a node will become faulty on the path from a source to destination the algorithm then founds the alternate path, incrementing the hop count avoiding the faulty node. In both the cases the algorithm finds the maximum used link of the network.that means through which link maximum number of light paths are passes.This has been shown in fig 4.

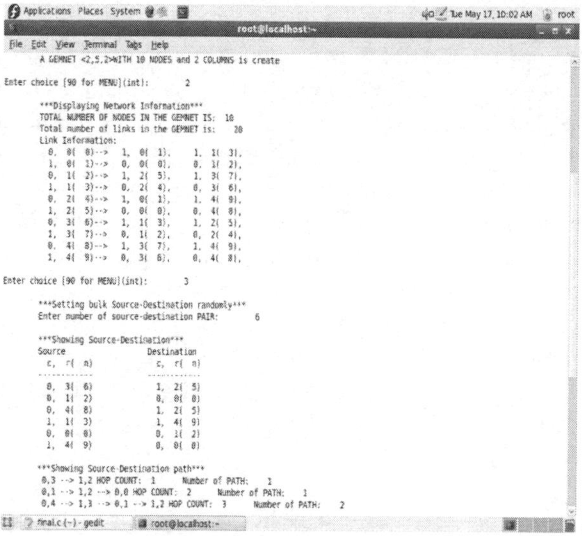
Applications Places System
Tue May 17, 10:02 AM root
root@localhost:~
File Edit View Terminal Tabs Help
A GEMNET <2,5,2>WITH 10 NODES and 2 COLUMNS is create
Enter choice [90 for MENU](int): 2
Displaying Network Information
TOTAL NUMBER OF NODES IN THE GEMNET IS: 10
Total number of links in the GEMNET is: 20
Link Information:
0, 0(0)--> 1, 0(1), 1, 1(3),
1, 0(1)--> 0, 0(0), 0, 1(2),
0, 1(2)--> 1, 2(5), 1, 3(7),
1, 1(3)--> 0, 2(4), 0, 3(6),
0, 2(4)--> 1, 0(1), 1, 4(9),
1, 2(5)--> 0, 0(0), 0, 4(8),
0, 3(6)--> 1, 1(3), 1, 2(5),
1, 3(7)--> 0, 1(2), 0, 2(4),
0, 4(8)--> 1, 3(7), 1, 4(9),
1, 4(9)--> 0, 3(6), 0, 4(8),
Enter choice [90 for MENU](int): 3
Setting bulk Source-Destination randomly
Enter number of source-destination PAIR: 6
Showing Source-Destination
Source Destination
c, r(n) c, r(n)
0, 3(6) 1, 2(5)
0, 1(2) 0, 0(0)
0, 4(8) 1, 2(5)
1, 1(3) 1, 4(9)
0, 0(0) 0, 1(2)
1, 4(9) 0, 0(0)
Showing Source-Destination path
0,3 --> 1,2 HOP COUNT: 1 Number of PATH: 1
0,1 --> 1,2 --> 0,0 HOP COUNT: 2 Number of PATH: 1
0,4 --> 1,3 --> 0,1 --> 1,2 HOP COUNT: 3 Number of PATH: 2
final.c (~) - gedit
root@localhost:~

Fig. 3.

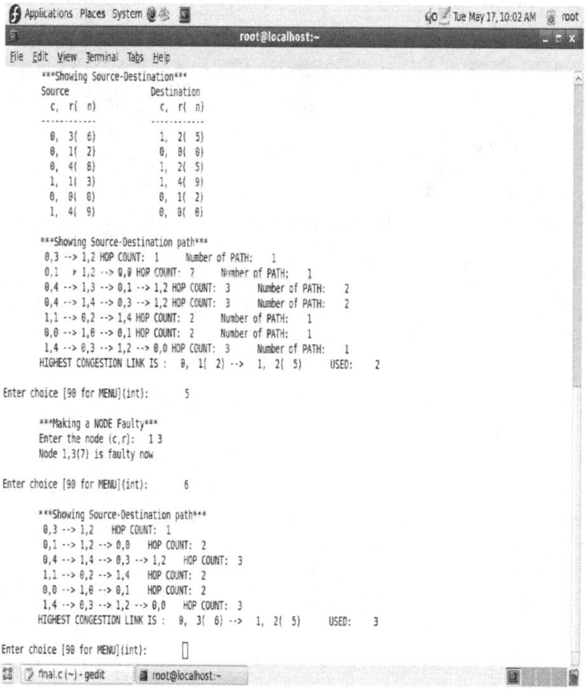
Applications Places System
Tue May 17, 10:02 AM root
root@localhost:~
File Edit View Terminal Tabs Help
Showing Source-Destination
Source Destination
c, r(n) c, r(n)
0, 3(6) 1, 2(5)
0, 1(2) 0, 0(0)
0, 4(8) 1, 2(5)
1, 1(3) 1, 4(9)
0, 0(0) 0, 1(2)
1, 4(9) 0, 0(0)
Showing Source-Destination path
0,3 --> 1,2 HOP COUNT: 1 Number of PATH: 1
0,1 --> 1,2 --> 0,0 HOP COUNT: 2 Number of PATH: 1
0,4 --> 1,3 --> 0,1 --> 1,2 HOP COUNT: 3 Number of PATH: 2
0,4 --> 1,4 --> 0,3 --> 1,2 HOP COUNT: 3 Number of PATH: 2
1,1 --> 0,2 --> 1,4 HOP COUNT: 2 Number of PATH: 1
0,0 --> 1,0 --> 0,1 HOP COUNT: 2 Number of PATH: 1
1,4 --> 0,3 --> 1,2 --> 0,0 HOP COUNT: 3 Number of PATH: 1
HIGHEST CONGESTION LINK IS : 0, 1(2) --> 1, 2(5) USED: 2
Enter choice [90 for MENU](int): 5
Making a NODE Faulty
Enter the node (c,r): 1 3
Node 1,3(7) is faulty now
Enter choice [90 for MENU](int): 6
Showing Source-Destination path
0,3 --> 1,2 HOP COUNT: 1
0,1 --> 1,2 --> 0,0 HOP COUNT: 2
0,4 --> 1,4 --> 0,3 --> 1,2 HOP COUNT: 3
1,1 --> 0,2 --> 1,4 HOP COUNT: 2
0,0 --> 1,0 --> 0,1 HOP COUNT: 2
1,4 --> 0,3 --> 1,2 --> 0,0 HOP COUNT: 3
HIGHEST CONGESTION LINK IS : 0, 3(6) --> 1, 2(5) USED: 3
Enter choice [90 for MENU](int):
final.c (~) - gedit
root@localhost:~

Fig. 4.

Discussions

In WDM optical network several wave-lengths are transmitted simultaneously through the same optical fiber. So we have to pay special attention during data transmission so that the data packet can reach at the destination safely. If any node is become faulty the data can't travel through that path where that faulty node resides. To reach at the destination it should follow another route avoiding the faulty node. We have also shown the link which carries the maximum number of light paths during data transmission for randomly generated source-destination pair. It is important to know that which link has the maximum traffic, so if the data is transmitted through that link the network become over-crowded .There are several physical topologies in WDM optical network for data transmission but here we deals with the physical topology , GEMNET. The survivable routing algorithm is done on GEMNET, & we can say that this survivable routing algorithm gives a new aspect for data communication in WDM optical network.

Future Work

As the algorithm has been modified deliberately to find the single node fault occurance,it cannot find the alternate paths when more than one node become faulty. Algorithm to find the alternate routes on occurrence of multiple node fault is under processing.

References

[1] Iness, J., Banerjee, S., Mukherjee, B.: GEMNET: a generalized, shuffle-exchange-based, scalable, and modular multihop network based on WDM lightwave technology. IEEE/ACM Transactions on Networking 3, 470–476 (1995)

[2] Chatterjee, M., Karmy, T., Dutt, S., Bhattacharya, S., Bhattacharya, U.: Reconfigurable Logical Topology Design for survivability in WDM networks. Department of computer science and engineering, Asansol engineering college, Asansol, West Bengal, India, Department of computer science and Technology, Bengal engineering and science university, Shibpur, Howrah, West Bengal, India National Institute of Technology, Durgapur, West Bengal, India

[3] Dissemination of Information in Optical Networks from Technology to Algorithms. Spin Springer's internal project number, if known– Monograph. Springer, Heidelberg (April 3, 2007)

[4] Bhattacharya, U., Datta, D., Chowdhury, B., Saha, G.C., Sikdar, B.K.: A congestion controlled logical topology for multihop optical network, Department of Computer Science & Technology, Bengal Engineering College (D.U.), Shibpur, Howrah-711103, West-Bengal, India

[5] Mukherjee, B.: WDM-Based Local Lightwave Networks, Part-II: Multihop Systems- As an alternative to single hop local lightwave networks, multihop systems have their own strength & limitations

[6] Siva Ram Murthy, C., Gurusamy, M.: WDM optical network: Concept, Design and Algorithms. Pearson Education

[7] Tridandapani, S., Mukherjee, B., Hallingstad, G.: Channel Sharing in Multi-Hop WDM Lightwave Networks: Do We Need More Channels? IEEE/ACM Transactions on Networking 5(5), 719–727 (1997)

[8] Borella, M.S., Jue, J.P., Banerjee, D., Ramamurthy, B., Mukherjee, B.: Optical Components for WDM Lightwave Networks, Computer Science Department, University of California, Davis Davis, CA USA

[9] Zhu, K., Mukherjee, B.: A review of traffic grooming in WDM optical networks, architectures and challenges: Computer Science Department, University of California, Davis Davis, CA USA

A Novel Approach for MIMO OFDM Systems to Estimate I/Q Imbalance, CFO, Channel Response Using Training Sequences

J. Tarun Kumar[1] and K. Anitha Sheela[2]

[1] Department of Electronics and Communication Engineering,
Ramappa Engineering College, JNT University, Warangal, India
tarunjuluru@yahoo.com
[2] Department of Electronics and Communication Engineering,
JNT University, Hyderabad, India
kanithasheela@gmail.com

Abstract. Systems using Orthogonal Frequency Division Multiplexing (OFDM) suffer with carrier frequency offset (CFO), in phase and quadrature phase imbalance (I/Q) due to which there will be large performance degradation. The CFO, I/Q imbalance are caused due to mismatch of carrier frequency at the transmitter and local oscillator frequency at the receiver. This paper presents a novel approach for joint estimation of I/Q imbalance, CFO and Channel Estimation for Multiple-Input Multiple-Output (MIMO) OFDM systems. A new energy parameter called φ is introduced, and from this parameter φ we can jointly estimate CFO, I/Q imbalance irrespective of channel estimation. The proposed method uses an optimal training block with one or two training sequences. For estimation of two repeated sequences, a two-step approach is proposed. From the simulation results we show that the Mean-Square Error (MSE) of this method is close to Cramer-Rao Bound (CRB).

Keywords: CFO, Channel response, I/Q imbalance, MIMO, OFDM.

1   Introduction

OFDM is the promising multiplexing scheme for future wireless communication for its good performance in terms of maintaining orthogonality between the cells, protection against inter-symbol interference, and effective utilization of band width. With the addition of MIMO causes high data rate and low complexity. These characteristics of OFDM are achieved when the receiver has exact channel information and the system parameters of transmitter and receiver are perfectly matched. But in real scenario these ideal condition does not prevail. Some of these non-idealities are I/Q imbalance and CFO. The I/Q imbalance is due to amplitude and phase mismatch of I phase and Q phase, where as the CFO is caused due to mismatch of carrier frequency at the transmitter and receiver. It is known from [1] that I/Q imbalance and CFO will cause severe Inter Carrier Interference (ICI) in OFDM which degrades the system performance. Several approaches are presented to compensate for

N. Meghanathan et al. (Eds.): CCSIT 2012, Part I, LNICST 84, pp. 146–158, 2012.
© Institute for Computer Sciences, Social Informatics and Telecommunications Engineering 2012

the I/Q imbalance and CFO[1]-[5]. The impact of I/Q imbalance and CFO on OFDM are estimated in [2]. A time domain method was proposed in [3], for the joint estimation of I/Q imbalance and channel response using one OFDM. In [4] maximum likelihood method was proposed for CFO estimation. Joint estimation and compensation of I/Q imbalance and CFO in frequency domain is proposed in [5].

To improve the data rates the MIMO system was combined with OFDM [6]. Several approaches are proposed to deal with the channel estimation of MIMO OFDM systems. One of these approaches is to send a optimal training sequence from different antennas which must be orthogonal [7].The I/Q imbalance for MIMO OFDM systems have been investigated in [8], which cause error flooring. A compensation of I/Q imbalance was proposed in [9] with more number of OFDM blocks. The authors derived Cramer – Rao Bound (CRB) for estimation of CFO and channel response for MIMO systems. Recently, researchers proposed a joint estimation of I/Q imbalance and channel response with only one OFDM training block [11].

In this paper we propose a novel method for joint estimation of I/Q imbalance, CFO and channel response in MIMO OFDM systems by introducing a new energy parameter φ. By minimising the φ we are able to estimate I/Q imbalance and CFO without knowing the channel response. From the estimated I/Q imbalance and CFO we can calculate the channel response easily. This method needs only one OFDM block for training. If the training data consists of two repeated sequences the above approach is to be performed on two training sequences and the average is calculated for estimation.

In Section 2 the MIMO OFDM system model is described. The channel estimation of MIMO is discussed in Section 3. The new method for estimation is studied in Section 4. In Section 5 the estimation for repetitive sequences are discussed. Simulations and results are discussed in Section 6 and we conclude the paper in Section 7.

2   System Model

The MIMO-OFDM transmission model used in this paper is shown in Fig. 1. A Nt-transmit / Nr-receive antenna configuration is considered. From the Fig.1 the input vector s_i is of Mx1 containing input symbols. To maintain the orthogonality between these symbols the input vector s_i are fed to IDFT of M-point. Then we obtain the Mx1 vector x_i . After insertion of a cyclic prefix (CP) of length L-1, the signal is transmitted through the ith transmit antenna. Let the channel impulse response of ith transmit antenna to the kth receive antenna be $h_{k,j}(n)$.The length of all the channels are

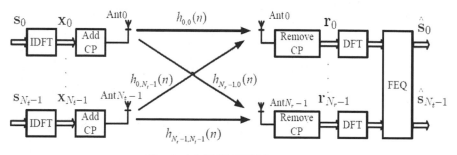

Fig. 1. A MIMO OFDM system

assumed to L , so there is no inter block interference .Then the received signal at the kth receiving antenna after removal of CP is given as

$$r_k = \begin{bmatrix} H_{K,0} & H_{K,1} & H_{K,2} & ....H_{K,N_t-1} \end{bmatrix} \begin{bmatrix} X_0 \\ X_1 \\ X_2 \\ . \\ . \\ X_{N_t-1} \end{bmatrix} + q_k \tag{1}$$

Where $H_{k,i}$ is an MxM circulant matrix with first column

$$h_{k,i} \equiv \begin{bmatrix} h_{K,i(0)} h_{K,i(1)} h_{K,i(2)} ...... h_{K,i(L-1)} 0 .... 0 \end{bmatrix}^T \tag{2}$$

And q_k is the channel noise vector of length Mx1.The output of the DFT block received vector is passed through a Frequency domain Equaliser (FEQ) to recover the transmit signals s_i.

If the system suffers with carrier frequency offset (CFO) Δf_k then the normalised frequency offset is given as

$$\theta_k = \frac{\Delta f_k}{\frac{1}{MT}} = \Delta f_k MT \tag{3}$$

Where M,T are given as the size of the DFT matrix and T sample spacing. The vector due to CFO is

$$y_k = E_k r_k \tag{4}$$

where r_k is desired vector and E_k is the MxM diagonal matrix given by

$$E_k \overset{\Delta}{=} diag \begin{bmatrix} 1 & e^{j\frac{2\pi}{M}\theta_k} & .... & e^{j\frac{2\pi}{M}(M-1)\theta_k} \end{bmatrix} \tag{5}$$

Suppose if there is I/Q mismatch at the receiver, then received vector due to it is

$$Z_k = \mu_k y_k + v_k y_k^* \tag{6}$$

Where μ_k and v_k are I/Q parameters due to amplitude mismatch ε_k, phase mismatch Φ_k and they are given as

$$\mu_k = \frac{1+\varepsilon_k e^{-j\phi_k}}{2} \text{. and } \quad v_k = \frac{1-\varepsilon_k e^{-j\phi_k}}{2}. \tag{7}$$

Substituting the value of y_k in (6)

$$Z_k = \mu_k E_k r_k + v_k E_k^* r_k^* \tag{8}$$

From (8) It is clear that the received vector consists of not only the desired base band vector r_k but also its complex conjugate r_k^*, and the E_k is due to CFO which also destroy the sub carrier orthogonality.

z_k is a received vector in the presence of I/Q imbalance and CFO. To recover r_k from z_k we define a parameter

$$\alpha_k = \frac{v_k}{\mu_k}. \tag{9}$$

If α_k is estimated correctly at the receiver then

$$\mu_k y_k = \frac{z_k - \alpha_k z_k^*}{1-|\alpha_k|^2}. \tag{10}$$

If the normalised CFO θ_k is known at the receiver then the recovered vector from the received vector is given by

$$\mu_k r_k = E_k^* \mu_k y_k = E_k^* \frac{z_k - \alpha_k z_k^*}{1-|\alpha_k|^2} \tag{11}$$

3   MIMO Channel Estimation

An MIMO channel is one where the antenna arrays are available at transmitter and receiver as shown in Fig.1. Channel estimation of these channels using training sequences are described in [7] If a MIMO channel with N_t transmit and N_r receiving antennas are selected then the received vector r is given as

$$r = \begin{bmatrix} X_0 & X_1 & \dots & X_{N_{t-1}} \end{bmatrix} \begin{bmatrix} h_o \\ h_1 \\ \vdots \\ h_{N_{t-1}} \end{bmatrix} + q \tag{12}$$

Where h_j is the Mx1 vector defined in (12). x_j is the first column of MxM circulant matrix . Let us define a MxL sub matrix A_j, which consist of the first L columns of x_j and c_j is defined as

$$c_j = [h_i(0)h_i(1) \ldots \ldots \ldots h_i(L-1)]^T \tag{13}$$

And

$$A = \begin{bmatrix} A_0 & A_1 \ldots \ldots \ldots \ldots & A_{N_{t-1}} \end{bmatrix} \tag{14}$$

The r may be re written as

$$r=Ac+q \tag{15}$$

In the above equation the channel vector c is identifiable if and only if M x LN_t matrix A has full column rank. Thus a necessary condition for channel identifiability is M≥LN_t. Then the least square estimator ĉ is given by

$$ĉ = (A^+A)^{-1} A^+ r \tag{16}$$

Then the error vector is defined as e= ĉ - c=$(A^+ A)^{-1}A^+$ q. The design of a optimal sequence that minimize the mean square error (MSE) $E\|e\|^2$ is given in [7].The optimal training sequence from different antennas must satisfy

$$A_k^+ A_i = \delta(k-i)I \tag{17}$$

That means the training sequence from different transmitter antenna must be orthogonal .When the training sequence are orthogonal the least square estimate of channel response becomes

$$ĉ = A^+ r \tag{18}$$

In this paper the above estimation is formulated in a different way, for joint estimation of I/Q imbalance, CFO and channel response that is

$$\rho = \frac{M}{Nt} \tag{19}$$

We assume that M is a multiple of N_t and also this can be further extended to the case where M is not a multiple of N_t by simple Modification. Furthermore we assume that $\rho \geq L$. To obtain the channel identifiability condition M≥N_t we add the (ρ-L)zeros to the length L vectors of c_i to obtain ρx1 vector given by

$$d_i = \begin{pmatrix} c_i \\ 0 \end{pmatrix} \qquad \text{for i=0,1,}\ldots\ldots\ldots.N_{t-1} \tag{20}$$

From all the vectors of d_i for $0 \leq i \leq N_t$ we form the Mx1 vector

$$d = \begin{bmatrix} d_0^T d_1^T \ldots \ldots \ldots \ldots d_{Nt-1}^T \end{bmatrix}^T \tag{21}$$

Let A_k^1 be any M x (ρ-L) matrix such that the following MxM matrix B is invertible

$$A = \begin{bmatrix} A_0 & A_0^1 & A_1 & A_1^1 & \ldots \ldots \ldots \ldots A_{N_{t-1}} & A_{N_{t-1}}^1 \end{bmatrix} \tag{22}$$

From (21)&(22) the vector can be rewritten as

$$r = Bd + q \tag{23}$$

The estimate MIMO channel response is given by

$$\hat{d} = \begin{bmatrix} \hat{d}_0^T & \hat{d}_1^T & \ldots \ldots \ldots \ldots \hat{d}_{Nt-1}^T \end{bmatrix}^T \tag{24}$$

$$= B^{-1} r \tag{25}$$

The estimated channel response $\hat{c}_j$ is given by the first L entries of $\hat{d}_j$. When the training sequences are orthogonal then the columns of A_k are orthogonal .Thus the channel estimate is given by $\hat{d}$ =B⁻¹r . It means the orthogonal sequences are the optimal sequences. B can be chosen to be unitary and circulant.

4   Proposed Joint Estimation Method

In this section we propose a new method to estimate the channel response in the presence of I/Q imbalance and CFO. The estimation done in two sections in section 4.1 we estimate channel response in the presence of I/Q imbalance and assume that no CFO is present. In section 4.2 we estimate channel response in the presence of CFO and I/Q imbalance. In both section we estimate the optimal solution α_k and θ_k from the received vector z_k at the kth receiving antenna. The estimation is performed for both simple sequence and repeated sequences.

4.1   Joint Estimation of Channel Response and I/Q Imbalance

In this section we assume that the carrier frequency at the transmitter and receiver are orthogonal means no CFO $\theta = 0$ and E = I in (11).Then the μr is related to the received vector and it is given as

$$\mu r = \frac{z - \propto z^*}{1 - |\propto|^2} \tag{26}$$

If α is known in (26) then the channel estimation can obtained as

$$\mu \hat{d} = \mu \begin{bmatrix} \hat{d}_0 & \hat{d}_1 & \ldots \ldots \ldots \ldots \widehat{d}_{Nt-1} \end{bmatrix}^T$$

$$= B^{-1} r$$

$$= B^{-1} \frac{z - \alpha z^*}{1 - |\alpha|^2} \tag{27}$$

In the above expression when α is estimated perfectly at the receiver then the L entries of the $\hat{h}_j$ gives channel estimation, and rest of the entries ρ-L of $\hat{d}_j$ are due to channel noise .To obtain adequate SNR the energy of the other entries must be small. Then defining a new energy parameter φ as

$$\varphi = \sum_{l=0}^{N_t-1} \sum_{i=L}^{\rho-1} \left| \left[\mu \hat{d}_l \right]_i \right|^2 \tag{28}$$

Where $\left[\mu \hat{d}_l \right]_i$ denotes the ith entry of $\mu \hat{d}_l$. If α is not estimated perfectly φ will increase. By minimizing the φ we can estimate α without knowing channel response .Let us define a new matrix S of $(M - N_t L) X N$ where

$$S = \begin{bmatrix} 0 & I_{\rho-L} & 0 & \cdots & 0 \\ 0 & \cdots I_{\rho-L} & & \ddots & \vdots \\ 0 & & & \cdots & I_{\rho-L} \end{bmatrix} \tag{29}$$

If $\rho > L$ then S is non zero matrix. Multiplying $\mu \hat{d}$ with S the φ can be given as

$$\varphi = \left\| S \mu \hat{d} \right\|^2 \tag{30}$$

$$\varphi = \left\| S B^{-1} \frac{z - \alpha z^*}{1 - |\alpha|^2} \right\|^2 \tag{31}$$

"α" is estimated in such a way to minimize the energy parameter φ. When the α is small, then φ is given as

$$\varphi \cong \left\| s B^{-1} (z - \alpha z^*) \right\|^2 \tag{32}$$

By this the optimal value of α which may minimize the φ is given by

$$\alpha_{opt} = \frac{(sB^{-1}z^*)(sB^{-1}z)}{\left\| sB^{-1}z^* \right\|^2} \tag{33}$$

4.2   Joint Estimation of Channel Response, CFO and I/Q Imbalance

If the CFO and I/Q imbalance both are present in the system then the received vector r in (11) is given as

$$\mu r = E^* \mu y = E^* \frac{z - \alpha z^*}{1 - |\alpha|^2} \tag{34}$$

Where E is due to CFO. Then the estimation of channel response can be obtained by

$$\mu \hat{d} = B^{-1} \mu r = B^{-1} E^* \frac{z - \alpha z^*}{1 - |\alpha|^2} \tag{35}$$

Similarly in the previous section if α and θ are estimated perfectly then ρ-L entries $\hat{d}_j$ are due to minimizing the φ is

$$\varphi(\alpha, \theta) = \left|\left|S\mu\hat{d}\right|\right|^2 \tag{36}$$

Substitute (35) in (36)

$$\varphi(\alpha, \theta) = \left|\left|SB^{-1}E^* \frac{z - \alpha z^*}{1 - |\alpha|^2}\right|\right|^2 \tag{37}$$

If $F = SB^{-1}E^*$ then it may be

$$\varphi(\alpha, \theta) = \left|\left|F \frac{z - \alpha z^*}{1 - |\alpha|^2}\right|\right|^2 \tag{38}$$

Here we can estimate α and θ by minimizing φ. We need to calculate first optimal α for a given θ and based on that optimized θ assuming α is small then

$$\varphi(\alpha, \theta) \approx \left|\left|Fz - \alpha Fz^*\right|\right|^2 \tag{39}$$

For given θ the optimal value of α is estimated as

$$\alpha_{\text{opt}}(\theta) = \frac{|Fz|^*(Fz)}{||Fz^*||^2} \tag{40}$$

$\alpha_{\text{opt}}(\theta)$ is a function of CFO(θ) ,because F depends on E substituting $\alpha_{\text{opt}}(\theta)$ in (39) φ can be written as

$$\varphi(\theta) = \left|\left|Fz^*\right|\right|^2 - \frac{|(Fz)^*(Fz^*)|^2}{||Fz^*||^2} \tag{41}$$

Then

$$\theta_{\text{opt}} = \min \ \varphi(\theta) \tag{42}$$

After obtaining α_{opt} and θ_{opt} ,the channel response estimation can be obtained by substituting these values in (39). In many practical applications the training data consists of repeated sequences so another approach is a two step approach for joint optimization.

5   Proposed Method for Repeated Sequence

If two repeated sequences are available in the in the training data [12] that means the block is of length (M+L-1)x1 vector. Out of which the training sequence x_i is of M/2 x1 vector and cyclic prefix of length L-1. If the above specified sequence suffers with I/Q imbalance, CFO then the channel estimation procedure is as follows.

There are two received vectors z_a, z_b and they are given as

$$Z_a = \mu y + vy^* + q_a \quad and \quad Z_b = \mu e^{j\pi\theta} y + v(e^{j\pi\theta} y)^* + q_b$$

(43)

Where a&b are OFDM blocks and y is an M/2 x 1 vector. For joint estimation of I/Q imbalance , CFO and channel Estimation we propose two cases

Case1: *Estimate CFO for given α.*

For a given value of α we can estimate CFO

$$\mu y = \frac{z_a - \alpha z_a^*}{1 - |\alpha|^2}$$

(44)

$$e^{j\pi\theta} \mu y = \frac{z_b - \alpha z_b^*}{1 - |\alpha|^2}$$

(45)

If α is given the CFO can be estimated

$$\hat{\theta} = \frac{1}{\pi} \text{angle}(z_a - \alpha z_a^*)(z_b - \alpha z_b^*)$$

(46)

Case2: *Estimate h(n),α for given θ*
From(35)

$$\mu \hat{d}_a = B^{-1} E^* \frac{z_a - \alpha z_a^*}{1 - |\alpha|^2} \quad and \quad \mu \hat{d}_b = e^{j\pi\theta} B^{-1} E^* \frac{z_b - \alpha z_b^*}{1 - |\alpha|^2}$$

(47)

Now for two repeated sequences the B and E are assumed to be of dimensions M/2 x M/2, and rest of the properties are same. Then the energy parameter φ is given as

$$\varphi_a = \left\| s\mu\hat{d}_a \right\|^2 \quad and \quad \varphi_b = \left\| s\mu\hat{d}_b \right\|^2$$

(48)

Similarly optimum value of α to minimize φ is

$$\hat{\alpha}_a = \frac{(Fz^*_a)^+(Fz_a)}{\|Fz^*_a\|^2} \quad and \quad \hat{\alpha}_b = \frac{(Fz^*_b)^+(Fz_b)}{\|Fz^*_b\|^2}$$

(49)

By taking average

$$\hat{\alpha} = \frac{1}{2}(\hat{\alpha}_a + \hat{\alpha}_b)$$

(50)

Substituting the value of $\hat{\alpha}$ in $\mu\hat{d}$ then the estimated Channel response is given as

$$\mu\hat{d} = \frac{1}{2}(\mu\hat{d}_a + \mu\hat{d}_b)$$

(51)

6   Simulations

In this paper the joint estimation of CFO, I/Q imbalance and channel response is proposed and these are performed on computer simulations. The simulations are conducted on MIMO OFDM systems with various parameters.

These simulations are performed on 64 random channels and the channel taps are assumed to be complex Gaussian random variables with variance equal to unity. The channel length is of L=65,CP length of L-1=64 and training data are QPSK symbols and channel taps are correlated, with 2 cases of parameters.

Case i: N_t=2, N_r=2with an amplitude mismatch ε=1, phase mismatch Φ=10^0 and CFO θ =1.

Case ii: *N_t=4, N_r=2with an amplitude mismatch of ε=1, phase mismatch Φ=10^0 and CFO θ =3*

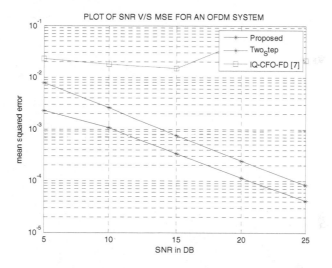

Fig. 2. MSE Vs SNR for I/Q in Case i

These two cases of simulations are conducted for both proposed models and compared with the method of IQ_CFO_FD [5]. Fig.2&3 shows the MSE of I/Q parameter estimation for case I &II. From these simulations it is clear that the proposed method provide good performance. In the result for IQ_CFO_FD the MSE [5] become flat, but for the proposed method the error flooring is reduced for high SNR values. Similarly Fig.4 &5. shows the MSE of CFO estimation for Case I &II and these simulations are very close to Cramer-Rao bound (CRB) [10]. The proposed method provides good estimation of CFO, whereas the method [5]cannot estimate the values of CFO greater than 1.In case II the CFO is considered to be 3. Fig.6&7 shows the MSE of channel estimation and the performance of this also close to CRB. If these are compared with IQ-CFO-FD for Case I parameters the MSE is good for less values of SNR but as the SNR increases the error flooring remains same, where as in case of proposed methods the error flooring reduces for high SNR values.

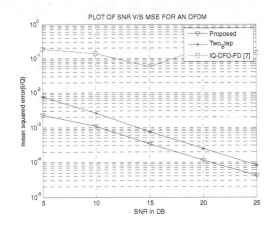

Fig. 3. MSE Vs SNR for I/Q in Case ii

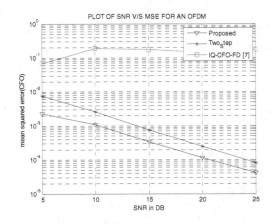

Fig. 4. MSE Vs SNR for CFO in Case i

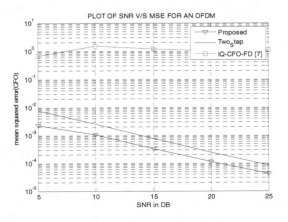

Fig. 5. MSE Vs SNR for CFO in Case ii

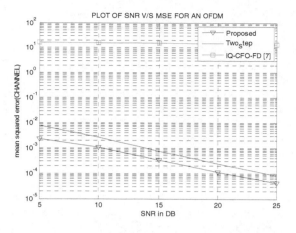

Fig. 6. MSE Vs SNR for Channel response in Case i

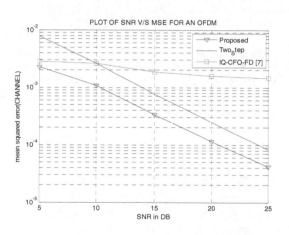

Fig. 7. MSE Vs SNR for Channel response in Case ii

7   Conclusion

In this paper, we propose a new parameter φ for joint estimation of CFO, I/Q imbalance and channel response for MIMO based OFDM systems. The proposed methods in section IV and V measure mean square error accurately compared with earlier approaches. Moreover, in this method the MSE's can be estimated for higher values of CFO. When the single OFDM block is available then the method proposed in section IV is suggested, if repetitive sequences are available then the method proposed in section V is suggested. In both the methods the simulation results shows that the MSE's are close to CRB.

References

1. Tarighat, A., Bahheri, E., Sayed, A.H.: Compensation schemes and performance analysis of I/Q imbalances in OFDM receivers. IEEE Trans. Signal Process. 53(8), 3257–3268 (2005)
2. Egashira, Y., Tanabe, Y., Sato, K.: A new IQ imbalance compensation method for OFDM systems. In: IEEE 64th Vehicular Technology Conference, VTC 2006 (2006)
3. Cho, W.-J., Chang, T.-K., Chung, Y.-H., Phoong, S.-M., Lin, Y.-P.: Frame synchronization and joint estimation of IQ imbalance and channel response for OFDM systems. In: Proc. IEEE ICASSP (March 2008)
4. Schmidl, T.M., Cox, D.C.: Robust frequency and timing synchronization for OFDM. IEEE Trans. Commun. 45(12), 1613–1621 (1997)
5. Chiu, Y.-J., Chen, C.-S., Hung, S.-P.: Adaptive estimation/compensation scheme of IQ imbalance with frequency offset in communication receivers. WSEAS Transactions on Communications (6) (June 2009)
6. Juluru, T.k., Kankacharla, A.S.: PHY Abstraction for MIMO Based OFDM Systems. In: Abraham, A., Mauri, J.L., Buford, J.F., Suzuki, J., Thampi, S.M. (eds.) ACC 2011. CCIS, Part VI, vol. 192, pp. 590–600. Springer, Heidelberg (2011)
7. Barhumi, I., Leus, G., Moonen, M.: Optimal training design for MIMO OFDM systems in mobilewireless channels. IEEE Trans. on Signal Processing 51(6), 1615–1642 (2003)
8. Lin, K.-H., Lin, H.-L., Wang, S.-M., Chang, R.C.: Implementation of Digital IQ Imbalance Compensationin OFDM WLAN Receivers. In: Proc. ISCAS 2006 (2006)
9. Simoens, S., de Courville, M., Bourzeix, F., de Champs, P.: New I/Q Imbalance Modelling and Compensation in OFDM Syatems with Frequency Offset. In: Proc. PIMRC 2002 (2002)
10. Li, J., Liao, G., Guo, Q., Besson, O., Stoica, P.: MIMO-OFDM channel estimation in the presence of carrier frequency offset. EURASIP Journal on Applied Signal Processing 5 (January 2005)
11. Chung, Y.-H., Phoong, S.-M.: Joint estimation of I/Q imbalance and channel response for MIMOOFDM system. In: Proc. EUSIPCO (September 2009)
12. Tian, Y., Lei, X., Xiao, Y., Li, S.: SAGE based joint timing-frequency offsets and channel estimation in distributed MIMO systems. Journal Computer Communications 33(17) (November 2010), http://dl.acm.org/citation.cfm?id=1864886
13. Tarighat, A., Sayed, A.H.: OFDM Systems with both transmitter and receiver IQ imbalances. In: Proc. of IEEE Workshop on Signal Processing and Advances in Wireless Communications (2005)
14. Bagadi, K.P., Das, S.: MIMO-OFDM Channel Estimation using Pilot Carriess. International Journal of Computer Applications 2(3), 81–88 (2010)

A Trust Based Routing Scheme
for Wireless Sensor Networks

Aveek Chakrabarti, Vishal Parekh, and Atin Ruia

Department of Computer Science and Engineering
Jadavpur University, India
{aveek.chakrabarti,vishal.jucse,atinruia.jucse}@gmail.com

Abstract. Wireless Sensor Networks are often deployed in unattended and hostile environments. These networks are susceptible to harsh physical conditions and attacks from adversaries. Sensor nodes have limited power, memory and computational ability and thus are vulnerable to capture. A few malicious adversaries can easily compromise sensor devices and inject false data to disrupt the integrity of the network. In this paper, we address this problem by proposing a three tiered architecture established upon a trust based framework which distinguishes illegal nodes from legal ones and filters out deceitful and forged data. Simulation results demonstrate that our trust based framework is an efficient approach to identify the trustworthiness of data.

Keywords: Wireless sensor network, Trust, Routing, Key management.

1   Introduction

Sensor nodes or motes are small devices with limited computing, communication and sensing capabilities. These nodes are typically deployed randomly over a specific area. They form an unattended wireless network, collect data, partially aggregate them and then sends this data to a base station for further processing. The deployment of sensor networks may contain tens to thousands of resource constrained nodes functioning collaboratively to perform a function [1]. Sensor nodes have applications in various areas such as – emergency response networks, energy management, logistics, medical, wildlife and climate monitoring, inventory support and battlefield management.

With the advent of new technology, sensor networks play a vital role in the age of pervasive computing, as personal mobile devices interact with sensor networks. However, security concerns constitute a potential stumbling block to the impending wide deployment of sensor networks. As sensor networks have mission-critical tasks, it is clear that security needs to be taken into account at design time. In an unattended and hostile environment, wireless sensor networks (WSNs) are vulnerable to various attacks such as physical node capture, eavesdropping and other sophisticated attacks [6]. As the main aim of WSNs is to gather sensory data an imminent threat from compromised nodes is the injection of false data. A major purpose of an attacker is to make the entire or partial network impractical or to gain control over individual

N. Meghanathan et al. (Eds.): CCSIT 2012, Part I, LNICST 84, pp. 159–169, 2012.

nodes. If an attacker gains control of a node it may send incorrect data, try to disrupt the transmission of aggregate data or not send any data at all.

In this paper we have proposed a systematic approach to identify the compromised nodes in a WSN and to circumvent these corrupted elements in order to ensure that the integrity of the network is not lost. This is done by calculating the trustworthiness or reputation of each element of the network which serves as a measure to gauge the credibility of that element. This trust value changes according to the data sent by each element. A three-tiered hierarchal architecture has been proposed and no assumptions have been made regarding which of the components can be compromised. The simulation results show that the proposed approach provides a constructive method for identifying corrupt nodes.

The rest of the paper has been organized as follows – Section 2 provides the related works. Section 3 describes the proposed network architecture with the trust based framework being explained in Section 4. Section 5 gives the experimental results and Section 6 concludes the article.

2   Related Work

There exists a large number of methods for securing aggregated information in literature. The basic approaches for security are to use Message Authentication Codes (MACs) and probabilistic key distribution schemes [7-8]. [10] and [11] proposes schemes to detect the compromised nodes by monitoring reported data. However in the schemes proposed in these papers the trust values of an entire network are stored by all the sensors of the network. These values are periodically circulated among themselves. This unnecessarily increases the network traffic and increases the workload on the sensors. There are centralized trust based systems for Internet such as [13]. These systems keep reputation values at a centralized trusted authority and therefore they are not feasible in wireless sensor network domain. Decentralized trust development systems are studied in mobile and ad-hoc networks [14]. These trust development systems are game theory based and try to counter selfish routing misbehavior of nodes by enforcing nodes to cooperate with each other. A trust based framework has been proposed in [12] which evaluates the trustworthiness of sensor nodes by extracting statistical characteristics from gathered information. However in this paper the sensor nodes have to take part in validation of aggregate nodes as well as send their sensed results. These nodes are typically low power nodes and the assignment of so much responsibility to these nodes is not feasible.

3   Network Architecture

Figure 1 depicts the network architecture in which we have implemented our scheme. Despite the popularity of flat wireless sensor networks, recent studies have revealed several limitations in these kinds of networks [2]. Flat networks have also been shown to have capacity limitations, and one approach to address this drawback is to employ a hierarchical architecture. In [3], it has been observed, when using the same amount of sensor nodes in a given coverage area for flat and hierarchical topologies, that the system throughput capacity increases, while system delay decreases. The main reason for these improvements is the reduced number of hops since most sensor data are destined for the Internet, which is reachable in a few hops in the hierarchical approach. Thus, we have implemented our scheme based on a hierarchical structure.

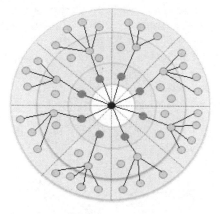

Fig. 1. Three tiered clustered architecture

In this paper we have used a three-tier clustered architecture. The sensor network is composed of densely deployed sensors which are organized into clusters. These clusters can be formed using an algorithm such as LEACH [4]. This architecture consists of three types of wireless devices: low power sensor nodes, aggregate nodes and cluster heads. The sensor nodes are responsible for sensing events and reporting these events to an aggregate node. As the name suggests, the aggregate node receives data from a certain number of sensors and aggregates this data into a single packet which is then forwarded to the cluster head. The cluster head receives data from all of the aggregate nodes within its cluster and forwards all of this data to the base station.

In Figure 1 the hierarchy of the WSN is shown. The entire network is partitioned into clusters. The node at the centre is the base station. The nodes situated one hop away from the base station are the cluster heads. Each of these nodes acts as a gateway to the base station for all the nodes in the cluster. The nodes present at the next hop are the aggregate nodes which relay the data sent by the sensor nodes to the cluster head. The nodes present at the last hop are the sensor nodes. These nodes report their sensed data periodically or by demand.

The three categories of nodes differ mainly in power, computation ability and communication. The sensor nodes are low power nodes with low computational power. The aggregate nodes are high power nodes. However as they are only responsible for forwarding data to their cluster heads, which are not located very far away, they do not require high computational ability. Cluster heads are nodes having the highest power capacity and also high computational power. The sensor nodes only communicate with the aggregate nodes. It is not required for them to be aware of the other sensor nodes or of the cluster head. The aggregate nodes communicate with both sensors and its cluster head. However, it is not aware of the base station. The cluster head can communicate with the aggregate nodes within its cluster and with the base station. Each cluster head is associated with a forwarding node. This node is only responsible for relaying data from the cluster head to the base station.

Certain assumption have been made about the network –

- The Base Station is fixed and may be located far away from the sensor network. The distances between the sensors are much smaller as compared to the distance between the sensor nodes and the Base Station.
- The sensor nodes are static and energy constrained with a uniform initial energy allocation.
- Initially none of the nodes are corrupt.
- Each sensor node is assumed to be either in transmitting mode, receiving mode or in sleep mode. It has been assumed that energy spent by the node in sleep state is negligibly small as compared to the amount spent while being in transmitting or receiving mode.

4   Trust Based Framework

In this section we discuss the framework and the functions of each step of the framework. A large number of sensor nodes are deployed densely in an area to form a wireless sensor network. These nodes are then partitioned into clusters using algorithms such as [4]. A cluster head is selected for each cluster. There may be more than one cluster head within a single cluster but only one such node will be active at any point. The cluster head will randomly select the aggregate nodes that are to be powered on. Each sensor node must be able to send data to at least one active aggregate node at all times. There will be more aggregate nodes present within the cluster but these will remain passive until activated by the cluster head.

4.1   Key Establishment

In critical applications, using incorrect or maliciously corrupted data can have disastrous consequences. Security services are essential to ensure the authenticity, confidentiality, freshness, and integrity of the critical information collected and processed by such networks. The authentication of the data source as well as the data is critical since adversaries might attempt to capture sensors and tamper with sensor data. A popular method for ensuring that the data sent by a node cannot be corrupted is encryption. Encryption is the process of transforming data to using a secret key or cipher. This makes the data it unreadable to anyone except those possessing special knowledge i.e. the key. The result of this process is encrypted data. At the other end the message is decrypted using the shared key to obtain the original message.

For two nodes to set up a secret and authenticated link, they need to establish a shared secret key. The key establishment problem studies how to set up secret keys between a pair of nodes in the network. A class of random key pre-distribution techniques that address the problem of key establishment has been discussed in [7-9]. Each sensor node shares a secret key with the base station. Whenever a sensor node sends data to an aggregate node it uses this key to encrypt the message it sends. This prevents eavesdropping and ensures that the aggregate node or the cluster head cannot tamper with the data and send incorrect readings. The sensor node forms a message with its id and its sensed reading. It then encrypts this message and sends it to an aggregate node which in turn forwards this message to the cluster head. Neither of these two nodes has the secret key and so they cannot decrypt this message. Thus they cannot intentionally change the data sent by the sensor node. If either the aggregate node or the cluster head try to alter the data, it can be easily recognised by the base station, as the changed data will produce gibberish or meaningless data on being decrypted.

4.1.1   Routing

The sensor nodes send data to the aggregate nodes at specific intervals of time. The sensors of a cluster encrypt their sensed data and send the encrypted message to one of the aggregate nodes in its cluster along with its id. An aggregate node accumulates all the data it receives from all of the sensors reporting to it and forwards it to the cluster head. The cluster head receives this message from all the aggregate nodes within its cluster and then forwards it to the base station. This operation within a cluster has been illustrated in Figure 2. An attacker may compromise a node at any level. Each attack must be detected and dealt with before the integrity of the data of the entire cluster is lost.

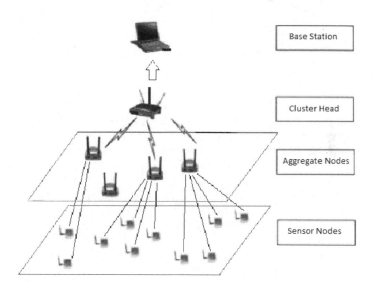

Fig. 2. Routing within a cluster

Sensor Node – If an aggregate node does not receive any data from a sensor node it sends all 1s in the corresponding field for that sensor in its message to signify an error. The base station maintains a trust index for all nodes in the sensor network. The trust value for a particular node gives the reputation of that node to the base station. The base station gives weightage to the data it has received from that node according to this value and changes its trust according to the data it receives. If the base station detects incorrect data sent by a node the trust value for that node is decreased. In the same way receiving correct data from a node increases its trust value. The decrease in the trust value of a node on receiving incorrect data is more than the increase in case of receiving correct data. Thus the reputation of a node decreases rapidly when it sends incorrect data but increases slowly for correct data. The method for calculating the change in trust values has been explained in the next section.

Aggregate node – If an aggregate node is compromised it could change the values of one or more of the fields of the message it sends. However as the aggregate node does not know any of the secret keys shared by the base station and the sensor nodes it cannot meaningfully change the values sent by the individual sensors. It can at most change some random bits of the message which it has received. This would transform the message into gibberish making it meaningless. On decrypting this message the base station could detect the change as the message will not make any sense. Thus the base station will be able to determine that the aggregate node has been compromised. The base station also keeps a trust value for all the aggregate nodes in the WSN. On receiving an incorrect message from any aggregate node it will decrease the trust value of that node. Once the trust value of a particular aggregate node is lowered beyond a threshold value then that aggregate node is deemed to be corrupt. When this occurs, the base station informs the cluster head. The cluster head switches off the compromised aggregate node and switches on one of the remaining passive aggregate nodes present within that cluster. For this purpose there are multiple aggregate nodes in the cluster of which some are kept passive. The base station updates the trust value of the new aggregate node and the cluster head broadcasts the id of the new node to all the sensors which were reporting to the previous one.

Cluster head – Each aggregate node also evaluates the honesty of its cluster head. The aggregate nodes can overhear the message sent from the cluster head to the base station. It in turn compares the fields of this message which it has sent, with the data which it had itself sent to the cluster head. If the corresponding fields do not match then the aggregate node deems the message sent by the cluster head to be dishonest. Each aggregate node stores a trust value for the cluster head. When this value is lowered below a threshold value then that aggregate node makes a vote to change the cluster head. When the majority of the aggregate nodes within a cluster vote for a change, the cluster head is deemed to be compromised. The aggregate nodes have the ability to switch off a cluster head and switch on one of the passive cluster heads present in the cluster. There are multiple cluster heads present in each cluster for this purpose. However, only one cluster head will be active at any particular time. The new cluster head informs the base station of the change and each aggregate node updates its trust value for the cluster head.

4.1.2   Trust Evaluation

The trust value denotes the confidence or reputation of one node with respect to another. In the proposed scheme the base station keeps track of the trust values or reputation of all the sensor nodes and aggregate nodes in the network while the aggregate nodes of a cluster keep track of trust values of its cluster head. The trust values change according to certain factors –

a. **Battery** – The battery factor represents the remaining lifetime of a node. We have chosen the discrete radio model [5] for estimating the power consumption of each node during the transmission and reception of data. This model is used for calculating power consumption and determining which links between sensor motes are available for transmission.

We have assumed that when a node is compromised, its battery usage is greater than an incorrupt node. This is because a compromised node will be executing extra lines of code and tries to interfere with the data sent by other nodes. Thus if the remaining battery of any node is much lower than the average remaining battery of the other sensors then that node has been compromised. Thus the battery factor of any sensor node in the WSN is given by:

$$\mathbf{b}_{\mathrm{f}} = \left\{ b - \left(\frac{\sum_{i=1}^{n} bi}{n} \right) \right\} / b \tag{1}$$

where, b_f is battery factor of the sensor node, b is the remaining battery of that node and n is the number of nodes. The value of b_f can range from 1 to -1. A negative value for this node indicates that the node has been using excessive power and hence is corrupt.

b. **Sensing Communication** – A node has a limited sensing range. Any event is said to be detectable if at least one node lies within its observable range. Now, the sensing models of sensor nodes can be broadly classified into two subcategories, the Boolean sensing model and the Probabilistic sensing model. The Boolean sensing model assumes the detection of an event if it occurs within the sensing radius of the node with equal probability (equal to one). However, it is not the case with the probabilistic sensing models, where the probability of detection of an event is a decreasing function of distance of the event from the sensor node.

Each sensor must send a data packet after a certain time interval. A node is deemed to be corrupt if it fails to send a packet within this interval. Thus the failure of a node, to send data, results in the decrease in its trust value. The sensing communication factor of any node in the sensor network is given by:

$$\mathbf{Sc} = \frac{\text{Struc} - \text{Sfalse}}{\text{Strue} + \text{Sfalse}} \tag{2}$$

where, S_c is the sensing communication factor for a sensor. S_{true} and S_{false} are values which give the number of times an event has been successfully sensed or not by that node. If the sensor node does not send data within the time period S_{false} is incremented by 1 and if it does send information S_{true} is decremented by 1.

c. **Variation** – This factor is used to determine the correctness of the data sent. A sensor node may report numerical values or boolean values. The validity of this data is determined by comparing this data with the data sent by four of its nearest neighbours within its cluster. The co-ordinates of each node in the WSN are stored by the base station. Thus on receiving the data of a sensor node, the base station can compare it with the data of its four nearest neighbours to determine the correctness of the data. The optimum result of any sensor node based upon the values sent by its four nearest neighbours is given by:

$$\text{optimum result of sensor } s = \frac{\sum_{i=1}^{4}(TVi * distancei * resulti)}{TVi * distancei} \qquad (3)$$

where, TV_i is the trust value of sensor node i, $distance_i$ is the distance between sensor i and sensor s and $result_i$ is the result sent by sensor i.

If this optimum result differs by the result sent by sensor s then var_{false} is incremented by 1 or else var_{true} is incremented by 1. The variation factor for sensor s is given by:

$$Vc = \frac{vartrue - varfalse}{vartrue + varfalse} \qquad (4)$$

Based on all these factors the trust value of a node is changed. The formula for this is given by:

$$TVnew = (TVold * 0.9) + \left(0.1 * \frac{(bf * k1 + Sc * k2 + Vc * k3)}{k1 + k2 + k3}\right) \qquad (5)$$

Thus using this formula we get the new trust value for a sensor node depending on its old trust value and the three factor factors. The values of the constants k1, k2 and k3 have been taken to be 0.2, 0.3 and 0.4 respectively. The battery of all the sensor nodes decreases with time and thus this factor has the least weightage. If a sensor sends incorrect data the value of the aggregate result could change drastically. As this sensor is trying to manipulate the end result it needs to be identified at the earliest possible moment. Thus the constant associated with variation of data, k3 is assigned the highest value. The sensing constant is assigned a value in between as a failure to report an event will not change the end result considerably. However if a node consistently fails to send data it could be faulty. In that case any data which it does send may not be accurate.

5   Results

In this section a set of simulations are presented to evaluate the performance of our framework against attacks. We have considered a network of twenty sensor nodes in our simulations. Of these twenty nodes four nodes are compromised. A compromised node may send correct or incorrect data. At times it may also send no data. Figure 3 shows the variation of the remaining battery of an uncompromised node and a compromised node with time. Initially the battery of both nodes are at 100 and as the number of iterations increase the battery consumption of the compromised node is observed to be much more than that of the uncompromised one.

Figure 4 shows the variation of the trust values of all the nodes in the network with time. Initially the trust values of all the nodes are 50. With the increase in time, the trust values of the nodes change according to the data it sends. As can be seen from Figure 4 the trust values for nodes numbered 8, 12, 16 and 19 decrease.

The plots for most of the uncompromised nodes overlap each other as they always send correct data and their trust values increase in the same way. As it can be seen from the graph in Figure 4 the trust values of all of the compromised nodes decrease

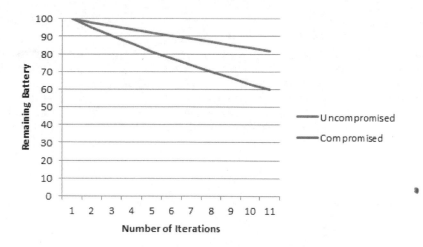

Fig. 3. Trust value of nodes vs. number of iterations

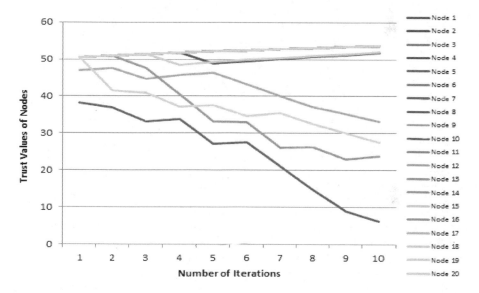

Fig. 4. Trust value of nodes vs. number of iterations

with time. However at some iteration the values also increase. This is because these nodes at times send correct data to delay their detection as much as possible. The trust values of some uncompromised nodes can also decrease at certain iterations. This is due to transmission errors or failure of a sensor to sense an event due to some fault. These changes are more noticeable as the decrease in the trust value of a node is much more than an increase in the trust value. This is to ensure that a compromised node can be detected as soon as possible. Thus in our framework with the reputation of compromised nodes decreasing, such corrupted nodes can be effectively identified and blocked to ensure that the true aggregation results are consistent.

6   Conclusions

In wireless sensor networks, compromised sensors can disrupt the integrity of data by intentionally sending incorrect data reports, by injecting fake data during data aggregation, and also by impeding the transmission of aggregated data. Since cryptographic solutions are not sufficient to prevent these attacks, general reputation based trust systems are proposed in the literature. This paper has presented a novel reliable data aggregation and transmission framework to provide a context-aware trust based security system for wireless sensor networks. A combination of context awareness and trust reasoning allows our system to calculate a trust value of a node based on the previous interactions with that node. As can be observed from the obtained simulation results, the framework proposed in this paper will provide a sound and complete security solution. It can be implemented to combat the inherent security weaknesses of a wireless sensor network.

References

1. Akyildiz, I.F., Su, W., Sankarasubramaniam, Y., Cayirci, E.: Wireless Sensor Networks: a survey. Computer Networks Journal 38, 393–422 (2002)
2. Gupta, P., Kumar, P.: The capacity of wireless networks. IEEE Transactions on Information Theory IT-46(2), 388–404 (2000)
3. Johnson, D., Maltz, D., Broch, J.: DSR: The dynamic source routing protocol for multihop wireless ad hoc networks. In: Perkins, C.E. (ed.) Ad Hoc Networking, pp. 139–172. Addison-Wesley (2001)
4. Heinzelman, W., Chandrakasan, A., Balakrishnan, H.: Energy efficient Communication Protocol for Wireless Micro sensor Networks. In: Proceedings of Hawaii International Conference on System Science (HICSS), Maui, Hawaii, pp. 3005–3014 (2000)
5. Hussain, S., Mallinson, M., Drane, P.: Discrete radio power level consumption model in wireless sensor networks. In: Workshop Proceedings of the Fourth IEEE International Conference on Mobile Ad-hoc and Sensor Systems, MASS (2007)
6. Kocher, P., Jaffe, J., Jun, B.: Differential Power Analysis. In: Wiener, M. (ed.) CRYPTO 1999. LNCS, vol. 1666, pp. 388–397. Springer, Heidelberg (1999)
7. Chan, H., Perrig, A., Song, D.: Random Key Pre-distribution Schemes for Sensor Networks. In: IEEE Symp. Security and Privacy (May 2003)
8. Du, W., et al.: A Pairwise Key Pre-distribution Scheme for Wireless Sensor Networks. In: Proc. 10th ACM Conf. Comp. and Commun. Security, pp. 42–51 (October 2003)
9. Eschenauer, L., Gligor, V.D.: A Key-Management Scheme for Distributed Sensor Networks. In: Proc. 9th ACM Conf. Comp. and Commun. Security, pp. 41–47 (November 2002)
10. Atakli, I., Hu, H., Chen, Y., Ku, W., Su, Z.: Malicious Node Detection in Wireless Sensor Networks using Weighted Trust Evaluation. In: The Symposium on Simulation of Systems Security (January 2008)
11. Hur, J., Lee, Y., Yoon, H., Choi, D., Jin, S.: The 7th International Conference on Advanced Communication Technology, ICAT 2005, pp. 491–496 (July 2005)

12. Zhang, W., Das, S., Liu, Y.: A Trust Based Framework for Secure Data Aggregation in Wireless Sensor Networks. In: IEEE Communications Society Conference on Sensor, Mesh and Ad Hoc Communications and Networks, SECON (2006)
13. Resnick, P., Zeckhauser, R.: Trust among strangers in Internet transactions: empirical analysis of eBays reputation system. In: Baye, M.R. (ed.) Advances in Applied Microeconomics, vol. 11. Elsevier Science (2003)
14. Xiong, L., Liu, L.: A reputation-based trust model for peer-to-peer ecommerce communities. In: Proc. of IEEE Conference on Ecommerce 2003, p. 275 (2003)

Survey of Trust Schemes on Ad-Hoc Network

Renu Dalal[1,*], Manju Khari[1], and Yudhvir Singh[2]

[1] Computer Science & Engg.Department, Ambedkar Institute of Technology,
New Delhi, India
[2] Department of Computer Science & Engg, U.I.E.T M.D University Rohtak,
India
dalalrenu1987@gmail.com

Abstract. MANET (Mobile Ad-hoc Network) is a structureless & dynamics network, which consist of mobile nodes without any physical link between them. MANET provides some basic functions like routing, communication, network management and packet forwarding etc over self organized network. Because MANET has not a fixed topology, in which mobile nodes comes and leaves the network within a random period of time. It effects energy, bandwidth and memory computations of network. Providing trust in MANET is such a crucial task because it doesn't having centralized infrastructure. In this paper, we survey the different trust model schemes of MANET with their unique features, merits and demerits.

Keywords: MANET, Cluster based, Maturity based, PKI, ABED, CORE.

1 Introduction

Security is an important issue in wired network (like LAN, WAN, Ethernet etc) as well as in wireless network (wireless sensor network, cognitive radio network, MANET etc).Trust models are necessary to provide security in networks. In MANET trust can be defined as a level of belief according to the behavior of nodes (or entities, agents etc) [1].The probability value of trust varying from 0 to1, where 0 represent DISTRUST and 1 represents TRUST [2]. According to Golybeck [3] trust has three basic properties: Transitivity, Asymmetry and Personalization (or personal opinion).

The different existing trust based schemes in Ad-hoc network were discussed in this paper as shown in fig. 1. *Section 2* Including Protocol based trust schemes (ABED, GRE, OTHER). *Section 3* presents seven different System level based trust models, *Section 4* will give the review of Cluster based trust model, *section 5* covers Maturity based trust model. PKI based trust model comes in *section 6* and conclusion in *section 7*.

---

* Corresponding author.

N. Meghanathan et al. (Eds.): CCSIT 2012, Part I, LNICST 84, pp. 170–180, 2012.

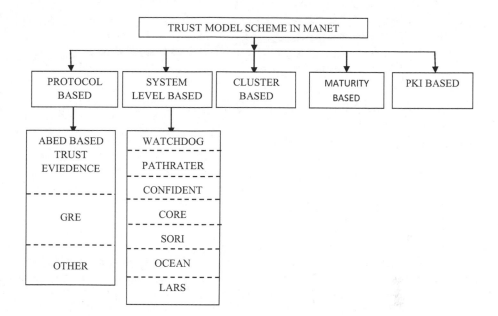

Fig. 1. Trust Based Schemes in MANET

2   Protocol Based Trust Schemes

2.1   ABED

ABED is Ant Based Evidence Distribution scheme, which was purposed by Jiang & Baras [4]. This scheme uses the concept of swarm intelligence paradigm. In this scheme, mobile nodes (in MANET) communicate indirectly with other mobile nodes through "agents" which called "ants" in ABED. Agents found the optimal path for evaluating trust evidence, through the information called "Pheromones" that is collected by "ants". Features of ABED: Easily adaptive to mobility, effectively work in structure less network. It can solve the problem of Dynamic optimization and combinatorial optimization. Work on Stigmergy principle.

2.2   GRE

Generalized Reputation Evidence (GRE) protocol based scheme is discovered by Buckerche & Ren [5]. The main feature of GRE is, it provide security to trusted community of MANET from malicious nodes because GRE scheme will not entered any suspicious node in trusted network. Merit of this scheme, neither attack is addressed on GRE model.

2.3   Other Scheme

Trust evidence evaluation scheme is discovered by Theodorakopoulos and Baras [4]. Features: Solving path problem in directed graph. Theory of Semirings is used for provide trust between nodes (where node as entities and link between two nodes as trust relationship) without using direct communication between them. This model is robust in nature in presence of Intruders. Binary variables (0 or 1) used as trust value. Trust is transistive according to this model.

3   System Level Based Trust Models

System level trust model is the combination of Individual level trust model and punishment or reward system. In this model, system will give punishment to those nodes which found as malicious or selfish in network and also give reward to those nodes which behave in a trustworthy way most of the time. The system level trust model includes "Trust evidence dissemination mechanism" [6].

3.1   Watchdog

In 2000, the Watchdog trust model was discovered by [7]. Watchdog mechanism find out the selfish node in MANET by observing each and every function (listening next node's transmission, exploiting promiscuous mode of operation etc) performed by mobile node. The mobile node considered as malicious node in the two cases and source is notified, *case 1*: if the packet is not forwarded by node within a certain period of time in network. *Case 2*: each node have a buffer for keeping recently sent packets, if overheard packet is not same as one stored in buffer.

3.2   Pathrater

Pathrater behaves as the Watchdog with including the feature of providing the" best route link (which is likely to be reliable) [7] for reliable data". For searching the best route for data, node calculates the path metric according to observe the rating for every neighboring node which is known in MANET. This scheme provides the shortest path selection when reliable information is not available. If negative value exists in path metric, it indicates one or more malicious node in the path.

3.3   CONFIDENT

CONFIDENT is a system level based trust model, which purposed in 2002 by [8]. Nodes are extracted in this model which does not behave normally in network. Implementation of Cooperation of Nodes Fairness in Dynamic Network (CONFIDENT) required four components: 1 Monitor:-The node found abnormal behavior by monitoring the transmission of next node or by behavior of route protocol. 2 Reputation System: - If any node found suspicious node in MANET, an ALARM message sent to the trust manager component. 3 Trust Manager: - It evaluates the trust of malicious node. The malicious node refers to as trustworthy node, if trust manager is not capable to prove malicious behavior (exceeding threshold to rule out coincidences etc). 4 Path Manager: - Each node having a list that contains the all malicious node and this list is interchanged at random period of time between other nodes.

3.4   CORE

Collaborative Reputation (CORE) trust scheme was founded in 2002 by [9]. CORE scheme differentiate the selfish node and malicious node. The nodes which not cooperate with other nodes in the MANET, for saving battery for its own communication is called "selfish node" while these nodes does not damage other node. The malicious node in MANET behaves abnormally and can damage other nodes by doing any suspicious activity. CORE purposed three different type of reputation: 1. Subjective Reputation: - Reputation value evaluated by giving priority to past observation of mobile node, rather than current one. If malicious node is found out then node's subjective reputation value is changed by using WD (watchdog) mechanism. 2. Indirect Reputation: - This value is calculated by providing reputation by one node to other node. Reputation value can be updated through reply message that contains the list of nodes which behaved normally in context of every function. If any node having negative reputation value all requested by that node will be rejected and this node works only as service provider not as requester. For long period of time if this node will provide correct services to all other nodes in MANET, node can achieved their reputation value again. When reputation value is above then the threshold reputation value, that node will again works as service provider as well as service requester. 3. Functional Reputation: - This reputation is the combination of indirect and subjective reputation value. The weight combine formula is used for calculation of functional reputation value.

3.5   OCEAN

Observation Based Cooperation Enforcement in Ad-hoc Network (OCEAN) trust scheme was discovered in 2003 by [10]. This scheme is not allowed to exchange the second hand knowledge about nodes to other nodes in MANET. OCEAN model has five components, 1. Neighbor Watch: - It will watch the behavior of neighboring node. 2 Route Ranker: - It maintains the route rank list for each of the neighboring node. 3 Rank based routing: - This component extracts those routes which contains malicious node. 4 Malicious Traffic Rejection: - All suspicious traffic is removed from node which consider as misleading by this component. 5 Second-chance Mechanism: - Malicious node is removed from the faulty list after a fixed duration of observation inactivity and constant value assigned to the node.

3.6   SORI

In 2004, Secure and Objective Reputation-based Incentive (SORI) scheme was discovered by [11]. SORI scheme takes concept of reputation rating which based on packet forwarding ratio of a node. It consists of three components, 1. Neighbors Monitoring, This component used to collect information of neighboring node about the behavior of packet forwarding. 2. Reputation Propagation: - It providing information sharing of other nodes with its neighbor. 3. Punishment: - It includes the process of removing the packet from the network. This scheme can't differentiate between the selfish and malicious node.

3.7   LARS

Locally Aware Reputation System (LARS) level trust model was purposed by [12] in 2006. It provides reputation value to its entire one hop neighboring node. This value can be changed on direct observation of neighbor node. The Warning message will be generated by the evaluator node (EN) to its neighbor, if EN founds any node's reputation value below to the threshold trustworthy value.

4   Cluster Based Trust Model

The cluster based trust model for MANET was introduced in 2008 by [13]. In this model, ad-hoc network divided into clusters. Important terms used in this model, 1. Direct trust value: - any two nodes in cluster calculate trust value between them according to recent transaction records. For ex.n2 and n3 takes α1 value as direct trust value in cluster c1. 2. Inter cluster trust value: - Cluster head collected the recommendation information from other nodes to compute the inter cluster trust value.3. Gateway: - It maintains interaction between MANET's node with adjacent cluster. 4. Routing:-Two type of cluster routing is used in this model. One is Intra-cluster routing, the routing with in a cluster. Another is Inter-cluster routing, the routing between two different clusters. Zone routing protocol is used in cluster based model, which is combination of "Proactive" (intra-cluster routing) and "Reactive" (inter-cluster routing).

(A) Direct trust Representation & Its Computation [13, 14, 15]
From Node N_J to N_i direct trust represented as TR^{ij}_D calculation of direct trust:

$$TR^{ij}_D = \frac{t_m + a/2}{t + a} \qquad t_m, t \geq 0, a > 0 \tag{1}$$

In case, when there is no previous interaction between mode N_J and N_i.

t is the time transactions, t_m is time success and a is a positive real number. a is inversely proportional to evidence in this model.

(B) Intercluster Recommendation Trust Value's Representation & Its Calculation
It is denoted as TR^j_r and calculated as:

$$TR^j_r = \frac{\sum_{i=1}^{t} TR^{hi}_D . TR^{ij}_D}{\sum_{i=1}^{t} TR^{hi}_D} \qquad \text{Where } TR^{hi}_D > H, \ i \neq j. \tag{2}$$

TR^{hi}_D is aggregation weight (direct trust value of node N_i, computed by CH), TR^{ij}_D is direct trust recommendations information and n is the number of nodes in current cluster.

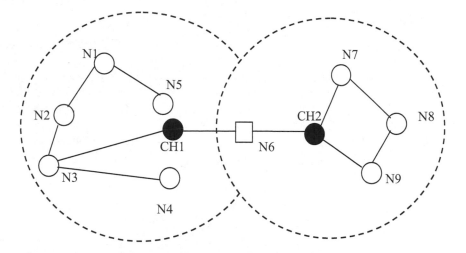

Fig. 2. Cluster Based Trust Model in MANET

●   CLUSTER-HEAD

□   GATEWAY

○   MANET'S NODE

(C) Total trust representation & computation

It is represented as $\Gamma(N_i, N_j)$ and computed as:

$$\Gamma(N_i, N_j) = \alpha \ TR^{ij}_D + \beta TR^i_r \qquad (3)$$

Where α, $\beta \geq 0$ and $\alpha + \beta = 1$. TR^{ij}_D is the direct trust between nodes N_i and N_j, α is the impact weight of direct trust and β is the impact weight of recommendation trust.

(D) Cross cluster trust

The cross cluster trust between nodes N3 & N7 can be calculated as:

$$\Gamma(N3, N7) = \Gamma(N3, N6). \ \Gamma(N6, N7) \qquad (4)$$

N3 node is in cluster c1 and N7 is in c2, through node N6 (gateway) both nodes are connected. Γ(N3, N6) is the global trust of node N6 by node N3.This trust value is calculated in c1 because node N3 and N6 locates in c1. Γ(N6, N7) is global trust, which calculates in cluster c2 because node N6 and N7 comes in cluster c2. Merits of cluster based trust model: No need of personal or past experience of any node in MANET for evaluation of trust value on nodes. Effective work in a small scale Ad-hoc network. Cluster head (CH) and gateways used in this model. There is no need of centralized infrastructure. Demerits: The performances will be degraded when cluster based model used in larger size MANET.

5   Maturity Based Trust Model

It was disclosed in 2010 by [16], figure [4] shows Maturity based trust model. Its features are as follows: This trust model introduces the concept of relationship maturity in Ad-hoc network. Trust increases between people as times goes by, same concept is used in maturity based model for MANET. Every node takes direct recommendation value to its neighborhood node only. This value will be decreased if new neighbor comes in network. This model purposed the REP (recommendation exchange protocol) for interchanging recommendation value for their neighbors.

(A) Calculation of recommendation value in Ad-Hoc

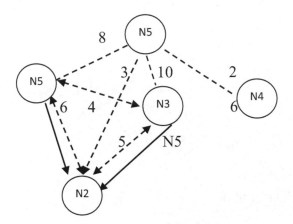

Fig. 3. Evaluation of recommendation value

In fig. [3], Decimal digits show how long the nodes know each other. Dotted arrows are used for connecting the neighboring nodes. Normal arrow indicates recommendation. Here N5 is neighboring node of N2, N1 & N3. Nodes N1 and N3 send recommendation value of N5 to N2. N2 consider the recommendation value (5) of N3 more important than N1 because node N3 knows node N5 as longer period of time also N3 having more older experience to interact with N5 as compared to N1.

(B) Maturity Based Trust Model Operation Modes
This model defines three types of operation modes. These are as follows: (i) Simple Mode, in which node using trust table and REP protocol optional. Nodes operated in less power capacity. (ii) In Intermediate Mode, nodes are operated in medium capacity and takes recommendations of other nodes. (iii)Advanced Mode, nodes are operated in higher power capacity & developed the system with all features. REP protocol is used for providing interface between network (TCP/IP) and trust, learning plan of System.

(C) Evaluation of Trust in Maturity Based Model
The evaluation of trust from node a to b is denoted as Ta (b). It takes the concept of T a (b) evaluation from [1]. Ta (b) = (1-α) Q_a (b) + α R_a (b); α ranges from 0 to 1, parameter in this model, that permits node to take most relevant factor. Q_a(b) lies

from 0 to 1 and presents direct value of node a to b. $R_a(b)$ lies between 0 to 1 and represents aggregate recommendation value of all other neighbors.

$Q_a(b) = \beta E_a(b) + (1-\beta) T_a(b)$; β lies between 0 to 1 and presents different weights for the factor of eq. & select best relevant at instance. $E_a(b)$ evaluates trust value by classifier components and $T_a(b)$ is the last trust value stored in trust table.

$$R_a = \frac{\sum_{i \in K_a} T_a(i) M_i(b) X_i(b)}{\sum_{j \in K_a} X_i T_a(j) M_j(b)} \tag{5}$$

Where $X_i(b)$ according to [18].

$X_i(b) = N(T_i(b), \sigma_i(b))$; $R_a(b)$ defined as recommendation value from all nodes, $i \in K_a$ about node b, $X(i)$ is the accuracy, $M(i)$ is the relationship maturity and value in a trust table of node i to b.

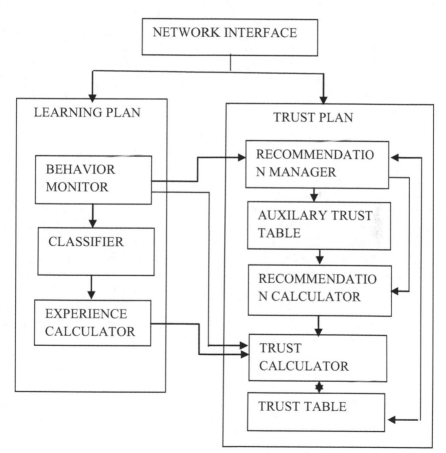

Fig. 4. Maturity Based Trust Model

(D) Working of REP in MANET

This protocol permits the nodes to interchange recommendations value between neighboring nodes. REP uses 3 messages, (i) Trust request (TREQ) (ii) Trust reply (TREP) (iii) Trust advertisement (TA)

Step 1 when new nodes (TN) come in network it sends TREQ message with IP address to each node

(- - - ➤)

Step 2 now neighboring node will only sends TREP with its recommendation value to

TN (target node) (——➤)

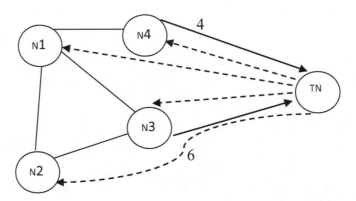

Fig. 5. Working of REP Protocol

Advantages: In this model no need of authentication mechanism. There is low vulnerability to false recommendation attack. It requires less resource consumption. This model is robust to slander colluding attack and tolerates up to 35% of liars. Any change in behavior of node can be easily identified by this model.

6   PKI Based Trust Model Scheme

The PKI approach in MANET can be implemented using either distributed certification or self organized public key management. In distributed certification scheme, by using a threshold digital signature, which provides facility of renewing & issuing, certificates [19-21]. Demerits: Needed additional storage requirement of public key. DOS attack not surely eliminated by this approach.

The self organized approach using centralized CA (certification authority) as self organized scenario [22]. Each node trusts on its neighboring node and stores information. The certificates receive trough chain of certificates which issued by nodes. According to [23], it uses this approach because of these reasons. All mobile nodes have equal roles. It requires less maintenance overhead. Simple bootstrap mechanism used in this scheme.

In This Approach, Each Node in MANET Performs These Tasks

Certificate Management: (i) Key generation, development of key pair (public key, private key) by node themselves (ii) Certificate issuance, public key with nodes identity binds in certificates, which issued by nodes it. (iii) Updated Certificate Repository, it is developed by node. (iv) Certificate exchange, non updated repository constructed by interchanging the certificates with other nodes.

Public Key verification: Searching and comparing the certificates in the chain. In algorithm, MPR technology used which was proposed by [23]. In MPR, the redundancy of messages can be decreased at local level. It search minimum number of nodes those required for reaching whole network, when applied recursively. For finding smallest number of certificates chain that is necessary to reach the node, algorithm: MPR Gout heuristic is used. This algorithm [23] defines re- transmission set for each vertex in certificate graph. Merits: Increment of certificate rate by using MPR technology. It reduced the length of certificate chain. Efficient verification procedure and authentication needs less communication between nodes.

7   Conclusion

In this paper, we surveyed existing trust schemes for mobile ad-hoc network to achieve the security and trustworthiness. It is concluded that, Protocol based trust scheme evaluate the trust through indirect communication but System level trust scheme is more feasible as compared to Protocol based. System level trust model uses concept of punishment or reward for nodes and it calculates trust value on the basis of direct communication. Cluster based and Maturity based model using standard eq. (1), (2) & (3) to find out trust value of node. Maturity based model is best as compared to Cluster based. In PKI based schemes, self organized scheme is more efficient than Distributed scheme of PKI. Some schemes like individual level trust model CRFSN, PTM etc, threshold cryptography, and cluster & non cluster based certification schemes in MANET are not covered in this paper. In future work, we plan to continue towards with unified trust model scheme.

References

1. Capra, L.: Toward a Human Trust Model for Mobile Ad-hoc Network. In: Proc. 2nd UK-UbiNet Workshop, May 5-7. Cambridge University, Cambridge (2004)
2. Jøsang, A., Presti, S.L.: Analyzing the Relationship between Risk and Trust. In: Jensen, C., Poslad, S., Dimitrakos, T. (eds.) iTrust 2004. LNCS, vol. 2995, pp. 135–145. Springer, Heidelberg (2004)
3. Golbeck, J.: Computing with Trust: Definition, Properties and Algorithm. In: Securecomm and Workshops- Security and Privacy for Emerging Areas in Communication Networks, Baltimore, MD, August 28-September 1, pp. 1–7 (2006)
4. Theodorakopoulos, G., Baras, J.S.: On Trust Models and Trust Evaluation Metrics for Ad-hoc Networks. IEEE Journal on selected Areas in Communications 24(2), 318–328 (2006)

5. Boukerche, A., Ren, Y.: A Security Management Scheme using a novel Computational Reputation Model for Wireless and Mobile Ad hoc Networks. In: Proc. Int'l. Workshop on Modeling Analysis and Simulation of Wireless and Mobile System, Vancouver, British Columbia, Canada, pp. 88–95 (2008)

6. Yu, H., Shen, Z., Miao, C., Leung, C., Niyato, D.: A Survey of Trust and Reputation Management System in Wireless Communications. In: Proc. of the IEEE (2010)

7. Marti, S., Giuli, T.J., Lai, K., Baker, M.: Mitigating Routing Misbehavior in Mobile Ad-hoc Networks. In: ACM MobiCom Conference (2000)

8. Buchegger, S., Le Boudec, J.-Y.: Performance analysis of the confident protocol "(cooperation of nodes: fairness in dynamic ad-hoc networks)". In: IEEE/ACM Symposium on Mobile Ad-hoc Networking and Computing, MobiHoc 2002 (2002)

9. Michirardi, P., Molva, R.: Core: A collaborative reputation mechanism to encode node cooperation in mobile ad-hoc networks. In: CMS 2002 Communication and Multimedia Security Conference (2002)

10. Bansal, S., Baker, M.: Observation –based Cooperation Enforcement in Ad-hoc Networks, arxiv:cs/0307012v2 (2003)

11. He, Q., Wu, D., Khosla, P.: SORI: A Secure and Objective Reputation- based Incentive Schemes for Ad-hoc Networks. In: WCNC 2004 IEEE wireless Communications and Networking Conference (2004)

12. Hu, J., Burnmester, M.: LARS: a locally aware reputation system for mobile ad-hoc networks. In: 44th Annual ACM Southeast Regional Conference (2006)

13. Chen, A., Xu, G., Yang, Y.: A Cluster Based Trust Model For Mobile Ad-hoc Networks. IEEE (2008)

14. Cramp, R.: Logical foundations of probability. University of Chicago press (1950)

15. Cramp, R.: Replies and systematic expositions. In: Schilpp, P.A. (ed.) The Philosophy of Rudolf Carnap, pp. 966–998. Open court, La Salle (1963)

16. Velloso, P.B., Laufer, R.P., Cunha, D.d.O., Duarte, O.C.M.B., Pujolle, G.: Trust Management In Mobile Ad hoc Networks Using a Scalable Maturity Based Model. IEEE Transactions on Networks and Service Management 7(3), 172–185 (2010)

17. Virendra, M., Chanddrasekaran, M., Upadhyaya, S.: Quantifying trust in mobile ad-hoc networks. In: Proc. IEEE International Conf. Integration Knowledge Intensive Multi-Agent Syst., Waltham, USA (April 2005)

18. Theodorakopouls, G., Baras, J.S.: Trust Evaluation in ad-hoc networks. In: ACM Workshop Wireless Security (October 2004)

19. Saxena, N., Tsudik, G., Yi, J.H.: Threshold Cryptography in P2P and MANETs: the case of access control. Computer Networks 51(12), 3632–3649 (2007)

20. Wu, B., Wu, J., Fernadez, E.B., Ilyas, M., Magliveras, S.: Secure and efficient key management in Mobile ad hoc networks. Journal of Network Computer Applications 30(3), 937–954 (2007)

21. Joshi, D., Namuduri, K., Pendse, R.: Secure, redundant, and fully distributed ket management scheme in mobile and ad- hoc networks: an analysis. EURASIP Journal on Wireless Communications and Networking (4), 579–589 (2005)

22. Capkun, S., Buttyan, L., Hubaux, J.P.: Self-organized public key management for mobile ad-hoc networks. Mobile Computing and Communication Review 6(4) (2002)

23. Caballero-Gill, P., Herandez-Goya, C.: Efficient Public Key Certificate Management for Mobile Ad Hoc Networks. EURASIP Journal on Wireless Communications and Networking 2011, 1–10 (2010)

Improve Service Discovery Performance over Different Networks Utilization and Sizes

Intisar Al-Mejibli, Martin Colley, and Salah Al-Majeed

Department of Computer Science and Electronic Engineering, University of Essex,
Colchester, UK
{ialmej,martin,ssaleha}@essex.ac.uk

Abstract. Service discovery requests' messages have a vital role in sharing and locating resources in many of service discovery protocols. Sending more messages than a link can handle may cause congestion and loss of messages which dramatically influences the performance of these protocols. Re-send the lost messages result in latency and inefficiency in performing the tasks which user(s) require from the connected nodes. *This issue become a serious problem in two cases: first, when the number of clients which performs a service discovery request is increasing, as this result in increasing in the number of sent discovery messages; second, when the network resources such as bandwidth capacity are consumed by other applications. These two cases lead to network congestion and loss of messages.* This paper propose an algorithm to improve the services discovery protocols performance by separating each consecutive burst of messages with a specific period of time which calculated regarding the available network resources. In addition, this paper explains the impact of increasing the number of clients and the consumed network resources on the proposed algorithm.

Keywords: Dropped messages, Service discovery protocols & Network Utilization.

1   Introduction

The home network has become recognized as the forefront of the networking revolution, where consumer technology and Internet infrastructure intersect to change the way we lead our lives. A fast growing increase in the uses of home networks has been noticed, for example recent research from Pike Research predicts a strong growth in the intelligent lighting control market. Global revenue is expected to increase from $1.3 billion to $2.6 billion by 2016 in intelligent lights [1].

In fact, home network would consist of everything a homeowner could imagine, ranging from large domestic appliances such as the fridges, microwaves, audio-visual equipment to the lightweight temperature and smoke sensors. In addition to mobile devices, smart cards, bar codes in grocery packages and little chips in clothing and accessories. The main goal of interconnecting the home devices together is to share the network services and resources, and to invoke them remotely. Many protocols have been proposed to achieve this purpose which is locate and invoke the services

N. Meghanathan et al. (Eds.): CCSIT 2012, Part I, LNICST 84, pp. 181–192, 2012.

and resources in network known as services discovery protocols [2]. Most of the service discovery protocols rely on the exchange of messages to locate remote services and to provide access to them. Sending too many messages into the network from multiple nodes at the same time, could cause congestion which will lead to router queue overflow and the loss of messages. Accordingly, more messages must be sent to discover the services in the network and this causes more latency in discovery process and greedy consumption of the network resources.

This paper discusses how to avoid dropped messages during service discovery process in small networks which fall in (local Area Network) LAN category such as a networked office building, or home. In addition, it proposes an algorithm to overcome this significant issue, in order to make the discovery process perform smoothly and seamlessly. Further it explains the impact of increasing the number of clients and rate of consumed network resources on the proposed algorithm results.

This paper is structured as follows. Section 2 introduces the related work which includes service discovery protocols and available mechanisms and algorithms that have been proposed to avoid or minimize the number of dropped messages. Section 3 introduces the proposed algorithm. The simulation results are detailed in section 4. Finally, the conclusion and future work are given in section 5.

2   Related Work

We should introduce service discovery protocols and the relevant work mechanism in order to understand the subsequent sections. Service discovery protocols acts vital role in sharing and locating resources in network and many of these protocols depend on messaging to achieve their process. From this point of view, it is a significant to introduce service discovery protocols to understand the proposed algorithm properly.

2.1   Service Discovery Protocol (UPnP)

Service discovery protocols enable devices to discover all services in a network and some of them allow devices that provide services to announce their services. Each service discovery protocol must have two components: a client which is the component that has a set of requirements that form the services it needs, and a device which is the component that offers its service(s) and is requested by client. Accordingly, any node in a network may be a client, a device, or a client and device at same time. Service discovery protocols can be classified into two types: Registry-based such as Jini [4][5] and Peer-to-Peer like UPnP [3]. Registry-based can be classified into centralized registry like Jini and distributed registry like Service Location Protocol (SLP) [4][6]. The Registry-based and Peer-to-Peer approaches both have advantages and drawbacks. For example: Registry-based is well organized and managed, but the registry node could cause a bottle neck problem for the entire network since if this node is damaged for any reason the clients are not able to access the required services. While in the Peer-to-Peer type all services send messages regularly even if there isn't a target client and this causes an unnecessary consumption for the networks' resources. Some protocols consider the announcement as an essential principle in service discovery issue such as UPnP whereas others protocols do not use the announcement approach such as Bluetooth [4] [7]. A selection technique should be used to select the most appropriate service when the discovery phase results in two or more identical services. There are two selection modes: manual and automatic modes. In manual mode, service selection is the responsibility of the user entirely. This mode has drawbacks: users may not know enough about the services to distinguish among them and too much user involvement causes inconvenience. This mode is applied in all the investigated service discovery protocols. In automatic mode, the service discovery protocol selects the service this simplifies client programs. On the other hand automatic selection may not be select the choice that user wants.

Each service discovery protocol has a specific features and philosophy which are different from other protocols. Here we will explain UPnP in more details as it is used in our simulated model.

UPnP is proposed for use in home and small office environments and targets device and service discovery. It has the capability of automatically assigning IP addresses to networked devices. The components considered in UPnP are control points (clients) which are optional and devices (offers service(s)). Service discovery in UPnP is depends on the Simple Service Discovery Protocol (SSDP) [5]. SSDP was proposed to discover devices and services in a network easily, quickly, dynamically, and without any a priori knowledge. It uses HTTP over unicast and multicast UDP packets to define two functions: search the services of a network and announce the availability of services in a network. UPnP cannot scale well since it uses multicasting extensively (multicasting is used both for service advertisements and service requests) [6]. When a control point is connected to network, it starts requesting the required service(s) by sending multicast message over UDP transport protocol. The service(s) that match the required criteria responds by sending unicast message to requested control point. Consequently, the control point gets information about the requested service. On the other hand, when the device is connected to network, it starts announcing its service(s) regularly by sending multicast message (over UDP). Figure 1 shows multicast M-SEARCH format of UPnP protocol.

```
M-SEARCH * HTTP/1.1
HOST: 239.255.255.250:1900
MAN: "ssdp:discover"
MX: seconds to delay response (MUST be greater than or equal to 1 and
SHOULD be less than 5 inclusive)
ST: search target
USER-AGENT: OS/version UPnP/1.1 product/version
```

Fig. 1. Multicast M-SEARCH format of UPnP protocol

MX field value contains maximum wait time in seconds. Device responses should be delayed a random duration between 0 and this many seconds in order to balance load for the control point (client) when it processes responses. The devices may assume an MX field value less than that specified in the MX header field. In another words, if the MX header field specifies a field value greater than 1, the device should assume that it contained the value 1 or less. Devices must not stop responding to other requests while waiting the random delay before sending a response.

2.2   Techniques and Methods

There are a number of techniques have been proposed to avoid dropping packets such as the approach which suggested by Parry and Gangatharan. The principle of their idea is the packet size of each source should be adjusted according to the network bandwidth to optimize the network utilization and also to avoid packet overflow at the client buffer. Their approach is based on a controller which is used to trace the data transmission rate at the router. When the total transmission rate is higher than the network bandwidth, the transmission controller adjusts the packet size of the source nodes so that the transmission rate is equal to the network bandwidth. [8].

Jacobson suggested an end-to-end congestion avoidance mechanism as used in Transmission Control Protocol (TCP). These mechanisms have worked well on low bandwidth delay product networks, while with newer high-bandwidth delay networks they have shown to be inefficient and prone to be unstable [9].

Jin proposed an alternative to the end-to-end congestion avoidance mechanism, named Network Lion and used in Transmission Control Protocol (TCP) too. Network Lion is developed as a part of a new network transmission protocol. His method uses a packet drop avoidance (PDA) mechanism which is based on the maximum burst size (MBS) theory. In addition, he uses a real-time available bandwidth algorithm. Network Lion does redesign the transmission control, as well as separating the pacing control in layer 3 and retransmission control in layer 4. [10].

Kevin Mills and Christopher Dabrowski [11] proposed four Algorithms for adaptive-jitter control depending on network size, in order to minimize the dropping of messages from the message queues in the UPnP protocol. In fact, UPnP permits clients to include a jitter bound in multicast (M-Search) queries in order to limit implosion. Qualifying devices use the jitter bound to randomize timing of their responses. Kevin Mills and Christopher Dabrowski's algorithms depend on the principle of this bound. All four of these algorithms are based on making each root device independently estimate the time it will take for all root devices to respond to each M-Search query. Each root device then uses its estimate to determine a time to send its own responses (if any). Each response message includes a value recommending how long the control-point M-Search task should listen for responses, so M-Search task does not need to guess an appropriate required maximum time for listening.

All root devices must send and listen to Notify messages (which include a caching time or *max-age*). When all root devices receives these messages, they should build a map (*NM*) of devices and services in the network. Consequently, a root device could use its *NM* to estimate how many response messages will be sent by all root devices. They assume that the messages will be sent consecutively at rate *R and* root devices will send messages sequentially in the ascending order of their unique identities.

3   The Proposed Algorithm

The aims of the proposed algorithm are: determines the required sending queue space and the required time for the routers to forwards all the messages of burst mode before receiving the next burst of messages. The proposed algorithm explains the relation between the required queue sizes and the interval separating two consecutive bursts of messages, to avoid dropping messages. The following rules must be applied to compute the sending queue size in each router or the space which required being available in the sending queue of each router at the sending time and calculate the best interval for each router. The algorithm was tested when the routers were connected in a decentralised configuration.

3.1   Queue Size Algorithm

The Algorithm which is used to calculate the size of the sending queue for each router is illustrated in Figure 2. The values m and n represent the number of clients and services that connected to Ri respectively, where i=1, 2 … No. of routers.

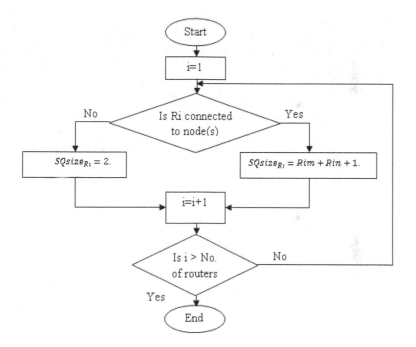

Fig. 2. Flowchart of Queue Size Algorithm

3.2   Best Interval Algorithm

The best interval algorithm is explained in figure 3. In the suggested network topology any chosen router will divide the network into two parts, left and right. Equation (1) which is mentioned in figure 3, guarantees that a specific router would forward all the receiving messages to their destination (client) before receiving the next burst of messages. It can be developed and take into consideration the available sending queue size for the specified router, as it represents the sharing space between

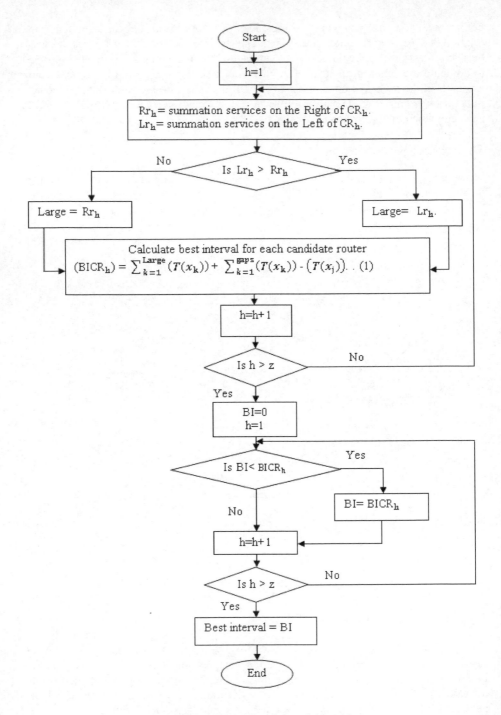

Fig. 3. Flowchart of Best interval Algorithm

all the clients (receivers) connected to that router so an overlap between two or more consecutive burst of messages can be achieved in order to minimize the required interval. Note z is the number of candidate routers.

Where, $(T(x_k)) = \dfrac{Message\ Size\ of\ service_{\ k}}{Bandwidth\ that\ message\ would\ use}$

In Formula (1) the $(T(x_j))$ value is the biggest among $(Time(x_k))$, $k = 1,2,...Large$. $(T(x_j))$ represents the time the message utilizes the link.

$\sum_{k=1}^{gaps}(T(x_k))$: represents the number of message times during which a specific router doesn't receive any service messages from nearest router(s). Here the average message size and average bandwidth is used. When there is a service connected directly to the nearest router, it would need at least two message times to reach the evaluated router.

The flowchart in fiure4 shows how to calculate the Overlapped space (OS):

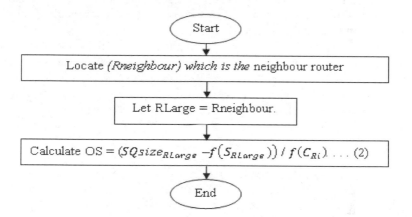

Fig. 4. Flowchart of OS Calculation Steps

Where $f(S_{RLarge}) = \sum_{k=1}^{n}(S_k)$ is number of all services that connected to the RLarge and

$f(C_{Ri}) = \sum_{k=1}^{m}(C_k)$ is number of all clients that connected to the and Ri.

Equation (1) could use OS value and could be written as:

The best interval (BI) $= \sum_{k=1}^{Big} T(x_k) + \sum_{k=1}^{gaps} T(x_k) - T(x_j) - \sum_{k=1}^{OS} T(x_k)$. . . (1)

The question now, must each router in a network be evaluated in order to identify the best interval for entire network? And which interval would be used for the network? The answer is: Not all routers in a network must be evaluated instead some of them would be candidate to be evaluated and the longest interval will be used at the end, because, logically using the longest interval will avoid dropping messages at all other routers.

There are some conditions that help to identify which router will have the most impact in determining the best interval.

3.3   Choosing Candidate Router Rules

1- Identify the longest path between a service and a client. Then the router which connected to this client must be selected.
2- Identifying the router that connected to the largest number of clients and receives the largest number of services from one side of the network.
3- Identifying the router that connected to one or more clients and located nearest the end of the network.
4- If the chosen router is connected to one client then the nearest router connected to client too must be chosen, in order to compare between two consecutive burst of messages reach these routers consecutively.

In case that the two (or more) consecutive burst of messages were sent to the same client and this client is the lonely client connected to router, this means logically there are two (or more) receivers connected to that router and this should be taken into consideration in calculating the (OS) value.

One client may satisfy more than one of the previous conditions, in other words the client that has longest path with a service could be the same client that connected to a router which receives largest number of services and this wouldn't cause any problem.

All the candidate routers must be evaluated and the longest interval is the best interval for the network which would guarantee no losing messages.

4   Simulation Results

The applied simulated model clarifies the influence of increasing the proportion of consumed network resources and the number of clients on the performing of UPnP. It has been compared between the algorithm and normal cases over UPnP. The network design includes 4 routers (R0, R1, R2, and R3) connected in decentralized manner where each router is connected to 3 services (S0, S1..., and S9) except R2 which connected to six clients (C0, C1... C5). Network parameters have been shown in table 1.

Table 1. Network Parameters

Parameter name	Value
Bandwidth among routers (Main links)	512Kb
Bandwidth between routers and other nodes (Sub links)	256Kb
Delay in main and sub	0ms
Queue Type	Drop Tail
Routing Protocol	DSDV
Message Length of discovery (Multicast)	64 bytes
Message Length of discovery reply (Unicast)	128 bytes
Message Length of backward traffic	100, 200, 300 bytes
Simulation Time	100.0 seconds

The applied scenario is:

1. (C0, C1... C5) send multicast messages to discover all the services in the network, then,
2. All services send reply messages to the requested clients. In algorithm each service separates any consecutive replying messages with a specific period of time. While, in normal case service replies to the discovery requested dependently.
3. There is a UDP background traffic (S0 with S8) and (S1 with S7), where S0, S1 are connected to R0 and S7& S8 are connected to R3. The rate of the backward traffic is 0.01 and the messages size is different.
4. In all tests the algorithm used the same interval regardless the backward traffic.

Figures (5, 6, 7, 8, 9 and 10) explain the impact of increasing the consumption of network resources such as bandwidth on the performing of suggested algorithm and normal case over UPnP. This has been achieved by increasing the size of backward traffic messages.

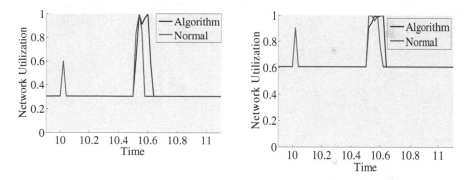

Fig. 5. Main link Utilization when backward traffic is 30%

Fig. 6. Main link Utilization when backward traffic is 62%

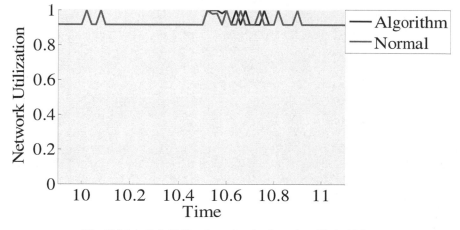

Fig. 7. Main link Utilization when backward traffic is 92%

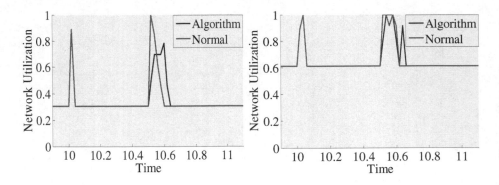

Fig. 8. Sub link Utilization when backward traffic is 30%

Fig. 9. Sub link Utilization when backward traffic is 62%

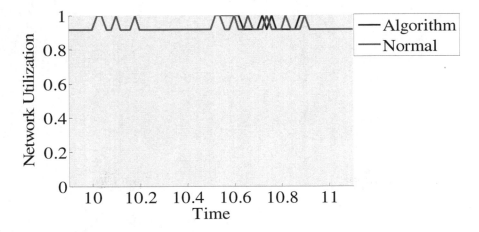

Fig. 10. Sub link Utilization when backward traffic is 92%

The network utilization peaks in figures (5, 7..., and 10) can be explained by their causes. The cause of first peak(s) which start at 10th second of simulation time is the clients' discovery requests' messages and the second peak(s) which start at 10.5th second of simulation time is the services replying messages. The waiting interval in algorithm gives more time for the routers to submit the available messages to their destination and this is clear in the previous figures (in second peak(s)).

As the backward traffic increasing, the available bandwidth decreasing result in more time required to deliver the messages. When the messages incoming rate is more than the available of link capacity the messages will be dropped caused reduction in network utilization after it has been reached the maximum usage. This is attributed to the routing management mechanism too, which it could produce bursty losses during congestions and high delays (by dividing the sending rate into half) [12]. Consequently, the network utilization is reduced when it is reach the maximum usage.

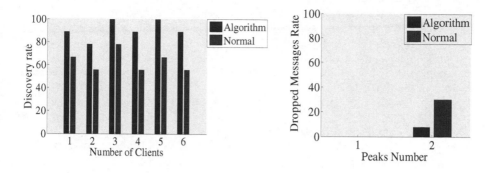

Fig. 11. discovery rates for each client when backward traffic is 30%

Fig. 12. Dropping rate in two when backward traffic is 30%

Figure 11 and 12 represent the discovery rate and the dropping rate in algorithm and normal case.

In algorithm case the discovery rate was ranging between 78% and 100%, while in normal case it was between 56% and 78%. There were not dropped messages in both algorithm and normal case in clients discovery phase, but there were dropped messages in services' replying messages phase. The dropping rate in normal case was more than four times as dropping rate in algorithm. The algorithm guarantees reasonably high discovery rate for all the involved clients and less dropped messages. The implementations show that if the number of clients is increased to be 8 clients the discovery rate would be in the same range in algorithm, but it would reduce in normal case to be between (45% and 78%). On the other hand the number of dropped messages will increase in both cases, but it is relatively increasing in algorithm case.

5   Conclusion

The aims of the proposed algorithm is to used the maximum of the available network resources and achieve optimal results by avoid dropping messages and speedily in performing the discovery process in services discovery protocols. The results show the delay in sending services response messages produce smoothing and speedily in discovery procedure. In addition they clarify improving in discovery rate and in dropping rate when the algorithm is employed. Further, the increasing in the number of clients does not affects the performance of the suggested algorithm, but it is influenced by the proportion of consumed network resources and this reveal the need for providing additional/different parameters in the suggested algorithm to cope with the changing in the available network resources.

References

[1] Edwards, J., Murtha, S.: DLNA Home Networked Interoperability Guidelines, Expanded (2006)
[2] Al-Mejibli, I., Colley, M.: Evaluating Transmission Time of Service Discovery Protocols by using NS2 Simulator. In: 2010 6th Conference on Wireless Advanced (WiAD), London (2010)

[3]   Members of the UPnP Forum, UPnP^{TM} Device Architecture 1.1 (2008)
[4]   Ververidis, C.N., Polyzos, G.C.: Service Discovery for Mobile Ad Hoc Networks: A Survey of Issues and Techniques (November 14, 2006),
      `http://mm.aueb.gr/publications/2008-SD-SURVEY-COMST.pdf`
[5]   Barbeau, M., Kranakis, E., Luo, H.: Strategies for Service Discovery over Ad Hoc Networks (May 4, 2006),
      `http://www.engineeringletters.com/issues_v13/issue_1/`
      `EL_13_1_2.pdf`
[6]   Novell Documentation: Novell eDirectory 8.7 - How SLP Works,
      `http://www.novell.com/documentation/edir87/?page=/documenta`
      `tion/edir87/edir87/data/a60jiyy.html`
[7]   Gryazin, E.A.: Service Discovery in Bluetooth. Helsinki University of Technology
[8]   Custine, C.: Introduction to OSGi, Denver Java User Group (November 12, 2008)
[9]   OSGi Alliance, About the OSGi Service Platform, Technical Whitepaper, Revision 4.1 (June 7, 2007)
[10] Mills, K., Dabrowski, C.: Adaptive Jitter Control for UPnP M-Search. In: IEEE International Conference, ICC 2003 (May 2003)
[11] Mills, K., Dabrowski, C.: Adaptive Jitter Control for UPnP M-Search. In: IEEE International Conference, ICC 2003 (May 2003)
[12] Kasera, S.K., Ramjee, R., Thuel, S., Wang, X.: Congestion Control Policies for IP-based CDMA Radio Access Networks, Holmdel, New Jersey (2005)

Adaptive K-Means Clustering to Handle Heterogeneous Data Using Basic Rough Set Theory

B.K. Tripathy[1], Adhir Ghosh[1], and G.K. Panda[2]

[1] VIT University, School of Computer Science and Engineering, Vellore, India
[2] Department of CSE and IT, MITS, Rayagada, Odisha, India
{tripathybk,adhir39}@rediffmail.com, gkpmail@sify.com

Abstract. Several cluster analysis techniques have been developed till the present to group objects having similar property or similar characteristics and K-means clustering is one of the most popular statistical clustering techniques proposed by Macqueen [12] in 1967. But this algorithm is unable to handle the categorical data and unable to handle uncertainty as well. But after proposing the rough set theory by Pawlak [15], we have an alternative way of representing sets whose exact boundary cannot be described due to incomplete information. As rough set has been widely used for knowledge representation, hence it can also be applied in classification and very helpful in clustering too. In real life data mining applications we do not have the crisp boundaries for clusters. So, in 2007 and 2009 Parmar et al [14] and Tripathy et al [16] proposed two algorithms MMR and MMeR using rough set theory but these two algorithms have the stability problem due to multiple runs and higher time complexity. In this paper we are proposing a new approach of k-means algorithm using rough set which can handle heterogeneous data and uncertainty as well.

Keywords: Classification, Cluster, Crisp boundaries, Heterogeneous data, Uncertainty.

1 Introduction

Cluster analysis is an important task in data mining. It is widely used in a lot of applications, including pattern recognition, data analysis, image processing, etc. By clustering, one can discover overall pattern distributions and interesting correlations among data attributes. Basically cluster analysis is applied on large heterogeneous data sets to make it into a smaller homogeneous data subsets that can be easily managed, separately modeled and analyzed [8]. For example, Wu et al. [18] developed a clustering algorithm specifically designed to handle the complexities of gene data that can estimate the correct number of clusters and find them. Jiang et al. [9] analyzed a variety of cluster techniques for complex gene expression data. Wong et al. [17] presented an approach used to segment tissues in a nuclear medical imaging method known as positron emission tomography (PET). Mathieu and Gibson [13] used cluster analysis as a part of a decision support tool for large-scale research and development planning to identify programs to participate in and to determine resource allocation. Finally, Haimov et al. [5] used cluster analysis to segment radar signals in

N. Meghanathan et al. (Eds.): CCSIT 2012, Part I, LNICST 84, pp. 193–202, 2012.
© Institute for Computer Sciences, Social Informatics and Telecommunications Engineering 2012

scanning land and marine objects. But all these algorithms are very specific. There are some general clustering algorithms like K-means [12], K-modes, fuzzy centroids etc. These algorithms suffer from problems like; they don't work when we have large data sets, missing value attributes and have irregular data shapes. Also, these algorithms can handle only numerical attributes. However, there are other algorithms like those proposed by Huang et al. [8], Gibson et al. [3], Guha et al. [4], Ganti et al. [2] and Dempster et al. [1]. These algorithms are not designed to handle uncertainty in data, which is a common issue in many real life applications. Using the concept of rough sets two algorithms were developed in 2007 and 2009 by Parmar et al. [14] and Tripathy et al. [16] respectively, which can handle both uncertainty and heterogeneous data. The time complexity of these two methods is high due to lots of calculations. So, in this paper we are proposing a new algorithm using general K-means methods and rough set theory in order to get the adaptive K-means algorithms using rough set which can handle hybrid data and uncertainty as well as its complexity is relatively low.

1.1   Basic Methods for Handling Categorical Data

Dempster et al. [1] presented a partition based clustering method, called the Expectation-Maximization (EM) algorithm. EM first randomly assigns different probabilities to each class or category, for each cluster. Then it successively adjusts the probabilities for maximizing the likelihood data those are given in the each cluster. After a large number of iterations, EM terminates at a locally optimal solution. Han et al. [6] proposed a clustering algorithm to cluster related items in a market database based on an association rule hyper graph. Also, we have some other categorical algorithms including K-modes [8] which extend the K-means algorithm. One advantage of K-modes algorithm is it is useful in interpreting the results [8]. However, these algorithms suffer from the problem of not being able to deal with uncertainty.

1.2   Handling Uncertainty

One of the first algorithms to deal with uncertainty is fuzzy K-means [11]. In this algorithm, each pattern or object is allowed to have membership functions to all clusters rather than having a distinct membership to exactly one cluster. Krishnapuram and Keller [10] propose a probabilistic approach to clustering in which the membership of a feature vector in a class has nothing to do with its membership in other classes and modified clustering methods are used to generate membership distributions. Krishnapuram et al. [11] have presented several fuzzy and probabilistic algorithms to detect linear and quadratic shell clusters. It may be noted that the initial work in handling uncertainty was based on numerical data. As they are unable to handle uncertainty in categorical data we cannot apply those algorithms in our real life applications as most of them depend on categorical data. Rough set theory has been used to develop clustering algorithms which handle uncertainty as well as deal with both categorical and numerical data [14, 16]. We shall discuss these approaches in the next section.

In real life situations, we find data with uncertainty, which may be numerical or categorical and so we need algorithms in order to deal such situations. Our effort in this paper adds one more algorithm in this direction, which is relatively faster than most of the other existing algorithms in this direction.

2   Rough Sets on Information Systems

Two of the most fruitful methods in dealing with uncertainty in data are the notion of Fuzzy Sets, introduced by Zadeh [19] and the notion of Rough Sets, introduced by Pawlak [15], which complement each other instead of being rivals. We formally introduce the notion of basic rough sets on information systems below.

Let U be a universe and X is a subset of U. Let $\mathbf{A}$ be the set of all the attributes of objects in U and $\mathbf{B}$ is a non-empty set of $\mathbf{A}$. (U, A) is called an information system.

Definition 1 (Indiscernibility relation)
Given two tuples x, y $\in U$ we say that x and y are indiscernible by the set of attributes $\mathbf{B}$ in $\mathbf{A}$ if and only if a(x) = a(y) for every a $\in \mathbf{B}$. This relation is an equivalence relation on U and decomposes into disjoint equivalence classes and is denoted by Ind($\mathbf{B}$). For any x $\in$ U, the equivalence class of x with respect to the set of attributes in $\mathbf{B}$ is denoted by $[x]_{Ind(\mathbf{B})}$.

Definition 2 (Approximation)
For any subset B of A and a set of objects X in U, the lower approximation of X with respect to B and the upper approximation of X with respect to B are defined as

$$\underline{X_{\mathbf{B}}} = \bigcup\{x/[x]_{Ind(B)} \subseteq X\} \tag{1}$$

$$\overline{X_B} = \bigcup\{x/[x]_{Ind(B)} \cap X \neq \varnothing\} \tag{2}$$

Definition 3 (Roughness)

The accuracy of estimation, is denoted by $R_B(X)$ and is defined by

$$R_B(X) = 1 - \left(\left|\underline{X_B}\right| / \left|\overline{X_B}\right|\right) \tag{3}$$

If $R_B(X) = 0$, X is crisp with respect to B, in other words, X is precise with respect to B. If $R_B(X) < 1$, X is rough with respect to B, That is, B is vague with respect to X.

Definition 4 (Relative roughness)
Given $a_i \in$ A, X is a subset of objects having one specifics value α of attribute a_i, $\underline{X_{a_j}}(a_i = a)$ and $\overline{X_{a_j}}(a_i = a)$ refer to the lower and upper approximation of X with respect to $\{a_j\}$, then $R_{a_j}(X)$ is defined as the roughness of X with respect to $\{a_j\}$, i.e.,

$$R_{a_j}(X/a_i = \alpha) = 1 - \left(\left| X_{a_j}(a_i = \alpha) \right| / \overline{\left| X_{a_j}(a_i = \alpha) \right|} \right) \quad \text{where } a_i, a_j \in A \text{ and } a_i \neq a_j. \tag{4}$$

Definition 5 (Mean relative roughness)
Let **A** have n attributes and $a_i \in A$. X be the subset of objects having a specific value α of the attribute a_i. Then we define the mean roughness for the equivalence class $a_i = \alpha$, denoted by MeR ($a_i = \alpha$) as

$$MeR(a_i = \alpha) = \left(\sum_{\substack{j=1 \\ j \neq i}}^{n} R_{a_j}(X/a_i = \alpha) \right)/(n-1) \tag{5}$$

Definition 6 (Relative distance)
Given two objects P and Q of categorical data with n attributes, the relative distance of P and Q is denoted by RD(P, Q) and is defined as follows:

$$RD(P,Q) = \frac{1}{n}\sqrt{\sum_{i=1}^{n} RD(p_i, q_i)^2} \tag{6}$$

Here, p_i and q_i are values of P and Q respectively, under the ith attribute a_i. We have, If cluster C_j has single object or in 0th iteration, then

$$\left. \begin{aligned} RD(p_i, q_i) &= 0, \, if \, p_i = q_i \\ RD(p_i, q_i) &= 1, \, if \, p_i \neq q_i \end{aligned} \right\} \tag{7}$$

Else

$$RD(p_i, q_i) = \left| avg \, centroid \, of \, p_i \, in \, C_j - number \, of \, occurences \, in \, corresponding \, objects \, in \, q_i \right| \tag{8}$$

When P and Q are numerical valued attributes, we have,
If the cluster C_j has single object or in 0th iteration, then

$$\left. \begin{aligned} RD(p_i, q_i) &= 0, \, if \, p_i = q_i \\ RD(p_i, q_i) &= \left| values \, of \, p_i \, in \, C_j - values \, of \, q_i \right|, \, if \, p_i \neq q_i \end{aligned} \right\} \tag{9}$$

Else

$RD(p_i, q_i)$ is given by (8).

3   Generalized K-Means Method

K-means clustering is one of the most popular statistical techniques [7, 12]. Here we take, $X = \{x_1, x_2....x_n\}$. We now present the generalized K-means method.

GKM   : A generalized algorithm of *K*-means clustering

GKM 1 : Give initial cluster centers $v_1, \ldots, v_k$. Let the cluster represented by v_i be G_i or $G(v_i)$.

GKM 2 : Reallocate each object x to the nearest center v_i. $i = \min_{1 \leq j \leq k} d(x, v_j)$

GKM 3 : After all objects are reallocated, update the cluster center.

$$v_i = \min_v \sum_{x_k \in G_i} d(x_k, v) \tag{10}$$

GKM 4 : Check for the convergent criterion. If not convergent, go to **GKM 2.**
End of GKM

The convergence criterion of K-means is when all the centroids of each cluster stabilize.

Incorporation of rough sets into K-means clustering requires the addition of the concept of lower and upper bounds. Calculation of the centroids of clusters from conventional K-Means needs to be modified to include the effects of lower as well as upper bounds. The modified centroid calculations for rough sets are presented in section 3.1.

3.1   Adaptation of K-Means to Rough Set Theory

As rough set needs the calculation of equivalence classes and lower and upper approximations, we need to calculate the upper and lower approximation of each cluster to update its centroid. The new centroid is as follows:

If Avg $\underline{R}X$ (of ith attribute of cluster C$_j$) = $\varnothing$, then

$$v_i(C_k) = \dfrac{\dfrac{1}{\#(distinct\ objects)} \cdot \sum_{for\ each\ distinct\ object} \left\{ \sum_{\substack{j=1 \\ j \ne i}}^{n} \left(R_{a_j}(X / a_i = \alpha) \right) / (n-1) \right\}}{\dfrac{1}{\#(distinct\ objects)} \left(\sum_{For\ each\ distinct\ object} \overline{R}X \right)} \tag{11}$$

Else

$$v_i(C_k) = \dfrac{\dfrac{1}{\#(distinct\ objects)} \cdot \sum_{for\ each\ distinct\ object} \left\{ \sum_{\substack{j=1 \\ j \ne i}}^{n} \left(R_{a_j}(X / a_i = \alpha) \right) / (n-1) \right\}}{\left| \left\{ \dfrac{1}{\#(distinct\ objects)} \left(\sum_{For\ each\ distinct\ object} \underline{R}X \right) \right\} - \left\{ \dfrac{1}{\#(distinct\ objects)} \left(\sum_{For\ each\ distinct\ object} \overline{R}X \right) \right\} \right|} \tag{12}$$

The new centroid v_i of ith attribute of cluster C$_K$ is determined by the above equation. If the average of lower approximation is equal to null then the average mean roughness is divided by average upper approximation otherwise it is divided by absolute average difference of the lower and upper approximation. The mean roughness of attribute a$_i$ is determined by the predefined value of α with respect to all other attributes in the cluster. Whether the object belongs to the lower approximation of the cluster or upper approximation of the cluster can be checked by the formula

$$\textbf{If}\ \left\{ \left\{ \frac{1}{n} \sum_{j=1}^{n} \left(\frac{1}{l} \sum_{i=1}^{l} \underline{R}_j(X_i) \right) \right\} - RD(V, X) \right\} < \left\{ \left\{ \frac{1}{n} \sum_{j=1}^{n} \left(\frac{1}{l} \sum_{i=1}^{l} \overline{R}_j(X_i) \right) \right\} - RD(V, X) \right\} \tag{13}$$

Then, the object X belongs to the lower approximation of the corresponding cluster. Here, l = #(distinct objects).

Else The object belongs to the upper approximation of the cluster. In case of a tie the object belongs to both the approximations.

4   Proposed Algorithm

In this section we propose our algorithm which is known as "Adaptive K-Means Clustering to Handle Heterogeneous Data" and is as follows:

```
Procedure RBKM (U,k)
1.   Begin
2.      Set current number of cluster CNC = k;
3.      Set ParentNode =U;
4.      Assign randomly selected objects to each cluster Cₖ;
5.      Label 1:
         Reallocate each object x to the nearest cluster Cₖ;
```

$$K = \min \frac{1}{n} \sqrt{\sum_{i=1}^{n} RD(v_i, x)^2}$$

```
         //Updation of cluster centroids;
6.       Update cluster();
         //Check for the convergent criterion;
  7.     If all the newly updated centroid value ≠ previous
         centroids value
8.       Goto Label 1
9.   End
```

```
Update cluster ()
1.   Begin
2.   For each aᵢ∈ A (i = 1 to n, where n is the number of
     attributes in A and j≠i)
         Calculate Roughₐⱼ(aᵢ);
```

$$MeR(a_i = \alpha) = \left(\sum_{\substack{j=1 \\ j \neq i}}^{n} R_{a_j} \left(X / a_i = \alpha \right) \right) / (n - 1)$$

```
3.   Next
     //Mean (MeR (aᵢ = α)) for each α;
4.   Find the lower approximation of each aᵢ;
5.   Make the average of lower approximation of each aᵢ
     for different α value;
6.   Find the upper approximation of each aᵢ;
7.   Make the average of upper approximation of each aᵢ
     for different α value;
8.   If average of lower approximation = null, then
```

$$v_i(C_k) = \cfrac{\cfrac{1}{total\ distinct\ objects} \cdot \displaystyle\sum_{for\ each\ distinct\ object} \left\{ \sum_{\substack{j=1 \\ j \neq i}}^{n} \left(R_{a_j}(X / a_i = \alpha) \right) / (n-1) \right\}}{\cfrac{1}{total\ distinct\ object} \left(\displaystyle\sum_{For\ each\ distinct\ object} \overline{RX} \right)}$$

9. Else

$$v_i(C_k) = \cfrac{\cfrac{1}{total\ distinct\ objects} \cdot \displaystyle\sum_{for\ each\ distinct\ object} \left\{ \sum_{\substack{j=1 \\ j \neq i}}^{n} \left(R_{a_j}(X / a_i = \alpha) \right) / (n-1) \right\}}{\left\{ \cfrac{1}{total\ distinct\ objects} \left(\displaystyle\sum_{For\ each\ distinct\ object} \overline{RX} \right) \right\} - \left\{ \cfrac{1}{total\ distinct\ objects} \left(\displaystyle\sum_{For\ each\ distinct\ object} \overline{RX} \right) \right\}}$$

10. End

5 Empirical Analysis

The study data was obtained is a random dataset and has only 15 objects in it. This dataset has eight attributes including the object identifier as "Row". From the rest of seven attributes six are categorical and the other one is numerical. We choose the total number of cluster as four and initially we will pick the object number 3, 7, 10 and 13 as the initial centroids and will assign all the rest of the objects by the measure of relative distance

$$Min \left(\frac{1}{n} \sqrt{\sum_{i=1}^{n} RD(v_i, x)^2} \right)$$

So, after 0th iteration the cluster structure will look like as follows:

Table 1. Cluster I

Row	A1	A2	A3	A4	A5	A6	SIZE
3	Small	Yellow	Soft	Fuzzy	Plush	Positive	2
4	Medium	Blue	Moderate	Fuzzy	Plastic	Negative	3
6	Big	Green	Hard	Smooth	Wood	Positive	17
8	Small	Yellow	Soft	Indefinite	Plastic	Positive	7
9	Big	Green	Hard	Smooth	Wood	Neutral	10

Table 2. Cluster II

Row	A1	A2	A3	A4	A5	A6	SIZE
7	Small	Yellow	Hard	Indefinite	Metal	Positive	14
1	Big	Blue	Hard	Indefinite	Plastic	Negative	4
5	Small	Yellow	Soft	Indefinite	Plastic	Neutral	21
11	Small	Yellow	Soft	smooth	Wood	Neutral	18
14	Small	Green	Hard	Metal	Wood	Neutral	7
15	Large	Yellow	hard	Metal	Plush	Negative	8

Table 3. Cluster III

Row	A1	A2	A3	A4	A5	A6	SIZE
10	Medium	Green	Moderate	Smooth	Plastic	Neutral	19
2	Medium	Red	Moderate	Smooth	Wood	Neutral	5

Table 4. Cluster IV

ROW	A1	A2	A3	A4	A5	A6	SIZE
13	Small	Red	Moderate	Indefinite	Wood	Neutral	5
12	Medium	Red	Moderate	Indefinite	Plastic	Positive	22

After this step we need to update the center of each cluster using the above proposed algorithm. Let us consider Table 1 for updating purpose. First we will calculate the mean roughness of each α (Big, Small and Medium) of attribute a_i as A1 with respect to the all other attributers and hence here total α is 3. To calculate roughness we need to calculate lower and upper approximations of a_i for each α and then need to find out the average to update the cluster center. This process will continue for each of the attributes with respect to the other attributes. After calculating the average roughness we will update the each cluster by the given equation (12) and (13). After all the calculations we get the final four clusters which are as follows:

Table 5. Final cluster I

Row	A1	A2	A3	A4	A5	A6	SIZE
4	Medium	Blue	Moderate	Fuzzy	Plastic	Negative	3
12	Medium	Red	Moderate	Indefinite	Plastic	Positive	22
15	Large	Yellow	hard	Metal	Plush	Negative	8
7	Small	Yellow	Hard	Indefinite	Metal	Positive	14

Table 6. Final cluster II

Row	A1	A2	A3	A4	A5	A6	SIZE
11	Small	Yellow	Soft	smooth	Wood	Neutral	18
14	Small	Green	Hard	Metal	Wood	Neutral	7
10	Medium	Green	Moderate	Smooth	Plastic	Neutral	19
3	Small	Yellow	Soft	Fuzzy	Plush	Positive	2
8	Small	Yellow	Soft	Indefinite	Plastic	Positive	7

Table 7. Final cluster III

Row	A1	A2	A3	A4	A5	A6	SIZE
5	Small	Yellow	Soft	Indefinite	Plastic	Neutral	21
13	Small	Red	Moderate	Indefinite	Wood	Neutral	5

Table 8. Final cluster IV

ROW	A1	A2	A3	A4	A5	A6	SIZE
1	Big	Blue	Hard	Indefinite	Plastic	Negative	4
6	Big	Green	Hard	Smooth	Wood	Positive	17
9	Big	Green	Hard	Smooth	Wood	Neutral	10
2	Medium	Red	Moderate	Smooth	Wood	Neutral	5

These are the final clusters those we got after the convergence criterion. For the experimental purpose we have used the small data set but it can be applied to the large data bases also to make the heterogeneous dataset into smaller homogeneous set.

6   Conclusions and Further Enhancement

In this paper we described modifications of K-means algorithm based on the concept of lower and upper bounds. This algorithm can handle databases with missing attribute values, hybrid type of values and having uncertainty. We have found it as an efficient method from empirical analysis. But, actual implementation and testing by using standard databases is likely to establish its position with respect to other related algorithms. Further enhancement can be done by providing better measure of relative distance (RD) and other measures of central tendency like standard deviation instead mean while computing relative roughness. Hybrid techniques like combinations of rough and fuzzy may improve the performance of this algorithm also.

References

1. Dempster, A., Laird, N., Rubin, D.: Maximum likelihood from incomplete data via the EM algorithm. Journal of the Royal Statistical Society 39(1), 1–38 (1977)
2. Ganti, V., Gehrke, J., Ramakrishnan, R.: CACTUS – clustering categorical data using summaries. In: Fifth ACM SIGKDD International Conference on Knowledge Discovery and Data Mining, pp. 73–83 (1999)
3. Gibson, D., Kleinberg, J., Raghavan, P.: Clustering categorical data: an approach based on dynamical systems. The Very Large Data Bases Journal 8(3-4), 222–236 (2000)
4. Guha, S., Rastogi, R., Shim, K.: ROCK: a robust clustering algorithm for categorical attributes. Information Systems 25(5), 345–366 (2000)
5. Haimov, S., Michalev, M., Savchenko, A., Yordanov, O.: Classification of radar signatures by autoregressive model fitting and cluster analysis. IEEE Transactions on Geo Science and Remote Sensing 8(1), 606–610 (1989)
6. Han, E., Karypis, G., Kumar, V., Mobasher, B.: Clustering based on association rule hypergraphs. In: Workshop on Research Issues on Data Mining and Knowledge Discovery, pp. 9–13 (1997)
7. Hartigan, J.A., Wong, M.A.: Algorithm AS136: A K-Means Clustering Algorithm. Applied Statistics 28, 100–108 (1979)
8. Huang, Z.: Extensions to the k-means algorithm for clustering large data sets with categorical value. Data Mining and Knowledge Discovery 2(3), 283–304 (1998)

9. Jiang, D., Tang, C., Zhang, A.: Cluster analysis for gene expression data: a survey. IEEE Transactions on Knowledge and Data Engineering 16(11), 1370–1386 (2004)
10. Krishnapuram, R., Keller, J.: A possibilistic approach to clustering. IEEE Transactions on Fuzzy Systems 1(2), 98–110 (1993)
11. Krishnapuram, R., Frigui, H., Nasraoui, O.: Fuzzy and possibilistic shell clustering algorithms and their application to boundary detection and surface approximation. IEEE Transactions on Fuzzy Systems 3(1), 29–60 (1995)
12. MacQueen, J.B.: Some Methods for classification and Analysis of Multivariate Observations. In: Proceedings of 5th Berkeley Symposium on Mathematical Statistics and Probability, pp. 281–297. University of California Press (1967)
13. Mathieu, R., Gibson, J.: A Methodology for large scale R&D planning based on cluster analysis. IEEE Transactions on Engineering Management 40(3), 283–292 (2004)
14. Parmar, D., Teresa, W., Jennifer, B.: MMR: An algorithm for clustering categorical data using Rough Set Theory. Data & Knowledge Engineering, 879–893 (2007)
15. Pawlak, Z.: Rough Sets- Theoretical Aspects of Reasoning about Data. Kluwer Academic Publishers, Norwell (1992)
16. Tripathy, B.K., Kumar, P.: MMeR: An algorithm for clustering Heterogeneous data using rough Set Theory. International Journal of Rapid Manufacturing (special issue on Data Mining) 1(2), 189–207 (2009)
17. Wong, K., Feng, D., Meikle, S., Fulham, M.: Segmentation of dynamic pet images using cluster analysis. IEEE Transactions on Nuclear Science 49(1), 200–207 (2002)
18. Wu, S., Liew, A., Yang, M.: Cluster analysis of gene expression data based on self-splitting and merging competitive learning. IEEE Transactions on Information Technology in Bio Medicine 8(1), 5–15 (2004)
19. Zadeh, L.A.: Fuzzy Sets. Information and Control 11, 338–353 (1965)

Different Types of Attacks Mitigation in Mobile Ad Hoc Networks Using Cellular Automata

Himadri Nath Saha[1], Debika Bhattachayya[1], and P.K. Banerjee[2]

[1] Department of Computer Science and Engineering,
Institute of Engineering & Management, West Bengal, India
[2] Department of Electronics and Telecommunication Engineering, Jadavpur University,
West Bengal, India

Abstract. Many security schemes for mobile ad-hoc network(MANET) have been proposed so far but none of them has been successful in combating the different types of attacks that a mobile ad-hoc network often faces. This paper is providing one way of mitigating attacks in mobile ad-hoc networks by authenticating the node who tries to access this network .This scheme has been applied by using cellular automata (CA). Our simulation results show how cellular automata(CA) is implemented for user authentication and secure transmission in MANET.

Keywords: Ad hoc network, User authentication, Node capturing, Shared key mechanism, Cellular automata.

1   Introduction

Wireless ad-hoc network[2] is a decentralized wireless network which comprises of a large number of sensor nodes. The network is ad-hoc because it does not rely on a pre-existing infrastructure, such as routers in wired networks or access points in managed (infrastructure) wireless networks. Instead, each node participates in routing by forwarding data for other nodes, and so the determination of which nodes forward data is made dynamically based on the network connectivity. Each node has certain computational ability and comprises of a processor, communicational module and a battery supply. These nodes are small, low cost, low power and has functionalities such as communicate over short distances, perform data processing, sense environmental data, etc.

Wireless ad-hoc network has a   wide range of applications. [3,5,15,16] It is used in the military field, in ecological survey, in health related cases such as human physiological data monitoring and many other miscellaneous applications. Most applications where these nodes are used are very critical and the data gathered from them are valuable and confidential therefore needs to be protected from outside attacks. There are many possible attacks that one can expect in an wireless environment. A subset of such threats includes Denial of Services (DoS), node capturing, time synchronizing attacks, injecting malicious traffic as well as routing threats. These outside security issues can only be handled by authenticating outside user /nodes. The main aim of authentication is to let sensor nodes themselves detect

N. Meghanathan et al. (Eds.): CCSIT 2012, Part I, LNICST 84, pp. 203–212, 2012.
© Institute for Computer Sciences, Social Informatics and Telecommunications Engineering 2012

maliciously injected or spoofed packets. But due to limited resources available in each node it is very challenging to apply user authentication scheme in each node. For this reason we propose to use cellular automata (CA) based components to implement the user authentication scheme in wireless ad-hoc network.

Rest of the paper is organized as follows. We explain related work in section 2 and describe details of proposed security scheme in section 3,simulation results in section 4 ,analysis in section 5 and finally we present our conclusions in section 6

2   Related Work

There are many possible attacks which can be expected in a common channel wireless environment. A subset of such threats would include DoS attacks [9], node capturing [18], blackhole attacks [20,21],grayhole attacks[20,21],sybil attacks[22], time synchronization attacks [14], injecting malicious traffic as well as routing threats [12],.Key pre-distribution is an important issue in WSN security. A number of literature is already devoted to secure distribution of keys in WSNs, include [6,8,10,11]. Now a days cellular automata is often used to set a defence mechanism for wireless sensor networks. In a wsn network the nodes are backed up with small memory size, low battery storage and weak processors. There are other ca based schemes which are proposed to develop a wsn security scheme. One of them is CAB which is a cellular automata based key management system that allows sensors to establish pair wise keys during any stage of the network operation using preloaded CAs. It uses simple bitwise OR and XOR. So its computation is very simple. It also has rekeying capabilities and achieves quasi-perfect resilience against node compromise. It considers a large-scale homogeneous sensor network whose nodes are randomly distributed over a region. There is no neighbourhood information available to any sensor before deployment. So a sensor discovers its neighbours and their CA information via local wireless broadcast after deployment.

The broadcast feature of wireless communication allows adversaries to perform a variety of passive and active attacks. In passive listening mode, adversaries silently listen to radio transmissions in order to capture data, security credentials, or other relevant information. For active attacks, adversaries may insert, modify, replay, or delete traffic, or jam part of the network. As a result, adversaries are capable of performing attacks that include session hijacking and man-in-the-middle attacks. Adversaries equipped with powerful communication devices may access any spot of the network from a remote location. However, they cannot monitor the entire deployment region simultaneously at all times. They can gain mobility through the use of robotics or vehicles, and can move inside or outside the network. Also, adversaries can deploy their own sensors and base stations in uncontrolled wireless environments. Further, they are able to capture, replace, compromise, and physically damage existing sensors.

Another scheme that uses CA is LISA or Lightweight Security Algorithm for wsn. This paper is tailored to implement resource restrained sensor node. This scheme can be used to get data authentication and data confidentiality both.

3   Proposed Security Scheme

It is clear that ad-hoc networks are spread over a field and it is possible to capture a node by an adversary. That is why we need to have some authentication before any data communication. To employ the proposed scheme we need to have a base station which will take care of initialization of authentication. As there is no base station in an ad-hoc network thus we need to have some scheme to determine one of the nodes as the base station. After that CA is applied for the authentication purpose. As we have seen this CA mechanism shows high randomness thus it is very difficult to breakdown and also CA involves very little computations like bit wise XOR , AND operations and also storage required is not high. First phase involves choosing of a base station.

Setting Up the Network

Before setting up a wsn , we must consider some key factor. As the connection is wireless, every node has to broadcast whatever it wants to send. In ad-hoc network there is no base station. But to make things easier we will select one of its nodes as base station .we will discuss the process of selection later on. In an ad-hoc network nodes can be captured or damaged frequently. So we need an efficient algorithm to select base stations when the current base station goes out of control.

A node in an ad-hoc network generally means an electronic device backed up by a battery. So we should not put excess load on a particular node to save battery power. We will set up our network by following some steps :

The first node wants to communicate becomes current base station. It gets marked with a serial number (for first node it is 0, it's an unique number) and starts counting it's age from 0.The base station always stores the serial number of the last node(sln) joined and when another node comes its serial no should be sln+1.The age of each node gets incremented after a specific amount of time that amount of time is constant for the entire network. Base station should keep sending an is-alive packet after a fixed time slot to inform the other nodes that it is alive.

When a node wants to communicate it broadcasts a hello message. The base station receives it and acknowledges it and also sends its serial number. New node gets its new serial no and starts its age counting.

When base station wants to shut down it broadcasts a message to inform it to other nodes. The base station searches for the alive node with lowest serial number and sends a packet to that node to let it know that it is the current base node.

If the base station gets captured or damaged and goes off without notifying other nodes then other nodes stops receiving is alive packets from the base station. At this point base station is selected by broadcasting their own serial numbers.

The base station also checks continually whether any node is showing any kind of malicious activities or not.[1]

Registration Phase. STEP 1:   Base Station(BS) chooses a secret key SB. We consider that each node has its own identity IDi and BS distributes an secret key to each node computing

$$Ski = H(IDi \oplus SB).$$

Whenever a node which was dead earlier has some data to send or receive it needs to register under BS. It sends its identity to the BS. Then BS again computes,

$$Si = H(IDi \oplus SB)$$

and sends it to the node via a secure channel.

STEP 2: Then the node broadcasts its identity to all the nodes. Each node after getting this message generates a Nonce Nik corresponding to IDi and keeps it for a definite time period in its memory. Then it sends Esk(Nik ‖ IDi ‖ IDk), IDk to the BS using the symmetric key cryptography.

STEP 3: BS on receiving the messages from the nodes computes SKk using its own SB. SKk= H(IDk $\oplus$ SB) and then decryptes the received message. If the IDk after decryption matches with the received one then BS computes (N1',N2'......Nk') using

$$(N1',N2'......Nk') = RCApq(N1,N2...Nk)$$

Then BS sends these values to the node along with their IDk.

STEP 4: The newly alive node receives those values and computes the nonce values using

$$(N1,N2......Nk) = RCApq(N1',N2'...Nk')$$

The node then generates a random Nonce N and sends Nki, ID to corresponding sensor with IDk encrypted with the nonce Nik. for mutual authentication.

STEP 5: Each sensor   node after receiving decrypts to get the ID and Nki. If the ID matches with the corresponding Nik then node authenticates the new node. If it does not match then node discards the requests from that node and marks the node as the malicious node reports to the BS. These Nonce values are kept for a definite time period after that re-authentication is required.

Shared key mechanism. At this point any node in the network has the Nonce of the newly alive node and as this process gets repeated for each node in the network each pair of node is aware of their own unique (Ni,Nj). Now in case of data transmission these nodes use CA rule and q th evolution on the nonce pair to generate a shared key. While transmitting data it encrypts using the shared key and sends own identity along with it . Node after receiving ·the message gets the nonce corresponding to the ID from memory. And it computes the shared key using same CA rule again this operation is simple and not time consuming but highly random. Any eavesdropper in the middle can get the identity of the sender and if also knows one of the nonce values cannot compute the key or cannot decrypt the message.

4   Simulation Results

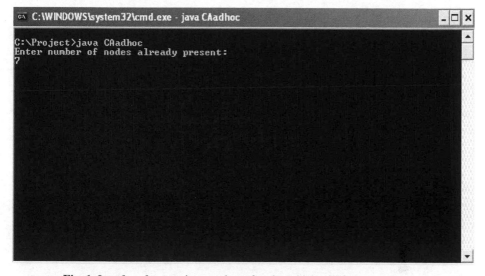

Fig. 1. Interface for entering number of nodes which will form the network

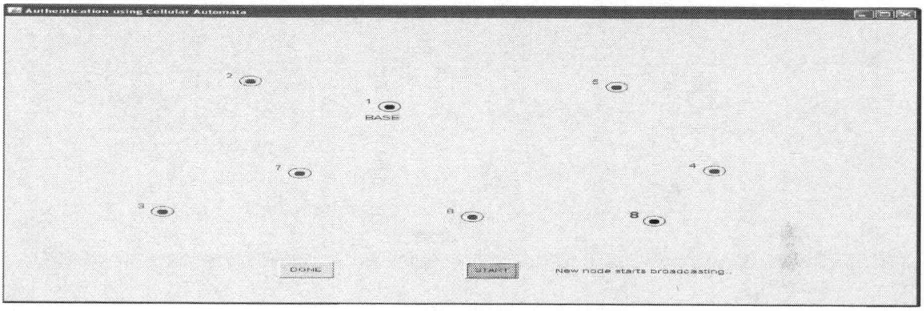

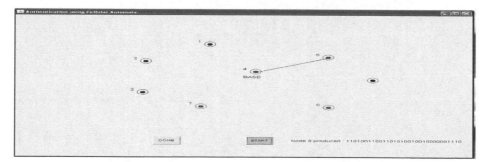

Fig. 2. New node starts broadcasting

Fig. 3. Node 5 produced 110100110011010100100100000001110

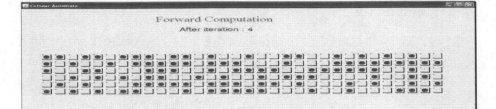

Fig. 4. Forward computation after iteration 4

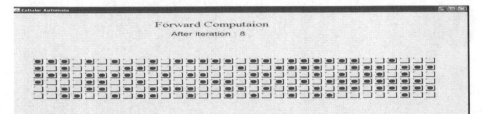

Fig. 5. Forward computation after iteration 8

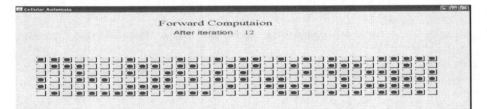

Fig. 6. Forward computation after iteration 12

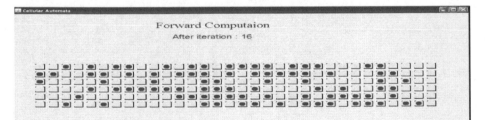

Fig. 7. Forward Computation after iteration 16

Fig. 8. Backward computation after iteration 0

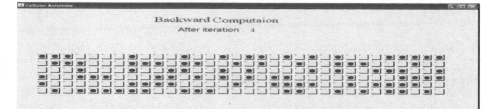

Fig. 9. Backward computation after iteration 4

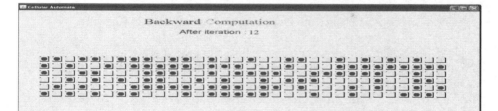

Fig. 10. Backward computation after iteration 8

Fig. 11. Backward Computation after iteration 12

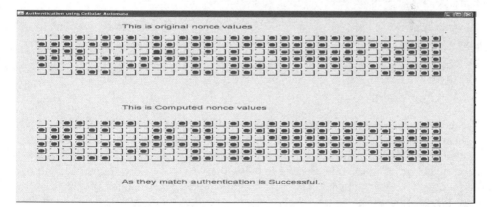

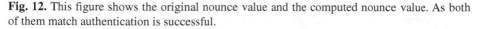

Fig. 12. This figure shows the original nounce value and the computed nounce value. As both of them match authentication is successful.

5   Analysis

In this scheme we have a group key authentication initially. Node is authenticated by several nodes. Again CA provides enough randomness thus it is really impossible for attackers to break the keys using dictionary methods, moreover, this is session key implementation so even if attackers able to crack the key, it won't be valid for long enough time. This CA based calculations are very simple and hence less time consuming.

The proposed security component is robust against the following attacks:

Node capturing attack. If an attacker captures a few nodes; the actual information can not be determined. This is because of lack of all correct information from different nodes. In the other way, it is infeasible for an attacker to determine to authenticate itself not knowing nonce values of other nodes.

Denial of service (DoS) attack. DoS is the most generous attack and adversary can disrupt the network services by draining the battery power. It is very difficult to avoid in the environments where, resource constrained devices like sensor nodes are involved. As the computational requirement in our proposed scheme is negligibly small at sensor nodes, attacker cannot make the node busy with computational intensive operations and hence the scheme avoids this form of DoS attack.

Replay attack. The entries in sensor node buffer are valid for a small period of time and therefore, reject the replayed message. On the other hand, the session key established between the sensor nodes is a nonce (number used for once only a standard term in cryptography), so the node also be able to identify the replayed data.

Sink hole or Black hole attack. As there is an strong authentication mechanism thus attacks like sink hole, worm hole are not feasible.

Eavesdropping. All the messages are being encrypted by session keys which are purely random and if nonce values are of 160 bits then It is impossible to break down the system by guessing attack.

6   Conclusion

In this paper we have described what an mobile ad hoc network is. After that we have discussed the different types of attacks that are likely to happen in a wireless ad hoc network. Following that we have introduced the concept of one-dimensional reversible 3-neighbourhood automata for securing wireless ad hoc networks from the previously discussed attacks. The next topic is about the analysis of the network securing schemes. Finally we conclude by saying that work is going on for further improvements in the necessary areas for a better and highly effective protection scheme against outside attacks and remarkable results may be anticipated. This proposed scheme can be further improved by introducing new mathematical concepts.

References

1. Saha, H.N., Bhattacharyya, D., Banerjee, P.K.: A Distributed Administration Based Approach for Intrusion Detection in Mobile Ad Hoc Networks. In: IEEE Int. Conference on Science,Technology and Sprituality, Mumbai (2010)
2. Hill, J., Culler, D.: Mica: a wireless platform for deeply embedded networks. IEEE Micro. 22(6) (2002)
3. Arora, A., Dutta, P., Bapat, S., Kulathumani, V., Zhang, H., Naik, V., Mittal, V., Cao, H., Demirbus, M., Gouda, M., Choi, Y., Herman, T., Kulkurni, S., Arumugam, U., Nesternko, M., Vora, A., Miyastha, M.: A line in the send: a wireless sensor network for target detection, classification and tracking. Comput. Networks 46(5), 605–634 (2004)
4. Benenson, Z., Gedicke, N., Raivio, O.: Realizing robust user authentication in sensor networks. In: Proc. Workshop on Real-World Wireless Sensor Networks REALWSN 2005 (2005)
5. Burne, R.A., Buczak, A.L., Jamalabad, V.R., Kadar, I., Eadan, E.R.: Selforganizing cooperative sensor network for remote surveillance improved target tracking results. In: Proc. SPIE, vol. 4232, pp. 313–321 (2001)
6. Chadha, A., Liu, Y., Das, S.K.: Group key distribution via local collaboration in wireless sensor networks. In: Proc. IEEE SECON 2005, pp. 46–54 (2005)
7. Chowdhury, A.R., Tripathy, S., Nandi, S.: Securing wireless sensor networks against spurious injections. In: Proc. IEEE Int. Conference on Communication System Software and Middleware OMSWARE 2007 (2007)
8. Delghosa, F., Fekri, F.: Key pre-distribution on wireless sensor networks using multivariate polynomials. In: Proc. IEEE SECON 2005, pp. 118–129 (2005)
9. Deng, J., Han, R., Mishra, S.: Defending against path-based DoS attacks in wireless sensor networks. In: Proc. ACM Workshop on Security of Ad Hoc and Sensor Networks SASN 2005, pp. 89–96 (2005)
10. Du, W., Deng, J., Han, Y.S., Varshney, P.K.: A pairwise key predistribution scheme for wireless sensor networks. In: Proc. ACM Conference Computer Communication and Security (CCS 2003), pp. 42–51 (2003)
11. Ito, T., Ohta, H., Matsuda, N., Yoneda, T.: A key pre-distribution scheme for secure sensor networks using probability density function of node. In: Proc. ACM Workshop on Security on Ad Hoc and Sensor Networks, SASN (2005)
12. Karlof, C., Wagner, D.: Secure routing in wireless sensor networks: attacks and countermeasures. In: Proc. IEEE Intl. Workshop on Sensor Network Protocols and Applications (SNPA 2003), pp. 113–127 (2003)
13. Luk, M., Perrig, A., Whillock, B.: Seven cardinal properties of sensor network broadcast authentication. In: Proc. ACM Conference on Security of Ad Hoc and Sensor Networks (SASN 2006), pp. 147–156 (2006)
14. Manzo, M., Roosta, T.: Time synchronization attacks in sensor networks. In: Proc. ACM Workshop on Security of Ad Hoc and Sensor Networks (SASN 2005), pp. 107–116 (2005)
15. Martinez, K., Hart, J.K., Ong, R.: Environmental sensor networks. IEEE Comput. 37(8), 50–56 (2004)
16. Martinez, K., Ong, R., Hart, J.: Glacsweb: a sensor network for hostile environments. In: Proc. IEEE SECON 2004, pp. 81–87 (2004)
17. Pal Chaudhuri, P., Chowdhury, D.R., Nandi, S., Chatterjee, S.: Additive Cellular Automata Theory and Applications, vol. 1. IEEE Computer Society Press (1997)
18. Perrig, A., Stankovic, J., Wagner, D.: Security in wireless sensor networks. Commun.+ ACM 47(6), 53–57 (2004)

19. Wolfram, S.: A New Kind of Sciences. Wolfram media Inc. (2002)
20. Saha, H.N., Bhattacharyya, D., Banerjee, P.K.: A Priority Based Protocol for Mitigating Different Attacks in MANET. International Journal for Computer Science and Communication I(2), 299–302 (2010)
21. Saha, H.N., Bhattacharyya, D., Banerjee, P.K.: A Distributed Administration Based Approach for Detecting and Preventing Attacks in MANET. International Journal for Scientific and Engineering Reasearch 2(3), 1–11 (2011)
22. Saha, H.N., Bhattacharyya, D., Banerjee, P.K.: Semi-Centralized Multi-Authenticated RSSI Based 'Solution to Sybil Attack. International Journal of Computer Science and Emerging Technologies I(4), 338–341 (2010)

A Location Dependent Semantic Cache Replacement Strategy in Mobile Environment

Kahkashan Tabassum, Mahmood Quadri Syed, and A. Damodaram

kahkashan@mjcollege.ac.in, syedmahmood.q@gmail.com,
adamodaram@jntuh.ac.in

Abstract. Mobile computing is developing fast and one of its major services is location dependent information services (LDIS).The dependence of the results of a query on the present location of the mobile user leads to such services. The query is called Location Dependent Query and the resultant data is called Location Dependent Data (LDD).The caching scheme often used in these services is semantic caching where information about data is stored along with data in cache. In this paper, we have added a new dimension, segment frequency (S_F) to the Semantic segment. The cache replacement policy takes this dimension into consideration when replacing the cache. The prediction algorithm Enhanced RBFNN (ERBFNN) takes the future location of neighbors into account. The existing FAR algorithm is modified taking into account the new dimension to replace items from cache. The proposed system is called Enhanced RBF-FAR (ERBF-FAR) algorithm. The experimental results show that the proposed system performs better and yields better results.

Keywords: Mobile Computing, LDIS, LDQ, LDD, Semantic Caching, FAR, ERBFNN.

1 Introduction

The development of high speed wireless network and the increasing use of portable wireless devices have led to the development of mobile computing. The ability to move and know your \own location has given rise to services known as Location Dependent Information Services (LDIS).A Location Dependent Data (LDD) is the data whose value depends on the current location of the mobile user [1]. The queries used to process these kind of data is known as Location Dependent Query (LDQ).Location Dependent Querying is gaining increasing popularity in mobile computing systems. Mobile users in wireless communications face several difficulties like low bandwidth, frequent network disconnection, etc. So, Data caching is needed [2]. When the mobile user cache gets full then data items from cache has to be removed to accommodate new item [3]. This is known as cache replacement [4].The scheme that fits exactly for the purpose of Location dependent Querying is the Semantic caching scheme. The basic idea of semantic caching is that the information about the data should be stored along with the data in the cache [3]. For improved performances, several semantic caching models have been proposed. Whenever a new Location dependent query is generated, the system checks whether it can be

N. Meghanathan et al. (Eds.): CCSIT 2012, Part I, LNICST 84, pp. 213–224, 2012.
© Institute for Computer Sciences, Social Informatics and Telecommunications Engineering 2012

responded by the information stored in cache. If yes, then the answer is then and there. If no, then if the query is query is partially answerable then the only a trimmed part of query is sent to the server. Semantic caching this way helps to reduce the network load by decreasing the amount of data that is transferred over the network.

In this paper, we study a semantic caching model. The definition of semantic segment that was proposed previously is enhanced to accommodate a new dimension Segment Frequency (S_f).This factors plays an important role when the decision has to be taken for which item has to be replaced in cache to accommodate a new item. We also study the existing cache replacement polices like Furthest Away Replacement (FAR) where the data item that is furthest is away from cache is removed first form cache. This cache replacement policy also predicts the clients future movement based on velocity. Another existing cache replacement policy that improves upon FAR known as RBF-FAR is also studied which predicts the client's future location using a RBF Network [11]. We then Propose a new scheme which an improvement on existing RBF-FAR scheme known as Enhanced RBF-FAR (ERBF-FAR).The proposed scheme improves upon the existing scheme where the cache replacement policy and the prediction architecture has been improved to provide better performance. We then simulate the existing system with proposed system and produce results.

2   Literature Survey

In this section, we first introduce the semantic caching model. This model uses the select and projects queries on a Database D, which has Relations R1, R2, . . . , Rn, i.e., D = {Ri,1 <= i <= n} [11].An Attribute set A is also defined where A= UARi,1 <= i <= n [11].With this, We define The term semantic segment and query.

Semantic Segment. Given a database D = {Ri,1 <= i <= n}and its attribute set A= UARi,1 <= i <= n , a semantic segment, S [11], is a tuple <SR,SA,SP,Sm,SC,ST>,where $Sc= \Pi SA\sigma Sp(SR)$, SR ε D , SA ε ASR and SP indicates the select condition that the tuple in S satisfy, SC represents the actual content of S. The Sm represents the MU user coordinate that helps to predict future location of moving objects and used to new replacement policy. ST is the timestamp for semantic segment.

Query. A Query Q is a semantic segment, <Q_R,Q_A,Q_P,Q_m,Q_C> [11].The Parameter S_T is removed as this parameter is only used for taking replacement decision. The storage of segments in the memory is done by a technique called paging [1]. Every page has a segment which connects to other pages and has a variable which holds the address and refers to the starting first page. An index is used to structure the cache memory in an organized manner which maintains the semantic descriptions and storage information for each segment in the cache. An example structure of index can be shown by taking two relations: Hospital (Hno, Hname, Hx, Hy), Petrol Pump ((Pno, Pname, Px, Py). We assume that the mobile user gives queries at different locations on his way. The current location of mobile user is designated using M(x, y).we issue two queries Q1, Q2 respectively,

Q1 - MU (30, 40): Show all hospitals within 25 km.
Q2 - MU (10, 30): Show all Petrol pumps within 7 km.

Table 1. An Example of semantic cache index

S	SR	SP	Sm	Sc	ST
S1	Hospital	(MUx-25<=Hx<=MUx+25)^(MUy-25<=Hy<=MUy+25)	(30,40)	2	T1
S2	Petrol Pumps	(MUx-7<=Px<=MUx+7)^(MUy-7<=Py<=MUy+7)	(10,30)	5	T2

Query Processing. Whenever a query is issued, we first check whether it can be answered by the cache. If yes, then the results are then and there. If the query can only be partially answered, we trim the original query by removing the presently answered parts and send it to the server for processing. The issue related processing query is the development of semantic segment. To prevent repeated data we cannot keep S and Q in the cache. Whenever a query is issued, if it overlaps a semantic segment in cache different techniques can be used to evaluate them. There no coalescing approach generates three disjoint parts: $(Q \cap S)$, $(S \wedge \neg Q)$ and $(\neg S \wedge Q)$ [9].Problem with this approach is that it may result in a many smaller segments. Complete coalescing approach is better for small queries but not for replacement [5]. The "partial coalescence in query" technique is the best [3]. The segment is decomposed in two parts: the overlapped part and the no overlapped part [6]. In this paper, we use the "partial coalescence in query" technique [5].

3   Existing System

In this section we will discuss the existing replacement policies and the existing prediction architecture. Furthest Away Replacement (FAR) policy is an existing policy which replaces the items which is furthest away from mobile client's present location. It also predicts the mobile client's future location using velocity. However, the FAR has its own problems which can be demonstrated by the following figure.

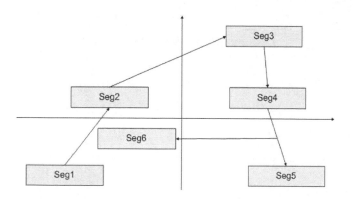

Fig. 1. Problems with FAR

In the figure above, Seg1, Seg 2, Seg 3, Seg 4, are semantic segments. Seg 5 and Seg 6 are assuming to be future semantic segments. We assume that, the Present timestamp is T4 of Seg 4, and T1<T2<T3<T4. Seg 5 or Seg 6 will be the semantic segment accessed if a new query is issued. When FAR algorithm is used, in Seg 4, the result that we get should be stored in cache but the space is not enough to store the result. Hence we have to remove an item from cache to accommodate the new item. Using FAR algorithm, the future location would be Seg 5 based on current velocity of Seg 4. So FAR replacement policy will remove Seg 1. But, if the mobile user changes its direction to Seg 6 half way then the next query will be generated on Seg 6 rather than Seg 5.Hence the Seg 1 which was removed was useful and should not have been removed. This was the result of inaccurate prediction by FAR algorithm. To overcome the problems with FAR, A new prediction model was developed which used RBF-Network to predict mobile user's future location [7]. The RBFNN is self learning model which takes the current location of mobile user M(x, y) using the S_m of Semantic segment and the timestamp S_t as input to the prediction architecture which gives the future location of mobile user $M_{fl}(x, y)$.The algorithm was called RBF-FAR [11].it uses RBF-Network to predict future location and based on that FAR replacement policy is used to replace the items in cache. The prediction architecture can be illustrated through the figure below.

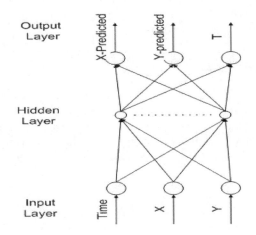

Fig. 2. Prediction Architecture

The whole description of how the RBF-FAR Replacement policy works is given by the following algorithm [11].

```
1:    Algorithm RBF-FAR(C, M)
2:    {
3:    In-Direction ←NULL;
4:    Out-Direction←NULL;
5:    Call RBFNN to predicate location;
6:    Mfl= (x-predicated, y-predicated);
7:    for every segment seg in C
```

```
8:   {
9:   if Distance(segL, MfL) ≤ Distance(segL, ML)
10:  then In-Direction ←In-Direction +{seg};
11:  else Out-Direction ← Out-Direction +{seg};
12:  }
13:  while ( Out-Direction != Empty )
14:  {
15:  seg ← the segment in Out-Direction which is the furthest from M;
16:  discard seg from C;
17:  remove seg from Out-Direction;
18:  add free space;
19:  if ( free space is enough )
20:  return (Success);
21:  }
22:  while ( In-Direction != Empty )
23:  {
24:  seg ← the segment in In-Direction which is the furthest from M;
25:  discard seg from C;
26:  remove seg from In-Direction;
27:  add free space;
28:  if ( free space is enough )
29:  return (Success);
30:  }
31:  return (Fail);
32:  }
```

The RBF-FAR algorithm should be trained for good performance. However if the training data is not sufficient then the RBFNN will give a lower performance [11].

4   Proposed ERBF-FAR Scheme

The existing RBF-FAR scheme needs to be trained for good performances and requires good amount of training data to perform well. The proposed ERBF-FAR scheme extends the RBF-FAR scheme for acquiring good performance. A new dimension S_f is added to the existing semantic segment which is used for cache replacement decision. The future location of the neighboring mobile users is given as input to the RBF-Network which improves the quality of prediction. The improvements in proposed scheme are discussed one by one in this section.

Proposed Semantic Segment. Given a database D = {Ri,1<=i<=n}and its attribute set A= UARi,1 <=i<=n, a semantic segment, S, is a tuple <SR,SA,SP,Sm,SC,ST,**SF**>, where $Sc = \Pi SA\sigma Sp(SR)$, SR ε D , SA ε ASR and SP indicates the select condition that the tuple in S satisfy, SC represents the actual content of S. The Sm represents the MU user coordinate that helps to predict future locations of moving objects and used to new replacement policy. ST is the timestamp for semantic segment; **Sf** is the frequency of the semantic segment.

Proposed Replacement Policy. The cache replacement policy takes the newly proposed dimension S_f into consideration for replacing an item from cache. The S_f denotes number of time the semantic segment was accessed. Whenever a new query results are obtained then an item in the cache has to be replaced to accommodate new results if the cache is full. According to FAR the items that are furthest away from current location should be removed. However In the proposed scheme we take the average of value of S_f of all semantic segment called S_{favg}. When the cache replacement decision is to be taken then we remove only the segment which has S_f less than S_{favg} and furthest away from current location. If a data item is furthest away from current location but its s_f is greater than or equal to average S_f then its should be removed from cache. The immediate next segment which is less further but has S_f less than S_{favg} should be removed. If all the items in cache have S_f greater then s_{favg} then the item with lowest S_f value should be removed.

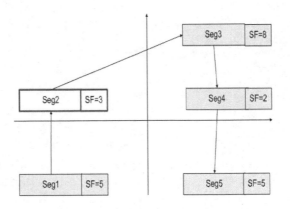

Fig. 3. ERBF-FAR Cache Replacement Scheme

In the above figure, a new query is issued at seg 4 and the results are obtained. We assume the cache is full so we need to replace an item from cache.seg 1 is the farthest away segment from seg 4 but it has S_f value 5 which is greater that average frequency 4.so the next farthest segment seg 2 is removed as it has S_f less than average frequency.

Prediction Architecture. The prediction architecture in the proposed system takes into account the future locations of neighboring mobile clients. The proposed prediction architecture is called Enhanced RBFNN (ERBFNN) which is an extension to RBFNN. The proposed prediction architecture will give improved performance. A new mobile user will not have any training data based on which prediction can be done. So training data can be taken from neighboring mobile clients who have good training sets and future locations can be accurately predicted.

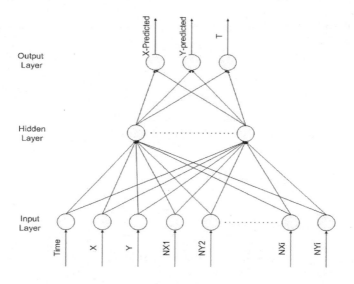

Fig. 4. Proposed Prediction Architecture

The whole description of how the ERBF-FAR Replacement policy works is given by the following algorithm.

```
1:   Algorithm ERBF-FAR(C, M)
2:   {
3:     In-Direction ←NULL;
4:     Out-Direction←NULL;
5:     Call ERBFNN to predicate location;
6:     Mfl= (x-predicated, y-predicated);
7:     for every segment seg in C
8:     {
9:     if Distance(segL, MfL) ≤ Distance(scgL, ML)
10:    then In-Direction ←In-Direction +{seg};
11:    else Out-Direction ← Out-Direction +{seg};
12:    }
13:    Favgi = average Sf of all segments in In-Direction.
14:    Favgo = average Sf of all segments in Out-Direction.
15:    while ( Out-Direction != Empty )
16:    {
17:    seg ← the segment in Out-Direction which is
18:    the furthest from M;
19:    while ( Out-Direction != Empty )
20:    {
21:    if(seg.Sf<Favgo)
22:    {
23:    discard seg from C;
```

24: remove seg from Out-Direction;
25: add free space;
26: if (free space is enough)
27: return (Success);
28: }
29: Else
30: {
31: Move to next furthest segment in Out-Direction
32: Repeat 19.
33: }
34: }
35: Seg ← segment with lowest Sf in Out-Direction.
36: Goto step 23
37: }
38: while (In-Direction != Empty)
39: {
40: seg ← the segment in In-Direction furthest from M;
41: while (In-Direction != Empty)
42: {
43: if(seg.Sf<Favgi)
44: {
45: discard seg from C;
46: remove seg from In-Direction;
47: add free space;
48: if (free space is enough)
49: return (Success);
50: }
51: Else
52: {
53: Move to next furthest segment in In-Direction
54: Repeat 41.
55: }
56: }
57: Seg ← segment with lowest Sf .
58: Goto step 45
59: }
60: return (Fail);
61: }

In this algorithm, if the mobile user moves in a well known location the replacement technique has a good performance. If user M moves to a new area, the FAR and RBF-FAR will be low effective whereas ERBF-FAR is more effective as takes neighbors into consideration for future location prediction.

5   Implementation Results

The design of our simulation scenario consists of one server, one mobile user and a wireless channel between them to communicate. The mobile user issues queries and the server responds to the queries by maintaining a database containing information to serve the mobile user. We consider that the mobile client has one of the three cache replacement policies i.e., FAR, RBF-FAR and ERBF-FAR. In the mobile client simulation scenario, we have LDQ which is generated on the basis of workload, A Semantic cache manager which manages the semantic cache memory and a semantic cache query processor which processes the queries. The system parameters are displayed in the following table.

Table 2. System parameter

Parameter	Description	Value
MUProcessor	Mobile user CPU speed	500(Mips)
MUcach	Mobile client cache size(KB)	512
BW	Wireless channel bandwidth	32 K
LenPage	Size of the data page(bytes)	4096
MsgFC	Fixed part protocol cost to send/receive message	10000
MsgPB	Size-dependent part protocol cost to S/R message	500
AttrSel	The attributes to be queried	AX,AY
QSel	Query selection	4 sets

The working design of the simulation scenario made up of three relations. One relation is a 1000 set and other two relations are 2000 set. We take two important attributes AX and AY. AX is indexed and unclustered and AY is indexed and clustered. We use select queries to generate LDQ's. We use location as predicate. AttrSel is used to specify attributes upon which query is generated and QSel is used to specify the query. The queries are generated using five random sets consisting of 1000 LDQ's. In Each set, the starting 100 queries are used as warm-up data and the rest 900 queries are used as test data. The LDQ's are well defined. The average time and network load is tested to show the effectiveness and efficiency of the model.

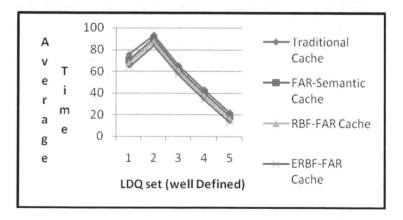

Fig. 5. Average response time vs well-defined paths

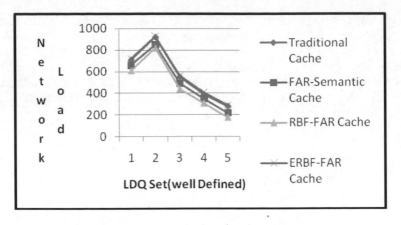

Fig. 6. Network-load vs. well-defined paths

The experimental results show that the semantic cache has less average response time than the traditional cache. The ERBF-FAR gives a good average response time performance than others. The network load has increased in the proposed system as the communication overhead has increased due to high communication with neighboring mobile clients for accessing their future locations. We also define LDQ's where mobile user is not well defined which means that the mobile user moves to a new location every time which it has previously not visited. The ERBF-FAR gives a good performance as it incorporates the future location of neighboring mobile users which increases the quality of future location prediction. The proposed scheme gives a better average response time than other schemes and the network load is increased due to communication overhead. But still it's sacrificed due good quality of prediction.

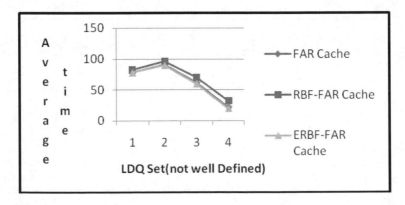

Fig. 7. Average time of response vs. poor-defined paths

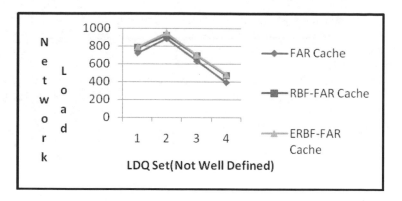

Fig. 8. Network-load vs. poor-defined paths

The main characteristics of a good cache replacement policy are that it will maintain a high cache hit ratio to improve the system performance. The ERBF-FAR shows an improved performance over other cache replacement policy and gives a high cache hit ratio. The addition of factor S_f to the semantic segment and its influence on the cache replacement decision has led to the increased cache hit ratio. The results are shown as following.

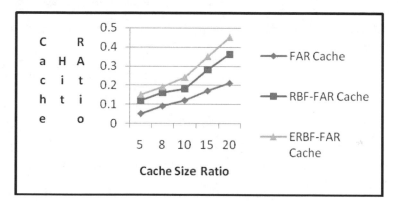

Fig. 9. Cache hit ratio vs. cache sizes

Hence the ERBF-FAR shows an improved performance and high cache hit ratio and is twice better than RBF-FAR and thrice better than FAR.

6   Conclusion

In this paper, we have discussed various cache management issues for location dependent data. We also defined the existing semantic segment, query and semantic segment index. The existing cache replacement policies were also discussed. The FAR cache replacement policy replaces the furthest away item and uses velocity for prediction of future location. The RBF-FAR uses FAR policy for replacement and RBF-Network for prediction of future location. The Proposed ERBF-FAR scheme proposes a new semantic segment which adds a new dimension Segment frequency (S_f) which is used for taking cache replacement decision. The prediction architecture is improved by adding future location of neighboring mobile users as input to the RBF-Network which gives an improved performance.

However, the introduction of future location of neighboring mobile users as increased the network load but has improved the quality of future location prediction. Hence, the Experimental results shows that, ERBF-FAR shows an improved performance over existing policies and gives better average response time and cache hit ratio.

References

1. Ren, Q., Dunham, M.H.: Using Semantic Caching to Manage Location Dependent Data in Mobile Computing. ACM (2000) 1-58113-197-6
2. Franlin, M.J.: Client Data caching. A Foundation for High Performance Object Database systems. Kluwer Academic (1996)
3. Dar, S., Franklin, M.J., Jonsson, B.T., Srivatava, D., Tan, M.: Semantic Data Caching and Replacement. In: Proc. VLDB Conf., pp. 330–341 (1996)
4. Ren, Q., Dunham, M.H.: Semantic Caching and Query Processing. IEEE Transactions on Knowledge & Data Engg. 15(1) (January 2003)
5. Dar, S., Franklin M.J., Johnson, B.T., Srivastav, D., Tan, M.: Semantic Data Caching and Replacement. In: Proc. - 22nd VLDB Conf., Mumbai, India (1996)
6. Manica, H., de Camargo, S.M.: A new Model for Location-Dependent Semantic Cache Based on Pre-Defined Regions. CLEI (2004)
7. Bilurkar, P., Rao, N.: Application of neural network techniques for location prediction in mobile networking. In: Proceedings of the 9th International Conference on Neural Information Processing, vol. 5, pp. 2157–2161
8. Wu, T.-T., Su, W.-Y., Zhou, X.-M.: Mobile Query Through Semantic Cache. Journal of Computer Research and Development 41(1)
9. Chen, C.M., Roussopoulos, N.: The Implementation and Performance Evaluation of the ADMS Query Optimizer: Integrating Query Result Caching and Matching. In: Jarke, M., Bubenko, J., Jeffery, K. (eds.) EDBT 1994. LNCS, vol. 779, pp. 323–336. Springer, Heidelberg (1994)
10. Gray, J.: The Benchmark Handbook. Morgan Kaufmann (1993)
11. Li, Z., He, P., Lei, M.: Research of Semantic Caching for LDQ in Mobile Network (2005)

Connectivity of Autonomous Agents Using Ad-Hoc Mobile Router Networks

Emi Mathews and Ciby Mathew

Heinz Nixdorf Institute
University of Paderborn
Paderborn, Germany
{emi,ciby}@hni.upb.de
http://wwwhni.uni-paderborn.de/eps

Abstract. Maintaining connectivity among a group of autonomous agents exploring an area is very important, as it promotes cooperation between the agents and also helps message exchanges which are very critical for their mission. Creating an underlying Ad-hoc Mobile Router Network (AMRoNet) using simple robotic routers is an approach that facilitates communication between the agents without restricting their movements. We address the following question in our paper: How to create an AMRoNet with local information and with minimum number of routers? We propose an agent-assisted router deployment algorithm for creating AMRoNet which is a localized, distributed router placement algorithm. The algorithm has a greedy deployment strategy for releasing new routers effectively into the area and a triangular deployment strategy to connect different connected components created by the agents exploring from different base stations. Empirical analysis shows that the agent-assisted router deployment algorithm is one of the best localized approaches to create an AMRoNet.

Keywords: Mobile Routers, Ad-hoc Network, Robotic network, Connectivity, Localized deployment.

1   Introduction

We envision a scenario with several *agents* which are humans or powerful robots moving autonomously on a terrain represented by a plane. These autonomous agents begin their exploration from one or more stationary base camp(s). We are looking for local and distributed strategies for maintaining the *connectivity* of the agents with the base station(s) and the other agents, as it promotes cooperation between the agents and also helps message exchanges which are very critical for their mission. These strategies must not restrict agent movements for the sake of maintaining connectivity.

Scenarios such as urban search and rescue and exploration of an unknown terrain are good examples, where we often have several exploring agents and one or more base station(s). In urban search and rescue scenarios, due to the aftermath

N. Meghanathan et al. (Eds.): CCSIT 2012, Part I, LNICST 84, pp. 225–237, 2012.

of natural or manmade disasters such as earthquakes, tsunamis, hurricanes, wars or explosions, the fixed communication infrastructure that could support communication between the agents are often destroyed. In other scenarios such as exploration of unknown terrains, e.g. subterranea or remote planets, no such infrastructure to support communication exist. A line of sight communication between the agents is not possible in such complex scenarios as the distance between the agents are often very large due to the large area to be explored. The presence of obstacles makes it difficult even at shorter inter-agent distance.

A stable and high bandwidth communication is feasible if we employ a multi-hop ad-hoc networking strategy for the agents. However, in such scenarios the number of agents is often very limited. Hence the agents themselves could not form a connected network always. Moreover, if they try to keep the network connected, it would restrict their movements.

We propose an alternate solution to maintain connectivity of the agents, i.e. deploy cheap router nodes that are mobile and create a network that acts as an infrastructure to support the communication of the agents. Thus we have a two tier network, with the agents and base stations lying at the upper layer and the routers deployed at the lower layer. The lower layer created to facilitate the communication between upper layer members is called Ad-hoc Mobile Router Network (AMRoNet). This network, in addition to supporting upper layer members' communication, provides various services to the agents, such as location information, topological maps and shortest path to base stations, and can also assist the search and rescue operation of the agents. The main advantage of this network is that the routers could relocate and maintain the connectivity in case of failures which are very common in scenarios described above.

In this paper, we address the following question: How to create an AMRoNet with local rules and with minimum number of routers? The remainder of this paper is organized as follows: Section 2 introduces the scenario and notations used in this paper. Related approaches known from the literature are discussed in Section 3. In Section 4 we present our new algorithm for creating AMRoNet with local information and discuss about the optimal solution. Next, in Section 5 we present a simulation based performance evaluation and analysis of the proposed algorithm. Finally, Section 6 summarizes the main results of this work and provides an outlook on possible future research.

2   Preliminaries

We have a two tier network, with the agents and base stations forming the upper layer. The environment where the agents explore is a 2-D area denoted as A and has n base stations. There are N_a agents which are humans or robots capable of performing tasks such as urban search and rescue. As the focus of this paper is mainly on the AMRoNet, we do not specify the requirements of the agents and the base stations, which vary according to the scenario considered. The only assumption we make is that they have a wireless devices to support communication.

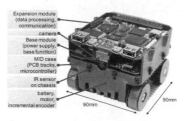

Fig. 1. Bebot mini-robot

The lower layer forming the AMRoNet consists of total N_r routers. The routers denoted by R, are very simple robots compared to the agents with limited sensing capabilities with which they avoid obstacles and perform local navigation. Routers are equipped with wireless transceivers for communication.

We assume the unit disk graph wireless model [2] for communication, where each node (agent, router or base station) can communicate with others located within a circle of radius r_c. We also assume that the communication area of one node πr_c^2 is much less than A. Hence, the agents have to send packets over several routers to reach a particular destination (other agent or base station).

We are interested in maintaining connectivity of the agents with minimum number of routers. Hence our objective is to find a strategy to create AMRoNet that provides *optimal coverage* with respect to the total *communication area*.

Mini-robots such as Bebots [7], shown in figure 1 are suitable candidates for routers. These robots are equipped with a camera with which they can assist agents in search and rescue operations. They have an infrared sensor ring for obstacle avoidance and wifi, zigbee and bluetooth modules for communication.

3   Related Work

Existing approaches to create AMRoNet are mostly based on *mobile routers making a chain*. In [3,10] the authors present different strategies such as Manhattan-Hopper, Hopper, Chase explorer and Go-to-The-Middle for maintaining the connectivity of an explorer with a base station. In [12] depending on whether the knowledge of the agent's trajectory is available or not, the trajectories for the routers are estimated.

The multi-robot spreading algorithms [6,8,14], though not meant for maintaining the connectivity of agents, could also be used for AMRoNet robots. In these algorithms, mobile robots spread out based on local rules. If the routers also move out of the base stations pro-actively and spread in the environment, using these algorithms they can form the AMRoNet for agents' communication.

Maintaining the connectivity of a group of robots while rendezvous, flocking, formation control etc. by controlling their motion pattern has been addressed in [4], [13], [11]. However, the agents we consider move independently and cannot be controlled for maintaining the connectivity.

4   Ad-Hoc Mobile Robotic Networks

Existing approaches to create AMRoNet presented in Section 3, maintain connectivity of the agents, if the routers move as fast as the agents. However, this assumption is not valid in our case as the routers used to create AMRoNet are very simple robots and their speed is usually very small compared to the speed of the agents. The *chain based* approach needs routers that can move faster than the agents [3, 10] and [12] needs twice the speed of the agent, to keep the chain connected. Existing chain based approaches cannot support connectivity of multiple exploring agents. Hence they are not useful in our scenario. The proactive spreading using *multi-robot spreading* algorithm also needs router moving as fast as the agents to keep them connected. Using simple routers that are slower than the agents, the multi-robot spreading algorithms based approaches work only if the deployment phase is finished prior to the exploration of the agents. However, in scenarios such as urban search and rescue, such pre-deployment is not feasible.

We propose a new approach called *agent-assisted router deployment* for AMRoNet creation which doesn't need any fast moving routers or pre-deployment phase. In agent-assisted router deployment, the agent carries the routers during the exploration. When they are at the verge of disconnection, they release a new router into the area. Routers move locally to maximize coverage. Such an approach is feasible, as our robots are very small [7] and the agents can carry several robots during their exploration.

4.1   Agent-Assisted Router Deployment Algorithm

Let the N_a agents begin their exploration from n base stations. Each base station has a unique id and one reference node which acts as a base station server for all communication. The base station i, for all $i \leq n$, is denoted as BS_i and its reference node as R_i. We set the *status* of R_i and the agents moving out of BS_i to i. Routers are denoted as R_{ij} and agents as A_{ij}, where i is their status and j indicates their unique id. The agents explore the area based on their own navigational algorithm. Figure 4.1 shows a schematic representation with two base stations and two agents (one agent per base station) exploring an open area.

Initially an agent A_{ij} has wireless links to R_i and other agents A_{ik} for any $k \leq N_a$. As the link between A_{ij} and R_i is initialized, A_{ij} asks R_i about its

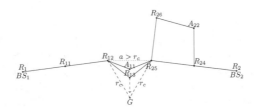

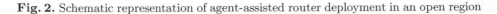

Fig. 2. Schematic representation of agent-assisted router deployment in an open region

position and stores this information. If A_{ij} is about to lose its connection to R_i, it places a new router with its status set to i and position set to A_{ij}'s current position. The new router R_{ik}, for any $k \leq N_r$, is placed very close to the current location of A_{ij} in the direction towards R_i. Agents use the position information of R_i for estimating the direction. This ensures that R_{ik} released is always connected to R_i. R_{ik} becomes the new reference for A_{ij} and for all other agents within R_{ik}'s communication rage. During the navigation, A_{ij} may move inside the range of a router R_{pq} for any $p \leq n$ and $q \leq N_r$ that has already been deployed. In this case R_{pq} becomes A_{ij}'s current reference. A_{ij} asks R_{pq} for its status and repeats the placement steps when it is about to lose its connection to R_{pq}. If an agent has wireless links to many reference robots, any one of them acts as the agent's current reference. The agent releases a new router only when it loses connection to the last reference node in its communication range. We call this placement strategy as *greedy deployment*.

The greedy agent-assisted router deployment builds a graph G with the nodes at the base stations and with routers released during agents' exploration as its vertices. Agents exploring from one base station form a connected component, denoted as CC, of G. However, such CCs created from multiple base stations are not connected. When an agent A_{ij} enters into the range of R_{pq} for $i \neq p$ from the current reference R_{ik}, CC_i and CC_p are temporarily connected. During the navigation, if A_{ij} loses it connection to R_{ik} but still has connection to R_{pq}, A_{ij} does not place another router, as it has R_{pq} as its current reference. In this case, A_{ij} loses connection to its original base station BS_i and CC_i and CC_p get disconnected again.

To solve the disconnection problem, in such situations we adopt another deployment strategy called *triangular deployment*. In triangular deployment, when an agent enters into the range of R_{pq} for $i \neq p$ from its current reference R_{ik}, it releases a new router with its status set to i and it moves to a point that keeps R_{ij} and R_{pq} connected and maximizes the local coverage. The goal point of the new router for maximizing the local coverage can be calculated as follows: If a is the distance between $R_{i_{ref}}$ and $R_{j_{ref}}$, the goal point lies at a distance $d = \sqrt{r_c^2 - (\frac{a}{2})^2}$ from the midpoint of the line joining R_{ij} and R_{pq} on the same side of the agent as shown in Figure 4.1. During the *goto goal* behavior, if the new router encounters an obstacle that cannot be avoided in few steps, it stops navigating to the goal location, as the obstacle could be too large to overcome without disconnecting R_{ij} and R_{pq}.

To optimize the number of robots used during the triangular deployment, we propose the following strategy. The agent A_{ij} performs the triangular placement only when it enters into the range of the first R_{pq} with $i \neq p$ and connects CC_i and CC_p. A_{ij} then disables triangular placement to all R_{pk}, for any $k \leq N_r$. If there are multiple agents and multiple base stations we propose two strategies for the triangular deployment. The first one needs global communication and the second one needs only local communication.

In the first strategy, when an agent A_{ij} entering into the range of R_{pq} with $i \neq p$, checks with R_{pq} if any other agent has already made CC_i and CC_p

connected. If not, it performs a triangular deployment to connect them and sends a message to all other agents and references that are connected to it either directly or by multi-hop networking. All these agents and references update their information about the connected components in G.

In the second localized strategy, the router released during the triangular deployment set the references R_{ij}, R_{pq} and itself as *disabled* for further triangular deployment. When an agent entering into the range of R_{pq} from the current reference R_{ij} with $i \neq p$, it checks if both R_{ij} and R_{pq} has already been disabled from triangular deployment. This ensures that CC_i and CC_p always get connected and prevents redundant deployment at the locations of triangular placements.

4.2   Optimal Deployment

We can find the optimal router location of an AMRoNet from the static optimal placement strategies used in the area coverage problems. The objective of these problems is to place minimum number of nodes in an environment such that, every point is optimally covered. If we look at the *optimal coverage* with respect to the total sensing area, the robots could form a triangular grid as shown in Figure 3(a). When the inter-robot distance $d = \sqrt{3}.r_s$, where r_s is the sensing radius, 100% coverage is attained with minimum number of robots. This approach creates a connected network if $r_c/r_s \geq \sqrt{3}$.

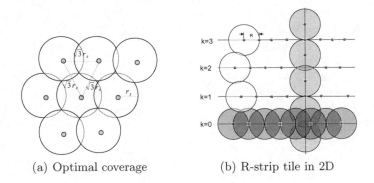

(a) Optimal coverage   (b) R-strip tile in 2D

Fig. 3. Coverage and Connectivity

We are interested in maintaining the connectivity of the agents with minimum number of routers. Hence the optimal coverage we refer to is the coverage with respect to the total communication area. A triangular grid with the inter-robot distance $d = \sqrt{3}.r_c$ cannot provide 100% *communication area coverage*, as robots cannot communicate when $d > r_c$. So a coverage and connectivity $(C - C)$ constraint arises and our objective is to maximize the communication area coverage with connectivity.

If we create a triangular grid with reduced inter node distance $d = r_c$, it is not optimal according to the $C - C$ constraint. What is optimal in 1-D, is an r-strip shown at the bottom row of Figure 3(b), where $d = r_c$. In 2-D, the lower

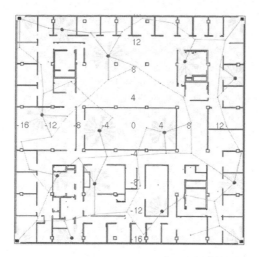

Fig. 4. An example scenario with 12 agents and 4 base stations

bound on node density for optimal $C - C$ is $d_{OPT} \geq \frac{0.522}{r^2}$ [9]. The optimal solution that achieves communication coverage with 1-connectivity in 2-D is the r-strip tile shown in the figure 3(b) [1]. It has a spatial density $d_{STR} = \frac{0.536}{r^2}$ [9]. The r-strip tile in 2-D is created as follows: for every integer k place a strip horizontally such that there is one node positioned at $(0, k(\frac{\sqrt{3}}{2} + 1)r_c)$ for every even k, and one node positioned at $(\frac{r_c}{2}, k(\frac{\sqrt{3}}{2} + 1)r_c)$ for every odd k. Finally place some nodes vertically in the following way. For every odd k, place two nodes at $(0, k(\frac{\sqrt{3}}{2} + 1)r_c \pm \frac{\sqrt{3}}{2})$. The purpose of this vertical strip is to connect the horizontal strips and thus ensure connectivity between all nodes.

A more commonly used regular patterns are hexagonal grid which has $d_{HEX} = \frac{0.77}{r^2}$ and square grid which has $d_{SQR} = \frac{1}{r^2}$ [9]. In triangular grids, the number of nodes in a $D \times D$ square area is $\frac{2D}{\sqrt{3}r} \cdot \frac{D}{r} \approx 1.155 \frac{D^2}{r^2}$ and hence the density $d_{TRI} = \frac{1.155}{r^2}$.

5   Performance Evaluation and Analysis

5.1   Simulation Setup

We evaluate the proposed agent-assisted router deployment algorithm using a simulation based empirical analysis. We use the Player robotic interface and Stage 2D simulator for our experiments [5]. The area considered is a $32m \times 32m$ square area which maps the floor plan of our institute as shown in Figure 4. In our simulations, the agents are modeled as Pioneer2dx robots, routers as Bebot robots and base stations as Amigobot robots. All robots are equipped with WiFi modules for communication. The base station robots are located at the corner of the simulation environment and are immobile. The scenario shown in Figure 4 has 4 base stations and 12 agents (3 per base station). The agents start their exploration from a point very close to the base station robots and are initially connected to them. We have chosen a random exploration strategy for the agents. They detect obstacles using their sonar sensors which have maximum range of 2 m and avoid them using the *obstacle avoidance* behavior implemented. The release of a new router by the agent is implemented by moving a router located outside the simulation environment to its placement point by the simulator. Routers released during the triangular placement use the *goto* behavior to navigate towards the goal points. They avoid collisions using their IR sensors which have maximum range of 14 cm.

5.2 Performance of Agent-Assisted Router Deployment Algorithm

To analyze the performance of the agent-assisted router deployment algorithm, we vary parameters such as r_c and N_a. Figure 5 shows the result of the algorithm, when r_c is varied from 4 to 10 in a square area of size $32m \times 32m$. The graph plot with label ARD shows the average number of routers (including the reference robot in the base station) deployed to cover the entire region, when all agents begin their exploration from one base station. Here, N_a is varied from 1 to 4. For each N_a, the simulation is repeated 5 times and the agents are assigned different start locations. So the graph plot with label ARD given in Figure 5 is the average of 20 simulations with confidence interval at 95%.

To compare the performance of the algorithm, we calculate the number of robots required, by the static placement strategies of the commonly used regular patterns such as r-strip tile, hexagonal grid, square grid and triangular grid. The estimated number of robots required to cover the area can be calculated using the spatial density of the patterns, i.e $d_{STR} = \frac{0.536}{r^2}$, $d_{HEX} = \frac{0.77}{r^2}$, $d_{SQR} = \frac{1}{r^2}$ and $d_{TRI} = \frac{1.155}{r^2}$. Since the area is bounded, the minimum number of robots actually required to cover the entire region is often higher than the estimated values. This is clearly visible in the example figures Figure 6(a) and Figure 6(b), where the estimated number of robots needed for the r-strip $RSTR_{est}$ is 35 and

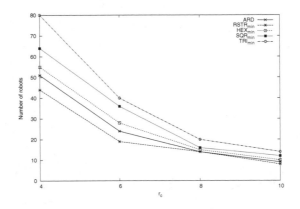

Fig. 5. Comparison of performance of router deployment algorithms

the hexagonal grid HEX_{est} is 50, but the minimum required number for r-strip tile $RSTR_{min}$ is 44 and the hexagonal grid HEX_{min} is 55. The figures also show that there are still uncovered areas, e.g. the location of the robots highlighted with circles. We cannot place additional routers to cover these areas, as they would be placed outside the specified area according to the regular placement pattern.

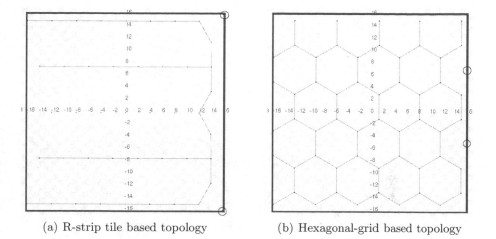

(a) R-strip tile based topology   (b) Hexagonal-grid based topology

Fig. 6. Static placement of regular pattern

Figure 5 also shows the plot of the minimum required values for r-strip tile $RSTR_{min}$, hexagonal grid HEX_{min}, square grid SQR_{min} and triangular grid TRI_{min} in the specified square area, when r_c is varied from 4 to 10. It shows that the proposed algorithm is better than TRI_{min}, SQR_{min}, and HEX_{min} placement strategies. The number of robots needed by the proposed algorithm is close to the $RSTR_{min}$ values which are the actual optimal values.

5.3   Effect of Number of Agents and Base Stations

To analyze the effect of number of agents and base stations on the agent-assisted router deployment algorithm, we now vary number of agents per base station N_{apbs} and the number of base stations n, for a fixed r_c. Figure 7 shows the average number of robots (including the base station robots) needed to cover the square area of size $32m \times 32m$ for $N_{apbs} = 1, 2$ and 3, when n is varied from 1 to 4.

Increasing the number of agents without increasing n do not affect the performance, as the deployments performed by the agents are based on the local rules which are in turn based only on losing or establishing connection with other routers and not with other agents. Hence the number of routers deployed is independent of the number of agents. The data points for a particular n shown in Figure 7 with different N_{apbs} confirm this.

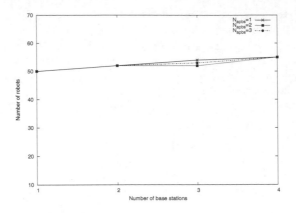

Fig. 7. Effect of number of agents and base stations on the performance

Increasing the number of base stations may result in more triangular deployments. The total area covered by three robots in a triangular deployment is usually lesser than the total area covered by them in an optimal deployment. The largest overlap in a triangular deployment occurs when two references are separated by a distance slightly greater than r_c. However, such deployments do not increase the number of routers considerably. Even the greedy deployment may produce similar less optimal overlapping regions, e.g. when an agent connected to two references move out of the communication radius of both references simultaneously.

Figure 8 shows a scenario where three routers are released during the triangular deployment. Actually at most 2 routers are needed to make the four chains connected. Such redundant deployment increases with the number of base stations. We could add more local rules to make the increase bounded, but this is not actually needed as the agents move independently (in our experiments, they move randomly) and the structures similar to the one shown in Figure 8 occur very rarely. The graph plots for $N_{apbs} = 1$ and $N_{apbs} = 2$ depicted in Figure 7 also show that the total number deployed is more or less the same for different base station counts.

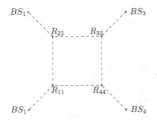

Fig. 8. Redundant router deployment during local triangular deployment

5.4   Localized r-Strip Tile Creation Algorithm

From the evaluation of the proposed agent-assisted router deployment algorithm, we see that it performs better than all other regular pattern based static placements except the r-strip tile in 2-D. Let us now look at a localized agent-assisted r-strip tile creation algorithm that does not restrict agent movements or causes disconnections. A straight forward extension of the agent-assisted router deployment algorithm for r-strip creation is: Agents release routers as per the greedy deployment strategy and the routers move to the goal points that create r-strip tiles locally.

During this localized r-strip creation the following problems arises: The routers released move to their goal point very slowly compared to the agent speed. If the agents use these moving routers as their references, to prevent disconnections they may have to release new routers before their current references reach their goal points. Hence more routers than the static optimal r-strip tiles are needed for this localized solution. Another problem is the presence of obstacles which prevents the routers from reaching the ideal optimal goal point. A third problem occurs when we have multiple base stations. The pattern created from one base station may not be aligned with the other from another base station. This also affects the optimality of the localized r-strip creation algorithm. These problems are not specific to the localized r-strip tile creation algorithm. The localized algorithms for creating regular patterns like hexagon, square or triangular grids also suffers these problems. Another problem that is specific to r-strip tile creation algorithm is: Non-optimal placement of the vertical strip that is needed to connect different horizontal r-strips. In the ideal case, it needs only one router to connect two horizontal strips. However, if the agents move in a adversarial manner, it needs one router per every second router in the horizontal strip.

5.5   Analysis of Agent-Assisted Router Deployment Algorithm

The localized r-strip creation without restricting agent movements or causing disconnection is not an optimal solution due to the problems mentioned above. Hence the actual number of robots needed for localized r-strip creation is much more than the estimated static r-strip tile value. Figure 5 shows that the agent assisted router deployment algorithm's performance is quite close to the actual static r-strip tile $RSTR_{min}$ value. Hence it is one of the best localized approaches to create an AMRoNet.

If we calculate the estimated number of robots needed for the hexagonal grid HEX_{est} in the specified square region for different r_c values, we observe that they are very close to the average number of routers used by the proposed algorithm. Hence we could use the equation $ARD_{est} = \frac{0.77}{r^2} * A$ to get an approximate estimate of the total number of routers needed to cover a given area A. This helps the agents in making an estimate on the numbers routers they need to carry, before beginning their exploration.

In our experiments, where we used the floor plan of our institute, we found that the proposed algorithm performed equally well, irrespective of the obstacles present in the area. The presence of obstacles affects the performance of other localized agent-assisted regular pattern creation algorithms, as they prevent the routers from reaching the optimal goal point. Our approach even works in area where we do not have any prior model or map of the environment. It could be extended to make it work without any location information, where we need just the link quality estimate provided by the WiFi devices. In such cases, the greedy deployment strategy is performed when the link quality drops below a threshold. Routers deployed during the triangular deployment, move in the direction where the link quality tends to be weak, in order to maximize the coverage area.

6   Conclusion

We have presented a new localized and distributed algorithm for creating an ad-hoc mobile router network that facilitates communication between the agents without restricting their movements. The agent-assisted router deployment algorithm has a greedy deployment strategy for releasing new routers effectively into the area and a triangular deployment strategy for connecting different connected components created by the agents exploring from different base stations. Empirical analysis shows that the number of routers deployed by the agent-assisted router deployment algorithm is close to the optimal static r-strip tile values. The performance of the algorithm is not affected by the number of agents or obstacles present in the environment. Increase in the number of base stations did not make any noticeable performance difference either.

We plan to verify the performance of the proposed algorithm in real life scenarios. The performance of the algorithm with link quality estimate needs to be validated with more quantitative results. We conclude that localized algorithms for achieving optimal *communication area coverage* are worth exploring more.

References

1. Bai, X., Kumar, S., Xuan, D., Yun, Z., Lai, T.H.: Deploying wireless sensors to achieve both coverage and connectivity. In: Proceedings of the 7th ACM International Symposium on Mobile Ad Hoc Networking and Computing, MobiHoc 2006, pp. 131–142. ACM, New York (2006)
2. Clark, B.N., Colbourn, C.J., Johnson, D.S.: Unit disk graphs. Discrete Mathematics 86(1-3), 165–177 (1990)
3. Dynia, M., Kutylowski, J., auf der Heide, F.M., Schrieb, J.: Local strategies for maintaining a chain of relay stations between an explorer and a base station. In: Proceedings of the Nineteenth Annual ACM Symposium on Parallel Algorithms and Architectures, SPAA 2007, pp. 260–269. ACM, New York (2007)
4. Ganguli, A., Cortes, J., Bullo, F.: Multirobot rendezvous with visibility sensors in nonconvex environments. IEEE Transactions on Robotics 25(2), 340–352 (2009)
5. Gerkey, B., Vaughan, R.T., Howard, A.: The player/stage project: Tools for multi-robot and distributed sensor systems. In: ICAR 2003, Proceedings of the 11th International Conference on Advanced Robotics, New York, NY, USA, pp. 317–323 (June 2003)

6. Heo, N., Varshney, P.: A distributed self spreading algorithm for mobile wireless sensor networks. In: IEEE Wireless Communications and Networking, WCNC 2003, vol. 3, pp. 1597 –1602 (March 2003)
7. Herbrechtsmeier, S., Witkowski, U., Rückert, U.: Bebot: A Modular Mobile Miniature Robot Platform Supporting Hardware Reconfiguration and Multi-Standard Communication. In: Kim, J.-H., Ge, S.S., Vadakkepat, P., Jesse, N., Al Manum, A., Puthusserypady K, S., Rückert, U., Sitte, J., Witkowski, U., Nakatsu, R., Braunl, T., Baltes, J., Anderson, J., Wong, C.-C., Verner, I., Ahlgren, D. (eds.) Progress in Robotics. CCIS, vol. 44, pp. 346–356. Springer, Heidelberg (2009)
8. Howard, A., Mataric, M.J., Sukhatme, G.S.: Mobile sensor network deployment using potential fields: A distributed, scalable solution to the area coverage problem. In: DARS: 6th International Symposium on Distributed Autonomous Robotics Systems, pp. 299–308 (June 2002)
9. Iyengar, R., Kar, K., Banerjee, S.: Low-coordination topologies for redundancy in sensor networks. In: Proceedings of the 6th ACM International Symposium on Mobile Ad Hoc Networking and Computing, MobiHoc 2005, pp. 332–342. ACM, New York (2005)
10. Kutyowski, J., auf der Heide, F.M.: Optimal strategies for maintaining a chain of relays between an explorer and a base camp. Theor. Comput. Sci. 410, 3391–3405 (2009)
11. Lin, Z., Broucke, M., Francis, B.: Local control strategies for groups of mobile autonomous agents. IEEE Transactions on Automatic Control 49(4), 622–629 (2004)
12. Tekdas, O., Wei, Y., Isler, V.: Robotic routers: Algorithms and implementation. Int. J. Rob. Res. 29, 110–126 (2010)
13. Zavlanos, M., Jadbabaie, A., Pappas, G.: Flocking while preserving network connectivity. In: 46th IEEE Conference on Decision and Control, pp. 2919–2924 (December 2007)
14. Zou, Y., Chakrabarty, K.: Sensor deployment and target localization based on virtual forces. In: Twenty-Second Annual Joint Conference of the IEEE Computer and Communications, INFOCOM 2003, March-April 3, vol. 2, pp. 1293–1303. IEEE Societies (2003)

A New Approach to Stegnography

Soumik Mukherjee, Moumita Deb, Pratik Kumar Agarwal, and Abhinava Roy

RCC Institute of Information Technology

Abstract. Steganography hides the fact that a message is being sent. It provides security. In this world full of intruders, security of information is the most vital concern. In this paper, we present a Steganography algorithm. Our approach is based on hiding message in an image file by selecting pixels using some mathematical formulation and replacing the last few bits of the pixel. The bit selection is also not obvious; the selection is decided again by some calculation. In our algorithm we try to ensure that there is minimum amount of distortion from the original image. We also use a symmetric key to ensure security of the message. To the best of our knowledge this approach can be used to hide data in an image file with great security and with a very small chance of detection.

Keywords: Steganalysis, Carrier File, Stego-Medium, Redundant bits, Payload, Steganographic Algorithm.

1   Introduction

Steganography[1] is the art and science of writing hidden messages in such a way that no one, apart from the sender and intended recipient, suspects the existence of the message, a form of security through obscurity. Generally Steganography has been derived from the Greek words Stegos (covered) [1] and Grafia (writing) [1].The main objective of Steganography is to communicate securely in such a way that true message is not visible to the observer, that is the unwanted parties should not be able to distinguish in any sense between the covered image (image not containing any secret message) and stego image (modified cover image that containing secret message). However Steganography differs from Cryptography[6] in the sense that the former focuses on concealing the existence of a message while the latter focuses on concealing the contents of a message. However Steganography differs[7] from Cryptography in a sense that former hides without altering the bits while the latter alter the bits without hiding. There is another difference between Steganography and Cryptography, Steganography is the process of embedding information within other seemingly harmless information in such a way that no one but the intended can retrieve it while cryptography is the process of transforming information into other unintelligible such that no one but the intended recipient can able to retrieve it.

Generally, Steganography was thrown into light by first Greek Historian Herodotus (485-525 B.C) [4]who shaved up the head of the messenger and then wrote the message into his scalp and then waited for the hair to regrow.The messenger apparently carrying nothing contentious, could travel freely. Arriving at his

N. Meghanathan et al. (Eds.): CCSIT 2012, Part I, LNICST 84, pp. 238–247, 2012.
© Institute for Computer Sciences, Social Informatics and Telecommunications Engineering 2012

destination, he shaved his head and pointed it at the recipient Steganography works as given below in the diagram.

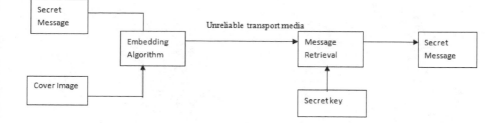

Fig. 1. Block diagram of Steganography process

   To hide a secret message in an image without changing its visible properties, the cover image can be altered in the "noisy" regions with many colour variations, so as to reduce the attention drawn towards the altered location. The most common methods of alteration include changing, masking, filtering and transformation of the bits is carried out at the least significant bit (LSB), developed by Chandramouli and others [2].Later came the construction of an algorithm for detecting LSB steganography. There is continuous changes[5] in the cutting edge world of steganography and the large amount of data involved, so steganalysists have tried to design algorithms to improve the hiding capacity of images and lowering the detecting rates.

   If we use a 24-bit image, a bit from each red, green and blue component can be used. So for an image of 500x400 pixel image can contain a total of 1600000 bits and a secret message of 600000 bits (75000 bytes).But using just 3 bits out of every 24 bits is waste of huge amount of space. So the main objective of the current work is to insert the message in more than one bit in each byte of the pixels of the cover image and still get a result similar to the LSB substitution (imperceptible to the naked eye). This objective is achieved by using a new steganography algorithm by hiding a large amount of data in bitmap images by using maximum number of bits per byte in each pixel. We can discuss two types of attacks to be sure that our process for embedding data is working efficiently. The first attack concerns to work against visual attacks,to make use of the ability of humans to unclearly discern between noise and visual patterns, and the second attack concerns to work against statistical attacks to make it much difficult to automate.

2   Our Idea Behind Steganography

Our main aim of this algorithm is to pass a secret message (within an image) with minimum distortion of the image so as to increase security and to reduce the chances of detection. But before going onto the main algorithm part, let us overlook some of the important concepts :-

a) Segmentation of the cover image: -We segment the image into blocks of 24 bytes each. We use uniform segmentation [3] because it saves space and there is less amount of wastage in this kind of segmentation.(Fig.2).

Uniform Segmentation   Non Uniform Segmentation

Fig. 2. Different way of segmentation of cover image

b) Pixel Selection: - This is another layer of security in the algorithm; we perform almost random selection of pixels based on their colour component and a secret key.

c) Bit Infection: -This is third layer of security in the algorithm; we insert three bits in place of a single bit but instead of adding more information we add more security. For a'0' we inject '101' and for '1' we inject '010'.Moreover if a specific pattern of bit is absent we spread these three bits into three different bytes.

2.1   Description of Our Algorithm

The present algorithm has two parts: one is the message hiding part at the receiver's end and another is the message extraction part at the receiver's end. These parts are developed and implemented for the following reasons stated below:-

1. This algorithm reduces the chances of statistical detection.
2. The algorithm must provide robustness against a variety of image   manipulation attacks.
3. The stego-image must not have any distortion.
4. The algorithm must not sacrifice security to achieve extra capacity for image storing.

The first part of the algorithm is to store the message in the cover image; it is achieved by the following steps:

- Accept an image from the sender, to be used as a cover image.
- Accept a secret two digit key from the sender.
- Embed the key in the cover image.

- Perform the required calculations as described in the algorithm (section 3 of this document).
- Take the secret message from the sender and embed it into the cover image according to the procedure stated in the section 3.
- Save the image.

While the second part of the algorithm is retrieve the message from the received image. It can be achieved by following steps:

- Accept the image received by the receiver.
- Accept the secret key from the receiver.
- Check whether the key entered by the receiver is the same as the encrypting key or not.
- If the keys match extract the message.

3   Algorithm

Consider the image(I) and convert it to its corresponding binary format bin[ ].
1. Calculate prominent color component of I, i.e. if prominent color is red or blue or green then comp=0 or 1 or 2.
2. Calculate the most frequent color byte of the color component (comp) ; in max.
3. Accept secret key and convert it into its binary format in key[ ].
4. Calculate the block increment value in incr ,

   incr = (Number of bytes in I) % Integer(key[ ])
   if incr > 11
   incr = incr % 11
5. Store the pattern '0011001100110011' in the image
   for denoting the presence of a message in the image.

   Consider bytes bi[ ], i = 1 to 8;
   if(i % 2 = =0)
   Replace (bi[6-7] ,11)
   else
       Replace (bi[6-7] ,00)
6. For the next 8 bytes consider each byte as bk[ ],

   vary i = 0 to 7
   Replace (bk[7] , key[i])
7. Consider the message in its binary format as message[ ] and its length in binary format as len[ ].

   Now for the next 8 bytes consider each byte as bk[ ],
   vary i = 0 to 7
   Replace (bk[7] , len[i])
8. Now consider 8x3 byte block cover from next sets of
   bytes ,each block denoted by Ni . Repeating the set of processes based on i,
   Where i = i +24 + (incr * 3) [incrementing and repeating till the message length number of times] Considering Ni,
   8.1   Search for the presence of max in the prominent

color components (comp) in Ni.

8.2   if max is present , replace the last bit of the first byte and the last bit of the last
      byte of the block with 1,consider the max byte as bk[] ,
      if(message[j] = =0)
      Replace(bk[5-7] , 101) [type-I byte]
      And check the previous existence of a byte of type –II, if present then flip the
      last bit and save it.
      else
      Replace(bk[5-7] , 010) [type-II byte]
      And check the previous existence of a byte of type –I, if present then flip the
      last bit and save it.
      else if max not present, replace the last bit of the
      first byte and the last bit of the last byte of the block with 0.
      Find byte closest to max, say bx[ ]
      if(message[j] = =0)
        Replace(bx-1[7] , 1), Replace(bx[7] , 0),
        Replace(bx+1[7] , 1),
      else
        Replace(bx-1[7] , 0), Replace(bx[7] , 1),
        Replace(bx+1[7] , 0)

9.   Save the new image .

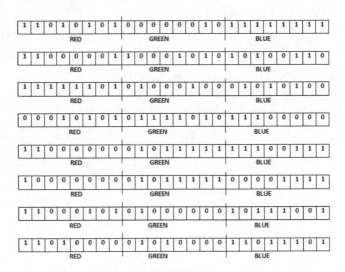

Fig. 3. A block of the image in binary format(with max)

3.1   Storing of Bits in an Image

Let us consider the prominent color component being BLUE and the max =
11111111.Following our algorithm for the above example, the max byte is searched
and found within the block.Now the last bit of the first byte and the last bit of the last
byte of the block is changed accordingly (Fig. 4).

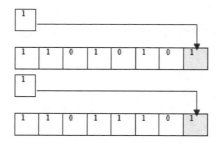

Fig. 4. Bit substitution of the first and last byte

Now if the message bit is 0, then we replace the 3byte of our block. (Fig. 5).

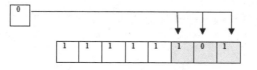

Fig. 5. Substituting the last 3bits as per the bit representation format

Now considering a situation when a block does not contain the max =11111111 byte in its color component (blue here) in Fig. 6.

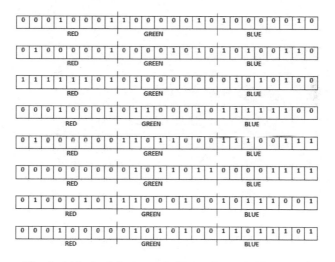

Fig. 6. A block of the image in binary format(without max)

Following our algorithm for the above example, the max byte is searched and it is not found within the block. Now the last bit of the first byte and the last bit of the last byte of the block is changed accordingly (Fig. 7).

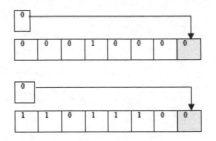

Fig. 7. Bit substitution of the first and last byte

Now if the message bit is 1, then we replace the last bit of the 12th byte of our block (Fig.8) with the message bit i.e. 1 and the previous byte or the 11th byte is transformed accordingly (Fig. 9) by replacing the last bit of the byte with 0. Moreover the 13th byte or the byte after the byte under consideration is modified by replacing the last bit of the block with 0(Fig. 10).

Fig. 8. Last bit substitution of the 12th byte

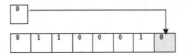

Fig. 9. Last bit substitution of the 11th byte

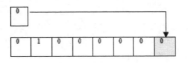

Fig. 10. Last bit substitution of the 13th byte

3.2   Retrieval of the Message

Consider the image(I) and convert it to its corresponding binary format bin[ ].
1. Calculate prominent color component of I, i.e. if prominent color is   red or blue or green then comp=0 or 1 or 2.
2. Calculate the most frequent color byte of the color component (comp) ; in max.
3. Accept secret key and convert it into its binary format in key[ ].
4. Check the pattern '0011001100110011' in the image

for denoting the presence of a message in the image.

Consider bytes bi[ ], i = 1 to 8;

Check if pattern exists considering the last two bits of the bytes all together, if present then proceed

Else , notify the user about the image being void of any message.

5. For the next 8 bytes consider each byte as bk[ ],

vary i = 0 to 7

Check(bk[7] , key[i])

If found correct then proceed , else allow two more chances to the user to enter the correct secret key.

6. Calculate the block increment value in incr ,

incr = (Number of bytes in I) % Integer(key[ ])

if incr > 11

incr = incr % 11

7. Extract the length of the message from the image data in the binary format in len[] ;

vary i = 0 to 7

Extract(bk[7] , len[i])

8. Now consider 8x3 byte block cover from next sets of bytes ,each block denoted by Ni repeating the set of processes based on i,

Where i = i +24 + (incr * 3)[incrementing and repeating till the message length number of times]

Considering Ni ,

8.1 Check if last bit of the first byte of Ni block is '1' or the last bit of the last byte is '1'or not. If it's '1' then consider the max byte as bk[] ,

Search for type-I byte (last three bits of bk[] replaced by '101') or

type –II(last three bits of bk[] replaced by '010') byte in the prominent color components (comp) in Ni

8.2 if type-I byte is present , store message[ ] bit as '0'

Or if type-II byte present ,store message[ ] bit as '1'

else Notify the user of the block data being tampered and Search for the byte nearest to the max byte in bx[ ]

Search for the two bit pattern within the last 3 bits of the byte that corresponds to a message bit representation and extract the message bit accordingly.

8.3 If last bit of the first byte or the last bit of the last byte of Ni block is '0'.

Search for the two bit pattern within the last 3 bits of the byte that corresponds to a message bit representation and extract the message bit accordingly.

9. Display the extracted message.

4   Results and Discussion

Specifications of a good Steganography algorithm depend on the following :

- Comparison between the present work and the previous work.
- Human vision scale (to avoid visual attack), message can be embedded in a cover image in such a manner that it is imperceptible to the human eye(Fig. 11).

- Security, if the attacker gets the hint of a hidden message in the cover image, even then he must not be able to extract it and use it for his personal gain.

Before Encryption   After Encryption

Fig. 11. Comparison between Images before and after encryption

Considering the above criterions our algorithm was found to be quite satisfactory since as relevant from the Fig. 11, the distortion in the image after undergoing the data embedding is negligible and due the features like spreading the data and variable bit embedding, the extraction of data by an unintended receiver is also quite difficult.

5   Future Prospects

In our algorithm we will like to modify certain things which includes using of asymmetric key instead of using symmetric key during pixel selection and we will try to embed secret message bits in image formats other than bitmap as well .Also we will try make our algorithm compatible for Video Steganography[8] and Audio Steganography[5] as well .Also we will try to reduce the distortion in the image when asymmetric keys will be used in our algorithm.

6   Conclusion

Steganography has its place in security. It is not intended to replace cryptography but supplement it. Hiding a message with Steganography method reduces the chance of a message being detected. However, if that message is also encrypted, if discovered, it must also be cracked (yet another layer of protection). In this work we have tried to develop a new algorithm for Steganography and the main objective of the algorithm is not only to hide the data but also to make sure that the data remains hidden and even if by some means an attacker get to know about the presence of data in the cover image even then he must not get the message itself.

References

1. The Wiki (2008), http://www.en.wikipedia.org/wiki/Steganography
2. Chandramouli, R., Memon, N.: Analysis of LSB based image steganography techniques. In: Proc. of ICIP, Thessaloniki, Greece (2001)

3. The Wikipedia,
   http://www.en.wikipedia.org/wiki/Steganography_tools
4. http://www.ims.nus.edu.sg/Programs/imgsci/files/memon/sing_s
   tego.pdf
5. Johnson, N.F., Duric, Z., Jaljodia, S.: Information Hiding – Steganography and
   Watermarking – Attacks and counter measures, USA (2001)
6. The Gary Kessler, http://www.garykessler.net/library/crypto.html
7. The Difference between,
   http://www.differencebetween.com/difference-between-
   cryptography-and-vs-steganography/
8. The Connect geeks, http://www.connectgeeks.com/?p=589

Survey on Key Pre Distribution for Security in Wireless Sensor Networks

T.P. Rani[1] and C. Jaya Kumar[2]

[1] Faculty, Department of Information Technology, Sri Sairam Engineering College
Sai Leo nagar, west Tambaram Chennai-44
ranitp.2010@gmail.com
[2] Faculty, Department of Computer Science and Engineering, R.M.K. Engineering College
Kavarapettai, Chennai
Cjayakumar2007@gmail.com

Abstract. Wireless sensor networks (WSNs) consists of small nodes with constrained capabilities to sense, collect, and disseminate information in many types of applications. As sensor networks become wide-spread, security issues become a central concern. In this paper, we identify the Security requirements of key management in WSN. The secure management of the keys is one of the most critical elements when integrating cryptographic functions into a system. An outline of hybrid cryptography, one way hash and Key infection schemes are discussed in this paper. Along the way we analyze the advantages and disadvantages of current secure schemes. Finally, we aim to provide efficient key management operations for secure communications in WSN.

Keywords: Security, Key management, Wireless Sensor Networks.

1   Inroduction

Sensors are inexpensive, low-power devices which have limited resources [1]-[2]. They are small in size, and have wireless Communication capability within short distances. A sensor node typically contains a power unit, a sensing unit, a processing unit, a storage unit, and a wireless transmitter / receiver. A wireless sensor network (WSN) is composed of large number of sensor nodes with limited power, computation, storage and communication capabilities. In recent years, major advances have been made in the development of low-power micro sensor nodes. The emergence of such sensor nodes has allowed practitioners to envision networking a large set of nodes scattered over a wide area of interest into a wireless sensor networks (WSNs) [1] for Large-scale event monitoring and data collection and filtering. So when WSNs are deployed in a hostile management plays a central role in data encryption and authentication. The prime problem in key management is to establish the secure keys between the sensor nodes. This problem is known as the key agreement problem.

Key agreement protocol of WSNs includes three types in the existing schemes: trusted server, public key, and key predistribution.

N. Meghanathan et al. (Eds.): CCSIT 2012, Part I, LNICST 84, pp. 248–252, 2012.
© Institute for Computer Sciences, Social Informatics and Telecommunications Engineering 2012

1)   Third Party Trusted Server protocols depend on a trusted server (also called a base station) for key agreement between the sensor nodes.

2)   Public-key Cryptography requires a public-key infrastructure that would impose additional computational costs as well as increased storage requirements. However, the limited computational and communication resources of nodes make it infeasible to use public-key protocols in WSN.

3)   Key pre-distribution: The third strategy to establish the   secret keys is key predistribution, where keys are distributed to all sensor nodes prior to deployment. Such schemes are proved to be most appropriate for WSNs

2   Key Management

The Sensor nodes cannot practically use a third party trusted server because of the high communication cost and deployment cost. The Public Key protocols involve high computation cost. Hence the Symmetric Key Cryptography involving is considered to be the better method of cryptography system in WSN. Sensor network dynamic structure, easy node compromise and self organization property increase the difficulty of key management and bring a broad research issues in this area. Due to the importance and difficulty of key management in WSNs, there are a large number of approaches focused on this area. Based on the main technique that these proposals used or the special structure of WSNs, we classify the current proposals as key predistribution schemes, hybrid cryptography schemes, one way hash schemes, key infection schemes, and key management in hierarchy networks, though some schemes combine several techniques.

A. KEY PRE-DISTRIBUTION SCHEMES

In the key predistribution schemes, sensor nodes store some initial keys before they are deployed. After deployed, the sensor nodes can use the initial keys to setup secure communication. This method can ease key management especially for sensor nodes that have limited resource.

Two types of key predistribution schemes suited for WSNs have been developed: random key predistribution and deterministic key predistribution.

1) Random Key Predistribution

According to this scheme, each sensor node receives a different random subset of keys from a large key pool as the node's key ring before deployment and then stores the key ring in its memory [3]-[5]. After sensor nodes have been deployed in the designated area, secure direct communication between two nodes requires that they share at least one common key.

2) Deterministic Key Predistribution

Combinatorial designs [6]-[9] are applied to key predistribution. They presented two classes of combinatorial designs. The combinatorial designs are associated with the distinct key identifiers and nodes, respectively. Though the probability of key establishment has been increased, this scheme is limited in network resiliency and network size.

B.HYBRID CRYPTOGRAPHY SCHEMES

Though most framework use one type of cryptography, there still exist some schemes that use both asymmetric-key and symmetric-key cryptographs. For example, a hybrid scheme proposed by Huang[11], balances public key cryptography computations in the base station side and symmetric key cryptography computation in sensors side in order to obtain adorable system performance and facilitate key management. On one hand, they reduce the computation intensive elliptic curve scalar multiplication of a random point at the sensor side, and use symmetric key cryptographic operations instead On the other hand; it authenticates the two identities based on elliptic curve implicit certificates, solving the key distribution and storage problems, which are typical bottlenecks in pure symmetric-key based protocols.

C. ONE WAY HASH SCHEMES

To ease key management, many approaches use the one-way key method that comes from one-way hash function technique. For example, Zachary[12] propose a group security mechanism based on one-way accumulators that utilizes a pre-deployment process, quasicommutative property of one-way accumulators and broadcast communication to maintain the secrecy of the group membership. Another group security mechanism proposed by Dutta, also use one-way function to ease group node joining or revocation. Their scheme has self-healing feature, a good property that makes the qualified users recover lost session keys over a lossy mobile network on their own from the broadcast packets and some private information, without requesting additional transmission from the group manager. The one-way hash function can also adapt to conduct public key authentication. To ease the joining and revocation issues of membership in broadcast or group encryption, many approaches use predistribution and/or a local collaboration technique.

D.KEY INFECTION SCHEME

Contrary to most of key management using pre-loaded initial keys, Anderson[13], propose a key infection mechanism. In a key infection scheme, different from key pre-distribution schemes, no predistribution key is stored in sensor nodes. This type of schemes establishes secure link keys by broadcasting plaintext information first. This type of schemes is not secure essentially. However, Anderson, show that their key infection scheme is still secure enough for non- critical commodity sensor networks after identifying a more realistic attacker model that is applicable to these sensor networks. Their protocol is based on the assumption that the number of adversary devices in the network at the time of key establishment is very small.

E. KEY MANAGEMENT IN HIERARCHY NETWORKS

In this type of key management, some use the physical hierarchical structure of networks, while others implement their hierarchy key management logically in physical flat structure sensor networks[14], which only include a base station and sensors. For example, LKHW (Logical Key Hierarchy for Wireless sensor networks), proposed by Pietro [16]-[18], integrates directed diffusion and LKH (Logical Key Hierarchy) where keys are logically distributed in a tree rooted at the key distribution center

(KDC). A key distribution center maintains a key tree that will be used for group key updates and distribution, and every sensor only stores its keys on its key path, i.e. the path from the leaf node up to the root. In order to efficiently achieve confidential and authentication, they apply LKHW: directed diffusion sources are treated as multicast group members, whereas the sink is treated as the KDC.

3   Conclusion

Thus, we provide features of various key management schemes for establishing secure communication in a wireless sensor network .Security can be accomplished by adapting the type of Key Management based on the environment of WSN. In this paper, efficient cryptographic techniques have been proposed which ensures confidentiality, authenticity, availability and integrity of wireless sensor network that are deployed in hostile environment. Since key management plays a major role in encryption and authentication various schemes have been summarized by us. We have presented a nearly comprehensive survey of security researches in wireless sensor networks.

References

[1] Akyildiz, I., Su, W., Sankarasubramaniam, Y., Cayirci, E.: A survey on sensor networks. IEEE Commun. Mag. 40(8), 102–114 (2002)
[2] Perrig, A., Szewczyk, R., Wen, V., Culler, D., Tygar, J.D.: SPINS: Security protocols for sensor networks. Wireless Netw. 8(5), 521–534 (2002)
[3] Eschenauer, L., Gligor, V.D.: A key-management scheme for distributed sensor networks. In: Proc. 9th ACM Conf. Comput. Commun. Secur., New York, USA, pp. 41–47 (2002)
[4] Chan, H.W., Perrig, A., Song, D.: Key distribution techniques for sensor networks. Wireless Sensor Networks (2004)
[5] Chan, H.W., Perrig, A., Song, D.: Random key predistribution schemes for sensor networks. In: Proc. IEEE Symp. Res. Secur. Privacy, pp. 197–213 (2003)
[6] Du, W., Deng, J., Han, Y.S., Varshney, P.K., Katz, J., Khalili, A.: A pairwise key predistribution scheme for wireless sensor networks. ACM Trans. Inf. Syst. Secur. 8(2), 228–258 (2005)
[7] Blom, R.: An optimal class of symmetric key generation systems. In: Proc. EURORYPT 1984 Workshop Adv. Cryptol.: Theory Appl. Cryptographic Tech., pp. 335–338 (1985)
[8] Liu, D.G., Ning, P., Li, R.F.: Establishing pairwise keys in distributed sensor net-works. ACM Trans. Inf. Syst. Secur. 8(1), 41–77 (2005)
[9] Çamtepe, S.A., Yener, B.: Combinatorial Design of Key Distribution Mechanisms for Wireless Sensor Network. In: Samarati, P., Ryan, P.Y.A., Gollmann, D., Molva, R. (eds.) ESORICS 2004. LNCS, vol. 3193, pp. 293–308. Springer, Heidelberg (2004)
[10] Chakrabarti, D., Maitra, S., Roy, B.: A Key Predistribution Scheme for Wireless Sensor Networks: Merging Blocks in Combinatorial Design. In: Zhou, J., López, J., Deng, R.H., Bao, F. (eds.) ISC 2005. LNCS, vol. 3650, pp. 89–103. Springer, Heidelberg (2005)

[11] Huang, Q., Cukier, J., Kobayashi, H., Liu, B., Zhang, J.: Fast authenticated key establishment protocols for self-organizing sensor networks. In: Proc. 2nd ACM International Conf. Wireless Sensor Networks Applications, pp. 141–150 (2003)
[12] Zachary, J.: A decentralized approach to secure group membership testing in distributed sensor networks. In: Proc. IEEE Military Commun. Conf. (2003)
[13] Anderson, R., Chan, H., Perrig, A.: Key infection: Smart trust for smart dust. In: Proc. 12th IEEE International Conf. Network Protocols (ICNP) (2004)
[14] Eltoweissy, M., Younis, M., Ghumman, K.: Lightweight key management for wireless sensor networks. In: Proc. IEEE International Conf. Performance, Computing, Commun., pp. 813–818 (2004)
[15] Shi, E., Perrig, A.: Designing secure sensor networks. IEEE Commun. Mag. 11, 38–43 (2004)
[16] Djenouri, D., Khelladi, L., Badache, N.: A survey of security issues in mobile ad hoc and sensor networks. IEEE Commun. Surveys Tutorials 7, 2–28 (2005)
[17] Wang, Y., Attebury, G., Ramamurthy, B.: A survey of security issues in wireless sen-sor networks. IEEE Commun. Surveys Tutorials 8, 2–23 (2006)
[18] Carman, D.W., Kruus, P.S., Matt, B.J.: Constraints and approaches for distributed sensor network security, NAI Labs Technical Report (2000)

A Link Distance Ratio Based Stable Multicast Routing Protocol for Mobile Ad Hoc Networks

Natarajan Meghanathan

Jackson State University
Jackson, MS 39217, USA
nmeghanathan@jsums.edu

Abstract. We present the design and development of a new multicast routing protocol, referred to as the Multicast Link Distance Ratio (MLDR) routing protocol, which yields stable trees with longer lifetime and without incurring any substantial increase in the number of edges and the hop count per source-receiver path. The proposed multicast protocol is based on the idea of assigning each link a weight, called the Link Distance Ratio (LDR), corresponding to the ratio of the actual physical Euclidean distance between the constituent nodes of the link to that of the maximum transmission range per node. The multicast tree construction procedure of MLDR focuses on discovering source-receiver paths that have the lowest sum of the LDR values of the constituent links. An aggregate of all such source-receiver paths yields the MLDR multicast tree. The lifetime of MLDR multicast trees is 25% - 63% longer than that of the well-known minimum hop based Multicast Ad hoc On demand Distance Vector (MAODV) routing protocol and at the same time the number of edges per tree and hop count per source-receiver path are slightly larger than that of MAODV, by factors of 11% and 8% respectively.

Keywords: Multicasting, Routing Protocol, Link Distance Ratio, Simulation, Stability, Mobile Ad hoc Networks

1   Introduction

A Mobile Ad hoc Network (MANET) refers to wireless networks whose topology dynamically changes with time owing to node mobility, bandwidth and energy constraints. MANETs are deployed for military, mission-critical, disaster-relief and emergency management applications. One characteristic nature of all of these applications is one-to-many communication, referred to as multicast, between the participating nodes. Multicasting can be more formally defined as the communication between a source node and a set of receiver nodes, the latter constituting what is called a multicast group. The source node need not be a member of the multicast group, as is the case in this paper. MANET multicasting is done via a tree or a mesh, determined in an on-demand fashion (i.e., only when a source node has data to be sent to the receiver nodes of the multicast group) through a global broadcast query-reply cycle, often called flooding. A multicast tree connects the source node to all of the

N. Meghanathan et al. (Eds.): CCSIT 2012, Part I, LNICST 84, pp. 253–262, 2012.

receiver nodes of the group such that there is exactly one path between the source node and each of the receiver nodes; some receiver nodes could also end up serving as intermediate nodes of the multicast tree. A multicast mesh connects the source node to the receiver nodes such that there are often more than one source-receiver paths. A multicast mesh is typically an extended multicast tree wherein all the links that exist among the tree nodes are considered to be part of the mesh.

Multicast trees are considered more efficient with respect to link usage, bandwidth and energy consumption as only one copy of the data packet reaches each receiver node of the multicast group and there are no redundant transmissions, unlike meshes. However, a multicast tree is considered broken even if one of the constituent links of the tree is broken. Frequently reconfiguring a communication structure using flooding is an expensive operation in MANETs, owing to their resource constraints. The advantage with meshes is that they are more robust to link failures and provide prolonged connectivity between the source node and the receiver nodes without requiring to be frequently rediscovered. But, there will be redundant transmissions of data packets through more than one path from the source to each receiver node.

The motivation for this research is to determine stable multicast trees that exist for a relatively longer time so that the number of tree discoveries in the network can be minimized and at the same time the link efficiency advantage with trees is retained. Multicast trees have been traditionally determined to be minimum-hop trees connecting the source node with each of the receiver nodes through minimum hop paths. When we analyze for the critical factors that trigger link failures (leading to tree failures) in such minimum hop-based multicast trees, the edge effect [6] has been observed to be a significant factor. In order to connect the source and receiver nodes with the minimum number of hops, the number of intermediate nodes added to the source-receiver path is as minimal as possible; however, this leads to a longer physical distance between the constituent end nodes of the links. As a result, for any given link on a minimum-hop path, the probability that the two end nodes of the link would move away from the transmission range of each other at any time is quite high. To counter the edge effect problem, it would be more prudent to construct the source-receiver paths by including those links whose constituent end nodes are not close to the boundary of the transmission range of each other. Accordingly, we define the Link Distance Ratio as the ratio of the physical Euclidean distance separating the two end nodes of a link and the transmission range of the nodes. Smaller the LDR value, we conjecture the link will be more stable. Likewise, a path with the minimum sum of the LDR values of the constituent links is likely to be more stable than minimum hop paths. This forms the hypothesis of our paper and our hypothesis has been proven to be correct through extensive simulation analysis.

The rest of the paper is organized as follows: Section 2 discusses related work. Section 3 describes in detail, the working of the proposed LDR-based stable multicast routing protocol (MLDR), including the packet structures and the sequence of different phases of tree construction and maintenance. Section 4 describes the simulation environment and presents the simulation results obtained when the MLDR is implemented and run in the ns-2 simulator [7]. We also compare the performance of MLDR with the well-known minimum-hop based Multicast Ad hoc On-demand Distance Vector (MAODV) routing protocol [9]. Section 5 concludes the paper and also outlines future work planned for extending our research on MLDR.

2   Related Work

In this section, we discuss related work in the literature on signal strength based routing in conjunction with stable path routing. The Signal Stability-based Adaptive (SSA) unicast routing protocol [1] characterizes the MANET links into two classes: strong and weak links. Nodes are required to periodically exchange beacons in the neighborhood. The network operates with two thresholds for signal strength: threshold for strong links P_{th}^{strong} and threshold for signal reception P_{th}^{rec}, with P_{th}^{strong} > P_{th}^{rec}. If the strength of beacon signal received from a neighbor node exceeds P_{th}^{strong}, then a node categorizes the link with the neighbor as a strong link. If the strength of the beacon is below P_{th}^{strong}; but above P_{th}^{rec}, the link is characterized as a weak link. SSA attempts to discover a stable route comprising only of strong links and if not successful, determines a route considering all the links in the network.

The Route-lifetime Assessment Based Routing (RABR) unicast protocol [2] works by computing a metric called "link affinity" for each link based on the average change in the signal strength of the beacons received within a time window during the recent past. If the average change in the signal strength is positive, then the nodes are assumed to be approaching each other and the affinity of the link is assigned to a high value (theoretically, ∞). If the average change in the signal strength is negative, then the affinity value of the link is the ratio computed by dividing the difference between the minimum threshold for the signal strength required for a link between two nodes to exist and the signal strength of the most recently received beacon with the average change in the signal strength. The affinity value for a path is the minimum of the affinity values of its constituent links.

In [5], the authors propose a signal strength-estimate driven stable path routing protocol wherein the estimated signal strength of the Route Request (RREQ) packets is recorded in the RREQ packets itself at each forwarding node. The estimated signal strength of a path is the minimum of the estimated signal strength of the constituent links on the path as included by the forwarding nodes. The destination chooses the path with the largest estimated signal strength and sends back a Route Reply (RREP) packet on the chosen path. A similar Min-Max approach for stable path routing based on the predicted link expiration time (LET) has been proposed in [3] and [4].

3   Design of the Multicast Link Distance Ratio (LDR)-Based Routing Protocol

The objective of the multicast link distance ratio (MLDR) based routing protocol for MANETs is to determine stable multicast trees that have a longer lifetime and at the same time incur a minimal increase in the number of edges per tree and hop count per source-receiver paths as part of the tree. The key assumptions behind the design and working of MLDR are as follows: (i) MLDR assumes the network is homogeneous in nature and that all nodes operate with an identical and fixed transmission range; (ii) MLDR requires nodes to periodically exchange beacons in the neighborhood so that a node can estimate the distance between itself and each of its neighbors by measuring the strength of the signal received from the neighbor. The signal propagation model used is the "two-ray ground reflection" model [8]; (iii) The Link Distance Ratio (LDR) is computed as the distance between a node and its neighbor node divided by the transmission range of the nodes. At any moment, every node maintains a LDR-table comprising of estimates of the LDR values to each neighbor node based on the latest beacons received from the node; (iv) The LDR of a path is sum of the LDR values of the constituent links of the path and (v) An aggregate of all the paths, with the least sum of the LDR values, connecting a source node to the receiver nodes leads to the desired stable multicast tree.

3.1   Propagation of the Multicast Tree Request (MTREQ) Messages

When a source node has data to send to the multicast group and is not aware of the next hop downstream nodes that are part of the multicast tree, the source node broadcasts a Multicast Tree Request (MTREQ) message to all of its neighbors as an attempt to reach out to the receiver nodes of the multicast group. The structure of the MTREQ message is shown in Figure 1. The sequence number field is used to avoid any loops in the broadcast of the MTREQ message and is a monotonically increasing quantity, incremented by 1, for every MTREQ message originating from the particular source node. The Route Record field stores the IDs of nodes through which the message has propagated, starting from the source node. The Link Distance Ratio field stores the cumulative value (sum of the LDR values) of the constituent links through which the MTREQ has propagated, starting from the source node. The source node initializes the LDR value in the MTREQ message to zero and inserts its own ID in the Route Record field. When an intermediate node receives a MTREQ message of a particular broadcast tree construction process (identified using a combination of the Source Node ID and the Sequence Number fields) for the first time, the intermediate node updates the LDR value in the MTREQ by adding to it the LDR value of its link to the upstream neighbor node from which the message was received. The intermediate node then inserts its node ID to the Route Record field and the MTREQ message is further broadcast to all the neighbor nodes. When an intermediate node receives a MTREQ message that it has already seen, the message is dropped.

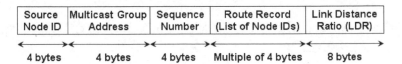

Fig. 1. Structure of the Multicast Tree Request (MTREQ) Message

3.2   Route Selection and Propagation of Multicast Tree Reply (MTREP) Messages

When a member node (of the multicast group) receives a MTREQ message for a particular broadcast multicast tree construction process, the node updates the LDR value in the message by adding to it the LDR value of the link to the upstream node from which the message was received. After waiting for a certain amount of time to receive the MTREQ messages from one or more paths, the node selects the MTREQ message that has the minimum LDR value. The receiver node then generates a Multicast Tree Reply (MTREP) message (shown in Figure 2) that propagates on the reverse path of the sequence of node IDs listed in the Route Record field of the chosen MTREQ message. The MTREP message propagates from the receiver member node to the source node of the multicast process.

Source Node ID	Originating Receiver	Multicast Group Address	Sequence Number	Route Record (List of Node IDs)	Link Distance Ratio (LDR)
4 bytes	4 bytes	4 bytes	4 bytes	Multiple of 4 bytes	8 bytes

Fig. 2. Structure of the Multicast Tree Reply (MTREP) Message

When the MTREP message reaches an intermediate node, the intermediate node checks whether it has an entry for the *<Source Node ID, Multicast Group Address>* in its multicast routing table, which is an ordered entry of *<key, value>* pairs, where the *<key>* is the tuple *<Source Node ID, Multicast Group Address, MTREP Sequence Number>* and the *<value>* is the tuple *<Upstream Node, List of Downstream Nodes>*. The structure of the multicast routing table maintained at an intermediate node is shown in Figure 3. The *Upstream Node* and the *List of Downstream Nodes* are part of the multicast tree rooted at the Source Node ID. After the *<key>* part of the multicast route entry is properly created or updated based on the most recent value of the MTREP Sequence Number, the intermediate node updates the *<value>* part of the multicast route entry by including the neighbor node from which the MTREP message was received into the *List of the Downstream Nodes* and the next hop neighbor node (that has been listed as the next hop node on the Route Record from the receiver node towards the source node) is included as the *Upstream Node*. If the *Upstream Node* is already listed in the multicast route entry, the MTREP message is just dropped and not forwarded as it would be only tracing a sub-path of the already established optimal path from the intermediate node to the source node. If the next hop neighbor node has been just then updated as the *Upstream Node* in the multicast routing table, the intermediate node sends the MTREP message to that upstream node.

Key			Value	
Source Node ID	Multicast Group Address	MTREP Sequence Number	Upstream Node ID	List of Downstream Nodes

Fig. 3. Structure of the Multicast Routing Table at an Intermediate Node

The source node maintains a multicast routing table of *<key, value>* pairs, where the *<key>* is the tuple *<Multicast Group Address, MTREQ-MTREP Sequence Number>* of the latest tree discovery process; the *<value>* is the *List of Downstream Nodes* that includes the neighbor nodes that sent it the MTREP messages.

3.3   Multicast Tree Acquisition, Data Transmission and Maintenance

After broadcasting the MTREQ messages, the source node waits for a certain time, called the Tree Acquisition Time, to receive the MTREP messages (originating from the multicast group members) through one or more neighbor nodes. If no MTREP message is received within the Tree Acquisition Time, the source node broadcasts the next MTREQ message (Sequence Number incremented by 1) to its neighborhood. If one or more MTREP messages are received within the Tree Acquisition Time, the source node starts transmitting the data packets through the multicast tree established as part of the MTREQ-MTREP cycle. After the first successful tree discovery procedure, the Tree Acquisition Time is dynamically reset depending on the time incurred to receive the MTREP messages from the multicast member nodes.

A multicast tree is broken even if one of the constituent links of the tree is broken. When an intermediate node could not forward a data packet to even of its downstream nodes in the tree, the intermediate node generates a Multicast Tree Error (MTERR) message and sends it to the source node of the multicast session. In this pursuit, the intermediate node sends the MTERR message (structure shown in Figure 4) to the immediate upstream node in its routing table entry for the particular source and multicast group address. The entry is also then removed from the table. The above process is repeated at every intermediate node (starting from the upstream node of the broken link all the way to the source node) in the tree, as the MTERR message propagates all the way back to the source node. The multicast routing table entries at nodes starting from the downstream node of the broken link, all the way to one or more receiver nodes of the multicast group, are flushed during the propagation of the MTREP message as part of the next broadcast tree construction process.

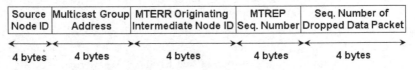

Source Node ID	Multicast Group Address	MTERR Originating Intermediate Node ID	MTREP Seq. Number	Seq. Number of Dropped Data Packet
4 bytes	4 bytes	4 bytes	4 bytes	4 bytes

Fig. 4. Structure of the Multicast Tree Error Message (MTERR)

4   Simulations

The performance of MLDR has been compared with that of the well-known minimum-hop based Multicast Extension of the Ad hoc On-demand Distance Vector (MAODV) routing protocol [9]. We implemented both the multicast routing protocols (MLDR and MAODV) in the ns-2 simulator (v. 2.32) [7]. The network dimensions are 1000m x 1000m. The transmission range per node is 250m and is the same for all the nodes in the network. The network density is varied by conducting simulations with 50 nodes (low density) and 100 nodes (high density). The nodes are initially assumed to be uniform-randomly distributed in the network.

Nodes move according to the Random Waypoint mobility model [10] with each node moving independent of the other nodes in the network. A node starts moving from an arbitrary location to a randomly chosen destination location within the range [0...1000m, 0...1000m], and moves to the chosen location at a speed uniform-randomly chosen from the range [0,..., v_{max}] where v_{max} represents the maximum node velocity. The v_{max} values used in the simulations are 5 m/s, 25 m/s and 50 m/s representing scenarios of low, moderate and high node mobility respectively. Pause time is 0 seconds. For a given condition of network density and v_{max} values, 5 different mobility profiles were generated. Simulation time is 1000 seconds.

Simulations are conducted with a multicast group size of 3 (small size) and 18 (larger size) receiver nodes. The source node is not part of the multicast group. For each group, we generated 10 lists of receiver nodes and conducted simulations with each of these 10 lists. So, basically, 10*5 = 50 multicast session simulations were run for every combination of network density, mobility (v_{max}) and multicast group size values. Each data point in the plots for the performance metrics illustrated in Figures 5 through 7 are an average of the metric values obtained for these 50 simulations. The traffic model assumed is Constant Bit Rate (CBR); the size of the data packets is 512 bytes and the source sends 4 data packets per second to the multicast group.

The performance metrics evaluated through the simulations are the following:

- **Lifetime per Multicast Tree:** For every multicast tree used during the simulation session, we keep track of the duration the tree exists. The lifetime per multicast tree is the average value of the duration of the multicast trees, over the entire simulation time, across all the simulation conditions corresponding to a particular combination of network density, node mobility and multicast group size.
- **Number of Edges per Multicast Tree:** This is the time averaged value of the number of edges in the multicast trees discovered and used over the entire simulation session (i.e., taking into consideration the duration of the trees).
- **Hop Count per Source-Receiver Path:** This is the time averaged value of the hop count of the paths from the source node to each of the receiver nodes of the multicast group, computed over the entire multicast simulation session.

4.1   Lifetime per Multicast Tree

For a fixed multicast group size, as the node velocity increases, the gain in the multicast tree lifetime incurred with MLDR over MAODV, decreases. However still, the lifetime of multicast trees incurred with MLDR is at least 25% more than that of the lifetime per multicast tree determined using MAODV. Thus, MLDR yields stable multicast trees compared to the minimum hop based well-known MAODV under all the simulation conditions tested. For a given v_{max}, the gain in the lifetime of multicast tree determined using MLDR compared to MAODV increases with multicast group size. For a given group size, the lifetime per multicast tree determined using both MLDR and MAODV decrease with increase in the v_{max} value. For a given v_{max} value, the multicast tree lifetime for both protocols decreased with increase in group size.

For a fixed v_{max} value and multicast group size, the lifetime per multicast tree determined using MLDR decreases slightly when the network density is doubled. The lifetime of MAODV multicast trees decreases rather more aggressively when the network density is doubled. In the case of both MLDR and MAODV, for fixed node mobility, the decrease in the multicast tree lifetime with increase in network density is more dominant when the multicast group size is larger. But, for both the protocols, for fixed multicast group size, the decrease in the multicast tree lifetime with increase in network density is more dominant in the presence of low node mobility (v_{max} = 5 m/s).

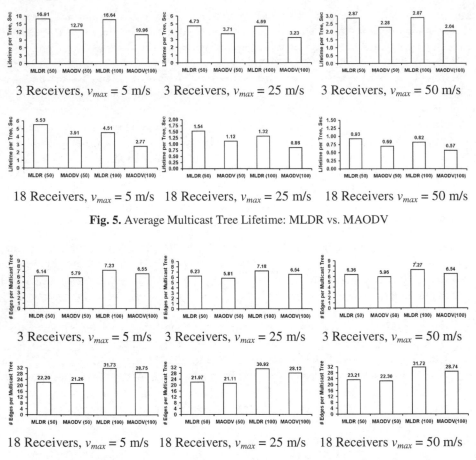

Fig. 5. Average Multicast Tree Lifetime: MLDR vs. MAODV

Fig. 6. Average Number of Edges per Multicast Tree: MLDR vs. MAODV

4.2   Number of Edges per Multicast Tree

The tradeoff that we observe for the gain obtained with multicast tree lifetime is a slight increase in the number of edges per multicast tree determined using MLDR compared to that of MAODV. But, the increase is very minimal and when considered over all the simulation conditions, the increase in the number of edges is not beyond 11%. Actually, for low-density networks the difference in the number of edges incurred by the multicast trees of both the protocols is not beyond 7%. For a fixed multicast group size and v_{max} value, both MAODV and MLDR incur lot more edges when operated in networks of high density (100 nodes) compared to that of low density (50 nodes). This can be attributed to the larger connectivity obtained in high-density networks and to connect the multicast source nodes to all the receiver nodes at the maximum percentage of connectivity, more edges are required. For larger multicast group sizes, there is a larger increase in the number of edges per multicast tree with increase in network density. For a given multicast group size, the number of edges incurred by both the MLDR and MAODV multicast trees does not significantly change with node mobility. The increase in the number of edges per multicast tree with increase in the multicast group size is sub-linear and actually the rate of increase in the number of edges gets reduced for larger values of multicast group sizes.

4.3   Hop Count per Source-Receiver Path

The tradeoff that we observe for the gain obtained with multicast tree lifetime is a slight increase in the hop count per source-receiver path on the multicast trees determined using MLDR compared to that of MAODV. But, the increase is very minimal and when considered over all the simulation conditions, the increase in the hop count per source-receiver path is not beyond 8%. Actually, for low-density networks the difference in the hop count per source-receiver path incurred with the multicast trees determined using MLDR and MAODV is not beyond 5%. For a given multicast group size, the hop count per source-receiver path incurred for the multicast trees determined using both MLDR and MAODV does not significantly change with node mobility. For fixed multicast group sizes and maximum node velocity, the hop count per source-receiver paths on the multicast trees slightly increase with increase in network density.

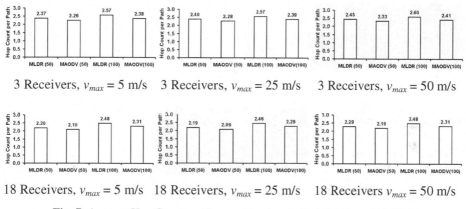

3 Receivers, v_{max} = 5 m/s   3 Receivers, v_{max} = 25 m/s   3 Receivers, v_{max} = 50 m/s

18 Receivers, v_{max} = 5 m/s 18 Receivers, v_{max} = 25 m/s   18 Receivers v_{max} = 50 m/s

Fig. 7. Average Hop Count per Source-Receiver Path: MLDR vs. MAODV

5   Conclusions and Future Work

Stability of the communication structures is critical to reduce the control overhead of the MANET routing protocols. In this pursuit, we have proposed a stable multicast routing protocol based on the Link Distance Ration (MLDR). The LDR of a link is the ratio of the distance between the constituent end nodes of the link and the transmission range per node. MLDR connects the source node to each of the receiver nodes of the multicast group through paths that have the lowest sum of the LDR values of the constituent links. MLDR has been observed to yield a 23-62% longer lifetime than the well-known minimum hop based MAODV routing protocol. At the same time, MLDR does not incur any significantly higher values for the number of edges per tree (at most 11% more edges) and the hop count per source-receiver path (at most larger by 8%), compared to those incurred with MAODV. MLDR requires periodic beacon exchange in the 1-hop neighborhood of nodes and this is a commonly used mechanism in MANETs for nodes to learn about their neighbor nodes. MLDR does not require any additional information to be included in these beacon messages. As part of future work, we intend to study the performance of MLDR, MAODV and some of the other stability-based multicast routing protocols under different mobility models [11] for ad hoc networks.

References

1. Dube, R., Rais, C.D., Wang, K., Tripathi, S.K.: Signal Stability-based Adaptive Routing for Ad hoc Mobile Networks. IEEE Personal Communications, 36–45 (1997)
2. Agarwal, S., Ahuja, A., Singh, J.P., Shorey, R.: Route-lifetime Assessment Based Routing Protocol for Mobile Ad hoc Networks. In: International Conference on Communications, vol. 3, pp. 1697–1701. IEEE, New Orleans (2000)
3. Su, W., Lee, S.-J., Gerla, M.: Mobility Prediction and Routing in Ad hoc Wireless Networks. International Journal of Network Management 11(1), 3–30 (2001)
4. Meghanathan, N., Thomas, D., Addison, E.S.: Multicast Extensions to the Flow-Oriented Routing Protocol and Node Velocity-based Stable Path Routing Protocol for Mobile Ad hoc Networks. In: International Conference on Ultra Modern Telecommunications and Workshops, St. Petersburg, Russia (2009)
5. Mamoun, M.H.: A Novel Technique for the Route Selection in DSR Routing Protocol. International Journal of Video and Image Processing and Network Security 11(3), 1–4 (2011)
6. Jiang, S., He, D., Rao, J.: A Prediction-based Link Availability Estimation for Mobile Ad hoc Networks. IEEE Transactions on Networking 13(6), 1302–1312 (2005)
7. Fall, K., Varadhan, K.: NS Notes and Documentation. The VINT Project at LBL, Xerox PARC, UCB, and USC/ISI (2001), http://www.isi.edu/nsnam/ns
8. Goldsmith, A.: Wireless Communications. Cambridge University Press (2005)
9. Royer, E., Perkins, C.E.: Multicast Operation of the Ad hoc On-demand Distance Vector Routing Protocol. In: The 5th International Conference on Mobile Computing and Networking, pp. 207–218. ACM, Seattle (1999)
10. Bettstetter, C., Hartenstein, H., Perez-Costa, X.: Stochastic Properties of the Random-Way Point Mobility Model. Wireless Networks 10(5), 555–567 (2004)
11. Camp, T., Boleng, J., Davies, V.: A Survey of Mobility Models for Ad hoc Network Research. Wireless Communication and Mobile Computing 2(5), 483–502 (2002)

A New Security Solution Architecture (SSA) for MANETS against Network Layer Attacks

G.S. Mamatha

Department of Information Science and Engineering, R.V. College of Engineering,
Bangalore, India
Mamatha.niranjan@gmail.com

Abstract. Mobile Ad hoc Networks (MANETS) are a group of large autonomous wireless nodes communicating on a peer-to-peer basis in a heterogeneous environment with no pre-defined infrastructure. The special characteristics of MANETS make them highly susceptible to security attacks than the wired networks. The paper presents a novel Security Solution Architecture (SSA) which is used to evaluate the newly proposed protocol, report on the behaviour of MANETS against attacks and then accomplished with the corrective measures to avoid malicious nodes in the routes. Our security solution architecture presented here mainly concentrates on security levels, security attacks and evaluation procedures for SSA.

Keywords: MANETS, Security, Attacks, SSA, Level, TODV.

1 Introduction

The salient characteristics of MANETS, such as broadcast radio channels, lack of central authority, lack of association, limited resources availability, physical vulnerability etc;, makes such networks highly vulnerable to security attacks when compared with wired, infrastructure-based wireless networks and even normal ad hoc networks. The paper concentrates on coming out with security solution architecture with an encryption technique to safe guard the data. In any of the systems, one cannot expect the three components I.e. providing security, detection and correction and recovery for transmission to be present; consequently, dealing with an infrastructure-less MANETS will be a dilemma, yet the approach presented for each of these components is independent in nature, providing unusual solutions for each one of them but concentrating mainly on the detection and correction category using a newly proposed protocol TODV (Time On Demand Distance Vector). The contributions of this paper are threefold. First, we define a *MANETS Security Solution Architecture (SSA)*. The proposed security solution architecture is a comprehension model which strives to provide end-to-end security for not only MANETS, but all kind of wireless networks for predicting, detecting and correcting security vulnerabilities that may be faced during data communications. As a main step to SSA, it identifies the required security requirements based on their objectives and also describes how they can be applied to MANETS and also taking in to account the types of network layer attacks they may face in networking sessions. Second, realization of different levels applied to SSA and illustration of the security requirements confined to these levels such as

N. Meghanathan et al. (Eds.): CCSIT 2012, Part I, LNICST 84, pp. 263–271, 2012.

authentication, availability, data confidentiality and data integrity. The proposed protocol TODV is illustrated to show how it selects the route for communication. The novel combination of ACK, PFC (Principle of flow conservation) and TODV is applied to one of the levels to ensure high security against threats. Through the real time simulation we can test the performance of the proposed security mechanism and demonstrate its effectiveness. Our architecture strives to provide a new novel security protocol that provides a high level of secure, available, scalable, flexible and efficient management services for MANETS. The third contribution is realizing the security attacks which lies within the detection component, which is represented by intentionally launching an attack and identification of the type of attack. This mechanism will be useful to detect malicious nodes which try to bring the system down. The approach presented in the paper as a part of detection level and correction levels can also be applied by varying the network density to study the impact of performance which is validated using an attacks case.

In this paper the proposed SSA for MANETS provides a comprehensive, end-to-end security solution that could be applied to every wireless network that satisfies the MANETS requirements. This solution allows us to predict, detect and correct security vulnerabilities that any system might face. The paper is organized as follows: in section 2 the MANETS Security Architecture is proposed. The security solution architecture identifies the newly proposed novel protocol TODV, security requirements, and security levels and proposes an end-to-end security solution for MANETS. Section 3 shows the security attacks the system might face. Section 4 shows the security solution in tabular form. Section 5 explains evaluation of SSA. In Section 6, the conclusions will be drawn.

2   Security Solution Architecture (SSA)

It becomes very crucial to consider security along with the design of the system, rather it should be considered as an inseparable aspect in the development of the system as it is learnt from the history of security attacks [1]. This criterion makes the proposed security architecture design to address the global security challenges of consumers, users, services and other applications. In order to prevent any type of attacks, external or internal, passive or active, a set of requirements must be identified in MANETS as shown in Figure 1.

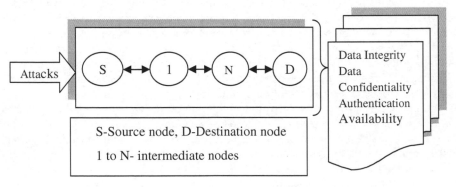

Fig. 1. Security Architecture for MANETS

2.1   Security Requirements

A set of security requirements are used to address and measure a particular aspect of network security, which is governed by a specific set of security policies. In the mentioned security architecture 4 major requirements that protect the MANETS against all major network layer security threats have been addresses; these requirements are:

- *Authentication* is one of the security measures which reveal the correct identity to both the communicating parties. The verification of communicating parties' identity is a must to confirm that the right parties are on the line.
- *Availability measure ensures* that entities, services and resources are available against all kinds of attack.
- *Data Confidentiality* measure means that the messages or packets are secured from any unauthorized access. Using this kind of security measure it can be easily understood that the information cannot reach the unauthenticated nodes. This can be achieved by applying any of the available encryption techniques.
- *Data Integrity* measure ensures that the messages are unaltered during any communication. The data in communication is protected against unauthorized modification, deletion, creation and replication.

The security requirements illustration is highly important to show how they can protect our system against all major security threats, to provide a comprehensive, end-to-end security solution for MANETS.

2.2   Network Security Levels

The proposed MANETS solution is logically separated into 4 architectural components called network security levels. The OSI [2] model which is useful in designing network protocols is a good example to follow in designing security protocols. This type of component architecture can provide advantages such as modularity, simplicity, flexibility and standardization of protocols. Figure 2 depicts the four network security architecture levels for MANETS, which are built upon one another to provide a network-based solution. The functionality of each level is explained belowDisplayed equations or formulas are centered and set on a separate line (with an extra line or halfline space above and below).

Network Topological Level: The level represents a fundamental building block of the network, consisting of the basic connections between nodes. The first node selected for communication becomes the source node and all the nodes in the middle till they reach the destined node will be the intermediate nodes. The node mentioned in the packet header of the source node will be the destination node. All these nodes identity will be shown clearly using the topological information with indicating the nodes with different colors. This level outlines our assumptions regarding the properties of the physical and network layers. Throughout this paper, an assumption is

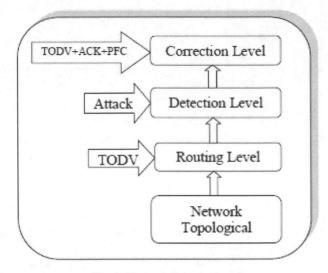

Fig. 2. Network Security Levels

made for bidirectional communication. Such symmetry of links is needed for the transmission of the designed ACK packets. Our scheme works with on demand routing protocols, such as the proposed TODV (Time on Demand Distance Vector Protocol), AODV [3] [4]. Further assumption is made that there will be no collusion among misbehaving nodes. A panel will be selected in the terrain area of the simulation environment which displays the number of nodes across the area randomly with incorporated mobility feature. This particular level incorporates the *availability* security requirement feature, with network available for communication as and when needed.

Routing Level: The routing level consists of basic transports and connectivity security mechanisms applied to routing protocols as well as the individual nodes. Every node in the ad hoc network acts as host and router and henceforth the considered solution is not different from that perspective. Moreover, nodes must exchange information about their neighbors to construct the network topology in order to apply any of the ad hoc routing protocols (Proactive, Reactive and Hybrid) [5]. All the nodes in the network must participate in the routing activity, which makes the network connected. Routing security level involves two aspects: secure routing and secure data forwarding. In secure routing all the nodes should cooperate in order to share correct routing information, thus keeping the network connected efficiently, whereas in secure data forwarding, data packets must be protected from message tampering, eavesdropping, and replicating by any of the unauthenticated party [6]. This marks as a route discovery phase in the architecture level and is carried in accordance with the data forwarding protocol employed. In this proposed architecture, a newly proposed on demand protocol TODV (Time On Demand Distance vector) loosely based on AODV is suitable because, TODV is a hop-by-hop routing protocol, which introduces a more dynamic strategy to discover and repair route on the par to other on-demand protocols. Instead of destination sequence numbers as in AODV, here we have time concept applied based on first come first served basis. The employed protocol TODV strives to maintain only needed routes in order to reduce the network overheads and to control the network traffic. This situation is applicable for network scenarios where mobility and density are having a moderate picture [7]. The explanation of TODV protocol is as follows:

A slighter modification to the existing AODV protocol has been considered in this paper. The RREQ carries Source Identifier (SID), Destination Identifier (DID) and a Route Node Collection packet (RNC). The SID denotes the source address, DID denotes the destination address and the RNC packet contains the intermediate node IDs address through number of hops as shown in figure 3. That is the RNC packet gives the route definition with total number of hops defined to every node it has visited. As mentioned earlier the limit for RREQ is 3 set for any of the source node, which starts flooding RREQs through the network. Once the RREQ reaches every node, it checks the DID with itself and if not matched forwards further to the next neighboring nodes. In this modified protocol version the RNC packet has different route node collection information. Every node maintains route information about the neighboring nodes. Every RREQ to a destination node generates a Route Reply (RRPLY) packet. The RRPLY packet contains a SID, DID and a RNC packet. Here the notations change, as the SID denotes the destination node address, DID refer to the source node address and RNC again gives the route information it has collected through the RREQ process. In RRPLY DID takes data from RNC to which node it has to pass the RRPLY until it reaches source node. The RRPLY will come from different routes to source node. The first come first served basis is applied here instead of considering the destination sequence number concept. The RRPLY which arrives first, means which takes minimum time to reach source node will be the shortest path in that instance of time; this is because the MANET topology is dynamic in nature. To count the time of every RRPLY that arrives back to source node a clock will be set at the chosen source node. As the next step the path chosen will be considered for data communication between source and destination nodes. Parallely the other alternative routes possible will also be maintained in database, in case if first route is proved to be malicious.

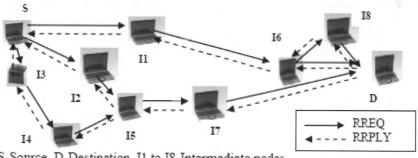

S-Source, D-Destination, I1 to I8-Intermediate nodes
Consider RREQ1 from S to I1:
RREQ1: (SID, DID, RNC= ({S⟶I1⟶D}, 3Hops))
RREQ1: (SID, DID, RNC= ({S⟶I1⟶I6⟶D}, 4Hops))
RRPLY1: ((DID, SID), {D⟶I6⟶I1⟶S})
RRPLY1: ((DID, SID), {D⟶I8⟶I6⟶I1⟶S})

Fig. 3. A Scenario of MANET showing the contents of RNC Packet

Detection Level: This level outlines the detection procedure proposed according to the architecture and levels presented in figure 1and 2 respectively. At first the route discovery will be done and then the packets in the information will be get divided in to 48 bytes each. With the fields like SID, DID, the original message with decryption algorithm details, which is protected and can be extracted only when the DID matches with node having the same DID and encrypted message the data frame is constructed. The encrypted information can be accessed by all the intermediate nodes that appear in the route selected for communication. A simple encryption method with replacement of characters by the next alphabet is employed in the proposed detection level of the architecture. In order to count the number of sent packets and number of missed/received packets two counters have been kept at sender node (Cpkt and Cmiss). If the adversary tries to tamper the message, even a small change will be reflected when comparing with the original message at the destination node. Once the data reaches destination, the addresses are matched and only then the fields in the data frame are extracted by the receiver node and decrypts it with the information available in one of the fields in the extracted header. Then the decrypted message is matched with the original message sent. In case both the messages matches, then destination node prepares an acknowledgement frame with an "ACK" field and sends back to the sender through the same intermediate nodes. Such nodes can be called genuine nodes. Else the data frame with "CONFIDENTIALITY LOST" field is sent back to the sender node and indicates the tampering of message. Such a link reveals that an intermediate node is acting as an adversary. Then the RTT (round trip time) is calculated as the difference between the end and starting time of data forwarding for each of the messages sent in milliseconds [7]. The current level mentions the three of the security requirements, authentication, and data integrity and data confidentiality. If there is a violation in these requirements as the next step a corrective measure is taken to identify the type of attacks and choose an alternative link in the correction level.

Correction Level: A time limit for RTT is set to 20ms or more according to the application. If the sender node gets the acknowledgement back exceeding the time limit, it indicates of packet losS. On the other end of the sender node parallely a counter to keep track of lost packets (Cmiss) is kept and incremented if an acknowledgement reaches exceeding time limit. The procedure is repeated for all the data packets sent. Later based on the principle of flow conservation a ratio of Cmiss/Cpkt will be calculated [8]. The threshold value for evaluating the ratio is set to 20% (0.2) called limit of tolerance ratio. The route chosen is evaluated for the ratio after completing the transmission. If the ratio exceeds the limit set then it is said to be misbehaving link. The further communication happens by choosing the alternative link available in the data base within few milliseconds. If sender finds the "CONFIDENTIALITY LOST" field in the acknowledgement frame then it comes to know about the malicious node from the routing table information which has tampered the message, maintained by the sender node. Such links which exceeds limit of tolerance ratio and has the above information in their acknowledgement is discarded for further session [7].

3   Network Security Attacks

The security plays a vital role in ad hoc wireless networks, especially in military applications. The lack of any central association makes MANETS more vulnerable to attacks than wired networks. Consequently, the network security attacks in MANETS are generally divided into two broad categories, namely, Passive and Active attacks. A passive attack refers to the attempts that are made by malicious nodes to perceive the nature of activities and to obtain information transacted in the network without disrupting the operation. For example, eavesdropping, active interference, leakage of secret information, data tempering, impersonation, message replay, message distortion and denial of service. Detection of passive attacks is complicated, since the network operation is not affected. One good solution to overcome such problems is through encryption methods, encrypting the data being transmitted, thereby making it hard for eavesdroppers to gain any active information from the data being transmitted. An active attack refers to the attacks that attempt to alter, inject, delete or destroy the data being exchanged in the network. These attacks can be prevented by using regular security mechanisms such as encryption techniques and firewalls. Internal attacks are more serious and difficult to detect than external ones. The brief descriptions of some of the main active attacks known in most networks [9, 10, 11, 12, 13 and 14] [15] are described in the paper [16]. The attacks that occur in the network layer, when several types of attacks are mounted on the routing protocols which are aimed at disrupting the operation of the network. Some of the major routing layer attacks are described briefly in the paper [16].

4   Evaluation of SSA

The section mainly discusses the methodology used to evaluate the performance of the proposed security mechanism of SSA. It explains the different evaluation metrics and the simulation environment used to test them, as shown in Figure 4. The behavior of the SSA in real time simulation network environments needs to be tested, the overhead caused by the proposed security protocol is to be measured and the time

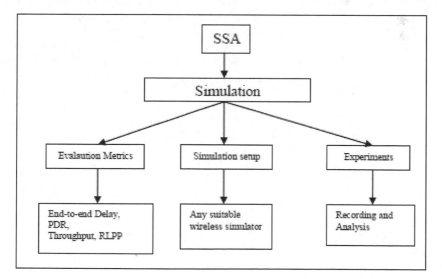

Fig. 4. Evaluation of SSA

needed to perform successful simulation without attacks is to be calculated. Therefore, a suitable network simulator must be chosen to provide the communication performance of the proposed security mechanism. This section will justify the application of the real time simulator used and developed at the par to standard simulators to simulate the security mechanism, as well as showing how the simulation environment is set, what are the simulation metrics and the network metrics used to measure performances [15].

5   Conclusion

Designing a clear line of defence in MANETS is a very tough task. Herewith we have come with a possible security solution in the form of architecture known as SSA. This SSA fulfils some of the main security requirements as we mentioned, further it can be extended to more also. The security and encryption mechanisms can also be varied according to the simulation environments. We are also ensuring that the protocol mentioned namely TODV also works at the par to satisfy the MANET requirements. As a next step to towards the research work simulation experiments are to be conducted and tested with results. This ensures that the proposed architecture guarantees the security objectives for MANETS.

References

1. Chandra, P.: Bulletproof Wireless Security GSM, UMTS, 802.11 and Ad Hoc Security. Elsevier (2005)
2. Carrieri, E., Rpcchini, C.A., Fioretti, A., Haylett, A.J.: An OSI Compatible Architecture for Integrated Multichannel Metropolitan and Regional Networks. In: Integrating Research, Industry and Education in Energy and Communicational Engineering, MELECON 1989, Mediterranean, April 11-13, pp. 639–643 (1989)
3. Capkun, S., Hubaux, J., Buttyan, L.: Mobility helps security in ad hoc networks. In: Proceedings of ACM Symposium on Mobile Ad Hoc Networking and Computing (June 2003)
4. Capkun, S., Hubaux, J., Buttyan, L.: Mobility helps peer-to-peer security. IEEE Transactions on Mobile Computing 5(1), 43–51 (2006)
5. Royer, E.M.: A Review of Current Routing Protocols for Ad Hoc Mobile Wireless Networks. IEEE Personal communication, 46–55 (April 1999)
6. Perkins, C.E., Royer, E.M.: Ad-hoc on-demand distance vector routing Mobile Computing Systems and Applications. In Proceedings IEEE Workshop, WMCSA 1999, February 25-26, pp. 90–100 (1999)
7. Mamatha, G.S., Sharma, S.C.: A Highly Secured Approach against Attacks in MANETS. International Journal of Computer Theory and Engineering 2(5) (October 2010)
8. Oscar, F.G., Ansa, G.W., Howarth, M., Paylou, G.: Detection and Accusation of Packet Forwarding Misbehavior in Mobile Ad hoc networks. Journal of Internet Engineering 2, 1 (2008)
9. Al Jaroodi, J.: Security Issues in wireless mobile ad hoc networks. Technical Report TR02-10-07, University of Nebraska-Lincoln (2002)

10. Siva Ram Murthy, C., Manoj, B.S.: Ad Hoc wireless networks, architecture and Protocols. Prentice hall communications, Engineering and Emerging technologies series, Upper Saddle River (2004)
11. Fokine, K.: Key Management in Ad Hoc Networks. Master Thesis, Linkping University (2002)
12. Mishra, A., Nadkarni, K.: Security in wireless ad hoc networks. In: Hand Book of Ad Hoc Networks, pp. 479–490. CRC Press, FL (2003)
13. Fei, X., Wenye, W.: Understanding Dynamic DoS Attacks in Mobile ad hoc Networks. In: Proceedings of MILCOM, pp. 1–7 (October 2006)
14. Wen-Guey, T.: A secure fault-tolerant conference-key agreement protocol. IEEE Transactions on Computers 51(4), 373–379 (2002)
15. Al-Bayatti, A.H.: Security Management for Mobile Ad Hoc Network of Networks (MANON). Thesis presented (February 2009)
16. Mamatha, G.S., Sharma, S.C.: Network Layer Attacks and Defense Mechanisms in MANETS- A Survey. International Journal of Computer Applications (0975 – 8887) 9(9) (November 2010)

Analysis of Different Associative Memory Neural Network for GPS/INS Data Fusion

S. Angel Deborah

Abstract. Aircraft navigation relies mainly on Global Positioning System (GPS) to provide accurate position values consistently. However, GPS receivers may encounter frequent GPS outages within urban areas where satellite signals are blocked. To overcome this drawback generally GPS is integrated with inertial sensors mounted inside the vehicle to provide a reliable navigation solution. Inertial Navigation System (INS) and GPS are commonly integrated using a Kalman filter (KF) to provide a robust navigation solution, overcoming situations of GPS satellite signals blockage. This work presents New Position Update Architecture (NPUA) for GPS and INS data integration. The NPUA has an Artificial Neural Network (ANN) block that uses Associative memoy Neural Networks like Bidirectional Associative Memory Neural Network (BAM-NN) and Hetero Associative memory Neural Network (HAM-NN). The performances of GPS/INS data integration are computed by using HAM-NN and BAM-NN. The performances of both networks are analysed using real time data in terms of Mean Square Error (MSE), Performance Index (PI), Number of Epochs and Accuracy. It is found that HAM is better than BAM in terms of accuracy, MSE, and PI whereas BAM is better than HAM in terms of Number of epochs.

Keywords: HAM-NN, BAM-NN, GPS, INS, KF, ANN, DR.

1 Introduction

1.1 Global Positioning System

The Global Positioning System (GPS) is part of a satellite-based navigation system developed by the U.S. Department of Defense under its NAVSTAR Satellite program. The fully operational GPS includes 24 or 28 active satellites approximately uniformly dispersed around six circular orbits with four or more satellites each. Theoretically, three or more GPS satellites will always be visible from most points on the earth's surface, and four or more GPS satellites can be used to determine an observer's position anywhere on the earth's surface 24 hours per day [14]. The GPS is accurate and the accuracy does not degrade with time but still it suffers from its own drawbacks and errors. It uses the energy of the radio waves for obtaining the navigation parameters hence it is prone to jamming. Also the signal may get obstructed in urban areas due to tall buildings and other obstacles [2]. GPS provides three positional components. The three positional components are along the East direction (corresponding to the vehicle's longitude), the North direction (corresponding to the vehicle's latitude) and the vertical direction (corresponding to the vehicle altitude h).

N. Meghanathan et al. (Eds.): CCSIT 2012, Part I, LNICST 84, pp. 272–284, 2012.

1.2 Inertial Navigation System

An Inertial Navigation System (INS) is a self-contained system that integrates three acceleration and three angular velocity components with respect to time and transforms them into the navigation frame to deliver position, velocity, and attitude components [2]. The three orthogonal linear accelerations are continuously measured through three-axis accelerometers while three gyroscopes monitor the three orthogonal angular rates in an inertial frame of reference. In general, inertial measuring unit (IMU), which incorporates three-axis accelerometers and three-axis gyroscopes, can be used as positioning and attitude monitoring devices. However, INS cannot operate appropriately as a stand-alone navigation system. The presence of residual bias errors in both the accelerometers and the gyroscopes, which can only be modeled as stochastic processes, may deteriorate the long-term positioning accuracy. Therefore, the INS/GPS integration is the adequate solution to provide a vehicular navigation system that has superior performance in comparison with either a GPS or an INS stand-alone system.

1.3 Existing INS/GPS Data Fusion Techniques

In order to overcome the problems associated with the operation of GPS and INS on their own, the two systems are integrated together so that the drawbacks associated with each system are eliminated. The INS/GPS data integration is commonly performed in real time using a Kalman filter (KF) [10]. This method requires a dynamic model of both INS and GPS errors, a stochastic model of the inertial sensor errors, and *a priori* information about the covariances of the data provided by both systems. Data fusion employing a KF has been widely used and is considered the benchmark for INS/GPS integration [11].

There are, however, several considerable drawbacks to its use [10]. These include the following: (1) the necessity of accurate stochastic modeling, which may not be possible in the case of low cost and tactical grade sensors; (2) the requirement for *a priori* information of the system and measurement covariance matrices for each new sensor, which could be challenging to accurately determine; (3) relatively poor accuracy during long GPS outages; (4) the weak observability of some of the error states that may lead to unstable estimates of other error states ; and (5) the necessity to tune the parameters of the stochastic model and the *a priori* information for each new sensor system. The above drawbacks can be overcome by using intelligent networks or Artificial Neural Networks (ANN) ([3], [4]). Other than Kalman filter there are also number of paper works related to GPS and INS data integration using soft computing techniques. GPS and INS data integration has been performed using Radial Basis Function Neural Network, Back Propagation Neural Network and Fuzzy system.

Radial Basis Function Neural Network (RBF-NN) generally has simpler architecture and faster training procedure than multi- layer perceptron neural networks ([1], [2], [6], [8], [10]). Though it has simple architecture and faster training procedure, it only has fixed topology, so it lacks dynamicity. Back Propagation Neural Network is one of the Multi-Layer Feed Forward Networks. Although it has batch update of weight which provides smoothing effect on the weight correction terms it only has fixed topology, so it lacks dynamicity ([1], [5]). It also consumes longer training time for complex problems. Fuzzy system can also be used to integrate

GPS and INS data but it does not have much learning capability [7]. It cannot examine all input and output for complex problems. It needs human operator to tune fuzzy rules and membership function.

1.4   Proposed GPS/INS Data Fusion Technique

The proposed data fusion technique introduces New Position Update Architecture (NPUA) which involves Artificial Neural Network in it. It is derived from the concept of Position Update Architecture (PUA) [5]. The NPUA can act in both prediction mode and training mode.

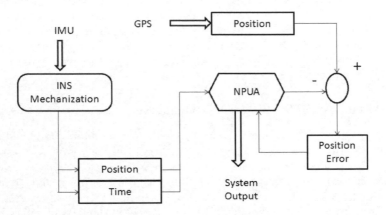

Fig. 1. System Configuration of Proposed Scheme

The NPUA receives input like position and time through INS Mechanization. Desired outputs are provided by the system in training mode when there is no GPS blockage with the help of the appropriate training algorithm. During the training mode of NPUA the initial error is stored the network. When there is GPS signal blockage, the system output operates in prediction mode. During the prediction mode of NPUA , the system makes use of the initial error stored and thereby predicts the accurate position values. The proposed system configuration is shown in Figure 1. The HAM-NN and BAM-NN are used in NPUA.

2   Neural Networks Used in GPS/INS Data Fusion

There are many different types of ANN according to its inherent structure and learning algorithms. The choice of the type of ANN depends on its suitability to a particular application. In this work, HAM-NN and BAM-NN have been implemented using Delta Learning Rule (DR).

2.1   Hetero Associative Memory Neural Network

Associative memory neural networks are networks in which the weights are determined in such a way that the net can store a set of P pattern associations.

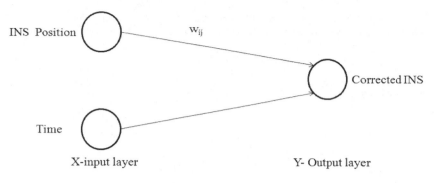

Fig. 2. GPS/INS Data Fusion using HAM

Hetero associative networks are static networks. No non-linear or delay operations can be done using hetero associative networks. The weights may be found using the Hebb rule or the delta rule. Hetero Associative Memory Neural Network is a Two - layer network with input and output layer. The design of a HAM-NN in its most basic form consists of two separate layers as shown in Figure 2 is used in GPS/INS data fusion.

It consists of only one layer of weighted interconnections. There exist 'n' number of input neuron in input layer and 'm' number of output neurons in the output layer. The training process is based on the Hebb learning rule. This is a fully inter-connected network, wherein the inputs and the output are different, hence it is called a hetero associative network.

2.2   Application Algorithm for HAM

The weights of the network are obtained using the training algorithm. These weights are used along with the testing data and the performance of the network is tested by applying the following application procedure ([12], [13]). The application procedure of a hetero associative net is as follows:

Step 1: Weights are initialized using Hebb or delta rule.
Step 2: For each input vector do steps 3 to 5.
Step 3: Set the activation for input layer units equal to the current vector x_i.
Step 4: Compute net input to the output units

$$Y\text{-}inj = \Sigma\ xiwij \tag{1}$$

Step 5: Determine the activation of the output unit.

The simple and frequently used method for determining the weights for an associative memory neural network is Hebb rule(HR). The other learning rule that can be used Associative memory is Delta Learning Rule (DR). The algorithm for DR is as follows:

Step 1: Initialize all weight to random values.
Step 2: For each training input-target output vector, do steps 3-5.
Step 3: Set activations for input units to present training input.

Step 4: Set activations for output units to current target output.
Step 5: Adjust the weights.

$$wij(new) = wij(old) + \Delta w \qquad (2)$$

Weight correction

$$\Delta w = \alpha(tj - y\ inj)xi \qquad (3)$$

Where i= 1 to n, j= 1 to m
   t- target vector,
   y_{inj} – actual output vector
   α- learning rate.

2.3   Bidirectional Associative Memory Neural Network

BAM-NN is a hetero associative recurrent neural network consisting of two layers. The net iterates by sending a signal back and forth between the two layers until each neuron's activations remains constant for several steps ([9], [15]).

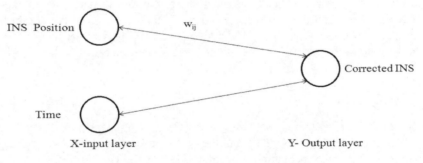

Fig. 3. GPS/INS Data Fusion using BAM

The hetero associative BAM network has 'n' units in X-layer and 'm' units in the Y-layer. The connections between the layers are bidirectional i.e. if the weight matrix for signals sent from the X-layer to Y-layer is W, the weight matrix for signal sent from Y-layer to X-layer is W^T . The architecture is shown in figure 3 is used in GPS/INS data fusion.The weights are adjusted between X-layer to Y-layer and also from Y-layer and X-layer.

2.4   Application Algorithm for BAM

The application procedure of bi-directional memory net is as follows:

Step 1: Initialize all weight to store a set of P vectors. Initialize all activations to 0.
Step 2: For each training input-target output vector, do steps 3-8.
Step 3: Set activation of X-layer to current input pattern.
Step 4: Input pattern y is presented to the Y-layer.

Step 5: While activations are not converged follow steps 6-8.
Step 6: Activation unit in Y-layer and net input are computed.

$$\text{Net Input, } y_{-inj} = \sum_i w_{ij} x_i \qquad (4)$$

$$\text{Activation } y_i = f(y_{-inj}) \qquad (5)$$

Send signals to the X-layer.
Step 7: Update activation unit in X-layer.

$$\text{Net input, } x_{-inj} = \sum_i w_{ij}^T y_j \qquad (5)$$

$$\text{Activations } x_i = f(x_{-inj}) \qquad (6)$$

Send signals to the Y-layer
Step 8: Test for convergence.

3   Simulation Results

3.1   Experimental Setup

In this experiment, the training mode and prediction mode of HAM-NN and BAM-NN were utilized in NPUA. During the presence of GPS signal, the proposed system relies on GPS position information to train the network. During the training stage, the HAM-NN module and is trained to mimic the latest vehicle dynamic, determine the INS position error, and correct the corresponding INS position component. The data is processed as follows: first, the INS and GPS signals are taken as input vector and target vector respectively. The INS position and time are then used as the input to HAM-NN and BAM-NN respectively. Then training is done until the output nearly equals the target GPS position. The training procedure continues working until GPS signal blockage is detected. When blockage is detected, the proposed system works in the prediction mode where the HAM-NN module and BAM-NN module predicts the corresponding INS position error based on the knowledge stored during the training procedures. Then with the help of the INS position error obtained during the training mode the corresponding corrected INS position is obtained during the absence of GPS, i.e, during the prediction mode.

3.2   Simulation Results

GPS position value is used as target vector value and INS position value is used as input vector in Mat lab. By training the HAM-NN module and BAM-NN module for latitude component figure 4 and 5 are obtained. In figure 4 and 5 latitude component is taken as x-axis and time is taken as y-axis. By comparing the actual output and target output the weight values all ANN values are updated using DR. Further the training is done if the actual output is not closely equal to the required target output. After each epoch the weight values are updated. The training proceeds until the stopping condition is reached. The stopping conditions can be number of epochs or minimum error.

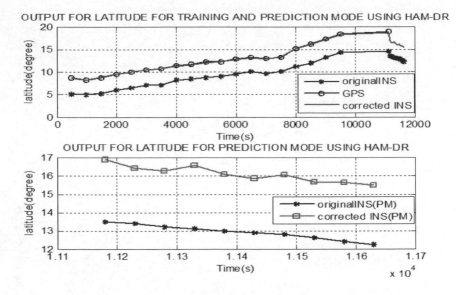

Fig. 4. Output of latitude component using HAM-NN

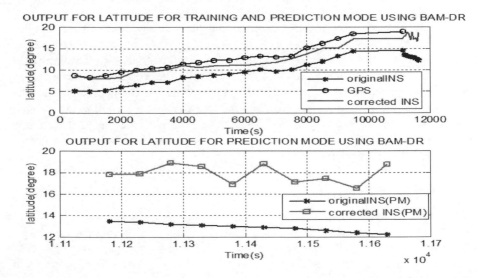

Fig. 5. Output of latitude component using BAM-NN

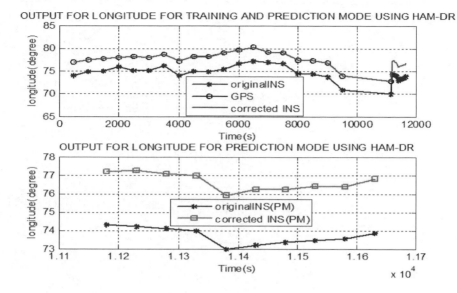

Fig. 6. Output of longitude component using HAM-NN

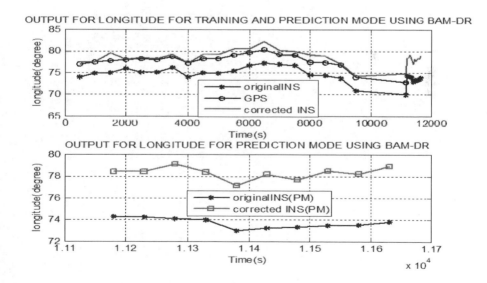

Fig. 7. Output of longitude component using BAM-NN

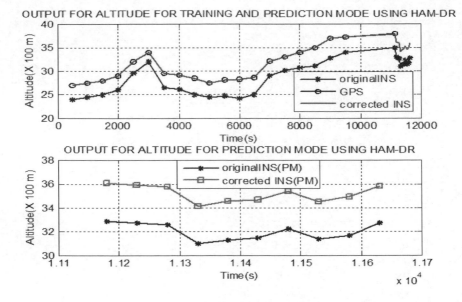

Fig. 8. Output of altitude component using HAM-NN

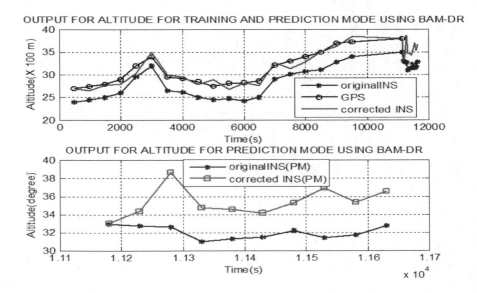

Fig. 9. Output of altitude component using BAM-NN

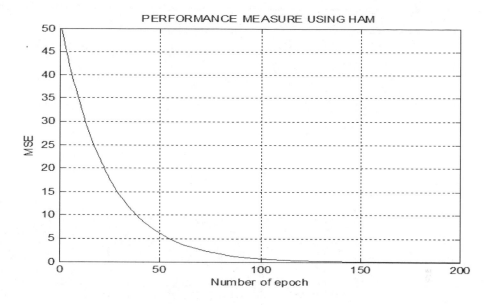

Fig. 10. HAM Performance for latitude component using TM

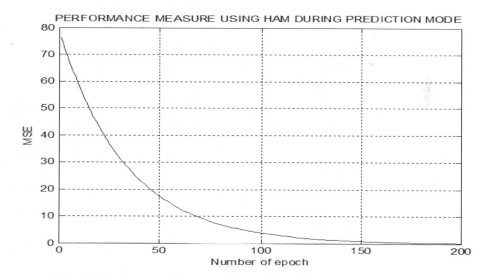

Fig. 11. HAM Performance for latitude component using PM

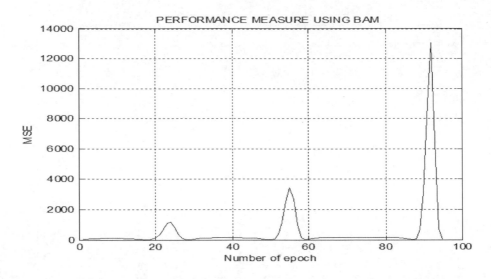

Fig. 12. BAM Performance for latitude component using TM

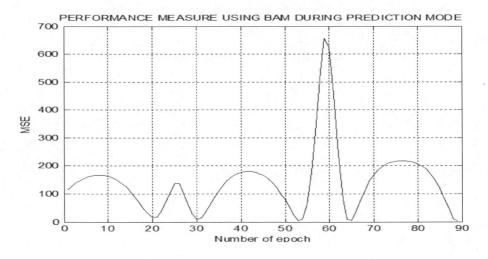

Fig. 13. BAM Performance for latitude component using PM

Similar to latitude component, the longitude component and altitude component is trained using HAM-NN, BAM-NN by choosing the appropriate weight factor and same learning rate value as used for latitude component. The output of longitude and altitude component obtained using HAM-NN and BAM-NN are given in figure 6, 7, 8 and 9 respectively. After each and every epoch error between the original GPS position   and corrected INS are calculated in both ANN modules.

Table 1. Numerical values of analysis

Criteria	HAM-NN (TM)	HAM-NN (PM)	BAM-NN (TM)	BAM-NN (PM)
Latitude MSE	0.0096	0.1859	1.4105	2.5449
Longitude MSE	0.0010	0.0048	1.1411	2.9511
Altitude MSE	0.0012	0.0031	0.9534	2.6700
Latitude PI	0.0053	0.0074	0.1120	0.1543
Longitude PI	$2.999e^{-5}$	$3.0297e^{-5}$	0.0147	0.0385
Altitude PI	$4.0645e^{-5}$	$4.9147e^{-5}$	0.0306	0.0759
Latitude NE	200	200	95	89
Longitude NE	12	10	6	6
Altitude NE	49	49	14	15

The mean square error value for each epoch is also calculated. The mean square error graphs using HAM and BAM for latitude component are given in figure 10, 11, 12, 13, respectively. In these graphs number of epochs is taken as x-axis and MSE value is taken as y-axis. The MSE, PI and Number of Epochs for all the three components are given in Table 1. In HAM-NN, it is found that more number of epochs is needed when compared to that of BAM-NN. Whereas BAM-NN is less accurate when compared to HAM-NN. It is also found that as the number of epochs increases the actual output i.e., CINS value of ANN training comes closer to the target output i.e., GPS value.

4 Conclusion

Thus from the results it was found that INS and GPS data Fusion can be performed by using Associative memory NN. HAM-NN using DR gives higher accuracy in both Training Mode (TM) and Prediction Mode (PM) when compared to BAM-NN using DR. Similarly HAM-NN using DR gives lesser MSE value in both Training Mode (TM) and Prediction Mode (PM) when compared to BAM-NN using DR. In terms of Performance Index (PI), HAM-NN using DR has lesser PI value, whereas BAM-NN using DR has higher PI value than PI values of HAM-NN using DR. Only the neural network lesser PI value can show better performance, so it can be found that HAM-NN using DR is better in terms of performance. Though HAM-NN using DR is good in terms of MSE, PI and accuracy, but it consumes more number of epochs. Thus, by considering MSE, PI and accuracy, it can be concluded that HAM-NN using DR can be used to fuse GPS and INS data. If the data fusion system requires lesser number of epochs, BAM-NN using DR can be used to fuse GPS and INS data.

References

1. Malleswaran, M., Vaidehi, V., Manjula, S., Angel Deborah, S.: Performance comparison of HONNs and FFNNs in GPS and INS integration for vehicular navigation. In: International Conference on Recent Trends in Information Technology (ICRTIT), 223–228. IEEE Xplore (June 2011)

2. Malleswaran, M., Vaidehi, V., Angel Deborah, S., Manjula, S.: Integration of INS and GPS Using Radial Basis Function Neural Networks for Vehicular Navigation. In: 11th International Conference on Control, Automation, Robotics and Vision, Singapore, December 5-8, pp. 2427–2430. IEEE Xplore (2010)

3. Chiang, K.W., Noureldin, A., El-Sheimy, N.: Constructive Neural-Networks-Based MEMS/GPS Integration Scheme. IEEE Transactions on Aerospace and Electronics Systems 44(2), 582–594 (2008)

4. Huang, Y.-W., Chiang, K.W.: An Intelligent and autonomous MEMS IMU/GPS integration scheme for low cost land navigattion applications. In: GPS Solutions, vol. 12, pp. 135–146. Springer, Heidelberg (2008)

5. Chiang, K.W., Huang, Y.W.: An intelligent navigator for seamless INS/GPS integrated land vehicle navigation application. Applied Soft Computing 8, 722–733 (2008)

6. Sharaf, R., Noureldin, A.: Sensor Integration for Satellite-Based Vehicular Navigation Using Neural Networks. IEEE Transactions on Neural Networks 18(2) (March 2007)

7. Wang, J.-H., Gao, Y.: The Aiding of MEMS INS/GPS Integration Using Artificial Intelligence for Land Vehicle Navigation. IAENG International Journal of Computer Science 33(1), IJCS_33_1_11 (February 2007)

8. Sharaf, R., Noureldin, A., Osman, A., EI-Sheimy, N.: Online INS/GPS Integration with a Radial Basis Function Neural Network. IEEE Systems Magazine 20(3), 8–14 (2005)

9. Singh, Y.P., Yadav, V.S., Gupta, A., Khare, A.: Bi-Directional Associative Memory Neural Network Method in the character recognition. Journal of Theoritical and Applied Information Technology, 382–386 (2005)

10. Sharaf, R., Noureldin, A., Osman, A., EI-Sheimy, N.: INS/GPS Data Fusion Technique Utilizing Radial Basis Functions Neural Networks. IEEE Xplore (2004)

11. Hosteller, L., Andreas, R.: Nonlinear Kalman filtering techniques for terrain-aided navigation. IEEE Transactions on Automatic Control 28(3), 315–323 (1983)

12. Sivanandam, S.N., Sumathi, S., Deepa, S.N.: Introduction to Neural Networks Using Matlab 6.0. Tata McGraw-Hill publication

13. Kumar, S.: Neural Networks: A Classroom Approach. Tata McGraw Hill publication (2004)

14. Tsui, J.B.-Y.: Fundamentals of Global Positioning System Receivers: A Software Approach. John Wiley and Sons Publication (2000)

15. Hagan, Demuth, Beale: Neural Network Design. Cengage Learning India edn. (1996)

Handover Latency Measurement of Mobile IPv6 in a Testbed Environment

Muhammad Arif Amin, Kamalrulnizam Bin Abu Bakar,
Abdul Hanan Abdullah, Mahesh Nair, and Rashid Hafeez Khokhar

Universiti Teknologi Malaysia, Johor, 81310 Skudai, Malaysia
mamin@hct.ac.ae
http://www.hct.ac.ae

Abstract. The emergence of wireless networking necessitates continuous time connectivity to support end-to-end TCP or UDP sessions. Wireless networking does not provide reliable connections to mobile users for real-time traffic such as voice over IP, audio streaming and video streaming. Handover latency in Mobile IPv6 poses many challenges to the research world in terms of disconnecting users while roaming. Many efforts have been made to reduce the handover latency with focus either on layer 2 or layer 3. This paper presents the handover procedure of Mobile IPv6 and investigates various factors affecting the delay during network switch over. In this paper, a testbed environment is presented that includes two different wireless LAN networks using Universal Mobile IP for Linux (UMIP) implementation and Cisco routers. The aim is to present handover latency caused by multiple signals at layer 2 and layer 3 and make recommendations on how to reduce the total handover latency experienced by the MIPv6 protocol.

Keywords: Handover, IPv6, WLAN, Mobile IPv4, Mobile IPv6.

1 Introduction

The exponential growth of wireless devices in the last few years demand continuous connectivity to the Internet. Mobile users require constant communication with others while moving from one place to another. To be able to reach others during motion, a node must have a unique public Internet Protocol (IP) address so that the traffic can be sent to others [1]. IP version 4 (IPv4) was originally proposed in the late '70s and was capable of allocating 32-bit addresses, which in total could provide approximately 4.3 billion addresses in the world. Since private IPv4 addresses does not follow the Internet hierarchy for address allocation, therefore it does not allow all the nodes to communicate on the Internet. To provide mobility to fixed nodes with IPv4, mobile IPv4 protocol [2] was introduced. However, due to the address space restriction, the protocol failed to gain popularity in the Internet world. The address space restriction in IPv4 led the Internet Engineering Task Force (IETF) to begin work on the new protocol called IPv6 [3], which is capable of providing 128-bit addresses to all IPv6-capable devices.

N. Meghanathan et al. (Eds.): CCSIT 2012, Part I, LNICST 84, pp. 285–299, 2012.
© Institute for Computer Sciences, Social Informatics and Telecommunications Engineering 2012

IPv6 follows the Internet hierarchical structure to assign IPv6 addresses to the nodes that allows any node to communicate with another node over the Internet. However, based on the experience with IPv4, the mobility functionality in IPv6 was kept from the beginning. Therefore, an extension to the IPv6 header was introduced to provide mobility to wireless users and thus named Mobile IPv6 (MIPv6) [4]. The potential use of the MIPv6 protocol is in smart phones, wireless laptops and many other devices. Typically, when the mobile node (MN) changes its location from one network to another, the IP address of the MN must change accordingly, this process is called the handover. However, with this process, the MN loses connectivity from the previous network, and the application in use disconnects. Although the TCP application can tolerate disturbance in connection and request retransmission, the UDP protocol cannot. Most of the real-time applications rely on UDP for fast communication. In this paper, we present experimental results in order to characterize and quantify the handover latencies of Mobile IPv6. Multiple experiments are set up to measure layer 2 and layer 3 handover delays independently in order to measure disruption due to the movement between different networks. In order to evaluate and quantify the results, an open source implementation environment is used, in particular Debian 5.0.1 and an open source MIPv6 application for Linux called Universal Mobile IP "UMIP 0.4" [5]. A deep analysis of the results are presented by comparing multiple methods that a mobile node may use to switch between networks.

Many articles propose new techniques and research to reduce the handover latency in MIPv6 by modifying the protocol, or propose methods to enhance either layer 2 or layer 3. This paper focuses the standard MIPv6 implementation on a Linux platform. Previous work has been done by many people to measure the performance and delays in MIPv6 using a testbed environment. In [6,7], the author used MIPL on RedHat 8.0, but the author did not implement route optimization. Another implementation done by [8], which includes Fedora Core and MIPL installation, movement detection, duplicate address detection (DAD)and effect of router advertisement (RA), is studied. However, the author used Linux machines as access routers and a Cisco router only for routing between networks. In [9], MIPv6 testbed is set up using FreeBSD and KAME to demonstrate the handover latency and the effect of RA is studied to reduce the handover latency. Using another Linux-based testbed for Linux [10,11], in which the authors have measured the handover latency, TCP and UDP protocols performance. A recent study includes performance of transport protocols in a testbed [12]. The rest of the paper is organized as follows: Section 2 presents the detailed Mobile IPv6 handover process and its components. In section 3 layer 2 experimentation and results are presented. Layer 3 experiments and results are presented in section 4 and the conclusion is presented in section 5.

2   Mobile IPv6 Handover Process

The Mobile IPv6 handover process provides the mechanism for users to roam between different networks; however, in order to roam freely a user should not disconnect from the current network. To achieve this, network entities should communicate with each other and be able to transfer information while the mobile node (MN) is moving from one network to another. A MN is allocated an IPv6 address from the home network called the home address (HoA). The MN is always addressable using this address by the communicating nodes called the correspondent node (CN); however, when it moves to a foreign network, the CN must form another IPv6 address called a care of address (CoA). Packets can still be routed to the MN by using a mechanism in which network entities such as access routers communicate with each other and forward traffic [13]. To perform the handover process, the access router must be configured with additional feature which allow packets to move continuously to the foreign network keeping the MN in contact.

- A MN must be able to detect the change in the network; i.e., the MN has moved to a new network.
- The MN must be able to inform its home network and other nodes communicating with it.
- The handover process should be performed efficiently so that upper layers do not disconnect.

A complete MIPv6 handover process consists of the layer 2 and layer 3 handover process [13]. However a layer 3 process cannot start unless the layer 2 process is completed by the MN. The Layer 2 process includes scanning, authentication and association to wireless access point. The Layer 3 process includes discovering new routers, address configuration, movement detection and then IP registration as shown in Figure 1.

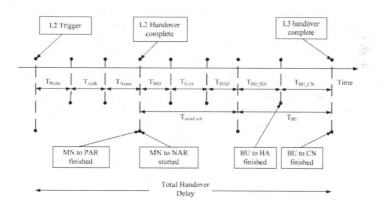

Fig. 1. Handover Delay Time Line for Mobile IPv6

The MIPv6 handover process mainly consists of the following components:

- Movement detection time (T_{mvd}): This is the time the MN uses to detect IPv6 router advertisements and neighbor discovery to find out if the MN has moved to a new network.

- Duplicate address detection time (T_{DAD}): This is the time take by the MN to form a CoA and perform duplicate address detection to confirm the uniqueness of the IPv6 address.
- Binding Update time (T_{BU}): This is the time taken by the MN to get acknowledgment from CN and HA after sending binding update (BU) signals.

The mathematical representation of the L2 and L3 handover is shown below.

$$T_{hand} = T_{L2} + T_{L3} \tag{1}$$

$$T_{L2} = T_{scan} + T_{auth} + T_{assoc} \tag{2}$$

$$T_{L3} = T_{mvd} + T_{DAD} + T_{BU} \tag{3}$$

$$Total_{hand} = T_{scan} + T_{auth} + T_{assoc} + T_{mvd} + T_{DAD} + T_{BU} \tag{4}$$

3 Layer 2 Handover Experiments

In the initial experimental setup, it is an obvious choice to link the IEEE 802.11-based mobile node in an environment that is independent of Mobile IPv6 protocol to test the link layer handover. The IEEE 802.11b wireless network specification has obtained significant acceptance in the industry and research; therefore, the specification is chosen as a layer 2 protocol over which to run Mobile IPv6. The aim of this first experiment is to evaluate the 802.11b handover time independent of Mobile IPv6, as a basis for later evaluating the component of handover time that occurs at the IP layer. In this experiment, the layer 2 and layer 3 handover delays are added to determine the total handover latency.

3.1 Methodology

Link layer or layer 2 handover in an IEEE 802.11b wireless network occurs when an 802.11b-based mobile node changes its point of connection from one network to another, usually characterized by a move from one access point to another. In order to experimentally quantify the average handover time of an 802.11b network, a simple IP network is built, consisting of two independent 802.11b Local Area Networks (LANs) linked by a regular Ethernet backbone. A single 802.11b mobile node is forced to move back and forth between the two access points, creating the kind of link layer move that would trigger a Mobile IPv6 handover event.

There are three methods for triggering a switch between access points:

1. Method 1: By decreasing the transmission power of the access point: In this method, the transmission power of the access point is decreased to which MN is currently connected. The MN will detect the degraded signal strength and switch to another access point, provided they both have the same SSID.

2. Method 2: Configure both access points with the same SSIDs and the same channel: In this method, both access points are configured with 100% transmission power. The MN will switch to another AP when not available. However, this is done by manually shutting down the wireless card of the access point to which the MN is currently attached.

3. Method 3: Configure both access points with different SSIDs and different channels: In this method, the MN will go through all the channels available before attaching to the other AP. This will consume more time and generate delay and more packet loss. To perform the test, the wireless card is manually shut down in the access point to which the MN is currently attached, forcing it to switch to another access point. This will require the MN to be configured with both SSIDs manually. However, a MN can also perform probes to detect another SSID in range and attach if open system authentication is used.

In this experiment, only methods 2 and 3 are used to obtain results and compare for consistency since it is not easy to switch the MN to another access point based on the power level in a lab environment. It is observed that when high-power access point is switched on, the MN immediately attaches to the access point regardless of forcing it to do so. However this experiment can be tested in a large area with no interference and the presence of other access points in the environment. In order to measure the handover latency at the link layer, a packet sniffing tool such as Wireshark [14] is used to record the time when MN disassociates from the old access point and associates with the new one.

3.2   TestBed Setup

A simple Ethernet network is established as shown in Figure 2. Two access points are connected to an Ethernet switch and are located close to each other. One node with the Debian 5.0.1 operating system is installed and configured with a wireless network card to act as a mobile node switching between access points. Another node with a wireless network card configured in monitor mode and installed with a packet sniffing tool called Wireshark is used to capture packets from the mobile node. The captured packets are then analyzed, and the individual delay related to the probe, authentication and association process is measured. The MN is initially attached with an old access point and then a switches over to the new access point. This is done by either reducing the transmitting power of an access point or by shutting down the old access point.The equipment used in the testbed setup is shown in Table 1.

Method 2. Triggering Handover by Configuring Both Access Points with the same SSIDs and same Channel:

   In this method, both access points are configured with channel 6 and the SSID "Home", the transmission power of both access points is kept to 100%. The configuration of the testbed is shown in Table 2. Initially, the mobile node is attached to access point 1 and SSID 'Home', and then the handover is triggered by shutting down the wireless card of access point 1. Since the network is set up

Table 1. Layer 2 Experiment Equipment Details

Hardware	Operating System	Interface	RAM	CPU
Cisco 2960 Switch	Cisco IOS 12.2	24 10/100 Ethernet	64 MB	IBM Pow-erPC405
2 X Dell Laptop D505	Debian 5.01	1 10/100 Ethernet, 1 Cisco WiFi 802.11b	2 GB	1.5 GHz
2 X Cisco Access Points 1200	Aironet 12.2(13)JA3	1 Ethernet, 802.11 b/g	16 MB	IBM Pow-erPC405 200 MHz

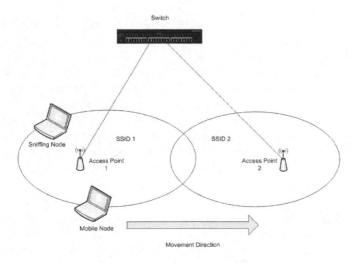

Fig. 2. Layer 2 TestBed Setup

with similar SSID and the same channle, the mobile node will switch to access point 2 in the area immediately. The handover delay is measured by sniffing the mobile node using wireshark program running on the sniffing node.

Method 3. Triggering Handover by Configuring Both Access Points with Different SSIDs and Different Channels:

In method 3, both access points are configured with the same power level, but with a different channel number and SSID. Access point 1 is set to channel 1 with SSID "Home" and access point 2 is set to channel 6 with SSID "Foreign". The configuration of the testbed is shown in Table 3. Initially the mobile node is attached with access point 1 and SSID "Home" and then the handover is triggered by shutting down access point 1. Since the network is setup with a different SSID, the mobile node will perform the probe scan, authentication and

Table 2. Testbed Configuration: Method 2

Access Point	Power Level	SSID	Power	Channel
Access Point 1	100 mW	Home	100%	6
Access Point 2	100 mW	Home	100%	6

Table 3. Testbed Configuration: Method 3

Access Point	Power Level	SSID	Power	Channel
Access Point 1	100 mW	Home	100%	1
Access Point 2	100 mW	Foreign	100%	6

association process to switch to access point 2 in the area. The handover delay is measured by sniffing the mobile node by using wireshark program running on the sniffing node.

3.3   Results

Method 2. Triggering Handover by Configuring Both Access Points with the Same SSID and the Same channel:

Figure 3 shows a scan, authentication and association delay as measured with experiments. A total of 15 different tests were conducted to analyze the signal pattern and delays. The graph shows that the highest delay is caused by the scan process and the lowest by the association process. The maximum value for scan delay is 0.069 sec, and the minimum is 0.0003 sec and the mean scan delay is approximately 0.01678 sec. The sudden increase in the scan delay could also be due to the interference from the other access points. However, since both access points were kept on the same channel, the MN does not scan when moving to the other access point because the MN will initially look for an access point on the same channel. The authentication delay minimum is 0.0004 sec, the maximum is 0.0357 sec and the mean 0.0033 sec. There is only one sudden authentication increase during the experiment in test 4 when the access point delayed the response to the MN. The association delay minimum is 0.0002 sec, the maximum 0.0089 and the mean is 0.0026 sec. The association delay does not take much time when the MN is already authenticated. The association step makes the MN and the access point start exchanging data packets.

Based on the mathematical equation (2) in section 2, the total layer 2 handover delay is the sum of scan, authentication and association delays. The layer 2 handover delays are measured as minimum of 0.0027 sec, maximum 0.0722 sec and the mean is 0.022 sec. The layer 2 handover largely depends on the individual signals. If any signal causes more delay, it will create impact on the total handover. In some cases where multiple authentications are used to secure the wireless networks, the layer 2 handover delay increases drastically.

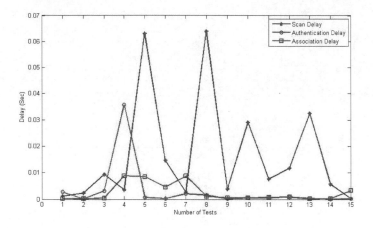

Fig. 3. L2 Signal Delays, Same SSID

The experimental result is shown in Figure 4 in which the minimum handover delay is 0.606 sec, the maximum is 0.687 sec and the mean is 0.630 sec. The large delay in the layer 2 handover depends on the scan delay, but if the scan delay is reduced, the total L2 handover can also be decreased. The Layer 2 handover constitutes part in the total handover delay in MIPv6; thus, if the layer 2 handover increases, then the total handover increases as well.

Method 3. Triggering Handover by Configuring Both Access Points with Different SSIDs and Different Channels:

Method 3 is similar to method 2, but with access points on different channels (access point 1 on channel 1 and access point 2 on channel 6). Figure 5 shows a plot of individual layer 2 signals. There is no difference in the authentication and association delay; however, the scan delay has increased compared to method 1.

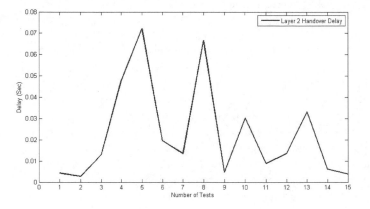

Fig. 4. L2 Handover Delay, Same SSID

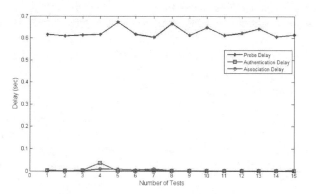

Fig. 5. L2 Signal Delays, Different SSID

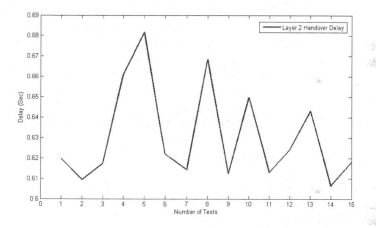

Fig. 6. L2 Handover Delay, Different SSID

The reason for the increase in the scan delay is because of scanning channels starting from channel 1 to channel 6. This has generated additional delay for the MN to send the authentication request signal. The increase in scan delay was measured from the time the MN has sent the de-authentication signal to the access point 1 and received a probe response signal from the access point 2. The minimum time for scanning is measured as 0.6003 sec, maximum at 0.6194 and the mean delay as 0.6079 sec. Since the scan delay has increased, it has impacted on the total layer 2 handover delay; thus, the minimum delay is 0.606 sec, maximum 0.6817 and the mean is 0.630 sec as shown in Figure 6.

4 Handover Delay on MIPv6

This section presents multiple experiments conducted to measure handover delays in standard Mobile IPv6 network using routers, access points, a mobile node and a correspondent node. The total handover delay in MIPv6 is the sum of the layer 2 and layer 3 delays, so the results obtained from the previous section allow an estimate of the contribution of the layer 2 handover time to the total handover time when using Mobile IPv6 over the 802.11b network.

4.1   Methodology

In order to experimentally measure the average handover delay of a Mobile IPv6 network, a physical network including IPv6 and Mobile IPv6 is built in a lab environment. Two different IPv6 networks are built using access routers configured to support IPv6 and MIPv6 functionality in order to send and receive signals from the mobile node. The access router at the home network is configured with home agent functionality, and the access router at the foreign network is configured with standard IPv6 functionality. The mobile node and correspondent nodes are installed with the Debian 5.0.1 operating system. The MN is running UMIP 0.4 application to support Mobile IPv6 functionality and is used to switch between the two different networks to measure the handover delay. Each network contains one access point configured with different SSID and auto channel selection to avoid interference. To trigger the handover, the MN is moved from "Home" network to "Foreign" and then back to "Home". In order to observe the effect of switching between the two networks and to measure the handover time, an Internet packet generator software called Distributed Internet Traffic Generator (D-ITG) is installed on the MN and correspondent node [15]. The software is used to simulate the different type of traffic; D-ITG support IPv4 and IPv6 protocols for simulation purpose. A large size UDP traffic is generated to measure various parameters such as MIPv6 delay, packet delivery rate and packet loss. The Mobile IPv6 handover time is determined by measuring the delay time when the MN loses communication and restarts communication with the CN. A sniffing computer at the foreign network is used to continuously sniff the MN traffic so that the tcpdump files can be used to investigate the details of the Mobile IPv6 handover procedure used by the UMIP implementation. A total of 15 tests were carried out to collect the results for analysis purpose and delay accuracy.

4.2   TestBed Setup

This section explains the testbed setup and relevant hardware in a lab environment for experimentation. It is important to discover the tools and equipment needed with compatibility with mobile IPv6 features. It has been discovered that Cisco 2600 routers with IOS version "c2600-advipservicesk9-mz.123-11.T3" and above support IETF RFC 3775 for Mobile IPv6 protocol. These routers support Mobile IPv6 features such as Binding Update, Binding Cache, Neighbor discovery, Duplicate address detection and Binding acknowledgment. The routers are configured with two different IPv6 networks to support the IPv6 routing feature. Since all the operating systems do not support Mobile IPv6 protocol, a careful study has shown that an open source mobility application called UMIP

0.4 can be installed on a Linux Kernel to provide mobility functionality through Ethernet or wireless network interface cards. Therefore, both MN and CN nodes are installed with the Debian 5.0.1 operating system with Linux Kernel version 2.6.30.1 and a UMIP 0.4 application to enable Mobile IPv6 functionality. The equipment list is shown in Table 5, network configuration in table 6 and the network topology in Figure 7.

Table 4. Layer 3 Experiment Equipment Details

Hardware	Operating System	Mobility Software	Interface
3 X Cisco 2611XM	c2600 IOS 12.4	IOS	2 10/100 Ethernet
Dell Laptop D505	Debian 5.0.1, Kernel 2.6.30.1	UMIP 0.4	1 10/100 Ethernet, 1 Cisco WiFi 802.11b
Dell Laptop D505	Debian 5.0.1, Kernel 2.6.30.1	UMIP 0.4	1 10/100 Ethernet, 1 Cisco WiFi 802.11b
2 X Cisco Access Points 1200	Aironet 12.2(13) JA3	None	1 Ethernet, 802.11 b/g

Figure 7 shows the network topology, in which access point 1 and router 1 are part of home network for the MN and access point 2 and Router 2 are part of foreign network. Router 1 acts as a home agent since it is configure as home agent. However, router 3 is connected with both router 1 and 2 with serial links to simulate WAN and is configured to do routing between all the networks. Hence, the routing table contains all the routes that exist in the network. This is required when the MN moves to a new network, it has to send the binding update signals to the home agent. A correspondent node is attached to router 3 for communication purpose, the MN will send all the traffic to CN while moving between the home and foreign network. The mobile node's IPv6 address at the home network is aaaa:0:1:0:aaa:ff:fe00:8 and the home agent's IPv6 address is aaaa:0:1:0:aaa:ff:fe00:2. Access point 1 is configured to broadcast SSID "Home" and access point 2 is configured to broadcast SSID "Foreign"; are configured to accept open authentication, so that no extra delays is encountered during the motion. The mobile node starts its movement from the home network and moves towards the foreign network and returns home.

Experiment 1. Moving the Mobile node from Home Network toward Foreign Network.

In this experiment, the mobile node is initially connected to the home network, and the packet generator is configured with a constant stream of UDP traffic of 1000 packets per second and 512 bytes of packet size. The correspondent node

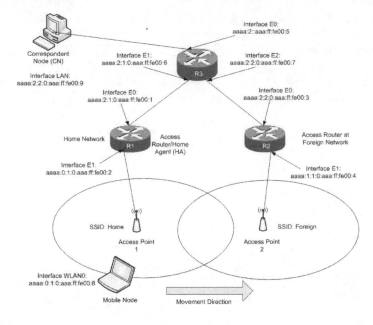

Fig. 7. Layer 3 TestBed Setup

is configured with the same packet generator in the receiver mode. The G.711 Voice specification traffic with 100 packet/sec and 120 bytes/packet is configured on the MN using the DITG generator to send VoIP traffic to the CN. When the MN is moved from the home to foreign network, it initially performs many tasks such as layer 2 handover, movement detection, IPv6 address configuration and then duplicate address detection. Once all these steps are done, then it starts to send binding, Home Test and Correspondent Test signals to the home agent and correspondent node, respectively. This is to inform the HA and the CN about the new IPv6 address so that they can continue communication. However, this process causes delays since the packets sent to the CN are lost until the MN gains re-connectivity. During the trial, the router advertisement interval is set to the standard 30-70 ms.

Experiment 2. Moving the Mobile node from Foreign Network toward the Home Network.

In experiment 2, the method used as exactly as experiment 1 except that the MN was moved from foreign network towards the home network while executing the same VoIP application. However, this process will have less latency, since the MN is returning home and has most of the information configured on it such as the home IPv6 address and the home agent address. Figure 8 shows the total MIPv6 delay for both experiments 1 and 2; it is observed that a maximum of 7 sec and minimum of 4.8 sec delay with the average of 5.6 sec has occurred when moving the MN from the home to the foreign network compared to maximum of 2.16 sec and minimum of 0.932 sec and average of 1.43 sec delay from the foreign to the home network. This is because when the MN moves from the home to the foreign network it performs Layer 2 handover which constitutes 0.6 sec, and then movement detection (MvD), IP address configuration (IPad), duplicate address detection (DAD) and binding update (BU). All these processes constitute individual delays, in which the DAD is the highest. However, it is also difficult for a MN to detect it has changed the network; this can be done only by listening to the router advertisements (RA) from the new router and sensing that it has moved. This becomes difficult for the MN to decide, because it can still receive RA from the old router as well from the new router.

4.3   Results

The analysis of trial 1 shows that the MIPv6 has higher delays and greater packet loss compared to trial 2.

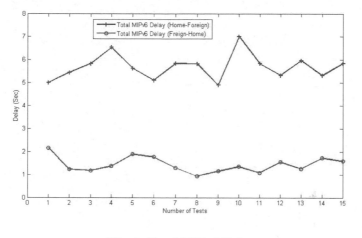

Fig. 8. Total MIPv6 Delay

The packet delivery rate is shown in Figure 9 and packet loss in Figure 10. It is observed that the packet delivery is much lower when the MN moves from home to foreign network. This is due to the large delay and large packet loss. Both the home router and MN are not configured to buffer packets; as soon the MN changes its location, the Home router stops sending packets to the CN and the MN. The maximum packet delivery rate from the home to the foreign is 13.4 packet/sec and minimum 3.2 packets/sec with average of 8.4 packets/sec. However, from the Foreign to the home network, the maximum is 62 packets/sec and the minimum is 31 packets/sec with an average of 43 packets/sec. It has been observed that at certain events when the MIPv6 delay is higher than the usual, even after receiving the minimum of three RA signals by the MN, it does not configure the IPv6 address. However, it starts sending the neighbor solicitation and router solicitation signals to the routers. This produces additional delay on the MN, and occurred only once or twice during the test runs.

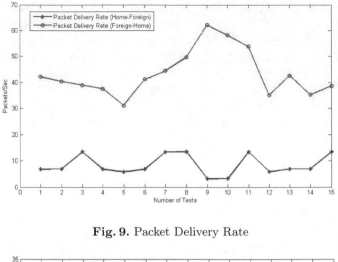

Fig. 9. Packet Delivery Rate

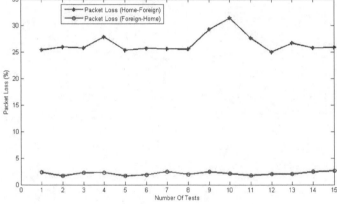

Fig. 10. Packet Loss

5   Conclusion

The handover process in Mobile IPv6 is a composition of layer 2 and layer 3 delays. Theoretically, the layer 2 delays consist of scanning, authentication and association. The layer 3 handover process consists of movement detection, IPv6 address configuration, duplicate address detection and binding update process. A layer 3 handover cannot begin until the layer 2 handover process finishes. Both layer 2 and layer 3 constitute delays that add up and produce a large handover delay for the MIPv6 protocol. In this paper, layer 2 and layer 3 delays have been analyzed individually through experimentation in a lab environment. A testbed is set up with routers, access points, a mobile node and a correspondent node. The mobile node is moved from one network to another while executing VoIP traffic and the delays are measured at the MN and the CN.

The test results show that the MIPv6 protocol experiences large handover delays, when the MN moves from the home network towards the foreign network compared to the reverse direction, the percentage difference of 42% is observed. The same is true for the packet delivery and packet loss. The packet delivery ratio between both movements is 1 to 5, where 5 is from the foreign to the home network and 1 is from the home to the foreign network. This is mainly because of large packet loss during movement. It has been observed that a large number of RS signals are sent by the MN rather than listening to the RA signals and detect a new network. In the future more realistic experiments will be performed to measure handover latency, in particular changing parameters such as the router advertisements and router solicitation. A number of applications such video, audio streaming and different standard of VoIP will be used to measure the packet loss and throughput.

References

1. Postel, J.: Internet Protocol, RFC 791 (Standard), Updated by RFC 1349 (September 1981)
2. Perkins, C.: IP Mobility Support for IPv4, RFC 3344 (Proposed Standard), Updated by RFC 4721 (August 2002)
3. Deering, S., Hinden, R.: Internet Protocol, Version 6 (IPv6) Specification, RFC 2460 (Draft Standard), Updated by RFCs 5095, 5722, 5871 (December 1998)
4. Johnson, D., Perkins, C., Arkko, J.: Mobility Support in IPv6, RFC 3775 (Proposed Standard) (June 2004)
5. Umip: Usagi-patched mobile ipv6 for linux,
   http://umip.linux-ipv6.org/index.php?n=main.homepage
6. Werapun, W., Unakul, A.: An experimental mobile ipv6 for linux testbed system, King Mongkut's Institute of Technology Ladkrabang, Bangkok, Thailand, NCS 2003 (September 2003)
7. Antoine, S., Wei, M., Aghvami, A.H.: Mobicom poster: impact of mobile ipv6 handover on the performance of tcp: an experimental testbed. SIGMOBILE Mob. Comput. Commun. Rev. 7, 31–33 (2003)
8. Busaranun, A., Pongpaibool, P., Supanakoon, P.: Handover performance of mobile ipv6 on linux testbed, Specialized Systems Consultants, Inc. (2004)
9. Stewart, L., Armitage, G., Banh, M.: Implementing an ipv6 and mobile ipv6 testbed using freebsd 4.9 and kame, Centre for Advanced Internet Architectures, Technical Report 040331A (March 2004)
10. Chen, J.-L., Lee, Y.-F., Chang, Y.-C.: Mobile ipv6 network: implementation and application. Int. J. Netw. Manag. 16, 29–43 (2006)
11. Xie, G., Chen, J., Zheng, H., Yang, J., Zhang, Y.: Handover latency of mipv6 implementation in linux. In: Global Telecommunications Conference, IEEE GLOBECOM 2007, pp. 1780–1785 (November 2007)
12. Dhraief, A., Chedly, Z., Belghith, A.: The impact of mobile ipv6 on transport protocols an experimental investigation. In: 2010 International Conference on Communication in Wireless Environments and Ubiquitous Systems: New Challenges (ICWUS), pp. 1–8 (October 2010)
13. Koodli, R., Perkins, C.: Mobile Internetworking with IPv6. John Willey & Sons (2007)
14. Wireshark, http://www.wireshark.org
15. D-itg: Distributed internet traffic generator,
    http://www.grid.unina.it/software/itg

Different Strategy for Data Management
in Mobile Computing

Chandrani Chakravorty and J. Usha

Department of MCA, R.V. College of Engineering,
Bangalore, India
{c.chandrani,ushajayadevappa}@yahoo.co.in

Abstract. Mobile computing is a revolutionary technology which enables us to access information, anytime and anywhere. Recently, there has been many research area found in mobile computing area. In this paper, we have discussed about different strategies that mobile computing has had in the area of data management. In wireless communication the data availability is the most important problem, so we have focused on the problem of data availability and discussed about replicating mobile databases.

Keywords: Cache Consistency, Cache Invalidation, Cache Management, Cache Replacement, Data Management.

1   Introduction

Mobile infrastructure has enabled to introduce of new mobile applications which are ranging from simple ones to many commercial transaction. From business and technology perspectives, data management technology that can support easy data access from and to mobile devices is among the main concerns in mobile information systems. Due to mobile behavior, it is difficult to employ the currently available database solutions ,because most of them had developed for the use on the fixed network environment.

Mobile database is popular terminology which is having the attributed to the data management technology that help to help to the use of databases on the mobile computing environment. This database is more advanced and challenging. Budiarto, Shojiro Nishio et.al[1] explain major challenges of the data management which are given below[1] .

1.Data are available anywhere independent of the availability of the fixed network connection :
With a help of mobile- devices, users can store a part of database and use it while being mobile. When a mobile user needs data which is not available locally, he can raise the request of for activating of the wireless communication of his device and initiate connection to the network via the closest mobile support station (MSS). Once it is connected, he can access the data from the data base which can be a part of

N. Meghanathan et al. (Eds.): CCSIT 2012, Part I, LNICST 84, pp. 300–305, 2012.
© Institute for Computer Sciences, Social Informatics and Telecommunications Engineering 2012

distributed database .mobile users can virtually access any data, anywhere and anytime, even in the absence of fixed network connection.

2. Databases on both mobile and fixed hosts are sharable in seamless way:
In mobile information systems, databases expended on both mobile and fixed hosts which is forming a distributed database system. There are many techniques are existing which use for data sharing in distributed databases .They are more complex than those algorithm which existing for centralized databases. In a mobile environment, use of wireless network which is known to be prone of frequent disconnections and the period of disconnection is also unpredictable.

2   Mobile Architecture

The architecture of the mobile environment is given in Fig 1. Mobile Environment consists of two distinct sets of entities: mobile units and fixed hosts. This fixed host are called Mobile Support System (MSS).This Mobile Support System are enhanced the wireless interface to Communicate with mobile units known as cell. This cell can be a part of cellular communication network or a wireless local area network within the area of building [3].In the Cellular Communication Network the bandwidth will be limited. It Supports data rates from 10 to 20 Kbits/sec . In the Wireless network the bandwidth is much wider up to 10 Mb/sec. Fixed hosts will communicate with the fixed network, while mobile units will communicate with other hosts via wireless channel .This host can be mobile or fixed [2].

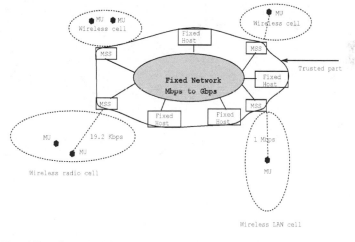

MU   **Mobile unit** (can be either dumb terminals or walkstations)
MSS **Mobile Support Station (has a wireless interface)**
Fixed Host **(no wireless interface)**

Fig. 1. A Mobile Computing Environment [2]

In this architecture, all units will be tied with the wireless interface .This unit are provide the services for which mobile users are client. Due to mobile property client can change the location as well as the network connection. While changing the location it is necessary for /mobile Host to maintain the connection. For this it will take a support of fixed host /stationary host with the wireless communication abilities which will be provided by Mobility support System(MSS). In a cell ,each MSS will communicate with all its mobile Hosts. At any point Mobile host can communicate with only those MSS which is responsible for that area. Movement of a MH (Mobile Host) from one cell to another is known as Handoff [2].

The mobile database will exchange the information with host database .It helps mobile database to keep update its information. While communication, it is not necessary that mobile host and database host should be connected with the same network .Communication can be done at   irregular intervals and for very short span of time. While using the mobile devices for storing the database it is very difficult to decide which part of the data can be stored in to the device and which part is required to be replaced. Maintaining the connectivity is also a big problem in mobile computing which can be intentional or unintentional [13].

The wireless medium will provide a powerful new method of disseminating information to a large number of users. New access method, algorithms and data paradigm have to be developed for broadcasting the data for the recipients [14].

Daniel Barbará [2] has suggested some characteristic features that make the mobile computing system unique and explore the fertile area of research. These are:

1. Skewness in the communications:
The bandwidth for the downstream direction i.e. servers-to-clients is much greater than that in the upstream direction i.e. clients-to-servers. Even some times clients will be not having capacity to send messages to the servers.

2. Ubiquitous disconnections:
Due to mobile property mobile unit do not stay connected with the network continuously. They regularly switch their unite on and off.

3. Power limitations:
Some time portable units will be limited battery backup. They frequently need to be recharged.

4. Screen size:
Portable units like the Personal Digital Assistants ,Mobiles are having very small screens.

Some time portable units will be limited battery backup. They frequently All the above features has an equally impression for data management in mobile computing. These help to effectively mange the data into the system.

3   Data Dissemination

Mobile Computing environments are normally known as slow wireless links and relatively underprivileged hosts with limited battery powers, are prone to frequent disconnections. Caching data at the hosts in a mobile computing environment can solve the problems which are associated with slow, limited bandwidth wireless links, by reducing latency and conserving bandwidth [10]. Cache replacement, Cache Consistency, Cache Invalidation are the most frequent technique used for data management in wireless network.

3.1   Cache Invalidation

Frequently needed data items in the database server are cached to improve transaction throughput [4]. It is necessary to maintain the data in the cache. It must be properly invalidated, to ensure consistency of data. For this technique most of the time the data base server involved is cache invalidation, by sending Invalidation report (IR) to all the mobile clients. It is necessary to develop the effective cache invalidation strategies that ensure the consistency between the cached data in the mobile clients and the original data stored in the database server. There are three basic ways to design invalidation strategies [3]:

1. Invalidation with Stateful Server:
The server knows which data are cached by which mobile clients. Whenever a data item is changed, the server will send an invalidation message to those clients which cached that particular item. This method necessitates the server to locate the clients. Since disconnected mobile clients cannot be contacted by the server, the disconnection of a mobile client automatically assumes that its cache is no longer valid upon reconnection. Also the mobile client needs to notify the server of its relocation. The mobility, disconnection of the clients and updation of data items will increase uplink and downlink messages.

2. Validation of cache data by mobile client:
The clients that have cached the data items normally query the server to verify the validity of their caches, whenever any cached data is used or on reconnection after disconnection if any. This method generates lot of uplink traffic in the network.

3. Invalidation with stateless Server:
The server is not aware of the state of the client's cache. The server simply periodically broadcasts an invalidation report containing the data items that have been updated recently. The client assures the validity of the data item by listening to the report, going uplink only if the cache validity is no longer guaranteed.

Among all this cache invalidation technique stateless technique found more suitable. There are many algorithms has suggested for the invalidation. Bit Sequence algorithm suggested by the Jin Jing et al. [11] which use a static bit mapping scheme.

3.2   Cache Replacement

Caching frequently accessed data items on the client side can be considered to improve the performance in a mobile environment [4]. But due to the limitations of the cache size, it is difficult to store all the accessed data items in the cache. Hence, cache replacement algorithms can be used effectively to improve the cache management. Most of the existing cache replacement policies use cost functions to incorporate different factors including access frequency, update rate, size of objects ,location and movement of the mobile clients [5]. Cache replacement policies such as LRU, LFU and LRU-k [7,9,10], considered the temporal feature of data access, while policies such as FAR [9] only deal with the location dependent aspects of cache management but neglect the temporal properties. PAID policy [7] and MARS [8] considered both spatial and temporal behavioral, even it accounts updates to data .PRRP which takes consideration of the access probability, valid scope area, data size in cache and data distance ,based on the predicted square region [6].

3.3   Cache Consistency

Caching frequently accessed data objects at the local buffer of a mobile user (MU) can significantly improve the performance of mobile wireless networks [5]. Marinating the cache consistency in mobile environment is a challenging task due to frequent disconnections and mobility of MUs. Several cache consistency maintenance schemes have been proposed for the for mobile wireless environments. The goals of these schemes and algorithms are to ensure valid data objects in the cache to enhance their availability and minimize overhead due to consistency maintenance.   Major cache consistency algorithm are depend on two property 1.Stateful where server will be unaware of cache content of mobile users   2.Stateless approaches are scalable.Scalable   Asynchronous Cache Consistency (SACCS) designed by Zhijun Wang et al. support scalable mechanism [11]. Sumit Khurana et. al. [12] had uses asynchronous call-back method for maintaining the cache consistency.

4   Conclusion

Management of the massive data in wireless mobile computing creates the new challenges. In this paper we have discussed about Data Management issues in the context of Mobile Computing. Cache Management approach like cache replacement, cache invalidation ,and cache consisting method are suggested to use for data management. Due to mobility feature of clients ,they can have different movement patterns,. It is necessary we should develop some adaptive techniques that can Consider that clients can move, and still o stay temporarily fixed.

References

1. Budiarto, Nishio, S., Tsukamoto, M.: Data management issues in mobile and peer-to peer environments. Data & Knowledge Engineering 41, 183–204 (2002)
2. Barbará, D.: Mobile Computing and Databases:A Survey. IEEE Transactions on Knowledge and Data Engineering 11(1) (January/February 1999)

3. Miraclin Joyce Pamila, J.C., Thanushkodi, K.: Performance Analysis of Improved Cache Invalidation Scheme in Mobile Computing Environment. JCSNS International Journal of Computer Science and Network Security 9(9) (September 2009)
4. Wang, Z., Kumar, M., Das, S.K., Shen, H.: Dynamic Cache Consistency Schemes for Wireless Cellular Networks. IEEE Transactions on Wireless Communications 5(2) (February 2006)
5. Yin, L., Cao, G., Cai, Y.: Generalized Target-Driven Cache Replacement Policy for Mobile Environment. In: Proceedings of the 2003 Symposium on Applications and the Internet, SAINT 2003 (2003) 0-7695-1872-9/03
6. Kumar, A., Misra, M., Sarje, A.K.: A New Cost Function based Cache Replacement Policy for Location Dependent Data in Mobile Environment. In: The 5th Annual Inter. Research Institute Student Seminar in Computer Science, Iriss 2006 (2006)
7. Zheng, B., Xu, J., Lee, D.L.: Cache Invalidation and Replacement Strategies for Location-Dependent Data in Mobile Environments. IEEE Trans. on Comp. 51(10) (2002)
8. Lai, K., Tari, Z., Bertok, P.: Location–Aware Cache Replacement for Mobile Environments. In: IEEE Globecom 2004, pp. 3441–3447 (2004)
9. Lai, K., Tari, Z., Bertok, P.: Location–Aware Cache Replacement for Mobile Environments. In: IEEE Globecom 2004, pp. 3441–3447 (2004)
10. O'Neil, E., O'Neil, P.: The LRU-k page replacement algorithm for database disk buffering. In: Proceedings of the ACM SIGMOD, pp. 296–306 (1993)
11. Wang, Z., Das, S., Che, H., Kumar, M.: Dynamic Cache Consistency Schemes for Wireless Cellular Networks. IEEE Transactions on Wireless Communications 5(2) (February 2006)
12. Kahol, A., Sandeep, K.S., et al.: A Stretegy to manage cache consistency in a disconnected Distributed Environment. IEEE Transactions on Parallel and Distributed System 12(7) (July 2001)
13. Khan, I., Touheed, N.: Physiology of Mobile Database: An Unconventional Database. In: Iadis International Conference Www/Internet (2004)
14. Imielinski, T., Badrinath, B.R.: Mobile Wireless Computing: Solutions and challenges in DataManagement. ACM Publishers

Generic Network Visualization Tool
for Monitoring Adhoc Wireless Networks

Girish Revadigar[1] and Chitra Javali[2]

[1] AllGo Embedded Systems, Bangalore, India
girishrevadigar@gmail.com
[2] PES Institute of Technology, Bangalore, India
chitra.javali@gmail.com

Abstract. Adhoc sensor network consists of dense wireless network having tiny, low-cost sensor nodes. Examples include military applications, and acquiring sensing information from inhospitable locations like thick forests, active volcano regions etc. Since the devices are scattered in a complex sensor network, It is very difficult to locate each node, know about its status and the topology of the wireless network. Hence the need of developing a system to visualise, control and monitor such networks arises. This paper presents implementation issues and author's contribution to design and implement a generic framework of the 'Network Visualization tool' to monitor adhoc wireless networks. The paper also elaborates system architecture, hardware and software organizations, and integration details of the proposed system with an exemplary wireless network based on standard IEEE 802.15.4 MAC protocol.

Keywords: Adhoc Wireless Networks, IEEE 802.15.4 MAC, Network Visualization.

1 Introduction

Recent advancements in wireless networking technology has enabled us to use wireless connectivity in almost all our applications. The ease of integration, support from multiple platforms, interoperability and co-existence with other technologies have made these more popular. At the same time, as the complexity of such networked systems increases, the effort required to monitor and control such systems also increases. For critical applications, if a single node is not working, then the loss of data from the node may cause serious complications.

In this paper, we describe our design, implementation and integration details of a 'Generic Network Visualization tool' for monitoring adhoc wireless networks.The implementation is based on IEEE 802.15.4 MAC protocol using AllGo's wireless nodes on Freescale's MC1321X MCU.

Section 2 explains the system architecture, section 3 describes target subsystem representing a wireless network. In section 4, the Host subsystem part featuring a PC based application details are present. Section 5 describes the integration and testing of our Network Visualization tool. Section 6 concludes the paper.

N. Meghanathan et al. (Eds.): CCSIT 2012, Part I, LNICST 84, pp. 306–315, 2012.

2   Network Visualization Tool Architecture

The framework of Network Visualization tool is designed in a generic way such that it can be easily integrated with any type of existing wireless network protocols like IEEE 802.15.4 MAC, SMAC, ZigBee[4]/ZigBee Pro[5] etc. Figure 1 shown below describes the system architecture.

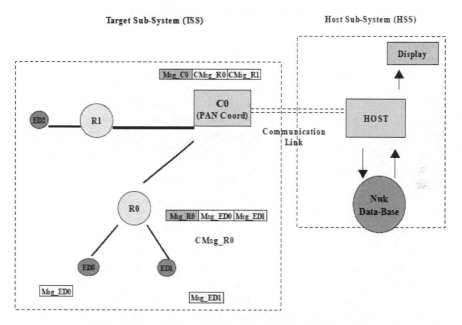

Fig. 1. Generic Network Visualization Tool Architecture

The tool consists of two mutually communicating components, a Target subsystem(TSS) and Host subsystem(HSS). Target subsystem resides on all the wireless nodes of the network viz. Coordinator, routers and end devices. The coordinator performs the task of sending network related information to the host. Host subsystem resides on the host PC/Laptop and is responsible for processing and displaying the network related information. Since the information received from target subsystem will be in a distributed form, host subsystem performs the function of analyzing and interpreting the information received from the coordinator and display it .

Since it is a visualization tool, most of the traffic will be from target subsystem to host subsystem. However a low bandwidth reverse flow is also required to configure target subsystem behavior based on user inputs provided to the host subsystem.

3   Target Subsystem (TSS)

Target subsystem is the most basic component of our visualization tool, since all the messages and information related to network are all constructed and sent to the host subsystem for interpreting the same. The different design constraints of target subsystem are explained in detail in the following sub sections.

The target subsystem is the actual network that is being visualized. Hence the target subsystem should be least intrusive to the actual network functioning, ex. In a multi priority system, message logging by the target subsystem will be the lowest priority task. In a single priority system, logging by the target subsystem will be the task executed after the devices have completed all the pending items. A target subsystem consists of various components which are described below.

3.1   Bridge Node (TSS-BN)

This is the node in the wireless network that communicates with the host subsystem(HSS) and all the other nodes in the TSS send (over the air) the data to be logged to this particular node. It can be any node but the main network coordinator device is a preferred choice for TSS-BN. In most of the applications network coordinator should have lot of network information that has to be logged. In such a case the tool bandwidth requirements will be greatly reduced by having coordinator perform as a TSS-BN also.

3.2   TSS Message Types

The messages exchanged between TSS and HSS are classified as below

1. Information Logs (Tx): These are the logs for network visualization. Two sub-types of logging are possible - event based logging and periodic logging,
2. Debug Logs (Tx): Software debug logs
3. Configuration Msgs (Rx): Used by host to configure logging parameters (log frequency, debug logs ON/OFF, Control signals etc.)

During the initial network configuration the HSS will require information about neighbours/child devices for each device in the network. Subsequently, only 'differential configuration information' will be sent to HSS. This can be viewed as an event based logging. Event based logging is made possible by the use of TSS-Call Back (TSS-CB) functions provided by the TSS to the network application.

To display certain network attributes (average LQI, network statistics, average_ON_Time) a periodic logging is required. This implies a timer based logging of the required attribute.

To allow a limited debugging each device can log data independently that will not be interpreted by HSS. It will be displayed as it is, in a separate window and can be turned ON/OFF dynamically on user requests. (It can be used to track the progress of any individual device as if the device itself is connected to serial link).

3.3   TSS Message Structures

To facilitate all the requirements at the target side, generic message structures are designed which can be used for specific purposes, for example, the Coordinator Device can use a structure called "DevInitMsg_t" as shown below to log its initial data to the host when it enters the TSS state machine's START_LOG state for the first time.

```
typedef struct DevInitMsg_tag
{
uint8_t devid[2];        // variable to hold the device id (short address)
uint8_t devtype;         // variable to hold the device type
uint8_t numchilddev;    // variable to hold the number of child devices.
} DevInitMsg_t;
```

3.4   Classification of TSS Messages and Functions

The messages used in TSS are classified into two types as 'Control Messages' and 'Log Messages'. Also there are two types of functions used with these message structures, viz 'APIs' and 'Callback functions'.

Control messages are those which are used by the devices in the network for the purpose of keeping track of the Host Subsystem. These can be as follows,

1. Control messages Request type - used by the end devices most of the time for querying the coordinator about the Host subsystem status
2. Control Messages Response type – used by the coordinator device to send the response back to the end devices in the network which send the query requests.

Log messages are the types of messages used by all types of devices in the network. There can be different types of log messages like the ones listed below,

1. The log message used by the coordinator and other devices in the network for logging their initial data,
    ```
    typedef struct DevInitMsg_tag
    {
            uint8_t devid[2];
            uint8_t devtype;
            uint8_t numchilddev;
    } DevInitMsg_t;
    ```
2. End device can log its Link quality using a specific log structure as shown below.
    ```
    typedef struct LinkQualityMsg_tag
    {
            uint8_t len;
            uint8_t lqi;
    } LinkQualityMsg_t;
    ```
3. Similar message structures can be used for different application purposes also, for example, for logging the temperature value received from a sensor etc.

```
        typedef struct AppTemperatureMsg_tag
        {
                uint8_t len;
                uint8_t temperature;
        } AppTemperatureMsg_t;
```

3.5   TSS Messages Operations

TSS consists of all the devices in the network including Pan coordinator, and End devices, routers. Each device in the TSS has a basic state machine for their functionality but the individual functionality of the devices varies in different states based on the device type, viz Coordinator/End device or router. The basic state machine and also different functionalities of the devices in these states are explained in the subsections of this chapter.

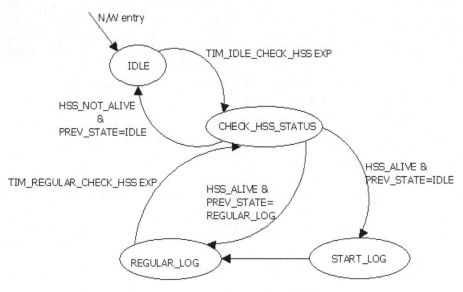

Fig. 2. TSS device state machine

The device will be in the state called "INVALID_STATE" until it joins the network, after it joins the network, the first state it enters is IDLE. The subsequent state transitions are explained as follows.

1. **State IDLE:** In this state the device will not do anything except waiting for the HSS to become active. A timer is set to expire every 10 seconds and is used to change the device tool state to a state called 'CHECK_HSS_STATUS' where the actual polling for HSS status happens. The device stays in this state until it receives 'HSS alive' response for the query of HSS status.

2. **State CHECK_HSS_STATUS:** In this state the device sends a query for HSS status and according to the present status receives one of the three

possible responses as 'HSS alive', 'HSS not alive', or 'Refresh log'. According to the type of response obtained for the query of HSS status the device then decides its next state . If the response is 'HSS not alive' then the device returns to 'IDLE' state. If the response is 'HSS alive', then the device chooses its next state as 'START_LOG' if the initial log is not complete(ie, if the previous state from which it entered the current state was 'IDLE'.), or the device may directly enter another state called 'REGULAR_LOG' if the initial log is already completed.(ie, if the previous state from which it entered the current state was 'REGULAR_LOG'.)

3. **State START_LOG:** In this state the device just does its initial log where it logs all its data related to network configuration and other useful information maintained by the device.

4. **State REGULAR_LOG:** In this state the device keeps waiting for any change of event to occur in the network and if it finds one, it just logs that data. Also the periodic logging is provided by means of a timer set for a particular time (say every 5 seconds). To keep track of HSS status, a timer is set to expire at every 20 seconds, after each time the timer expires, the device state changes to 'CHECK_HSS_STATUS' where the actual polling for HSS status happens. If the response for the HSS status query is 'HSS alive' and the 'Initial log complete bit' in the device tool status register is set, (ie, the previous state from which it entered the current state was 'REGULAR_LOG') the device then enters 'REGULAR_LOG' state again.

3.6   Data Logging Mechanism

To reduce the number of air accesses and the logging latency, a buffer based logging mechanism is employed by the TSS. The information to be logged will be stored in a 'log/dump-buffer' in an appropriate message structure:DEV-SINGLE-MSG. Multiple such messages will be collected in the 'log-buf'. Then either timer-based or total-message length based (or both) logic will be employed to actually send this information over the air to the parent/coordinator. This message will be sent via another message structure:DEV-OTA-MSG. A few benefits of such a mechanism are:

1. Better control for over-the-air message lengths and frequency.
2. Better control over the logging latency.

A priority logging can be easily introduced by having a higher priority buffer that has to be flushed out first.

3.7   Timer Based Activities in TSS

All the timer based activities in TSS are specified in terms of 'TimeTicks' of a specified duration. The 'TimeTick' duration can be quite flexible if a regular processor timer is selected to provide the basic 'TimeTick'. But since an application will require the end-devices to sleep it might not be appropriate to use the regular processor timer. In such a case a basic 'TimeTick' will be equal to 'sleep duration' of the device. Thus, to be able to efficiently handle both these cases the period based events will be tracked using the 'TimeTicks' instead of the amount of time (s or ms).

3.8   TSS Interactions with Application

TSS, a part of wireless device will be at the same level as the 'APP' layer in the application domain. Figure 3. shows the TSS interactions with the application. As mentioned earlier, TSS needs to be easily integrated onto existing application and hence the interfaces between TSS domain and Application domain needs to be well defined. TSS will need NWK APIs to send (Tx) log messages over the air, to query some typical parameters from the network data-base (Neighbour tables, routing tables etc.) or to receive (Rx) some configuration parameters/control signals over the air from coordinator.

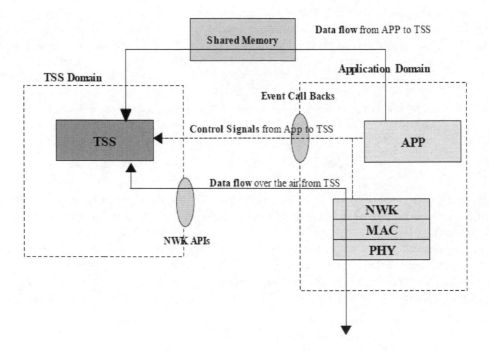

Fig. 3. TSS and application interactions

On the other hand the application might also need to interact with TSS. For ex. to inform TSS about network configuration change (association successful, addition/removal of node), register a data structure to log (actual data transfer takes place through shared memory) etc. Interactions between tool domain and application domain will be through 3 mechanisms: NWK APIs, Event Call Backs and Shared Memory.

1. **Event-CB Functions:** Call-back functions for application to inform TSS task of different events. Application will need to use these call-back functions whenever any event takes place that needs to be communicated to TSS.

2. **Network-Usage APIs:** APIs for using network/applications services. These APIs will be using the network service provided by the application and hence will need to be adapted based on the network we are integrating the TSS with.
3. **Shared Memory:** To share application data structures to be logged. To share data received over the air meant for TSS.

4   Host Subsystem

The host subsystem essentially consists of the following parts,

1. A host Pc/Laptop on which the network visualization tool runs
2. A serial port configuration module and Interpreter written in Java,
3. A database for storing the data
4. Prefuse tool kit – A Java based GUI tool (Graph visualization tool),

Steps include - Get the messages from network through Pan Coordinator using serial port, interpret the incoming messages and update the data structure which stores the current graph.

5   Integration and Testing

We have tested the tool by integrating with a simple star network based on standard IEEE 802.15.4 MAC protocol.

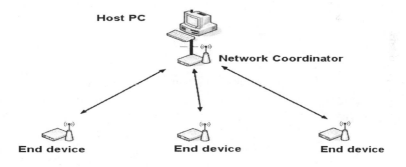

Fig. 4. Example network : Star network based in IEEE802.15.4 MAC

Following are the hardware and software used for the integration and testing:

1. A PC for development and using as a host system,
2. AllGo's wireless modules based on Freescale's MC1321x MCU, an 8 bit microcontroller of HCS08 family,
3. P&E USB multilink debugger,

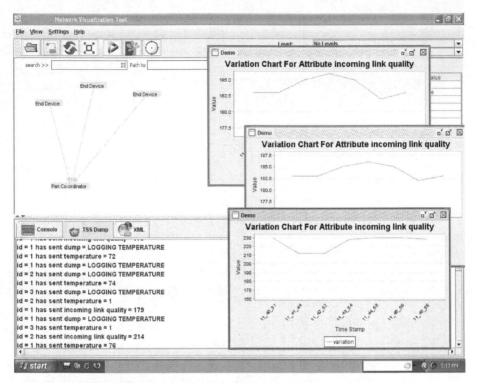

Fig. 5. Tool snapshot showing the link quality variations for each connected device

    4.   IEEE802.15.4 MAC code base for HCS08 generated from Freescale's Beekit,

    5.   JDK 1.5,

    6.   Prefuse toolkit for java.

A simple star network set-up as shown in Figure 4. was used for integration and testing. The network coordinator is connected to host Pc via serial port. All other devices in the network are connected to the coordinator through wireless network.

    Each phase of development of this project has undergone various types of testing from the beginning of high level design till the the end of interfacing the Target Sub System part with the Host Sub System for its proper functionality. Fig.5 shows the snapshot of the tool after set up of the network.

6　Conclusions

Thus the tool can easily communicate with the application for its different purpose,. like obtaining the short address of the device, or obtaining the link quality at the data indication, or obtaining the app specific data such as temperature or other parameter to be logged etc. The tool requires the basic essential network functionality and builds its structure based on the protocol stack information. Since there is only change in the network specific API's and Callback functions needed for the integration, this tool developed finds great importance with focus on future types of sensor networks also. The tool developed is presently tested by integrating with an IEEE802.15.4 MAC[1] based star network configuration. The following features of tool are verified systematically by the test results:

1. The basic state machine of each device is tested for proper functionality, which is the basic requirement for the tool to operate for any type of network since this is network platform independent.
2. The generic message structures developed are functioning as desired for the specific build used (802.15.4 MAC[1]). This proves the approach of designing platform specific API's and Callbacks.

Thus, this network visualization tool can become a standard framework for developing the network visualization and monitoring tool for any of the future network types also.

References

1. Wireless Medium Access Control (MAC) and Physical Layer (PHY) Specifications for Low- Rate Wireless Personal Area Networks (LR-WPANs), Institute of Electrical and Electronics Engineers, IEEE 802.15.4 (2003)
2. ISO/IEC 10039:1991, Information technology-Open systems interconnection-Local area networks- Medium Access Control (MAC) service definition (1991)
3. ISO/IEC 15802-1:1995, Information technology-Telecommunications and information exchange between systems-Local and metropolitan area networks-Common specifications-Part 1: Medium Access Control (MAC) service definition (1995)
4. ZigBee Specification, ZigBee Standards Organization, 053474r06 Version 1.0 (June 2005)
5. ZigBee Network layer specifications, revision 10, version 1.00, ZigBee document (2004)
6. Bulusu, N., Heidemann, J., Estrin, D.: GPS-less Low Cost Outdoor Localization For Very Small Devices. IEEE Personal Communications, Special Issue on Smart Spaces and Environments 7(5), 28–34 (2000)
7. ISO/IEC 8802-2:1998 (IEEE Std 802.2^{TM}, 1998 Edition), Information technology-Telecommunications and information exchange between systems - Local and metropolitan area networks-Specific requirements-Part 2: Logical link control (1998)
8. ISO/IEC 9646-1:1994, Information technology-Open systems interconnection-Conformance testing methodology and framework- Part 1: General concepts (1994)
9. ISO/IEC 9646-7:1995 (ITU-T Rec. X.296 (1994)), Information technology- Open systems interconnection-Conformance testing methodology and framework-Part 7: Implementation conformance statements (1995)

Adaptive MMSE Equalizer through LMS Algorithm Based CMA Channel Equalization

R. Nirmala Devi[1], Tara Saikumar[2], and K. Kishan Rao[3]

[1] Dept of EIE, KITS- Warangal, India
[2] Dept of ECE, CMR Technical Campus, Hyderabad, India
[3] Vaagevi Group of Institutions,Warangal, India
tara.sai437@gmail.com, nimala123@yahoo.com,
prof_kkrao@rediffmail.com

Abstract. The adaptive algorithm has been widely used in the digital signal processing like channel estimation, channel equalization, echo cancellation, and so on. One of the most important adaptive algorithms is the LMS algorithm. We present in this paper an multiple objective optimization approach to fast blind channel equalization. By investigating first the performance (mean-square error) of the standard fractionally spaced CMA (constant modulus algorithm) equalizer in the presence of noise, we show that CMA local minima exist near the minimum mean-square error (MMSE) equalizers. Consequently, CMA may converge to a local minimum corresponding to a poorly designed MMSE receiver with considerably large mean-square error. The step size in the LMS algorithm decides both the convergence speed and the residual error level, the highest speed of convergence and residual error level.

Keywords: CMA, LMS Algorithm, MMSE.

1 Introduction

Blind equalization has the potential to improve the efficiency of communication systems by eliminating training signals. Difficulties of its application in wireless communications, however, are due largely to the characteristics of the propagation media - multipath delays and fast fading. The challenge is achieving blind equalization using only a limited amount of data. A widely tested algorithm is the constant modulus algorithm (CMA). In the absence of noise, under the condition of the channel invertibility, the CMA converges globally for symbol-rate IIR equalizers and fractionally spaced FIR equalizers . It is shown in [9] that CMA is less affected by the ill-conditioning of the channel. However, Z. Ding *et. al*, showed that CMA may converge to some local minimum symbol rate for FIR equalizer. In the presence of noise, the analysis of convergence of CMA is difficult and little conclusive results are available. Another drawback of CMA **is** that its convergence rate may not be sufficient for fast fading channels. Another approach to the blind equalization is based on the blind channel estimation. Some of the recent eigen structure-based channel estimations require a relatively smaller data size comparing with higher-order statistical methods.

N. Meghanathan et al. (Eds.): CCSIT 2012, Part I, LNICST 84, pp. 316–324, 2012.
© Institute for Computer Sciences, Social Informatics and Telecommunications Engineering 2012

However the asymptotic performance of these eigen structure-based schemes is limited by the condition of the channel [12, 13]. Specifically, the asymptotic normalized mean square error (ANMSE) is lower bounded by the condition number of the channel matrix. Unfortunately, frequency selective fading channels with long multipath delays often result in ill-conditioned channel matrices. The key idea of this paper is to combine the approach based on minimizing the constant modulus cost and that based on matching the second-order cyclostationary statistics. The main feature of the proposed approach **is** the improved convergence property over the standard CMA equalization and the improved robustness for ill-conditioned channels.

2   Blind Channel Equalization and Types

The field of blind channel equalization has been existence for a little over twenty years. Research during this time has centered on developing new algorithms and formulating a theoretical justification for these algorithms. Blind channel equalization is also known as a self recovering equalization.. The objective of blind equalization is to recover the unknown input sequence to the unknown channel based solely on the probabilistic and statistical properties of the input sequence. The receiver synchronizes with the received signal and adjusts to equalizer without any training sequences. The term blind is used in this equalizer because it performs the equalization on the data without a reference signal. Instead, the blind equalizer relies on knowledge of the signal structure and its statistic to perform the equalization.

1. Blind signal is the unknown signal which would be identified in output signal with accommodated noise signal at receiver. 2. Channel equalization uses the idea & knowledge of training sequences for channel estimation where as Blind channel equalization doesn't utilizes the characteristics of training sequences for frequency and impulse response analysis of channel. 3. Blind Channel Equalization differs from channel equalization and without knowing the channel characteristics like transfer function & SNR, it efficiently estimate the channel and reduces the Inter Symbol Interferences (ISI) by blind signal separation and also eliminating noise at the receiver.

3   CMA-(Constant Modulus Algorithm)

In digital communication, equalizer was designed to compensate the channel distortions, through a process known as equalization. Equalization are categories in to

1) Trained equalization, 2) Blind (self-recovering) Equalization
Blind equalization finds important application in data communication system. In data communications, digital signals are generated and transmitted by the sender through an analog channel to the receiver. Linear channel distortion as a result of limited channel bandwidth, multipath and fading is often the most serious distortion in digital communication system. Blind equalization improves system bandwidth efficient by avoiding the use of training sequence. The linear channel distortion, known as the Inter-symbol interference (ISI), can severely corrupt the transmitted signal and make it difficult for the receiver to directly recover the transmitted data. Channel equalization and identification has proven to be an effective means to compensate the linear distortion by removing much of the ISI.

Channel Equalization

A typical communication system design involves first passing the signal to be transmitted through a whitening filter to reduce redundancy or correlation and then transmitting the resultant whitened signal. At the receiver, the recorded signal is passed through the inverse whitening filter and the original signal is thus restored. However, the channel will affect the transmitted signal because of a) Channel noise b) Channel dispersion leading to inter symbol interference. It is necessary to pass the received signal through a so called equalizing filter to undo the dispersion effect as shown in figure 2 below. Equalization compensates for Inter symbol Interference (ISI) created by multi path within time dispersive Channel message signal whitening signal receiver.

Blind Channel Equalization

The field of blind channel equalization has been existence for a little over twenty years. Research during this time has centered on developing new algorithms and formulating a theoretical justification for these algorithms. Blind channel equalization is also known as a self-recovering equalization. The objective of blind equalization is to recover the unknown input sequence to the unknown channel based solely on the probabilistic and statistical properties of the input sequence. The receivers synchronize to the received signal and adjust the equalizer without the training sequence. The term blind is used in this equalizer because it performs the equalization on the data without a reference signal. Instead, the blind equalizer relies on knowledge of the signal structure and its statistic to perform the equalization. A natural question from for direct adaptive equalization with training is, ``How can we adapt our filter F, without the use of a training signal?''. Figure 2 shows such a system. There has been extensive research on this subject for single user applications as well as multi-user applications. The Constant Modulus Algorithm is one such algorithm employed for the blind adaptation problem.

4   LMS Algorithm

Usually, the adaptive algorithm consists of a transfer filter for processing the input single and an algorithm unit for update the transfer filter's coefficients. $x(n)$ is the input signal; $w(n) = [w_0, w_1, w_2, \ldots . w_l]$ is the vector of the transfer filter's coefficients; $d(n)$ is the desired output of the transfer filter; $y(n)$ is the output of the transfer filter; $e(n)$ is the error value, and it can be written as:

$$e(n) = d(n) - y(n) \tag{1}$$

The Adaptive algorithm unit represents some algorithm to update the coefficients of the transfer filter. For LMS algorithm, the method to update the coefficients of the transfer filter is given as follows:

$$w(n) = w(n+1) + \mu^* x(n) * e(n) \tag{2}$$

μ, is the step of LMS algorithm.

5   Adaptive MMSE Equalizer

The Sampled signal after MMSE Equalizer can be expressed in matrix form as

$$\hat{s}(i) = w^H y(i) \tag{3}$$

$$\text{Where } y(i) = H^T(i)s(i) + n(i), \tag{4}$$

is the length of the MMSE Equalizer: $w = [w_1, w_2, w_3, w_4, w_5 .... w_M]^T$ is the equalizer coefficients vector; Then the error signal $e(i)$ is given

$$M \quad \text{by } e(i) = d(i) - \hat{s}(i) \tag{5}$$

where $d(i)$ is the desired response. For MMSE equalizer, $d(i) = s(i+D)$, D is a time delay parameter which is $L+1$ usually. The MMSE criterion is used to derive the optimal equalizer coefficients vector w :

$$w = \min imizeE\left\{|e|^2\right\} \tag{6}$$

We make the assumption that signal $s(i)$ and noise $n(i)$ are independent identity distribution stochastic

Variable and uncorrelated each other, then the equalizer coefficients vector w can be expressed as[2]:

$$w = (H^H H + \frac{1}{SNR} I)^{-1} H^H \delta_D \tag{7}$$

Where $\delta_D = [0 .... 1_D; 0 .... 0]^T_{1X(L+M-1)}$ $SNR = \frac{\sigma_s^2}{\sigma_n^2}$ denotes the signal noise

ratio I is MxM identity matrix.

To reduce the complexity caused by matrix inversion of ideal MMSE equalizer, we propose an adaptive MMSE equalizer algorithm. In code-multiplexed pilot CDMA systems, conventional adaptive equalizer is difficult to implement for lack of reference signal. In this paper, the steepest descent method [4] is used to derive adaptive equalizer algorithm in code-multiplexed pilot CDMA systems.

According to Eqn.3 and Eqn.5, the mean square error (MSE) J can be expressed as

$$J(w) = E[e(i)e(i)^*] = \sigma_s^2 - w^H p - p^H w + w^H Rw \tag{8}$$

where autocorrelation matrix $R = E[y(i)y^H(i)]$; cross-correlation vector $p = E[y(i)d^*(i)], \sigma_s^2$ denotes the signal power; $(.)^*$ represents conjugate operation. Because the wireless channel is time-varying, the equalizer coefficients vector w must be updated real time. Conventional adaptive algorithm requires reference signal $d(i)$, while in the downlink of code-multiplexed pilot CDMA systems, $d(i)$ is difficult to distill. To resolve this problem, the steepest decent method is used. From Eqn.8, the gradient vector is

$$\frac{\partial J(w)}{w} = -2p + 2Rw \tag{9}$$

then the equalizer coefficients updating equation is

$$w(i+1) = w(i) + 2\mu[p - Rw(i)] \tag{10}$$

where parameter μ is a positive real-valued constant which controls the size of the incremental correction applied to the equalizer coefficients vector.

For the autocorrelation matrix:

$$R = E[y(i)y^H(i)]$$

$$R = E[s(i)s^H(i)]\{H^H(i)H(i)\}^T + E[n(i)n^H(i)]$$

$$R = \sigma_s^2\{H^H(i)H(i)\}^T + \sigma_n^2 I \tag{11}$$

the cross-correlation vector

$$p = E[y(i)d^*(i)] = E[(H^T(i)s(i) + n(s))s^*(i-D)]$$

$$p = \sigma_s^2 H^T(i)\delta_D \tag{12}$$

From Eqn.7,8,9, we can obtain the time recursive equation of MMSE equalizer by:

$$w(i+1) = w(i) + 2\mu\sigma_s^2[H^T(i)\delta_D - (\{H^H(i)H(i)\}^T + \frac{1}{SNR}Iw(i)] \tag{13}$$

As can be seen from Eqn.13, the updating process avoids the matrix inversion operation. On the other hand, the updating process abstains the requirement to store the autocorrelation matrix $R(i)$ and only the equalizer coefficients vector of last time is needed. From Eqn.13 we know, the channel convolution matrix $H(i)$ is required to update the equalizer coefficients vector.

For CMA , channel response can be estimated through code-multiplexed pilot. In this paper, the low complexity sliding-window method is used to estimate the channel coefficients, which can be expressed

$$\text{as } \hat{\beta}_l(i) = \frac{1}{2\sqrt{\alpha p w(i+1)T_s}} \int_{\tau_l+(i-\frac{w}{2})T_s}^{\tau_l+(i+\frac{w}{2})T_s} y(t)c_p^*(t-\tau_l)dt \tag{14}$$

where $\hat{\beta}_l(i)$ is estimation of the complex gain of l-th path; w is the length of sliding-window in symbols and should be selected properly according to the varying speed of the channel.

6   Experimental Result

The Simulation Results shows that CMA Algorithm offers substantial performance gains over the traditional Adaptive MMSE and LMS algorithm, figures from 1-8.

It is observer from these plots that perform of the channel estimation is analyzed by transmitter and a receiver bit which shows the equalizers convergences.

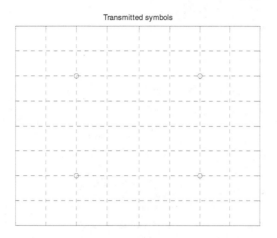

Fig. 1. Transmitter side of Adaptive CMA

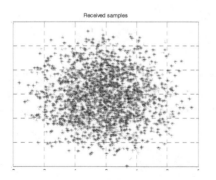

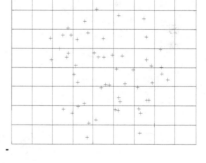

Fig. 2. Receiver side of Adaptive CMA   **Fig. 3.** Adaptive CMA Equalizer

The figures from 1-4 are obtained for Adaptive CMA Equalizer, with more efficient for equalization and convergences. Secondly from figure 5-8 are obtained for an Adaptive MMSE equalizer through LMS algorithm. The efficient of equalization and convergences is too good. The time complexity is very less and more efficient for advance communication systems.

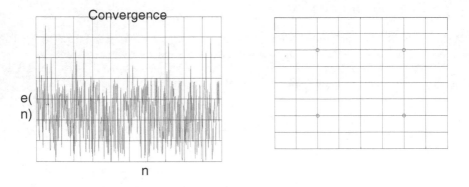

Fig. 4. Convergence of Adaptive CMA equalizer **Fig. 5.** Transmitter side of   Adaptive MMSE Equalizer

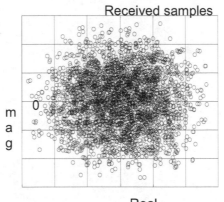

Fig. 6. Receiver side of Adaptive MMSE Equalizer

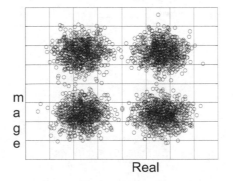

Fig. 7. Adaptive MMSE Equalizer through LMS

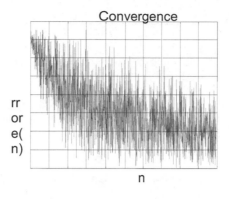

Fig. 8. Convergence of Adaptive MMSE Via LMS algorthim

7 Conclusion

In this paper, Aim at conventional Rake receiver can't satisfy the performance requirement in high data rate transmission, while ideal MMSE equalizer is difficult to real-time implement because its large computational complexity, a low complexity adaptive MMSE equalizer algorithm is proposed. In future conclusion, the proposed low complexity adaptive MMSE equalizer in code-multiplexed CDMA system can be proposed and this system has better practical application value.

References

[1] Krauss, T.P., Zoltowski, M.D., Leus, G.: Simple MMSE equalizers for CDMA downlink to restore chip sequence: Comparison to Zero-Forcing and Rake. In: ICASSP, vol. 5, pp. 2865–2868 (May 2000)

[2] Hooli, K., Latva-aho, M., Juntti, M.: Multiple access interference suppression with linear chip equalizers in WCDMA downlinkreceiver. In: General Conference (PartA), GLOBECOM, pp. 467–471 (December 1999)

[3] Mailaender, L.: Low-complexity implementation of CDMA downlink equalization. 3G Mobilec Communication Technologies (477), 396–400

[4] Haykin, S.: Adaptive Filter Theory, 3rd edn. Prentice Hall (1996)

[5] Golub, G.H., Van Loan, C.F.: Matrix Computation, 3rd edn., 728 pages. Johns Hopkins University Press (1996) ISBN:0801854148

[6] Shynk, J.J.: Frequency-domain and multirate adaptive filtering. IEEE Signal Processing Magazine 9(1), 14–37 (1992)

[7] Godard, D.N.: Self-recovering equalization and carrier tracking in two-dimensional data communication systems. IEEE Trans. on Communications 28, 1867–1875 (1980)

[8] Fijalkow, I., Manlove, C.E., Johnson Jr., C.R.: Adaptive fractionally spaced blind CMA equalization: Excess MSE. IEEE Trans. on Signal Processing 46(1), 227–231 (1998)

[9] Ding, Z., Kennedy, R.A., Anderson, B.D.O., Johnson Jr., C.R.: Ill-convergence of godard blind equalizers in data communication systems. IEEE Trans. on Communications 39, 1313–1327 (1991)

[10] Johnson Jr., C.R., Dasgupta, S., Sethares, W.A.: Averaging analysis of local stability of a real constant modulus algorithm adaptive filter. IEEE Trans. on Acoustics, Speech, and Signal Processing 36, 900–910 (1988)

[11] Brown, D.R., Schniter, P.B., Johnson Jr., C.R.: Computationally efficient blind equalization. In: 35th Annual Allerton Conference on Communication, Control, and Computing (September 1997)

[12] Casas, R.A., Johnson Jr., C.R., Kennedy, R.A., Ding, Z., Malamut, R.: Blind adaptive decision feedback equalization: A class of channels resulting in illconvergence from a zero initialization. International Journal on Adaptive Control and Signal Processing Special Issue on Adaptive Channel Equalization

[13] Johnson Jr., C.R., Anderson, B.D.O.: Godard blind equalizer error surface characteristics: White, zeromean, binary source case. International Journal of Adaptive Control and Signal Processing 9, 301–324

Weighted Angle Based Approach for Face Recognition

M. Koteswara Rao[1], K. Veeraswamy[2], K. Anitha sheela[3], and B. Chandra Mohan[4]

[1] QIS College of Engineering & Technology
[2] Qis College of Engineering & Technology
[3] JNTUH, Hyderabad
[4] Bapatla Engineering College
koteshproject@gmail.com, kilarivs@yahoo.com,
kanithasheela@gmail.com, chadrabhuma@gmail.com

Abstract. A Face recognition scheme using weighted angle based approach is proposed in this paper. In content based image retrieval, Face recognition system performs fast and accurate detection from database. Feature vector based on Eigen vectors of sub images is used for recognition. Image is partitioned into sub images. Sub parts are rearranged into rows and column matrices. Eigenvectors are computed for these matrices. Global feature vector is generated and weighted angle distance is used for face recognition. Experiments performed on benchmark face database (YALE) indicated that the proposed weighted angle based approach has better recognition performance in terms of average recognized rate and retrieval time compared to the existing methods.

Keywords: Sub-pattern, Eigenvectors, Weighted angle.

1 Introduction

In recent years, face recognition has been the subject of intensive research. With the current perceived world security situation, governments as well as businesses require reliable methods to accurately identify individuals, without overly infringing on rights to privacy or requiring significant compliance on the part of the individual being recognized. Face recognition provides an acceptable solution to this problem. A multitude of techniques have been applied to face recognition and can be separated into two categories geometric feature matching and template matching. Geometric feature [1] matching involves segmenting the distinctive features of the face – eyes, nose, mouth, etc – and extracting descriptive information about them such as their widths and heights. Ratios between these measures can then be stored for each person and compared with those from known individuals. Template matching is a non-segmentation approach to face recognition. Each face is treated as a two dimensional array of intensity values, which is then compared with other facial arrays. Earliest methods treated faces as points in very high dimensional space and calculated the Euclidean distance between them

Basically geometric feature images can be partitioned into three categories: In the first type holistic matching [2] method (HMM), an image of the whole face is used for pattern recognition [5] One of the most popular is actually the Eigen faces technology. In the second method, it involves local features and their relationship

N. Meghanathan et al. (Eds.): CCSIT 2012, Part I, LNICST 84, pp. 325–333, 2012.

used for classification. In the Third type hybrid method [3] it is also called as human perception system. It involves combined process is whole image Eigenfaces technology and local features of images.

In the mathematical terms of pattern recognition [4], the eigenvector of the co-variance matrix of the set of eigenface images [5], treating as an images of a point (or vector) in a very high dimensional space. The eigenvectors are ordered, each one accounting for a different amount variation among the face images. These eigenvector can be thought of a set of features, which together characteristics the variation among face images. Each image contribute some amount each eigenvector, so that the eigenvector formed from an ensemble of face images appear as a sort of ghostly face images.

Fundamentals of face recognition are discussed in section 2. Proposed algorithm is discussed in section 3. Experimental results are presented in section 4. Concluding in section 5.

2   Face Recognition Concept

The concept of the proposed work is to study the use of texture orientation as face image features in face based image retrieval. The basic architecture of Face recognition system is shown in figure. An improved method based on hybrid approach for face recognition system is proposed in this work.

There are two issues in building a face recognition system.

a) Every face image in the face image data base is to be represented efficiently by extracting significant feature.

b) Relevant face images are to be recognized using similarity measure between query and every face image in the face image data base.

The performance of the proposed face recognition system can be tested by retrieving the desired number of face images from the database. Advantage of weighted angle approach recognition rate and recognition time.The average recognition rate is known as the average percentage number of images belonging to the same face image as the query face image in the top 'N' matches. 'N' indicates the number of recognized images.

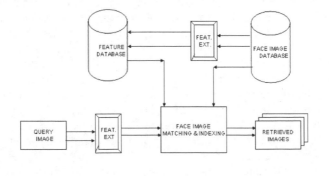

(FEAT EXT.-FEATURE EXTRACTION)

Fig. 1. Face recognition system Architecture

3   Proposed Algorithm

The basic steps involved in the proposed face recognition algorithm as follows.

1. There are N face images belonging to M persons in the training set; N = $N_1+N_2+N_3+...N_M$. Images size is represented as no. of rows and columns (A1×A2). By using sub-pattern method Each face image is first partitioned into S equally sized, these sub-pattern images are transformed   into corresponding column vectors with dimensions of d = (A1×A2)/S using non-overlapping method.

2. In the first step calculate mean value of sub-pattern images. Each of them can be expressed in the form of a d-by-N Column data matrix

$$C_i = \{c_{i1}+c_{i2}+c_{i3}+...c_{iN}\} \text{ with } i = 1, 2,........ S \quad (1)$$

Each column of column data matrix must be removed its mean value. After this obtain the vertically centered column data matrix

$$C_{vi} = \{\hat{c}_{i1}+\hat{c}_{i2}+\hat{c}_{i3}+...\hat{c}_{iN}\} \text{ with } i = 1, 2,........S. \quad (2)$$

Similarly

In the second step calculate mean vector $m_i = 1/N\sum_{j=1}^{N}c_{ij.}$ Where $^C{}_{ij}$ denotes the ith sub-pattern image of the jth face image then obtain centered column data matrix   in horizontal direction, i.e., $\hat{c}_{ij} = c_{ij} - m_i$.

After this step, obtain the horizontally centered column data matrix

$$C_{Hi} = \{\hat{c}_{i1}+ \hat{c}_{i2}+ \hat{c}_{i3}+......+ \hat{c}_{iN}\} \text{ with } i = 1, 2,....S. \quad (3)$$

3. Each of them can be expressed in the form of a d-by-L   eigenvector matrix.

$$P_{Vi} = \{P_{i1}+ P_{i2} +P_{i3}+......+ P_{iL}\} \text{ with } i = 1,2,....S. \quad (4)$$

The orthogonal eigenvectors $P_{i1,}P_{i2,}P_{i3}........P_{iL}$ corresponding to first L largest positive eigenvalues. The corresponding sub-feature weights based on P_{Vi} are computed as

$$G_{vi} = P_{Vi}^{T} C_{vi} = \{G_{i1}+ G_{i2}+......+ G_{iN\}, i} = 1,2,...S. \quad (5)$$

Similarly

Horizontally centered column data matrix for first L

Largest positive eigenvector..

$$P_{Hi} = \{ P_{i1,} P_{i2,............} P_{iL}\}, \text{ with } i = 1,2,......S. \quad (6)$$

$$P_{Ab} = diag(Pi1,Pi2,....PiL) \text{ with } I = 1,2,......S. \quad (7)$$

The orthogonal eigenvector $P_{i1,} P_{i2,......} P_{iL}$ correspond to first L largest positive eigenvalues $\lambda_{i1}\geq \lambda_{i2}\geq.....\geq \lambda_{iL}$.

Then, the whitening matrix is computed as

$$P_{wi} = P_{Hi}\lambda^{-1/2}, i=1,2,.....S. \quad (8)$$

Where $\lambda_I = diag(\lambda_{i1,} \lambda_{i2,.....} \lambda_{il})$.

Therefore, the sub-pattern weights based are computed as

$$G_{Hi} = P_{Wi}^T C_{Hi} = \{G_{i1}, G_{i2}, \ldots G_{iN}\}, \quad i = 1, 2, \ldots S \tag{9}$$

4. Afterwards, S extracted local sub feature weights of an individual vertically are synthesized into a global feature denoted as

$$G_{Vj} = (G_{1j}^T, G_{2J}^T, \ldots G_{Sj}^T)^T, j = 1, 2, \quad N. \tag{10}$$

Where G_{Vj} denotes the (L×S)-by-1 global feature vector of the jth face image.
Similarly
Av individual horizontal are synthesized into a global feature denoted as

$$G_{Hj} = (G_{1j}^T, G_{2j}^T, \ldots G_{Sj}^T)^T, j = 1, 2 \ldots \ldots N. \tag{11}$$

Where G_{Hj} denotes the (L×S)-by-1 global feature vector of the jth face image.

5. At final stage necessary to identify a new test image, this image also partitioned into S sub-pattern images. Each of them is represented as $C_{test\ i}$ and its vertically centered is as $C_{test\ vi}$ with i = 1, 2 .... S.
The corresponding sub-pattern image are computed as

$$G_{test\ i} = P_{Vi}^T C_{test\ vi}$$

Then global feature of the test image is obtained as

$$G_{test\ V} = (G_{test\ i}^T G_{test\ i}^T \ldots G_{test\ i}^T)^T \tag{12}$$

Finally, the identification of the test image is done by using nearest neighbor classifier with cosine measure, in which the cosine of the angle between the test image and each training image in the database is defined as

$$Z_{Ab} = \sqrt{1/P_{Ab}} \tag{13}$$

Where Z_{Ab} is the weighted angle

$$Rvj = G_{test\ v} \cdot Gvj \cdot Z_{Ab} / \| G_{test\ v} \| \| Gvj \|. \tag{14}$$

Where size of Rvj is (L×S)-by-1 of the jth face image.

$$R_{Hj} = G_{test\ v} \cdot G_{Hj} / \| G_{test\ v} \| \| G_{Hj} \| \tag{15}$$

Where size of R_{Hj} is (L×S)-by-1 of the jth face image.

$$Rj = Rvj + R_{Hj}. \tag{16}$$

4   Experimental Results

Recognition performance in terms of average recognition rate and recognition time of the proposed face recognition system is tested by conducting an experiment on hybrid approach face database. A face database [6] test set was constructed by selecting 100 images of 10 individuals, ten images per person. These images of a person used for training and testing. the experimental results are tabulated in Table 1. Since the recognition accuracy of the sub-pattern image, several sizes of sub-pattern images were used in our experiments as shown below: 56×46(S=4), 28×23(S=16), 14×23(S=32), 7×23(S=64), and 4×23(S=112). Result has been presented in hybrid approach with S<64.

4.1   Feature Selection

A sample image from face database and by using sub-pattern technique it can be divided by equal parts. Feature of the query image size is (64×1) by using sub-pattern method.

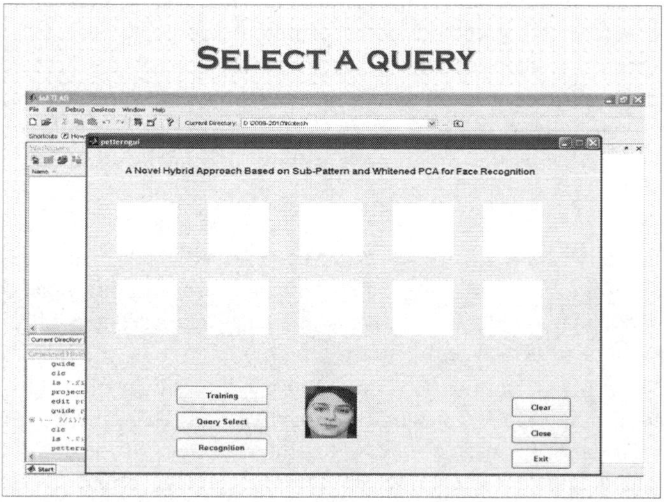

Fig. 2. Sample image from face database

Some of the recognized results when all the 10 images (N=10) in one subject of the image database are recognized are shown in figure 3. From the query image feature is taken based on sub-pattern method .After that in this paper we take only 64 feature of this query image. That may be depends up on the sub-parts of this image(S=16). For each sub-pattern we consider four positive eigenvectors that is largest eigenvector of

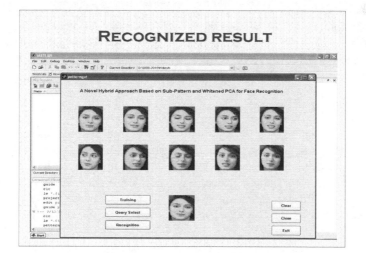

Fig. 3. Recognized images

the sub-part. It is represented as only local feature of the query image. After that combination of all sub-parts local feature it can be represented as global feature of the query image. Comparative performance of all training global feature with this query image finally recognized results images with top left image as query image.

From the experimental results, conclude that: when testing images under varying illumination, sub-pattern method and principal component analysis [8] can significantly improve the recognition accuracy of sub-pattern vertically centered method. Since the vertical centering process centers the data by removing the mean of each image, it can be used to eliminate the effect of the values. In other words, the property of vertical centering process [9] can be helpful in eliminating the shifted values of original-pixels. Further, the sub-pattern technique can be utilized to encourage the efficiency of the vertical centering process. Therefore, sub-pattern technique is actually useful to vertical centering process of sub-pattern technique. The vertical centering may benefits for the recognition in varying illumination. Now, we have confirmed this possible forecast and strongly increased the efficiency of the vertical centering process by sub-pattern technique in this paper. From the total experimental results, it can also be seen that for expression variant test, sub-pattern technique and Eigen vector can slightly improve weighted angle based approach classifier, the similarity between a test image and training image is defined as

In the weighted angle based approach method cosine measurement

$$Rvj = G_{test\ v} . Gvj. Z_{Ab} / \| G_{test\ v} \| \| Gvj \|$$

Where size of Rvj is (L×S)-by-1 of the jth face image.

$$R_{Hj} = G_{test\ v} . G_{Hj} / \| G_{test\ v} \| \| G_{Hj} \|$$

Where size of R_{Hj} is (L×S)-by-1 of the jth face image.

$$Rj = Rvj + R_{Hj.}$$

The experimental results of this weighted angle based approach when compared with vertically centered values and horizontally centered values. In which recognition rates of the sub-pattern based approaches were obtained using S = 16. as can be seen from the results, weighted angle based approach method has best recognition accuracy.

4.2   Average Recognized Rate

The average recognized rate for the query is measured by counting the number of images from the same category which are found in the top 'N' matches. From below table, we can observe that the recognition rates of five methods. Compared with other process we can get efficient recognized result, here we are comparing local and global feature [10] of the images. Comparative recognition performance of the proposed face recognition system on the face database using hybrid approach feature is shown in table 1.

(1, 3, 5,7,10 are Top 'N' recognized images)

Table 1. Recognized rate on face database

Methods	Number of top matches				
	1	3	5	7	10
Mean value	100	77.5	71	65	58
Variance	100	58.5	50.5	44.2	36.25
Diagonal (SVD)	100	60	54.5	48.2	42.25
Hybrid Approach	100	99.16	95.5	87.4	78.75
Weighted angle based Approach (L=Largest four) PROPOSED	**100**	**99.16**	**96.5**	**87.85**	**79.25**

In the hybrid approach method cosine measurement

$$Rvj = G_{test\ v} . Gvj / \| G_{test\ v} \| \| Gvj \|$$

Where size of Rvj is (L×S)-by-1 of the jth face image.

$$R_{Hj} = G_{test\ v} . G_{Hj} / \| G_{test\ v} \| \| G_{Hj} \|$$

Where size of R_{Hj} is (L×S)-by-1 of the jth face image.

$$Rj = Rvj + R_{Hj.}$$

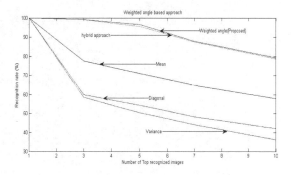

Fig. 4. Comparative recognition rates

Comparative performance in terms of average recognized rate is shown in figure 4 indicates the superiority of the weighted angle based for face recognition system with largest four eigenvectors when compared to largest all positive eigenvector and also be observed over remaining methods in terms of average recognized rate.

4.3   Recognized Time

Face recognition system with weighted angle based approach technique for largest four eigenvector recognized time is 51.84 seconds (training time is 51.42 seconds and recognized time is 0.42 seconds), hybrid approach technique for all positive eigenvector recognized time is 52.23 seconds, Diagonal value method in SVD recognized time is 1.65 seconds, variance time is 2.90 seconds and mean value method recognized time is 2.72 seconds.

5   Conclusions

Weighted angle based approach for face recognition is presented in this paper. Global feature vector is generated and used for face recognition. Horizontal and vertical variations are considered in feature vector. Weighted angle based approach for face recognition gives better performance in terms of average recognized rate and retrieval time compared to existing methods.

Acknowledgement. Authors would like to thank the Dr.S.Srinivas Kumar, Director Sponsered Research, JNTU, Kakinada for his valuable suggestions. Authors thank the Dr.Ch.Srinivasa Rao, Principal, Sai Aditya Engineering College, Surampalem for his support to finish this work.

References

1. Smeulders, A.W.M., Worring, M., Satini, S., Gupta, A., Jain, R.: Content – Based Image Retrieval at the end of the Early Years. IEEE Transactions on Pattern analysis and Machine Intelligence 22(12), 1349–1380 (2000)
2. Gupta, A.: Visual Information Retrieval Technology: A Virage perspective, Virage Image Engine. API Specification (1997)
3. Hsieh, P.-C., Tung, P.-C.: A Novel Hybrid Approach Based On Subpattern Technique and Whitened PCA for Face Recognition. Pattern Recognition 42, 978–984 (2009)
4. Perlibakas, V.: Distance measures for PCA based face recognition. Pattern Recognition Letters 25, 711–724 (2004)
5. Choi, S.I., Kim, C., Choi, C.H.: Shadow compensation in 2D images for face recognition. Pattern Recognition 40, 2118–2125 (2007)
6. Turk, M., Pentland, A.: Eigenfaces for recognition. J. Cognitive Neurosci. 3(1), 71–86 (1991)
7. Yalefacedatabase,
   http://cvc.yale.edu/projects/yalefaces/yalefaces.html

8. Yang, J., Zhang, D., Yang, J.Y.: Is ICA significantly better than PCA for face recognition? In: Proceedings of IEEE International Conference on Computer Vision, vol. 1, pp. 198–203 (2005)

9. Phillips, P.J.: Face recognition: a literature survey. ACM Computing Surveys, 399–458 (2003)

10. Hart, P.E., Stork, D.G., Duda, R.O.: Pattren Classification. John Wiley and Sons, Inc., New York (2001)

11. Chen, S., Zhu, Y.: Subpattern-based principle component analysis. Pattern Recognition 37, 1081–1083 (2004)

Multiple Mobile Agents based Data Dissemination Protocol for Wireless Sensor Networks

Govind P. Gupta[1], Manoj Misra[1], and Kumkum Garg[2]

[1] Department of Electronics & Computer Engineering
Indian Institute of Technology, Roorkee, India
{gpg09dec,manojfec}@iitr.ernet.in
[2] Manipal Institute of Technology, Manipal, India
kumkum.garg@manipal.edu

Abstract. Energy Efficient and reliable data dissemination in wireless sensor network is an important research issue since the network consists of low cost nodes with limited resources. Mobile agent-based data dissemination (MADD) approach that deploys multiple mobile agents for the data gathering task is a flexible, robust, and distributed solution to the data dissemination problem in wireless sensor networks. However the manners in which mobile agents follow the itineraries (order of visited sensor nodes) have an impact on the efficiency of the data gathering. In this paper, we propose a multiple mobile agents with dynamic itineraries based data dissemination (MMADIDD) protocol that not only adapts to unexpected node failures but also prolongs the network lifetime.

Keywords: Wireless sensor network, Data Dissemination, Mobile agent.

1   Introduction

Recent advances in embedded micro-electro-mechanism system (MEMS) and wireless communication technologies have enabled the development of small size, low-cost sensor nodes with sensing, computation and wireless communication capabilities [1].Wireless sensor networks (WSNs) consist of a large number of these tiny sensor nodes that cooperatively monitor and react to physical or environmental phenomenon and send the collected data to a sink using wireless channels. WSNs have found many applications in areas such as battlefield surveillance, industrial process monitoring and control, environmental and habitat monitoring, home automation, traffic control, and healthcare applications [2], [3]. Sensor nodes are usually battery powered and they are left unattended after the initial deployment and it is difficult to recharge them. So an important issue in the design and efficient implementation of wireless sensor networks is to optimized energy consumption and keep the network functional for as long as possible.

Recently, mobile agent based computing paradigm has been proposed in the field of WSNs [4], [5], [6], [7], [12]. A mobile agent[7] is a special kind of software process that has ability to migrate from one node to another following certain itinerary and perform data aggregation locally at each node. Mobile agent based computing paradigm presents several important benefits [5]. First, it can significantly reduce bandwidth consumption by moving the computation process to the location of the sensed data; otherwise its transmission in raw form would consume more energy of the node. In addition, mobile agent computing paradigm also provides stability and fault-tolerance since it can be dispatched when the network connection is alive and return results when the connection is re-established. Finally, mobile agent can also extend the functionality of network by carry task-adaptive processing code [5], [6].

Mobile agent based data dissemination process in WSN largely depends on the planning of the mobile agent itinerary (order of sensor nodes to be visited during the mobile agent migration) [7].Itinerary planning can be classified as static or dynamic according to place where mobile agent routing decisions are made [7]. A dynamic itinerary planning scheme determines the route on the fly at each hop of the mobile agent, while a static scheme derives the route at the mobile agent dispatcher (i.e. sink) node before mobile agent is dispatched and it is based on global information of network topology. A mobile agent with dynamic itinerary is more flexible, and can adapt to faults during its traversal by changing its itinerary on the fly [7]. However, the node or link failures may invalidate the static itineraries determined centrally at the sink. In static scheme, sink node require to maintain global information of network topology for determining the itineraries of mobile agents. While in dynamic scheme, sink does not require to maintain global information of network topology [13].

In this paper, we propose a multiple mobile agents with dynamic itineraries based data dissemination protocol (MMADIDD) that uses multiple mobile agents for data dissemination task and each mobile agent is responsible for collecting sensed data from a particular area and determines its route on fly at each hop using local information. Our protocol not only adapts to unexpected node failures but also prolongs the network lifetime. The proposed protocol is designed for monitoring applications to obtain the periodically sensed data, such as temperature, humidity, and pressure, from the surrounding environments. The performance of our protocol is evaluated through a number of simulation results, which show that our protocol performs better than static itinerary based protocol when node or link failures occur en route.

The rest of the paper is organized as follows: we briefly describe works related to the research presented herein in Section 2. In Section 3, we present system model and list the assumptions in our work. In Section 4, we describe our proposed MMADIDD protocol in detail. Section 5 describes our simulation environment in detail and compares the performance of our protocol with other protocols with respect to the selected metrics of interest. Finally, Section 6 concludes this paper.

2   Related Work

Recently, mobile agents [4], [5], [6], [8], [11], [12], [13] have been proposed for data dissemination task in wireless sensor networks. In [4], H. Qi et al. proposed two heuristic protocols, Local Closest First (LCF) and Global Closest First (GCF) to derive the itinerary of mobile agent for performing data gathering task. In LCF, mobile agent starts its route from the sink and searches for next destination with shortest distance to its current location. In GCF, each mobile agent also starts its route from the sink and selects the next closest node to the sink as its next destination. The performance of LCF depends on current location of mobile agent. Wu et al. [7] proposed a genetic algorithm (GA) for computing itinerary of mobile agent .It uses global network topology information to derive the static itinerary of mobile agent and provides better performance than LCF and GCF protocols in terms of energy consumption. The protocols proposed in [4] and [7] use single mobile agent to visit all sensor nodes and their performance is reasonable for small network; however, it declines as the network size grows. This is because mobile agent's size increases as network size increases resulting in more energy consumption and more time to finish the data gathering task.

In [11], M. Chen et al. proposed multi agent Itinerary Planning (MIP) algorithm. MIP is a centralized algorithm executed at sink and divides the deployed sensor nodes into different groups and in each group, single agent based protocol like LCF, GCF or GA is used to derive the itineraries of mobile agents. This approach reduces the task completion time than single agent based approach. In [13], Charalampos et al. proposed a tree based itinerary design (TBID) algorithm that employs multiple mobile agents for data gathering task in WSNs. In this method, it is assumed that sink knows the geographic location of all the sensor nodes. TBID algorithm is a centralized algorithm and is executed at sink. After processing, it determines the number of mobile agent used for data gathering and its itineraries. This algorithm follows greedy methods for grouping sensor nodes in multiple mobile agent itineraries. Basically, it builds a spanning forest of binary trees rooted at sink in network and calculates itineraries by post order traversal of binary trees and finally, assigns these itineraries to individual mobile agents. In this scheme, each mobile agent carries the pre-computed itinerary that determines the order of sensor nodes to be visited. The main limitation of static itinerary based approach is that mobile agent cannot complete its data dissemination task if a node or link fails en route.

3   System Model

In this paper, we consider a sensor network consisting of N sensor nodes uniformly distributed in a circular monitoring area of radius R, as in [16], as shown in Figure1(a). There is only one sink node that is located at the centre of the area. We make the following assumptions:

- All the sensor nodes are static, homogeneous and have the same computational and communication capabilities.
- Initially all nodes are charged with the same amount of energy.
- Wireless links are bidirectional.
- Sink node is static and uses a directional antenna for equiangular wedge setup and to dispatch mobile agent. However, its receiving antenna is omni-directional.
- Each node is assigned a unique identifier (ID).

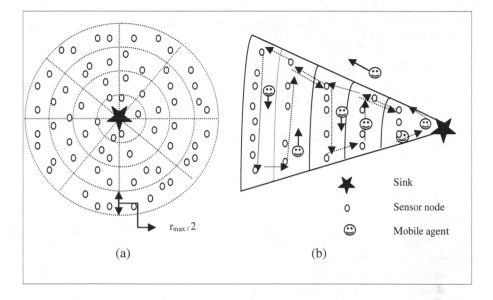

Fig. 1. (a) Network structure model. (b) Mobile Agent Migration Process

4   Proposed Data Dissemination Protocol

In this section, we present our proposed MMADIDD (multiple mobile agents with dynamic itinerary based data dissemination) protocol. Our protocol consists of two phases: initialization process and mobile agent migration process.

4.1   Initialization Process

This process is further divided into two sub processes: circular coronas and equiangular wedge setup process and neighbor discovery process. In circular coronas and equiangular wedge setup process, we aim to divide whole circular monitoring area into coronas and wedges. The width of each corona is $r_{max} / 2$ as shown in Figure 1(a), where r_{max} is the maximum transmission range of any sensor node. The angle of each wedge is 45 degree i.e. whole monitoring area is divided into eight equiangular wedges centered at sink. After this phase, each node knows its corona and wedge number and also sets its boundaryState field if it is located at boundary of wedge. The main aim of this process is to determine the visiting area of each mobile agent. Since circular sensing area is divided into eight equiangular wedges, for data gathering from each wedge, sink dispatches eight mobile agents in parallel, one for each corresponding wedge. The pseudo code for coronas and wedge construction phase is given in Algorithm 1 and 2.

Algorithm 1. Concentric Coronas Creation

For the Sink:
1: R = radius of circular monitoring area
2: r = the maximum transmission range of sensor node
3: CN = corona number
4: i=1
5: for R <= 0 do
6:     sink node create a CoronasCreationPkt packet with CN field set to i
7:     adjust the transmission power equivalent to transmission range i× r/2
8:     Broadcast CoronasCreationPkt (sinkID, CN)
9:     R = R – r/2;
10:    i = i + 1
11:   wait for time t_1
For any sensor node (i):
1: Initialize: corona state cn = 0
2: if (receive CoronasCreationPkt and cn = =0)
3:     set cn by CN field of received CoronasCreationPkt

Algorithm 2. Equiangular Wedge Creation

For the Sink:
1: WN = wedge number
2: j=1
3: θ = 45 // set angle of directional antenna
4: adjust the transmission power equivalent to transmission range R
5: while (θ < = 360)
6:     sink create a WedgeCreationPkt   packet with WN field set to j
7:     adjust angle of directional antenna by θ
8:     Broadcast WedgeCreationPkt (sinkID, WN)
9:     θ = θ + 45
10:    j = j+1
11:   wait for time t_2
For any sensor node (i):
1: Initialize: wedgeNo state wn = 0
2: if (receive WedgeCreationPkt and wn = =0)
3:     set wn by WN field of received WedgeCreationPkt

In one-hop neighbor discovery process, each node is made to broadcast HELLO packets only once, which includes their nodeID, remaining energy, start time, wedge Number and coronas number. All one hope neighbors of any node that receive HELLO packet update their neighbor table. The neighbor table at each node maintains information – nodeID of the neighbor node from which it has received the Hello packet, the remaining energy at the neighbor node, distance of neighbor node, corona and wedge number of the neighbor node from which it has received the Hello packet. This phase is invoked by sink node. The pseudo code for neighbor discovery phase is given in Algorithm 3.

Algorithm 3. Neighbor Discovery

For the Sink:
1: sink node create a HELLO packet
2: Broadcast HELLO packet to its 1-hop neighbor
 3: if (receive HELLO packet)
4:   Update Neighbor table
For any sensor node (i):
1: Initialize: timeOn = false
2: boundaryNode = false
3: outerNode = false
4: if (receive HELLO packet from own Wedge)
5:   Update Neighbor table
6: else
7:     set boundaryNode = true
8: if (timeOn is false)
9:      create HELLO packet
10:     set timeOn = true
11.   Broadcast HELLO packet

4.2   Mobile Agent Migration Process

Mobile agent migration process is divided into two phases. In first phase, mobile agent is forwarded by boundary nodes of wedge W_i until it reaches to outer ring or corona. In second phase, mobile agent starts its data aggregation and gathering task from sensor nodes of outer corona C_k to next inner corona C_{k-1} of same wedge W_i and so on until it reaches at sink as shown in Figure 1(b). In each sector S_{ij} , mobile agent starts its data collection from one boundary node to another by using least-cost based multi-hop routing scheme i.e. it migrates to node which is nearest and has highest enough node energy . The cost function for mobile agent forwarded from node N_i to node N_j is derived from [6]:

$$C_{ij} = w \cdot \frac{d}{R} + (1-w) \cdot \frac{E}{E_{max}} \tag{1}$$

Where d is the distance between sensor node N_i and N_j, R is the maximum transmission range of sensor node, E is the remaining energy of node N_j, E_{max} is the initial energy of sensor node, w is used to adjust the importance between distance and energy component, and $0 < w < 1$.The pseudo code for mobile agent itinerary computation phase is given in Algorithm 4.

Algorithm 4. Mobile Agent Migration

Initialize: sink know its 1-hop neighbor say N_1
k: no of mobile agent used for data collection task, initial value is 1
CN: concentric coronas number
C: no of coronas
i=1
For the Sink:
1: while (k <=8)
2:      sink create mobile agent packet with MA-id = k
3:      send to Groupleader of wedge k
For any sensor node (i)
1: if (receive MobileAgentpkt packet)
2:   {   if (node is Groupleader and MA_direction is DOWN)
3:            send   MobileAgentpkt to boundary node of next corona
4:          else { if (boundaryNode and CN < = C)
5:                        send   MobileAgentpkt to boundary node of
                           next corona
6:                      else   set MA_direction to UP
7:                              send MobileAgentpkt to its
                               nearest neighbor of same CN_i
8:                }
9:       if (receive MobileAgentpkt packet and MA_direction is UP
             and !boundaryNode)
10:        send MobileAgentpkt to its nearest neighbor of same CN_i
11   else   send MobileAgentpkt to its nearest neighbor node
             of CN_{i-1} coronas

---

5   Simulation Results and Discussion

In this section, we present and discuss simulation results of our proposed data gathering protocol MMADIDD and compare the performance of MMADIDD with TBID, LCF and GCF algorithms in terms of total energy consumption, response time. We used Castalia [19] simulator to implement and conduct a set of simulation experiments. Castalia is a simulator for wireless sensor network and body area network which is built and based on the OMNeT++ [18] discrete event simulation platform.

Our simulation scenarios consist of a circular monitoring area of radius 100 m containing five different scales (25, 50,100,150, and 200) of sensor nodes randomly deployed. All nodes are identical with a radio transmission range set to 25m. The sink node is situated at the centre of the simulation field. The simulation time was set to 1000s.

5.1   Performance Metrics

We use three metrics, energy consumption, response time and success rate of itinerary of mobile agent, to compare the performance of the protocols.

a) *Energy consumption:* A sensor node has three main units [14] namely the processing units (PU), the transceiver unit (TU) and the sensor board unit (SU). Each of these units consumes a certain amount of energy while operating. The energy consumed by a sensor node can be defined as[14][17]:

$$E_{SN} = E_{PU} + E_{TU} + E_{SU} \tag{2}$$

Where E_{PU}, E_{TU} and E_{SU} represent the energy consumed by the processing unit, the transceiver unit and the sensor board unit respectively. Energy consumed [9], [14] by the transceiver unit (E_{TU}) can be further defined as

$$E_{TU} = E_{TU_{TX}}(d) + E_{TU_{RX}} \tag{3}$$

Where E_{TUtx} represents the energy consumed by the transceiver unit (TU) to transmit a bit of data for a distance d and E_{TUrx} represents the energy consumed by the transceiver unit (TU) to receive a bit of data. The total energy consumed by a sensor node is represented as [14],[17]:

$$E_{SN} = E_{PU} + E_{TU_{TX}}(d) + E_{TU_{RX}} + E_{SU} \tag{4}$$

Generally, E_{PU}, E_{TUrx} and E_{SU} are constant and sum of these represented as C and E_{TUtx} is a function of d which depends on network topology. In other way, equation (6) can be written as:

$$E_{SN} = C + E_{TU_{TX}}(d) \tag{5}$$

For mobile agent based data dissemination protocols, energy consumption at a sensor node i (E_{SN_MAi}) can be represented as

$$E_{SN\_MA_i} = E_{DA} + E_{Rx\_MA} + E_{Tx\_MA} \tag{6}$$

Where E_{DA} is energy spent for data aggregation at sensor node, $E_{Rx\text{-}MA}$ is energy spent at a node by receiving mobile agent and $E_{Tx\text{-}MA}$ for energy required to transmit mobile agent. So for mobile agent based data dissemination protocols, total energy consumption E_{total_MA} can be represented as

$$E_{total\_MA} = \sum_{i=1}^{N} E_{SN\_MA_i} = \sum_{i=1}^{N} \left(E_{DA} + E_{Rx\_MA} + E_{Tx\_MA} \right) \tag{7}$$

Normally, E_{DA} is constant for all source nodes visited by the mobile agent. $E_{Rx\text{-}MA}$ and $E_{Tx\text{-}MA}$ depends on size of mobile agent received and transmit respectively. This metric is important because the energy level that a network uses is proportional to the network's lifetime. The lower the energy consumption the longer is the network's lifetime. E_{total_MA} depends on itinerary length traveled by mobile agent during data dissemination process.

b) *Response time:* Response time is calculated as the time spent to finish a data collection task from all source nodes to sink. For agent-based data dissemination protocols, it consist of four components [12], [13],[17] time spent in mobile agent instantiation (T_{inst}), time spent for mobile agent to complete its data aggregation task at a node (T_{proc}), time spent in mobile agent transmission (T_{trans}) and time spent in mobile agent propagation (T_{prop}). So response time ($T_{responsetime\_MA}$) is represented as :

$$T_{responsetime_{MA}} = T_{inst} + \left(T_{proc} + T_{trans} + T_{prop}\right) \times n \qquad (8)$$

Where n is number of sensor nodes visited by mobile agent. In general, T_{inst} is constant and assumed as 5 ms in our experiments. T_{proc} is also constant and assumed as 25ms. T_{trans} depends on the mobile agent size and network transfer rate. T_{prop} depends on the overall itinerary length that is the distance covered in successive mobile agent migrations. In a single agent based protocol, the response time is equivalent to the average reporting delay, from the time when a mobile agent is dispatched by the sink to the time when mobile agent returns to the sink. In a multi agent based protocol, since multiple agents is used for data gathering in parallel, there must be a mobile agent which is last one to return to the sink. Then, the response time of multi agent based protocol is delay of that mobile agent.

c) *Success rate of itinerary:* This metrics is used to evaluate the reliability of mobile agent's data collection process in presence of faulty or dead nodes. It is evaluated as percentage ratio of number of sensor nodes visited by mobile agent to total number of nodes.

5.2   Performance Analysis

In this section, we investigate the performance of the protocols in a multi-hop network topology. We study the impact of the number of deployed sensor nodes on energy consumption per round, overall response time and success rate of itinerary of mobile agent in presence of faulty or dead nodes. From the analysis of the simulation results, we have the following observations:

Figure 2 shows the performance comparison of the two single agent based data gathering protocol (LCF and GCF) and the two multi agent based protocol (TBID and MMADIDD) in terms of overall energy consumption per round .When the number of nodes is increased, energy consumption per round is also increases in all of the four protocols as shown in Fig. 2. Our proposed MMADIDD protocol consumes slightly (approx. 5%) more energy than TBID. This is due to the use of dynamic itinerary where mobile agent uses local information to determine the next source node. However, MMADIDD performs better than single agent based data gathering protocols (LCF and GCF) in terms of energy consumption. The reason of this outcome is that in LCF and GCF, a single mobile agent has to visit all nodes distributed in the network.

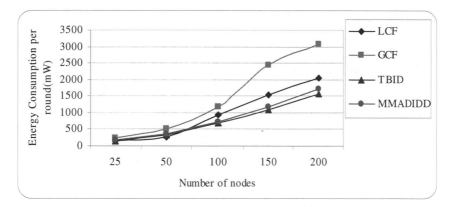

Fig. 2. Energy consumption per round

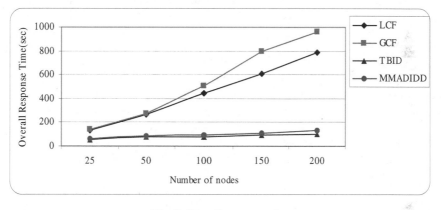

Fig. 3. Overall response time

Figure 3 shows the performance of LCF, GCF, TBID and MMADIDD protocols in terms of their respective overall response time. Overall response time increases as the number of deployed sensor nodes increases. Our proposed MMADIDG protocol takes slightly (approx. 3%) more time to complete the data dissemination task than TBID. This is because MMADIDD derives next destination of mobile agent on the fly based on local information. However, overall response time of MMADIDD and TBID are much lower than LCF and GCF. This is because of MMADIDD and TBID both dispatch multiple mobile agents in parallel to complete data dissemination task and each of them visits a small number of sensor nodes. While, LCF and GCF employ a single mobile agent to visit all deployed sensor nodes thereby increasing mobile agent's state size, significantly increasing the associated transmission delay.

As shown in Figure 4, MMADIDD protocol has absolute gain in terms of success rate of itinerary. The performance of MMADIDD protocol is better than static itinerary based protocol (LCF, GCF and TBID) because statically determined order of sensor nodes to be visited during the mobile agent migration may fail when node or link failure occurs on some nodes en route.

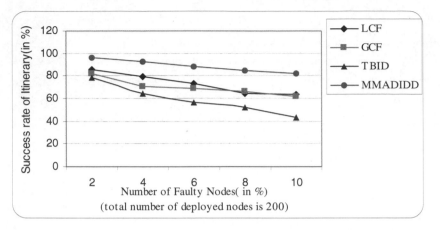

Fig. 4. Success rate of itinerary

6   Conclusion

In this paper, we have proposed a multiple mobile agent based data dissemination protocol that dynamically determines the order of sensor nodes to be visited during the mobile agent migration. It divides the circular sensing area into number of equiangular wedge centred at sink. In each wedge, we employ a mobile agent for data dissemination task. We have demonstrated through simulation results that our proposed protocol performs better than static itinerary based protocol when node or link failure occurs en route.

References

1. Akyidiz, I.F., et al.: Wireless Sensor Network: A survey. Computer Networks 38, 393–422 (2002)
2. Alemdar, H., et al.: Wireless sensor networks for healthcare: A survey. Elsevier Computer Networks Journal (2010)
3. Anastasi, G., et al.: Energy conservation in wireless sensor networks: A survey. Elsevier Ad Hoc Networks Journal (2009)
4. Qi, H., Wang, F.: Optimal itinerary analysis for mobile agents in ad hoc wireless sensor networks. In: Proceedings of the IEEE International Conference on Communications (ICC 2001), Helsinki, Finland (2001)
5. Qi, H., Wang, X., Iyengar, S.S., Chakrabarty, K.: Multisensor data fusion in distributed sensor networks using mobile agents. In: Proceedings of 5th International Conference on Information Fusion (2001)
6. Qi, H., Xu, Y., Wang, X.: Mobile-Agent-Based Collaborative Signal and Information Processing in Sensor Networks. Proc. IEEE 91(8), 1172–1183 (2003)
7. Wu, Q., Roa, N., Barhen, J., Iyengar, S., Vaishnavi, V., Qi, H., Chakrabarty, K.: On Computing Mobile Agent Routes for Data Fusion in Distributed Sensor Networks. IEEE Transactions on Knowledge and Data Eng. 16(6), 740–753 (2004)

8. Chen, M., Gonzalez, S., Leung, V.: Applications and Design Issues of Mobile Agents in Wireless Sensor Networks. IEEE Wireless Communications Magazine (WCM), Special Issue on Wireless Sensor Networking 14(6), 20–26 (2007)
9. Biswas, P.K., Qi, H., Xu, Y.: Mobile agent based collaborative sensor fusion. Elsevier Journal of Information Fusion (9), 399–411 (2008)
10. Chen, M., Kwon, T., Yuan, Y., Choi, Y., Leung, V.C.M.: Mobile agent-based directed diffusion in wireless sensor networks. EURASIP Journal on Advances in Signal Processing (2007), doi:10.1155/2007/36871
11. Chen, M., Gonzalez, S., Zhang, Y., Leung, V.C.M.: Multi-Agent Itinerary Planning for Wireless Sensor Networks. In: Bartolini, N., Nikoletseas, S., Sinha, P., Cardellini, V., Mahanti, A. (eds.) QShine 2009. LNICST, vol. 22, pp. 584–597. Springer, Heidelberg (2009)
12. Mpitziopoulos, A., et al.: Deriving Efficient Mobile Agent Routes in Wireless Sensor Networks with NOID Algorithm. In: Proc. IEEE 18th Annual IEEE Inter. Symp. Personal, Indoor, and Mobile Radio Comm. (PIMRC 2007), pp. 1–5 (September 2007)
13. Konstantopoulos, C., et al.: Effective Determination of Mobile Agent Itineraries for Data Aggregation on Sensor networks. IEEE Transaction on Knowledge and Data Engineering 22(6), 1679–1693 (2010)
14. Heinzelman, W.B., Chandrakasan, A., Balakrishnan, H.: An application specific protocol architecture for wireless microsensor networks. IEEE Transactions on Wireless Communications 1, 660–670 (2002)
15. Liu, A.F., et al.: Research on the energy hole problem based on unequal cluster-radius for wireless sensor networks. Elsevier Journal of Computer Communications, 302–321(2010)
16. Olariu, S., Stojmenovic, I.: Design Guidelines for Maximizing Lifetime and Avoiding Energy Holes in Sensor Networks with Uniform Distribution and Uniform Reporting. In: Proc. IEEE INFOCOM 2006, April 1-12 (2006)
17. Gupta, G.P., Misra, M., Garg, K.: Performance Evaluation of Agent and Non-Agent based Data Dissemination Protocols for Wireless Sensor networks. In: Proc.17th IEEE Conference on Network (ICON 2011) (to be appear, 2011)
18. http://www.omnetpp.org/
19. http://castalia.npc.nicta.com.au/

Enhanced Cluster Based Routing Protocol for MANETS

Kartheek Srungaram and M.H.M. Krishna Prasad

Department of Information Technology,
JNTUK-UCEV, Vizianagaram, A.P, India
{kartheek588,krishnaprasad.mhm}@gmail.com

Abstract. Mobile ad-hoc networks (MANETs) are a set of self organized wireless mobile nodes that works without any predefined infrastructure. For routing data in MANETs, the routing protocols relay on mobile wireless nodes. In general, any routing protocol performance suffers i) with resource constraints and ii) due to the mobility of the nodes. Due to existing routing challenges in MANETs clustering based protocols suffers frequently with cluster head failure problem, which degrades the cluster stability. This paper proposes, Enhanced CBRP, a schema to improve the cluster stability and in-turn improves the performance of traditional cluster based routing protocol (CBRP), by electing better cluster head using weighted clustering algorithm and considering some crucial routing challenges. Moreover, proposed protocol suggests a secondary cluster head for each cluster, to increase the stability of the cluster and implicitly the network infrastructure in case of sudden failure of cluster head.

Keywords: MANETS, Cluster, CBRP.

1 Introduction

Mobile ad-hoc networks (hereinafter, MANETs) are infrastructure less self organizing networks, formed arbitrarily by mobile hosts using wireless links, and the union of which forms a communication network. Routing protocol provides communication beyond the physical wireless range of nodes by relaying on intermediary nodes [1]. Due to the mobility of nodes, the network topology changes frequently, hence, nodes do not familiar with topology of their network. Each node learns about neighbor nodes by listening announcements (using broadcasting of packets) of other nodes [2]. Due to the existing constraints of MANETs, routing should be resource saving. Clustering is one approach to reduce traffic during the routing process, and several authors proposed cluster based routing protocols [1, 3-5]. All the nodes are grouped into clusters and each cluster has one cluster head in addition to many gateways; the cluster head is responsible for its cluster member, whose rebroadcast can cover all nodes in that cluster.

One of the leading protocols in MANET is Cluster Based Routing Protocol (CBRP), proposed by [3]. CBRP is an on demand routing protocol, where nodes are divided into clusters. Initially each node in the network has undecided state. Node starts timer and broadcasts HELLO packet. If it receives a Hello reply from any

N. Meghanathan et al. (Eds.): CCSIT 2012, Part I, LNICST 84, pp. 346–352, 2012.
© Institute for Computer Sciences, Social Informatics and Telecommunications Engineering 2012

cluster head then sets it state as cluster member else it makes itself as cluster head but only when it has bidirectional links with one or more neighbor nodes. Otherwise it repeats the procedure with sending HELLO packets.

Clustering is the process that divides the network into interconnected substructures, called clusters. Each cluster has a cluster head and act as a coordinator within the substructure. Each cluster head, in other terms acts as a temporary base station within its zone or cluster and communicates with its peers. Clustering algorithm used in CBRP is a variation of simple "lowest ID" clustering algorithm in which the node with a lowest ID among its neighbors is elected as the Cluster head. Each Node maintains neighbor table and cluster adjacency table which help to has knowledge of network topology.

This paper proposes a new schema for electing cluster heads by considering factors viz., node mobility, power, transmission range and degree of node, and also suggests a secondary cluster head which improves the performance of CBRP, to make the system fault tolerant.

The rest of paper is organized as follows: section 2 presents related work on routing protocols. Section 3 describes the proposed Enhanced CBRP (hereinafter, ECBRP) algorithm and section 4 presents ECBRP evaluation and results analysis. Finally section 5 concludes and directs for future study.

2   Related Work

Ref. [6] proposed a new approach to improve cluster stability, namely Smooth and Efficient Re-Clustering (SERC) protocol. In SERC, every cluster head known as primary cluster head (PCH). Each PCH elects secondary cluster head (SCH). When PCH no longer be a cluster head SCH will be cluster head. Since SCH known to all cluster members, the cluster leadership will be transferred smoothly. Each node has four battery power levels when battery power of PCH at critical threshold it transfers its responsibilities to SCH. This approach improves cluster stability and reduces cluster communication overhead.

Ref. [7] proposed Vice Cluster Head on Cluster Based Routing Protocol (VCH-CBRP) by enhancing CBRP specifically designing self-healing of clusters. To enable self-healing they introduced a vice cluster heads concept. In this, after election the cluster head the cluster head sends a notification to each node about this vice cluster head. If the primary cluster head dies for some reason, then vice cluster head advertises itself as cluster head, which reduces the frequency of calling cluster formation algorithm due to mobility/crash of cluster head. So it increases the performance of clustering.

Ref. [1] proposed Cluster Based Trust-aware Routing Protocol (CBTRP), which is a reactive protocol. CBTRP aimed to work in presence of malicious nodes. In CBTRP each node establishes trust among them and maintains it in a trust table. When establishing a route CBTRP ensure that all nodes in the path are trust worthy. If any node detected as malicious, then it will be isolated from the network such that no packets are forwarded through or from it. As mentioned earlier, one of the problems with any cluster based protocol is cluster head failure, which causes frequent execution of cluster formation algorithm. To avoid frequent execution of cluster formation algorithm one solution is secondary cluster head schema. When primary cluster head fails the secondary cluster head takes primary cluster head responsibilities. CBTRP uses local cluster formation algorithm to increase the cluster stability. In local cluster formation algorithm whenever a cluster head detected as malicious the next best trustworthy node in cluster, will be elected as cluster head. This algorithm considers only malicious cluster heads case. But there are other chances to cluster head failure which yields to frequent execution of cluster formation algorithm like cluster head moved away from the cluster and died due to lack enough energy. Therefore, ECBRP handles cluster head failure caused by node mobility and due to lack enough energy.

3   Enhanced CBRP

CBRP is a source routing protocol that works based on dynamic source routing. The main idea of CBRP is to divide the network into overlapped or disjoint clusters. Initially each node starts timer and broadcasts HELLO message, which carries neighbor table and cluster adjacency table. Neighbor table contains information about neighbor nodes id, status and link status, where cluster adjacency table has information about adjacent cluster head id and gateway nodes to reach that cluster head.

In CBRP, routing has mainly two phases: Route discovery and Data packets transmission. When source node wants to send data to destination node, source node broadcasts route request (RREQ) packet to cluster heads. After receiving RREQ packet it checks whether destination node is in its cluster or not. If destination node available sends request directly to it else broadcasts to neighbor cluster heads. Before broadcasting each node adds their node id to packet so it may drop packets with its id. When destination node receives RREQ packet it reply to source with route reply (RREP) packet through the nodes which are recorded in RREQ   packet. If source doesn't receive RREP from destination within some time period, it tries to send RREQ again. When source receives RREP it starts sending data packets.

Many researchers concentrated their studies on CBRP to improve its performance in different factors. The challenges for any routing in MANETs are mobility, resource constraints. Because of these factors the Cluster head may move away from the cluster or die lack of sufficient energy. So, original cluster head election algorithm of CBRP may not gave a better solution to the problem. Hence, this paper presents Enhanced CBRP (ECBRP) algorithm designed to provide a better solution for this problem. Main motivation for this research is to achieve significant impact in the performance of CBRP by improving the cluster stability. This proposed schema improves and develops performance of clustering algorithm than in CBRP.

ECBRP makes use of Weighted Clustering algorithm (WCA) for electing cluster heads [8] adopts a combined weight metric that takes some parameters like ideal node degree, transmission power, mobility and the battery power of the nodes to elect cluster heads. Each node calculates its weight as follows:

$$W_v = w_1\Delta_v + w_2D_v + w_3M_v + w_4P_v \ . \tag{1}$$

Parameter Δ_v represents degree-difference for every node v. Degree of the node is nothing but number of neighbors of that node (i.e., nodes within its transmission range), D_v is sum of the distances with all its neighbors. The running average of the speed for every node till current time T gives a measure of mobility and is denoted by M_v. P_v implies how much battery power has been consumed.

In equation 1, the first component, $w_1\Delta_v$, helps to avoid MAC layer problems because it is always desirable for a cluster head to handle up to a certain number of nodes. The second component is related to energy consumption because to communicate for a longer distance it requires more power. Hence, it would be better if the sum of distances to all neighbors of a cluster head is less. The third component, mobility of the node, a cluster head having less mobility shows grater improvement on stability of cluster. Last component, P_v, is the total (cumulative) time a node act as cluster. Battery drainage will be more for cluster heads comparing to cluster members. WCA also provides the flexibility to adjust the weighting factors according to our network requirements.

Initially each node in undecided state and calculates its weight Wv, then broadcasts their ids along with Wv values. When a node received it, it checks for the node with smallest W_v in its list and sets it as its cluster head and makes itself as cluster member. All nodes broadcast their weights along with ids in Hello message. Before every broadcast a node should calculate its weight. Whenever a cluster head received a broadcast message from an undecided node, it will reply with a Hello message immediately. After receiving reply from a cluster head, the undecided node changes its status as cluster member. When a node elected as cluster head it checks for next best node (i.e. node with smallest W_v) among cluster members, and broadcasts it as secondary cluster head to cluster members. So when a cluster head dies for some reason, secondary cluster head takes responsibilities of primary cluster head and improves the cluster stability by avoiding frequent execution of cluster formation algorithm. When two cluster heads move next to each other, then one of them will lose its cluster head position. i.e., whenever a cluster head receives a broadcast message from another cluster head, it checks its own weight with that of the other cluster head's. The one with smaller weight will be cluster head and another one with larger weight makes itself as a cluster member. If any node falls under the transmission range of two cluster heads, then the node joins to the cluster, which having a cluster head with smallest weight (W_v). Each cluster is identified by its cluster head id.

Every node maintains data structures to store information about network. Each node has two tables: Neighbor table and Cluster Adjacency table. Neighbor table contains the information of neighbor node id and status (i.e., cluster head or cluster member), whereas cluster adjacency table consists of neighbor cluster id, ids of the gateway node through which the neighboring cluster head could be reached. Note that there may be many gateways to reach neighbor cluster. These tables are updated periodically by Hello messages.

While coming to route discovery and transmission of data, the process is same as CBRP. ECBRP differs with CBRP when a routing failed because of cluster head failure. In CBRP, while transmitting data from source to destination, if route error occurred because of some reason (i.e., the next node in the path may died or moved away from the transmission range of the node which is currently forwarding the packets), the node which found route error will try to salvage the route. Otherwise, it generates route error packet and tells to source. But in ECBR, if route error occurred, the current node first checks whether the next node is cluster head or not. If it is a cluster head, then in the path the cluster head will be replaced by the secondary cluster head of that cluster.

For evaluating the proposed algorithm i.e., ECBRP, is experimented with authors own java simulation framework and performance is compared with original CBRP protocol.

4   Evolution and Results Analysis

In this section, the proposed protocol is evaluated using authors own java simulation framework, and compared with CBRP. In this phase of research, authors concentrated mainly in the packet delivery ratio (PDR) of the network to measure the network performance. PDR is defined as the ratio of the number of packets received at the destination to the number of packets sent by the source. In this paper, authors adopted the weighing factors from WCA [8] to compute Eq. 1, as follows: $w_1 = 0.7$, $w_2 = 0.2$, $w_3 = 0.05$ and $w_4 = 0.05$.

Authors assumed that all nodes initially having equal power and power of the node will be reduced when a node transmits (sending its own packets or forwarding) packets and all nodes are having bidirectional links. We have simulated a wireless ad hoc network with 30 nodes in general but nodes may vary up to 100 in some Experiments. The area of simulation is 400mX400m and the transmission range of the node is assumed as 80m. During the simulation the source and destinations were randomly chosen among all the nodes in the network. While coming to node mobility, destination position of each node selected randomly and moves toward the destination with 20mps with 100sec of pause time.

Figure 1, shows the experimental framework, where nodes are distributed randomly and cluster heads and cluster members are represented with blue and black colors respectively, and the dead nodes are represented with red color.

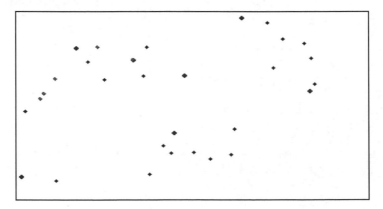

Fig. 1. Randomly distributed nodes

As discussed earlier, initially each node calculates its weight using equation 1, and broadcasts it along with their ids. The node having minimum weight will be elected as cluster head and next best one is secondary cluster head, which will be announced by cluster head. Figure 2, shows that a node broadcasting its weight to other nodes which falls within its transmission range.

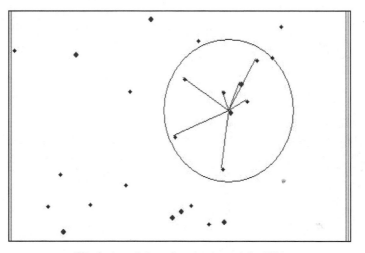

Fig. 2. A node broadcasting its weight (Wv)

The experimental results obtained with ECBRP are compared with the results (PDR) of CBRP, for various numbers of nodes (from 5 to 60), which is presented in Figure 3. For each data point in the result, 5 simulation results were performed, then the average value is computed. From figure 3, one can observe that the Enhanced CBRP performs well than the CBRP at all cases, its due to increase of cluster stability and implicitly reducing the process of cluster reformation.

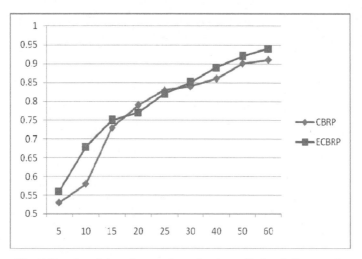

Fig. 3. Results of changing number of nodes to Packet delivery ratio

5   Conclusion and Future Work

In this paper, authors proposed an Enhanced Cluster Based Routing Protocol (ECBRP) technique, designed to improve the performance of CBRP. ECBRP makes use of the Weighted Clustering algorithm; ensures the election of best cluster head and improves the cluster stability by replacing cluster heads with the help of secondary cluster heads, leading to rare execution of recreation of clusters. As the performance of network is tightly coupled with the frequency of cluster reorganization, the proposed algorithm helps to reduce the frequency of cluster reorganization and increases the network performance. From the experimental observation it is clear that the Enhanced CBRP performs well, when compared with traditional CBRP.

In general, Intrusion Detection System (IDS) requires support of a good routing protocol. In cluster based IDSs, cluster head runs IDS, which imposes routing and IDS overhead on cluster heads. Due to this phenomenon the cluster head drains quickly. ECBRP helps in a way to decide which node should run the IDS. Authors suggest running IDS on secondary cluster head, which reduces the overhead on cluster head.

References

1. Safa, H., Artail, H., Tabet, D.: A cluster-based trust-aware routing protocol for mobile ad hoc networks. J. Wirel. Netw. 16, 969–984 (2010)
2. SECAN lab- Cluster Based Routing Protocol, `http://wiki.uni.lu/secan-lab/Cluster+Based+Routing+Protocol.html`
3. Liu, W., Chiang, C., Wu, H., Gerla, C.: Routing in Clustered Multihop, Mobile Wireless Networks with Fading Channel. In: Proc. IEEE SICON 1997, pp. 197–211. IEEE Press, Piscataway (1997)
4. Jiang, M., Li, J., Toy, Y.C.: Cluster Based Routing Protocol (CBRP) Functional Specification Internet Draft. IETF Draft (1999), `http://tools.ietf.org/html/draft-ietf-manet-cbrp-spec`.
5. Gerla, M., Tsai, J.T.C.: Multicluster, mobile, multimedia radio network. J. Wireless Networks 1, 255–265 (1995)
6. Al-kahtani, S.M., Mouftah, H.T.: Enhancements for clustering stability in mobile ad hoc networks. In: Proceedings of the 1st ACM International Workshop on Quality of Service & Security in Wireless and Mobile Networks, pp. 112–121. ACM, New York (2005)
7. Yassein, M.B., Hijazi, N.: Improvement on Cluster Based Routing Protocol by Using Vice Cluster Head. In: NGMAST 2010 Fourth International Conference on Next Generation Mobile Applications, Services and Technologies, pp. 137–141. IEEE Computer Society, Washington (2010)
8. Chatterjee, M., Das, S.K., Turgut, D.: WCA: A Weighted Clustering Algorithm for Mobile Ad Hoc Networks. J. Cluster Computing 5, 193–204 (2002); Smith, T.F., Waterman, M.S.: Identification of Common Molecular Subsequences. J. Mol. Biol. 147, 195–197 (1981)

Soft Computing Technique Based Call Admission Control Decision Mechanism

H.S. Ramesh Babu[1], Gowrishankar[2], G. Mahesh[3], and P.S. Satyanarayana[4]

[1] Department of Information Science and Engineering,
Acharya Institute of Technology
Bangalore, India
rameshbabu@acharya.ac.in
[2] Department of Computer Science and Engineering,
B.M.S. College of Engineering
Bangalore, India
s.gowrishankara@gmail.com
[3] Department of Information Science and Engineering,
Acharya Institute of Technology
Bangalore, India
maheshg@acharya.ac.in
[4] Department of Electronics and Communication Engineering,
B.M.S. College of Engineering
Bangalore, India
pssvittala.ece@bmsce.ac.in

Abstract. The decision Mechanism is the concluding phase of any decision making process. This paper discusses on the different methodologies available for implementing the decision mechanisms. The paper preambles with a brief description on set of conventional Multi criteria Decision Mechanisms (MCDM) like Analytical Hierarchy Process (AHP), Simple Additive weighting Method (SAW) and Technique for Order Preference by Similarity to Ideal Solution (TOPSIS), Grey Rational Analysis (GRA) along with benefits and limitations of each technique. The different intelligent/soft computing techniques that are widely used in decision making processes like fuzzy logic, neural networks are discussed and finally confines the discussions to the different neural network (NN) based decision support systems. The paper proposes a fuzzy neural network based architecture for call admission control decision mechanism in a heterogeneous wireless network environment.

Keywords: Analytical Hierarchy Process, TOPSIS, Grey Rational Analysis, Fuzzy neural networks.

1 Introduction

The MCDM system is an analytical technique that analyzes the complex problem of with contradicting constraints and assists in finding best possible solution by bringing all deciding factors together. The MCDM systems are extensively used in many fields

N. Meghanathan et al. (Eds.): CCSIT 2012, Part I, LNICST 84, pp. 353–367, 2012.
© Institute for Computer Sciences, Social Informatics and Telecommunications Engineering 2012

like engineering and technology fields like environmental study, reliability of systems, study of social issues, financial analysis and analyzing political scenarios. The MCDM system will involve different conflicting interests in obtaining an optimal or near optimal solution to the multi constraint problem. The MCDM approach has been very widely used in the recent past for RRM mechanisms [1, 2]. The MCDM methods can be classified as conventional and evolutionary methods [3]. Some of the conventional methods used often are The Analytical Hierarchy Process (AHP), Simple Additive weighting Method (SAW) and Technique for Order Preference by Similarity to Ideal Solution (TOPSIS), Grey Rational Analysis(GRA). The evolutionary approaches are based on soft computing techniques like Genetic algorithms (GA), Fuzzy logic, Neural Networks (NN).

2   Conventional Decision Mechanisms

The Simple Additive weighting Method (SAW), Analytical Hierarchy Process (AHP), Grey Rational Analysis (GRA), and Technique for Order Preference by Similarity to Ideal Solution (TOPSIS) are widely used conventional methods.

A. Simple Additive Weighting Method

SAW is undoubtedly the one of the best MCDM method. It is simple and easy to understand [4].In SAW the score is obtained from adding the contributions from each attribute The Normalization is applied to add two items with different measurement units as we will not be able to add two attribute values directly. In this method the overall score of an alternative is computed by multiplying the comparable rating for each attribute based on the importance of the weight assigned to the attribute and then summing these products over all attributes. [5].

Formally, score of an alternative in the SAW method can be expressed as

$$V(A_i) = V_i = \sum_{j=1}^{n} w_j v_j(x_{ij}), \quad i = 1, 2, 3 \dots m \qquad (1)$$

Where $V(A_i)$ is the value function of alternative A_i ; w_j and $v_j(.)$ are weights and value functions of attribute x_{ij} respectively. Through the normalization process, each incommensurable attribute becomes a pseudo-value function, which allows direct addition among attributes. The value of attribute A_i can, then, be rewritten as

$$V_i = \sum_{j=1}^{n} w_j r_{ij}, \quad i = 1, 2, 3 \dots m \qquad (2)$$

Where, r_{ij} is the comparable scale of x_{ij}, which can be calculated by normalization process [5].

The calculation of r_{ij} can be done using either linear normalization or vector normalization. In linear normalization, it adopts a simple procedure of dividing the rating of an attribute by its maximum value. The normalize value of the x_{ij} for a benefit attribute is given by

$$r_{ij} = \frac{x_{ij}}{x_j^{\max}} \quad i = 1,....m, \quad j = 1,...n \tag{3}$$

For instance, if bandwidth and performance are benefit attributes of the network in CAC and need to have larger values then such networks are ideal for CAC. In case of cost attributes, lesser the cost more the weightage/preference to the network for CAC decision in the HWN environment. Hence for cost attributes the r_{ij} is calculated by:

$$r_{ij} = \frac{x_j^{\min}}{x_{ij}} \quad i = 1,....m, \quad j = 1,...n \tag{4}$$

Finally, by applying the weight factors for individual attributes, the weighted average value V is calculated for each alternative.

B. AHP: Hierarchical SAW Method

AHP was developed by Saaty in 1980.This is the formalization of our intuitive understanding of a complex problem in a hierarchical structure.AHP develops a goal of hierarchy to solve the decision problem with a large number of attributes. It is best suited for finding optimal solution for complex decision making problems. In AHP the final objective of the problem is analyzed until the problem acquires a hierarchical structure. This step of structuring a problem as a hierarchy of multiple criteria is the first step of implementing the AHP.

A hierarchy should have at least three levels: focus or overall goal of the problem at the top, multiple criteria that define alternatives at middle and in this hierarchical structure the lowest level will have the alternative solutions of the problem found. The elements of each level of hierarchy are compared pair wise as far as the degree of preference of one against the other [6].The required comparison between the pair is realized via matrices. After comparison the next step is the assignment of preference for each pair of decision elements. The values assigned could be the Saaty numerical gradationvalues1,2,3,4,5,6,7,8,9,1/,2,1/3,1/4,1/5,1/6,1/7,1/8,1/9.The final stage of AIIP is to compute the contribution of overall goal by aggregating the resulting weights vertically.

C. TOPSIS

The TOPSIS method was developed by Hwang and Yoon (1981). This method is based on the idea that the chosen alternative need to have the shortest distance from the ideal solution and the farthest distance from the negative ideal solution. The ideal solution is a theoretical solution for which all attribute values correspond to the maximum attribute values in the database comprising the satisfying solutions; the negative ideal solution is the hypothetical solution for which all attribute values correspond to the minimum attribute values in the database. TOPSIS thus gives a solution that is not only closest to the hypothetically best, that is also the farthest from the hypothetically worst [7]. TOPSIS then defines an index called similarity or relative closeness to the positive ideal solution and the remoteness from the negative ideal solution. Then it chooses an alternative with the maximum similarity to the positive ideal solution. TOPSIS assumes that each attribute takes either monotonically increasing or monotonically decreasing attribute. That is larger the attribute outcome greater the preference and this is applicable to benefit attributes for ex. Coverage, bandwidth etc.. But in case of the cost attributes lesser attribute more the preference.

D. Grey Rational Analysis

GRA builds the grey relationship between the individual elements of two series under comparison .The one of the two series used in GRA consists of best quality elements and the other series contains comparative elements. The less difference between these two series will help in drawing better comparison series. Taking the similarity and variability between two series is defined by Grey relational Coefficient (GRC).

There are 6 steps in implementing GRA[8].

Step 1 classifying the elements of series by three situations. The situations are larger-the –better, smaller-the-better and nominal the best
Step 2 defining upper bound, lower bound, and middle /moderate bounds of series elements
Step 3 Normalizing Individual entities
Step 4 defining the ideal series
Step 5 calculating the grey relational coefficient
Step 6 selecting the alternative with the largest grey relational coefficient

3   Intelligent Techniques in Decision Making

The application of intelligent/soft computing techniques has become wide spread for nonlinear time varying and complex problems that were posing a great challenge to researchers when they used the conventional methods. The partial list of soft computing techniques includes techniques such as such as Genetic algorithms, fuzzy logic systems, artificial neural networks and the hybrid systems like fuzzy neural networks have outperformed the conventional algorithmic methods. The advantages of these methods are many, which include most notably learning from experience, scalability, adaptability, moreover the ability to extract the rules without the detailed or accurate mathematical modeling. Soft Computing deals with data that is imprecise, data that are uncertain and partial correct   to achieve controllability, robustness and low cost. All these features make the soft computing techniques the best candidates for solving the complex problems in any domain.

Intelligence is defined as the competence of understanding or the ability to perceive and comprehend meaning [9]. Majority of researchers immaterial of the field of research are attempting to design and develop intelligent systems and intelligent methods to solve complex problems. The term intelligent describes a system or method that is able to modify its action dynamically based on the ongoing events. These systems are adaptive and give the appearance of being intelligent as they change their behavior without the intervention of a user. The Intelligent systems can be classified into two categories: rule based techniques and non–rule based techniques [9]. The methods under rule-based methods include fuzzy logic and genetic algorithms. The non-rule based group comprises of techniques such as neural networks which aim to perceive and comprehend the significance of the data with which they are trained. Neural networks are best distinguished from other intelligent techniques in that they are non rule-based and can additionally be made stochastic so that the same action does not necessarily take place each time for the same input. This capability of stochastic behavior of   neural network makes it to explore its environment more fully and potentially to arrive at a better solution than linear methods might allow.

The categorization of the intelligent techniques into rule-based and non-rule-based categories helps in understanding better how these systems work and where they may be applied. The rule based techniques will often have wider acceptance than the non-rule based methods. This is for the obvious reasons as it is fairly easy to understand how the rule-based intelligent system arrives at its solution and this can be used to analyze   that this system will operate within definite set of input parameters.

A. Genetic Algorithms

The concept of GA originated in early 70s and was developed by Holland and his colleagues. The Genetic algorithms are based on the principles of evolution of natural genetics theory. As per the principles of evolution of natural genetics, the weak and unfit species within their environment are faced with extinction by natural selection. The strong ones have greater opportunity to pass their genes to future generation via reproduction. The notion of the GA is survival of the fittest, the individual who are fittest are likely to survive and have chance of passing their characteristics to next generation.

In GA terminology, a solution vector $x \in X$ is called an individual or a chromosome. The chromosomes are made of discrete units called Genes. Each of the gene controls one or more characteristics of chromosome. Initially Holland assumption of genes as binary numbers initially but in later implementation varied type of genes were introduced. In general, a chromosome is considered as a unique solution x in the solution space. This requires a method to map between the solution space and chromosomes. This mapping function is called as encoding.GA actually works with encoding of the problem and not the problem itself.

The GA operates with randomly initialized population which is formed by a group of chromosomes. As the search progress with the filter solutions, the population finally converges to a single solution. The crossover and mutation are the two operators used to find new solution from the existing solutions.

The parent chromosomes are combined together to form new chromosomes called offspring in crossover operation. The parents are selected among existing chromosomes in the group of chromosomes by giving preference for the fitness of the chromosome so that offspring is expected to inherit a good gene. By repeated application of crossover operation, the percentages of genes of good chromosomes are expected to increase in the population, which leads to an overall good solution. The mutation operator introduces random changes in characteristics of chromosomes. Mutation process is normally applied at the gene level. In typical implementation of GA, the mutation rate is very small which may be less than 1%. Therefore, the new chromosomes produced by mutation will not be very different from the original ones. The purpose of mutation operation is to reintroduce genetic diversity back into the population, and to overcome local optimal solution.

Among the various artificial intelligence techniques, GAs has been widely used in optimization tasks, including numerical optimization and combinatorial optimization problems as well as admission control in wireless systems. Its ability for parallel searching and fast evaluation distinguish itself from other decision and optimization algorithms. In parallel searching, a distributed GAs (DGA) is well known to be a smarter search algorithm compared to traditional GAs. In order to solve the CAC problem, several GA based approaches have been proposed for specific wireless network architectures [10][11]. Although these schemes are promising, they do not specifically consider admission control policies as a means to provide a unified scheme for maximum network utilization, minimum handoff latency and QoS.

B. Fuzzy Logic

The concept of Fuzzy logic has been extensively applied in characterizing the behavior of nonlinear systems. The nonlinear behavior of the system can be effectively captured and represented by a set of Fuzzy rules [12]. In other words fuzzy logic can be viewed as a theory for dealing with uncertainty about complex systems, and as an approximation theory. Many engineering and scientific applications including time series are not only nonlinear but also non-stationary. Such applications cannot be represented by simple fuzzy rules, because fixed number of rules can describe time invariant systems only and cannot take in to account the non-stationary behavior. Recently, a new set of Fuzzy rules have been defined to predict the difference of consecutive values of non-stationary time series [13].

Fuzzifier is the first step in the Fuzzy Logic (FL) and control decision making system. The objective of this process is to assign, for each input linguistic variable, a value between 0 and 1 corresponding to the degree of membership of this input to a given Fuzzy Subset or Term. The fuzzifier transforms the crisp inputs into degrees of match with linguistic values. A Fuzzy Subset is a linguistic subjective representation of the input variable. The linguistic variables are denoted by LV_i. The fuzzification is performed by the fuzzifier and is the process that transforms crisp data into fuzzy sets. A fuzzy set is characterized by a membership function μF which takes values in the interval [0, 1], namely, $\mu F: U \rightarrow [0, 1]$. Thus, a fuzzy set may be represented as a set of ordered pairs of a generic element u and its grade of membership function $F= \{(u, \mu F(u))|u \in U\}$ [14].

The Inference engine and fuzzy rule base is the second step of the fuzzy logic and control decision making system .In a FC, the dynamic behavior of the system is characterized by a set of linguistic rules based on expert knowledge. The expert knowledge is expressed in If-Else form:

Since the antecedent and the consequent parts of these IF–THEN rules are associated with fuzzy concepts, they are called fuzzy inference rules or fuzzy control rules. Several linguistic variables might be involved in the antecedents and conclusions of these rules, thus providing a convenient way for expressing control/decision policies and simplifying complex decision problems. The total of the fuzzy inference rules forms the fuzzy rule base, the inference engine is the control mechanism that applies fuzzy control rules contained in the fuzzy rule base.

Defuzzification is the next step in the FL based decision control system .The defuzzification process is executed by the defuzzifier and consists of the transformation of the outputs of the inference process, which are so far fuzzy sets, into non-fuzzy (crisp) control value. The defuzzification method considered is the center-of-area method [15].

The advantages of fuzzy logic approach [16] are easy to understand and build a predictor for any desired accuracy with a simple set of fuzzy rules, no need of mathematical model for estimation and fast estimation of future values due to the less computational demand. The limitation of fuzzy logic approach is that it works on single step prediction and it does not have learning capability. In general the methods based on fuzzy logic are cumbersome to use, which requires exercise knowledge and user involvement in order to make decision rules .This makes fuzzy logic solutions applicable and more convenient when the problem dimension is very small. Bringing in the learning abilities of neural networks to fuzzy logic systems may provide a more promising fuzzy logic approach.

C. Neural Networks

Neural networks have large number of highly interconnected processing elements called 'node'. These nodes demonstrate the ability to learn and generalize from training patterns or data. The neural networks are low-level computational elements that exhibit good performance when they deal with sensory data. They can be applied to the situation where there is sufficient observation data available. The NN method is used in any problem related to control, prediction and classification. NNs are able to gain this popularity because of the commanding capacity they have in modeling exceptionally complex nonlinear functions. NNs have a biggest advantage in terms of easy to use which is based on training-prediction cycles. Training the NN plays crucial role in the system usage of NNs. The training pattern that contains a predefined set of inputs and expected outputs is used to train the NN. Next, in prediction cycle, the outputs are supplied to the user based on the input values. To make NNs to behave like a physical system or predict or control the training set used in the training cycle shall consist of enough information representing all the valid cases [17-19]. NNs are flexible soft computing frameworks for modeling a broad range of nonlinear problems [20]. One significant advantage of the neural network based approach over other classes of nonlinear models is that NNs are universal approximation tools that can approximate large class of functions with a high degree of accuracy [21]. This approximation power of NN model comes from several parallel processing elements, called as 'neurons'. No prior assumption of the model form is required in the model building process. Instead, the network model is largely determined by characteristics of the data.

The benefits of neural network approach [22] are as follows. First, the NN Prediction accuracy is much superior to conventional approaches. Second, NN Model can be used for single and Multi-step forecasting. Third, they are capable of learning the system and demands low computation structures. The limitations of NN approach are: The optimal choice of number of layers and number of neurons in each layer is a heuristic process and it requires expertise in the field of NNs for a model designer. Deciding of the weights to the non-cyclic links will determine the accuracy of forecasting. However, deciding the appropriate weights to the link is once again a heuristic process.

D. Recurrent Neural Networks

The Recurrent Neural Network (RNN) architecture can be classified into fully interconnected nets, partially connected nets and Locally Recurrent & Globally Feed-forward (LRGF) nets [23]. The recurrent neural networks (RNNs) have superior capabilities than the feed forward neural networks [24][25]. Since a recurrent neuron has an internal feedback loop to capture the dynamic response of a system without external feedback through delays. The RNNs have the ability to deal with time-varying input or output through their own natural temporal operation [24]. In addition to all these , the RNNs have dynamic mapping and demonstrate good control performance in the presence of un-modeled dynamics, parameter variations, and external disturbances [24][26]. Since, a recurrent neuron has the internal feedback loop to capture the dynamic response of the system without external feedback through delays; the RNNs have superior capabilities than the non-recurrent feed forward neural networks [27].

E. Radial Basis Function Networks

A fuzzy system maps an input fuzzy set into an output fizzy set. The characteristics of this mapping are governed by fuzzy rules in the fuzzy system. One of the important design issues of fuzzy systems   construction a set of fuzzy rules which plays vital role in the system performance of the fuzzy systems. Where the construction of rules can be implemented using either manual or automatic rule generation. The manual approach becomes more difficult if the required number of rules increases or if there is lack of domain knowledge which may is not easily available .This not only limits applications of fuzzy systems, but also forces system designers to spend tough time to fine tune fuzzy rules abstracted from the knowledge of domain experts.

These difficulties motivate researchers to automate the process of fuzzy rule extraction. The basic idea behind the automatic design approaches is to estimate fuzzy rules through learning from input and output sample data. The functional equivalence between radial basis function networks and fuzzy systems with some restrictions was shown in [28]. The Radial Basis Function Network (RBFN) proposed in [29]is a type of neural networks which employ local receptive fields to perform function mappings, demonstrated that RBFNs and their usefulness in a variety of applications including classification, prediction, and system modeling.

The RBFN has a faster convergence property than a multilayer Perceptron (MLP) because of its simple structure and simple learning process. Additionally, the RBFN has a similar feature to the fuzzy system. First, the output value is calculated using the weighted sum method. Then, the number of nodes in the hidden layer of the RBFN is same as the number of if–then rules in the fuzzy system. Finally, the receptive field functions of the RBFN are similar to the membership functions of the premise part in the fuzzy system. Therefore, the RBFN is very useful to be applied to time variant systems [30] [31].

The implementation of RBFN bases for recurrent RBFN based FNN improves the accuracy of the approximation function. Based on the architecture of the conventional RBFN, the Recurrent Radial Basis Function network (RRBFN) have input looped neurons with sigmoid activation functions. These looped neurons represent the dynamic memory of the RRBF, and the Gaussian neurons represent the static one. The dynamic memory enables the networks to learn temporal patterns without an input buffer to hold the recent elements of an input sequence. The recurrent or dynamic aspect is obtained by cascading looped neurons on the first layer. This layer represents the dynamic memory of the RRBF network that permits to learn temporal data. The RRBFN architecture is able to learn temporal sequences and RRBFN network is based on the advantages of Radial Basis Function networks in terms of training process time.

4   Intelligent Methods in CAC Decision Mechanisms

Fuzzy logic based CAC is excellent in dealing with real world imprecision and has a greater ability to adapt itself to dynamic, imprecise and burst traffic environments. But Fuzzy logic is incompetent in learning capabilities needed to automatically construct its rule structure and membership functions which is mandatory to achieve optimal performance.

Neural network based CAC provides learning and adaptation capabilities which reduce the estimation error of conventional CAC and achieve performance similar to that of a fuzzy logic based call admission controller. However, for obvious reasons it is difficult to incorporate the knowledge embodied in conventional methods into the design of neural networks. From the above discussion it is clear that the fuzzy logic is easy to understand and uses simple linguistic terms and if-then rules and NNs are smart enough to learn the system characteristics. Therefore the Fuzzy Neural Networks (FNN) combines the benefit of both NNs and fuzzy systems to solve the CAC problem. This research work proposes an ICACM based on Fuzzy Neural Call Admission Control (FNCAC) developed using RRBFN to handle the complex problem of CAC in HWNs supporting multimedia traffic. The advantages of RRBFN have already been discussed in the previous chapter. FNCAC is a hybrid model and it is a combination of fuzzy logic and NN that succeeds in absorbing the benefits of all the three approaches discussed i.e. Conventional, Fuzzy logic and NN based CAC while minimizing their drawbacks for HWNs for supporting multimedia traffic.

5   FNCAC Controller for ICACM

The fuzzy neural call admission control (FNCAC)of the intelligent call admission controller mechanism (ICACM) utilizes the learning capability of the NN to reduce decision errors of conventional CAC policies that is generally resulted from modeling, approximation, and unpredictable traffic fluctuations of the system. FNCAC also employs the rule structure of the fuzzy logic controller which is easy to learn and requires less learning time and prevents operating errors. Further, the neural fuzzy network is a simple structured network which needs proper selection of input variables and design the rule structure for the FNCAC scheme so that it not only provides a robust framework to mimic experts' knowledge embodied in existing traffic admission control techniques but also constructs an intelligent computational algorithm for CAC.

The FNCAC controller with its other processors for HWNs is as shown in Figure 1. The peripheral processors are traffic estimator of the incoming traffic, and a network resource estimator of the HWN environment. The network character estimator will provide the information about the available network resources in the system. The Incoming traffic requirement estimator collects the incoming traffic requirements like BER, required bandwidth/data rate of the incoming traffic/user request through the network resource manager. The network resource manager plays an important role in Resource provisioning.

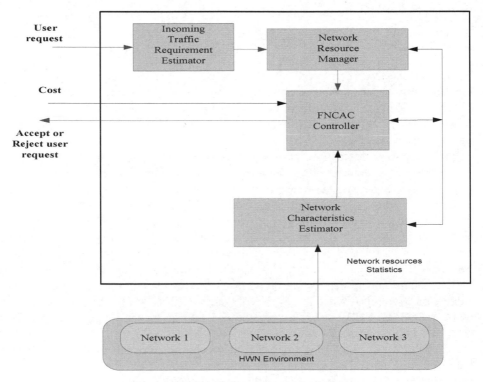

Fig. 1. Architecture of FNCAC based ICACM

The FNCAC also takes price as one of the input. The FNCAC will take the decision of admitting/ rejecting the user request based on the user QoS requirements and networks resource constraints and the economic input like cost which will act as bias. The FNCAC based ICACM meets the interest of the network service provider by increasing the radio resource utilization which results in increased revenue. It improves the user's satisfaction by enhanced QoS provisioning and overall network stability.

The proposed ICACM particularly use the feed forward neural networks which has the ability to map any nonlinear and non-stationary function to an arbitrary degree of accuracy. One such popular feed-forward network is the Radial Basis Function Network(RBFN).

It is a single hidden layer feed-forward network. Each node in the hidden layer has a parameter vector called as Centre. These centres are used to compare with network input and produce radically symmetrical response. These responses are scaled by connection weights of the output layer and then produce network output, where Gaussian basis function is used and is represented as

$$\hat{y} = \sum_{i=1}^{n} w_i \exp\left(-\frac{\|y - \mu_i\|}{2\sigma_i}\right) \qquad (5)$$

Recurrent Radial Basis Function Network is a class of Locally Recurrent and Globally Feed-Forward(LRGF) RNN. In LRGF network the recurrent/self-connection is either in the input layer or in the output layer. RRBFN is having recurrent connection at the input layer. Where i is the dimension of the influence field of hidden layer neuron, y and i are input and prototype vector respectively.

The proposed architecture of RRBFN based FNCAC for ICACM is shown in Figure 2. The FNCAC takes the characteristics of the three different networks for the study and the requirements of the incoming traffic are taken as inputs. The cost is considered as the bias input. The NN based Call admission control   involves training and testing of RRBFN based CAC controller.

6   Validation of FNCAC

The training and testing samples are randomly picked from the sample size of 3000. The second phase of simulation is training and testing of the RRBF network. The RRBF network has 500 neurons in input layer with sigmiodal activation function with recurrent connection the range of recurrent weights are -1 to +1, the hidden RBF layer has 375 neurons with RBF activation and output layer has single neuron with linear activation. Input weights are in the range of - 0.40 to + 0.40, recurrent weights are in the range of - 0.6 to +0.6. All the layers except input layer neurons have radial activation function.

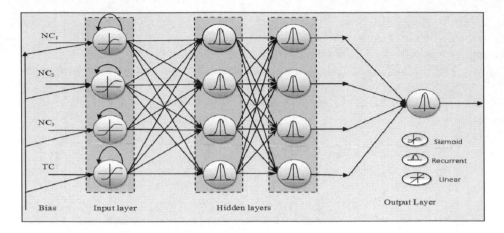

Fig. 2. Architecture of RRBFN based FNCAC for ICACM

The set of experiments were conducted with varying the aggregate traffic and individual traffic of the network and the call blocking probability of Fuzzy neural technique was compared with the conventional CAC and Fuzzy based CAC.

The performance of RRBFN based FNCAC system for next generation networks is compared and validated with the performance of fuzzy based CAC and conventional Guard channel based CAC. The Performance of FNCAC model in an heterogeneous RATs supporting multimedia traffic is studied pitching upon the call blocking probability by varying the utilization rate of the aggregate traffic and the individual traffic and is indicated in Figure 3.

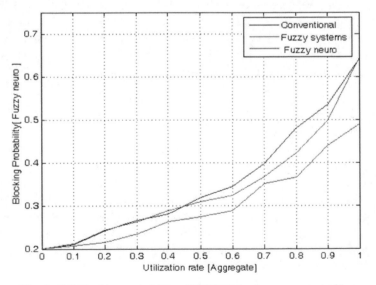

Fig. 3. Call blocking probability of FNCAC for the aggregate traffic

The simulation study conducted records the following observations.

The concept of minimizing the call blocking probability is an optimization technique to provide fair QoS to the set of users in the wireless network and there is a need of intelligent call admission control strategy in the admission control mechanism to make the decision of accepting are rejecting a call, keeping the blocking probability minimal in an HWNs was clearly indicative.

The increase in the utilization rate of the aggregate traffic in the network increases the call blocking probability of the system. The important observation made from the Simulation results reveal that the FNCAC scheme achieves superior system utilization and high learning speed while keeping the QoS contract, compared with the conventional CAC and fuzzy logic based CAC scheme.

7   Conclusion

The analysis made in the work makes RBFN-based FNN is the right tool for implementing the CAC decision in this study. In addition, the structure and the parameter learning phases are preformed concurrently and on line in the Recurrent RBFN based NN makes RRBFN the better choice for CAC Mechanism. The soft computing techniques based decision making system is widely implemented. In our future work we are planning to implement the soft computing based decision mechanism radio resource management techniques in fourth generation networks.

References

[1] Song, Q., Jamalipour, A.: A Network Selection Mechanism for Next generation Networks. In: IEEE International Conference on Communications, vol. 2, pp. 1418–1422 (2005)

[2] Tawil, R., Salazar, O., Pujolle, G.: Vertical Handoff Decision Scheme Using MADM for Wireless Networks. In: IEEE Wireless Communication and Networking Conference, pp. 2789–2792 (2008)

[3] Marler, R.T., Arora, J.S.: Survey of Multi-objective Optimization Methods for Engineering. Structural and Multidisciplinary Optimization 26(6), 369–395 (2004)

[4] Zhang, W.: Handover Decision Using Fuzzy MADM in Heterogeneous Networks. In: WCNC (2004)

[5] Pual Yoon, K., Hwang, C.-l.: Multi attribute decision making. An Introduction series: Quantitative applications in the social sciences

[6] Charilas, D., Markaki, O., Nikitopoulos, D., Theologou, M.: Packet –Swithced network selection with the highest QoS in 4G networks. Elsevier Computer Networks 52, 248–258 (2008)

[7] Venkata Rao, R.: Decision Making in the Manufacturing Environment Using Graph Theory and Fuzzy Multiple Attribute Decision Making Methods. Springer series in advanced manufacturing

[8] Chalmers, D., Soloman, M.: A Survey of Quality of service in Mobile computing Environments. IEEE Communication, Tutorials and Surveys, 2nd qtr. (1999)

[9] Clarkson, T.: Applications of Neural Networks in Telecommunications, white paper, King's College London (1999)

[10] Xiao, Y., Chen, C.L.P., Wang, Y.: A Near Optimal Call Admission Control With Genetic Algorithm For Multimedia Services In Wireless/Mobile Networks. In: IEEE Nat. Aero. Elec. Conf., pp. 787–792 (October 2000)

[11] Zomaya, A.Y., Wright, M.: Observations on Using Genetic- Algorithms for Channel Allocation in Mobile Computing. IEEE Transactions on Parallel and Distributed Systems 13(9), 948–962 (2002)

[12] Takagi, T., Sugeno, M.: Fuzzy Identification of Systems and its Application to Modeling and Control. IEEE Transaction on System, Man and Cybernetics 15, 116–132 (1985)

[13] Kim, I., Lee, S.: A Fuzzy Time Series Prediction Method Based on Consecutive Values. In: IEEE International Conference on Fuzzy Systems, vol. 2, pp. 703–707 (1998)

[14] Giupponi, L., Agusti, R., Perez-Romero, J., Sallent, O.: A Framework for JRRM with Resource Reservation and Multiservice Provisioning in Heterogeneous Networks. Mobile Networks and Applications 11, 825–846 (2006)

[15] Ross, T.J.: Fuzzy logic with engineering applications. McGraw-Hill (1995)

[16] Cheok, A.D., Ertugrul, N.: Use of Fuzzy Logic for Modeling, Estimation and Prediction In switched Reluctance Motor Device. IEEE Transaction on Industrial Electronics 46(6), 1207–1224 (1999)

[17] Wolpert, D.H.: The mathematics of generalization. In: Proceedings of the SFI/CNLS Workshop on Formal Approaches to Supervised Learning. Santa Fe Institute Studies in the Sciences of Complexity, vol. 20. Addison-Wesley, MA (1994)

[18] The lack of A priori distinctions between learning algorithms. Neural Computation 8(7), 1341–1390 (1996)

[19] The existence of A priori distinctions between learning algorithms. Neural Computation 8(7), 1391– 1420 (1996)

[20] Zahang, P., Qi, G.M.: Neural Network Forecasting for Seasonal and Trend Time Series. European Journal of Operational Research 160, 501–514 (2005)

[21] Chen, A., Leung, M.T., Hazem, D.: Application of Neural Networks to an Emerging Financial Market: Forecasting and Trading the Taiwan Stock Index. Computers and Operational Research 30, 901–923 (2003)

[22] Li, M., Huang, G., Saratchandran, P., Sundarajan, N.: Performance Evaluation of GAP-RBF Network in Channel Equalization. Neural Processing Letters 22(2), 223–233 (2005)

[23] Elman, J.L.: Finding Structure in Time. Cognitive Sciences 14(2), 179–211 (1990)

[24] Jordan, M.I.: Generic Constraints on Underspecified Target Trajectories. In: International Joint Conference on Neural Networks, vol. 1, pp. 217–225 (1989)

[25] Campolucci, P., Uncini, A., Piazza, F., Rao, B.D.: Online learning algorithms for locally recurrent neural networks. IEEE Transactions on Neural Networks 10(2), 340–355 (1999)

[26] Lin, C.H., Chou, W.D., Lin, F.J.: Adaptive hybrid control using a recurrent neural network for a linear synchronous motor servo-drive system. IEE Proceedings of Control Theory Applications 148, 156–168 (2001)

[27] Campolucci, P., Uncini, A., Piazza, F., Rao, B.D.: On-line learning algorithms for locally recurrent neural networks. IEEE Trans. Neural Networks. 10(2), 340–355 (1999)

[28] Jang, J.S.R., Sun, C.-T.: Functional equivalence between radial basis function networks and fuzzy inference systems. IEEE Trans. Neural Networks 4(1), 156–159 (1993)

[29] Moody, J., Darken, C.: Fast learning in networks of locally-tuned processing units. Neural Computation 1, 281–294 (1989)
[30] Swevers, J., Al-Bender, F., Ganseman, C.G., Prajogo, T.: An integrated friction model structure with improved presliding behavior for accurate friction compensation. IEEE Trans. Autom. Contr. 45(4), 675–686 (2000)
[31] Park, E.C., Lim, H., Choi, C.H.: Position control of X-Y table at velocity reversal using pre-sliding friction characteristics. IEEE Trans. Contr. Syst. Technol. 11(1), 24–31 (2003)

Mechanisms Supporting Mobility in WSNs

Saimadhavi[1] and Y.S. Kumarswamy[2]

[1] CSE Dept, RYM Engg college, Bellary
[2] MCA Dept, Dayanand sagar college, Bangalore

Abstract. Applications of todays world require to have dynamic features like mobility support,In this paper we proposed and evaluated a comprehensive set of mechanisms essential to assure the support of mobility in WSNs,by providing energy efficiency mechanism for a node and a mechanism for soft handoff,based on link quality.

1   Introduction

wsns are viewed with an angle to suite the most basic requriments suitable for various applications.

In this paper we propose a set of mechanisms to turn sensor networks into an adaptable and flexible solutions,so as to provide solution to most applications .Here we basically focus on node mobility which is categorized based on whether the node is moving within the same network domain or whether it is moving between domains. Based on the specific properties of WSNs, the requirements of Mobility and the demand for critical applications, we propose a model for the support and deployment of mobility-aware wireless sensor networks.

2   Related Work

So far we have seen S-MAC and WiseMAC which use different duty cycles.some of the ideas which could be used for adapting neighbor discovery protocol to WSNs.

Load adhoc routing[1]- defines a method called LOAD to provide route discovery,for maintaining data structures and maintaining local connections.

Hierarchial routing[2]- introduces issue of dynamic address assignment with self configuration.

lowPAN neighbor discovery extension[3]-proposes optimized methods,minimizing the multicast of router solicitations.

[4]-neglects unnecessary information of global address,instead previous L2 address is replaced with (RA)router advertisement.

[5]-this new mechanism allows the use of stateless address assignment,neighbor discovery proxy,and optimization of RA also introducing concept of (RE),router edge per network.

To support mobility in WSNs it was need to combine a method for node discovery with a method for handoff management [9].

N. Meghanathan et al. (Eds.): CCSIT 2012, Part I, LNICST 84, pp. 368–371, 2012.
© Institute for Computer Sciences, Social Informatics and Telecommunications Engineering 2012

Wireless communication consumes more energy,especially in broadcast,which is unavoidable since broadcasting helps in establishing a network,node discovery,access points and neighbours,looking above protocol for neighbor discovery is presented where in a periodic broadcast of of router advertisements messages to present an overview of the complete protocol.

When a new node is deployed, it broadcasts a Router Solicitation. Then, all sinks in the area answer with a Router Advertisement, and the node selects the best one to connect based on the Received Signal Strength Indication (RSSI) value. The selection is confirmed by a accept message. After receiving the accept message,the Sink Node computes a Time-to-Live value. Then, it sends this value to the mote, which, in turn, confirms the procedure with an acknowledgement. During the Registration procedure, the ack message contains the list of supported services in the data field.

While performing this procedure, the Sink Node saves all information in a local database, so that it can be made available to applications if needed. In turn, when it receives the TTL value, the mote self configures its address with the network prefix. This means that a force is made to use global addresses based on Router Advertisements. This procedure does not require an additional message to announce it. Once registered in a network, it must guarantee the connections even for high mobility motes.

mobility is crucial to apply WSN in the most critical and demanded environments. Mobile nodes should not be physical constrained and we must assume the possibility to occur not only intra-mobility, but also inter-mobility where motes must reboot the transceiver during the handoff process. To control the communication during the handoff, including latencies and packet losses. To do so, it needed to provide a mechanism to detect on time if the mote is moving away or if it is arriving. In order to detect movement, a study based on the RSSI value, which is the link metric [7] provided by

IEEE802.15.4 to detect when the mote is moving by comparing the RSSI of the exchanged messages. In [6] it concluded that independently of the environment conditions and the achieved distance, the lowest acceptable RSSI value is -88dBm. After that point the connection is lost. Therefore, it defined this point as the rupture point, Rpoint. However, nodes must connect to another Sink before reaching that point, at a point that we call the critical point,C-point. Naturally, the difference between C and R – which we denote Δc – depends on the average time taken by the handoff process and on the rate of RSSI degradation experienced by the mote. If the sensor node is experiencing a decrease in RSSI of Ei dB during a time interval T and it takes an average t seconds to perform the handoff procedures, then:

$$\Delta c = k \times t \times Ei \, / \, T \, (1)$$

Where k is a constant used to adjust the handoff policy. Naturally, Δc is always an estimation, as there is no way to determine future RSSI values. A conservative approach would use $k > 1$, and an optimistic approach would use $k < 1$. Based on the above formula, nodes, or any other responsible 'entity, can decide if and when to handoff, according to their movement. Once detected that the mote is within the critical area Δc, the handoff process must start.

Based on mobility model, nodes were able to determine when they should look for another sink. In addition, nodes were enabled with the proposed soft handoff capabilities. following experiments measured the elapsed time from the moment the node detects a bad connection until the moment the node connects to a new parent and reports that to the Home Agent via a Binding Update. To perform this evaluation a scenario was implemented with two Sink Nodes, each one in a different domain, programmed with the NoDiS server module, and one mobile node, programmed with NoDiS mote module. The applications were developed in C and nesC respectively, as extensions to the ones used in the previous experiments. To force the handoff, a micaZ was installed on a radio-controlled model car moving along the corridor at a constant speed of 1.5 m/s.

According to the experiments[ ], the time it takes since the node detects a bad connection until it connects to a new Sink and sends the Care-of Address, through the Binding Update, to the Home Agent, is approximately 2.106 seconds. For handoff time this is a considerable long period, in which several packets might be lost. Therefore, even considering soft-handoff mechanisms, we must improve this value.

3   Proposed Model

By analyzing previous papers we found that the relay nodes are selected randomly. But there may be a situation that randomly selected relay node may be overloaded or it can be moving, leading to data loss and repeated retransmissions. So it is necessary to develop an efficient technique for relay node selection.

Hence we propose an optimal load and mobility aware MAC protocol with efficient relay node selection, for wireless sensor network.

Mobility prediction
Each node measures the received signal strength (RSS) from the receiver by monitoring the acknowledgement (ACK) packets and based on the RSS value the link quality and mobility of the node can be predicted. When the link quality is below a minimum value, then relay node selection (RNS) is done.

Relay node selection
The node broadcasts RNS request message to all its neighbors at time T1. Upon receiving the RNS message, the nodes recovers from sleep state to awake mode and it compute their current load. Within the time T2, each neighbor should reply back with RNS reply message along with its load value. On receiving the RNS reply message from its neighbors, the source node computes the RSS of nodes. When more than one RNS reply are received, the node with minimum load and best RSS is chosen as relay node. This procedure reduces the packet drop due to overloading and weak link quality. When no RNS reply is received within T2, source node enters into sleep state in order to avoid inefficient communication and to save energy.

Through this approach, the frequent link failure can be avoided thus reducing packet drop. Further the proposed technique minimizes the energy consumption.

4   Conclusions

Hence a dynamic frame time ,that is inversely proportional to level of mobility is required to cope with these problems we introduce a mobility-adaptive frame time that enables the protocol to dynamically adapt to changes in mobility patterns,making it suitable for sensor environments with both high and low mobility. the above presented mechanisms,though assure mobility support,we aim to improve them,in order to optimize the handoff time so as to control latencies and packet losses.

References

[1] Yoo, S., et al.: 6lowpan ad hoc on-demand distance vector routing (load), draft-daniel-6lowpan-load-adhoc-routing (December 2007)

[2] Kim, K., Yoo, S., Park, S.D., Lee, J., Mulligan, G.: Hierarchical routing over 6lowpan (hilow), draft-daniel-6lowpan hilow hierarchical- routing (December 2007)

[3] Chakrabarti, S., Nordmark, E.: Lowpan neighbor discovery extensions draftchakrabarti-6lowpan-ipv6-nd-05.txt (2008)

[4] Toutain, L., Chelius, G., Lee, Y., Dong, Y.: Neighbor discovery suppression draft-toutain-6lowpan-ra-suppression-00.txt (2008)

[5] Shelby, Z., Thubert, P., Hui, J., Chakrabarti, S., Nordmark, E.: Neighbor discovery for 6lowpan draft-ietf-6lowpan-nd-02 (2009)

[6] Silva, R., Silva, J.S., Simek, M., Boavida, F.: A new approach for multi-sink environments in wsns. In: 11th IFIP/IEEE International Symposium on Integrated Network Management (June 2009)

[7] Srinivasan, K., Levis, P.: RSSI is Under Appreciated. In: Proceedings of the Third Workshop on Embedded Networked Sensors, Cambridge, MA (2006)

[8] Pham, H., Jha, S.: Addressing mobility in wireless sensor media access protocol. In: Proceedings of the 2004 Intelligent Sensors, Sensor Networks and Information Processing Conference, pp. 113–118 (December 2004)

An Optimal RPC Based Approach to Increase Fault in Wireless Ad-Hoc Network

Rabindra Kumar Shial, K. Hemant Ku Reddy, and K.L. Narayana

Dept. of Computer Science & Engineering
National Institute of Science & Technology, Odisha
rkshial@yahoo.com, khemant.reddy@gmail.com,
lakshmi2912@hotmail.com

Abstract. In wireless network, fault tolerant topology control is an important and a challenging task. The wireless nodes and links could experience frequent failures since Wireless networks are usually deployed under extreme environments. Therefore, fault tolerance must be considered for many applications. In wireless network Topology control has been proved effective in saving node power. The main idea of topology control is that instead of using its maximal transmission power, each node sets its power to a certain level such that the global topology satisfies a certain constraint. To increase fault tolerance, nodes in the network will consume more power. Here we need to give the optimum distance between the nodes of the wireless network in order to reduce the consumption of the power of each node.

This paper deals with the approach for the finding the minimum distance between the nodes of the wireless network by the use of mat lab coding through the graph theory considering the minimum weight based algorithm.

Keywords: Ad-hoc wireless network, RPC, graph theory, spinning tree, fault tolerance, PSO, WMA.

1 Introduction

Basically in wireless networks [8, 15], the communication models can be categorized into four classes namely all-to-all communication network, which represents end-to-end communication of every pair of nodes in the network. Secondly one-to-one in which the communication from a given source node to a given destination node can be done. The other way of wireless communication model all-to-one, which indicates the communication from all nodes to a given (root) node. And in one-to-all, which indicates the communication from the root to all the other nodes.

The rest of the paper is organized as follows: section 2 describes power assignment to nodes in a typical power system and its network topology. Section 3 describes an approach to minimize the weight and find the minimum distance between nodes in a network. Section 4 describes power optimization using Particle swarm optimization. Section 5 summarizes the simulation result. Section 6 describes the conclusion and future developments.

N. Meghanathan et al. (Eds.): CCSIT 2012, Part I, LNICST 84, pp. 372–382, 2012.
© Institute for Computer Sciences, Social Informatics and Telecommunications Engineering 2012

2   Power Assignment to Node

Considering a set $V = \{v_1, v_2, v_3, \ldots, v_n\}$ of n wireless nodes distributed in a 2D plane. Let w_{uv} is the power [10] needed to support the communication between two nodes u and v is a monotone increasing function of the Euclidean distance $\|uv\|$. In other words, $w_{uv} > w_{xy}$ if $\|uv\| > \|xy\|$ and $w_{uv} = w_{xy}$ if $\|uv\| = \|xy\|$. $w_{uv} = c + \|uv\|^\beta$, where c is a positive constant real number, and real number $\beta \in \{2; 5\}$ depends on the transmission environment, and $\|uv\|$ is the Euclidean distance between points u and v. Assuming all nodes have omni-directional antennas, i.e., if the signal transmitted by a node u can be received by a node v, then it will be received by all nodes x with $\|ux\| \leq \|uv\|$. In addition, we assumed that all nodes can adjust the transmission power dynamically. The present work represents the minimum distance and the minimum distance path of one to all communication network model.

2.1   Network Topology

The network considered in this case is a wireless network consisting of N nodes each is equipped with an omni-directional antenna with a maximal transmission range of r_{max}. The power required for a node to attain a transmission range of 'r' is at least Cr^α, where C is a constant, α is the power attenuation exponent and usually chosen between 2 and 4. For any two nodes u and v, there exists a link from u to v if the distance $d(u, v) \leq r_u$, where r_u is the transmission range for node u, determined by its power level. If the links are asymmetric, the existence of a link from u to v does not guarantee the existence of a link from v to u. The network is assumed to have symmetric links and is static, i.e., the nodes in the network are stationary. Given the coordination of the nodes in the plane and the transmission power of the nodes, the network can be mapped into a cost graph G = (V, E, c), where V denotes the set of wireless nodes, E denotes the set of wireless links induced by the transmission power, and the weight c for a given edge (u, v) is computed as $C_d(u, v)^\alpha$, where d is the distance. By this mapping, a symmetric wireless network is represented by an undirected graph.

Wireless Network [7] have an important feature called Wireless Multicast Advantage (WMA) because of its broadcast media. WMA is often utilized to save power. For a node to send data to multiple nodes (one to all) in its transmission range, instead of sending data multiple times, it only needs to send it once and all nodes in its transmission range can receive the same data. In light of WMA, the power and weight are different in wireless networks, where weight is link based, while power is node based.

2.2   Graph Theory

A simple graph G is a pair G = (V, E) where 'V' is a finite set, called the vertices of G, 'E' is a subset of $P_2(V)$ (i.e., a set E of two-element subsets of V), called the edges of G [4], where the notation $P_k(V)$ stands for the set of all k-element subsets of the set V. A graph is triple G = (V, E, φ) where 'V' is a finite set, called the vertices of G, 'E' is a finite set, called the edges of G, and 'φ' is a function with domain E and co domain $P_2(V)$. Given the coordination of the nodes in the plane and the transmission power of the nodes, the network can be mapped into a cost graph G = (V, E, c), where V denotes the set of wireless nodes, E denotes the set of wireless links induced by the transmission power, and the weight c for a given edge (u, v) is computed as $C_d(u, v)^α$, where d is the distance. By this mapping, a symmetric wireless network is represented by an undirected graph.

3   Minimum Weight Based Approach

The main idea of Minimum Weight Based Algorithm (MWBA) is to construct a k-out connected [1] sub-graph with the goal to minimize its weight, and then analyze its performance for minimum power k-out connectivity problem. Given G = (V,E), k, and root node r ∈ V, MW utilizes FT which constructs a minimum weight directed k-out connected sub-graph for a directed graph as follows:

1. Construct G' by replacing each edge in G with two opposite directed edges. The weight of each directed edge is the same weight as the original edge.
2. DFT = FT (G', k, r), DFT is the directed k-out connected sub-graph with optimal weight.
3. Construct the undirected version of DFT, called GFT. An undirected graph is constructed from a directed graph as follows: if there is a directed edge *uv* in DFT, then there exists an undirected edge *uv* in GFT. It is obvious that GFT is an undirected k-out connected sub-graph.

Example: Let us consider a network graph as shown in figure 1.

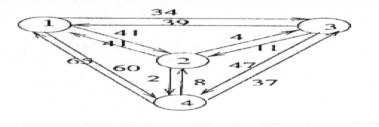

Fig. 1. Network Graph with node weights

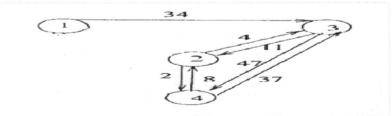

Fig. 2. Sub-Graph after 1st Iteration

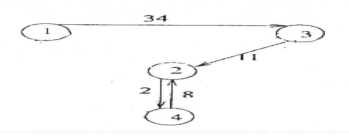

Fig. 3. Sub-Graph after 2nd Iteration

Fig. 3. Sub-Graph after 2nd Iteration

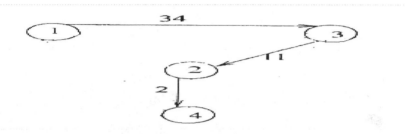

Fig. 4. Sub-Graph after 3rd Iteration

As explained in the graph theory the following figures 2, 3 and 4 are the direct k-out connected sub-graphs [2, 3] which are represented as iterations.

After 3rd iteration: Since all nodes are traversed after the third iteration in the figure-4 which is the required optimum network.

3.1 Approach: Optimum Distance

In this section we considered six node wireless networks as shown in figure-5 for complexity and of course it can be more than six which we considered as 'N' node for the simulation results.

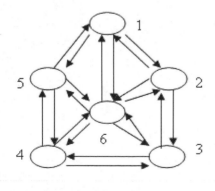

Fig. 5. Wireless Network

Table 1. Power vs. No. of Nodes

Nodes	1	2	3	4	5	6
1	0	10	12	5	2	6
2	8	0	11	10	16	20
3	18	26	0	3	5	31
4	14	15	7	0	9	1
5	23	24	4	6	0	17
6	19	30	14	15	36	0

The distances between the nodes 2 and 1 is 8 as shown by the arrows in the table-1, which are the inputs for the logic based on the minimum weight based approach for which the algorithm has been used.

3.2   Algorithm: Minimum Distance Calculation

START:

1.   Set N:= Input the number of nodes.

2.   Find D:= Distance between all the nodes & D_i : is the distance of node N_i

3.   Find MAX:=Maximum distances among all nodes.

$$MAX=\max\left\{d\left(N_1\right),d\left(N_2\right),d\left(N_3\right),.....,d\left(N_n\right)\right\}$$

4.   Set Max=Max+1;

5.   Replace the distance of unconnected nodes with Max.

6.   Level : L1

7.   Min:= Minimum distance of connected node with node 1.

$$MIN=\min_i\left\{d\left(N_i\right)\right\},i=1,2,....,n$$

8.   Display the node

9.   goto node having minimum distance

10. If(all nodes are visited)

   exit(0);

11. else

   goto L1;

12. STOP.

4   Optimizing Power

A wireless network consists of N nodes, each of which is equipped with an omni-directional antenna with a maximal transmission range of r_{max}. The power [11] required for a node to attain a transmission range of r is at least Cr^{α}, where C is a constant, α is the power attenuation exponent and usually chosen between 2 and 4. For any two nodes u and v, there exists a link from u to v if the distance d(u, v) $\leq r_u$, where r_u is the transmission range for node u, determined by its power level. If the links are asymmetric, the existence of a link from u to v does not guarantee the existence of a link from v to u. In this paper, we consider symmetric links and assume the wireless network is static, i.e., the nodes in the network are stationary. Given the coordination of the nodes in the plane and the transmission power of the nodes, the network can be mapped into a cost graph $G = (V, E, c)$, where V denotes the set of wireless nodes, E denotes the set of wireless links induced by the transmission power, and the weight c for a given edge (u, v) is computed as $Cd(u, v)^\alpha$, where d is the distance. By this mapping, a symmetric wireless network is represented by an undirected graph.

4.1   Particle Swarm Optimization (PSO)

PSO is a method for doing numerical optimization without explicit knowledge of the gradient of the problem to be optimized. PSO is due to Kennedy, Eberhart and Shi was originally intended for simulating social behaviour, but the algorithm was simplified and it was realized that the particles were actually performing optimization. The book by Kennedy and Eberhart describes many philosophical aspects of PSO and swarm intelligence. PSO optimizes a problem by maintaining a population of candidate solutions called particles and moving these particles around in the search-space according to simple formulae. The movements of the particles are guided by the best found positions in the search-space, which are continually being updated as better positions are found by the particles.

Explanation: Evolutionary computation exploit a set of potential solutions and detect the optimal ones through cooperation and competition among the individuals of the population. Particle swarm optimization (PSO) is one of the population based stochastic optimization technique inspired by social behavior of "bird flocking". PSO shares many similarities with evolutionary computation techniques such as Genetic Algorithm(GA). A population of random individuals is initially generated and these individuals probe the search space during their evolution to identify the optimal solution. Compared to GA, PSO does not employ evolution operators such as cross over and mutation and does not need information about the objective function gradient. Other advantages characterized by PSO such as the easy implementation and the low requirement of computational resources. In PSO, the individuals, called the particles, are collected into a swarm and fly through the problems by following the optima particles. Each individual has a memory, remembering the best position of the search space it has ever visited. In particular, particle remembers the best position among those it has visited, refer to as a *pbest*, and the best position by its neighbors. There are 2 versions for keeping the neighbors best position, namely *lbest* and *gbest* . The first(*lbest*) is related to the best position of the particle in the neighbors of the particle itself while *gbest* refers to the best position recorded by the entire swarm. Each individual of the population has an adaptable velocity (position change), according to which it moves in the search space. Thus, its movement is an aggregated acceleration towards its best previously visited position and towards the best individual of a topological neighborhood. Compared to GA, the information sharing mechanism of PSO is notably different. Chromosomes share information and the entire population evolves towards an optimal area in compact manner. The evolution of particles, guided only by the best solution, tends to be regulated by behavior of the neighbors. In the simplest form, the position S and velocity V of each particle are represented by the following equations by considering lbest rather than gbest as the best position of the particle referred to the neighbours.

4.2   Basic PSO Equations

The particle velocity is expressed as

$V(t) = W*V(t-1)+C_1*r_1{}^{(lbest-S(t-1))} +C_2*r_2{}^{(gbest-S(t-1))}$

And the particle displacement is expressed as

$S(t) =S(t-1)+V(t)$, Where V =particle velocity

S =particle displacement

Lbest =local best

Gbest =global best

W =inertial weight

C_1 and C_2 are acceleration constants =2.0

r_1 and r_2 are random variables{0,1}

t =current iteration

4.3   Application of PSO in Power Calculations

The power is expressed as:

$$P(i) = w* P(t-1)+C_1 *r_1^{(L_{best}-S(t-1))} +C2* r_2^{(G_{best}-S(t-1))}$$

The distance is expressed as:

$$S(t) = S(t-1)+P(t),$$ Where P is power, S is distance.

L_{best} =Local best , G_{best} =Global best

W =Inertial weight and C_1, C_2 are acceleration constants=2.0

r_1 , r_2 are random variables & i=current iteration

L_{best} :Optimum power obtained locally & G_{best} :Optimum power obtained globally

The values taken for the power: W=unifrnd(0.8, 1.1) ,   r1= unifrnd(0.26,0.3)

r2=1-r1 & L_{best} =10, G_{best} =12 & $C_1= C_2$ =2.

When any signal is transmitted from one to another the signal gets attenuated due to various atmospheric factors like temperature, pressure, rain, wind etc. Hence attenuation factor should be taken into account while establishing a network. Since the signal gets attenuated the signal needs to be amplified at every node of the network. But the signal cannot be amplified if the signal gets attenuated below a certain level. Therefore amplification factor should also be considered.

$$Amp = unifrnd(1, 1.3), Attn = unifrnd(0.35, 0.5)$$

Since the attenuation and amplification vary from place to place and time to time so it is appreciable to use random functions to obtain their value.

5   Results Discussion

Let us consider any network with 4 nodes: The distance matrix of the given network is given by:

Table 2. Node distance matrix

Nodes	1	2	3	4
1	0	21	27	32
2	40	0	38	12
3	16	20	0	18
4	39	27	10	0

Using the minimum weight based approach we get the optimum path as 1→2→4→3. The power for the above path can be obtained using PSO. The power so obtained will be the optimum power for the network.

Table 3. Node optimum power list

Nodes	Power
1	0.1
2	0.06819
3	0.057233
4	0.055203

The number of paths traversing all the nodes are=3! =6, The paths are shown below:

Table 4. Node traversal path list

Slno/paths				
1	1	4	3	2
2	1	4	2	3
3	1	3	4	2
4	1	3	2	4
5	1	2	3	4
6	1	2	4	3

The power at all nodes along different path are given below:

Table 5. Node power with different path

Path/nodes	1	2	3	4
1	0.1	0.087509	0.055662	0.0659130
2	0.1	0.087509	0.077178	0.092966
3	0.1	0.077533	0.063871	0.076513
4	0.1	0.077533	0.066371	0.057204
5	0.1	0.06819	0.10187	0.064347
6	0.1	0.06819	0.057233	0.055203

From the above table we can conclude that the power is maximum in case of path 2. The power variation with respect to the distance for path 2 is shown in the below figure.

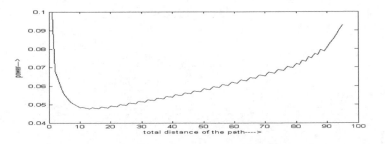

Fig. 6. Power vs total distance of the path

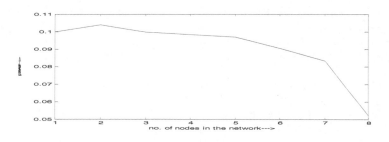

Fig. 7. Power vs. No. of Nodes in network

Therefore we can infer from the above plot that as the number of nodes in a network increases the power at the end node of each network decreases [13]. From the plot we can observe that if the number of nodes in a network is more than 8 then the power at the end node of the network drops off below the threshold value for which it cannot be amplified. So it is desirable to take into consideration the number of nodes in a network while establishing the network physically

6   Conclusions

In this paper, we propose the use of Particle Swarm Optimization technique to minimize the distance and consumption of power in wireless ad-hoc network environment by increasing the fault tolerance of any network. The network achieved by this way is an optimized network covering optimized area with minimum power consumption. Our proposed approach starts by taking nodes in a network to be used as a network group. We also explored the results of the performance evaluation of four extensions to the standard Particle Swarm Optimization algorithm in order to reduce the energy consumption in Wireless Ad-hoc Networks. Communication distance is an important factor to be reduced in ad-hoc networks. We have simulated in mat-lab and simulation result shows an exciting result. The result of the proposed technique is also compared with two other well-known clustering algorithms for power consumption [11, 13] though the framework of our work different then the existing two technique. The results exhibit the promising capability of the proposed technique and clearly show that it works better than the other two clustering techniques.

References

[1] Wang, F., Thai, M.T., Li, Y., Cheng, X., Du., D.-Z.: Fault tolerant topology control for all to one and one to all communication in wireless network
[2] Lavaul, C., Valencia-Pabon, M.: A distributed approximation algorithm for the minimum degree minimum weight spanning trees
[3] Greenberg, H.J.: Greedy Algorithms for Minimum Spanning Tree
[4] Harju, T.: Graph Theory

[5] Fault-Tolerant Topology Control for All-to-One and One-to-All Communication in Wireless Networks. IEEE Transactions on mobile Computing 7(3)

[6] Basile, C., Killijian, M.-O., Powell, D.: A Survey of Dependability Issues in Mobile Wireless Networks, cbasile@uiuc.edu, marco.killijian, david.powell_@laas.fr (February 21, 2003)

[7] Akyildiz, I., Su, W., Sankarasubramaniam, Y., Cayirci, E.: Wireless sensor networks: A survey. Computer Networks Journal 38(4), 393–422 (2002)

[8] Su, W., Lee, S.-J., Gerla, M.: Mobility prediction and routing in ad hoc wireless networks. Int'l. Journal of Network Management (2000)

[9] Singh, S., Woo, M., Raghavendra, C.S.: Power aware routing in mobile ad hoc networks. In: Proc. ACM Mobicom, pp. 181–190 (1998)

[10] Monks, J.P., Bhargavan, V., Hwu, W.M.: A power controlled multiple access protocol for wireless packet networks. In: Proc. IEEE INFOCOM, pp. 219–228 (2001)

[11] Shahzad, W., Khan, F.A., Siddiqui, A.B.: Weighted Clustering using Comprehensive Learning Particle Swarm Optimization for Mobile Ad Hoc Networks

[12] Obaidy, M.A., Ayesh, A.: The Implementation Of Optimization Algorithm For Energy Efficient Dynamic Ad Hoc Wireless Sensor Networks

[13] Bandyopadhyay, S., Coyle, E.J.: An energy efficient hierarchical clustering algorithm for wireless sensor networks. In: Proceedings of the IEEE Conference on Computer Communications (INFOCOM 2003) (2003)

[14] Laurent Chalard, L.V.A.W., Helal, D., Zory, J.: Wireless sensor networks devices: Overview, issues, state of the art and promising technologies. ST Journal of Research 4(1), June 8 (2007)

Location Management and Resource Allocation Using Load Balancing in Wireless Heterogeneous Networks

G. Adiline Macriga[1] and V.S. Surya[2]

[1] Department of Information Technology,
Sri Sai Ram Engineering College, Chennai
[2] Department of Computer and Communication,
Sri Sai Ram Engineering College, Chennai

Abstract. In the next generation of wireless networks, the entire network operating on different radio frequencies under wireless mode will be available for communication. The rapidly growing demand for "any service – anywhere - anytime" high-speed access to IP-based services is becoming one of the major challenges for mobile networks. However, in several situations, mobile terminals tend to associate with networks guaranteeing the best performances to stay "Always Best Connected" which leads to overload the most attractive technology while keeping the others technologies underutilized. As a recent research focus, load balancing is one of the key technologies in the convergence of heterogeneous wireless networks. Load balancing is a significant method to achieve the resource sharing over heterogeneous wireless networks, and it can improve resource utilization, enlarge system capacity, as well as provide better services for users. When dealing with high speed traffic over heterogeneous, we propose a load balancing algorithm using novel approach. For wireless packet network, this novel load metric is based on the packet scheduling and the radio link quality information. The solution can be used in on-line system because it requires less computation time and it operates in a distributed way instead of a usual centralized way. The two main targets of the proposed algorithm are the admission control and the network initiated handover. Further we have to investigate the joint load balancing and resource allocation optimization in heterogeneous networks.

Keywords: Heterogeneous, load balancing, admission control, handover.

1   Introduction

In the heterogeneous networks, generally the available networks in the transmission path (e.g., WLAN, 3G, 3GPP, UTRAN, WiMax) operating on the Radio frequencies under wireless mode available for communication are brought under a single head, based on their common operating procedures and functions such as request – acknowledge - response. As the radio access network is considered the parameters such as - signal strength, maximum coverage, power level, network load, flow rate, traffic rate are taken as the major factor. Along with the increase of multimedia and data-intensive applications, future networks will experience an extremely high load.

N. Meghanathan et al. (Eds.): CCSIT 2012, Part I, LNICST 84, pp. 383–393, 2012.

This load metric definition takes into account not only the user's required resource but also the radio link quality between the user and the BS. An operator can deploy different technologies or interwork with other technologies owned by other operators to enable the global roaming capability through a coordinated heterogeneous access network environment. Load balancing plays an important role in the Common Radio Resource Management (CRRM). It is defined as a platform to gather information from the Base Stations (BS) of different Radio Access Technology (RAT), and to control the resource allocation of all BSs to optimize the overall system performance.

An advanced Common RRM (CRRM) is a motivation for interworking among these networks, and also a challenge to overcome the existing load balancing techniques. The load balancing algorithm consists of accepting or denying a new incoming network request and forcing users connected to a heavily loaded BS to hand over to a lightly loaded one considering the loosely coupled architecture as shown in fig 1. The stronger the coupling is, the more efficient the resource can be utilized. In other words the balancing scheme is based on the load values of different access nodes regardless of underlying technologies and underlying scheduling schemes.

In the proposed model, load balancing is divided into two parts: network architecture and load balancing algorithm. The former is the foundation of load balancing, and a good network architecture can improve the efficiency of load balancing. In the perspective of control mode, load balancing mechanisms can be classified as centralized, distributed and semi-centralized and semi-distributed. A few problems are faced in the first two mechanisms: the centralized one is relatively low reliability, while the distributed one has a huge overhead. This solution can be used to rectify the above mentioned problems and can be used in on-line system because of its less computation time and the way it operates in a distributed way instead of a usual centralized way.

The remainder of this paper is organized as follows. In Section 2 we briefly discuss the related researches into overhead and reliability of network architectures. Section 3 introduces the system model we proposed. In Section 4, the proposed model is presented followed in Section 5 by our simulation and the results. Finally in Section 6 we conclude this paper with discussion of our work.

2   Related Work

The authors of [14] developed a mathematical framework that can be used to compactly represent and analyze heterogeneous networks that combine multiple entity and link types. They generalized Bonacich centrality, which measures connectivity between nodes by the number of paths between them, to heterogeneous networks and used this measure to study network structure. The authors of [9] proposed a semi-centralized and semi-distributed architecture (SCSDA), in which a BS just exchanges load information with several neighboring BSs. Although the architecture can reduce the overhead of control signaling, the authors neither expressed the overhead in mathematical formula, nor proved it by simulation. Reference [15] designed hybrid wireless network architecture, [16] proposed a multiple mobile routers based network architecture to support seamless mobility across heterogeneous networks, and they both tested the overhead by NS2 simulator. However, the model of the overhead was derived in neither [4] nor [12]. Route overhead was analyzed in theory in [8], by calculating the number of control messages generated in a BS/AP service area due to maintaining route. Nevertheless, the simulation for overhead was not given. The communication overhead of the scheme presented in [6] was calculated, and an algorithm for minimizing the communication overhead was given, which was proved to be effective through simulation. The authors of [15] considered a general heterogeneous network architecture with two basic entities in the system: mobile nodes (MNs) and access points (APs). They formulated the overhead of AP discovery which is divided into hello messages and RREQ messages, and gave the simulation results. Reference [2] proposed a hierarchical and distributed (HD) architecture with three hierarchical levels of mobility management being distinguished: end terminal remains connected to the same radio access network but it changes its point of attachments, end terminal changes its radio access network but it remains associated to the same operator and end terminal changes its operator network. And it also studied signaling cost generated by QoS negotiation during handover process in both theory and simulation. The research on reliability of telecommunication network starts at the study on switched telecommunication network by Li [10]. Li defined call blocking as the link failure, and measured reliability taking connectivity [13] as standard. Reference [12] mentioned the concept of integrated reliability, which took call loss as the evaluation indicator of network reliability, and proved that the integrated reliability can reflect the practical situation much better than taking connectivity as standard. The authors of [5] analyzed the reliability aspects of some access network topologies to insure a certain level of quality of service at the lowest cost for the end users.

Most of the previous work mainly focused on identifying the functionalities of the CRRM architectural components, and designing the protocols for control exchanges between these components. Besides, the resource allocation scheme which aims at quantifying the amount of resources allocated to each user in such a way to maximize the operator's revenue or the user's satisfaction has also been increasingly studied. However, the load balancing between different BSs and different RATs has not been sufficiently considered. Although the load balancing is much related to the resource allocation, they are two separable aspects. The load balancing can be considered on the one hand as an objective of the resource allocation scheme and on the other hand as a constraint for the resource allocation optimization. In this work, we only focus on the load balancing issue.

3   System Model

The load can be computed in different manners for different systems. As a result, the same load value for two different systems does not mean the same load situation. As such a comparison is the basis of any cross-system load balancing solution, having a same semantic of the load metric is mandatory. The existing load computation methods, which are based on the interference or the throughput, do not allow the load variation anticipation prior to the situation where a user moves into/out of a cell. The estimation of future interference or throughput values is really challenging. Accordingly, we will not be able to make the right decision to achieve an efficient resource balancing.

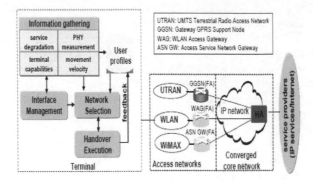

Fig. 1. Loosely Coupled Architecture

In order to solve the general load-balancing problem different algorithms have been proposed. Examples, mainly from the area of distributed computing, are diffusion algorithms, random matching algorithms, pre-computation based load distribution algorithms, algorithms based on microeconomics, force models (also called particles approach) and simple transmitter receiver-based algorithms. The force-based load-balancing algorithm introduced is a descriptive and easily extendable CRRM algorithm for combined UMTS/GSM networks.

A.   DISTRIBUTED Vs CENTRALIZED ARCHITETURE

The semi-centralized and semi-distributed architecture (SCSDA), in which a BS just exchanges load information with several neighboring BSs. Although the architecture can reduce the overhead of control signaling, it does not consider the load history of the neighboring nodes. The hybrid wireless network architecture (figure 2) comparatively distribute the load on multi tier mode.

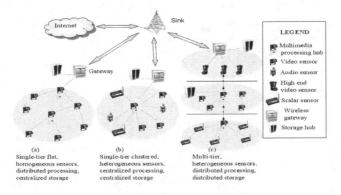

Fig. 2. Hybrid wireless network architecture

B.   HIERARCHICAL SEMI-CENTRALIZED ARCHITECTURE

The hierarchical semi-centralized architecture based on basic grids, which takes three different types of access networks (UMTS, WLAN and WiMax) for example. A basic grid is made up of several adjacent cells. IS (Information Server), RA (Resource Allotter) and RS (Resource Statistics) are collectively referred to as Resource Management Unit (RMU), which are responsible for managing the resources of basic grids. Installed in the access point, a RS is used to calculate resources of the cell administered by the RS. A RA collects load information from RSs, and balances the load according to the load and resources of the basic grid. Normally an IS allocates resources for the borders of basic grids and stores information of cell identification, location and load states. However, it can take over the broken RA immediately. In order to improve the system reliability, a main IS and a standby IS are set up. Once the main IS stops running, the standby one will take over it.

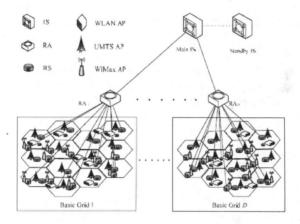

Fig. 3. Hierarchical semi-centralized architecture

4   Proposed Load Balancing Algorithm

The aim of the proposed work is to design a feasible and suboptimal solution for load balancing while minimizing the resource rearrangement and the computation effort. When a user initiates a connection, the end-user device selects a suitable access network among available ones using the network selection mechanism. The load value of each access node may be used in the network selection evaluation if the user has access to this information.

The user will not be allowed to select the heavily loaded access node. Besides, the access node may refuse the user's connection request based on its admission control policy if it is heavily loaded. Despite the use of an admission control, the overload of an access node still happens due to the transmission channel fluctuation, the mobility or the application data rate changes. To handle the load balancing, on-going calls will be transferred from an access network to another. The two main targets of our proposed algorithm are the admission control and the network-initiated handover.

A. ADMISSION CONTROL

The admission control is employed to admit or reject a new originating or handing over communication in order to avoid overload situations. A connection request to a specific BS will be accepted if the BS's load, including the contribution of the incoming communication, is below an admission threshold d_{th}. Otherwise, the new incoming communication will be redirected to the least loaded overlapped access network. If all BSs in the coverage area could not accommodate the new communication, the connection request is rejected. If the incoming communication is a handing over one, the admission threshold is greater than the one used for a new originating communication. It is generally preferable to refuse the new calls rather than to drop the on-going calls. That explains also why we choose a load balancing threshold $d < 1$. In our solution, we choose to always accept the handing over users.

However, the admission control is just a first step in the load balancing process as it only deals with incoming communications and it does not treat the load fluctuation of ongoing ones. Moreover, trying to redirect an originating communication to a less loaded access system (redirect from one technology to another) may not be possible if the communication is initiated from a single-mode terminal. In this case, it may be better to accommodate the originating single-mode user and to force a multimode user to make a vertical handover to a coordinated access system. That motivates the need to use handover enforcement to effectively distribute the load over the heterogeneous systems.

B. HANDOVER ENFORCEMENT

In addition to the admission control, it is essential to have a mechanism to detect and handle imminent overload situations. Such mechanism is known as the handover enforcement since its main role is to select suitable users in a heavily loaded access network and force them to handover. Instead of balancing the resources of the overall system as described in the optimal algorithm, our proposed solution aims at redistributing locally the load of a heavily loaded BS around its neighboring overlapped BSs. In turn, the neighboring BS will redistribute its load to its own neighboring BSs and so on. By doing so, the load of the overall system will be then balanced. In fact, the handover enforcement will be triggered when the load of a specific BS is greater than d. The algorithm execution is continued until $x2 = 0$ or we cannot find a handover to improve index $x2$. In our proposition we only consider one-move and two-move operations during the handover enforcement since considering more than two consecutive moves is not realistic in on-line system due to its computation time.

5   Simulation and Results

In this section, we derive an analytical model for reliability of handover procedure between UMTS and WLAN/WiMax network. The following notations are used in our analysis.

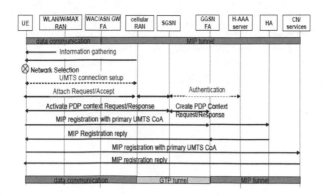

Fig. 4. Handover procedure from WLAN/WiMAX RAN to UMTS RAN

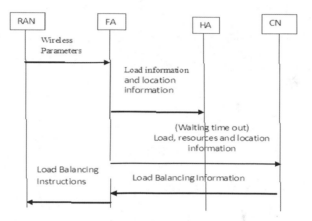

Fig. 5. Signaling Flow Chart

i: System type. i=1 denotes UMTS system; i=2 denotes WLAN system; i=3 denotes WiMax system.

b_{ij}: The traffic intensity between FA_i and HA_j.

c_j: The traffic intensity between HA_j and CN.

R_{CN}: The reliability of CN.

R_{HA}: The reliability of HA.

Rc: The reliability of junction line between CN and HA.

a_i: The signaling overhead of transferring load information once between one FA located in system type i and HA.

d: The signaling overhead of transferring load information once between one HA and CN.

e: The signaling overhead of transferring load information once between one main CN and standby CN.

A_i: The number of RANs in system type i.

D: The number of HAs.

A_{ij}: The number of RANs for system type i in the basic grid j.
λ_i: The traffic arrival rate of system type i.
μ_i: The service rate of system type i.
m_i: The cell capacity of system type i.
k_{i1}: The light threshold of system type i.
k_{i2}: The heavy threshold of system type i.
T: The period of transferring load information among RMU.
To facilitate the analysis, we assume that there are only one main CN and one standby CN.

A. Simulation Scenario

The scenario is a medium urban area, where both UMTS system and WiMax system cover the whole area while WLAN system covers the hot spots only. In order to reduce the complex of simulation, we assume that there are all the three types of APs in each basic grid, and the number of APs for the same system is equal in every basic grid.

The values of parameters used in simulation are as follows. $T=0.1$s, $A_1=600$, $A_2=900$, $A_3=600$; $R_{IS}=0.99$,

$R_{HA}=0.98$, $R_c=0.97$; $b_i=1e_{rl}$; $K_1=1$, $K_2=1$, $K_3=1$; $a_1=1$, $d=1$, $e=1$; $m1=60$, $m2=20$, $m3=80$; $\eta_{iTH1}=0.7$, $\eta_{iTH2}=0.9$; $\mu_i=1/180$s. Where $i=1, 2, 3$.

A. Simulation Results

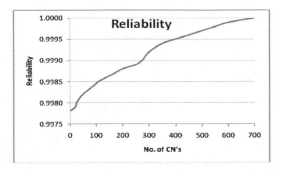

Fig. 6. Network Reliability in a Heterogeneous environment

Figure 6 gives the reliability while choosing the network. In the heterogeneous environment the reliability is high even when the number of nodes is high. The higher transmission latency experienced in the heterogeneous network can be observed in the graph provided (Figure. 6). On the transmit side, the transmission is performed with no silence period. On the receiver side, handing over to the cellular network introduces more latency, results in a silence period the order of magnitude of which is equal to the latency difference between both networks. The use of an adaptive buffer at the receiver side makes it transparent to the user which is reflected as a smooth seamless flow in the heterogeneous Networks. When considering the 3G/ Wimax cellular network, the number of users is high compared with the other networks and also had a wider coverage but there is a pitfall at the end, the bandwidth fluctuates

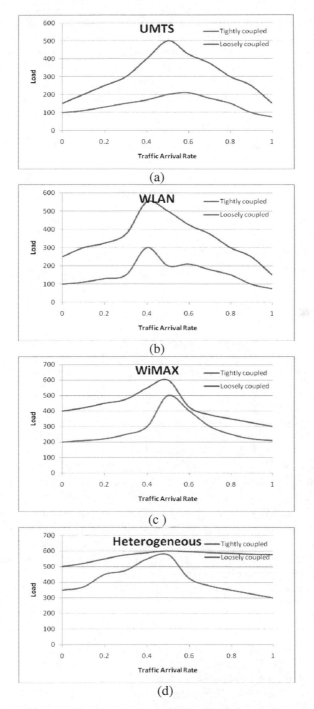

Fig. 7. (a, b, c, d). Load sharing in different networks

beyond 80%. At the time of mobility the network coverage is limited as shown in figure 7 (a,b,c,d). Load sharing in the Heterogeneous Network Environment, by considering the positive measures of the above mentioned networks and by having a thorough understanding between the available networks the heterogeneous network is designed. The heterogeneous network provides maximum throughput, minimum number of handoffs and maximum coverage at mobile. By designing a proper QoS standard and having proper understanding between the network the desires which are explained at the initial paragraph can be achieved. By improving the performance measures by deploying and allocating the code spectrum for the 3GPP network and by having proper power management in the 3G network and by making use of antennas with wider coverage in WLAN environment, the available bandwidth can be maximum utilized and also the number of handoffs can be reduced as the nature of the network present in the graphical architecture between the source and the destination is studied in advance, a maximum throughput can be achieved with minimum tolerable delay or no delay based on the nature of the information that is taken for transmission. The data rate of the heterogeneous network is very close to the available rate as shown in fig. 7.

6   Conclusion

In this paper, we have proposed a new load metric which makes it possible to formulate the load balancing as a classic optimization problem. This novel load metric for wireless packet networks is based on the packet scheduling and the radio link quality information. Thank to this new metric, the heterogeneity of different access technologies can be removed. It also facilitates the load balancing operations since it allows load variation anticipation. We introduced a new load balancing index to measure the overload degree of a system. This balancing index leads to minimize the overload degree of a system instead of equalizing the load among the access nodes within a system. We designed a load balancing scheme which consists of admission control and handover enforcement. The proposed handover enforcement based on one-move and two-move iterative search is one of the feasible suboptimal solutions to the problem. The solution can be used in on-line system because it does not require much computation time and because it operates in a distributed way instead of a usual centralized way. It was shown that our proposed approach outperforms the existing approaches. In the future work, we plan to investigate the joint load balancing and resource allocation optimization in heterogeneous networks.

References

[1] Yu, F., Krishnamurthy, V.: Optimal Joint Session Admission Control in integrated WLAN and CDMA Cellular Networks with Vertical Handoff. IEEE Transaction on Mobile Computing 6(1), 126–139 (2007)
[2] Holis, J., Pechac, P.: Elevation Dependent Shadowing Model for Mobile Communications via High Altitude Platforms in Built- Up Areas. IEEE Transactions on Antennas and Propagation 56(4) (2008)

[3] Imre, S.: Dynamic Call Admission Control for Uplink in 3G/4G CDMA-Based Systems. IEEE Transactions on Vehicular Technology 56(5) (2007)

[4] Zhang, Y., Fujise, M.: Location Management Congestion Problem in Wireless Networks. IEEE Transactions on Vehicular Technology 56(2) (2007)

[5] Morris, D., Hamid Aghvami, A.: Location Management Strategies for Cellular Overlay Networks—A Signaling Cost Analysis. IEEE Transactions on Broadcasting 53(2) (2007)

[6] Chen, H., Wu, H., Kumar, S., Tzeng, N.-F.: Minimum-Cost Data Delivery in Heterogeneous Wireless Networks. IEEE Transactions on vehicular Technology 56(6) (2007)

[7] Chen, Y.-S., Chuang, M.-C., Chen, C.-K.: DeuceScan: Deuce-Based Fast Handoff Scheme in IEEE 802.11 Wireless Networks. IEEE Transactions on Vehicular Technology 57(2) (2008)

[8] Olama, M.M., Djouadi, S.M., Papageorgiou, I.G., Charalambous, C.D.: Position and Velocity Tracking in Mobile Networks Using Particle and Kalman Filtering With Comparison. IEEE Transactions on Vehicular Technology 57(2) (2008)

[9] Misra, A., Roy, A., Das, S.K.: Information-Theory Based Optimal Location Management Schemes for Integrated Multi-System Wireless Networks. IEEE/ACM Transactions on Networking 16(3) (2008)

[10] Xiao, Y., Pan, Y., Li, J.: Design and Analysis of Location Management for 3G Cellular Networks. IEEE Transactions on Parallel and Distributed Systems 15(4) (2004)

[11] Huang, D.-W., Lin, P., Gan, C.-H.: Design and Performance Study for a Mobility Management Mechanism (WMM) Using Location Cache for Wireless Mesh Networks. IEEE Transactions on Mobile Computing 7(5) (2008)

[12] Zhu, Y.-H., Leung, V.C.M.: Optimization of Sequential Paging in Movement-Based Location Management Based on Movement Statistics. IEEE Transactions on Vehicular Technology 56(2) (2007)

[13] Rodríguez-Dagnino, R.M., Takagi, H.: Movement-Based Location Management for General Cell Residence Times in Wireless Networks. IEEE Transactions on Vehicular Technology 56(5) (2007)

[14] Ma, W., Fang, Y., Lin, P.: Mobility Management Strategy Based on User Mobility Patterns in Wireless Networks. IEEE Transactions on Vehicular Technology 56(1) (2007)

[15] Niyato, D., Hossain, E.: A Noncooperative Game-Theoretic Framework for Radio Resource Management in 4G Heterogeneous Wireless Access Networks. IEEE Transactions on Mobile Computing 7(3) (2008)

[16] Roberts, M.L., Temple, M.A., Raines, R.A., Mills, R.F., Oxley, M.E.: Communication Waveform Design Using an Adaptive Spectrally Modulated, Spectrally Encoded (SMSE) Framework. IEEE Journal of Selected Topics in Signal Processing 1(1) (2007)

Cross Language Information Retrieval Approach in Peer-to-Peer Network

M. Archana and K.A. Sumithra Devi

Department of MCA, RV College of Engineering,
Bangalore-59, India
archanams_m@yahoo.com, sumithraka@gmail.com

Abstract. Peer-to-Peer systems have emerged as popular way of sharing large volume of data. It is an application layer networks which enables network host to share resources in a distributed manner. The usability of these systems depends on effective search techniques to retrieve data. In this paper, an approach is made to list out some of the searching techniques that are applicable for the peer-to-peer network. However, most of the Peer-to-Peer information Systems is still unaware of some important features, such as cross-language information retrieval. Cross-language information retrieval is the state-of-art research area in the information retrieval research area.

Keywords: Peer-to-Peer, Cross-Language Information retrieval (CLIR), Search, Translation.

1 Introduction

Peer-to-Peer can be viewed as a communication model in which each computer has the same capabilities as the other. Any computers can initiate the communication session and it is implemented by giving each communication node both server and client capabilities, but in the recent years internet is used to exchange the information with each other directly or through an intermediate. Peer-to-Peer (P2P) networks are increasingly becoming popular because they offer opportunities for real-time communication, ad-hoc collaboration and information sharing in a large-scale distributed environment. The main advantages of the systems is its multi-dimensionality that is, they improve scalability by enabling direct and real-time sharing of services and information, enable knowledge sharing by aggregating information and resources from nodes that are located on geographically distributed and potentially heterogeneous platforms and provide high availability by eliminating the need for a single centralized component.

Peer to Peer (P2P) networks are very popular since they offer opportunities for real time communication. They also help to build adhoc network to collaborate and share information in a large scale distributed environment. Apart from this P2P is a multidimensional network where it improves scalability by enabling direct and real time sharing of services and information. It enables knowledge sharing by aggregating information and resources from nodes that are located on geographically

N. Meghanathan et al. (Eds.): CCSIT 2012, Part I, LNICST 84, pp. 394–401, 2012.

distributed and heterogeneous platforms. It also provides high availability by eliminating the need for a single centralized component.

Information retrieval is the process, where a prospective user of information is able to convert his need for information into an actual list of citations to documents in storage containing information useful to him. Information retrieval can be considered as a process where a user is able to convert the information in the form of list of citations to documents in a storage containing information useful to him. It can also be viewed as a software program that stores and manages information on documents. The system assists the users in finding the information that is needed. There are three basic processes an information retrieval system has to support. The following are the processes which an information retrieval system has to support.

- The representation of the content of the documents.
- The representation of the user's information need.
- The comparison of the two representations.
- The representation of the content of the documents and user's information need.
- The comparison of the content and user's information need.

Cross language retrieval backs the user of multilingual document collections by allowing them to submit queries in one language and retrieve documents in any of the language covered by the retrieval system. Considering the example of language1 (L1) queries on a language2 (L2) document collection. Cross-language retrieval can be achieved in three different ways [1]:

- Off-line document translation: translating L2 documents into L1 and then indexing in L1.
- Off-line index translation: indexing L2 documents in L2, then translating index into L1.
- On-line query translation: indexing L2 documents in L2 and translating L1 quires into L2.

Query translation can be applied in environment, where it would be impossible to produce translations for all available documents. In document translation, it is possible to present the user with a high quality preview of all the retrieved documents. Translating documents after they are retrieved, does not suffice because it will not help users to identify material that they wanted to be translated. Since it assumes that the user has already found the relevant document in its original foreign language, it fails to support exactly that part of a search in a multilingual environment which is the most difficult one, to formulate a query which will take the user to the foreign language document of interest.

2   Peer-to-Peer Network for CLIR

Peer-to-Peer network distinguishes itself by its distribution of power and function. They can form *ad hoc* connections between nodes for sharing all kinds of information and files. They can build connections between nodes by building adhoc connections between them. Peer-to-Peer discards hierarchical notions of clients and servers and replaces it with equal peer nodes that function similarly as clients and servers. Different software modules communicate with each other for processing the information required for the completion of the distributed application. Each computer can access services from the software modules on another computer, as well as providing services to the other computer. The discovery process in the peer-to-peer network is much more complicated than that of the client server. Each computer should know the network addresses of the other computers running the distributed application or at least of subset. And also propagating changes to the different software modules on all the computers would also be harder.

Every computer is capable of accessing services to and fro with other computers. Each computer should know the network addresses of other computers which run the distributed application. It should be able to propagate the changes to different software modules on all the computers. However, the combined processing power of several large computers could easily surpass the processing power available from even the best single computer, and the peer-to-peer network could thus result in much more scalable applications. Peer-to-peer architecture for cross language information system can be divided into two systems

- Cooperative- information is held in the central place (description, collection index, statistics).
- Uncooperative- peer is independent and does not have information about its neighbor, but it answers to the neighbors queries.

According to network structure, peer-to-peer systems can be classified as

- Centralized network
- Decentralized network

2.1   Centralized Network

Centralized network can be treated as a combination of client-server and peer-to-peer. Alike the client-server model, some nodes in the network will act as a server, providing only the directory services. All information resources are distributed among the other peer in the networks. Centralized network also come cross the same problem as the client-server model, single point of failure and scalability. It is observed that one directory server is capable of handling only few requests from the peers and the response time will increases, if more request are placed. In this network, failure of the server will result in the total system crash down; this can be overcome by adding more servers to the networks. Most of the real world peer-to-peer systems are based on this model; Bit Torrent and Edonkey network are the best examples. Some of the benefits can be list as [2]:

- Since it is combination of client-server, transferring to this network from the existing system is very easy.
- High scalability can be achieved by improving the network usage and reducing the broadcasting.
- Finally, it is easy to manage.

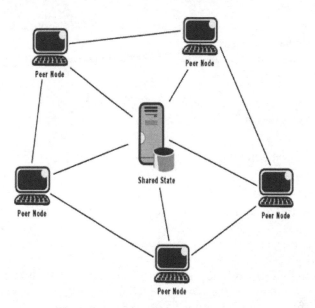

Fig. 1. Centralized peer-to-peer networks

2.2   Decentralized Network

Decentralized network is further sub divided into

1. Structured
2. Unstructured

Structured P2P also known as structured overlay networks or distributed hash tables, in which peers are grouped or clustered. In a common identifier space, each peer is responsible for a subset of identifiers and even the multiple peers are responsible for same space to acquire higher reliability. Overlay routing protocol are used by the peer to forward the messages, to carry out this process efficiently an routing table is maintained. Compared to the unstructured, the structured P2P overlay networks exhibit much lower bandwidth consumption for the search. The concept that can be used for designing the search engine for CLIR is[11]:

-Global index in structured P2P
In an unstructured system all the peers in the network are treated equally, that is they both can issue the request, respond to each other request and also route requests to other nodes. Peers flood search requests in the network, this approach is effective for the search of a popular content and performers poorly for a rare content. P2P search engine for cross language information retrieval can be designed such that:

-Local indexes in unstructured or hierarchical P2P networks
In this method documents are divided over the network and each peer maintain the list of its broadcast. To prevent the numerous documents held in the network, the queries can be answered in two different levels:

1. Peer level – which locate the group of peers with relevant document collections
2. Document level – the query is submitted to the peers and it is answered by querying the local index.

If you have more than one surname, please make sure that the Volume Editor knows how you are to be listed in the author index.

3   Search Mechanism in Peer to Peer Network

The main purpose of search mechanism in P2P network is to guide the query to the sources, so that the appropriate document can be retrieved and then translated back to the query language. The objective of this mechanism is to decrease the number of unrelated document retrieval per query and at the same time maintain a high recall rate.

In the centralized network, an index is maintained of all the documents by the participating peer. Some of the commercial information retrieval systems are web search engines and centralized P2P indexing systems. Usually in this method, all the peers in the network give the index of its entire shared document to the centralized repository, from which the required document can be retrieved. It appears as though two peers in the network are communicating directly. Any of the available translating method can be used if required.

For the decentralized network, some of the search mechanisms are [12]:

1.   Breath first search

It is a widely used method in the networks. When a node has to search for a information, it generates the query message and broadcast it to the other peers in the network. If some node has a match, it responds by generating the query hit message. When the sender receives the query hit from more the one peer, it tries to download the documents from the peer with the best connectivity. One of the major sang with this method is that, each query consumes excessive network because it is propagated along all links. Therefore a node with a lower bandwidth can cause bottleneck.

2.   Random Breadth-first-search (RBFS)

The drawback of the BFS is overcome in this method, here a peer which request for the information sends its search message to only a few of the peers in the network that are selected in random. In this method, a peer which request information sends messages to only a few other peers in the network which are selected randomly. It also eliminates all the disadvantages of the BFS method. Since this method randomly choices the peer, there are possibility that some of the peers in the network that contain the related information may be left unnoticed.

3.   Random walkers

This method is similar to the RBFS. Here the node that needs the information forwards a query message called walker to randomly selected peer. To reduce the time taken in getting the result, one walker is extended to n-walker, where n independent walkers are consecutively sent from the searcher. It is assumed that n-walker after T steps will reach the same number of peer as a one walker after nk steps.

4   Translation Technique

Any of the available translation methods can be used if required [9]

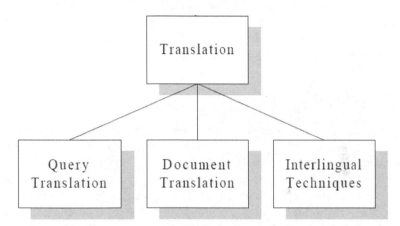

Fig. 2. Translation techniques [9]

1.   Query translation
Query translation is a most general strategy in which the query is automatically converted into every supported language and is relatively efficient. The principal limitation of query translation is that queries are often short and provide little context for disambiguation. Homonymous words produce undesirable matches. Translation ambiguity causes this problem, by potentially introducing additional terms that are themselves homonymous. For this reason, controlling translation ambiguity is a central issue in the design of effective query translation techniques.

2.   Document translation
Document translation is just the opposite of query translation, automatically converting all of the documents into each supported query language. It typically provides more context than queries, more effective strategies to limit the effect of translation ambiguity may be possible. Another potential advantage is that selected documents can be preseted to the user for examination without on-demand translation.

Document translation can be considered as a methodology of converting all the documents into each supported query language. The advantages of this method includes that the selected documents can be presented to the user for examination without on-demand translation. It also provides more contexts than queries, more effective strategies to limit the effect of translation etc.

3.   Interlingual techniques

Interlingual techniques convert both the query and the documents into a unified language-independent representation. Controlled vocabulary techniques based on multilingual thesauri are the best examples of this approach. Controlled vocabulary techniques based on Multi lingual thesauri can be considered as one of the best example for this method. Because each controlled vocabulary term typically corresponds to exactly one concept, terms from any language may be used to index documents or to form queries. Latent semantic indexing and the generalized vector space model both use a document aligned training corpus to learn a mapping from one or more languages into a language-neutral representation. Document and query representations from either language can be mapped into this space, allowing similarity measures to be computed both within and across languages.

5   Conclusion

Peer-to-Peer is a most important part of the computer networks. Some of the methods for the centralized and decentralized network are proposed that enables the retrieval of information in the Peer-to-Peer networks with some of the translation techniques that helps the user to retrieve the required document, in the understandable languages. There are several useful CLIR techniques are known for the information retrieval. Monolingual retrieval is still more effective for free text than CLIR. Query translation, document translation, and interlingual techniques provide a range of alternatives that can be tailored to specific applications. The proposed translation techniques for CLIR do have drawback, which can be overcome by selecting the appropriate algorithms, which can be carried ad the future work of the same paper.

References

1. Hiemstra, D.: Using Language Models for Information Retrieval (2003)
2. Sankar, K.: What is peer to peer (2003),
   http://p2p.inetrnet2.edu/documents/
   what%20is%20to%20peer-5.pdf
3. Callan, J., Powell, A.L., French, J.C., Connell, M.: The effects of query based sampling on automatic database selection algorithms. Technical report IR-181, center for intelligent information retrieval. Dept. of Computer Science, University of Massachusetts
4. Crespo, A., Garcia-Molina, H.: Routing Indices for Peer-to-Peer Systems. In: Proc. of ICDCS 2002, Vienna, Austria (2002)
5. Tang, C., Xu, Z., Dwarkadas, S.: Peer-to-Peer information retrieval using self-organizing semantic overlay networks. In: Proc. of ACM SIGCOMM 2003, Karlsruhe, Germany (2003)
6. Zeinalipour-Yazti, D.: Information retrieval in Peer-Peer Systems. M.Sc Thesis. Dept of Computer Science, University of California-Riverside (June 2003)
7. Ata, B.M.A., Mohd, T., Sembok, T., Yusoff, M.: SISDOM: acmultilingual document retrieval system. Asian Libraries 4(3), 37–46 (1995)

8. Fluhr, C.: Multilingual Information Retrieval. In: Cole, R.A., Mariani, J., Uszkoreit, H., Zaenen, A., Zue, V. (eds.) Survey of the State of the Art in Human Language Technology: Center for Spoken Language Understanding, Oregon Graduate Institute, pp. 391–305 (1995)
9. Oard, D.W.: Alternative Approaches for Cross-Language Text Retrieval. In: Cross-Language Text and Speech Retrieval, AAAI Technical Report SS-97-05
10. Dorrigiv, R., Lopez-Ortiz, A., Pralat, P.: Search Algorithms for Unstructured Peer-to-Peer networks
11. Chen, H., Gong, Z., Huang, Z.: Self-Learning Routing in Unstructured P2P network. International Journal of Information Technology 11(12)
12. Zeinalipour-Yazti, D., Kalogeraki, V., Gunopulos, D.: Information retrival in Peer-to-Peer networks
13. Bawa, M., Bayardo Jr., R.J., Rajagopalan, S., Shekita, E.: Make it Fresh, Make it Quick Searching a Network of Personal Webservers. In: Proc. of WWW 2003, Budapest, Hungary (2003)
14. Archana, M., et al.: Mining The Web Information For Cross Language Information Retrieval. In: Proceeding of ICMET 2011. ASME Press (2011)
15. Archana, M., et al.: Extracting web information for CLIR. International Journal of Modeling and Optimization (IJMO) (yet to be published)

Detecting and Avoiding Wormhole Attack in MANET Using Statistical Analysis Approach

Saurabh Upadhyay[1,*] and Brijesh Kumar Chaurasia[2]

[1] Sarvottam Institute of Technology and Management , Greater Noida, India
[2] Institute of Technology and Management, Gwalior, India
{saurabh.cse.cs,bkchaurasia.itm}@gmail.com

Abstract. A mobile ad hoc network (MANET) consists of a collection of wireless mobile nodes that forms a temporary network without having any fixed infrastructure or centralized administration. MANET is infrastructure-less, lack of centralized monitoring and dynamic changing network topology. MANET is highly vulnerable to attack due to open error prone shared wireless medium. In this paper, we proposed an algorithm for avoiding and preventing the wormhole attacks in MANET using statistical analysis approach. Simulation and results show that efficacy of proposed algorithm and the proposed heuristics provides better security and performance than conventional AODV in the presence of wormhole attack.

Keywords: MANET, Wormhole attack, Wormhole detection technique, Wormhole prevention, Statistical mechanism.

1   Introduction

A mobile Ad hoc network (MANET) is a collection of two or more devices or nodes equipped with wireless communication and networking capabilities [1], [2], [3].These node includes laptop, computers, PDAs and wireless phones etc, have a limited transmission range. Such a wireless ad-hoc network is infrastructure less, self-organizing, adaptive and does not require any centralized administration. If two such devices are located within transmission range of each other, they can communicate directly. Each node can communicate directly with only few nodes within the communication range and has to forward messages using the neighbor nodes until the messages arrive at the destination nodes. Since the transmission between sender and receiver may use several nodes as intermediate nodes, many routing protocols [3] have been proposed for the MANETS. Most of the protocol assumes that other nodes are trustable so they do not consider the security and attack issues. The lack of infrastructure, rapid deployment practices, and the hostile environments in which MANETS are deployed make them vulnerable to a wide range of security attacks that are presented in [4], [5], [6]. However most of these attacks are performed by a single malicious node. Many solutions exist to solve single node attacks [7], [8], [9], but they cannot prevent from the attacks that are executed by colluding malicious node

---

* Corresponding author.

N. Meghanathan et al. (Eds.): CCSIT 2012, Part I, LNICST 84, pp. 402–408, 2012.

such as wormhole attack. Wormhole attack is more dangerous than single node attacks. Analysis of wormhole attack is discussed in [10]. In [11], a wormhole, an attacker connects two distant points in the network, and then replays them into the network from that point. An example is shown in Fig. 1. Here S and D are the two end-points of the wormhole link (called as wormholes). In this diagram, wormhole attack is that all the nodes in area A assume that nodes in area B are their neighbors and vice versa.

The wormhole link can be established by many types such as long-range wireless transmission in wireless networks, by using an Ethernet cable, a long-range wireless transmission and an optical link in wired medium. Wormhole attack records packets at one end-point in the network and tunnels them to other end-point. These attacks are severe threats to MANET routing protocols. For example, when a wormhole attack is used against an on-demand routing protocol such as AODV/ DSR, than all the packets will transmit through this tunnel and no other route is discovered. If the attacker creates the tunnel honestly and reliably than it will not harm the network and also provides the useful service in connecting the network more efficiently. The attacker can perform the attacks even if the network communication provides confidentiality and authenticity. If single path on-demand routing protocol such as AODV [12] is being used in highly dynamic wireless ad hoc networks, a new route need to be discovered in response to every route break. Each route discovery is associated with high overhead and latency. This inefficiency will be reduced if there are multiple paths available and a new route discovery is required only in the situation when all paths break.

In this paper, we propose an approach to detect wormhole in MANET by using average time delay to detect anomalies based on statistical information of packets in the networks. Three features of the network are monitored including: the number of incoming packets, the number of outgoing packets and the average route discovery time related to each node. The network is having wormhole attacks if any abrupt change of one of these features is reported. The proposed algorithm is light weight and low computation overhead.

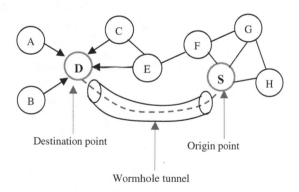

Fig. 1. Wormhole attack in a network

The rest of the paper is organized as follows. Section 2 describes proposed algorithm of wormhole detection model in MANET. Result and analysis is illustrated in section 3. Section 4 concludes the work.

2   Proposed Wormhole Attack Model

The proposed wormhole attack model method works without any extra hardware requirements, the basic idea behind this work is that the wormhole attack reduces the length of hops and the data transmission delay. The steps of proposed algorithm of wormhole attack are as follows:

1.   Randomly generate a node identity, number 0 to maximum number of nodes in the network.
2.   Make the node with same number as transmitter node.
3.   Generate the route from selected transmitting node to destination node.
4.   Start counter and send RREQ using reactive routing technique.
5.   Receive the RREP packet from the each path; associate it in route list with time delay.
6.   Now calculate the average time delay.
7.   Select the route within covariance range of average delay.
8.   The routes that are not within the covariance range are black listed hence they are not involved in future routes discovery.
9.   Whole process (from step1 to step9) is repeated for limited assumed time.

3   Simulation and Results

In this section simulation and results are illustrated. Node distribution scenario is depicted by Fig.2. There are 18 nodes in the network. Simulation parameters are given in Table 1.

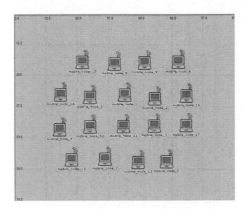

Fig. 2. Node distribution scanerio

Wormhole attack scenario is shown in Fig. 3. Wormhole attack is created in between *node 0* and *node 5* . Due to wormhole attack, all the traffic between *node 0* and *node 0* will go directly without using any nodes while other intermediate nodes are presented in the network.

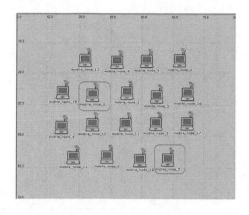

Fig. 3. A netwok affected by wormhole attack

Table 1. Simulation parameters

Parameters	Description
Examined Protocol	AODV
Simulation Time	1000 sec.
Simulation Area	80x80 m
Number of Nodes	18
Malicious Nodes	02
Number of Wormholes	01

Fig. 4 shows the average route length in terms of number of hops for all three conditions'. X direction shows the simulation time where as Y direction illustrates the number of hops. Normal condition is depicted by red color. As wormhole attack occurs wormhole affected node start sending packet by using the tunnel without using intermediate nodes so number of hopes reduces as shown by green color. Fig. 4 shows that at the time of 3 minutes the difference between the number of hops required in wormhole affected scenario and without wormhole scenario is maximum that means the minimum number of hops is required to transmit the data and most of the data is being transmitted involving the wormhole affected node. After the time of 6 min of our proposed algorithm reached very near to the without attack scenario in terms of number of hops required that means wormhole affected nodes is being avoided. By implementing the proposed algorithm wormholes are avoided in the route discovery process as number of hopes per route increases as shown by blue color.

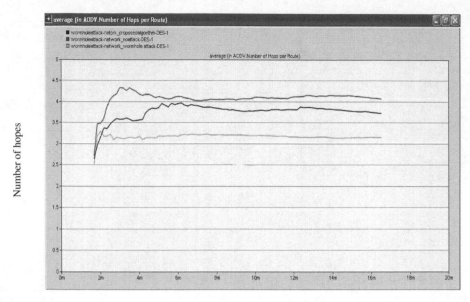

Simulation time

Fig. 4. Average number of hopes per route

Average route discovery time for all three conditions is depicted by Fig. 5. This results show that the wormhole tunnel is selected all the times by wormhole affected nodes so new routes are not discovered this will reduce the route discovery time. At

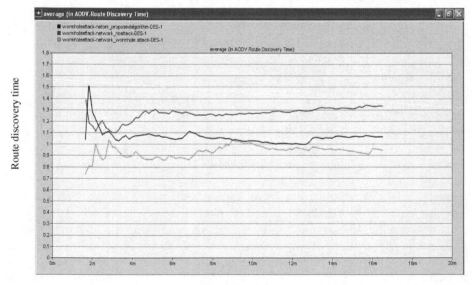

Simulation time

Fig. 5. Average route discovery time

the time of 3 minutes route discovery time of proposed algorithm almost equal to the route discovery time of without attack scenario that mean all the nodes are being checked for route discovery process. After 14 min, the route discovery time of proposed scenario has become almost steady. The proposed algorithm wormhole affected routes are avoided and the entire route is being checked so route discovery time may be increase.

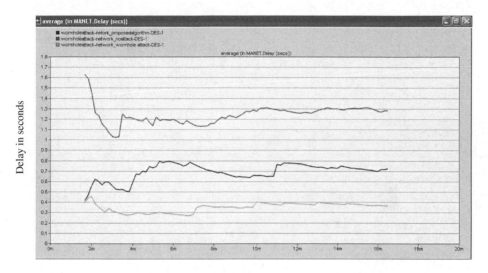

Simulation time

Fig. 6. Average delay in seconds

Fig. 6 shows, the average delay for all three conditions. Due to the wormhole attack the delay reduces because the packets are delivered without any intermediate nodes. The proposed algorithm is used the number of intermediate nodes to avoid wormhole tunnel, so delay is increased from without attack environment but it is very less from attack scenario. At the time of 3 minutes delay is around 0.5 sec. At the time of 5 minutes and after that delay is in between 0.7 to 0.8 sec of our proposed algorithm.

4   Conclusion

Statistical analysis is a technique used to detect routing anomaly as long as the sufficient information about the routes is available from the multi-path routing. Simulation results are shown that proposed algorithm is successful at detecting wormhole attacks and locating the malicious nodes. The simulation shows the avoidance of using the attacker nodes in data transmission. Security against wormhole attack can be provided by using our proposed algorithm. The algorithm performs better compared to existing routing protocols on three parameters hop count, route discovery time, delay. The proposed model is shown that algorithm is very light-weight and suited the security issues of MANET.

References

1. Perkins, C., Bhagwat, P.: Highly dynamic destination-sequenc distance-vector routing (DSDV) for mobile computers. In: Proceedings of ACM Conference on Communications Architectures, Protocols and Applications (ACM SIGCOMM 1994), London, UK, pp. 234–244 (1994)
2. Perkins, C., Royer, E.: Ad hoc on-demand distance vector routing. In: Proceedings of Second IEEE Workshop on Mobile Computing Systems and Applications, pp. 90–100 (1999)
3. Perkins, C.E.: Ad hoc Networking. Addison Wesley, Boston (2001)
4. Yang, H., Luo, H., Ye, F., Lu, S., Zhang, L.: Security in mobile ad hoc networks: challenges and solutions. IEEE Wireless Communications 11(1), 38–47 (2004)
5. Zhen, J., Srinivas, S.: Replay Attacks for Secure Routing in Ad Hoc Networks. In: Pierre, S., Barbeau, M., An, H.-C. (eds.) ADHOC-NOW 2003. LNCS, vol. 2865, pp. 140–150. Springer, Heidelberg (2003)
6. Hu, Y.-C., Perrig, A., Johnson, D.B.: Rushing attacks and defense in wireless ad hoc network routing protocols. In: Maughan, W.D., Perrig, A. (eds.) ACM Workshop on Wireless Security (WiSe), pp. 30–40 (2003)
7. Tamilselvan, L., Sankaranarayanan, D.V.: Prevention of impersonation attack in wireless mobile ad hoc networks. International Journal of Computer Science and Network Security (IJCSNS) 7(3), 118–123 (2007)
8. Papadimitratos, P., Haas, Z.J.: Secure routing for mobile ad hoc networks. In: Proceedings of SCS Communication Networks and Distributed Systems Modeling and Simulation Conference (2002)
9. Hu Y.-C., Johnson, D.B., Perrig, A.: SEAD: Secure efficient distance vector routing for mobile wireless ad hoc networks. In: IEEE Workshop on Mobile Computing Systems and Applications (WMCSA), pp. 3–13 (2002)
10. Upadhyay, S., Chaurasia, B.K.: Impact of Wormhole Attacks on MANETs. International Journal of Computer Science & Emerging Technologies 2(1), 77–82 (2011)
11. Yang, H., Luo, H., Ye, F., Lu, S., Zhang, L.: Security in mobile ad hoc networks: challenges and solutions. IEEE Wireless Communications 11(1), 38–47 (2004)
12. Perkins, C., Belding-Royer, E., Das, S.: Ad hoc On-Demand Distance Vector (AODV) Routing, RFC 3561 (2003)

Energy Efficient Hierarchical Clustering Routing Protocol for Wireless Sensor Networks

Diwakar Meenakshi and Sushil Kumar

School of Computer and Systems Sciences
Jawaharlal Nehru University, New Delhi, India
meenakshi.d02@gmail.com, skdohare@yahoo.com

Abstract. Advanced technology of Wireless Sensor Networks used in many applications like health, environment, battle field etc. The sensor nodes equipped with limited power sources. Therefore, efficiently utilizing sensor nodes energy can maintain a prolonged network lifetime. One of the major issues in sensor networks is developing an energy-efficient routing protocol to improve the lifetime of the networks. In this paper, we propose EEHCRP (Energy-Efficient Hierarchical Clustering Routing Protocol), a protocol for wireless sensor networks. Network partitioned into annular rings by using various power levels at base station and each ring having various sensor nodes. The mathematical formulae for choosing the cluster head are provided. The model developed is simulated in MATLAB. The results are obtained in terms of three metrics, lifetime of the network, and number of clusters and energy consumption of clusters heads. From the results of simulation, it is observed that the performance of EEHCRP is better in terms of energy consumption of CH, number of clusters and lifetime of network compared with LEACH.

Keywords: Wireless Sensor Network, Energy Efficiency, Network Lifetime, Clustering, LEACH protocol.

1   Introduction

Wireless Sensor networks (WSN) consist of large number of sensor nodes and these nodes are directly interacting with their environment by sensing the physical parameters such as temperature, humidity, etc[1]. All the sensor nodes send or receive data to/from a fixed wired station called base station (BS). The base station usually serves as a gateway to some other network. WSNs have a comprehensive range of applications in this field including [6, 9, 10]; environmental applications, military applications, home security, etc.

The main challenge is related to the limited, usually unrenewable energy supply of the sensor nodes. Hence, the available energy at the nodes should consider as a major constraint while designing the routing protocols.

Hierarchical-based routing protocols also known as cluster based routing protocols. This type of protocols enforces a structure on the network to use the energy efficiency, extend the lifetime and scalability. In this protocol, nodes of the network are organized into the clusters in which higher energy nodes (e.g. assume the job of the cluster

N. Meghanathan et al. (Eds.): CCSIT 2012, Part I, LNICST 84, pp. 409–420, 2012.
© Institute for Computer Sciences, Social Informatics and Telecommunications Engineering 2012

head)can be used to process and forwarding the information, while lower energy nodes can be used to do the sensing the target. Clustering is an efficient way to reduce energy consumption and extend the life time of the network, doing data aggregation and fusion in order to reduce the number of transmitted messages to the BS [2].

In this paper, we present EEHCRP (Energy Efficient Hierarchical Clustering Routing Protocol) based on different power levels for Wireless Sensor Networks. EEHCRP reduces the number of dead nodes and the energy consumption, to extend the network lifetime.

The rest of the paper is organized as follows. An overview of related work is given by section 2. In section 3, propose an energy efficient hierarchical clustering routing protocol. Simulations and results of experiments are discussed in the section 4. In section 5, concludes the work presented in this paper and the scope of further extension of this work.

2   Related Work

The first hierarchical routing protocol for WSN is Low Energy Adaptive Clustering Hierarchy (LEACH). LEACH is a cluster-based routing protocol which includes cluster formation in distributed manner. In LEACH [3], the nodes form themselves into local clusters, with one node acting as the local cluster-head. LEACH includes randomized rotation of the high-energy cluster-head position such that it rotates among the several sensors nodes in order to not deplete the battery of a single sensor. In addition, CHs performs local data fusion to "compress" the amount of data arriving from the nodes that belong to the respective cluster and transmit aggregate data to the base station, further reducing energy dissipation and enhancing system lifetime.

In LEACH, the cluster head receive data directly from each node and the sink uses single-hop routing. Therefore, it is not applicable for large networks. Also, it is not obvious how the number of predetermined number of cluster heads is going to be uniformly distributed through the network. Therefore, it is possible no or lots of CHs selected and also possible that too many CHs are located in a specific area. Furthermore, the dynamic clustering routing implemented with extra overhead, e.g. cluster head changes, advertisements etc., which consumed more energy.

LEACH-C protocol is the extended version of LEACH protocol. In which, all nodes in the network transmit their information to the BS, includes their ID, remaining energy, and position information. After this, the BS calculate the average energy of the network and select a set of CHs that have more energy than the average energy of the network and sends information about CHs ,their members and TDMA schedule. The member nodes decide own TDMA slot and transmit data in its time slot [4].A non-sovereign cluster-head selection is the main drawback of this protocol. Moreover, LEACH-C needs location information of all nodes in the network. However, the location information in wireless sensor networks is only available through GPS (Global positioning system) or a location sensing technique, such as triangulation which requires additional communication among the nodes [5].

Power-efficient gathering in Sensor Information Systems (PEGASIS) is an enhancement of the LEACH protocol. A single node in a chain is used by PAGASIS to send data to BS rather than multiple nodes. The chain is constructed in a greedy way. Each node only communicates with their closest neighbors along the communication chain. Gathered data moves from node to node, aggregated and finally transmit to the BS [6].In PAGASIS, Each sensor node is required to have additional local information about the wireless sensor network. When the PEGASIS protocol selects the head node, there is no consideration about the energy of nodes, location of the BS. This applies to the greedy algorithm for construct chain, some delay may occur. Since the head node is a single, it may happen to a bottleneck at the head node.

In [11], clustering of network is done symmetrically and cluster head node is selected by the comparisons of remaining energy and distance with the other nodes. Determine the cluster head of next hope by using the weight function in [12].

3   EEHCRP: Energy Efficient Hierarchical Clustering Routing Protocol

Hierarchical clustering algorithms are very important to increasing the lifetime of network. We propose EEHCRP (Energy Efficient Hierarchical Clustering Routing Protocol), which is a hierarchical clustering routing protocol. EEHCRP reduces the number of dead nodes and the energy consumption to extend the network lifetime. Before studying the details of the proposed algorithm, we define the expected network model and energy model.

3.1   Network Model

Let us consider a sensor network, consisting of n sensor nodes, which are randomly deployed over in an area of wireless sensor network. To prepare the network model, the following assumptions are made about sensor nodes.

Assumptions:

1. There is one base station which is fixed and located at middle in a given sensor network.
2. All sensor nodes are fixed and homogeneous with a limited stored energy.
3. Base station can transmit various power levels.
4. The sensed data by the sensor nodes are routed to the base station.
5. Each node is equipped with power constrain capabilities and vary their transmitted power.
6. Nodes are not equipped with GPS unit.

3.2   EEHCRP Algorithm

In this section, we describe our protocol in detail. This protocol is divided into three phases, setup phase, cluster setup phase and inter cluster routing phase.

3.2.1 Setup Phase
On the initial deployment, the base station (BS) transmits a level-1 signal with minimum power level. All nodes, which hear this message, set their level as 1. After that, the base station increases its signal power to attain the next level and transmit a level-2 signal. All the nodes that receive the massage but do not set the previous level set their level as 2.

This procedure continuous until the base station transmits corresponding massages to all levels. The total number of messages of levels is equivalent to the number of distinct transmit signal at which the BS can sends [7].

BS broadcast a hello massage, fig [1]. This massage contains the information of upper limit and lower limit of each level.

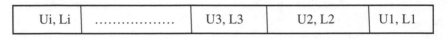

| Ui, Li | .... | U3, L3 | U2, L2 | U1, L1 |

Fig. 1. Structure of Hello message

Where
Ui: Upper limits of level i
Li: Lower limit of level i
Each node calculates the distance from the BS based on the received signal strength.

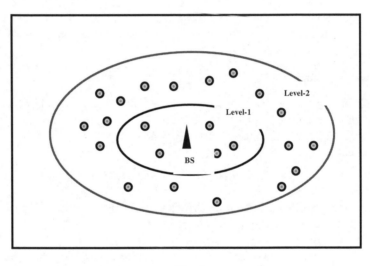

Fig. 2.

Algorithm 1. Setup phase

#No. of nodes N
BS can transmit i levels; i $\geq$ 1
1. For each level i, message transmitted by BS
2. If (Nodes does not assign previous level and hear new message or BS transmit level i = 1)
3. Assign level i
4. End if
5. End for
6. BS broadcast hello message, which contains the information of upper limit and lower limit of each level.
7. Each node calculates the distance from the BS based on received signal strength

3.2.2 Cluster Setup Phase

In this phase, each level is divided into clusters. The operation of cluster-setup phase is the same as LEACH [3] except the difference of threshold formula. For each level i, each node decide whether or not to become a cluster head for the current round by choosing a random number x between 0 and 1. The node becomes a cluster head for the current round if this number is less than the threshold $T_i(n)$. The threshold defined in ways. First approach is:

$$T_i = \begin{cases} \dfrac{P \times c}{1 - P \times \left(r \bmod \frac{1}{P}\right)} \times \dfrac{U_i - d(n, BS)}{(U_i - L_i)} & \text{if } n \in Z \\ 0 & \text{otherwise} \end{cases} \tag{1}$$

Where

P = the desired percentage of the cluster heads.
r = the current round.
Z = the set of nodes which have not been CHs in the last 1/P rounds.
c = the constant factor between the 0 and 1.
Ui = the upper limit of level-i.
Li = the lower limit of level-i.
d (n, BS) =the distance between node n and base station.

The second approach is

$$T_i(n) = \begin{cases} \dfrac{P \times c}{1 - P \times (r \bmod \frac{1}{P})} \times \left(\dfrac{U_i - d(n, BS)}{U_i - L_i}\right) \times \dfrac{E_{cur}(n)}{E_{ini}(n)} & \text{if } n \in Z \\ 0 & \text{Otherwise} \end{cases} \tag{2}$$

Where
$E_{cur}(n)$ n) = current energy of node n.
$E_{ini}(n)$ = initial energy of node n.

Each node that elected itself a cluster head for the current round, broadcast an advertisement message to the rest of the node by using CSMA Mac protocol. All cluster heads broadcast their advertisement message with the same transmit energy. All non- cluster head nodes receiving these messages from all cluster head nodes and each non-cluster node decided the cluster to which it will belong for the current round. This decision is based on received signal strength of the advertisement messages. Each node must inform to the cluster head that it will be a cluster member by using CSMA Mac protocol. After that, each cluster head creates a TDMA schedule for its cluster members. This information is broadcasted back to the nodes in the cluster. Once the clusters are created and TDMA schedule is fixed, data transmission can begin. Each cluster member can be turned off until the node's allocated time.

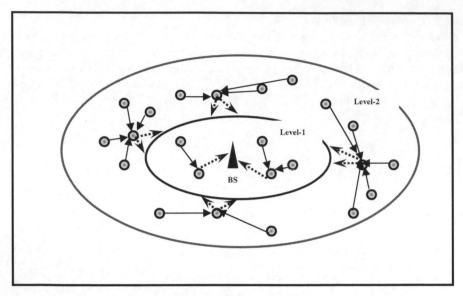

Fig. 3. Cluster formation

Each node sends data to its cluster heads with minimal transmission power. This power is estimated by received signal strength of the advertisement message. So that data transmission uses a minimal amount of energy.

When all the data has been received from the cluster members, then cluster head node perform data aggregation function to compress the data into a single signal. After a certain time the next round begin.

Algorithm 2. Cluster setup phase

1. for each (node N)
2. N selects random number x between 0 and 1.
3. If (x< T (n))
4. N becomes CH.
5. N broadcasts an advertising message for its CH status.
6. Else
7. N becomes a NCH node.
8. N chooses the CH, this selection is based on the received signal strength of advertise.
9. N informs the selected CH and become a member of its cluster.
10.End if.
11.for each (CH)
12.CH creates TDMA schedule for each cluster member.
13.Each cluster member communicates to the CH in its time slot.
14.End for

3.2.3 Inter Cluster Routing

After the cluster formation, the cluster heads broadcast the aggregate data to the next level. At the next level, the nodes aggregate their data and sends to their cluster heads.

In this manner the cluster heads at the last level transmit the final information to the BS.

Algorithm 3. Inter cluster routing

1. For each (level i)
2. for each CH
3. CH receives the data from the cluster member
4. Aggregate the data.
5. If (i ==1)
6. CH transmits data to the BS.
7. Else
8. CH broadcasts data in the next level.
9. End if
10. End for
11. End for

3.3   Energy Model

We use a free space model. This model is used to calculate the power of received signal of each packet. There is only one clear line of sight path between receiver and transmitter is assumed by the free space propagation.

The energy consumed during the transmission is the main part of the total energy consumption. The received signal power in free space at a distance r is calculated by using the following equation [8].

$$p_r dBm = p_t dBm + 10 \log_{10}(G_l) + 20 \log_{10}(\lambda) \\ - 20 \log_{10}(4\pi) - 20 \log_{10}(r) \tag{3}$$

Where the transmitted signal power is denoted by p_t, product of receive and transmit antenna field radiation patterns in the line-of-sight (LOS) direction is G_l and λ is the carrier wavelength.

The minimum transmission power level $p_{t\text{-min}}$ at the sender is calculated as.

$$p_{t\_min} dBm = p_{r\_min} dBm - 10 \log_{10}(G_l) - 20 \log_{10}(\lambda) + 20\log_{10} \\ + 20\log_{10}(r) \tag{4}$$

from (3) and (4), we obtain.

$$p_{t\_min} dBm = p_{r\_min} dBm - p_r dBm + p_t dBm \tag{5}$$

where $p_{r\text{-min}}$ is the receiver's sensitivity?

The non-cluster head nodes calculate the strength of the advertisement messages from equation (1) and join the cluster which has the maximum strength of the received signal. These nodes also calculate the minimum transmission power for sending data to the cluster head with the help of eqn (5).

In free space model, to transmit a 1 bit message over the distance r, transmission energy consumption $E_{T(x)}(1, r)$ [3] is-

$$E_{T(x)}(1, r) = E_{T(x-elec)}(r) + E_{T(x)-amp}(1, r) \tag{6}$$

$$E_{T(X)}(1, r) = E_{elec} * 1 + \varepsilon_{amp} * 1 * r^2 \tag{7}$$

where $E_{T(x)-elec}$ is the energy dissipated by the transmitter electronics and ε_{amp} is the energy dissipated by the transmit amplifier.

$$E_{R_x}(r) = E_{R_{x-elec}}(r) \tag{8}$$

$$E_{R_x} = E_{elec} * r \tag{9}$$

Where $E_{R_{(x)-elec}}$ denote the receiver electronics.

4   Simulation Results

In this section, the simulated results are obtained to evaluate the performance of EEHCRP using MATLAB. We simulated the energy consumption, number of clusters and resulting lifetime of the network. The results obtain in terms of three metric, energy consumption of CHs, number of clusters and life time of WSN are represented

Table 1. Shows the simulation parameter

Parameters	Value
Network size	100 x100 m
BS station	(50, 50)
Number of sensor nodes	100
Initial energy	.05 J
E_{elec}	50 nJ/b
ε_{mp}	10pJ/b/m^2
EDA	5nJ/b/signal
Data packet size	4000 bits
n (level)	3

in form of graphs. We define the two version of EEHCRP: EEHCRP-1 and EEHCRP-2. The only difference between these two versions is EEHCRP-1approch uses eqn (1) and EEHCRP-1 approach uses eqn (2).

We assume that 100 sensor nodes are randomly deployed over 100 x 100 m square area sensor field and the whole network is divided in three levels (n=3). The BS located at (50, 50). The initial energy of each node is .05 J and a node is considered dead when its energy is less than equal to 0.

A. Energy Consumption of Cluster Heads(CHs)

Fig.[4] shows the results for the energy consumed by CHs in EEHCRP by using both approaches eqn(1) and eqn(2) and LEACH protocol for 30 rounds. The energy consumed by CHs for each round in EEHCRP is much lower than that in LEACH. This is due to fact that in LEACH, CHs transmit their data direct to the BS. Therefore, the energy consumption is much higher. In EEHCRP, CHs sends their data to the BS through multihop communication. So a significant amount of energy is saved. For example, after the 25 rounds, the LEACH consumed the about 40% of the initial energy while in EEHCRP is about 12%.

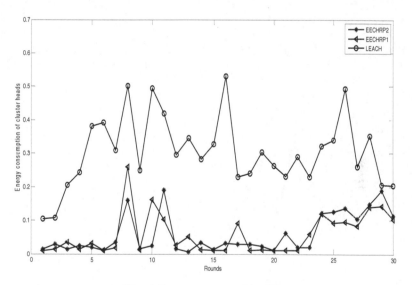

Fig. 4. Energy consumed by CHs

B. Number of Clusters

Fig [5] shows the distribution of the number of clusters in EEHCRP-1, EEHCRP-2 and LEACH for 25 rounds. Its shows that the number of clusters in EEHCRP-1 and EEHCRP-2 is fewer than LEACH. Further it is also observed the numbers of clusters in EEHCRP-2 are less that EEHCRP-1.

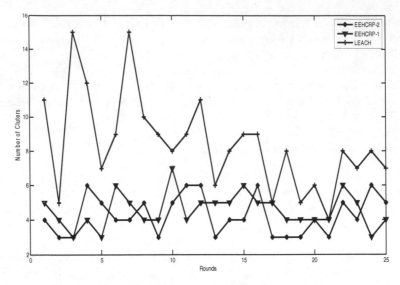

Fig. 5. Number of clusters

C. Lifetime of WSN

The result between the number of nodes alive and the number of rounds is shown by Fig [6]. The result obtained by measuring of time until the first node dies to time until

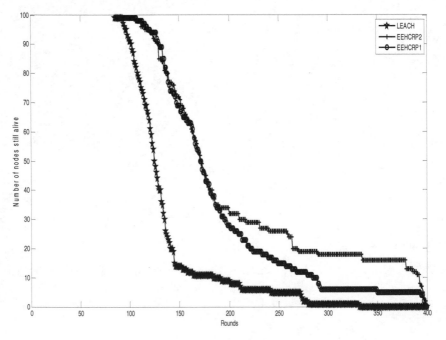

Fig. 6. Network lifetime

the last node dies for 400 rounds. The first dead node appeared in 90 rounds for EEHCRP-1 and in round 92 for EEHCRP-2, in 86 rounds for LEACH and the last dead node appeared in 393 rounds for EEHCRP-1,in 398 rounds for EEHCRP-2, in333 rounds for LEACH. It is observed that the EEHCRP much better improves the life time of network than the LEACH protocol. Further, it also observed that EEHCRP-2 improves the life time of the network better that EEHCRP-1.

5   Conclusion and Future Work

In this paper, a hierarchical clustering based routing protocol has been proposed. The network model based on power levels is being developed. The mathematical formulae for choosing the cluster head are provided. The model developed is simulated in MATLAB. The simulation results of energy consumption of cluster heads, numbers of clusters and network lifetime are provided. It has been observed that the energy consumed by CHs for each round in EEHCRP is much lower than that in LEACH. For example, after the 25 rounds, the LEACH consumed the about 40% of the initial energy while in EEHCRP is about 12%. It has been also observed that the number of clusters in EEHCRP-1 and EEHCRP-2 is fewer than LEACH and the numbers of clusters in EEHCRP-2 are lesser than that of using EEHCRP-1. Furthermore, It is observed that the EEHCRP much better improves the life time of network than the LEACH protocol and EEHCRP-2 improves the lifetime of the network better than that of using EEHCRP-1. Finally, it is concluded that the performance of EEHCRP is better than LEACH.

In future research, we will study to optimize the number of levels to efficiently consume the energy of all nodes and improve the network lifetime. We also want to extend our algorithm to heterogeneous WSNs.

Acknowledgement. This work was supported by council of scientific and industrial research, India for promotion of research and scientific excellence program.

References

1. Karl, H., Willig, A.: Protocols and Architecture for Wireless sensor networks. Wiley (2005) ISBN: 0470095105
2. Akkaya, K., Younis, M.: A survey on routing protocols for wireless sensor networks. Elsevier B.V (2003)
3. Heinzelman, W.R., Chandrakasan, A., Balakrishnan, H.: Energy-Efficient Communication Protocol for Wireless Microsensor Networks. In: Proceedings of the 33rd Hawaii International Conference on System Sciences (2000)
4. Heinzelman, W., Candrakasan, A., Balakrisnan, H.: AN Application-Specific Protocol Architecture for Wireless Microsensor Networks. IEEE Transaction on Wireless Networking 1(4), 660–670 (2000)
5. Fengjun, S.: A Distributed Clustering Algorithm for Wireless Sensor Networks. Wuhan University Journal of Natural Sciences 13(4), 385–390 (2008)

6. Akyildiz, I.F., Su, W., Sankarasubramaniam, Y., Cayirci, E.: Wireless sensor networks: a survey
7. Murthy, G.R., Iyer, V., Bhawani Radhika, V.: Level Controlled Clustering. IEEE Wireless Sensor Networks (2008)
8. Goldsmith, A.: Wireless Communications, pp. 28–29. Cambridge University Press (2005)
9. Akyildiz, F., Su, W., Sankarasubramaniam, Y., Cayirci, E.: A Survey on Sensor Networks. IEEE Communications Magazine (2002)
10. Tubaishat, M., Madria, S.: Sensor Networks: An Overview. IEEE Potentials 22(2), 20–23 (2003)
11. Lu, H., Li, J., Wang, G.: A Novel Energy Efficient Routing Algorithm for Hierarchically Clustered Wireless Sensor Networks. IEEE (2009)
12. Huang, W., Peng, Y., Wen, J., Yu, M.: Energy-Efficient Multi-hop Hierarchical Routing Protocol for Wireless Sensor Networks. IEEE (2009)

An Analysis on Energy Efficient System Design in Grid Computing

D. Ramesh[1] and A. Krishnan[2]

[1] Anna University of Technology, Tiruchirappalli
drameshphd@gmail.com
[2] K.S. Rangasamy College of Technology, Tiruchengode

Abstract. The primary focus of research in computing systems has been on the improvement of the effective designon system performance. In order to fulfil this objective, the performance has been steadily growing driven by more efficient system design and algorithms. The performance of grid is improved in many aspect based on various research direction of last few year. In grid computing, load sharing is the major research issue. In addition to the load sharing, at present, the power management is attracting current researchers. This paper further explains basic power management scheme in the general computing as well as grid computing. And this paper strongly performed an analysis on various categories of real time grid systems. The power consumption on various grid levels based on multiple volumes in the organization level is analysed. The conclusion is focused the future requirement of research direction in the energy efficient system design of grid computing.

Keywords: Grid Computing, Power Management, Energy Efficient System Design.

1 Introduction

The modern computing industry focus for grid computing as the requirement is over whelming. Although the performance per watt ratio has been constantly rising, the total power drawn by computing systems is hardly decreasing. Oppositely, it has been increasing every year that can be illustrated by the estimated average power use across three classes of servers presented in Table 1. The table describes the power consumption of every year from 2000 to 2006 on various grid levels and on various volumes. If this trend continues, the cost of the energy consumed by a server during its lifetime will exceed the hardware cost.

The problem is even worse for large-scale compute infrastructures, such as clusters and data centres. It was estimated that in 2006, IT infrastructures in the United States consumed about 61 billion kWh for the total electricity cost about 4.5 billiondollars. The estimated energy consumption is more than double from whatwas consumed by IT in 2000. Moreover, under current efficiency trends, theenergy consumption tends to double again by 2011, resulting in 7.4 billion dollarsannually.Energy consumption is not only determined by hardware efficiency, but it is alsodependent on the resource management system deployed on the infrastructure and theefficiency of applications running in the system.

N. Meghanathan et al. (Eds.): CCSIT 2012, Part I, LNICST 84, pp. 421–428, 2012.

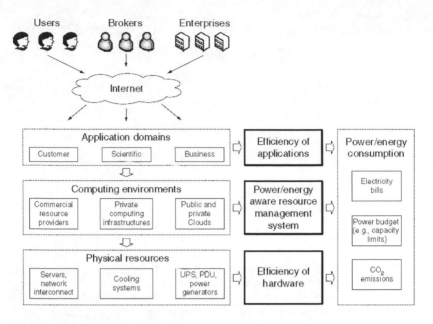

Fig. 1. General Overview of Energy Consumption in Computing Industry

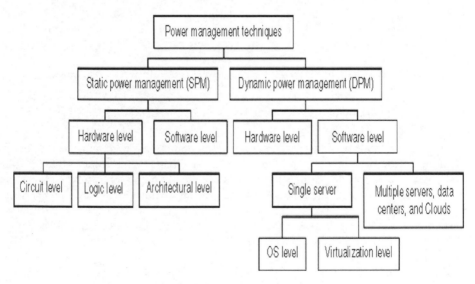

Fig. 2. Power Management

Table 1. Estimated Average Power Consumption / Grid Class

Grid Class	2000	2001	2002	2003	2004	2005	2006
Volume	186	193	200	207	213	219	225
Mid-Range	424	457	491	524	574	625	675
High-end	5534	5832	6130	6428	6973	7651	8163

The general overview of energy consumption in the various organization level of computing industry is explained in the figure 1. The power management with various factors of energy parameters is shown in the figure 2.

2   Related Work

There are a number of industry initiatives aiming at the development of standardized methods and techniques for the reduction of the energy consumption in computer environments. They include Climate Savers Computing Initiative (CSCI), Green Computing Impact Organization (GCIO), Green Electronics Council, The Green Grid, International Professional Practice Partnership (IP3), with membership of companies such as AMD, Dell, HP, IBM, Intel, Microsoft, Sun Microsystems, and VMware.

Energy-efficient resource management has been first introduced in the context of battery-powered mobile devices, where energy consumption has to be reduced in order to improve the battery lifetime. Although techniques developed for mobile devices can be applied or adapted for servers and data centres, this kind of systems requires specific methods.

To reduce the power and energy consumption in modern computing systems, as well as recent research works that deal with power and energy efficiency at the hardware and firmware, operating system (OS), virtualization, and data centre levels. The main objective of this work is to give an overview of the recent research advancements in energy-efficient computing, identify common characteristics, and classify the approaches. On the other hand, the aim is to show the level of development in the area and discuss open research challenges and direction for future work.

According to data provided by Intel Labs [1], the main part of power consumed bya server is accounted for the CPU, followed by the memory and losses due to thepower supply inefficiency. The data show that the CPU no longer dominatespower consumption by a server. This resulted from the continuous improvement ofthe CPU power efficiency and application of power-saving techniques (e.g., DVFS)that enable active low-power modes. In these modes, a CPU consumes a fraction ofthe total power, while preserving the ability to execute programs. As a result, currentdesktop and server CPUs can consume less than 30% of their peak power in lowactivitymodes, leading to dynamic power range of more than 70% of the peak power. In contrast, dynamic power ranges of all other server's components are muchnarrower: less than 50% for dynamic random access memory (DRAM), 25% for diskdrives, 15% for network switches, and negligible for other componentsPower supplies transform alternating current (AC) into direct current (DC) to feedserver's components. This transformation leads to significant power losses due to theinefficiency of the current technology.

Dhiman et al [2] have found that although regression models based on just CPU utilization are able to provide reasonable prediction accuracy for CPU-intensive workloads, they tend to be considerably inaccurate for prediction of power consumption caused by I/O- and memory-intensive applications. The authors have proposed a power modelling methodology based on Gaussian mixture models that predicts power consumption by a physical machine running multiple virtual machine

(VM) instances. The main reason of the power inefficiency in data centres is low average utilization of the resources.

3   Energy Management – Concepts and Theory

To understand power and energy management mechanisms, it is essential to clarifythe terminology. Electric current is the flow of electric charge measured in amperes.Amperes define the amount of electric charge transferred by a circuit per second.Power and energy can be defined in terms of work that a system performs. Power isthe rate at which the system performs the work, while energy is the total amount ofwork performed over a period of time. Power and energy are measured in watts (W)and watt-hour (Wh), respectively. Work is done at the rate of 1 W when 1 A istransferred through a potential difference of 1 V. A kilowatt-hour (kWh) is theamount of energy equivalent to a power of 1 kW (1000 W) being applied for onehour.

The difference between power and energy is very importantbecause a reduction of the power consumption does not always reduce the consumedenergy. For example, the power consumption can be decreased by lowering the CPUperformance. However, in this case, a programmay require longer time to complete itsexecution consuming the same amount of energy. On one hand, a reduction of the peakpower consumption results in decreased costs of the infrastructure provisioning, suchas costs associated with capacities of UPS, PDU, power generators, cooling system,and power distribution equipment. On the other hand, decreased energy consumptionleads to a reduction of the electricity bills. The energy consumption can be reducedtemporarily using dynamic power management (DPM) techniques or permanentlyapplying static power management (SPM). DPM utilizes the knowledge of the realtimeresource usage and application workloads to optimize the energy consumption.

However, it does not necessarily decrease the peak power consumption. In contrast,SPM includes the usage of highly efficient hardware equipment, such as CPUs, diskstorage, network devices, UPS, and power supplies. These structural changes usuallyreduce both the energy and peak power consumption.The main power consumption in complementary metal-oxide-semiconductor(CMOS) circuits comprises static and dynamic power.

The static power consumption,or leakage power, is caused by leakage currents that are present in any active circuit,independently of clock rates and usage scenarios. This static power is mainly determinedby the type of transistors and process technology. The reduction of the staticpower requires improvements of the low-level system design. Dynamic power consumption is created by circuit activity (i.e., transistorswitches, changes of values in registers, etc.) and depends mainly on a specificusage scenario, clock rates, and I/O activity. The sources of the dynamic powerconsumption are short-circuit current and switched capacitance. Short-circuit currentcauses only 10–15% of the total power consumption and so far no way has beenfound to reduce this value without compromising the performance. Switched capacitanceis the primary source of the dynamic power consumption.

The efficiency of power supplies depends ontheir load. They achieve the highest efficiency at loads within the range of 50–75%.However, most data centres normally create a load of 10–15% wasting the majority ofthe consumed electricity and leading to the average power losses of 60–80%. As aresult, power supplies consume at least 2% of the US electricity production. Moreefficient power supply design can save more than a half of the energy consumption.

Power efficiency and energy conservation are key design considerationsfor embedded systems. Various techniques have beenproposed over the years to reduce the energy consumption ofprocessor and memory subsystems as they are the two major contributorsof overall system energy dissipation. Dynamic voltagescaling (DVS) can be effectively used to reduce the power requirementquadratically while only slowing the processor performancelinearly. Recent studies show thatmemoryhierarchy, especially thecache subsystem, has become comparable to the processor in termsof energy consumption.

Dynamic cache reconfiguration (DCR)provides the ability to change cache configuration at run time sothat it can satisfy each application's unique requirement in termsof cache size, line size and associativity. By specializing the cachesubsystem, DCR is capable of improving cache energy efficiency aswell as overall performance

4   Energy Management – Grid Environment

4.1   Grid System Power Management

There are two main strategies for power reduction in *Grid*system: Dynamic Voltage/Frequency Scaling (DV/FS) and *Grid*number controlling: Vary-On Vary-Off (VOVF). DV/FS works by reducing the voltage and frequency, consequently saving energy at the cost of slower program execution. Researchers have developed various DV/FS scheduling algorithms to save energy under timing deadlines [3, 4]. Some researchers also utilized feedback control to dynamically adjust server frequency [5]. In these existing works, control variables can be either *Grid*frequency or application-level quality of service requirements [6-8]. VOVF is a major mechanism for power reduction applied in *Grid*clusters [5, 6, 7]. VOVF dynamically turns idle *Grid*off when the system experiences a light workload, and turns the appropriate *Grid*on when the system encounters a heavy workload. VOVF dramatically improves the system energy efficiency by reducing the idle *Grid*power consumption. Virtualization as a key strategy to reduce power consumption for application services is another way of VOVF. When applying virtualization, multiple virtual servers can be hosted on a smaller number of more powerful physical servers, using less electricity [9]. In [10], researchers demonstrated a method to efficiently manage the aggregate platform resources according to the guest virtual machine (VM) relative importance (Class-of-Service), for both the black-box and the VM-specific approach.

4.2   Cooling-Aware Power Management

Increasing computation capabilities in data centres has resulted in corresponding increases in rack and room power densities. How to cool these new higher-powered racks is a question that challenges all data centre managers [11]. There is several works attempting to reduce the energy consumption in the cooling sub-system. In [12], the authors explored the physics of heat transfer, and presented methods for integrating it into batch schedulers. It reduced the amount of heat recirculation in the data centre and improved the cooling subsystem efficiency. A mathematical scheduling problem is formulated in [13] to minimize the data centre cooling cost; they also provided two heuristic methods XInt-GA and XInt-SQP to solve the problem. In [14], researchers present a unified, coordinated, thermal-computational approach to the data centre energy management problem. Another group of researchers formulated an optimization problem to reduce the power consumption in servers and cooling system by selecting frequency level and cold air supply [15]. An integer linear programming was applied to solve the problem. Future work differs from these efforts: all of the above works focus on a single data centre, none of them considered multi-mirror services and their request distribution, and how they influence on the total cost for OSPs. In addition to these related work, there are few proposals which concentrates more on energy efficiency as well as effective system design. One such example in the computer network is energy efficient and reliable communication proposed by chandramohan et al [16-19], in which the author presented swarm intelligence based methodology.

4.3   Leveraging Variability Electricity Price in Reducing Cost

In [7], the researcher first considered the variable electricity prices for data centres and proposed a scheme to shut down the data centre when the electricity price is high. In [15],the author proposed a load dispatching strategy to reduce total electricity cost. An optimization problem was formulated in [8] to minimize the electricity cost in a multi-electricity-market environment. In [9], researchers considered the problem of capping the brown energy consumption of Internet services and interacting with the carbon market. However, existing efforts focus narrowly on electricity usage of the *Grid*subsystem without considering the dynamic behaviour of the cooling system and how to leverage it to reduce cost. Also, the network cost is not well studied in relation to reducing the total operational cost. The contribution of future work is that to provide a precise modelling of electricity usage in IDCs and provide energy-efficiency strategies in both *Grid*and cooling subsystems in addition to leveraging variability of electricity price. The net-work cost is also considered to obtain the optimal load dispatching among IDCs.

The motivation of this work is to help OSPs to conserve and manage their own electricity and network cost. Future work is directed to build by mainly exploring the following two opportunities:

1) Electricity market volatility: Electricity markets have been deregulated, attempting to create more economically desirable consumer markets. In the spot electricity markets, prices exhibit both location diversities and time diversities. If the electricity price is high in one region, dynamically route more requests to the regions with lower prices in order to save the total electricity cost.

2) Applying energy-efficiency strategies in IDCs: Two distinct sub-systems account for most of an IDC power draw: the *Grid*subsystem, which accounts for 56% of total power consumption of an IDC, the cooling subsystem, which accounts for about 30% of total power consumption.

These two subsystems dominate and their power draw can vary drastically with system workload. Applying energy-efficiency strategies in those two subsystems will contribute on both energy savings and electricity cost reductions in IDCs.

References

1. Minas, L., Ellison, B.: Energy Efficiency for Information Technology: How to Reduce PowerConsumption in Servers and Data Centers. Intel Press, USA (2009)
2. Dhiman, G., Mihic, K., Rosing, T.: A system for online power prediction in virtualizedenvironmentsusing gaussian mixture models. In: Proceedings of the 47th ACM/IEEE Design Automation Conference, Anaheim, CA, USA, pp. 807–812 (2010)
3. Vasic, M., Garcia, O., Oliver, J., Alou, P., Cobos, J.: A DVS system based on the trade-off between energy savings and execution time. In: 11th Workshop on Control and Modeling for Power Electronics, COMPEL 2008, pp. 1–6 (2008)
4. Pinheiro, E., Bianchini, R., Carrera, E., Heath, T.: Dynamic cluster reconfiguration for power and performance. In: Compilers and Operating Systems for Low Power (2001)
5. Wang, X., Chen, M.: Cluster-level feedback power control for performance optimization. In: Proc. of Symposium on High-Performance Computer Architecture (2008)
6. Sharma, V., Thomas, A., Abdelzaher, T., Skadron, K., Lu, Z.: Power-aware QoS management in web servers. In: 24th Annual IEEE Real-Time Systems Symposium (2003)
7. Dovrolis, C., Stiliadis, D., Ramanathan, P.: Proportional differentiated services: delay differentiation and packet scheduling. In: Proceedings of the Conference on Applications (1999)
8. Sharma, R., Bash, C., Patel, C., Friedrich, R.: Balance of power: dynamic thermal management for Internet data centers. IEEE Internet Computing (2005)
9. Murugesan, S.: Harnessing green it: principles and practices. IT Professional (2008)
10. Kesavan, M., Ranadive, A., Gavrilovska, A., Schwan, K.: Active CoordinaTion (ACT) – toward effectively managing virtualized multicore clouds. In: 2008 IEEE International Conference on Cluster Computing (2008)
11. Patterson, M.K., Fenwick, D.: The State of Data Center Cooling. A review of current air and liquid cooling solutions, Intel White Paper (2008)
12. Moore, J., Chase, J., Ranganathan, P., Sharma, R.: Abstract making scheduling cool: temperature-aware workload placement in data centers. In: Usenix Annual Technical Conference (2005)
13. Tang, Q., Gupta, S., Varsamopoulos, G.: Energy-efficient thermal-aware task scheduling for homogeneous high-performance computing data centers: a cyber-physical approach. IEEE Transactions on Parallel and Distributed Systems 19, 1458–1472 (2008)
14. Banerjee, A., Mukherjee, T., Varsamopoulos, G., Gupta, S.K.S.: Cooling-aware and thermal-aware workload placement for green HPC data centers. In: Proceedings of the International Conference on Green Computing, GREEN-COMP 2010, pp. 245–256. IEEE Computer Society, Washington, DC, USA (2010)
15. Pakbaznia, E., Pedram, M.: Minimizing data center cooling and server power costs. In: Proceedings of the 14th ACM/IEEE International Symposium on Low Power Electronics and Design, ISLPED 2009, pp. 145–150. ACM, New York (2009)
16. Chandra Mohan, B., Baskaran, R.: Reliable Transmission for Network Centric Military Networks. European Journal of Scientific Research 50(4), 564–574 (2011)

17. Chandra Mohan, B., Baskaran, R.: Survey on Recent Research and Implementation of Ant Colony Optimization in Various Engineering Applications. International Journal in Computational Intelligent Systems 7(4) (2011)
18. Chandra Mohan, B., Baskaran, R.: Energy Aware and Energy Efficient Routing Protocol for Adhoc Network Using Restructured Artificial Bee Colony System. In: Mantri, A., Nandi, S., Kumar, G., Kumar, S. (eds.) HPAGC 2011. CCIS, vol. 169, pp. 473–484. Springer, Heidelberg (2011)
19. Chandra Mohan, B., Sandeep, R., Sridharan, D.: A Data Mining approach for Predicting Reliable Path for Congestion Free Routing using Self-Motivated Neural Network. SCI, vol. 149, pp. 237–246. Springer, Heidelberg (2008)

Cluster-based Power Aware Scheduling (CPAS) Algorithm for Network Longevity in WSN

K. Arthi and P. Vanaja Ranjan

Department of Electrical Engineering, Guindy, Anna University, Chennai
arthimanivasakam@yahoo.co.in

Abstract. Efficient power utilization gains more importance for WSNs (Wireless sensor Network), since battery replacement is not possible in many sensor applications. Sensors consume energy when it changes from one radio state (transmission, reception, listen, sleep) to another. In this paper, a Cluster-based Power-Aware Scheduling (CPAS) algorithm is proposed to specifically design a low-data-rate WSNs to reduce the number of state transitions of a node, thereby efficiently maintaining the power level of the network. In CPAS, the nodes within the cluster are first synchronized to avoid collision during transmission. CPAS is based on IEEE 802.15.4 standard with dynamic routing ability based on the power level of the nodes. Performance evaluation is done by using simulation, and it has been showed that this cluster based algorithm considerably improves network lifetime when compared to non-cluster based network in WSN.

Keywords: EEE 802.15.4, Minimum Spanning Tree Algorithm, Power-Aware, Radio States, TDMA.

1 Introduction

Wireless sensor networks (WSNs), is a distributed collection of sensor nodes which forms network interconnected by wireless communication links. Sensor nodes are often powered by batteries and have limited computing and memory resources. Because of the limitations due to battery life, most sensor networks are built with power conservation in mind. WSNs can operate in an event-driven model or regular continuous monitoring model. Here, the protocol works for an event-driven model, where each sensor will monitor its vicinity and sends its information to the sink via the relay of other sensors nodes whenever an event occurs. There are various standards existing for wireless communication in industry. IEEE 802.15.4 standard is considered because it is specifically designed for low data rate applications. The 802.15.4 standard has many power management mechanisms, based on duty cycle, to minimize the activity of sensor nodes.

1.1 IEEE 802.15.4 Standard

IEEE 802.15.4 [1] is a standard for low-rate, low-power, and low-cost Wireless Personal Area Networks (WPANs). A PAN is formed by one PAN coordinator which

N. Meghanathan et al. (Eds.): CCSIT 2012, Part I, LNICST 84, pp. 429–436, 2012.

is in charge of managing the whole network, and, optionally, by one or more coordinators which are responsible for a subset of nodes in the network. Ordinary nodes must associate with a (PAN) coordinator in order to communicate. The supported network topologies are *star* (single-hop), *cluster-tree*, and *mesh* (multihop). The standard defines two different channel access methods: a *beacon-enabled* mode and a *nonbeacon-enabled* mode.

The beacon-enabled mode provides a power management mechanism based on a duty cycle. It uses a superframe structure (Figure 1) which is bounded by *beacons*, i.e., special synchronization frames generated periodically by the coordinator node(s). The time between two consecutive beacons is called *Beacon Interval (BI)*, and is defined through the *Beacon Order (BO)* parameter (BI=15.36*2^{BO}ms, with $0 \leq BO \leq$ 14). Each superframe consists of an active period and an inactive period. In the active period nodes communicate with the coordinator to which they are associated with, while during the inactive period they enter a low-power state to save energy. The active period is denoted as *Superframe Duration (SD)* and its size is defined by the *Superframe Order (SO)* parameter. It can be further divided into a *Contention Access Period (CAP)* and a *Collision Free Period (CFP)*. During the CAP, a slotted CSMA / CA algorithm is used for channel access, while in the CFP communication occurs in a Time-Division Multiple Access (TDMA) style by using a number of *Guaranteed Time Slots* (GTSs), reassigned to individual nodes.

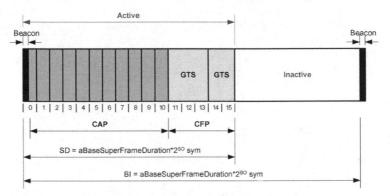

Fig. 1. IEEE 802.15.4 Superframe Structure

In the non beacon-enabled mode there is no superframe, nodes are always active (energy conservation is delegated to the layers above the MAC protocol) and use the unslotted CSMA/CA algorithm for channel access. The algorithm is based on beacon enabled IEEE 802.15.4 standard.

2   Power-Aware Scheduling Algorithm

A homogenous centralized scheduling of sensor activities is considered to minimize the energy cost and maintain the overall power level of the network. The tree T constructed based on Minimum Spanning Tree is considered as a cluster, with root node as the cluster head and the other nodes as the child nodes. The transmitting time slots for each individual child node and the cluster head is scheduled. The children will send their data in one period and the parent will receive the data when it is awake. Thus, the energy consumption due to the state transition will be definitely saved since each node needs only to wake up twice: once for receiving all data from its children and once for transmitting its data to its own parent.

TDMA is used for scheduling node activities in the CFP within the superframe structure.The time is logically divided into slots with slot size t_s, and time slots are synchronized among nodes. A schedule period T is composed of T consecutive time slots. The activities of every node are then repeated with period T. Assume that a node v_i will produce r_{vi} data packets per scheduling period T. When a node v_i is transmitting packets to a neighboring node v_j, some other neighboring nodes that are in the listening state will also consume energy. Therefore, the total energy consumption upon the scenario that node v_i transmits in L slots, while k neighboring nodes listening is $(P_{rcv}+P_{tx}+P_{lst}.K) \times L \times t_s$. To minimize the energy consumption, the activities of sensor nodes are scheduled to reduce state transitions.

Table 1. Energy Cost Symbols

Symbol	Meaning
P_{tx}	Energy consumption in transmitting
P_{rcv}	Energy consumption in receiving
P_{lst}	Energy consumption in listening
P_{slp}	Energy consumption in sleeping
t_p	Time needed to poll channel once
r_{vi}	Data packets per period by v_i

The scheduling of activities for all nodes is to assign each time slot $1 \leq t \leq T$ (scheduling period) to one of the four possible states: transmitting, receiving, listening, and sleeping. Since TDMA access method is used, no nodes need to be in listening state if all nodes are perfectly synchronized. If the synchronization is needed, nodes will also have additional state listening so that adjacent nodes can synchronize their activities. See Figure. 2.for an illustration. Here, the sender node will use a short preamble to synchronize the receiving node. In other words, when a sender wakes up, it will periodically send a message SYN (contains its address and the receiver's address, and the time slots needed for sending data) and listen for the ACK message from the receiver. When the receiver wakes up, it will listen for the message SYN and reply a message ACK if it gets one completed SYN message. After getting the correct ACK message, the sender starts sending data.

In a simple event-driven data collection, a sensor, which is triggered by an event, will wake up and monitor its vicinity, and then, produce some sample data. It will then wake up its parent node (called dominator node sometimes) and send data to it. However, when the dominator node dominates k sensors, it may need to wakeup k times to receive all the data from its children nodes in the worst case, which is energy

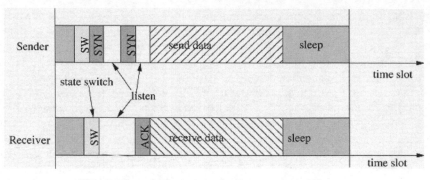

Fig. 2. Flow of Synchronization between two nodes

consuming because of multiple state transitions. Our objective is to schedule the activities of sensor nodes to minimize the states transitions (especially from sleeping state to active states), in the meanwhile, the data rate by all sensors is supported. In this paper, it is always been considered for low-data rate WSNs where in the majority of time slots, sensor nodes can sleep to save the energy. Notice that in low-data-rate WSNs, each sensor needs to switch from sleeping state to active state at least once. A schedule has been designed in which any sensor node only needs to wake up at most twice: once for receiving data from its children nodes and once for sending its data to its parent node as shown in Figure 3. This also dramatically reduces the cost of the clock synchronization.

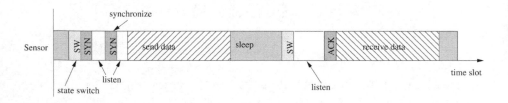

Fig. 3. Schedule for each node in a cluster

The clusters is scheduled in the decreasing order of their weight. Within the cluster, the child node or the leaf node need not use the same parent to send its data to the sink. Based upon the battery level they can share the neighboring parent to dynamically route the data to the sink. Our algorithm assumes that the nodes are first synchronized using a short preamble and it ensures that it will not cause any interference for the transmissions of any sensors in C_i.

2.1   Algorithm

Activity Schedule after constructing a Minimum Spanning Tree (MST)

Step 1: For each sensor v_i do
Step 2: Calculate its receiving-weight W_i
         (Based on amount of data)

Step 3: Sort the sensor in non-increasing order of weight W_i
Step 4: For i=1 to n do
Step 5: For i=1 to n do
Step 6: Sort the path for routing for each node based on the power level
Step 7: If power level is less than the threshold value
Step 8: Goto Step 9 else Goto Step 6
Step 9: Assign Cluster C_i (equivalently sensor node v_i for receiving) W_i earliest available time slots for transmitting that will not overlap with time slots assigned to conflicting clusters.
Step 10: Each sensor node v_j in C_i will be sequentially assigned w_j consecutive time slots for transmitting.

3 Proposed System Analytical Model

In this paper, the described cluster based power-aware scheduling (CPAS) algorithm which randomly selects a node as the cluster head (CH) from the group of sensor nodes (as it is done in the LEACH algorithm, in which the residual energy of sensor nodes to is used to select the cluster head), thereby avoiding unbalanced energy consumption of the sensor nodes. The main energy consumption of wireless sensor nodes is typically for the following operations: transmitting a packet, receiving a packet, listening radio signals, sampling the vicinity, reading sample data from the ADC, reading data from the flash, and writing / erasing data in the flash. In this project, it has been focused to synchronize the nodes within the cluster and efficiently schedule the timeslots for data transfer.

The radio is in any of the four states: transmitting, receiving, listening, and sleeping, each of which has different energy consumption (energy consumption per unit time) of P_{tx}, Prcv, P_{lst} and P_{slp}, respectively (as shown in Table 1). The model also consider the energy $E_{A,B}$ consumed by transiting from one state A to another state B for a sensor and other control units. Typically, the time to restart a sensor node from the sleep mode to active mode is about 4ms [11].For a node v_i, if it is scheduled to transmit at time slot t, denote it as $X_{i, S,t}=1$; otherwise denote it as $X_{i,S,t}= 0$. Variables $X_{i,R,t}\in\{0,1\}, X_{i,P,t}\in\{0,1\}$ and $X_{i,L,t}\in\{0,1\}$ to denote whether the node v_i is scheduled to receive, sleep, or listen at time slot t or not, respectively. Energy consumed by state transition is denoted as $E_{P, S}$, $E_{P,R}$ or $E_{P,l}$. See Table 2 for notations used.

In practice, the energy consumed for transition from an active state (such as transmitting, receiving, and listening) to an idle state (sleeping or deep sleeping) is often ignored. Notice that the energy cost by a node v_i in all states is

$$T = \sum_{t=1}^{T} (X_{i, S,t} \cdot P_{tx} + X_{i, R,t} \cdot P_{rcv} + X_{i,l,t} \cdot P_{lst} + X_{i,P,t} \cdot P_{slp}).t_s;$$

The energy cost for state transitions is

$$\sum_{t=1}^{T} (X_{i,P,t} \cdot X_{i, S,t+1} \cdot E_{P, S} + X_{i, P,t} \cdot X_{i, R,t+1} \cdot E_{P,R} + X_{i,P,t} \cdot X_{i, L,t+1} \cdot E_{P,L});$$

The objective of a schedule S is to minimize the summation of these two energy costs.

Table 2. Symbol Notations

Symbol	Meaning
$X_{i,S,t}$	Node v_i transmitting at time t
$X_{i,R,t}$	Node v_i receiving at time t
$X_{i,P,t}$	Node v_i sleeping at time t
$X_{i,L,t}$	Node v_i listening at time t
$E_{P,S}$	Energy consumed from sleeping to transmitting
$E_{P,R}$	Energy consumed from sleeping to receiving
$E_{P,L}$	Energy consumed from sleeping to listening

For a given data gathering tree T, the time slot needed to transmit and receive by an individual node is fixed because it only depends on the tree structure. So, the difference of the energy consumption from different schedules is the cost for the wake up and clock synchronization. In our scheduling, there are at most two state switches for each node. So, the total number of state switches is at most 2n times of the energy consumption for a node to switch the state. That is, $E_S \leq 2. n. E_S$, where E_S is the energy consumption for state switch of one sensor in our scheduling, and n is the number of sensors. Because there is at least one state switch for each node in any scheduling, $E^{opt}_S \geq n. E_S$, where E^{opt}_S is the optimal energy consumption for state switch. E_T is used to denote the total energy consumption in the active states by all nodes by our method; E as the total energy consumption in our scheduling and E^{opt} as the optimal energy consumption.

$$E = E_T + E_S \leq E^{OPT}_T + 2E^{OPT}_S < 2 E^{OPT}_T + 2E^{OPT}_S = 2E_{opt}.$$

Thus the energy consumption for the scheduling derived by algorithm is at most twice of the optimum.

4   Performance Evaluation

To perform our simulation analysis, ns2 simulation tool [16] is used. The algorithm is experimented with a single cluster, it is assumed the same performance with multiple clusters in a densely deployed network. In our experiments, construct two trees for the data collection using minimum spanning tree (MST) algorithm. The clustering concept is implemented to one tree and make the root node acts as the PAN coordinator and all other nodes operate with a duty cycle for power management. Assumed that in the considered radio model, all nodes are in the carrier sensing range of each other. This minimizes the probability of collisions due to the hidden node problem. The network uses the beacon-enabled mode. The duty cycle is set to about 1.5%, according to the typical values recommended by the ZigBee standard [3] which are in the range 0.1%–2%. Specifically, the Beacon Interval is 125.8 s, while the active period is 1.97s. Note that the active period is large enough to let every node send its data packets in all the analyzed scenarios, so that the enforced duty cycle does not harm the packet transmission process.

In this simulation, different data rates is used to study how the data rate can affect energy consumption. Based on the topology, a sink node (with a fixed position) will collect data from the other sensors in the network. Figure.4 show that energy consumption will decrease when the data rate increases, but the reduction is slower than the data rate increasing. Among different structures, it has been found that MST tree has the smallest time span, and therefore, the less energy consumption, when compared to non-tree node distribution. This is because MST tree structure has the shortest hops from all other nodes to the sink.

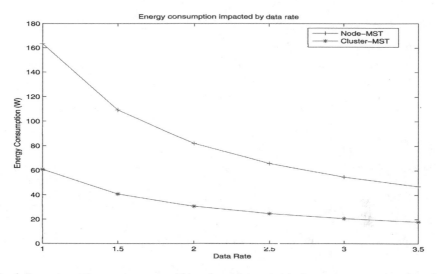

Fig. 4. Impact on the energy cost with various data rates in homogeneous networks using cluster based MST tree, and non cluster based MST tree

It is also found that the schedule by our cluster-based method performs much better than the node-based method. In cluster-based method, to avoid potentially delaying the transmission to the next scheduling period, time slots of a parent node after its children nodes' sending time slots is intentionally scheduled. That is, the transmissions are always within one scheduling period. The energy consumption is dramatically reduced when scheduling the node to wake up at most twice in a time period. The energy consumption in cluster-based method is also much better than node-based method, as shown in Figure.4.

5   Conclusion

In this paper, a algorithm has been proposed for efficient centralized scheduling that not only remove the unnecessary listening cost, but also reduce the energy cost for state switching and clock synchronization. In our protocol, every node needs only to wake up at most twice in one scheduling period: one for receiving data from its children and one for sending data to its parent. Dynamic routing ability based on the power level of the nodes is also been done to balance the overall network power level. The simulation result shows that the energy consumption is less for cluster-based nodes than non cluster based nodes. This work could also be enhanced for clusters with mobile sink.

Acknowledgements. I would like to acknowledge Dr.P.Vanaja Ranjan, Associate Professor, Department of Electrical and Electronic Engineering, Anna University, Chennai, for her valuable discussions and suggestions to development of this algorithm.

References

[1] IEEE Standard for Information Technology, Part 15.4; Wireless Medium Access Control (MAC) and Physical Layer (PHY) Specifications for Low-Rate Wireless Personal Area Networks (LR-WPANs). IEEE Computer Society (2006)

[2] Mainwaring, A., Culler, D., Polastre, J., Szewczyk, R., Anderson J.: Wireless Sensor Networks for Habitat Monitoring. In: Proc. First ACM Int'l Workshop Wireless Sensor Networks and Applications (WSNA 2002), pp. 88–97 (2002)

[3] ZigBee Alliance Official Site, http://www.zigbee.org

[4] IEEE: IEEE Std 802.15.4^{TM} (2003), http://standards.ieee.org

[5] Clendenin, M.: ZigBee's improved spec incompatible with v1.0, EE Times Europe, http://eetimes.eu/showArticle.jhtml?articleID=193006080

[6] Akyildiz, I.F., Su, W., Sankarasubramaniam, Y., Cayirci, E.: Wireless sensor networks: A survey. Computer Networks 38(4), 393–422 (2002)

[7] Anastasi, G., Conti, M., Di Francesco, M.: A Comprehensive Analysis of the MAC Unreliability Problem in IEEE 802.15.4 Wireless Sensor Networks. IEEE Transactions on Industrial Informatics 7(1) (February 2011)

[8] Lu, G., Krishnamachari, B., Raghavendra, C.: Performance evaluation of the IEEE 802.15.4 MAC for low-rate low-power wireless networks. In: Proc. Energy-Efficient Wireless Communications and Networks Conference (EWCN 2004), pp. 701–706 (2004)

[9] Zheng, J., Lee, M.J.: A comprehensive performance study of IEEE 802.15.4. IEEE Press (2004); Leibnitz, K., Wakamiya, N., Murata, M.: Modeling of IEEE 802.15.4 in a cluster of synchronized sensor nodes. In: Proc. 19th Int. Teletraffic Congr. (ITC-19), Beijing, China, pp. 1345–1354 (August 2005)

[10] Ergen, S.C., Varaiya, P.: TDMA Scheduling Algorithms for Sensor Networks, Technical report, Univ. of California, Berkley (2005)

[11] Koubaa, A., Alves, M., Tovar, E.: A comprehensive simulation study of slotted CSMA/CA for IEEE 802.15.4 wireless sensor networks. In: Proc. IEEE Int. Workshop on Factory Commun. Syst. (WFCS 2006), Torino, Italy, pp. 183–192 (June 2006)

[12] Rhee, I., Warrier, A., Aia, M., Min, J.: ZMAC: A Hybrid MAC for Wireless Sensor Networks. In: Proc. ACM Conf. Embedded Networked Sensor Systems (SenSys) (2005)

[13] Yedavalli, K., Krishnamachari, B.: Enhancement of the IEEE 802.15.4 MAC protocol for scalable data collection in dense sensor networks. In: Proc. Int. Symp. Modeling and Optimization in Mobile, Ad Hoc, and Wireless Networks (WiOpt 2008), Berlin, Germany, March 31-April 4, pp. 152–161 (2008)

[14] Pollin, S., Ergen, M., Ergen, S., Bougard, B., Van der Perre, L., Moerman, I., Bahai, A., Catthoor, F.: Performance analysis of slotted carrier sense IEEE 802.15.4 medium access. IEEE Trans. Wireless Commun. 7(9), 3359–3371 (2008)

[15] Park, P., Di Marco, P., Soldati, P., Fischione, C., Johansson, K.H.: A generalized Markov chain model for effective analysis of slotted IEEE 802.15.4. In: Proc. IEEE Int. Conf. Mobile Ad-Hoc and Sensor Systems 2009 (IEEE MASS 2009), Macau, China, pp. 130–139 (October 2009)

[16] Network Simulator Ns2, http://www.isu.edu/nsnam/ns

Development of System for GPS Data Transmission to Web Server for Online over Head Conductor Sag Measurement

Sangeeta Kamboj[1] and Ratna Dahiya[2]

[1] National Institute of Technology, Kurukshetra, Haryana, India
[2] Faculty, National Institute of Technology, Kurukshetra, Haryana, India
http://www.nitkkr.ac.in/

Abstract. This paper describes the design and testing of Web based system for online overhead conductor sag measurement of 11V power distribution line using Global Positioning System (GPS). The paper shows testing results of GPS data transmission from mid span of overhead conductor to substation. Maximum utilization of a power line may be achieved using dynamic rating algorithm for which conductor sag measurement is important. Raw GPS measurements are not so accurate that these are usable for overhead conductor sag evaluation. Further signal processing techniques such as bad data identification/modification, LSPE method and wavelet analysis required to improve accuracy of GPS measurements are discussed in the paper.

Keywords: GPS, LSPE method, Wavelet Analysis, Web Server, Overhead conductor sag, NMEA0183.

1   Introduction

GPS is satellite based radio positioning and navigation system. It provides position in three dimension and time information to users worldwide with twenty four hours a day [2]. It was declared operational for civilian users in December 1993. The developments in applications of GPS over last 10 years have done at higher rate than advancements in realization of GPS constellation. It is maintained by the United States government and every user can freely access this with a GPS receiver. According to W. Wooden, the detailed definition of GPS is "The Navstar GPS is an all-weather, space based navigation system under development by the Department of Defense to satisfy the requirements for the military forces to accurately determine their position, velocity, and time in common reference system, anywhere on or near earth on a continuous basis". A GPS receiver calculates its position by precisely timing the signals sent by GPS satellites. There may be visible more than four satellites but only four satellites are used in position calculation of GPS receiver [3, 9].The application market for vehicular tracking and monitoring, digital video processing, recording and transmission is nowadays considered one of the most promising in the security area [8]. Tracking systems were first developed for the shipping industry because they wanted to determine where each vehicle was at any

N. Meghanathan et al. (Eds.): CCSIT 2012, Part I, LNICST 84, pp. 437–444, 2012.

given time. But nowadays Automatic Vehicle Location system has been used which transmit the vehicle location information in real time. Real time vehicular tracking system incorporates a hardware device installed in the vehicle and a remote Tracking server [7]. The ability of GPS Technology to provide time synchronization in order of nanoseconds over wide area has opened up the usage of GPS in electric power systems for its reliable and secure operation [5, 6].

The most concerned issue about GPS application in measurement of overhead conductor sag is its accuracy. There are several factors that affect the accuracy of GPS [4]. Various signal processing techniques such as LSPE method and Wavelet Analysis using Haar wavelet to improve accuracy of GPS measurements are used in the paper. In the paper test system for GPS data transmission to Web Server at 66KV Grid Substation Idgah, sector6, Faridabad has been developed. The testing results of GPS data transmission from mid span of overhead conductor of 11KV Power distribution line, sector 6, Faridabad to substation for sag measurement are also shown in the paper.

2   Description of System

The overhead power distribution line online sag measuring system consists of GPS receiver at mid span of line, leaptop on earth below mid span of overhead conductor, Web Server e.g. at substation and data communication as shown in figure1.

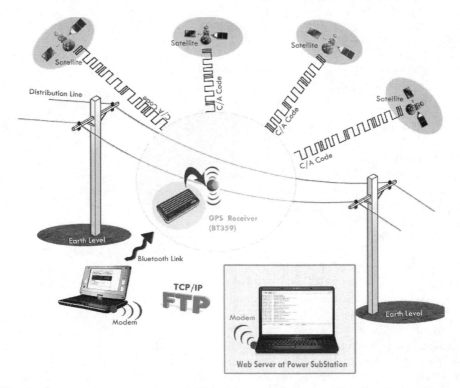

Fig. 1. Conceptual representation of GPS data transmission to Web Server for overhead conductor sag measurement

The GPS receiver BT359 with proper insulation has been hanged at mid span on 11KV power distribution line having span length of 60m. GPS data has been collected for approximately 300s. The lowermost single phase of line section is considered for GPS measurements. Bluetooth link is used to transfer GPS relevant information in standard NMEA0183 sentences from GPS receiver to the leaptop placed on earth where it is processed using GPS software "NMEA/GPS data logger" and gives the information of GPS receiver position in the form of latitude(x), longitude(y) and altitude (z). The Reliance Netconnect   modem is installed at leaptop placed on earth for data connection.

At substation, Reliance Netconnect   modem has also been installed at personal computer/laptop which is used as data collecting and Web Server system. The communication between GPS based overhead conductor sag measurement system and personal computer/laptop uses the TCP/IP protocol as shown in figure2.

3   11KV Power Distribution Line – Testing

The testing of system as shown in figure1 has been done at 66KV Grid Substation Idgah, sector6, Faridabad, Haryana, India and 11KV power distribution line, sector 6, faridabad is considered for overhead conductor sag measurement. The GPS data logging by NMEA/GPS data logger software in leaptop has been shown in following figure 2. The figure3 shows synchronization of this logged data to Web Server using File Transfer Protocol (FTP).

Fig. 2. Logging of GPS data

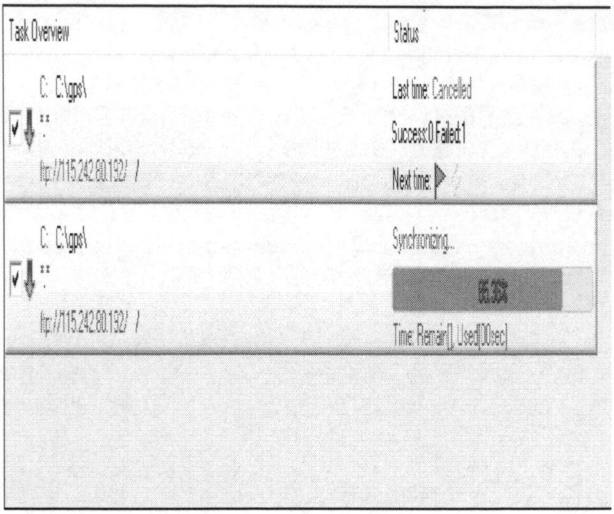

Fig. 3. Message Window showing GPS data Synchronization

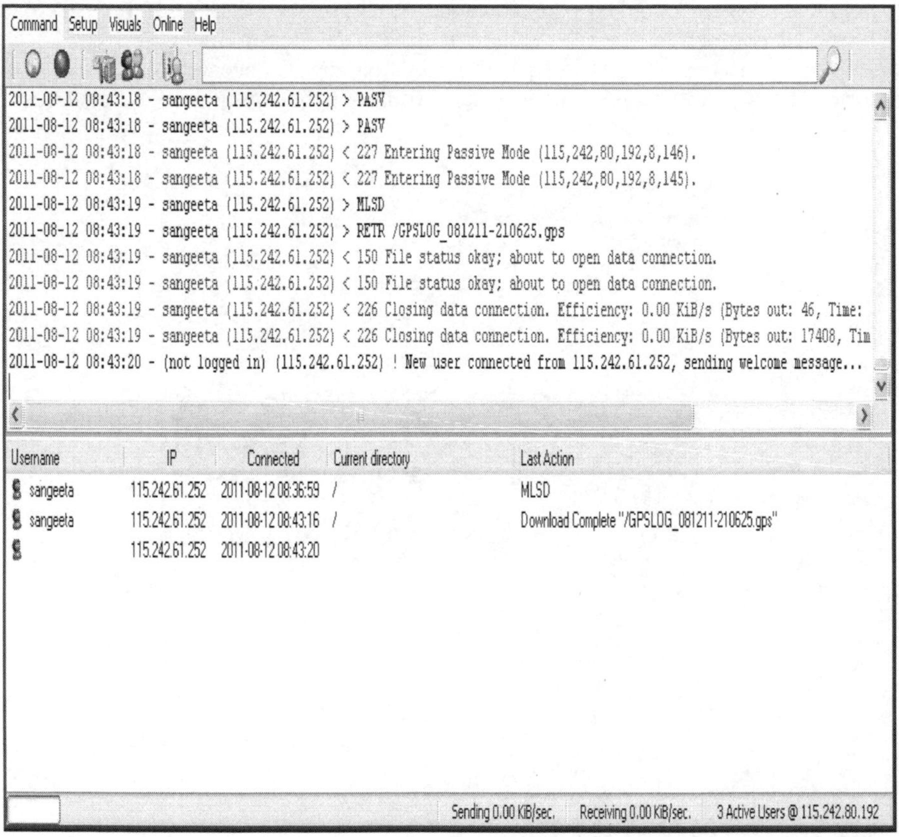

Fig. 4. Communication between Leaptop at field site and Web Server (at substation)

The GPS data from Leaptop placed on earth below mid span of overhead conductor of 11KV power distribution line has been transmitted to Web Server e.g. at 66KV Grid Substation Idgah, sector6, Faridabad, Haryana, India as can be seen from figure4.

4 Results and Discussion

At substation after collecting GPS data for some period of time, a module has been developed in MATLAB programming environment to process only raw GPS altitude data to obtain best estimate of GPS altitude data for particular time instance [9]. The altitude information is important for sag measurement. The Altitude obtained by GPS receiver is above mean sea level. It is required to take measurements with GPS at 2-3 places to improve accuracy of GPS measurements. The GPS measurements have been taken at mid span and its nearby places. An average of approximately 300 readings has been taken at each place. From these GPS altitude measurements taken at three places, more accurate measurements are used as controlled data in the LSPE method considered to obtain best estimate of raw GPS altitude measurements at mid span.

The figures 5, 6 & 7 show raw GPS altitude measurements taken at mid span and its nearby places (10cm towards right and 20cm towards left). The deviation of raw GPS altitude measurements from actual altitude is error in these raw GPS altitude measurements which can be seen in following figures 5, 6 & 7.

The error in raw GPS altitude measurements at mid span has been reduced using LSPE method and further reduced using Haar wavelet at level nine as can be seen in figure 8 [9]. Furthermore accuracy of GPS altitude measurements is more important to evaluate sag of power distribution line. The GPS altitude measurements obtained from Haar wavelet is closely matches to actual altitude as compared to those obtained from LSPE method. It can be seen from figure8. The wavelet analysis technique may be used to process raw GPS altitude measurements directly rather than estimated GPS altitude measurements resulting from LSPE method as can be seen from figure9.

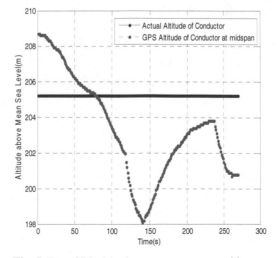

Fig. 5. Raw GPS altitude measurements at mid span

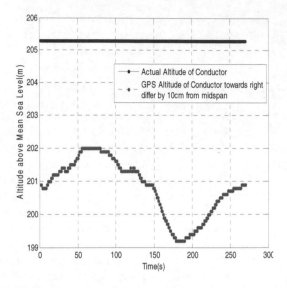

Fig. 6. Raw GPS altitude measurements towards right differ by 10cm from mid span

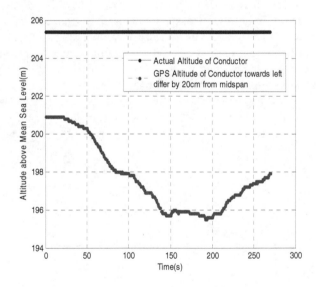

Fig. 7. Raw GPS altitude measurements towards left differ by 20cm from mid span

The accuracy of observed GPS altitude measurements has not been improved to such extent as improved using Haar wavelet to estimated GPS altitude measurements resulting from LSPE method as can be seen from figure9.

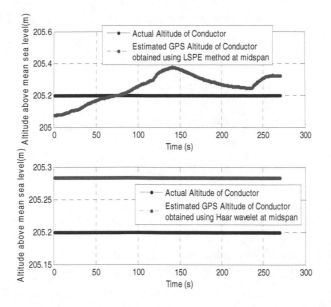

Fig. 8. Comparison of Estimated GPS altitude measurements resulting from LSPE method and further using Haar wavelet with actual altitude of conductor at mid span

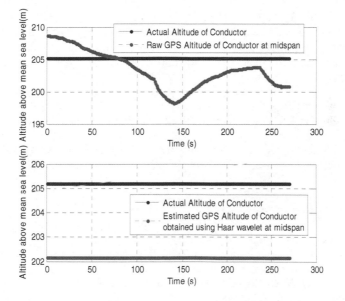

Fig. 9. Comparison of Estimated GPS altitude measurements resulting from Haar wavelet using raw GPS measurements with actual altitude of conductor at mid span

Thus use of Wavelet analysis to further reduce errors in estimated GPS altitude measurements resulting from LSPE method gives better accuracy of raw GPS altitude measurements taken for overhead conductor sag measurement in power distribution line.

5   Conclusion

It can be concluded that Web based system may be used for online overhead conductor sag measurement of 440V power distribution line using Global Positioning System (GPS) at substation. It is concluded from the test results that user can access GPS data transmitted using TCP/IP for overhead conductor sag measurement at anywhere in the world using internet connection. The Least Square Parameter Estimation and Wavelet Analysis methods have been used to improve accuracy of GPS altitude measurements. These methods reduce error significantly. Better results are found using wavelet analysis method if it is used to process estimated GPS altitude measurements resulting from LSPE method. The DGPS receiver may also be used to get better accuracy as compared to handheld GPS receiver.

Acknowledgement. We acknowledge the cooperation of Assistant Executive Engineer Hansraj, HVPNL, Faridabad, Haryana, India to carry out work.

References

[1] Mensah-Bonsu, C., Krekeler, U.F., Heydt, G.T., Hoverson, Y., Schilleci, J., Agarwal, B.A.: Application of the Global Positioning System to the Measurement of Overhead Power Transmission Conductor Sag. IEEE Transactions on Power Delivery 17(1), 273–278 (2002)

[2] Dana, P.H.: Global Positioning System (GPS) Time Dissemination for Real Time applications. Real Time Systems, 9–46 (1997)

[3] Pratt, T., Bostain, C., Allnutt, J.: Satellite communication. John Wiley & Sons, Singapore (2005)

[4] Introduction to the Global Positioning System for GIS and TRAVERSE, Corvallis Microtechnology, Inc. 413 S.W. Jefferson Avenue Corvallis, OR 97333, U.S. Publication (June 1996)

[5] Cory, B.J., Gale, P.F.: Satellites for Power System Applications. IEE Power Engineering Journal 7(5) (October 1993)

[6] Bo, Z.Q., Weller, G., Jiang, F., Yang, Q.X.: Application of GPS Based Fault Location Scheme for Distribution System. Powercon 1, 53–57 (1998)

[7] Muruganandham, Mukesh, P.R.: Real Time Web based Vehicle Tracking using GPS. World Academy of Science, Engineering and Technology (2010)

[8] Alberto J.: VideoMon Mobile – Vehicle Monitoring System Based on Video, GPS, GSM/GPRS/3G and Google Maps, Patent PI0605735-7A2, November 17 (2006)

[9] Kamboj, S., Dahiya, R.: Real Time Sag Measurement of Overhead Conductor for 11KV Power Line using Global Positioning system GPS). IJSAT 1(3) (May 2011)

A Comparative Study of Partitioning Algorithms
for Wireless Sensor Networks

Zeenat Rehena[1], Debasree Das[2], Sarbani Roy[2], and Nandini Mukherjee[2]

[1] School of Mobile Computing & Communication, Jadavpur University, Kolkata, India
[2] Computer Science & Engineering Department, Jadavpur University, Kolkata, India
zeenatrehena@yahoo.co.in, debasree.cse@gmail.com,
{sarbani.roy,nmukherjee}@cse.jdvu.ac.in

Abstract. In many applications large scale Wireless Sensor Networks (WSNs) use multiple sinks for fast data dissemination and energy efficiency. A WSN may be divided into a number of partitions and each partition may contain a sink, thereby reducing the distance between source nodes and sink node. This paper focuses on partitioning algorithms for WSN. Some existing graph partitioning algorithms are studied that can be applied for partitioning a WSN. A novel partitioning approach for WSN is proposed along with its modification. Simulation of the proposed algorithms has been carried out and their performances are compared with some existing algorithms. It is demonstrated that the proposed algorithms perform better than the existing algorithms.

Keywords: Partitioning Algorithms, WSN, Nearest Neighbour Graph.

1   Introduction

For early detection of critical events in large scale wireless sensor networks (WSNs), multiple sink nodes are required to be deployed. Routing the information regarding a critical event only from the source (the node that sensed the event) to its nearest sink also reduces energy consumption in an energy constrained WSN. We propose to partition the entire network into a number of sub-networks where each sub-network contains one sink node and all the sensor nodes in the sub-network forward the data sensed by them to the sink contained within it.

This paper focuses on algorithms for partitioning a network into smaller-sized sub-networks. A number of graph partitioning algorithms have been proposed in the literature. Some of them which are used for partitioning wireless sensor networks have been studied in this research work. We also propose a partitioning algorithm based on k-nearest neighbour. Another algorithm with some improvements over the former algorithm is also described. Both algorithms are implemented in a simulation environment and their performances are compared with the existing algorithms.

The rest of the paper is organized as follows. Section 2 presents the related works. The existing and the proposed partitioning algorithms are discussed in Section 3. Section 4 presents a comparative study of the existing and proposed algorithms and simulation results. Finally, we conclude the paper in Section 5.

N. Meghanathan et al. (Eds.): CCSIT 2012, Part I, LNICST 84, pp. 445–454, 2012.
© Institute for Computer Sciences, Social Informatics and Telecommunications Engineering 2012

2   Related Work

Conventionally, the objective of graph partitioning method is to separate the vertices of the graph into a predetermined number of sub-graphs, in which each sub-graph consists of an equal number of vertices and the cut sets among these sub-graphs are minimized. In the literature many heuristic graph partitioning algorithms have been proposed based on spectral, combinatorial, geometric and multilevel techniques.

Pothen, Simon, and Liou [1] introduce an approach to partition the input graph using the spectral information of Laplacian matrix. This technique is referred to as *recursive spectral bisection (RSB)*. Eigenvector of the Laplacian matrix is computed and using its component the graph is initially partitioned into two sets of vertices. Chan and Szeto [3] show the size of the cut sets can be minimized by using the second smallest eigenvalue of the Laplacian matrix. They have done this by introducing the concept of median cut RSB method. In this method the indices of vertices which have values above the median are mapped onto one part and which have values below the median are mapped onto the other part. The partitions are then further partitioned by recursive application of the same procedure. Another variation of RSB method is known as Modified RSB. Here instead of using median value, another statistical function quantile is used to split the graph into desired number of partitions. The authors in [7] use RSB method for partitioning a WSN into two halves and then apply this method recursively to obtain optimal number of clusters.

In [2], authors propose the approximation of the Maximally Balanced Connected Partition problem (MBCP). In [6], the authors used this MBCP to partition the entire WSN into 2^n equal sized sub-partitions where n is the number of iterations.

Both MBCP and RSB techniques finally produce 2^n equivalent smaller sub-networks where n is the number of iterations. But our objective is to partition the network into any desired number of sub-partitions according to the number of sinks available. Each sub-partition will be attached with a sink in the network, so that the nodes can interact with that associated sink only. In contrast to the above methods, we propose algorithms based on nearest neighbour computation. The main difference with the proposed algorithms with other algorithms is that here we make prior assumption regarding sink placement which is generally common in WSN.

3   Existing Partitioning Algorithms

In this section three popular graph partitioning algorithms are discussed. A novel algorithm is also proposed in this section which is based on the nearest neighbour [4] concept. Table 1 lists the notations used in different algorithms in this paper.

3.1   Recursive Spectral Bisection (RSB) [5]

RSB uses the Laplacian matrix of a graph. The construction of the Laplacian matrix is such that its smallest eigenvalue λ_1 is zero for connected graph and all the associated eigenvectors are equal to one. Except λ_1, all the other eigenvalues are greater than zero. The RSB method that we mention here is based on the Fiedler vector of the Laplacian matrix of a given graph.

In the RSB method, the spectral information is used to partition the graph. The RSB uses *Spectral Bisection* algorithm recursively. Initially the algorithm computes Laplacian matrix *LM* of the given graph and the eigenvectors *EV* corresponding to the second largest eigenvalue of *LM*. Then it computes the median *m* of *EV*. The nodes whose eigenvectors are less than median *m* are placed in one partition and the rest are placed in the other partition. The partitions are further partitioned by recursive application of the same procedure. Above method partitions a graph into power of 2.

Table 1. List of Notations used in all the algorithms

Symbol	Description
p	total number of sink nodes, SINK={SINK$_1$,.., SINK$_n$}
NextNode	the node used for finding its k-NNG in the next iteration
Flag	used to denote visited or unvisited node
pre_dist	previously stored distances of each node from *NextNode*
cur_dist	current distance of each node from the *NextNode* in each partition
Neighbor_list NN$_s$	a set of neighbour nodes of each node s generated from k-NNG, where k is the pre-defined number of nodes
dist	A vector storing distances of all neighbor nodes of a given node
Partition_list P	a set of sensor nodes for each partition P_p

3.2 Modified Recursive Spectral Bisection (M-RSB) [5]

Unlike RSB, the modified recursive spectral bisection algorithm partitions a graph into any number of sub-graphs. M-RSB also computes *LM* and *EV* and bisects the graph into two parts based on the value of quantile. In case of RSB, median is used to bisect the graph. In case of M-RSB, instead of median, the quantile percentage q of *EV* is calculated and used as the splitting value. The nodes whose eigenvector is less than q are placed in one partition and the rest are placed in the other partition. Each partition is then further partitioned by recursive application of the same procedure. Quantile percentage q of *EV* determines the number of nodes in each partition.

3.3 Maximally Balanced Connected Partition (MBCP) [6]

MBCP finds the maximally balanced connected partition for a graph $G(V, E)$. It results in a partition (V_1, V_2) of V composed of disjoint sets V_1 and V_2 such that both sub-graphs of G induced by V_1 and V_2 are connected.

The algorithm starts with two connected partitions V_1 and V_2 for G. Initially V_1 consists of the single vertex $v_1 \in V$ near the periphery of the network. V_2 consists {V - V_1}. In the next step, it creates a set V_0 by choosing a vertex u from V_2 such that $(V_1 \cup \{u\})$ and $(V_2 - \{u\})$ would also be a connected partition of G. From V_0, a vertex v_i is selected such that v_i is the closest element to V_1. This is done by sorting the list of candidates according to their distances from V_1. The algorithm repeats until the total number of vertices in V_1 is greater than or equal to half of the vertex in V.

3.4   Proposed Algorithm: FN_NNG (Farthest Node in Nearest Neighbor Graph)

The algorithm runs in two phases: Initial Phase and Incremental phase. Initially, there are p sink nodes and the algorithm outputs p partitions at the end. In the initial phase, each sink generates its k-nearest-neighbors, k-NNG. These are stored in its *Neighbour_list* as well as in the *Partition_list* associated with it. A Flag is used for each sensor node which is set to 'False' initially.

In the Incremental phase, the farthest neighbour node is found for each sink node. These nodes are set as *NextNode* and their neighbour nodes are found in the next step. The k-NNG of each *NextNode* is generated and these neighbour nodes are stored in the *Neighbour_list,* as well as in the *Partition_list.* This phase is repeated until the union of all the *Partition_lists* equals total number of nodes deployed. By setting the *Flag* of each sensor node when it is first visited, we can avoid duplication. Thus, each *Partition_list* contains disjoint set of nodes. Whenever a sensor node is included in a partition, it stores the *id* of the corresponding sink as the destination address. Algorithm for Incremental Phase is shown in the Fig. 1.

The following functions are used in FN_NNG algorithm:

FARTHEST selects the farthest neighbour node of $Root_p$, such that the returned node is not $SINK_p$ and it belongs to NN_p.

GENERATE returns the k nearest neighbours of a given node and place them in set *NN*.

FIND returns the $k + i^{th}$ nearest neighbour of a given node if such a node exists, else it returns null.

3.5   Improvement on FN_NNG

One major problem of using k-NNG is that the algorithm needs global information of sensor nodes such as location information. For this reason GPS enabled sensor nodes are required which increases the cost of the network. Furthermore, while searching k-Nearest Neighbour of a node in any partition, we may select a node u for partition P_1. Later if it is found that the node u is nearer to another node in partition P_2, it will not be included in partition P_2 according to the above algorithm. In such cases the region covered by partition P_1 is larger than other partitions. This scenario is depicted in Fig. 2.

Thus, some modifications on FN_NNG algorithm are suggested. Instead of using k-NNG, the concept of 1_Hop_Neighbour nodes is used. Here the algorithm only needs local information in the network. In order to overcome the second problem we use a variable *pre_dist* which stores the calculated distance of each node from the *NextNode*. This algorithm is also run in two phases: Initial Phase and Incremental phase. The Initial phase is similar to FN_NNG. The initial value of *pre_dist* is set to infinity. The incremental phase is shown in Fig. 3.

```
Input: NN_p, P_p, n, k, S'
Output: Partition P_p at each sink node SINK_p

Root_p = SINK_p, i=0
while |S'| ≠ n do
for each P_p do
     NextNode=FARTHEST (Root_p)
     NN_NextNode = GENERATE (NextNode)
        for each node q in NN_NextNode do
           if Flag_q = =true then
              i=i+1
              NN_NextNode =NN_NextNode - {q}
              r = FIND (NextNode, k+i)
              if r ≠ null
                 NN_NextNode =NN_NextNode U {r}
              end if
           else Flag_q = true
        end if
     end for
     P_p = P_p U NN_NextNode
     S' = S' U P_p
     Root_p = NextNode
end for
end while
Return P_p
```

Fig. 1. Algorithm of Incremental Phase

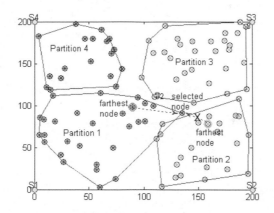

Fig. 2. Partitioning Scenario

In the 1_Hop_Neighbour function, for a particular *Neighbour_list p*, if the node *m* is not previously selected and the *cur_dist* is less than the *pre_dist* then the node is assigned into *Neighbour_p*. The *pre_dist* value is modified by *cur_dist* value. Now in the same iteration if *cur_dist* value of the node *m* in another *Neighbour_list q*, is less than *pre_dist* value, then the node *m* is deleted from previous *Neighbour_p* and included in new *Neighbour_q*. The algorithm for selecting 1_Hop_Neighbour is given in Fig. 4.

The following additional functions are used in M-FN_NNG algorithms:

SEARCH returns the 1-Hop *Neighbour_list* which are within the communication range of a node and current distance, *cur_dist* of each neighbour node.

GET picks up an element from distance vector *dist* that corresponds to the distance of node *m*.

GETPARTITION returns the partition *id* of the partition in which the node *m* has already been included.

```
Input: NNₚ, Pₚ, n, k, S'           Neighborₚ = = NULL
Output: Partition Pₚ at each         [Neighbor_list, dist] = SEARCH(Rootₚ)
        sink node SINKₚ              for each node m in Neighbor_list
                                         cur_distₘ = GET(dist, m)
Rootₚ = SINKₚ                            if Flagₘ= = False
while |S'| ≠ n do                            Neighborₚ = Neighborₚ U {m}
 for each Pₚ do                              pre_distₘ = cur_distₘ
   NextNode = FARTHEST (Rootₚ)           else
   NNₙₑₓₜₙₒ𝒹ₑ = 1-Hop_Neighbor(NextNode)    if (cur_distₘ <= pre_distₘ)
   for each node q in NNₙₑₓₜₙₒ𝒹ₑ do            q = GETPARTITION({m})
       Flag_y = true                          Neighbor_y = Neighbor_y - {m}
   end for                                    Neighborₚ = Neighborₚ U {m}
   Pₚ = Pₚ U NNₙₑₓₜₙₒ𝒹ₑ                       pre_distₘ = cur_distₘ
   S' = S' U Pₚ                            end if
   Rootₚ = NextNode                      end if
 end for                              end for
end while                             return Neighborₚ
Return Pp
```

Fig. 3. Algorithm of Incremental Phase   **Fig. 4.** Algorithm of 1_Hop_Neighbour

4   Comparative Analysis and Simulation Results

Spectral Bisection methods find good partitions and are used in many applications. But the calculations of the eigenvector in spectral methods involve expensive computation.

4.1   Comparative Analysis

Using RSB method the network is partitioned into 2^n sub-networks where *n* is the number of iterations. M-RSB partitions the network into any number of partitions. Fig. 5 shows the partitioning structure of a given network using RSB method having four parts. Fig. 6 shows that six partitions are created using M-RSB.

All the methods, except M-FN_NNG, need global information of the nodes. M-FN_NNG needs only 1-Hop neighbour information. Like M-RSB, our proposed methods also partition the network into any number of sub-networks. Fig. 7 depicts four sub-partitions using FN_NNG method and Fig. 8 shows four sub-partitions using M-FN_NNG methods. Fig. 9 and Fig. 10 show six sub-partitions using FN_NNG and M-FN_NNG of a given network respectively.

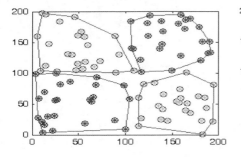

Fig. 5. 4-partitions using RSB   **Fig. 6.** 6-partitions using M-RSB

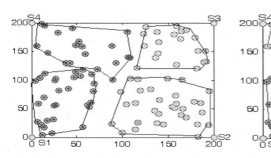

Fig. 7. 4-partitions using FN_NNG   **Fig. 8.** 4-partitions using M-FN_NNG

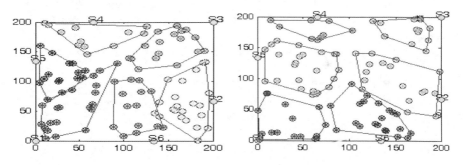

Fig. 9. 6-partitions using FN_NNG   **Fig. 10.** 6-partitions using M-FN_NNG

The MBCP method also partitions the network into 2^n sub-networks where n is the number of iterations. The authors in [6] have not mentioned clearly how the node u is chosen from set V_0. According to them, node u of V_0 is chosen in such a way that u is closest to the elements of V_1. Thus in most cases this partitioning method generates sub-partitions which are not physically separated. This situation is shown in Fig. 11.

While implementing MBCP, we have made some modifications in the strategy of choosing the node u from set V_0. We calculate the mean of distances between u and each element of V_1. Then we choose a node u which has least mean distance in V_0.

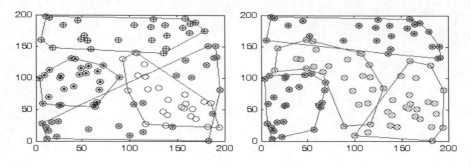

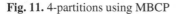

Fig. 11. 4-partitions using MBCP   **Fig. 12.** 4-partitions using M-MBCP

Using the new strategy (M-MBCP), the sub-partitions generated by MBCP are shown in Fig. 12. In the next section we describe the simulation environment and present the experimental results.

4.2   Simulation Environment and Metrics

The simulations of the above algorithms have been done in Matlab environment. A wireless sensor network deployed in a square region is considered.

We use four different sensor networks ranging from 100 nodes to 400 nodes. The 100 node field is generated by randomly placing the nodes in a 200 m x 200 m square area. We assume that the area contains homogeneous sensor nodes with a communication range of 45m. Other sizes are generated by scaling the square and keeping the communication range constant in order to keep average density of sensor nodes constant.

Following metrics are evaluated for performance analysis of the algorithms:

Average Execution Time for a particular method. Execution time needed for computation of the sub-partitions in a given network is measured. We have considered four sub-partitions for each of the algorithms.

Number of Edge cuts in a particular method. Edge cut is defined as follows:

$$E_C = | E' |$$, Where E' is the set of edges with one point in V_1 and the second point in V_2. V_1 and V_2 are the set of vertices of two sub-partitions.

4.3   Result Discussion

Execution times needed for partitioning using RSB, M-RSB, MBCP, M-MBCP, FN_NNG and M-FN_NNG are compared in Fig.13. It is clear from Fig.13 that MBCP needs highest execution time and M-FN_NNG needs lowest execution time. Execution time of RSB increases due to its computation of the eigenvalues and eigenvectors. M-RSB performs slightly better than RSB. Both MBCP and M-MBCP require higher execution time, because time is spent in checking connectivity while including a vertex in each partition. Thus, FN_NNG and M-FN_NNG give much better performance among all the methods. Fig.14 compares the number of edge cuts for the above mentioned algorithms. RSB and M-RSB return equal number of edge cuts. Fig.14 depicts that FN_NNG and M-FN_NNG also give low edge cut in comparison with other methods. Fig.15 demonstrates execution time needed to run all the methods with different sized networks. As expected, with the increased number of nodes, the execution time increases. However, in case of FN_NNG, M-FN_NNG, RSB and M-RSB methods, execution time increases slowly. But in case of MBCP and M-MBCP, the execution time increases rapidly with the increase in number of nodes.

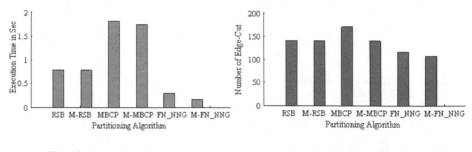

Fig. 13. Execution time   **Fig. 14.** Number of Edge-cut

5   Conclusion

This paper makes a comparative analysis of different graph partitioning algorithms and proposes novel algorithms which can be applied in wireless sensor networks. The existing partitioning algorithms partition the network into number of sub-partitions, whereas the proposed algorithms partition the network according to the available sinks. The simulation results demonstrate that the proposed algorithms have low execution time and low edge cut. Since WSN applications need fast response therefore the proposed algorithms are suitable for critical WSN applications, like disaster monitoring.

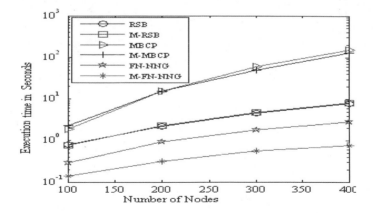

Fig. 15. Execution time with different sizes of network

References

1. Pothen, A., Simon, H.D., Liu, K.: Partitioning sparse matrices with eigenvectors of graphs. SIAM J. Matrix Anal. Appl. 11(3), 430–452 (1990)
2. Chlebikova, J.: Approximating the Maximally Balanced Connected Partition Problem in graphs. Information Processing Letters 60, 225–230 (1996)
3. Chan, T.F., Szeto, W.K.: On the Optimality of the Median Cut Spectral Bisection Graph Partitioning Method. SIAM J. Sci. Comput. 18(3), 943–948 (1997)
4. Eppstein, D., Paterson, M.S., Yao, F.F.: On Nearest-Neighbour Graphs (2000)
5. Kabelikova, P.: Graph Partitioning Using Spectral Methods. VSB - Technical University of Ostrava (2006)
6. Slama, I., Jouaber, B., Zeghlache, D.: Energy Efficient Scheme for Large Scale Wireless Sensor Networks with Multiple Sinks. In: Wireless Communications and Networking Conference, WCNC-IEEE (2008)
7. Elbhiri, B., El Fkihi, S., Saadane, R., Aboutajdine, D.: Clustering in Wireless Sensor Networks Based on Near Optimal Bi-partitions. In: Next Generation Internet (NGI) (2010)

Sensor-Cloud: Assimilation of Wireless Sensor Network and the Cloud

Sanjit Kumar Dash[1], Jyoti Prakash Sahoo[2], Subasish Mohapatra[2],
and Sarada Prasanna Pati[2]

[1] College of Engineering & Technology,
Biju Patanaik University of Technology,
Bhubaneswar, Odisha, India
[2] Institute of Technical Education and Research,
Siksha 'O' Anusandhan University,
Bhubaneswar, Odisha, India
{sanjitkumar303,sahoo.jyotiprakash,
subasish.mohapatra,saradapati78}@gmail.com

Abstract. A broad ranges of vital applications that acquire and process information from the corporeal world are in the extensive need of Wireless sensor networks. Similarly distributed resource sharing is also in the need of Cloud computing which serves as a standards-based approach. Extension of the Cloud computing paradigm to the sharing of sensor resources in wireless sensor networks results in a much promising technology called Sensor Clouds. The amount of data generated from these vast set of sensor applications is huge. These data if combined with various web-based virtual communities can prove to be beneficial in several significant areas like a virtual community of doctors monitoring patient healthcare for virus infection, portal for sharing real-time traffic information, real-time environmental data monitoring and analyzing, etc. To permit this study, all types of sensor data will require for an increasing capability to do analysis and mining on-the-fly. Since the applications provided by Cloud computing is plenty; it may be combined with Sensor network in the application areas such as environmental monitoring, weather forecasting, transportation business, healthcare, military application etc. The idea that WSNs deployed for various applications are brought under one roof and then seeing it as a distinct virtual WSN unit through cloud computing infrastructure is novel. Sharing and analysis of real time sensor data on-the-fly becomes easier when cloud is integrated with WSNs. Added to it is the benefit of providing sensor data or sensor event as a service over the internet. In this paper, we have addressed numerous issues and challenges in the design of Sensor Clouds and we propose a framework called sensor-cloud to enable this exploration by integrating sensor networks to the talented cloud computing.

Keywords: Sensors, Wireless Sensor Networks, Cloud Computing, Sensor-Cloud, Pub/Sub Agent, Internet.

1 Introduction

The mounting fashion of using cloud environments for storage and data processing needs has led to the ever-increasing popularity of cloud computing in distributed

N. Meghanathan et al. (Eds.): CCSIT 2012, Part I, LNICST 84, pp. 455–464, 2012.

computing environment. It is a new period of accessing shared computing resources through Cloud computing which provides applications, platforms and infrastructure over the internet. On the contrary, wireless sensor networks are being seen as one of the most crucial technologies for the 21st century where distributed spatially connected sensor node automatically forms a network for data transmission and receiving among themselves. This is popularly known as Sensor Network [1]. The applications that require the interaction between users and the physical world are deploying Wireless sensor networks as the main platform. Important applications of wireless sensor networks include environmental and habitat monitoring, healthcare monitoring of patients, weather monitoring and forecasting, military and homeland security surveillance, tracking of goods and manufacturing processes, safety monitoring of physical structures and construction sites, smart homes and offices, and many other uses. Another challenging issue is the communication among sensor nodes using Internet. It is quite sensible to integrate sensor networks with Internet [2]. Concurrently the accessibility of the data of sensor network should be made accessible at any time, at any place. Since the assignment of address to the sensor nodes of large numbers is complicated; so sensor node may not necessarily establish connection with internet exclusively. The rising domain of *Sensor Clouds* extends the Cloud Computing paradigm to the sharing of sensor resources in wireless sensor networks. A Sensor-Cloud is the result of the integration of wireless sensor networks with the cloud. There are several motivations for Sensor Clouds. First, on using the computational and data storage resources of the cloud the large amount of data collected by the sensors can be processed, analyzed, and stored. Secondly, under flexible usage scenarios the sensors can be efficiently shared by different users and applications. Users can be able to run a specific application, and to collect the desired type of sensor data by accessing a subset of the sensors during a particular time period. Third, it is more proficient to offload specialized tasks such as image and signal processing to the sensor devices as sensor devices with embedded processors become more computationally powerful. Lastly, access to a wide variety of resources in a pervasive manner is also seamlessly provided by the Sensor-Cloud.

This paper is organized as follows: Section 2 and Section 3 present an overview of Clouds and Sensor Network. Section 4 outlines various issues and challenges in designing sensor-cloud platform. Section 5 describes the proposed sensor-cloud architecture and design and finally section 6 concludes the paper.

2   Cloud: Overview

Cloud computing is a term used to describe both a platform and type of application. A cloud computing platform dynamically provisions, configures, reconfigures servers as needed. Servers in the cloud can be physical machines or virtual machines. It is an alternative to having local servers handle applications. The end users of a cloud computing network usually have no idea where the servers are physically located—they just spin up their application and start working. Advanced clouds typically include other computing resources such as storage area networks (SANs), network equipment, firewall and other security devices. Cloud computing also describes applications that are extended to be accessible through the Internet. These cloud applications use large data centers and powerful servers that host Web applications and Web services. Anyone with a suitable Internet connection and a standard browser can access a cloud application.

Many formal definitions have been proposed in both academia and industry, the one provided by U.S. NIST (National Institute of Standards and Technology) [3] appears to include key common elements widely used in the Cloud Computing community:

Cloud computing is a model for enabling convenient, on demand network access to a shared pool of configurable computing resources (e.g., networks, servers, storage, applications, and services) that can be rapidly provisioned and released with minimal management effort or service provider interaction [3].

3   Sensor Network: Overview

A wireless sensor network (WSN) consists of spatially distributed autonomous sensors to cooperatively monitor physical or environmental conditions, such as temperature, sound, vibration, pressure, motion or pollutants.[4,5] The development of wireless sensor networks was motivated by military applications such as battlefield surveillance. They are now used in many industrial and civilian application areas, including industrial process monitoring and control, machine health monitoring [6], environment and habitat monitoring, healthcare applications, home automation, and traffic control [4, 7].Each node in a sensor network is typically equipped with a radio transceiver or other wireless communications device, a small microcontroller, and an energy source, usually a battery. A sensor network is a computer network composed of a large number of sensor nodes. [8] The sensor nodes are densely deployed inside the phenomenon, they deploy random and have cooperative capabilities. Usually these devices are small and inexpensive, so that they can be produced and deployed in large numbers, and so their resources in terms of energy, memory, computational speed and bandwidth are severely constrained. There are different Sensors such as pressure, accelerometer, camera, thermal, microphone, etc. They monitor conditions at different locations, such as temperature, humidity, vehicular movement, lightning condition, pressure, soil makeup, noise levels, the presence or absence of certain kinds of objects, mechanical stress levels on attached objects, the current characteristics such as speed, direction and size of an object. Normally these Sensor nodes consist of three components: sensing, processing and communicating [9].

4   Design Issues and Challenges

This section discusses the important issues and challenges in the design of Sensor Clouds. Most of these design issues and challenges arise due to the inherent limitations of sensor devices such as limited processor performance, small storage capacity, limited battery power, and unreliable low-bandwidth wireless communication and some issue arise due issue de-facto standard of cloud such as reliability, back up, privacy, security ownership etc.

4.1   Sensor Issues

1) *Power Management*: Power management is a major concern as sensor nodes do not have fixed power sources and relies on limited battery power. Sensor applications executing on these devices have to make tradeoffs between sensor operation and conserving battery life. The sensor nodes should provide adaptive power management facilities that can be accessed by the applications. From the Sensor-Cloud perspective, the availability of sensor nodes is not only dependent on their load, but also on their power consumption. Thus, the Sensor Cloud's resource management component has to account for power consumption.

2) *Scalability:* Scalability is the ability to add sensor resources to a Sensor-Cloud to increase the capacity of sensor data collection, without substantial changes to its software architecture. The Sensor-Cloud architecture should allow multiple wireless sensor networks, possibly owned by different virtual organizations, to be easily integrated with compute and data cloud resources. This would enable an application to access sensor resources across increasing number of heterogeneous wireless sensor networks.

3) *Network Connectivity and Protocols:* The network connections are usually fast and reasonably reliable in cloud. On the other hand, the sensor nodes in Sensor Clouds are connected via wireless ad hoc networks which are low-bandwidth, high-latency, and unreliable. The network connectivity of sensor nodes is dynamic in nature, and it might be irregular and vulnerable to faults due to noise and signal degradation caused by environmental factors. The Sensor-Cloud has to gracefully handle unexpected network disconnections or prolonged periods of disconnection. Thus, efficient techniques to interface sensor network protocols with cloud networking protocols are necessary.

4) *Scheduling:* In wireless sensor networks, scheduling of sensor nodes is often performed to facilitate power management and sensor resource management. Researchers have developed algorithms to schedule the radio communication of active sensor nodes, and to turn off the radio links of idle nodes to conserve power. Similarly, for applications like target tracking, sensor management algorithms selectively turn off sensor nodes that are located far away from the target, while ` to improve the availability of sensor nodes are necessary. Sensor Clouds should support job and service migration, so that a job can be migrated from a sensor node that is running out of power or has failing hardware to another node.

4.2   Cloud Issues

1) *Reliability*: Stability of the data storage system is of important consideration in clouds. Generally, people worry about whether a cloud service provider is financially stable and whether their data storage system is trustworthy. Most cloud providers attempt to mollify this concern by using redundant storage techniques, but it is still possible that a service could crash or go out of business, leaving users with limited or no access to their data.

2) *Data Backup*: Cloud providers employ redundant servers and routine data backup processes, but some customers worry about being able to control their own back-

ups. Many providers are now offering data dumps onto media or allowing users to back up their data through regular downloads.

3) *Privacy:* The Cloud model has been criticized by privacy advocates for the greater ease in which the companies hosting the Cloud services control and monitor communication and data stored between the user and the host company lawfully or unlawfully. There have been efforts to "harmonize" the legal environment by deploying local infrastructure and allowing customers to select "availability zones."

4) *Security:* Cloud service providers employ data storage and transmission encryption, user authentication, and authorization. Many clients worry about the vulnerability of remote data to criminals and hackers. Cloud providers are enormously sensitive to this issue and apply substantial resources to mitigate this problem.

5) *Ownership*: Once data has been relegated to the cloud, some worry about losing their rights or being unable to protect the rights of their customers. Many cloud providers address this issue with well-skilled user-sided agreements. According to the agreement, users would be wise to seek advice from their favorite legal representative.

6) *Availability and Performance:* Business organizations are worried about acceptable levels of availability and performance of applications hosted in the cloud.

7) *Legal:* There are certain points of concern for a cloud provider and a client receiving the service like location of the cloud provider, location of infrastructure, physical location of the data and outsourcing of the cloud provider's services etc.

Sensor networks is an emerging area and there are many research issues pertaining to sensor networks such as energy management, coverage, localization, medium access control, routing and transport, security etc. Research in cloud computing is also in fantasy stage. It also has a number of research challenges such as efficient resource allocation, high resource utilization and security etc. Apart from the afore-mentioned research issues in sensor networks and cloud computing, sensor-cloud computing gives rise to additional research challenges, especially when it is used in mission-critical situations. These research challenges are: web services and service discovery which work across both sensor networks and the cloud, interconnection and networking, coordinated quality of service (QoS) mechanisms etc.

5   Sensor- Cloud Architecture and Design

5.1   Sensor-Cloud Organization

A Sensor-Cloud consists of wireless sensor networks (WSNs) and cloud resources like computers, servers and disk arrays for the processing and storage of sensor data. The resources in the Sensor-Cloud are shared by several Organizations and certain resources might also belong to more than one organization. Users from various organizations may access the resources in the Sensor Cloud, even if the resources are not owned by their organization.

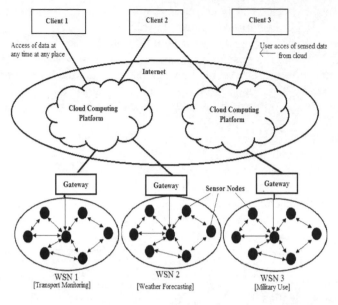

Fig. 1. Sensor-Cloud System Model

Figure 1 consists of WSNs (i.e. WSN1, WSN2, and WSN3), cloud infrastructure and the clients. Clients seek services from the system. WSN consists of physical wireless sensor nodes to sense different applications like Transport Monitoring, Weather Forecasting, and Military Application etc. Each sensor node is programmed with the required application. Sensor node also consists of operating system components and network management components. On each sensor node, application program senses the application and sends back to gateway in the cloud directly through base station or in multi-hop through other nodes. Routing protocol plays a vital role in managing the network topology and to accommodate the network dynamics. Cloud provides on-demand service and storage resources to the clients. It provides access to these resources through internet and comes in handy when there is a sudden requirement of resources. Combining WSNs with cloud makes it easy to share and analyze real time sensor data on-the-fly. It also gives an advantage of providing sensor data or sensor event as a service over the internet. Merging of two technologies makes sense for large number of application such as Transport monitoring, Weather Forecasting and Military Application etc [10].

5.2   Sensor-Cloud Platform

The proposed platform consists of Virtualization Manager, Pub/Sub Broker, Monitoring and metering, System Manager, Service Registry, Stream Monitoring and Processing Component and Application Specific Interface. Figure 2 gives an overview of the components that constitute the WSN-cloud platform.

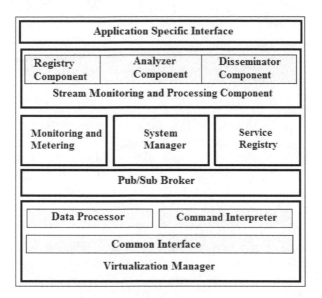

Fig. 2. Sensor-Cloud Platform

I. Virtualization Manager

This component is divided into three subcomponents. They are — Common Interface, Data processor and Command interpreter.

1) Common Interface: Sensor networks are connected with the gateway through common interface in different ways (serial, USB and Ethernet). Gateway receives the raw data from the communication ports and converts it to a packet. The packet is further kept in a buffer for further processing.

2) Data Processor: This component retrieves the packet from the buffer and processes according to its type. The packet type depends on the application being run on the platform.

3) Command Interpreter: This component is responsible for providing reverse communication channel from the gateway to the WSN and for processing and interpreting various commands issued from different applications and generates the code that is understood by the sensor nodes.

II. Publish/Subscribe Broker

This module is responsible for monitoring, processing and delivering events to registered users through SaaS applications.

III. Monitoring and Metering (MaM)

This module tracks the usage of the primary cloud resources. Consumer uses signed web service requests to access the data. Role of MaM deals with handling the request of consumers, checking of registry manager, keeps track of web services etc.

IV. System Manager

This module is responsible for processing and archiving the sensor data and also manages the system resources. Computation cycles are utilized internally to process the data that emanates from the sensors. Storing the sensor data will help to analyze the patterns in the data collected over a period of time.

V. Service Registry

It maintains the credentials of different consumers' applications register to publisher/subscriber system for various sensor data required. For each application, registry component stores user subscriptions, sensor data and sensor event types the application is interested in. Each application is associated with a unique application ID along with the service level agreement (SLA). SLA provides basis for metering and accounting of services to be used, by covering all the attributes of the service customs.

VI. Stream Monitoring and Processing (SMP)

SMP monitors the sensor streams comes in many different forms from different sources and invokes correct analysis method. This module is divided into three sub components — registry component, analyzer component and disseminator component.

1) Registry Component (RC): Registry component stores user subscriptions of different applications and user specific sensor data types of those users who register to Pub/Sub Agent. It also sends all user subscriptions along with application id to the disseminator component for event delivery.

2) Analyzer Component (AC): AC analyzes the incoming sensor data or event to match with user subscriptions in the Service registry. If the sensor data matches with the interest of the subscriber, the same is handed over to the disseminator component to deliver to the appropriate users.

3) Disseminator Component (DC): DC receives the data or event of interest from the analyzer component and delivers the data through SaaS interface to the subscribed applications.

VII. Application Specific Interface

The interfaces give access to the WSN cloud platform web services. Consumers can consume the services through web services that are often referred to as internet application programming interface (IAPI). This allows the users to access the remotely hosted services over network, such as internet. Consumers can build their customer applications by weaving the required services from the WSN cloud platform.

5.3   Sensor-Cloud Architecture

This framework aims at bringing sensor data to a pub/sub Agent through gateways. Pub/sub agent delivers information to the consumers of applications interfaces. The WSN cloud platform web services are granted access through the interfaces built with Web 2.0 technologies. The masking of the lower level details of each WSN cloud in terms of different platforms, sensors being used, and data being generated is done by the Virtualization Manager. The various SaaS applications transfer the information and subscriptions of the registered users to pub/sub Agent registry. Sensor data, on reaching the system from gateways, are then determined through stream monitoring and processing component (SMPC) in the pub/sub Agent as to whether they need processing or just have to be stored for periodic send or for immediate delivery. If in case sensor data need periodic/ emergency delivery, the analyzer determines which SaaS applications the events belong to and then pass the events to the disseminator. The disseminator then delivers the events for use by finding appropriate subscribers for each application with the help of event matching algorithm. Computational cycles are provided internally by SM as required to process the data emanated from the sensors. SRM manages the users' subscriptions and credentials. MaM calculates the price for the offered services.

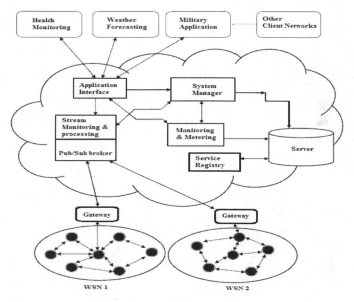

Fig. 3. Sensor-Cloud Framework

6   Conclusion

Combination of the two talented technologies, wireless sensor networks and cloud computing which further results in sensor clouds significantly enhances the prospective of these technologies for new and powerful applications. This further explains the reason of the widespread adoption of this technique in industries. Thus, we believe that sensor clouds will attract growing attention from the research community and the industry.

In this paper, we have examined the important design issues and challenges for sensor clouds. To address these design issues, we proposed a framework for Sensor-Cloud integration. The success of the sensor-cloud computing approach will depend on the ability of the sensor network and cloud computing research communities to work together to ensure compatibility in the techniques and algorithms that will be developed in the future.

References

1. Culler, D., Estrin, D., Srivastava, M.: Overview of sensor networks. IEEE Computer, 41–49 (August 2004)
2. Ulmer, C., Alkalai, L., Yalamanchili, S.: Wireless distributed sensor networks for in-situ exploration of mars, Work in progress for NASA Technical Report,
   http://users.ece.gatech.edu/
3. Mell, P., Grance, T.: Draft nist working definition of cloud computing - v15, August 21, 2005 (2009)
4. Römer, K., Mattern, F.: The Design Space of Wireless Sensor Networks. IEEE Wireless Communications 11(6), 54–61 (2004),
   http://www.vs.inf.ethz.ch/publ/papers/wsn-designspace.pdf,
   doi:10.1109/MWC.2004.1368897
5. Haenselmann, T.: Sensornetworks. GFDL Wireless Sensor Network textbook (April 05, 2006),
   http://pi4.informatik.uni-mannheim.de/~haensel/sn_book (retrieved August 29, 2006)
6. Tiwari, A., et al.: Energy-efficient wireless sensor network design and implementation for condition-based maintenance. ACM Transactions on Sensor Networks (TOSN),
   http://portal.acm.org/citation.cfm?id=1210670
7. Hadim, S., Mohamed, N.: Middleware Challenges and Approaches for Wireless Sensor Networks. IEEE Distributed Systems Online 7(3), 1 (2006),
   http://doi.ieeecomputersociety.org/10.1109/MDSO.2006.19 art. no. 0603-o3001, doi:10.1109/MDSO.2006.19
8. http://en.wikipedia.org/wiki/Sensor_Networks
9. Akyildiz, I.F., Su, W., Sankarasubramaniam, Y., Cayirci, E.: A Survey on Sensor Networks. IEEE Communications Magazine, 102–114 (August 2002)
10. Dash, S.K., Mohapatra, S., Pattanaik, P.K.: A Survey on Applications of Sensor Network using Cloud Computing. International Journal of Computer Science and Emerging Technologies 2(4), 50–55 (2010)

Game Theoretic Model for Selfish Node Avoidance in Ad Hoc Networks

Upasana Dohare, D.K. Lobiyal, and Sushil Kumar

School of Computer and System Sciences,
Jawaharlal Nehru University, New Delhi
{upasanadohare,skdohare}@yahoo.com, lobiyal@gmail.com

Abstract. In this paper, a Game Theoretic Model for selfish node avoidance routing is presented. A mathematical framework for rational node that maximizes its credits has been developed. Using game theory, it is verified that that this proposed model is robust and can achieve full cooperation among nodes. The proposed model is simulated using network simulator ns-2 The simulation results show that game theoretic model improves packet delivery ratio with the increase in number of the routes in the network. It is shown that game theoretic model with AODV can achieve higher packet delivery ratio for heavy traffic network in the presence of selfish nodes as compared to the original AODV. Further, it is observed that the packet delivery ratio of cooperative nodes decreases proportionally when the number of selfish nodes increases. Furthermore, it is also shown that game theoretic model with AODV gives low routing overheads.

Keywords: Game Theory, Nash Equilibria, Cooperation, Selfish Node, Ad Hoc Network.

1 Introduction

Mobile Ad-hoc Networks are infrastructureless networks. These networks have no fixed routers, every node could be router. All nodes are capable of free movement and can be connected dynamically in arbitrary manner. The responsibilities for organizing and controlling the network are distributed among the terminals themselves. In this type of networks, some pairs of terminals may not be able to communicate directly with each other and have to relay on some terminals so that the messages are delivered to their destinations. These terminals as an evolution of current mobile phones, laptops, iPAD and emerging PDAs equipped with wireless interfaces. The only external resource needed for their successful operation is the bandwidth. The nodes may be located in or on airoplanes, ships, trucks, cars, perhaps even on people or very small devices [1].

In the absence of a fixed infrastructure, the basic network operations of wireless ad hoc network rely on cooperation of the nodes. The delivery of packets from source node to destination node relies on the several others nodes to help in forwarding the packets since destination is the beyond the transmission range of a source node. To increase the life time and energy efficiency of the network, it is allowing packets to be

N. Meghanathan et al. (Eds.): CCSIT 2012, Part I, LNICST 84, pp. 465–476, 2012.

delivered over several short transmission links rather than one long transmission link. If the destination node is not directly approachable, the intermediate nodes between the source and destination make mutual contribution in the transmission by forwarding or relaying the packet along the route to the destination. However, the nodes in the ad hoc network may belong to different organization, company and person, so these nodes are autonomous and functioning for their own self-interest to minimize the use of their limited resources like energy, may refuse to forward packets for other nodes. This is the fundamental problem of the ad hoc network in which nodes are participating with selfish behavior. Selfishness of nodes may lead to inefficient use of the network resources since packets may have to be rerouted through alternative paths to the destination node or retransmitted when nodes dropped packets [2][3].

The researchers have addressed the several problems of inspiring the cooperation among nodes which promise to forward the packets but do not termed as misbehaving. They proposed many game theoretic solutions to enhance the efficiency of the networks with autonomous nodes acting on their self-interest to minimize the use of their limited resources. These solutions assumed to give nodes credit for packet forwarding or relaying for others node. The cooperative nodes earn credit through its behavior and use the accumulated credit to buying cooperative behavior from other nodes [4], [5] [6]. Another approach to inspiring the cooperation among nodes which agree to forward the packets based on the reputation of nodes gathered from neighboring nodes. These neighboring nodes continue to monitor the behavior of a node whether it is forwarding the packets or misbehaving with the packets [7], [8].

While the researcher provided many solutions to encourage the cooperation among nodes, still there are several possible drawbacks with these solutions. The monitoring nodes may be misinterpreting the behavior of nodes, increasing the computation to monitor the misbehaviors for other nodes, increasing the overhead on the network by consuming the channel capacity, forwarding the reputation information gathered from others nodes, and use its limited resources like energy for monitoring the misbehavior of others. In this paper, we proposed to use game theoretic approach to minimize the routing overheads and preventing the nodes becoming selfish in participating in routing.

2   Related Work

In the ad hoc networks, solutions for the problems of selfish nodes have been studied either using game theory or reputation systems. Recently there have been a sequence of research papers [2],[3],[4],[5],[6],[7], [9], and [10] published in the area of communication and ad hoc networks that made efforts to solve various problems introduced by selfish nodes. A node tries to select a strategy that maximizes its own gain called rational node. Some of these studies have a common approach of incurring the credits if they are considered to provide the service for others. While others have a common approach to motivate the cooperation among nodes by gathering secondhand information.   Based on this information of neighboring nodes, a source node decides to forward packets through a node having good reputation.

Authors in [2] provided an introduction to neutral cooperation in the ad hoc network which is based on game theoretic analysis of selfishness of the nodes with a focus on the packet forwarding and relaying scenarios. Authors explained the two-player packet forwarding scenario and more-player packet forwarding scenario. In [3] a context-free (COFFEE) protocol is presented that does not rely on past experience and selfish behavior detection. This protocol can send packets through a route without knowing whether the intermediate nodes are selfish or not. In paper [4], Wireless nodes are considered with the energy constraints. Nodes are assumed to rational. A rational node means that its actions are strictly determined by self-interest. Each node is associated with a minimum lifetime constraint. The throughput of each node is measured in terms of the ratio of the number of successful rely requests generated by the node. The optimal tradeoff between the throughput and lifetime of nodes are studied using the game theory. A distributed Generous TFT (tit for tat) algorithms was introduce which decides whether to accept or reject a rely request.

In [5] a game theoretic model to investigate the conditions for cooperation in wireless ad hoc networks, without incentive mechanisms has been presented. Several theorems for the strategy always defects (AIID) are stated and proved for cooperation, considering the topology of the network and the existing communication routes. It is concluded that with a very high probability, there will be some nodes that have AIID as their best strategy. In [6] a reputation-based system as an extension to source routing protocols for detecting and punishing selfish nodes has been introduced. It is shown that by punishing these nodes will not benefit them. Instead, being cooperative has a better chance to increase their benefit. In [7], the local reputation information is used to decide the reputation value of nodes. Author suggested that every node have knowledge of the reputation value of all its neighbor nodes. Three reputation thresholds are given to categorize as good, misleading. The reputation of node is increased if it forwards a packet otherwise it is decreased. When the route is initiated, a node with good reputation is chosen. Otherwise, if no node is available with good reputation, it prefers to choose misleading node.

In [9] a game theoretic reputation mechanism is introduced to incentivize nodes which forward the packet for others, where cooperation is induced by the threat of partial or total network disconnection if a node acts selfishly. It is shown that a node which is perceived as selfish node due to the problem of packet collisions and interference can be avoided. In [10], an approach for detection of selfish behavior in the wireless mobile ad hoc networks is presented. This approach is based on Dempster-Shafer theory (DST) named as Dempster-Shafer theory based selfishness detection framework (DST-SDF). After reviewing the related work, it is observed that game theory can be used as the tools for analyzing selfishness and complex interactions between nodes in ad hoc network. Above techniques can be combined with other schemes, algorithms and analytical tools to derive a new framework for routing in wireless ad hoc networks.

3   Game Theoretic Model for Selfish Node Avoidance

In this section, a game theoretic model for analyzing the selfishness of nodes in forwarding packets is presented. Application of Game theory in this model is based on the hypothesis that a node forwards the packets rationally. In other words, each node has a utility function that a node tries to maximize with imposed constraints on its choices of actions in the game.

3.1   Preliminaries

It is assumed that an ad hoc network consists of two types of nodes - non-selfish node and selfish node but not malicious. These nodes are equipped with a limited power battery. A selfish node is a rational user that wants to save its energy by not forwarding the packet for others. The packet forwarding through multi-hop routes from the originating node to destination node relies on the intermediate nodes. Wireless links are bidirectional. The node listens to all the transmitted packets from their neighbors. The dynamic nature of ad hoc networks leads to imperfection or noise in transmission observed by a node.

A node consumes its resources in packets forwarding for others. It is assumed that the forwarding/relaying cost is β where $\beta \geq 1$. A node receives a reward α when its packet is relayed where $\alpha \geq 1$. Any two neighbor nodes desired to send the packets to each other and also forward each other's packet. We can identify such pair of nodes and analyze interaction between them as a two-player game. It is reasonable to expect that the packet forwarding game between two players play several times since they decide whether to drop or forward their respective packets. It also assumed that time is divided into slots and a node is able to send sufficiently large number of packets in each slot. At the end of the each slot, the node monitors the throughput of its neighbor by overhearing. If throughput is below a certain threshold, it stops the transmitting packet. The node is denoted by a subscript i and its neighbor by a subscript $-i$.

3.2   Forwarding Game Formulation

This section describes a two player packet forwarding scenario for natural cooperation. The natural cooperation between a pair of nodes is affected by different assumptions about the selfishness in packet forwarding and noise observed while overhearing.

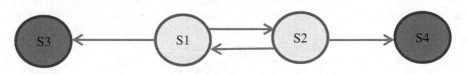

Fig. 1. A two player packet forwarding game scenario

This section describes a two player packet forwarding scenario for natural cooperation. In fig. 1, there are four nodes S1 to S4. S1 and S2 are willing to send packets to their destination S4 and S3 respectively. Without cooperation of S1, S2 is not able to send its packets to S3 and similarly, S1 can't send packets to S4. The set of actions are available to each player are as "forward" or "Do not forward" the packet of the other source. The payoff is defined as the difference between the reward of successfully delivered packets minus the cost of the forwarding a packet for the other sources. In this scenario, the payoff matrix of two player forwarding game is give in Table-1.

Table 1. Payoff Matrix of Two Player Forwarding Game

	S2 DOES NOT FORWARD(DNF)	S2 FORWARD(F)
S1 DOES NOT FORWARD(DNF)	(0, 0)	(α, -β)
S1 FORWARD(F)	(-β, α)	(α-β, α-β)

Packet drop due to selfishness in packet forwarding: - The packet forwarding through multi-hop routes from the originating node to destination node relies on the intermediate nodes. However, the intermediate nodes provide the packet forwarding, consume their limited energy resources. Therefore they, in order to conserve its limited energy resources could decide not to cooperate in the packet forwarding by switching off its interface. If many of them are acting selfishly by changing their behavior in this way, may lead to the collapse of the network. Nodes may choose to participate in packet forwarding but uses the minimum transmission power to deliver a packet acting as selfishly. Source node may not overhear this transmission, assumed that the packet is dropped by relay node. We define a drop probability $p_{-i}^{(t)}$ of node $-i$ as

$$p_{-i}^{(t)} = \begin{cases} 0 & if \ \frac{E_c}{E_f} < \theta_{E}, & \text{Packet is dropped} \\ \frac{E_c - \theta_{E} E_f}{E_f - \theta_E E_f} & if \ \frac{E_c}{E_f} \geq \theta_{E}, & \text{packet is forwarded} \end{cases} \quad (1)$$

where E_c is the residual energy, E_f is the full energy and θ_E is threshold energy ratio. The relay nodes monitor its energy level before forwarding a packet, if it is below θ_E then relay node drop the packet otherwise forward a packet. The θ_E may not be the same for all nodes.

Packet perceived to drop due to noise observed in overhearing:- The nodes overhear all the transmitted packets from their neighbors. Due to noise in transmission, it is not always possible to detect whether a relay node forwarded a packet or not. A packet may be perceived to drop by -i since node i is not completely overhear the packet transmission but it is not dropped. Let us assume that length of a packet is L bits. If node i did not overhear all L bits of a packet, it is assumed to be dropped by -i. it is assumed that the loss probability of a bit is $p_b = 10^{-4}$. Probability that node i overhear forwarded packet is $(1 - p_b)^L$. Probability that node -i drops a packet at time slot t is

$$p_e = 1 - (1 - p_b)^L. \quad (2)$$

A packet may be dropped either selfishness in packet forwarding or noise observed in overhearing. By overhearing the transmission, node i then estimates the perceived dropping probability $\hat{p}_{-i}^{(t)}$ of its neighbor at time slot t≥0. Further, It is assuming that in each slot t, node i wishes to send N packets through node $-i$ to its destination. The throughput of node $-i$ estimated by node i in time slot t is can be expressed as

$$\tau_{-i}^{(t)} = N\hat{p}_{-i}^{(t)} .$$

$$= N[p_{-i}^{(t)} + (1 - p_{-i}^{(t)})p_e] .$$

Substituting p_e form (2) in above expression, we get

$$\tau_{-i}^{(t)} = N\left[\left(p_{-i}^{(t)} + \left(1 - p_{-i}^{(t)}\right)\right)\left(1 - (1 - p_b)^L\right)\right] \qquad (3)$$

We defined the normalize throughput of node $-i$ as

$$\hat{\tau}_{-i}^{(t)} = \frac{node\ i\ estimate\ number\ of\ packet\ forwarded\ by - i}{actul\ number\ of\ packet\ send\ to - i}$$

$$\hat{\tau}_{-i}^{(t)} = \frac{\tau_{-i}^{(t)}}{N} = \left[\left(p_{-i}^{(t)} + \left(1 - p_{-i}^{(t)}\right)\right)\left(1 - (1 - p_b)^L\right)\right] . \qquad (4)$$

The normalize throughput $\hat{\tau}_{-i}^{(t)}$ will be used as input to strategies function of node i. The average payoff of the node i at time slot t using the table -1 can be expressed as:

$$\pi_i^t = (\alpha - \beta)(1 - p_i^{(t)})(1 - p_{-i}^{(t)}) + \alpha(1 - p_i^{(t)})p_{-i}^{(t)} - \beta(1 - p_{-i}^{(t)})p_i^{(t)} .$$

By simplifying:

$$\pi_i^t = (\alpha - \beta)\left[1 + \frac{\beta}{\alpha - \beta}p_i^{(t)} - \frac{\alpha}{\alpha - \beta}p_{-i}^{(t)}\right]. \qquad (5)$$

A player wishes to maximize its total discount payoff and is given by [2]

$$U_i = \sum_{n=0}^{\infty} \delta^n \pi_i^t . \qquad (6)$$

where $0 < \delta < 1$ is the discount factor. Substituting the π_i^t from (5), the total discount payoff of node i can be expressed as

$$U_i = \sum_{n=0}^{\infty} \delta^n (\alpha - \beta)\left[1 + \frac{\beta}{\alpha - \beta}p_i^{(t)} - \frac{\alpha}{\alpha - \beta}p_{-i}^{(t)}\right]. \qquad (7)$$

The payoff of node i can be calculated by using the actual value of $p_{-i}^{(t)}$ from equation (1). If the node i supposed to have many chances for future interaction, then δ will be close to one.

3.3   Trigger Strategy

In the repeated game, each player is permitted to use a strategy to deicide its action "do not forward" or "forward" packets for others on the information collected in past. We define the trigger strategy in the two player repeated packet forwarding game to provide cooperation $\bar{\bar{P}}_i^t$ of a node i in time slot t such that the cooperation of a node $-i$ is estimated based on normalized throughput $\hat{\tau}_{-i}^{(t)}$ in the time slot t-1. If the normalized throughput of a node is below a threshold τ_{th}, it is consider a selfish node and node i decided to not forward the packet of node $-i$. Mathematically the trigger strategy is defined as:

$$\bar{\bar{P}}_i^t = f_i\left(\hat{t}_{-i}^{(t-1)}\right).$$ (8)

where $f_i(.)$ is a strategy function of node i. There are many strategies possible. Few of them are given below:

$$\bar{\bar{P}}_i^0 = f_i\left(\hat{t}_{-i}^{(0)}\right) = 0, \quad \text{Use this function if node-i playing DNF in the first time slot}$$

$$f_i\left(\hat{t}_{-i}^{(t-1)}\right) = \begin{cases} 0 & if\ \hat{t}_{-i}^{(t-1)} \leq \tau_{th}, & use\ this\ if\ Node-i\ playing\ DNF \\ 1 & if\ \hat{t}_{-i}^{(t-1)} = 1, & use\ this\ funtion\ if\ Node-i\ playing\ F \\ \hat{t}_{-i}^{(t-1)} & if\ 1 < \hat{t}_{-i}^{(t-1)} < \tau_{th}, & use\ this\ TFT \end{cases}$$

where DNF means "DO NOT FORWARD", F means "FORWARD" and TFT (Tit-For-Tat). It is defined as a node i is playing this strategy start with F and then playing with the same throughput as of node-i in the previous time slot.

The strategy profile (DNF, DNF) is the only Nash equilibrium of the forwarding game with uncertain ending since neither player stands to improve their payoff from cooperation with an opponent that always do not forward. The dilemma of this game is that both players could receive a better payoff of α-β > 1 if they selected the strategy profile (F, F). This strategy profiles is Pareto optimal.

4   Simulation

In the simulations, our focus is to study the performance of proposed game theoretic model for selfish node avoidance using the AODV protocol. The model developed is simulated in network simulator ns-2.

4.1   Simulation Setup

We used the two rays ground radio-propagation model for wireless channel. The bandwidth of the wireless channel is 2 Mbps. To propagate the signal in all direction, Omni directional antenna has been used. The multiple accesses with collision avoidance protocol (802.11) was used at the MAC layer. The physical radio range of node is 200 meters. Routing was performed using the AODV protocol with selfish node. The simulation parameters used in the work are shown in table-2. Initially, in the simulation, 10 nodes are randomly placed in an area of 500×500 m². We have implemented the proposed game theoretic model. During the simulation run we randomly selected 2 nodes that do not implement game theoretic model and behave selfishly by dropping all packets that are destined for others. A selfish node means a node that drop the packet to save its energy by not forwarding packet for others. A cooperative node is one which forwards the packets. Thereafter 20, 30, and up to 80 cooperative nodes are randomly selected and same number of selfish nodes are also selected for the simulation.

Table 2. Simulation parameter and its value

PARAMETER	VALUE
Number of node	100
Number of selfish node	10%-90%
Cooperative node	10%-90%
Area	500x500 m^2
Packet size	512 bytes
CBR	5-30 packets/sec
Initial Energy E$_f$	1000 Joules
Threshold Energy ratio θ_E	.40
Threshold Normalize throughput τ_{th}	.60
Simulation time	500 s

To evaluate the performance of the network in which nodes implement two players game theoretic model, the number of forwarded packet are measured. We measured the following evaluation metrics - number of routes versus packet delivery ratio, CBR versus packet delivery ratio, and percentage of selfish nodes versus packet delivery ratio. Further, we also measured the metrics and percentage of selfish nodes versus routing overhead. *Packet Delivery Ratio* is defined as the ratio of the number of packet received at the destination node to the number of packets sent by the source node. *Routing Overhead is* defined as the ratio of the amount of routing related control packet in bytes (RREQ, RREP, RERR and Game Theoretic AODV) to the amount of data packet sent in byte in the network.

4.2   Simulation Results

Fig. 2 shows the simulation results obtained for Packet delivery ratio as the number of routes varies in the network where 10% nodes are selfish and 90% are cooperative

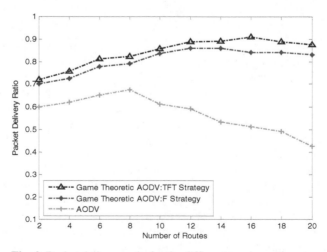

Fig. 2. Packet delivery ratio for the different numbers of routes

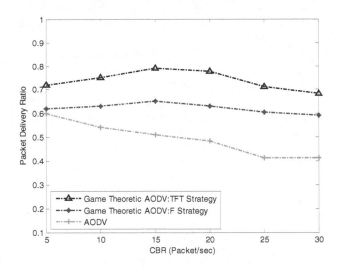

Fig. 3. Packet delivery ratio for the different packets rates

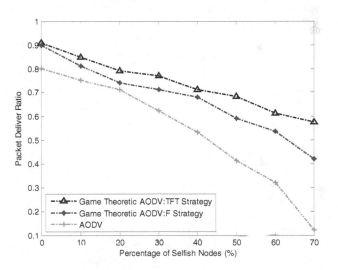

Fig. 4. Packet delivery ratio for the different number of selfish nodes

nodes. It is observed that the packet delivery ratio increases with the increase of the routes. This is due to fact that when there are more active routes, a node does not listen since it is busy in forwarding the increased number of packet. This is leading to consume more energy of node. Therefore cooperative nodes are supposed to be acting as selfish. This increases the level of retaliation situations in TFT strategies. When the number of route is more than 16, the packet delivery ratio starts decreasing since the packets are being forwarded by the originating node. But the packets are not overheard by the originating node due to bit error in packet overhearing which increases selfishness among the cooperative nodes. Further, packet delivery ratio of

AODV with selfish nodes falls drastically since nodes do not implement the game theoretic model for avoiding the selfishness.

Fig. 3 shows the simulation results for packet delivery ratios as the rate of CBR traffic of source nodes varies. It is observed that when CBR source generates more than 15 packets in one second, the packet delivery ratio start decreasing. . This is due to fact that when there are more cooperative nodes they might deviate from strategy F to strategy TFT to save their energy since forwarding of more packets consume more energy. Therefore cooperative nodes are supposed to be acting as selfish. Further, Packet delivery ratio for AODV decreases faster as the CBR increases compared to AODV with game theoretic model. It works efficiently in the heavy loaded network as compared to the original AODV in the presence of selfish nodes.

Fig. 4 shows the simulation results for packet delivery ratio as the percentage of selfish nodes and cooperative nodes varies in a network. The percentage of selfish nodes in the network is varied from 0 to 70%. The CBR for this simulation is 10 packets. It is observed that the packet delivery ratio for both strategy F and TFT is 0.90 and for AODV is 0.80 when none of the node is acting as a selfish node. Further, the packet delivery ratio of cooperative nodes decreases proportionally when the number of selfish nodes increases. This is happening because of two facts. First, as the number of selfish nodes increases, the total number of packets being dropped increases proportionally. Second, it decreases as the repeated route request is fired and the overheads for searching the alternative route are increased. Compared with the original AODV, the game theoretic modeled AODV protocol works better in situations where the selfishness among nodes is increasing. For example, there are 70% nodes are selfish, the game theoretic modeled AODV protocol delivers about 58% of the data traffic, while the original AODV protocol can only deliver 12%.

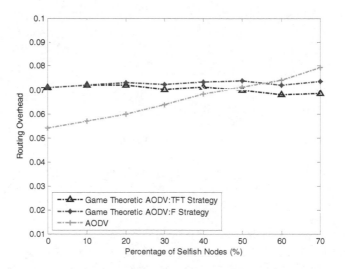

Fig. 5. Routing overhead for the different number of selfish nodes

Fig. 5 shows the simulation results for the routing overhead of the game theoretic modeled AODV for the different percentage of selfish nodes and cooperative nodes in the network. The percentage of selfish nodes in the network is varied from 0 to 70%. The CBR for this simulation is 10 packets. It is observed that the routing overhead increases to 7% approximately for the game theoretic modeled AODV while in the case of original ADOV it is 5.5% when no node is acting as selfish node. The routing overheads for the game theoretic modeled AODV increases very slowly with the increase of selfish nodes. While the routing overheads for the original AODV increases faster. This is due to fact that repeated route request are fired for route establishment and overheads are incurred in searching the alternative routes. For example when there are 70% selfish nodes, the overheads for the original AODV are 8.0%. While for the game theoretic modeled AODV protocol, it is only 7.5% since in the original AODV, the nodes do not implement the cooperation mechanisms.

5   Conclusion

We have studied how game theoretic model can help for selfish node avoidance routing by enforcing cooperation among selfish nodes. A mathematical framework for rational node that maximizes its credits has been presented. To enforce cooperation among the selfish nodes, two trigger strategies are used; game theoretic model with F (forward) and with TFT (Tit For Tat). Further, to explore the usability of this model simulations are carried out using NS-2. From the simulation results, the following observations are made: The gap between packet delivery ratio of the two cooperative nodes strategies increases with the increase in number of routes. This is happening since increase the level of retaliation situations in TFT strategies. The game theoretic modeled with AODV achieves higher packet delivery ratio for heavy traffic network in the presence of selfish nodes as compared to the original AODV. The packet delivery ratio of cooperative nodes decreases proportionally when the number of selfish nodes increases. This is happening because of two facts - first, the number of selfish nodes increases as the total number of packets being dropped increases, and second, firing of repeated route requests and overheads for searching the alternative route. The implementation of game theoretic modeled with AODV results in low routing overheads.

References

1. Aggelou, G.: Mobile Ad Hoc Networks: from wireless LANs to 4G networks. Tata McGraw-Hills (2009)
2. Yang, J., Klein, A.G., Richard Brown III, D.: Natural Cooperation in Wireless Networks. IEEE Signal Processing Magazine 26(5), 98–106 (2009)
3. Song, C., Zhang, Q.: Protocol for stimulating packet forwarding in wireless ad hoc networks. IEEE Wireless Communication 17(5), 50–55 (2010)
4. Srinivasan, V., Nuggehalli, P., Chiasserini, C.F., Rao, R.R.: Cooperation in Wireless Ad Hoc Networks. In: IEEE INFOCOM, vol. 2, pp. 808–817 (March 2003)

5. Jaramillo, J.J., Srikant, R.: A game theory based reputation mechanism to incentivize cooperation in wireless ad hoc networks. Ad Hoc Networks 8(4) (June 2010)
6. Felegyhazi, M., Hubaux, J.-P., Buttyan, L.: Nash equilibria of packet forwarding strategies in wireless ad hoc networks. IEEE Trans. Mobile Computing 5, 463–476 (2006)
7. Liu, F., Dong, R., Liu, J., Xu, X.: A Reputation Mechanism to Stimulate Node Cooperation in Ad Hoc Networks. In: Third International Conference on Genetic and Evolutionary Computing (2009)
8. Michiardi, P., Molva, R.: CORE: a collaborative reputation mechanism to enforce node cooperation in mobile ad-hoc networks. In: Proceedings of the 6th IFIP Conference on Security Communications, and Multimedia, pp. 1–15. CMS (2002)
9. Anantvalee, T., Wu, J.: Reputation-based System for Encouraging the Cooperation of Nodes in Mobile Ad Hoc Networks. In: IEEE International Conference on Communications (2007)
10. Jerzy, K., Rafal, O.: A framework for detection of selfishness in multihop mobile ad hoc networks. Journal of Telecommunications and Information Technology (2), 34–40 (2009)

Performance Evaluation of VANET Using Realistic Vehicular Mobility

Nidhi and D.K. Lobiyal

School of Computer and Systems Sciences,
Jawaharlal Nehru University, New Delhi-110067, India
nnidhi.malhotra@gmail.com, dkl@mail.jnu.ac.in

Abstract. Vehicular Ad-hoc Networks (VANETs) is attracting considerable attention from the research community and the automotive industry to improve the services of Intelligent Transportation System (ITS). As today's transportation system faces serious challenges in terms of road safety, efficiency, and environmental friendliness, the idea of so called "ITS" has emerged. Due to the expensive cost of deployment and complexity of implementing such a system in real world, research in VANET relies on simulation. This paper attempts to evaluate the performance of VANET in a realistic environment. The paper contributes by generating a real world road Map of JNU using existing Google Earth and GIS tools. Traffic data from a limited region of road Map is collected to capture the realistic mobility. In this work, the entire region has been divided into various smaller routes. Vehicular Traffic Flow on these routes has been created using MOVE. The traffic flow generator model of MOVE generates traces of the traffic flow. These traces of different traffic scenario are subsequently used in NS-2 which facilitated the simulation of traffic flow of region under study. The realistic mobility model used here considers the driver's route choice at the run time. Finally, the performance of the VANET is evaluated in terms of average delivery ratio, packet loss, and router drop as statistical measures. The maximum average delivery ratio for varying number of vehicles is observed to be very high as compare to the packet loss. Overall, this experiment has provided insight into the performance of real life vehicular traffic communication.

Keywords: Intelligent Transportation System, Vehicular Ad-hoc Networks, Geographical Information System, Mobility Model Generator for Vehicular Networks, Simulation of Urban Mobility, Network Simulator-2.34.

1 Introduction

As per the World Health Organization (WHO) statistics, more than 1.3 million people worldwide are estimated to be killed each year out of road accidents. According to an online article published in Deutsche Welle [1] by Murali Krishnan dated 29.04.2010, "India's record in deaths has touched a new low, as toll rose to at least 14 deaths per hour in 2009 against 13 the previous year". While trucks/lorries and two-wheelers were responsible for over 40% deaths, the rush during afternoon and evening hours

N. Meghanathan et al. (Eds.): CCSIT 2012, Part I, LNICST 84, pp. 477–489, 2012.
© Institute for Computer Sciences, Social Informatics and Telecommunications Engineering 2012

were the most fatal phases.[1,2]. Also, as per another article of WHO (article in Times of India, Dipak Kumar Dash, TNN, Aug 17, 2009, 04.10am IST) India leads the world in road deaths. In addition to this, some of the common problems to tackle with are the "Miles of Traffic Jam" on highway and the "Search for best Parking Lot" in an unknown city.

For all the above mentioned reasons, the Government and Automotive Industries today pay lot of attention towards traffic management and regulation of a smooth traffic. They are investing many resources to slow down the adverse effect of transportation on environment, thereby increasing traffic efficiency and road safety. The advancements in technology, in the areas of Information and Communications, have opened a new range of possibilities. One of the most promising areas is the study of the communication among vehicles and Road Side Units (RSUs), which lead to the emergence of Vehicular Network or Vehicular Ad-hoc Network (VANET) into picture. [3].

VANET is characterized as a special class of Mobile Ad hoc Networks (MANETs) which consists of number of vehicles with the capability of communicating with each other without a fixed infrastructure. The goal of VANET research is to develop a vehicular communication system to enable 'quick' and 'cost-efficient' transmission of data for the benefit of passenger's safety and comfort. Due to the expensive cost of deploying and complexity of implementing such a system in real world, research in VANET relies on simulation. However, the simulation depends on the mobility model that represents the movement pattern of mobile users including its location, velocity and acceleration over time. A mobility model needs to consider the characteristics of the real world scenario either by a real world MAP obtained from TIGER(Topologically Integrated Geographic Encoding and Referencing) database from U.S. Census Bureau or by taking Satellite images of Google Earth into consideration to simulate a realistic network.

VANET is the ultimate solution to the cooperative driving between communicating cars on road. It has particular features like "decentralized and self-organized network", composed of high speed moving vehicles. Here the vehicular speed and distribution of data are constrained by the underlying dynamic network topology. [4]

Related work is briefly described in Section 2. In Section 3, the methodology of proposed work is explained along with various tools which are used to carry out the work. Section 4 further discusses the simulation of established network, results & the analysis obtained through simulations conducted. Finally, Section 5 concludes the work presented in this paper..

2   Related Work

Research is being carried out in the field of VANET such as Analyzing data dissemination in VANETs, Identifying and studying routing protocols in VANET in terms of highest delivery ratio and lowest end-to-end delay etc. The issues of Security and Privacy also demands great attention. The study of Mobility Models and their realistic vehicular model deployment is a challenging task.[8] Random way Point(RWP)[9] is an earlier mobility model widely used in MANET in which nodes move freely in a predefined area but without considering any obstacle in that area. However, in a VANET environment vehicles are typically restricted by streets, traffic light and obstacles. GrooveSim [10] was the first tool for forecasting vehicular traffic flow and evaluating vehicular performance. It gives a traffic simulator environment which is easy to use for generating real traffic scenario for evaluation. But it fails to include network simulator as it was unable to create traces for network. David R. Choffnes et al. [11] proposed a mobility model named STRAW (Street RAndom Waypoint). This model has taken real map data of US cities and considered the node (vehicle) movement on streets based on this map. This model also has the functionality to simplify the traffic congestion by controlling the vehicular mobility. But still it lacks overtaking criteria that cause convey effect in street as it considered random method which is not realistic. Kun-chan Lan et al.[6] describes a realistic tool MOVE for generating realistic vehicular mobility model. It is built on top of an open source micro-traffic simulator SUMO and its output is a realistic mobility model that can immediately be used by popular network simulators such as ns-2 and qualnet.

3   Proposed Work and Methodology

To evaluate the performance of VANET, there is a need to deploy a real world scenario with all the vehicular constraints. In this paper the experiment was performed by taking a limited bounded region of a real world scenario i.e. "JAWAHARLAL NEHRU UNIVERSITY (JNU), NEW DELHI, INDIA" into consideration. The steps to implement a VANET simulation in this region are as follows:

- Generation of JNU Map
- Creation of Vehicular Traffic flow on this Map
- Simulation of established Network

The detailed procedure in implementing such above mentioned steps are explained in the rest of this paper.

3.1   JNU Map Generation

For creating a real world Map of JNU, Some of the existing tools have been used such as Google Earth, ArcGIS 9 (ArcMap version 9.1), MOVE Simulator (v 2.81)[5,6] and Adobe Dreamweaver CS4.

Satellite image of JNU has been taken from Google Earth shown in Figure 1. This image was further imported into ArcGIS 9 as depicted in Figure 2.

ArcGIS is basically a suite consisting of a group of Geographic Information System (GIS) software products.[12]

NOTE: Google Earth gives latitude and longitude of a particular location whereas ArcGIS maps those latitudes and longitudes to the required coordinate plane with the desired origin in a Two Dimensional Space.

Some of the 2-D Co-ordinates of this Map were not lying in the first quadrant of the 2-D Co-ordinate plane. In order to obtain all the co-ordinates in the first quadrant, the origin was shifted to an appropriate location. Shifting of the old Co-ordinates (x, y) to a new origin (h, k) is given by :

$$X = x + h; \quad Y = y + k ;$$

Where (X,Y) represents the translated Co-ordinates in the plane with new origin which is further used as the inputs to the Map Node Editor of MOVE Simulator as shown in Figure 3. After creating nodes using Map Node editor, numbers of parameters are defined such as edges between nodes, number of lanes, speed and priority of roads on which vehicle move, with the help of Road Editor of MOVE simulator as shown in Figure 4. Here, a multi-lane scenario of two lanes with 75% road priority has been set. The threshold speed has been considered for each lane in a region of JNU Map as 40m/s. Next a connection was established between nodes via edges by writing an XML code (**.con.xml**)[16] using Dreamweaver CS4. Finally the nodes, edges and connection files are configured into **.net.xml** by using NETCONVERT to create the MAP. Figure 5 depicts the JNU Map created by the above defined tools.

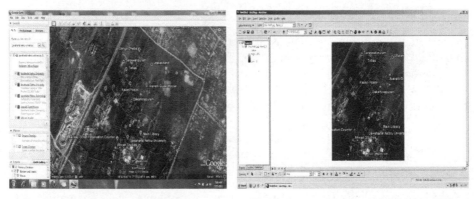

Fig. 1. Satellite Image of JNU   **Fig. 2.** Imported Image of JNU in ArcGIS

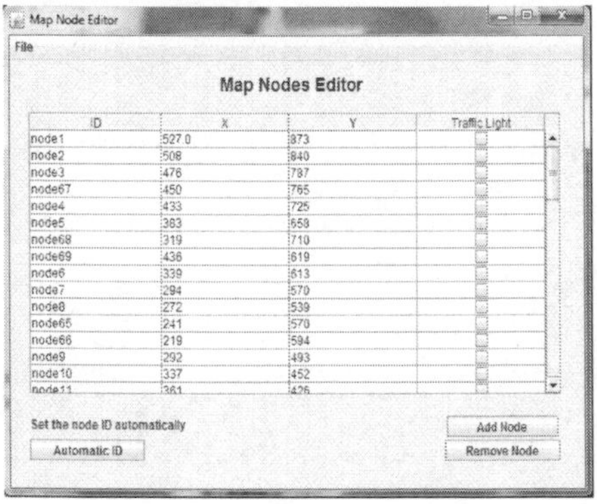

Fig. 3. Map Node Editor of MOVE 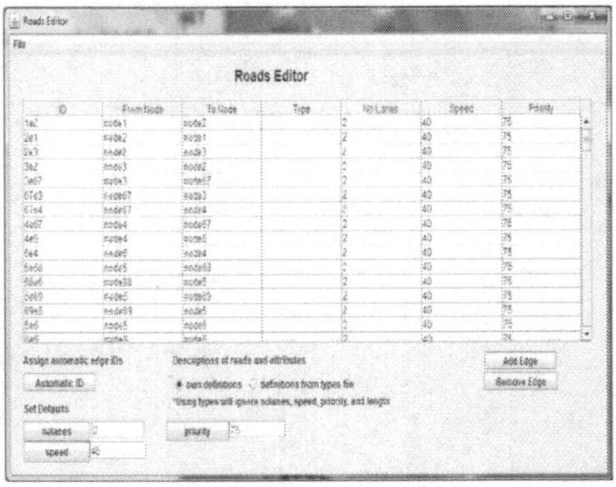   **Fig. 4.** Road Editor of MOVE

3.2   Traffic Flow

For generating a vehicular traffic flow on the above created Map, SUMO 0.12.3[17] simulator has been used in addition to MOVE simulator. Initially, the Route File in XML (**rou.xml**) was created, in which acceleration, deceleration, maximum speed, length and type of a vehicle were specified (see Table 1). In addition to this, the bounded JNU region has been divided into 36 smaller routes which the vehicles can take. Further, the departure time of a particular vehicle on a particular route which creates the vehicular traffic flow among the nodes has been specified. The vehicle's destination from the source and their turning directions at the intersections, such as right turn, left turn and straight as per their destination were also set as per the driver's route choice at intersection.

Table 1. Types of Vehicle and their Characteristics

Vehicle Type	Max.Acc. (m/s^2)	Max.Dec. (m/s^2)	Length (m)	Max. Speed (m/s)	Sigma
Car A	3.0	6.0	5.0	30	0.5
Car B	2.0	6.0	7.5	30	0.5
Car C	1.0	5.0	5.0	20	0.5
Car D	1.0	5.0	7.5	10	0.5

Different Route files have been created for varying traffic flow consisting of 20,40,60,80,100,120,140,160,180 vehicles. This varying flow has been set by keeping in mind, a constant deceleration and acceleration model in which vehicles do not move and stop abruptly. Map file (.net.xml) and the different Route files (rou.xml) of varying traffic flow were configured to create the corresponding trace files (**sumo.tr**) which can be visualized using SUMO simulator. These trace files basically shows the JNU Map as shown in Figure 5 and the flow of traffic as depicted in Figure 6. After setting the parameters of SUMO, the real world scenario of JNU region can be visualized with vehicles moving on it as depicted in Figure 6 (a), (b) & (c).

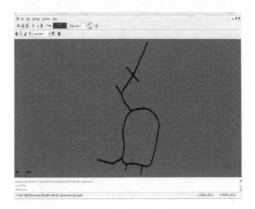

Fig. 5. SUMO visualization of JNU Map

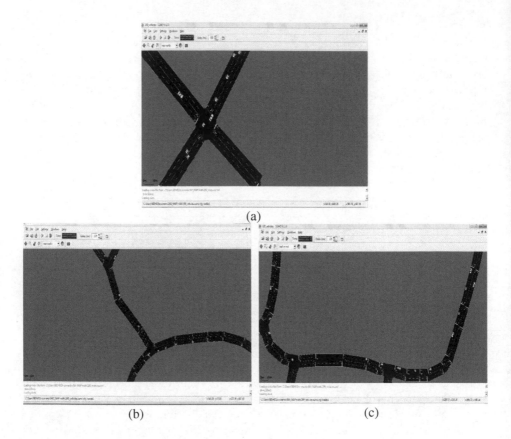

Fig. 6. (a) Vehicular Traffic at intersection, (b) and (c) Traffic Flow

4   Simulation

In order to simulate the established network, communication was established among the vehicular traffic flow, using Traffic Model Generator of MOVE and Network Simulator (NS2.34) [18].

The Traffic Model generator of MOVE simulator was used to create the **trace file** of the vehicular flow, by interfacing traffic flow created in section 3.2 with the JNU MAP created in section 3.1. The output was a trace file that contains the information of realistic vehicular flow of the map, which can be further used in NS2.

Various parameters were considered for establishing the communication among vehicles. For example, a vehicular traffic flow was deployed using 802.11 Ad-Hoc radio mode with transmission range of 250 meters. The other parameters used are discussed in Table 2.

Table 2. Network parameters

Parameters	Values
Channel Type	Wireless Channel
Propagation Model	Two Ray Ground Model
Network Interface Type	Wireless Phy
MAC Type	802.11
Interface queue	DropTail/Pri Queue
Link Layer Type	LL
Anetnna	Omni Antenna
Ifqlen	50
Varying No. of Nodes	20,40,60,80,100,120,140,160,180
Routing Protocol	AODV
Topology (X,Y) Co-ordinates	(659, 911)
Transmit Power, Pt	0.2818
Channel Frequency	2412e+6
RXThresh	3.65262e-10
CSThresh	(Expr 0.9 * RXThresh)

As mentioned above, the simulation was conducted using NS2. The simulation covers 600349 m^2 area and the following parameters has been setup for traffic flow between nodes.

Table 3. Parameters of Traffic Flow between nodes

Parameters	Values
Agent	UDP
Packet_size	1000
Application_Traffic	CBR
CBR Rate	64kbps
CBR_max_pkts	2280000
CBR interval	0.05micro sec
Different RNG seed	2,4,6,8,10

After setting up the network and traffic flow as discussed above, the simulation was conducted by taking 3 CBR's at three different nodes for a traffic scenario of 20 vehicles initially. Further, all the traffic parameters as given in table 3 were kept constant for varying traffic of 40, 60, 80,100,120, 140,160 and 180 vehicles.

4.1   Simulation Results

The impact of realistic vehicular mobility (using various tools as discussed in Section 3), on the performance of ad-hoc routing protocols has been evaluated in this section.

The driver route choice behavior has been simulated in a real world, where all possible routes from the source to destination are defined and the driver needs to decide about which route has to be taken from among all possible routes at any intersection. Our simulation concentrates on selecting the probability of choosing a route at the intersection. This probability directly determines the number of vehicles on a particular route. The data in terms of packets are transmitted to facilitate communication among vehicles. In order to study the behavior of communication, the parameters like delivery ratio, packet loss and router drop has been considered which are discussed in the subsequent sections.

4.1.1   Average Delivery Ratio
Delivery Ratio implies the ratio of number of packets successfully delivered to the number of packets sent.

For calculating delivery ratio with respect to the number of vehicles, different traffic scenarios were simulated with varying number of vehicles in multiples of 20. For each scenario, delivery ratio was calculated for 5 simulation runs by changing the seed in multiples of 2. The Average delivery ratio for each scenario was an average of 5 simulation runs and it is calculated as follows:

$$APR = \left(\sum_{k=1}^{5} PR \text{ for seed } (2k)\right)/5$$

$$APS = \left(\sum_{k=1}^{5} PS \text{ for seed } (2k)\right)/5$$

$$ADR \% = (APR/APS) * 100$$

Where, PR = Packet Received, PS = Packet Sent, APR = Average Packet Received and APS = Average Packet Sent.

The summary of results obtained is shown in table 4 and the results are further analyzed graphically in figure 7. It can be observed that the choice of route at intersection points can significantly affect the simulation results.

Table 4. Number of Traffic and Avg. Delivery Ratio (ADR) %

Vehicular Traffic	ADR %
20	96.6%
40	91.9%
60	91.3%
80	98.5%
100	95.5%
120	93.5%
140	96.7%
160	73.3%
180	95.9%

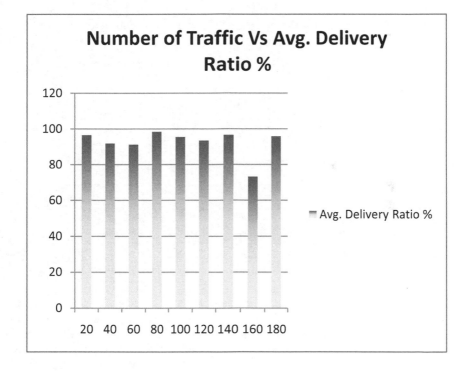

Fig. 7. Number of Traffic Vs Avg. Delivery Ratio%

4.1.2   Router Drop

Router Drop for each traffic scenario is calculated by taking the average of Router Drop to the packets sent with the multiples of seed values as shown below :

$$RD\ \% = \left(\sum\nolimits_{k=1}^{5} \frac{RD}{PS} \text{ for seed 2k}\right) * 100$$

Where, RD % = Router Drop %

4.1.3   Packet Loss

Packet loss is calculated by taking the average of packet loss to the packets sent with the multiples of seed values :

$$PL = \sum_{k=1}^{5}(PS - PR) \text{for seed 2k}$$

$$PL\ \% = \left(\sum\nolimits_{k=1}^{5} \frac{PL}{PS} \text{ for seed 2k}\right) * 100$$

Where, PL = Packet Loss.

The results obtained for Router Drop and Packet Loss are summarized in table 5 for varying vehicular traffic. This is further illustrated in figure 8.

Table 5. (Number of vehicular traffic) Vs (Router Drop and Packet Loss%)

No. of Vehicles	RD %	PL %
20	3.39%	3.39%
40	8.24%	8.12%
60	8.61%	8.61%
80	1.49%	1.40%
100	4.59%	4.54%
120	6.57%	6.50%
140	3.52%	3.33%
160	26.72%	26.68%
180	4.23%	4.01%

Our Simulation results suggest that increasing number of vehicular traffic may deteriorate packet transmission rate as in case of node 160 shown in Figure 7. This happens due to the random collision of packets. Further, it was observed that this scenario was not linearly increasing or decreasing since the collision of packets completely depends on the routes taken into consideration by the driver at run time. Packet delivery ratio was always more than 90% except for 160 nodes where the packet delivery ratio was observed to be as 73.3%. This phenomenon can be explained by deployment and movement of vehicles in a given scenario. It seems that the connectivity between the vehicles get reduced for this scenario.

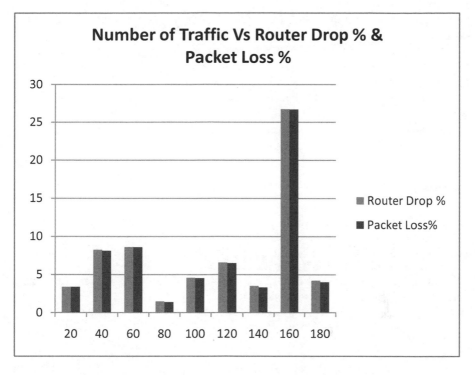

Fig. 8. Vehicular Traffic Vs (Router Drop% & Packet Loss%)

Figure 8 shows the effect of varying number of vehicles on packet loss and router drop together. A packet may be dropped by a vehicle or by a router. The packet loss percentage is considered as packets dropped by vehicles. Further in figure 8, it is quite evident that the percentage of packet loss was slightly more than router drops. This happens because of higher chances of packet being dropped at the end rather than being dropped at intermediate nodes. Here, again from the figure, it is quite evident that both the packet loss and router drops were below 10% except in the case of 160 nodes. As explained for the case of lower deliver ratio in Figure 7, the drop rate was higher due to low connectivity.

5   Conclusion

In this paper, we have obtained an in-sight idea of simulating real world scenario of VANET. As it is not easy to deploy and implement such a complicated system in real world before knowing the impact of all parameters used in VANET, a small real world area i.e. our University, JNU itself, was taken into consideration, for studying the impact of mobility in the VANET. Traffic movement has been deployed across the area under consideration using one of the realistic vehicular mobility models. The behavior of this network was simulated using NS2 to study the impact of driver's choice on packet transmission over V2V communication using AODV routing protocol and IEEE 802.11 standard.

The performance of the network has been evaluated by taking delivery ratio, packet loss and router drop as statistical measures. The average delivery ratio for various scenarios such as varying number of vehicles with constant power transmission range of 250m and frequency of 2.4GHz was observed to be 92.57% whereas packet loss was 7.39%. It is concluded from the results that with the increase in transmission range, there would be a corresponding marginal increase in delivery ratio and decrease in packet loss.

References

1. DW World-de: Deutsche Welle,
   http://www.dw-world.de/dw/article/0,5519345,00.html
2. Khairnar, V.D., Pradhan, S.N.: Comparative Study of Simulation for Vehicular Ad-hoc Network. IJCA (0975 – 8887) 4(10) (August 2010)
3. Olariu, S., Weigh, M.C.: Vehicular Networks, from theory to practice. Chapman & Hall/CRC computer and information science series (2009)
4. Huang, C.M., Chen, J.L., Chang, Y.C.: Telematics Communication Technologies and Vehicular Networks: Wireless Architectures and Applications. Information Science Reference, New York (2010)
5. Lan, K.C., Chou, C.M.: Realistic mobility models for Vehicular Ad hoc Network (VANET) simulations. In: 8th IEEE International Conference, pp. 362–366. ITS Telecommunication (2008)
6. Paier, A., Bernadó, L., Karedal, J., Klemp, O., Kwoczek, A.: Overview of vehicle-to-vehicle radio channel measurements for collision avoidance applications. In: 71st IEEE Vehicular Technology Conference, VTC Spring, Taipei (2010)
7. David, B., David, A.: Dynamic source routing in ad hoc wireless networks. Mobile Computing 35, 153–181 (1996)
8. Sichitiu, M., Kihl, M.: Inter-vehicle communication systems: a survey. IEEE Communications Surveys & Tutorials 10(2), 88–105 (2008)
9. David R.C., Fabián E.B.: An integrated mobility and traffic model for vehicular wireless networks. In: 2nd ACM International Workshop on Vehicular Ad Hoc Networks (VANET), Cologne, Germany (2005)
10. GIS Tutorial: How to Use ArcMap 9.1,
    http://www.trincoll.edu/depts/cc/documentation/GIS/
    HowToArcMap.pdf
11. Kim, J., Sridhara, V., Bohacek, S.: Realistic mobility simulation of urban mesh networks. Ad Hoc Networks (2008)
12. Djenouri, D., Nekka, E., Soualhi, W.: Simulation of Mobility Models in Vehicular Ad hoc Networks. In: 1st ICST on Ambient Media and Systems (Ambi-sys), Quebec, Canada (2008)
13. Härri, J., Filali, F., Bonnet, C.: Mobility Models for Vehicular Ad Hoc Networks: A Survey and Taxonomy, Technical Report RR-06-168, Institut Eurecom (2007)
14. Harold, E.R.: XML Bible, 2nd edn. Hungry Minds Inc. (2001)

15. SourceForge.net:sumo, Main Page,
    `http://sourceforge.net/apps/mediawiki/sumo/`
    `index.php?title=Main_Page`
16. Pall, K., Vardhan, K.: The ns Manual (formerly ns Notes and Documentation),
    `http://www.isi.edu/nsnam/ns/doc/ns_doc.pdf`
17. Härri, J., Fiore, M., Filali, F., Bonnet, C.: A Realistic Mobility Simulator for Vehicular Ad
    Hoc Networks, Technical Report RR-05-150, Institut Eurecom (2007)
18. XML Tutorial, `http://www.w3schools.com/xml/`
19. Preuss, M., Thomas, S.: Wireless, mesh & ad hoc networks; Military convoy location and
    situation awareness. In: IEEE Sarnoff Symposium, pp. 1–5 (2008)
20. Gainaru, A., Dobre, C., Cristea, V.: A Realistic Mobility Model Based on Social Networks
    for the Simulation of VANETs. In: 69th IEEE Vehicular Technology Conference, pp. 1–5
    (2009)
21. David, R.C., Fabián, E.B.: An integrated mobility and traffic model for vehicular wireless
    networks. In: 2nd ACM International Workshop on Vehicular Ad Hoc Networks (2005)
22. Meyer, H., Cruces, O.T., Hess, A., Hummel, K., Ordinas, J.M.B., Casetti, C.E., Karlsson,
    G.: VANET Mobility Modeling Challenged by Feedback Loops. In: 10th Annual Mediter-
    ranean Ad Hoc Networking Workshop (2011)
23. Sommer, C., Dietrich, I., Dressler, F.: Realistic Simulation of Network Protocols in
    VANET Scenarios. In: 26th IEEE INFOCOM, Mobile Networking for Vehicular Envi-
    ronments (MOVE), Poster Session, Anchorage, Alaska, USA (2007)
24. Xu, Y., Wu, Y., Wu, G., Xu, J., Liu, B., Sun, L.: Data Collection for the Detection of Ur-
    ban Traffic Congestion by VANETs. In: IEEE Services Computing Conference (APSCC),
    Asia-Pacific, December 6-10, pp. 405–410 (2010)
25. Mahajan, A., Potnis, N., Gopalan, K., Wang, I.A.: Urban Mobility Models for VANETs.
    In: 2nd IEEE (2006)
26. Hartenstein, H., Laberteaux, K.P.: VANET: Vehicular Applications and Inter-Networking
    Technologies. JohnWiley & Sons Ltd. (2010)
27. Kone, V.: Data Dissemination in Vehicular Networks,
    `http://www.cs.ucsb.edu/~vinod/docs/vinod_mae.ppt`
28. The Network Simulator- ns-2, `http://isi.edu/nsnam/ns/`

Ensuring Data Confidentiality and Privacy
in Mobile Ad Hoc Networks

Hamza Aldabbas[1], Helge Janicke[1], Radwan AbuJassar[2], and Tariq Alwada'n[1]

[1] Software Technology Research Laboratory (STRL), De Montfort University,
Leicester, United Kingdom
{hamza,heljanic,tariq}@dmu.ac.uk
[2] School of Computer Science and Electronic Engineering, University of Essex, Essex
{rabuja}@essex.ac.uk

Abstract. Mobile *ad hoc* networks (MANETs) are autonomous systems which are comprised of a number of mobile nodes that communicate between themselves by wireless communication in a peer-to-peer basis. They are self-organized, self-configured and self-controlled infrastructure-less networks. Nodes can communicate with each other without any pre-planned or a base station. Disseminating information securely between these nodes in such networks however is a challenging task, particularly when the information is confidential. Revealing such information to anyone else other than the intended nodes could be highly damaging, especially in military applications where keeping the message secret from adversaries is essential. In this paper we present our novel framework for privacy control in mobile *ad hoc* networks in which privacy policies are attached to messages as they are send between peers. We evaluate our framework using the Network Simulator (NS-2) to provide and check whether the privacy and confidentiality of the originator are met. For this we implemented the privacy enforcement as an NS2 agent that manages and enforces the policies attached to packets at every node in the MANET.

Keywords: MANETs, Policy Enforcement Point(PEP), Policy decision Point(PDP) and Discretionary Access Control (DAC).

1   Introduction

Recently, mobile *ad hoc* networks received extensive attention in both industrial and military applications, because of the striking property of creating a network while moving from one place to another and it does not require any pre designed infrastructure. The key challenges in designing (MANETs) come from the decentralised nature, self-organisation, and self-management, since the opportunity of the node movement is very high. On top of that, all communications are carried out through wireless medium in short-range communication. These unique characteristics present some security issues for (MANETs), so there have been concerted efforts by the research community [13,3,14] in message encryption, digital signature, key management etc. Many challenges especially related to the privacy of originator issues however remain to be solved.

N. Meghanathan et al. (Eds.): CCSIT 2012, Part I, LNICST 84, pp. 490–499, 2012.
© Institute for Computer Sciences, Social Informatics and Telecommunications Engineering 2012

These existing approaches in security which have been applied to MANETs such as access control, digital signature, and encryption focused only in securing the channel, however how these nodes act after these mechanisms is left.

In this paper we provide a review of the security issues in MANET and survey existing solutions for this problem and to highlight a particular area which has not been addressed up to now which is controlling the information flow in mobile ad hoc networks, and to provide an architecture that allows the policy-based control the dissemination of data that is communicated between nodes, in order to ensure that data remains confidential not only during transmission but also after it has been communicated to another peer, to keep message contents private to an originator defined subset of nodes in the MANET.

We will overview the characteristics in MANETs in Section 2, and focus on security issues in Section 3. In Section 4 we present the state of the art work on securing (MANETs) to which we relate our proposed policy-based architecture and the algorithim chart in Section 5, then the discussion will be presented in section 6. The paper concludes in section 7 where we summarise our findings and outline our future work in this area.

2   Characteristics of MANET

A mobile *ad hoc* network (MANET) is an independent system of mobile nodes linked by wireless connections. These nodes are thus free to move arbitrarily; therefore, the topology of wireless networks can be changed swiftly and in an unpredictable manner. MANETs have therefore many characteristics that make them are distinguished from other wireless and wired networks [1,9,12,4] which in detail are:

1. **Constrained Resources:** In general, most MANET devices are small handheld devices like personal digital assistants (PDAs), laptops and cell phones. These devices indeed have limitations because of their restricted nature battery-operated, small processing and storage facilities.
2. **Infrastructure less(Autonomous):** MANETs are created based on the teamwork between independent nodes, peer-to-peer nodes that need to communicate with each other for some aim. Without any pre-planned or base station.
3. **Dynamic Topology:** MANET nodes can move arbitrarily; thus the nodes can be dynamically inside and outside the network, continually changing its links and topology, leads to change in the routing information all the time due to the movement of the nodes. Consequently, the communicated links between nodes could be bi-directional or unidirectional.
4. **Limited Physical Security:** MANETs are in general more vulnerable to physical layer's attacks than wired network; the possibility of spoofing, eavesdropping, jamming and denial of service (DoS) attacks should be carefully considered. However the self-administration nature of MANET makes them more robust against single failure points.
5. **Short Range Connectivity:** MANETs rely on radio frequency (RF) technology to connect, which is in general considered to be short range communication. For that reason, the nodes that want to communicate directly need to be in the close

frequency range of each other. In order to tackle this limitation, multi-hop routing mechanisms have therefore to be used to link remote nodes through intermediary ones that operate as routers.

3 Network Security

The distinctive characteristics of MANETs bring a new set of essential challenges to security design, these challenges noticeably make the looking for security solutions that perform both data protection and applicable network performance are required [11]. Normally while we addressing the network security, we have to consider the security requirements to take account of the functionality required to provide a secure networking system.

3.1 Security Requirements

The security requirements specified below specified by International Telecommunications Union (ITU-T) represented in their recommendation X.805 and X.800 [8,7,11]:

1. **Authentication:** Authentication is very important to verify the identity of each node in MANET and its eligibility to access the network. This means that, nodes in MANETs are required to verify the identities of the communicated entities in the network, to make sure that these nodes are communicating with the correct entity.

2. **Authorisation and Access Control:** Each node in MANET is required to have the access to shared resources, services and personal information on the network. In addition, nodes should be capable of restricting each other from accessing their private information. There are many techniques that can be used for access control such as Discretionary Access Control (DAC), Mandatory Access Control (MAC) and Based Access Control (RBAC).

3. **Privacy and confidentiality:** Each node has to secure both the information that is exchanged between each other; and secure the location information and the data stored on these nodes. Privacy means preventing the identity and the location of the nodes from being disclosed to any other entities, while confidentiality means keeping the secrecy of the exchanged data from being revealed to those who have not permission to access it.

4. **Availability and survivability:** The network services and applications in MANET should be accessible, when needed, even in the presence of faults or malicious attack such as denial-of-service attack (DoS). While survivability means the capability of the network to restore its normal services under such these conditions. These two requirements should be supported in MANET.

5. **Data integrity:** The data transmitted between nodes in MANET should be received to the intended entities without been tampered with or changed by unauthorised modification. This requirement is essential especially in military, banking and aircraft control systems, where data modification would make potential damage.

6. **Non-repudiation:** This ensures that nodes in MANET when sending or receiving data-packets should not be able to deny their responsibilities of those actions. This

requirement is essential especially when disputes are investigated to determine the misbehaved entity. Therefore digital signature technique is used to achieve this requirement to prove that the message was received from or sent by the alleged node.

4   State of the Art

Existing approaches in security which have been applied to MANETs. For example, traditional cryptographic solutions are using public key certificates to maintain trust, in which a Trusted Third Party (TTP) or Certificate Authority (CA) certifies the identity associated with a public key of each communicated entities, therefore they can provide end-to-end secure communication channels. These approaches mainly focused on message confidentiality, integrity and non-repudiation, they do not consider however the trust management of the communicated entities, and how these certified entities act is left to the application layer [2]. Lidong Zhou et al [14] studied the security threats, variabilities and challenges which faces the ad hoc network, in their work they protected the packets sent between nodes by choosing the secure routing path to the destination node based on the redundancies routes between nodes to maintain the availability requirement, because of all key based cryptographic approaches such as digital signature needs a proper and secure key management scheme to bind between the public and private keys to the nodes in the network; Lidong Zhou used replication and new cryptographic technique (threshold cryptography) [6,5] to build a secure key management process to achieve the trust between a set of servers in ad hoc networks by distributing trust among aggregation of nodes to certify nodes are trustworthy.

Securing the routing in mobile ad hoc network has also given much interest by the researchers; therefore many approaches have been proposed to cope with external attack. Sirios and Kent [10] proposed an approach to protect the packet sent to multi receivers by using keyed one-way hash function supported by windowed sequence number to ensure data integrity . The trust issue systems like in mobile ad hoc network is a challenging task to achieve. Whilst Public Key Infrastructure (PKI) and cryptography are achieving kind of a quasi-trust before the communication is start. However how the nodes act after that will be controversial issue as you cannot predict who is going to be un trusted node only on the behaviour without using a tracing technique to prove some nodes are misbehaving in the network and thus they are un trusted anymore.

In our work we show how disclosing private information by a malicious node (inside the network) to unauthorised nodes will cause a fatal problem and data will be leaked. Therefore traditional encryption tools are widely used in security systems and it solved part of the problem by encrypting data exchanged between entities by encrypting in the public key of the destination node and then decrypting the packet by the destination's private key but how the distination behave after is left. However, using the mechanisim which using the access control to ensure confidentiality is still not been used, so our work intend to use access control mechanism especially Discretionary Access Control (DAC) to ensure data confidentiality and privacy of the originator node in MANETs.

5   Our Proposed Framework

5.1   Scenario

Protecting a message sent in wireless network such as in mobile *ad hoc* networks (MANETs) is a very difficult task. For example, in military alliance where some armies want to share tactical mission information only between themselves and not with other coalition members.

Considering three nodes A,B,C in Figure 1, where node A and B are allocated to British and US armies, and C is allocated to Afghan army. Node A wants to send a tactical message for the mission that says "'we are going to start the mission after 8 pm'" to node B, however node A does not want node B send the message to nodeC because node C is not trusted by A. How can node A trust node B not to send the message to node C?

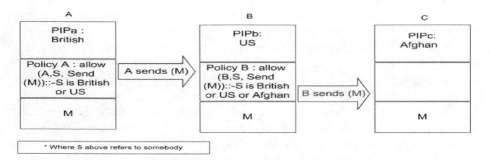

Fig. 1. node B disclose the message to C

Node A sends the message (M) to node B, node B now knows the message (M). However depend on its policy node B can send the message (M) and disclose it to node C. Which it is the problem of the node A privacy.

The goal of our proposed approach is to solve this problem by allowing the originator to specify a high level policy which will automatically apply and enforce itself to all the communicated entities on the network. This is done by attaching the policy of the originator (A) with the message (M) to control the access to it, which is capable to define who are allowed to access that message. In this way the policy of node A attached with the message (M), tells node B to which node can the message (M) be send to (only British or US armies can receive the message) as in Figure 2 :

Node A sends the message (M) + policy of node A which tells node B to allow sending the message (M) to any node if its British or US nodes. Here after node A sent the message (M) to node B attached by the node A policy. node B receives the packet and now knows the message (M) in addition of that it knows the policy of A':

Allow (Node B, Send(M) to S: if S is British or US, where S refers to somebody.

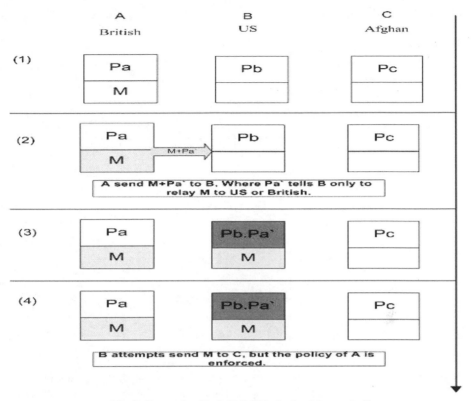

Fig. 2. Prevention Node B Of Disclosing M to node C

5.2   Our Framework

Figure 3 presents the proposed framework, where policies are used to enforce access control to such information sent by the originator to other entities in the system, our framework will be introduced in every entity in the communicated systems.

Our framework is composed of four components as they shown in the Figure 3:

1. policy enforcement point (PEP/OUT): executes and enforces policy decisions in the sender node, this component installed at the transmitter interface that does merge system's policy with the message sent to others systems. In our simulation we configured the send function to achieve the functionalities of this component.
2. policy enforcement point (PEP/IN): executes and enforces policy decisions in the receiver node, this component installed at the receiving interface that does inverse process at the receptive system, splitting and dividing the message from the policy attached. In our simulation we configured the receive function to achieve the functionalities of this component.
3. Policy decision point (PDP): plays a crucial role in both the sender and the receiver side in our framework, and helping other components to do their jobs. In our simulation we configured this function at the source to achieve the functionalities of this component.

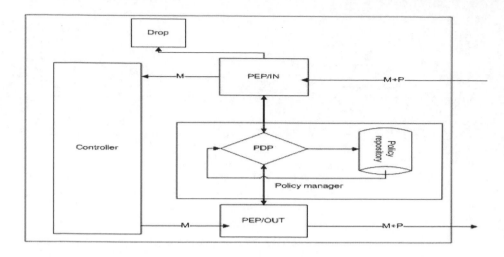

Fig. 3. The proposed framework

4. controller that process and store the information received from the other components.

In the Figure 4 we show an example of six nodes, assuming that each node in the system has a grouipid number, that means we are classifying the nodes in our work into different groups, which in such case are three groups: groupid1, groupid2, groupid3. The first group has n0,n2,n4 and n5. where as n1 and n3 are in groupid3 and groupid3 respectively. In our work we make n0 broadcast a message to all nodes in the groupid which specified in the policy file at file0.txt in node n0, and we call this grouipid in this situation is permitted group as shown in the algorithm chart in Figure 5. If file0.txt as in the example has 1 that means only nodes in the groupid1 can recieve the pkt.

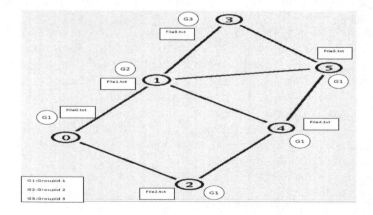

Fig. 4. Example illustrating the Algorithim chart

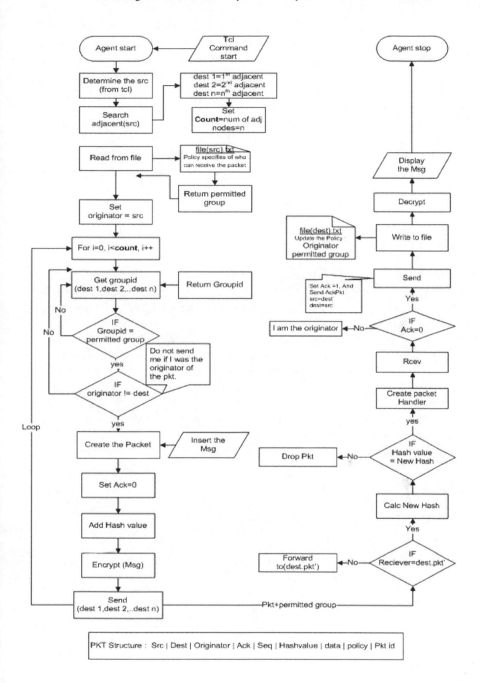

Fig. 5. Our Chart Algorithim and packet structure

Then n0 will start searching for the adjacent nodes in the range. In this example n0 will find n1 and n2. dest1=n1 dest2=n2. Now n0 will check if the dest1 in the permitted group or not and do the same to dest2 also. In the algorithm chart this depicted as Getgroupid (dest) process and check If groupid=permitted group or not. In this example it will be yes for n2 as n2 in the groupid1. n0 will send to n2 not only the pkt it also sends his policy which existed in file0.txt, where as n2 will create a packet handler to recieve the pkt, once it recieved the policy of n2 will be updated according to policy of n0 and deletes it's old policy becuasue it is the originator policy.

Now, when n2 at another time wants to broadcast the message again will start and do the same process like in n0, however this time n2 will send to n4 but not to n0 becasue n0 is the originator of the pkt as shown in the algorithm chart in Figure 5, and the system will continue in the same steps for other nodes.

6   Result and Discussion

In this work we used the Network Simulator (NS2) which is a real network environment simulator, which showed only intended nodes can recieve the packet which has been sent by the source. We simulated our approach into multi variable number of nodes where the originator node disseminate the packet(Data+Policy) to the other nodes. Our result from the tracing file and the nam showed that only nodes in the permitted groupid can recieve the packet, because of the restriction which has issued from the originator node 'not to send the packet to nodes in different groupid '.

We simulated our agent with the vary number of UDP agents together to check what if all agents are started in the simulation and how that will be affect the time taken for a packet to be transmitted across a network from source to destination. In Figure 6 we measured the delay time versus number of cbr traffics which depicted on the y-axis and x-axis respectively, the result of this figure showed that as the the number of cbr traffic

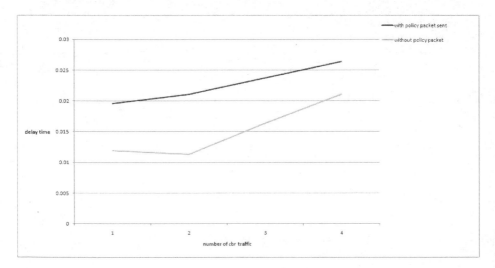

Fig. 6. Delay time

increase, the delay time of both agents will increase, we started with 1 cbr traffic, 2 3 and 4 with and without our agent be started at different sources and destinations to measure the average of the delay time between them.

7 Conclusion

In this paper we concluded that our framework acheived the source policy to send the packet for intended nodes only in the network, on top of that we highlighted the special considerations for security in MANETs and provided an extensive overview of related work and the state of the art in this area. To our knowledge, none of the related work addressed the issue of controlling the information flow in mobile *ad hoc* Networks. We presented a scenario drawn from the military domain, where the impact of this form of confidentiality breach is evident and a real risk. We provided an architecture that addresses this problem by automatically attaching policies to the messages that identify how the information can be used by the receiver, thus limiting the relay of messages based on the originator's confidentiality requirements.

References

1. Al-Jaroodi, J.: Security issues at the network layer in wireless mobile ad hoc networks at the network layer. Tech. rep., Faculty of Computer Science and Engineering, University of Nebraska-lincoln, Nebraska, USA (2002)
2. Blaze, M., Feigenbaum, J., Lacy, J.: Decentralized trust management. In: Proceedings of 1996 IEEE Symposium on Security and Privacy, pp. 164–173. IEEE (1996)
3. Burbank, J., Chimento, P., Haberman, B., Kasch, W.: Key challenges of military tactical networking and the elusive promise of manet technology. IEEE Communications Magazine 44(11), 39–45 (2006)
4. Chadha, R., Kant, L.: Policy-driven mobile ad hoc network management. Wiley-IEEE Press (2007)
5. Desmedt, Y., Frankel, Y.: Threshold Cryptosystems. In: Brassard, G. (ed.) CRYPTO 1989. LNCS, vol. 435, pp. 307–315. Springer, Heidelberg (1990)
6. Desmedt, Y.: Threshold cryptography. European Transactions on Telecommunications 5(4), 449–458 (1994)
7. Li, W., Joshi, A.: Security Issues in Mobile Ad Hoc Networks-A Survey (2008)
8. Menezes, A., Van Oorschot, P., Vanstone, S.: Handbook of applied cryptography. CRC (1997)
9. Murthy, C.S.R., Manoj, B.: Ad Hoc Wireless Networks: Architectures and Protocols. Prentice Hall PTR, Upper Saddle River (2004)
10. Sirois, K., Kent, S.: Securing the nimrod routing architecture. In: SNDSS, p. 74. IEEE Computer Society (1997)
11. Stallings, W.: Cryptography and Network Security: Principles and Practice, 4th edn. Pearson Education (2005)
12. Toh, C.: Maximum battery life routing to support ubiquitous mobile computing in wireless ad hoc networks. IEEE Communications Magazine 39(6), 138–147 (2001)
13. Yang, H., Luo, H., Ye, F., Lu, S., Zhang, L.: Security in mobile ad hoc networks: challenges and solutions. IEEE Wireless Communications 11(1), 38–47 (2004)
14. Zhou, L., Haas, Z.: Securing ad hoc networks. IEEE Network 13(6), 24–30 (1999)

Hiding Sensitive Association Rules without Altering the Support of Sensitive Item(s)

Dhyanendra Jain[1,*], Pallavi Khatri[1], Rishi Soni[1], and Brijesh Kumar Chaurasia[2]

[1] Institute of Technology and Management-Gwalior, (M.P.), India
[2] ITM University, Gwalior, (M.P.), India
{dhyanendra.jain,rishisoni17,bkchaurasia_itm}@gmail.com,
pallavi_magic@yahoo.com

Abstract. Association rule mining is an important data-mining technique that finds interesting association among a large set of data items. Since it may disclose patterns and various kinds of sensitive knowledge that are difficult to find otherwise, it may pose a threat to the privacy of discovered confidential information. Such information is to be protected against unauthorized access. Many strategies had been proposed to hide the information. Some use distributed databases over several sites, data perturbation, clustering, and data distortion techniques. Hiding sensitive rules problem, and still not sufficiently investigated, is the requirement to balance the confidentiality of the disclosed data with the legitimate needs of the user. The proposed approach uses the data distortion technique where the position of the sensitive items is altered but its support is never changed. The size of the database remains the same. It uses the idea of representative rules to prune the rules first and then hides the sensitive rules. Advantage of this approach is that it hides maximum number of rules however, the existing approaches fail to hide all the desired rules, which are supposed to be hidden in minimum number of passes. The paper also compares of the proposed approach with existing ones.

Keywords: Privacy preserving data mining, Association rule, Association rule hiding.

1 Introduction

Data mining is the knowledge discovery process of finding the useful information and patterns out of large database. In recent times data mining has gained immense importance as it paves way for the management to obtain hidden information and use them in decision-making. While dealing with sensitive information it becomes very important to protect data against unauthorized access [1], [2]. A key problem faced is the need to balance the confidentiality of the disclosed data with the legitimate needs of the data users. In doing this it becomes necessary to modify the data value(s) and relationships (Association Rules). Obtaining a true balance between the disclosure and hiding is a tricky issue [2], [4]. This can be achieved largely by implementing hiding of rules that

---

* Corresponding author.

N. Meghanathan et al. (Eds.): CCSIT 2012, Part I, LNICST 84, pp. 500–509, 2012.
© Institute for Computer Sciences, Social Informatics and Telecommunications Engineering 2012

expose the sensitive part of the data. One such method is hiding of association rule because association amongst the data is what is understood by most of the data users.

Such vulnerability of association rule posses' a great threat to the data if the data is in hands of a malicious user.

To prevent data from being misused two common strategies exist. First strategy alters the date before delivering it to the data miner [3]. Second strategy releases only a subset of the complete data using distributed databases approach.

Algorithms have been proposed in the literature for hiding of rules. The proposed algorithms are based on modifying the database transactions so that the confidence of the rules can be reduced. Hiding association rule by using support and confidence is discussed in [3], basically this approach algorithm hides a specific rule while association rule mining [4] algorithm hide rules with respect to sensitive item(s) either on the left or on the right of the rule. However, these approaches fail to hide all the desired rules, which are supposed to be hidden in minimum number of passes.

In this paper, we propose strategies and a suit of algorithms for privacy preserving and hiding knowledge from data by minimal perturbing values. The proposed approach uses the data distortion technique where the position of the sensitive item(s) is altered but its support is never changed however the size of the database remains the same. The proposed heuristics use the idea of representative rules to prune the rules first and then hides the sensitive rules. This approach results in a significant reduction of the number of rules generated, while maintaining the minimum set of relevant association rules and retaining the ability to generate the entire set of association   rules with   respect   to   the   given constraints [1], [2]. Advantages of the proposed approach is that the support of the sensitive item(s) is neither increased nor decreased as done in existing approaches and the size of the database is kept same while the previous approaches either increase or decrease the size of the database. Support of the sensitive item(s) is kept same and simply its position have been changed i.e. it is being deleted from one transaction and added to some other transaction in which it does not exist. Another advantage of this approach is that it hides maximum number of rules in minimum number of alterations in the database. An algorithm is also proposed for this work and demonstrated by example. The proposed approach is compared with previously existing approaches [5].

The rest of the paper is organized as follows. Section 2 describes the association rule mining. In section 3, the association rule is described. Problem definition is given in section 4. Proposed scheme is presented in section 5. The scheme is evaluated through simulation and results are in section 6; section 7 concludes the work.

2   Association Rule Mining

Let $I = \{i_1, i_2, \ldots\ldots i_m\}$ be a set of m distinct literals, called items. Given a set of transactions D, where each transaction T is a set of items such that $T \subseteq i$. An association rule is an implication of the form $X \rightarrow Y$ where $X \subset I, Y \subset I$ and

$X \cap Y = \phi$ X and Y are called antecedent/body and consequent /head of the rule respectively [6].

Strength of a rule whether it is strong or not is measured by two parameters called support and confidence of the rule. These two parameters help in deciding the interestingness of a rule [5], [7].

For a given rule $X \Rightarrow Y$

Support is the percentage of transaction that contains both X and Y or $X \cup Y$ is the proportion of transactions jointly covered by the LHS and RHS and is calculated as:

$$S = |X \cup Y|/|N|$$

Where, N is the number of transactions.

Confidence is the percentage for a transaction that contains X also contains Y or is the proportion of transactions covered by the LHS that are also covered by the RHS and is calculated as

$$C = |X \cup Y|/|X|$$

For the database given in Table1, with a minimum support of 33% and minimum confidence 70% following nine association rules could be found:

$$C \Rightarrow A(66.667\%, 100\%), A, B \Rightarrow C(50\%, 75\%),$$

$$B \Rightarrow C, A(50\%, 75\%), C, B \Rightarrow A(50\%, 100\%),$$

$$C => A, B\ (50\%, 75\%), C, A => B\ (50\%, 75\%),$$

$$B => C\ (50\%, 75\%), C => B\ (50\%, 75\%),$$

$$B => A\ (66.667\%, 100\%)$$

Table 1. Set of transactional data

TID	ITEMS
T1	ABC
T2	ABC
T3	ABC
T4	AB
T5	A
T6	AC

3   Representative Association Rule

Generally, number of association rules discovered in a given database is very large. It is observed that a considerable percentage of these rules are redundant and useless. A user should be presented with all of them, which are original, novel and interesting. To address this issue, [6] introduced a notion for concise (loss less) representation of association rules, called representative rules (RR). RR is a least set of rules that allow deducing all association rules without accessing a database. In a notion of cover operator was introduced for driving a set of association rules from a given association rule. The cover C of the rule $X => Y$, $Y \neq \phi$ is defined as follows:

$$C(X => Y) = \{X \cup Y => V/Z, V \subseteq Y \text{ and } Z \cap V = \phi \text{ and } V \neq \phi\}$$

Each rule in $C(X => Y)$ consists of a subset of items occurring in the rule $X => Y$. The number of different rules in the cover of the association $X => Y$ is equal to $3^m - 2^m, m = |Y|$.

In general, the process of generating representative rules may be decomposed in to two sub-processes: frequent item-sets generations and generation of RR from frequent item-sets. Let Z be a frequent itemset and $\phi \neq X \subset Z$. The association rule $X => Z/X$ is representative rule if there is no association rule $(X => Z'/X)'$ where $Z \subset Z'$, and there is no association rule $(X' => Z/X')$ such that $X \supset X'$. Formally, a set of representative rules (RR) for a given association rules (AR) can be defined as follows:

$$RR = \{r \in AR / \neg \exists r' \in AR, r \neq r' \text{ and } r \in C(r')\}$$

Each rule in RR is called representative association rule and no representative rule may belong in the cover of another association rule [8], [9].

4   Problem Definition

The expression 'Data Mining' indicates a wide range of tools and techniques to extract useful information, which can be sensitive (interesting rules) from a large collection of data. Objective of this work is to propose a new strategy to avoid extraction of sensitive data. Data should be manipulated /distorted in such a way that sensitive information cannot be discovered through data mining techniques. While dealing with sensitive information it becomes very important to protect data against unauthorized access. The key problem faced is the need to balance the confidentiality of the disclosed data with the legitimate needs of the data users. The proposed algorithm are based on modifying the data base transaction, so that, the confidence of the rules can be reduced for this both the approaches either pros or cons the support of the item.

Following section proposes a algorithm for hiding the sensitive rules (sensitive rules are those rules that contain sensitive item(s)).

5   Proposed Algorithm

In order to hide an association rule a new concept of '*not altering the support*' of the sensitive item(s) has been proposed in this work. Based on this strategy an algorithm has been proposed .in this assumed that a set of sensitive item(s) is passed and the proposed algorithm distorts the original database such that sensitive rules cannot be discovered through Association Rule Mining algorithms.

Input to proposed algorithm is a database, min_supp, min_conf, and a sensitive item(s) H(each sensitive item in H is represented by h) to be hidden and the goal is to distort the database D such that no association rules containing $h \in H$ either on the left or on the right can be discovered.

ALGORITHM:
```
Input
        (1)  A source database D
        (2)  A min_support.
        (3)  A min_confidence.
        (4)  A set of sensitive items H.

Output
      A transformed database D' where rules containing H
on RHS/LHS will be hidden
1.    Find all large itemsets from D;
2.    For each sensitive item h∈H   {
3.    If h is not a large itemset then H=H-{h};
4.    If H is empty then EXIT;
5.    Select all the rules containing h and store in U
                        //h can either be on LHS or RHS
6.    Select all the rules  from U with h alone on LHS
7.    Join RHS of selected rules and store in R;
                        //make representative rules
8.    Sort R in descending order by the number of sup-
      ported items;
9.    Select a rule r from R
10.   Compute confidence of rule r.
11.   If conf>min_conf then   {
                //change the position of sensitive item h.
12.   Find T₁={t in D|t completely supports r ;
13.   If t contains x and h then
14.   Delete h from t
15.   Else
16.   Go to step 19
17.   Find  T₁ ={t in D|t does not support LHS(r)  and
      partially supports x;
18.      Add h to t
19.      Repeat
20.      {
21.              Choose the first rule from R;
22.              Compute confidence of r ;
23.      } Until(R is empty);
```

```
24.        }                        //end of if conf>min_conf
25.        Update D with new transaction t;
26.        Remove h from H;
27.        Store U [i] in R;    //if LHS (U) is not same
28.        i++, j++;
29.        Go to step 7;
30.        }//end of for each h∈H
```

Output updated   as the transformed database   Proposed algorithm selects all the rules containing sensitive item(s) either in the left or right. Then these rules are represent in representative rules (RR) format. After this a rule from the set of RR's, which has sensitive item on the left of the RR is selected.

Now delete the sensitive item(s) from the transaction that completely supports the RR i.e. it contained all the items in RR selected and add the same sensitive item to a transaction which partially supports RR i.e. where items in RR are absent or only one of them is present.

For example in Table1 at a *min_supp of 33% and a min_conf* of 70 % and sensitive item $H=\{C\}$, choose all the rules containing 'C' either in RHS or LHS

$$C \Rightarrow A(66.667\%,100\%), A, B \Rightarrow C(50\%,75\%),$$

$$B \Rightarrow C, A(50\%,75\%), C, B \Rightarrow A(50\%,100\%),$$

$$C => A, B (50\%,75\%), C, A => B (50\%,75\%),$$

$$B => C (50\%,75\%), C => B (50\%,75\%),$$

and represent them in representative rule format.

Like $C \rightarrow A$ and $C \rightarrow B$ can be represented as $C \rightarrow AB$

Now delete C from a transaction where A, B and C are present and add C to a transaction where both of them (A and B) are either absent or only one of them is present. If transaction T_1 is modified to AB and transaction T_5 is modified to AC then the rules that will be hidden are:

$$C \rightarrow B, C \rightarrow A, C \rightarrow AB, B \rightarrow C, AB \rightarrow C, B \rightarrow AC, \text{and } AC \rightarrow B$$

i.e. seven rules out of eight rules containing sensitive item(s) are hidden.

6   Results and Analysis

We performed our experiments on a Intel PIV workstation with 1.8 GHz processorand with 512 MB RAM, under Microsoft Windows-xp operating system using α-minor tool. To demonstrate the working of the above algorithm for hiding sensitive items the following section shows some results.

6.1 For a given database in Table1 with a minimum support of 33% and minimum confidence of 70% we hide 7 rules out of 8 rules containing sensitive item(s), if transaction T_1 is changed to **AB** and transaction T_5 is changed to **AC**. This has been discussed in above section of the paper.

6.2 For database in Table1. if **H={B}** i.e. if sensitive item is **B** and the rule which is to be hidden is $B => C$ $(B => A \text{ and } B => C$ represented as $B => AC)$ then change transaction T_1 to **AC** and transaction T_5 to **AB**.

6.3 For a database given in Table2 with a minimum support of 33% and minimum confidence of 70% following association rules are mined:

$$A => B, A => C, B => C, B => A, C => A, C => B,$$

$$AD => C, CD => A$$

Select the rules containing sensitive items either in the LHS or in the RHS

$$A => C, B => C, B => A, C => A, C => B, AD => C, CD => A$$

Representation of rules in representative rule format is:

$$C => A, \text{ and } C => B \text{ can be represented as } C => AB$$

Delete **C** from a transaction in which **A** and **B** are present and add it in a transaction where both **A** and **B** are absent or only one of them is present

This results in modification of the database by changing the transaction T_2 to **ABD** and transaction T_5 to **CDE**.

Out of 6 rules containing sensitive items all of them are hidden.

6.4 Similarly for database in Table 2. if **H={B}** i.e. and the rule which is to be hidden is $B => C (B => A \text{ and } B => C$ represented as $B => AC)$ if sensitive item is **B** then change transaction T_2 to **ACD** and transaction T_5 to **BDE**.

Out of 4 rules containing sensitive items all of them are hidden.

6.5 Analysis: This section analyzes some of the characteristics of the proposed algorithm and it is compared with the existing algorithms.

First characteristic of proposed algorithm as described in previous section of the paper is that support of the sensitive item is not changed. The position of the sensitive item is changed only. This characteristic is demonstrated with examples in previous section and is summarized in Table 3 and 4.

The second characteristic we analyze is the efficiency of the proposed algorithm with previous approaches.

For proposed algorithm, the number of DB scans required for Table1 are 4 and number of rules pruned are 7.

Table 2. Set of transactional data

TID	ITEMS
T1	ABC
T2	ABCD
T3	BCE
T4	ACDE
T5	DE
T6	AB

Table 3. Database before and after hiding C and D

TID	D	$D_1(C$ sensitive$)$	$D_2(B$ sensitive$)$
T1	ABC	AB	AC
T2	ABC	ABC	ABC
T3	ABC	ABC	ABC
T4	AB	AB	AB
T5	A	AC	AB
T6	AC	AC	AC

Table 4. Database before and after hiding C and B

TID	D	$D_1(C$ sensitive$)$	$D_2(B$ sensitive$)$
T_1	ABC	ABC	ABC
T_2	ABCD	ABD	ACD
T_3	BCE	BCE	BCE
T_4	ACDE	ACDE	ACDE
T_5	DE	CDE	BDE
T_6	AB	AB	AB

In [3] algorithm DB scans are 4 and number of rules pruned are 0. For Wang's approach DB scans are 3 and number of rules pruned are 2. This characteristic is summarized in Table5 and the same characteristics for the database of Table2 is summarized in Table6 and it is clear from both the tables that the proposed algorithm prunes more number of rules in the same number of DB scans[3].

One of the reasons that the existing approaches fail is that the approach in tries to hide every single rule from a given set of rules without checking if some of the rules could be pruned after changing some transactions of all.

Approach in hides only those rules, which has sensitive item either in the right or in the left. It runs two different algorithms depending on the position of the sensitive item(s) (whether it is antecedent or consequent). This approach also fails to hide more number of rules.

Table 5. Database scans and rules pruned in hiding item *C* using proposed algorithm

	DB scans	Rules Pruned	
		Table1	Table2
Proposed algorithm	4	7	6
ISLF	3	2	3
[3] Dasseni *et al.*	4	0	1

Table 6. Database scans and rules pruned in hiding item *B* using proposed algorithm

	DB scans	Rules Pruned	
		Table1	Table2
Proposed algorithm	4	6	4
ISLF	3	2	2
[3] Dasseni *et al.*	4	1	1

However, proposed approach hides almost all the rules, which contain sensitive item(s) (either on the left or on the right[11], [12],[13], [14] and [15].

7   Conclusion

In this paper, we presented the threats to database privacy and security challenges due to rapid growth of data mining. An algorithm for this is also been proposed which is based on modifying the database transactions so that the confidence of the sensitive rules can be reduced but without altering the support of the sensitive item, which is in contrast with previous algorithms, which either decrease or increase the support of the sensitive item to modify the database transactions. The efficiency of the proposed approach is compared with the existing approaches. It is observed that number of DB scans required by proposed approach is same as in approach in and one more than the approach used in but it prunes almost all the desired rules which previous approaches fail to do.

References

1. Verykios, V.S., Elmagermld, A.K., Bertino, E., Saygin, Y., Dasseni, E.: Association Rule Hiding. IEEE Transactions on Knowledge and Data Engineering 6(4) (2004)
2. Wang, S.-L., Lee, Y.-H., Billis, S., Jafari, A.: Hiding sensitive items in privacy preserving association rule mining. In: IEEE International Conference on Systems, Man and Cybernetics, vol. 4, pp. 3239–3244 (2004)
3. Dasseni, E., Verykios, V.S., Elmagarmid, A.K., Hwang, J.: Hiding association rules by using confidence and support. In: Moskowitz, I.S. (ed.) IH 2001. LNCS, vol. 2137, pp. 369–383. Springer, Heidelberg (2001)
4. Verykios, V.S., Elmagarmid, A.K., Elisa, B., Elena, D., Saygin, Y.: Association Rule Hiding. IEEE Transactions on Knowledge and Data Engineering, 434–447 (2000)
5. Wang, S.-L., Jafari, A.: Using unknowns for hiding sensitive predictive association rules. In: IEEE International Conference on Information Reuse and Integration, pp. 223–228 (2005)
6. Agrawal, A., Thakar, U., Soni, R., Chaurasia, B.K.: Efficiency Enhanced Association Rule Mining Technique. In: Nagamalai, D., Renault, E., Dhanushkodi, M. (eds.) PDCTA 2011. CCIS, vol. 203, pp. 375–384. Springer, Heidelberg (2011)
7. Saygin, Y., Verykios, V.S., Clifton, C.: Using unknowns to prevent discovery of association rules. ACM SIGMOD Record 30(4), 45–54 (2001)
8. Huang, Y., Lu, Z., Hu, H.: A method of security improvement for privacy preserving association rule mining over vertically partitioned data. In: 9th International Database Engineering and Application Symposium, pp. 339–343 (2005)
9. Saygin, Y., Verykios, V.S., Elmagarmid, A.K.: Privacy preserving association rule mining. In: IEEE Proceedings of the 12th Int'l Workshop on Research Issues in Data Engineering, pp. 151–158 (2002)
10. Evfimievski, A., Srikant, R., Agrawal, R., Gehrke, J.: Privacy preserving mining of association rules. In: Proc. of the 8th ACM SIGKDD Int'l. Conference on Knowledge Discovery and Data Mining, Edmonton, Canada (2002)
11. Agrawal, R., Srikant, R.: Privacy preserving data mining. In: ACM SIGMOD Conference on Management of Data, Dallas, Texas, pp. 439–450 (2000)
12. Agrawal, R., Imielinski, T., Swami, A.: Mining Association Rules Between Sets of ITEMS in Large Databases. In: Proceedings of ACM SIGMOD International Conference on Management of Data, Washington, D.C., pp. 207–216 (May 1993)
13. Sun, D., Teng, S., Zhang, W., Zhu, H.: An Algorithm to Improve the Effectiveness of Apriori. In: The 6th IEEE Int. Conf. on Cognitive Informatics (ICCI 2007), pp. 385–390 (2007)
14. Ping, D., Yongping, G.: A New Improvement of Apriori Algorithm for Mining Association Rules. In: The International Conference on Computer Application and System Modeling (ICCASM 2010), pp. 529–532 (2010)
15. Lu-Feng, W.: Association Rule Mining Algorithm Study and Improvement. In: The 2nd International Conference on Software Technology and Engineering (ICSTE), pp. 362–364 (2010)

Dependable Solutions Design by Agile Modeled Layered Security Architectures

M. Upendra Kumar[1,*], D. Sravan Kumar[2], B. Padmaja Rani[3], K. Venkateswar Rao[4],
A.V. Krishna Prasad[5], and D. Shravani[6]

[1] CSE JNTUH and CSE MGIT, Hyderabad, A.P., India
uppi_shravani@rediffmail.com
[2] CSE KITE WCPES, Hyderabad, A.P., India
dasojusravan@gmail.com
[3] CSE JNTU CEH, Hyderabad, A.P., India
padmaja_jntuh@yahoo.co.in
[4] CSE JNTU CEH, Hyderabad, A.P., India
Kvenkateswarrao_jntuh@rediffmail.com
[5] S.V. University Tirupathi, A.P., India
kpvambati@gmail.com
[6] Rayalaseema University, Kurnool, A.P., India
sravani.mummadi@yahoo.co.in

Abstract. Our research entitled "Designing Dependable Agile Layered Security Architecture Solutions" addresses the innovative idea and novel implementations of Security Engineering for Software Engineering using Agile Modeled Layered Security Architectures for Dependable Privacy Requirements, with a validation of an exemplar case study of Web Services Security Architectures. Securing the Software Architecture in any application at design phase is known as Security Architectures, and we focus on authentication and authorization of the user. Now a day most of the applications are developed as a Layered Security Architecture Pattern, typically we have user presentation layer, Business Logic Layer and Database access layer. Now Agile modeling is used in all applications design (but Agile Modeled Architectures are given little importance) because of shortened developed time, with customer collaborations with developers and importantly with Test Driven Development approaches. Securing Agile Modeled architectures, which being an iterative development, will provide enhanced Dependable Security Requirements in terms of Privacy of user, in its successive iterations. All this research paves a way for Secure Web Engineering.

Keywords: Security Architectures, Agile Modeling, Layered Pattern, Designing Solutions, Dependable Privacy Requirements, Web Services.

---

* Corresponding author.

N. Meghanathan et al. (Eds.): CCSIT 2012, Part I, LNICST 84, pp. 510–519, 2012.

1   Research Methodology for Designing Dependable Agile Layered Security Architecture Solutions—Web Services Case Study

This paper discusses the latest and advantages in secure software development process in an early stage. The primary focus is on security considerations early in the life cycle, i.e. at the system architecture stage, which has the potential to improve the requirements engineering in software system. The ultimate goal is to have a better quality product. Initially we discuss about the Research Methodology for Designing Dependable Agile Layered Security Architecture Solutions. Later on we discuss about dependability of data and application layers by Agile Modeled Security Architectures, validated with a case study of Web Services Security Architectures.

Research on Security Architectures. Software Engineering covers the definition of processes, techniques and models suitable for its environment to guarantee quality of results. An important design artifact in any software development project is the Software Architecture. Software Architectures important part is the set of architectural design rules. A primary goal of the architecture is to capture the architecture design decisions. An important part of these design decisions consists of architectural design rules. In a Model Driven Architecture (MDA) context, the design of the system architecture is captured in the models of the system. MDA is known to be layered approach for modeling the architectural design rules and uses design patterns to improve the quality of software system. And to include the security to the software system, security patterns are introduced that offer security at the architectural level. More over, agile software development methods are used to build secure systems. There are different methods defined in agile development as eXtreme Programming (XP), scrum, Feature Driven Development (FDD), Test Driven Development (TDD), etc. Agile processing includes the phases as Agile Analysis, Agile Design, and Agile Testing. These phases are defined in layers of MDA to provide security at the Modeling level which ensures that, "Security at the system architecture stage will improve the requirements for that system".

Research Problem Statement. Our research entitled "Designing Dependable Agile Layered Security Architecture Solutions" addresses the innovative idea of Security Engineering for Software Engineering using Agile Modeled Layered Security Architectures for Dependable Privacy Requirements with a validation of case study of Web Services Security Architectures. The key research questions addressed are: How a failure addresses a specific security service at a specific layer impact other (interdependent) layers? Also how successful implementation of a security service had an affect on the rest of the system? [2] How can agile methods be used to generate effective security requirements? In what ways do these agile methods change the development of security requirements? How is the outcome of emergent security development different from more traditional forms? [3]

Organization of Research Methodology. First, we introduce to secure software engineering, security architectures design and development, introduction and overview of research title, software security architecture using Model Driven Architecture, Agile Methods, Case study of Web Services Security Architectures are discussed so that the problem statement can be designed. Second, a detailed literature survey was conducted on Secure Software Engineering, Model Driven Architecture, Agile methodology, Security Patterns for Agile Layered Security Architectures, UML 2.0, and Secure UML, Web Services Security Architectures, to find out basis for the thesis. Third, we design Agile Modeled Layered Security Architectures, with validations of case study for Web Services Security Architectures, with a initial case study validations using on simple secure Web Services Design using Agile Modeled Test Driven Development. Fourth, we design solutions using Agile Modeling for Layered Security Architectures with case study of Web 2.0 Services Security Architectures and its implementations. Fifth, Dependability (regarding Privacy requirements) Agile Modeled Layered Security Architectures with a case study of Web Services Security architectures are done, with implementation of a financial application for Secure Stock Market using Web Services.

2   Dependable Solutions Design by Agile Modeled Layered Security Architectures

Software Architecture: An important design artifact in any software development project, with the possible exception of very small Projects, is the Software Architecture. An important part of any architecture is the set of Architectural Design Rules. Architectural Design Rules are defined as the rules, specified by the architect(s) that need to be followed in the detailed design of the system. A primary role of the architecture is to capture the architectural design decisions. An important part of these design decisions consists of architectural design rules.

Security: Security ensures that information is provided only to those users who are authorized to possess the information. Security generally includes the following:

Identification: This assumes that system must check whether a user really is whom he or she claims to be. There are many techniques for identification and it is also called as authentication. The most widely used is "Username/Password" approach. More sophisticated techniques based on biometrical data are like retinal fingerprint scan.

Authorization: This means that the system should provide only the information that the user is authorized for, and prevent access to any other information. Authorization usually assumes defining "user access rights", which are settings that define to which operations, data, or features of the system the user, does have access.

Encryption: This transforms information so that unauthorized users (who intentionally or accidentally come into its possession) cannot recognize it.

Model Driven Architecture: Model-Driven Development (MDD) is a modeling approach. The basic premise of Model-Driven Development is to capture all important design information in a set of formal or semiformal models, which are kept consistent automatically. To realize full benefits of MDD, formalize architecture design rules, which then allow automatic enforcement of architecture on the system model. There exist several approaches to MDD, such as OMG's (Object Management Group) MDA (Model-Driven Architecture), Domain Specific Modeling (DSM), and Software factories fro Microsoft. Model-Driven Architecture prescribes that three models or sets of models shall be developed as:

The Computationally Independent Model(s) (CIM) captures the requirements of the system.

The Platform-Independent Model(s) (PIM) captures the systems functionality without considering any particular execution platform.

The Platform-Specific Model(s) (PSM) combines the specifications in the PIM with the details that specify how the system uses a particular type of platform. The PSM is a transformation of the PIM using a mapping either on the type level or at the instance level.

MDA does not directly address architectural design or how to represent the architecture, but the architecture has to be captured in the PIM or in the mapping since the CIM captures the requirements and the PSM is generated from the PIM using the mapping.

Agile Methods: Over the past few years, a new family of software engineering methods has started to gain acceptance amongst the software development   community. These   methods, collectively called Agile Methods, conform to the Agile Manifesto, which states "We are uncovering better ways of developing software by doing it and helping others does it. Through this work we have come to value: Individuals and interactions over processes and tools working software over comprehensive documentation customer collaboration over contract negotiation responding to   change over following a plan That is, while there is value in the items on the right, we value the items on the left more." The individual agile methods include Extreme Programming (XP), Scrum, Lean Software Development, Crystal Methodologies, Feature Driven Development (FDD), and Dynamic Systems Development Methodology (DSDM). While there are many differences between these methodologies, they are based on some common principles, such as short development iterations, minimal design up-front,   emergent design and architecture, collective code ownership and ability for anyone to change any part of the code, direct communication and minimal or no documentation (the code is the documentation),   and gradual building of test cases. Some of these practices are in direct conflict with secure SDLC processes.

Security Requirements: Agile information systems and software methods are characterized by nimbleness to rapid changes, multiple incremental iterations and a fast development pace. Agile development is defined as a set of principles and practices that differs as a whole from traditional planned development. The major principles for agile information systems and software methods include:

Accept multiple valid approaches: A stable architecture, a tool orientation and component based development combine to enable a "fluid view" of methodology and the value of tailoring the methodology for each development project. Improvisation in development approach will help match the methodology to the constraints of the project environment. Engage the customer: Close involvement of customers in the project enables accurate and fast requirements elicitation, and the customers again immediate satisfaction as their ideas and requirements arise in each new release.

Accommodate requirements change: Agility means that developers quickly and easily respond to the shifting requirements driven by the changing environment for which the software is intended. Build on successful experience: The "right" people are important for project success in order to foster innovation in software development. Courage, specific knowledge, intelligence, and commitment are needed for agile development. Develop good teamwork: The right mix of people operating with the right process framework means that the right mix of knowledge and working style will be present in the project. Agile development teams must often come together quickly and be immediately effective. Agile practices include:

Develop in parallel: Releases may be completely developed in parallel, or staged onto the market such that design, development, and quality assurance are all taking place simultaneously, but sequentially on different releases. Coding may even begin before the requirements are declared. Release more often: Releases are scoped to more frequently deliver small sets of new features and fixes. Constant re-prioritization of features enables responsiveness to changing requirements and enables features to easily slip from one release to the next. Depend on tools: Heavy use of development tools and environment that speed up the design and coding process offer much of the functionality that used to be custom built. Ideally, agile developers try to avoid wasting time repetitively building features others have already developed. Implant customers in the development environment: Fast and intimate access to customer views and opinions slashes time, and ensures the high-priority features are built first. When customers participate closely in all phases of development, cycle times shorten and teams can better chuck requirements into logical releases from customer views.

Establish a stable architecture: This anchors a rapid development process that is never quite stable, yet each release has some similarity and components reuse. Assemble and reuse components: Never unnecessarily build software from scratch when it can be assembled from existing components. It is quicker and equally effective to acquire, integrate, and assemble components with wrappers, including business logic software, interfaces and back-end infrastructure.

Ignore maintenance: Building components for short life spans eliminates the need for documentation. Assembled software can be thrown away and reassembled with greater ease than maintaining complex and custom-build components. Tailor the methodology daily: Operating with an overall development framework, but allowing project teams to adjust the exact approach to the daily situation, enabled teams to meet intense demands for speed by skipping unnecessary tasks or phases. Use just enough process to be effective, and no more.

Security requirements for Agile Security methods and Extant Security methods: Requirements for security methods that are targeted to be integrated into agile software methods: The security approach must be adaptive to agile software development methods. They must be simple; they should not hinder to the development project. The security approach, in order to be integrated successfully with agile development methods, should offer concrete guidance and tools at all phases of development (i.e., from requirements capture to testing).

A successful security component should be able to adapt rapidly to ever changing requirements owing to a fast-paced business environment, including support for handling several incremental iterations.

Key Security Elements in Agile Software Development. The key security element stems from information security "meta-notation", or notation for notations, and database security. Apply these key security elements to a process aimed at developing secure software in an agile manner. This generic security process consists of these key security elements in different phases of software development (requirements analysis, design, implementation and testing). These steps are not necessarily sequential and in any case, every step is optional.

Web Services Security Architectures Case Study. This case study is done with a research motivation for Secure Service Oriented Analysis and Design and Secure Service Modeling. "Designing Dependable Web Services Security Architecture Solutions" addresses the innovative idea of Web Services Security Engineering through (or using) Web Services Security Architectures with a research motivation of Secure Service Oriented Analysis and Design. It deals with Web Services Security Architectures for Composition and Contract Design in general, with authentication and authorization (access control) in particular, using Agile Modeled Layered Security Architecture design, which eventually results in enhanced dependable privacy requirements, Security Policies and Trust Negotiations. All the above findings are validated with appropriate case studies of Web 2.0 Services, BPEL for Role Based Access Control, a secure stock market financial application, and their extensions for spatial mobile application for cloud. All this research paves a way for Secure Web Engineering (or) Secure Web Science. Key research questions addressed here are: How can Agile Modeled Layered Security Architectures design be used for Web Services Security Architectures with a motivation of Dependable Privacy requirements? How can we extend the above approach for Web 2.0 Services Security Architectures? How can we validate this approach for Spatial Mobile Web Services Security Architectures for Cloud case study?

Further Extension of this Research Work. Mining approach for Business Intelligence to improve insights of Web Engineering applications deals with an innovative idea of Mining for Web Engineering with a case study of Business Intelligence Web application. Next generation Business Intelligence web application development uses integrated technologies like Web 2.0, Agile Modeling, and Service-orientation (using Web Services). We initially validated the Web 2.0 Services and Agile Modeling, for insights of Web application security in terms of authentication and authorization for Web Engineering. Applying Mining strategies to Web Services will provide valuable insights in terms of Service discovery, Service dependency, Service composition etc. This approach provides insights of Web application security for Web Engineering. These insights are important in maintenance of these developed applications and also in their scalability purposes. We validate our approach with a suitable exemplar Secure Web Services for Stock Market application.

3   Implementations and Validations

The section discusses about Implementations and Validations on Web Services Security Architectures Case Study.

SERVICE-ORIENTED computing (SOC) is an emerging paradigm for designing distributed applications. SOC applications are obtained by suitably composing and coordinating (that is, orchestrating) available services. Services are stand-alone computational units distributed over a network and are made available through standard interaction mechanisms. Composition of services may require peculiar mechanisms to handle complex interaction patterns (for example, to implement transactions) while enforcing nonfunctional requirements on the system behavior, for example, security, availability, performance, transactional, quality of service, etc. From a methodological perspective, Software Engineering should facilitate the shift from traditional approaches to the emerging service-oriented solutions. Along these lines, one of the goals of this paper is to strengthen the adoption of formal techniques for modeling, designing, and verifying SOC applications. In particular, we propose a SOC modeling framework supporting history-based security and call by contract.

The execution of a program may involve accessing security-critical resources and these actions are logged into histories. The security mechanism may inspect these histories and forbid those executions that would violate the prescribed policies. Service composition heavily depends on which information about a service is made public, on how those services that match the user's requirements can be chosen, and on their actual runtime behavior. Security makes service composition even harder. Services may be offered by different providers which only partially trust each other. On the one hand, providers have to guarantee that the delivered service respects a given security policy in any interaction with the operational environment, regardless of who actually called the service. On the other hand, clients may want to protect their sensitive data from the services invoked.

Our methodology for designing and composing services is to create new services, and to sell it by a package base through a secured media. In particular, we are concerned with Safety properties of service behavior. Services can enforce security policies locally and can invoke other services that respect given security contracts. This call-by-contract mechanism offers a significant set of opportunities, each driving secure ways to compose services. We discuss how we can correctly plan service compositions in several relevant classes of services and security properties. With this aim, we propose a graphical modeling framework in this project. Our formalism features dynamic and static semantics, thus allowing for formal reasoning about systems. Static analysis and model checking techniques provide the designer with useful information to assess and fix possible vulnerabilities.

Several approaches have been developed to support the verification of service-oriented systems. For example, dynamic bisimulation-based techniques have been adopted to analyze the consistency between orchestration and choreography of services whereas state-space analysis has been exploited to check the correctness of service orchestration. Our approach allows for synthesizing and checking the correctness of the orchestration statically.

In proposed system, we introduced a UML-like graphical language for designing and verifying the security policies of service oriented applications. Another feature offered by our framework is that of mapping high-level service descriptions into more concrete programs. This can be done with the help of simple model transformation tools. Such model-driven transformation would require very little user intervention. Here one new framework is introduced called Service Component Architecture (SCA). This framework aims at simplifying implementations by allowing designers to focus only on the business logic while complying with existing standards. Our approach complements the SCA view, providing a full-fledged mathematical framework for designing and verifying properties of service assemblies. It would be interesting to develop a (model-transformation) mapping from our formal framework to SCA. Refer to Figure 1 which provides class diagram for Web Services Design Application.

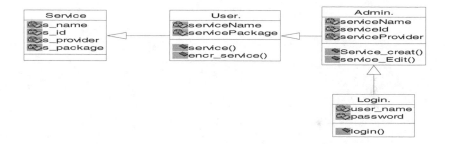

Fig. 1. Class Diagram for Web Services Application Design

Role Based Access Control for Web Services Security Policies

In the computerized world all the data are saved on electronically. It also contains more sensitive data. In computer systems security, role-based access control is an approach to restricting system access to authorized users. It is a newer alternative approach to mandatory access control and discretionary access control. Security critical business processes are mapped to their digital governments. It needs different security requirements, such as healthcare industry, digital government, and financial service institute. So the authorization and authentication play a vital role. Authorization constraints help the policy architect design and express higher level organizational rules. Access is the ability to do something with a computer resource (e.g., use, change, or view). Access control is the means by which the ability is explicitly enabled or restricted in some way (usually through physical and system-based controls). Computer- based access controls can prescribe not only who or what process may have access to a specific system resource, but also the type of access that is permitted. These controls may be implemented in the computer system or in external devices. Refer to Figure 2 and Figure 3which provides respectively class diagram and sequence diagram and execution screen shot for Role-based access control for Web Services policies.

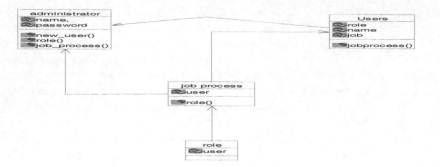

Fig. 2. Class Diagram for RBAC Web Services Security Policies

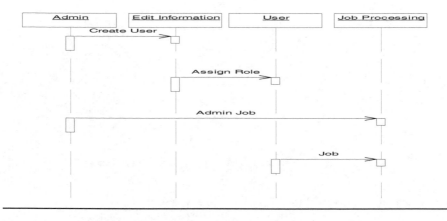

Fig. 3. Sequence Diagram for RBAC Web Services Security policies

4   Conclusions

This paper had discussed about Research Methodology on Designing Dependable Agile Layered Security Architecture Solutions – Web Services Case Study. In this research the major part is given to model architectural design rules using Model Driven Architecture (MDA) so that architects and the developers are responsible to automatic enforcement on the detailed design and easy to understand and use by both of them. This MDA approach is implemented in use of agile strategy in three different phases covering three different layers to provide security to the system. With this procedure a conclusion has been given that with the system security the requirements for that system are improved. This research summarizes that security is essential for every system at initial stage and upon introduction of security at middle stage must lead to the change in the system i.e. an improvement to system requirements.

References

1. Peterson, G.: Security architecture Blueprint. Arctec Group LLC (2007)
2. Tillwick, H., Olivier, M.S.: A Layered Security Architecture Blueprint. In: Proceedings of the Fourth Annual Information Security South Africa Conference (2004)
3. Baskerville, R.: Agile Security for Information Warfare: A call for research. Georgia State University, USA
4. Anderson, R.: Security Engineering: A guide to building Dependable Distributed Systems, 2nd edn. Wiley Publishers, USA (2008)
5. Bishop, M.: Computer Security. Art and Science. Pearson Education (2003)
6. Mao, W.: Modern Cryptography: Theory and Practice. Pearson Education (2004)
7. Gupta, V., et al.: Sizzle. A standard based end to end security architecture for the Embedded Internet. In: Pervasive and Mobile Computing. Elsevier (2005)
8. Pandian, D., et al.: Information Security Architecture – Context aware Access control model for Educational Applications. International Journal of Computer Science and Network Security (2006)
9. Whitmore, J.J.: A method for designing secure solutions. IBM Systems Journal 40(3), 747–768 (2001)
10. Smetters, D.K., Grinter, R.E.: Moving from the design of usable security technologies to the design of useful secure applications. In: ACM New Security Paradigms Workshop, pp. 82–89 (2002)
11. Cheng, B.H.C., Konrad, S., Campbell, L.A., Wasserman, R.: Using security patterns to model and analyze security requirements
12. Hunt, J.: Agile Software Construction. Springer, Heidelberg (2006)
13. Zelster, L.: Security Architecture cheat sheet for Internet applications
14. Harman, M., Mansouri, A.: Search based Software Engineering. Introduction to the special issue of the IEEE Transactions on Software Engineering, 737–741 (November/December 2010)
15. Spiekermann, S., Cranor, L.: Engineering Privacy. IEEE Transactions on Software Engineering 35(1), 67–82 (2009)
16. Mattsson, A., Lundell, B., Lings, B., Fitzgerald, B.: Linking Model-Driven Development and Software Architecture: A Case Study. IEEE Transactions on Software Engineering 35(1) (2009)
17. Douglass, B.P.: Real-time agility, the Harmony/ESW Method for Real-time and Embedded Systems Development. Pearson Education Inc. (2009)
18. Russo, B., Scotto, M., Silliti, A.: Agile Technologies in Open Source Development. IGI Global publishers (2010)
19. Keramati, H., Mirian-Hosseinabadi, S.-H.: Integrating Software Development Security Activities with Agile Methodologies. IEEE (2008)
20. Lazar, I., Parv, B., Motogna, S., Czibula, I.-G., Lazar, C.-L.: An Agile MDA approach for Executable UML Structured Activities. Studia Univ. Bases LII(2) (2007)
21. Gueheneuc, Y.-G., Antoniol, G.: DeMIMA: A Multilayered Approach for Design Pattern Identification. IEEE Transactions on Software Engineering 34(5) (2008)
22. Halkidis, S.T., Tsantalis, N., Chatzigeorgiou, A., Stephanides, G.: Architectural Risk Analysis of Software Systems Based on Security Patterns. IEEE Transactions on Dependable and Secure Computing 5(3) (2008)
23. Gamma, E.: Design Patterns Elements of Reusable Object Oriented Software. Addison Wesley Publishers (2009)
24. Siponen, M., Baserville, R., Kuivalainen, T.: Extending Security in Agile Software Development Methods, pp. 143–157
25. Peeters, J.: Agile Security Requirements Engineering, psu.edu 10.1.1.91.4183

Block Lanczos to Solve Integer Factorization Problem Using GPU's

Harish Malla[*], Vilas SantKaustubh, Rajasekharan Ganesh, and Padmavathy R.

National Institute of Technology
Warangal

Abstract. Public key cryptography is based on some mathematically hard problems, such as Integer Factorization and Discrete Logarithm problems. The RSA is based on Integer factorization problem. Number Field Sieve is one of the popular algorithms to solve these two problems. Block Lanczos algorithm is used in the linear algebra stage of Number Filed Sieve method for Integer Factorization. The algorithm solves the system of equations Bx=0 for finding null spaces in the matrix B. The major problems encountered in implementing Block Lanczos are storing the entire sieve matrix and solving the matrix efficiently in reduced time. Implementations of Block Lanczos algorithm have already been carried out using distributed systems. In the current study, the implementation of Block Lanczos Algorithm has been carried out on GPUs using CUDA C as programming language. The focus of the present work has been to design a model to make use of the high computing power of the GPUs. The input matrices are very large and highly sparse and so stored using coordinate format. The GPU on-chip memories have been used to reduce the computation time. The experimental results were obtained for the following problems; RSA100, RSA110, RSA120. From the results it can be concluded that a distributed model over GPUs can be used to reduce the iteration times for Block Lanczos.

Keywords: Public Key cryptography, RSA, Block Lanczos, GPUs.

1 Introduction

Public key cryptography is based on some mathematically hard problems. The popular RSA is based on integer factorization and the counterparts ElGamal and Diffie-Hellman are based on discrete logarithm problem. In number theory, integer factorization problem is to factor the given composite number into its factors. The problem is found to be hard when the factors are big primes. The best known method to solve the above problem is Number Field Sieve.

The Number Field Sieve consists of two steps, such as sieving and solving. The sieving phase generates a large and sparse matrix called as sieve matrix. The solving phase, first reduces the large size matrix into small and still sparse matrix and later solves the linear system of equations.

---

[*]Corresponding author.

N. Meghanathan et al. (Eds.): CCSIT 2012, Part I, LNICST 84, pp. 520–529, 2012.

The solving phase is the main bottle-neck in the overall process. In the literature, many algorithms are reported. The method proposed by Lanczos is widely known and attempted method, since it needs less memory and easily adoptable for large and sparse matrices.

Block Lanczos algorithm which is a modified version of Lanczos algorithm used in the linear algebra stage of Number Field Sieve (NFS) is proposed in [1]. This algorithm is one of the ideal candidates for parallelization. The algorithm uses subspaces instead of vectors for solving the sparse matrix generated in sieving stage, for finding null spaces. The subspaces are represented using matrices. The parallel implementation of Block Lanczos using Mondriaan partitioning for sparse matrices is discussed in [2]. In this he discussed about the global-local indexing mechanism, vector partitioning, sparse matrix partitioning, sparse matrix-vector multiplication, AXPY operations and dense vector inner product computation. Coppersmith et.el., discussed how Block Lanczos is much competitive than Gaussian Elimination for solving linear system of equations [4]. The paper also discusses that the block operations performed in Block Lanczos reduces the 32 matrix-vector operations to one. Nathan Bell et. el., reported the different format of representation for sparse matrix to store and perform matrix operations on them efficiently [6]. The different formats given by the author are DIA, ELL, CSR, COO, hybrid format. The use of COO format shows very little variance in efficiency over different data and applications. They also discussed about how matrix operations can be performed efficiently on different matrix formats that have been discussed in their previous work [7].

In the present study Block Lanczos is implemented on GPUs. The GPUs have larger number of cores on a chip when compared to CPUs. Also the Arithmetic Logical Units (ALUs) in case of GPUs are much more than in CPUs. Many-coreprocessors, especially the GPUs, have high floating-point performance. As discussed in [4], Block Lanczos algorithm is one of the ideal candidates for parallelization. Also from [6] and [7] it can be inferred that the sparse matrix operations of Block Lanczos can be performed efficiently on GPUs using CUDA. These ideas provided the motivation for implementing the Block Lanczos algorithm on GPUs using CUDA C.

1.1   Integer Factorization

There are different methods for Integer Factorization like continued fraction method, quadratic sieve, and number field sieve. Integer factorization algorithms require several nonzero vectors x belonging to Galoise field ($GF(2)^n$) such that a system of equations Bx= 0 is obtained, where B is a given m×n matrix over the field GF(2). This matrix B is called sieve matrix and is usually very large and highly sparse with m < n. Suppose, an integer M is to be factored, the quadratic sieve method finds congruence's between a_j^2 and product of p_i raised to some exponents b_{ij}, modulus M. Here p_i are primes or -1 and the b_{ij} are exponents, which are mostly zeroes. The quadratic sieve method then tries to find S $\in$ { 1, 2, - - ,n } such that both sides of the congruence.

$$\prod_{j \in S} a_j^2 = \prod_{j \in S} \prod_{i=1}^{m} p_i^{b_{ij}} \ (\text{mod M}) \tag{1}$$

are perfect squares. The left hand side product is automatically a square, but the right hand side product is a square only if all exponents are even, i.e., if $\prod j \in S$ $b_{ij} \equiv 0$ (mod 2) for $1 \leq i \leq m$. This is equivalent to the system of equations $Bx \equiv 0 (\mathrm{mod}\ 2)$, where B $= (b_{ij})$, and $x = (x_j)$, and where $x_j = 1$ if $j \in S$ and $x_i = 0$ if $j \in S$.

The matrix B that arises in the sieving stage of factoring has a specific structure. This matrix is extremely sparse, with around 60-80 non-zero entries per row. It is divided into dense block and sparse block. The dense parts in columns correspond to smaller primes and very sparse parts in columns correspond to larger primes. The best way to solve the matrix is the combination of Structured Gaussian elimination with Lanczos or Wiedemann. The Structured Gaussian elimination algorithm is applied first to reduce the large matrix to a comparatively smaller matrix which is still sparse. This step is called filtering. After getting the filtered matrix, the Block Lanczos or Wiedemann iterations can be applied efficiently on a smaller matrix.

Wiedemann is found to be slower compared to Lanczos and hence, Block Lanczos algorithm is chosen as the best method for finding the required linear dependencies [5, 8, 9, 13].

1.2   Block Lanczos

The Lanczos method is used for solving linear equations Ax=b for finding eigenvectors. But the algorithm fails in GF(2) due to the self orthogonality property of the binary vectors. To eliminate this problem, a set of vectors(representing subspaces) instead of a single vector were used. Each subspace is represented by a matrix. The matrix-vector products in Lanczos are replaced by matrix-matrix products in $GF(2^n)$. The matrix A can be applied to N (generally 32 or 64) different vectors in $GF(2^n)$ at once using bitwise operators. This modification is called Block Lanczos.

The Block Lanczos method, which is a variation of the Lanczos procedure uses block versions of the three-term recursions. As a general thrust, block algorithms substitute matrix block multiplies and block solvers for matrix-vector products and simple solvers in unblocked algorithms. In other words, higher level block arithmetic operations are used in the inner loop of the block algorithms. This decreases the I/O costs essentially by a factor of the block size. In addition, the block algorithms are generally more robust and efficient for matrices with multiple or closely clustered eigen values.

Suppose A is a symmetric n × n matrix over the field GF(2). The Block Lanczos algorithm produces a sequence of subspaces $\{W_i\}_{i=0}^{m-1}$ of GF (2^n) which are pair wise A−orthogonal. The properties of vectors w_i in the Lanczos algorithm ensures the finding of a solution vector. These properties were generalized to a A-orthogonal subspaces W_i to ensure a solution in the modified sequence of iterations.

The condition $w_i^T A w_i \neq 0$ in Lanczos is replaced by a requirement that no non-zero vector in W_i be A−orthogonal to all of W_i. The subspace W satisfying this property is said to be A− invertible.(A subspace $W \in K^n$ is said to be A-invertible if it has a basis W of column vectors such that $W^T AW$ is invertible). It will have a basis W of column vectors such that $W^T AW$ is invertible.

The property of being A-invertible is independent of the choice of basis, since any two bases for W are related by an invertible transformation. If W is A-invertible, then any u $\in K^n$ can be uniquely written as v + w where w $\in$ W and WAv = (0). The generalization to subspaces can be given as, W_i is A-invertible , $W_j^T A W_i = \{0\}$ for i $\neq$ j , and AW $\underline{C}$ W, where W=W_0+W_1+...+W_{m-1} .

Assuming the above statement, given b $\in$ W, an x $\in$ W can be constructed such that AX = b. Let x = $\sum w_j$, where $w_j \in W_j$ is chosen so that Aw_j - b is orthogonal to all of W_j. If the columns of W_j form a basis for W_j, then x can be given as

$$x = \sum_{j=0}^{m-1} W_j (W_j^T A W_j)^{-1} W_j^T b \tag{2}$$

Now fix N > 0. At certain step i, an n x N matrix Vis generated, which is A-orthogonal to all earlier W_j. The initial V_0 is taken to be arbitrary. W_i is selected using as many columns of V_i as can be possible, subject to the requirement that W_i be A-invertible. The Lanczos iterations are replaced by

$$W_i = V_i S_i, \tag{3}$$

$$V_{i+1} = A W_i S_i + V_i - \sum_{j=0}^{i} W_j C_{i+1,j} \quad (i \geq 0) \tag{4}$$

$$w_i = <W_i> \tag{5}$$

Iterations are stopped when $V_i^T A V_i = 0$. suppose this occurs for i = m. In the above equation S_i is an N x N_i projection matrix which has been chosen so that $W_i^T A W_i$ is invertible while making $N_i \leq N$ as large as possible. The matrix S_i should be zero except for exactly one 1 per column and at most one 1 per row. These ensure that $S_i^T S_i = I_{N_i}$ and that $S_i S_i^T$ is a sub matrix of I_N reflecting the vectors selected from V_i. The equation V_{i+1} tries to generalize while ensuring that $W_j A V_{i+1} = \{0\}$ for j $\leq$ i, if the earlier W_j exhibits the desired property of A-orthogonality. Then the following expression can be used

$$C_{i+1,j} = (W_j^T A W_j)^{-1} W_j^T A (A W_i S_i^T + V_i) \tag{6}$$

The terms V_i -$W_i C_{i+1,i}$ select all the columns of V_i not used in W_i; those columns are known to be A-orthogonal to W_0 through W_{i-1}, and the choice of $C_{i+1,i}$ adjusts them so they are A-orthogonal to W, as well. Without the V_i term, rank (V_{i+1}) would be bounded by rank($A W_i S_i^T$) $\leq$ rank(V_i), and would soon drop to zero. After further simplification,

$$V_{i+1} = A V_i S_i S_i^T + V_i D_{i+1} + V_{i-1} E_{i+1} + V_{i-2} F_{i+1} \tag{7}$$

2   Review of Basic Operations Involved in Block Lanczos Algorithm

2.1   Block Lanczos Algorithm

The Block Lanczos algorithm is used to solve the linear system of equations $Bx=0$ for finding the null spaces in matrix B. This is achieved by decomposing $GF(2)^n$ into several subspaces of dimension almost N which are pair wise orthogonal with respect to the symmetric n x n matrix $A = B^T B$. In each of the iteration the matrices B and B^T are applied to an n xN matrix and then a few supplementary operations are performed [12].

The pseudo-code for the algorithm is given as Algorithm 1.

Algorithm 1: Block Lanczos

Input:Matrices B of size $n_1 \times n_2$ and Y of size $n_2 \times N$

Output:The matrices X and V_m

1: Initialization: $X = 0$ 2: $V_0 = AY = B^T * (BY)$

3: $C_0 = V_0^T A V_0 = V_0^T (B^T B) V_0 = (BV_0)^T * BV_0$ 4: Compute $AV_0 = B^T * (BV_0)$

5: $i = 0$

6: while $C_i \neq 0$ do

7: compute $V_i^T A^2 V_i = (AV_i)^T * (AV_i)$

8: $[W_i^{inv}, SS_i^T] = $ Inverse $(V_i^T AV_i, SS_{i-1}^T, N)$

9: $X = X + Vi * (W_i^{inv} * (V_i^T * V_0))$ 10: $Z_i = (V_i^T A^2 V_i) * (SS_i^T) + C_i$

11: $D_{i+1} = I_N - W_i^{inv}(Z_i)$ 12: $E_{i+1} = -W_{i-1}^{inv}(C_i * SS_i^T)$

13: $F_{i+1} = -W_{i-2}^{inv}(I_N - C_{i-1} + W_{i-1}^{inv})(Z_{i-1}) SS_i^T$

14: $V_{i+1} = AV_i S_i S_i^T + V_i D_{i+1} + V_{i-1} E_{i+1} + V_{i-2} F_{i+1}$

15: compute BV_{i+1}

16: $C_{i+1} = V_{i+1}^T AV_{i+1} = (BV_{i+1})^T * (BV_{i+1})$ and $AV_{i+1} = B^T * BV_{i+1}$

17: $i = i + 1$

18: end while

19: Return X and V_m

The experimental results are carried out on a machine with following characteristics:-
A system with following configurations

- Intel i7 740QM processor
- 4GB DDR3 RAM
- NVIDIA Ge Force 330M GPU (1 GB)
- Another system for debugging using SSH portal.

Software Requirements

- Operating System: Ubuntu 10.10
- NVIDIA Developer Driver for Linux (260.19.26)
- CUDA 3.2 Toolkit
- SSH server on system with GPU and SSH client on another system

3   Implementation

3.1   Distribution of Data

The typical matrices for which the Block Lanczos algorithm is applied are very large
and mostly sparse. Taking advantage of the latter, the matrix can be stored in a way
that is much more clever than just explicitly storing every entry in the matrix. Storing
each entry is already infeasible for a matrix with n of size 500,000, since that would
need about 32 GB of RAM to store it. Note that this requirement is much too large to
be fulfilled by the RAM of today's typical machine. Also the typical n may be two to
twenty times larger than this, increasing the RAM requirement substantially.

The matrix corresponding to the system of equations that is generated from the
number field sieve follows a very predictable pattern. The matrix that is obtained
from sieving stage is stored by collections of columns, each collection may form a
dense block or a sparse block. The number field sieve (much like the quadratic sieve)
uses three factor bases (rational, algebraic, and quadratic characters) in sieving as part
of the process of factoring a large number. Dense rows of the matrix correspond to the
smaller primes, and sparse rows correspond to larger primes. These first few rows are
called dense since they have relatively higher non-zero entries. Once sparsity of the
matrix increases, it is more worthwhile to store the locations of these entries rather
than storing all the particular entries.

The sizes of the sieve matrices are too huge. Hence sometimes it may not be possible to store the entire matrix on a single device. Hence the need to keep the matrix on
several devices is arising. So storing the matrix on many number of devices and dealing with them efficiently is necessary. Distributing the matrix uniformly over the
devices is necessary so as to distribute the computation load uniformly.

Therefore the matrix B is stored in co-ordinate form with each entry giving the indices of row and column to which then on-zero element belong. The use of coordinate
format greatly reduces the memory requirements, which is directly proportionate to

number of non-zero entries in the matrix. Also an advantage of storing the matrix in coordinate format was that no extra memory was used to store the transpose of memory. Only a slight change in the logic for multiplication of transpose of matrix was required. The matrix is being stored in global memory on GPU because this matrix is used in all the iterations twice. The matrix is also divided into strips of size which depends on shared memory restrictions of GPU. The strip size of the matrix depends on the shared memory because the output of the multiplication of the matrix with column vector is being stored in shared memory which greatly reduces the write access time costs. The offsets of these strips have also been stored in global memory on GPU. These offsets are used in relation to transpose of matrix B. The dense part of matrix is stored as an array of bit strings. The data distribution can be found in [3]. Programming massively parallel processors is reported in [10] and the GPU programming is illustrated in [11]

3.2   Basic Functions Implemented Using CUDA C on GPUs

The following are some of the main operations to be computed to carry out the block lanczos algorithm.

Random Vector Y, Computation of V_0, Computation of C_i, Computation of V_i. $^TA^2V_i$ and Computation of V_{i+1}

3.2.1   The List of Functions Written in CUDA C

The algorithm is implemented in CUDA C. The implementation consists of different functions on device based on operations that are to be performed in the algorithm. The word-size N is 32 bits. A brief description of functions is given below:

rand_gen( ) This function randomly generates vector Y of size of n x N which is represented as n words. To increase the randomness of the data used Y is divided into 3 blocks and each block uses a different seed.

strip_mul ( ) This function performs the operation in1 for a block of matrix B of size m x n with column vector Y of size n words on the device. The output of this function is a partial matrix product that is passed to the reduce() function to get final product.

reduce( ) This function takes the partial products and performs the XOR operation on them to get the final result.

productBY( ) This function performs the multiplication of matrix B (size m x n) with vector Y (size n x N) by calling the function strip_mul( )for each strip in B. It also makes use of pthreads and parallely reduces the outputs of strip_mul( ) for the previous strip. The same function is used for calculating product BV (size m x N) during each iteration of the algorithm.

dense_mul( ) This function computes the product of the dense block of matrix B and vector Y which is later on combined with product of sparse block of B with Y.

strip_trans_mul( ) This function performs the operation in2 for block of matrix B of size m x n with vector V of size n words. The output of this function is a partial matrix product that is passed to the reduce( ) function to get final product.

productV( ) This function performs the multiplication of matrix B^T with vector V by calling the function strip_trans_mul( ) for each strip. The same functionis used for calculating the product AV during each iteration of the algorithm.

dev_trans_dense_mul( ) This function computes the product of the dense block of matrix B^T(size m × n) and vector Y (sizen × N) which is later on combined with product of sparse block of B^T with Y.

device_mul_NnnN( ) This function performs operation op2 for matrix AV and its transpose.

dev_mul_nNNN( ) This function performs operation op1.

mul_NNNN( ) This function performs the operation op3.

inverse( ) This function implements the algorithm given in algorithm 4 to compute W_i^{inv}, SS_i^T

The inputs were generated using msieve 1.48 which is developed for factoring RSA numbers. Msieve is implemented on pthreads and MPI that make use of multi-core architecture of CPUs. These matrices that were obtained from Msieve were in column-major order format for the sparse part and in bit string representation for the dense part of the sparse matrix. These matrices were later on reordered to suit the implementation model that was followed in the current work. Block Lanczos was carried out for three different matrices that are obtained in three different RSA numbers. Details of which are tabulated in following table.

Table 1. Input matrices dimensions.

Input Matrix	Number of rows	Number of columns
RSA100	186821	186999
RSA110	346763	346940
RSA120	736255	736431

The operations were carried out by varying the number of blocks in the grid and also number of threads in each block. The results obtained were as follows:

Table 2. Experimental results obtained by varying the number of blocks keeping the number of threads constant

Input Matrix	Number of Blocks (Number of threads=512)				
	8	16	32	64	128
RSA100	1922	1924	1866	1855	1941
RSA110	3303	3213	3129	3102	3271
RSA120	6053	5994	5865	5847	6175

These results are single iteration times in milliseconds.

Table 3. Results obtained on varying the number of threads keeping the number of blocks constant

Input Matrix	Number of threads (Number of blocks=64)			
	64	128	256	512
RSA 100	2077	1996	2007	1855

These results are also single iteration times in milliseconds.

It can be seen that by varying the number of blocks and threads in all the three cases best results are obtained by keeping number of blocks as 64. Also, the number of threads to get the least time possible for this implementation is 512.

From the results above, it can be concluded that the single iteration times increase by a factor of less than 2 for each increase of 10 digits in the RSA number factored. Also it was found that the optimum time was reached when the program was executed using 64 blocks each of 512 threads. In this way it was found that by focusing on the architecture of device an efficient implementation of Block Lanczos algorithm on GPUs can be carried out.

References

[1] Montgomery, P.L.: A Block Lanczos Algorithm for Finding Dependencies over GF(2). In: Guillou, L.C., Quisquater, J.-J. (eds.) EUROCRYPT 1995. LNCS, vol. 921, pp. 106–120. Springer, Heidelberg (1995)

[2] Bisseling, R.H., Flesch, I.: Mondriaan Sparse Matrix Partitioning for Attacking Cryptosystems by a Parallel Block Lanczos Algorithm -a case study. In: Proceeding of International Conference on Parallel Computing: Current and Future Issues of High-End Computing, ParCo 2005. NIC Series, vol. 33, pp. 819–826 (2006) ISBN 3-00-017352-8

[3] Vastenhouw, B., Bisseling, R.H.: A Two Dimensional Data Distribution Method for Parallel Sparse Matrix-Vector Multiplication, Preprint 1238, Department of Mathematics, Utrecht University, Utrecht, Netherlands (May 2002)

[4] Coppersmith, D.: Solving Linear Equations over GF(2): Block Lanczos Algorithm. Linear Algebra Application 192, 33–60 (1993)

[5] Cullum, J.K., Wiloughby, R.A.: Lanczos Algorithm for Large Symmetric Eigenvalues Computation. Theory, vol. 1. Birkhauser, Boston (1985)

[6] Bell, N., Garland, M.: Implementing Sparse Matrix-Vector Multiplication on Throughput-Oriented Processors. In: Proceedings Supercomputing 2009 (November 2009)

[7] Bell, N., Garland, M.: Efficient Sparse Matrix-Vector Multiplication on CUDA, NVIDIA Technical Report, NVR-2008-004 (December 2008)

[8] Coppersmith, D.: Solving Homogenous Linear Equations over GF(2) via Block Wiedemann Algorithm. Mathematics of Computation 62, 333–350 (1994)

[9] Montgomery, P.L.: Square roots of product of algebraic. In: Gautschi, W. (ed.) Proceedings of Symposia in Applied Mathematics. Mathematics of Computation 1943-1993: a Half Century of Computational Mathematics, pp. 567–571. American Mathematical Society (1994)

[10] Sanders, J., Kandrot, E.: CUDA by Example-An Introduction to General Purpose GPU programming (2011)

[11] Kirk, D., Hwu, W.-M.W.: Programming Massively Parallel Processors- A Hands on Approach (2010)

[12] Ramanjulu, M.: Parallel Computations for the Matrix stage of Integer factorization, M.Tech thesis (2008)

[13] LaMacchia, B.A., Odlyzko, A.M.: Solving Large Sparse Linear Systems Over Finite Fields. In: Menezes, A., Vanstone, S.A. (eds.) CRYPTO 1990. LNCS, vol. 537, pp. 109–133. Springer, Heidelberg (1991)

Lattice Based Tools for Cryptanalysis
in Various Applications

R. Santosh Kumar[1], C. Narasimham[2], and S. Pallam Setty[3]

[1] Department of Information Technology, MVGR College of Engg., Vizianagaram, India
santu_hcunitk@yahoo.co.in
[2] Department of Information Technology, VR Siddhartha Engineering College,
Vijayawada-7, India
narasmham_c@yahoo.com
[3] Dept. of Computer Science & Systems Engineering, Andhra University,
Vishakhapatnam, India
drspsetty@yahoo.com

Abstract. Lattice reduction is a powerful concept for solving diverse problems involving point lattices. Lattice reduction has been successfully utilizing in Number Theory, Linear algebra and Cryptology. Not only the existence of lattice based cryptosystems of hard in nature, but also has vulnerabilities by lattice reduction techniques. In this survey paper, we are focusing on point lattices and then describing an introduction to the theoretical and practical aspects of lattice reduction. Finally, we describe the applications of lattice reduction in cryptanalysis like subset sum problem of low density, modular equations, Attacking RSA with small e by knowing parts of the message and Diophantine Approximation using LLL algorithm.

Keywords: attices, Lattice Reduction, RSA, Coppersmith, Subset Sum, Simultaneous Diophantine, Merkle-Hellman.

1   Introduction

Lattices are periodic arrangements of discrete points. Apart from their wide-spread use in pure mathematics, lattices have found applications in numerous other fields as diverse as cryptography/cryptanalysis, the geometry of numbers, factorization of integer polynomials, subset sum and knapsack problems, integer relations and Diophantine approximations, coding theory. In this paper, we survey the main tools which can be used to the verify vulnerabilities of different cryptosystems.

Lattice reduction is concerned with finding improved representations of a given lattice using algorithms like LLL (Lenstra, Lenstra, Lov´asz) reduction .There are some versions for lattice reduction, but people are using the LLL algorithm for theoretical and practical purposes. It is a polynomial time algorithm and the vectors are nearly orthogonal. In section II, we briefly discuss the complexity issues of LLL algorithm and its properties. In section III, we discuss the subset sum problem and how lattice reduction has been used to get a solution in some instances. This technique, in turn can be applied

N. Meghanathan et al. (Eds.): CCSIT 2012, Part I, LNICST 84, pp. 530–537, 2012.
© Institute for Computer Sciences, Social Informatics and Telecommunications Engineering 2012

to break knapsack cryptosystems like Merkle-Hellman knapsack cryptosystem. In section IV, we discuss Univaraite polynomial congruence problem and how lattice reduction was used to get a solution. This technique, in turn can be applied to check vulnerabilities of RSA cryptosystem. In section V, we discuss simultaneous Diophantine approximation problem and vulnerabilities of knapsack cryptosystem.

2   Terminology

2.1   Lattices

A lattice is a discrete subgroup of $\mathbb{R}^n$. Equivalently, given $m \leq n$ linearly independent vectors $b_1, b_2, b_3, \ldots, b_n, \in \mathbb{R}^n$, the set $\mathcal{L} = \mathcal{L}(b_1, b_2, b_3, \cdots, b_m)$ $= \{\sum_{i=1}^m \alpha_i b_i \mid \alpha_i \in \mathbb{Z}\}$, is a lattice. The b_i are called basis vectors of $\mathcal{L}$ and $\mathcal{B} = \{b_1, b_2, \cdots, b_m\}$ is called a lattice basis for $\mathcal{L}$. Thus, the lattice generated by a basis $\mathcal{B}$ is the set of all integer linear combinations of the basis vectors in $\mathcal{B}$. The determinant of a lattice, denoted by $vol(\mathcal{L})$ is the square root of the gramian nant$det_{1 \leq i,j \leq m} \langle b_i, b_j \rangle$, which is independent of particular choice of basis. A general treatment of this topic see [1].

2.2   Lattice Reduction

Lattice reduction techniques have a long tradition in mathematics in the field of number theory. The goal of lattice basis reduction is to find, for a given lattice, a basis matrix with favorable properties. Usually, such a basis consists of vectors that are short and therefore this basis is called reduced. Unless stated otherwise, the term "short" is to be interpreted in the usual Euclidean sense. There are several definitions of lattice reduction with corresponding reduction criteria, such as Minkowski reduction, Hermite-Korkine-Zolotareff reduction, Gauss reduction, Lenstra-Lenstra-Lov´asz (LLL) reduction, Seysen reduction. The corresponding lattice reduction algorithms yield reduced bases with shorter basis vectors and improved orthogonality; they provide a tradeoff between the quality of the reduced basis and the computational effort required for finding it. Here we consider the LLL reduced, because there is a polynomial time algorithm exists and vectors are near orthogonal and the first vector solves the   approximate SVP problem. For good survey on lattice reduction algorithms refers [4].

2.3   LLL Reduced

The following LLL reduced version given by Lenstra, Lenstra, Lovasz[1],[2],[3].

LLL reduced: A basis $b_1, b_2, b_3, \cdots, b_m$ of a lattice $\mathcal{L}$ is said to be Lovasz-reduced or LLL-reduced if

$$|\mu_{i,j}| \leq \frac{1}{2} \text{ for } 1 \leq j < i \leq n$$

$\left|b_i^* + \mu_{i,i-1}b_{i-1}^*\right|^2 \geq \frac{3}{4}|b_{i-1}^*|^2$ for $1 < i \leq n$. where the b_i^* and $\mu_{i,j}$ are defined by the Gram-Schimdt orthogonalization process acting on the b_i. Above in place of ¾ one can replace any quantity $\frac{1}{4} < \delta < 1$.

2.4   LLL Algorithm

The Lenstra –Lenstra -Lov´asz (LLL) algorithm [1][2][3] is an iterative algorithm that transforms a given lattice basis into an LLL-reduced one. Since the definition of LLL-reduced uses Gram-Schmidt process, the LLL algorithm performs the Gram-Schimdt method as subroutine.

LLL Algorithm with Euclidean norm

Input: $b_1, b_2, b_3, \cdots, b_n \in \mathbb{Z}^m$
Output: LLL reduced basis $b_1, b_2, b_3, \cdots, b_n$
1: Compute the Gram-Schimdt basis $b_1^*, b_2^*, \cdots, b_n^*$ and coefficients $\mu_{i,j}$ for $1 \leq j < i < n$.
2: Compute $B_i = \langle b_i^*, b_i^* \rangle = \|b_i^*\|^2$ for $1 \leq i \leq n$
3: k=2
4: while $k \leq n$ do
5:       for $j = k - 1$ downto 1 do
6:           let $q_j = \mu_{k,j}$ and set $b_k = b_k - q_j b_j$
7:           update the values $\mu_{k,j}$ for $1 \leq j < k$ and B_k
8:       end for
9:       if $B_k \geq (\frac{3}{4} - \mu_{k,k-1}^2)B_{k-1}$ then
10:          $k = k + 1$
11:      else
12:          Swap b_k with b_{k+1}
13:              Update the values $b_k^*, b_{k-1}^*, B_k, B_{k-1}, \mu_{k-1,j}$ and $\mu_{k,j}$ for $1 \leq j < k$ and
                 $\mu_{i,k}$ and $\mu_{i,k-1}$ for $k < i \leq n$.
14:          $k = \min\{2, k - 1\}$
15:      end if
16: end while

Let $b_1, b_2, b_3, \cdots, b_m$ be an LLL reduced basis of a lattice $\mathcal{L}$ and $b_1^*, b_2^*, \cdots, b_m^*$ be it s Gram-Schimdt orthogonalization. Then $|b_1| \leq 2^{\frac{m-1}{2}}$ for every $x \in \mathcal{L}$ and $x \neq 0$. It can be proven that the LLL algorithm terminates a finite number of iterations. Let $\mathcal{L} \subset \mathbb{Z}^n$ be a lattice with basis $\{b_1, b_2, b_3, \cdots, b_m\}$, and $C \in \mathbb{R}$, $C \geq 2$ be such that $\|b_i\| \leq \sqrt{C}$ for $i = 1, 2, \cdots, n$. Then the number of arithmetic operations needed for the algorithm $O(n^4 \log C)$ on integers of size $O(n \log C)$ bits.

3 Solving Subset Sum Problem of Low Density

Let $\{a_1, a_2, a_3, \ldots, a_n\}$ be distinct positive integers. The subset sum problem is, given an integer s obtained as a sum of elements a_i, to find $x_i \in \{0,1\}$ for $i = 1,2, \cdots n$ such that $\sum a_i x_i = s$. The density of S is defined to be $d = \dfrac{n}{\max\{\log a_i | 1 \le i \le n\}}$. The subset sum problem is $\mathcal{NP}$-complete.

3.1 LLL Algorithm Solution

Using LLL algorithm one can find a particular short vector in a lattice[4]. Since the reduced basis produced by LLL algorithm includes a vector of length which is guaranteed to be within a factor of $2^{\frac{n-1}{2}}$ of the shortest non-zero vector of the lattice. In practice, however, the LLL algorithm usually finds a vector which is much shorter than what is guaranteed. So the LLL algorithm can be expected to find the short vector which yields a solution to the subset sum problem provided that this vector is shorter than most of the non zero vectors in the lattice.

3.2 Justification

Consider the matrix $(n + 1) * (n + 2)$ matrix $B =$
$$\begin{bmatrix} 2 & 0 & 0 & & 0 & ma_1 & 0 \\ 0 & 2 & 0 & \cdots & 0 & ma_2 & 0 \\ 0 & 0 & 2 & & 0 & ma_3 & 0 \\ & \vdots & & \ddots & & \vdots & \\ 0 & 0 & 0 & \cdots & 2 & ma_n & 0 \\ 0 & 0 & 0 & & 1 & ms & 1 \end{bmatrix}$$

Let the rows of the matrix B be $b_1, b_2, b_3, \ldots, b_n, b_{n+1}$ and L be the lattice generated by these vectors. If $x_1, x_2, x_3, \ldots, x_n$ is a solution to the subset sum problem, then we have

$$y = \sum_{i=1}^{n} x_i b_i - b_{n+1}$$

$$= (x_1 b_1 + x_2 b_2 + x_3 b_3 + \ldots + x_n b_n - b_{n+1})$$

$$= (2x_1 - 1, 2x_2 - 1, \ldots, 2x_n - 1, m(a_1 x_1 + a_2 x_2 + \ldots + a_n x_n - s), 1)$$

Since $(x_1, x_2, x_3, \ldots, x_n)$ is a solution and each x_i $(1 \le i \le n)$ is either 0 or 1, we have $y_i \in \{-1,1\}$ and $y_{n+1} = 0$. Since $\|y\| = \sqrt{y_1^2 + y_2^2 + \ldots + y_{n+1}^2 + y_{n+2}^2}$, the vector y is a vector of short length in L. If the density of the knapsack set is small, i.e the a_i are large, then most vectors in L will have relatively large lengths, and hence y may be unique shortest non zero vector in L. If this is indeed the case then there is a good possibility of the algorithm finding a basis which includes this vector. Above algorithm is not guaranteed to succeed. Assuming that the LLL algorithm always produces a basis which includes the shortest non zero lattice vector, then algorithm succeeds with high probability if the density of the knapsack set is less than 0.9408.

3.3   Application

This is most powerful general attack known on knapsack encryption schemes[5]. It is typically successful if the density of the knapsack set is less than 0.9408. This is significant because the density of a Merkle-Hellman knapsack[6] set much be less than 1, since otherwise there will be many subsets of the knapsack set with the same sum, in which case some cipher texts will not be uniquely decipherable.

4   Solving Modular Equations

It is easy to compute the integer roots of a polynomial in a single variable over the integers. But the related problem of solving modular equations can be hard. We have different tools to solve $f(x) = 0$. But one cannot solve $f(x) = 0 \ (mod \ n)$ efficiently. The solution for the above equation was proposed by Coppersmith in the year 1997[7]. Here we present simple version of Howgrave-Graham[8].

Let N be an integer and $f \in \mathbb{z}[x]$ be a monic polynomial of degree d. Set $X = N^{\frac{1}{d} - \varepsilon}$ for some $\varepsilon \geq 0$. Then given $\langle N, f \rangle$, one can efficiently find all integers $|x_0| < X$ satisfying $f(x_0) = 0 (mod \ N)$ using the LLL algorithm. This fact claims the existence of an algorithm which can efficiently find all roots of f modulo N that are less than $X = N^{\frac{1}{d}}$. As X gets smaller, the algorithm's runtime decreases. This theorem's strength is the ability to find out all small roots of polynomials modulo a composite N. The idea is simply reducing the root finding problem in modular equations to the case of root finding equations over the integers. Thus one has to construct from the polynomial $f_b(x)$ with the root $x_0 \leq X$ modulo b a polynomial of $f(x)$ which has the same root x_0 by applying standard root finding algorithms to $f(x)$. But how can be transform $f_b(x)$ into $f(x)$?. This transform is exactly the core of the Coppersmith's method. He defines the matrix which has the elements of the form $g_{i,j}(x) = N^{m-i} x^j f_b^i(x)$ for $i = 1, \cdots m$ and some choice of j and it has a root $x_0 mod \ b^m$. Then every integer linear combination $f(x) = \sum_{i,j} g_{i,j}(x), \ a_{i,j} \in \mathbb{z}$ of polynomials in G also has the root $x_0 mod \ b^m$. Our goal is to find among these linear combinations one which has the root x_0 not just modulo b^m but also over the integers. For this one can choose coefficients of $f(x)$ satisfies the relation $f(x_0) < b^m$. This is where the lattice reduction algorithm such as LLL comes into the picture. The first vector of a reduced basis satisfies the above inequality.

4.1   Application 1: Attacking RSA with Small e by Knowing Parts of the Message

Suppose that $m = M + x$ for some known part M of the message and some unknown part $x \leq N^{\frac{1}{e}}$. Now one can recover m from above scenario. This situation occurs in the case of stereotyped messages. Let (N, e) be a public key in RSA public key crypto system[7]. Furthermore, let $C = (M + x_0)^e mod \ N$ be an RSA encrypted message with known M and unknown x_0, where $|x_0| \leq N^{\frac{1}{e}}$. Then one can find x_0 in time polynomial in $\log N$ and e. The above fact is direct application of Coppersmith's method.

4.2 Application 2: Repeated Message and Short Pad Attack

Consider the situation when Bob sends two messages to Alice that only differ by a small amount. Also assume that sender is using a public exponent 3. In this case $M^3 = c_1 (mod\ N)$ and $(M + x)^3 = c_2 (mod\ N)$. One can eliminate the M from above two equations by using resultants, and is left with the equation $x^9 + 3(c_1 - c_2)x^6 + 3(c_2^2 + 7c_1 c_2 + c_1^2)x^3 + (c_1 - c_2)^3 = 0 (mod\ N)$, so one may discover the padding as long as $|x| \leq N^{\frac{1}{9}}$. It is not obvious that recovering M from the knowledge of x, but this is true due to clever trick of Franklin and Reiter[9].

5 Simultaneous Diophantine Approximation

Simultaneous Diophantine approximation is concerned with approximating a tor $\left(\frac{q_1}{q}, \frac{q_2}{q}, \cdots, \frac{q_n}{q}\right)$ of rational numbers by a vector of $\left(\frac{p_1}{q}, \frac{p_2}{q}, \cdots, \frac{p_n}{q}\right)$ of rational numbers with a smaller denominator p. Algorithms for finding simultaneous Diophantine approximation have been used to break some knapsack public key cryptosystems. The vector $\left(\frac{p_1}{q}, \frac{p_2}{q}, \cdots, \frac{p_n}{q}\right)$ of rational numbers is said to be a simultaneous Diophantine approximation of δ-quality to the vector $\left(\frac{q_1}{q}, \frac{q_2}{q}, \cdots, \frac{q_n}{q}\right)$ of rational numbers if $p < q$ and $\left|p\frac{q_i}{q} - p_i\right| \leq q^{-\delta}$ for $i = 1, 2, \cdots, n$. One can reduce the problem of finding a δ-quality simultaneous Diophantine approximation to the problem of finding a short vector in a lattice [2]. The latter problem can be solved using LLL algorithm. Consider the (n+1) dimensional matrix $A_{i,j}$ as

$$= \lambda q \text{ if } i = j \text{ and } 1 \leq i \leq n,$$

$$= 0 \text{ if } i \neq j \text{ and } i \leq i \leq n,$$

$$= -\lambda q_j \text{ if } i = n + 1 \text{ and } j \neq n + 1,$$

$$= 1 \text{ if } i = n + 1 \text{ and } j = n + 1 \text{ where } \lambda \approx q^\delta.$$

5.1 Justification

Apply LLL algorithm to above matrix and let the rows of the matrix A be denoted by $(b_1, b_2, \cdots, b_n, b_{n+1})$. Suppose that $\left(\frac{q_1}{q}, \frac{q_2}{q}, \cdots, \frac{q_n}{q}\right)$ has a δquality approximation $\left(\frac{p_1}{q}, \frac{p_2}{q}, \cdots, \frac{p_n}{q}\right)$. The vector $x = p_1 b_1 + p_2 b_2 + \cdots + p_n b_n + p_{n+1} b_{n+1} = (\lambda(p_1 q - pq_1), \lambda(p_2 q - pq_2), \cdots, \lambda(p_n q - pq_n), p)$ is in L and has length less than approximately $\sqrt{n+1}q$. Thus x is short compared to the original basis vectors, which are of length roughly $q^{1+\delta}$. Also, if $v = (v_1, v_2, \cdots, v_n, v_{n+1})$ is a vector in L of length less than q, then the vector $\left(\frac{p_1}{q}, \frac{p_2}{q}, \cdots, \frac{p_n}{q}\right)$ defined as above is a δ quality approximation.

5.2   Application

Given the public knapsack set, this technique finds a pair of integers U', M' such that $\frac{U'}{M'}$ is close to $\frac{U}{M}$ where U and M are part of the private key of the Merkle-Hellman Cryptosystem and $U = W^{-1} mod\ M$ and such that the integers $b_i' = U' a_i mod\ M, 1 \leq i \leq n$ form a super increasing sequence. This sequence can then used by an adversary to decrypt messages [2].

6   Conclusions

In this survey paper, we have discussed some Cryptographic attacks using some tricky lattice techniques. First one, we solved subset sum problem of low density. Then we observe vulnerabilities of Merkle-Hellman knapsack cryptosystem which is based on subset sum problem. Second one, we solved univaraite modular polynomial equations. Using this we check the pitfalls of RSA function in two cases. Finally we discuss the problem of Simultaneous Diophantine Approximation problem. Again we observe vulnerabilities of Merkle-Hellman Cryptosystem. All are implemented in NTL number theory [12] library maintaining by victor shoup.

References

1. Cohen, H.: A Course in Computational Algebraic Number Theory, 2nd edn. Springer, Heidelberg (1995)
2. Menezes, A.J., van Oorschot, P.C., Vanstone, S.A.: Hand book of Applied Cryptography. CRC Press (1997)
3. Lenstra, A.K., Lenstra Jr., H.W., Lovasz, L.: Factoring polynomials with rational coefficients. Mathematische Annalen 261(4), 515–534 (1982)
4. Schnorr, P., Euchner, M.: Lattice basis reduction: Improved practical algorithms and solving subset sum problem. Math. Prog. 66, 181–199 (1994)
5. Shamir, A.: A polynomial-time algorithm for breaking the basic Merkle-Hellman cryptosystem. IEEE Transactions on Information Theory (1984)
6. Merkle, R.C., Hellman, M.E.: Hiding information and signatures in trapdoor knapsacks. IEEE Transactions on Information Theory IT-24(5), 525–530 (1978)
7. Rivest, R.L., Shamir, A., Adleman, L.: A method for obtaining digital signatures and public key cryptosystems. Commun. of the ACM 21, 120–126 (1978)
8. Coppersmith, D.: Finding a Small Root of a Univaraite Modular Equation. In: Maurer, U.M. (ed.) EUROCRYPT 1996. LNCS, vol. 1070, pp. 155–165. Springer, Heidelberg (1996)

9. Howgrave-Graham, N.A.: Finding Small Solutions of Univaraite Modular Equations Revisited. In: Darnell, M.J. (ed.) Cryptography and Coding 1997. LNCS, vol. 1355, pp. 131–142. Springer, Heidelberg (1997)
10. Coppersmith, D., Franklin, M., Patarin, J., Reitert, M.: Low Exponenet RSA with related messages
11. Kannan, R.: Algorithmic geometry of numbers. Annual Review of Computer Science, 231–267 (1987)
12. Victor Shoup. NTL: A library for doing number theory,
    http://www.shoup.net/ntl/

Securing the National Knowledge Network

S.V. Nagaraj

RMK Engineering College, Kavaraipettai, 601 206, India
svnagaraj@acm.org
http://www.rmkec.ac.in

Abstract. The National Knowledge Network is an important initiative of the Government of India approved in the year 2010. This network is expected to connect over 1500 institutions specializing in higher education, research and development, health care, agriculture and governance and provide multi-gigabit connectivity. It is expected to create a revolution by ushering in technological progress through the rapid spread of knowledge. We look at ways of securing this network. We also study various security challenges it is likely to face and suggest remedial measures.

Keywords: Security, Knowledge Network, NKN, REN, Computer Networks.

1 Introduction

The Government of India approved in March 2010 the setting up of the National Knowledge Network (NKN). According to experts, this network is expected to be fully operational in 2 or 3 years time. It is currently being built by the National Informatics Center (NIC). A knowledge network may be considered as a center of knowledge which helps in the best utilization of available knowledge in order to bring benefits to its users. Many countries have high speed networks which connect various organizations and universities. Such networks are known as research and education networks (RENs). They have become indispensable all over the world. There are many national research and education networks. We give a few examples of such specialized networks.

The Internet2 is an American network that connects several thousand colleges, universities, government organizations, research institutes, libraries as well as schools and museums. Within the USA, there is another such network known as the National Lambda Rail. In Canada, there is a REN known as CANARIE. In Netherlands, the REN is known as SURFnet. In the UK, the REN is the JANET. In South Africa, there is a South African National Research Network (SANReN). ERNET is India's REN. Japan's REN is known as SINET. There are some RENs that span various countries. For example, the GLOBAL RING NETWORK FOR ADVANCED APPLICATIONS DEVELOPMENT (GLORIAD) network connects scientists in US, Russia, China, Korea, Canada, Netherlands, India, Egypt, Singapore, and Nordic Countries. The Trans Eurasia Information Network (TEIN3) connects researchers in China, India, Indonesia, Japan,

N. Meghanathan et al. (Eds.): CCSIT 2012, Part I, LNICST 84, pp. 538–541, 2012.

Korea, Laos, Malaysia, Nepal, Pakistan, the Philippines, Singapore, Sri Lanka, Taiwan, Thailand, Vietnam and Australia. Other countries such as Bangladesh, Bhutan and Cambodia are in the process of joining TEIN3. The GEANT is a pan-European REN. Such RENs may also have connectivity to other RENs. For example, TEIN3 has connectivity to GEANT.

2 Architecture of the NKN

The NKN will have three layers: a high-speed core (supporting speeds in excess of 10 Gbps), a distribution layer (to support the core), and an edge layer having more than 1500 nodes. The connections to the NKN will be provided through either the core layer or through the distribution layer. NKN will connect educational institutions (such as IITs), research and development institutions (such as CSIR), libraries, laboratories, and nuclear, space and defense research organizations (such as BARC, ISRO, DRDO). NKN will provide a variety of services including Internet, intranet, e-mail, messaging and caching gateways, Domain Name System, Web hosting, Voice over IP, video portals and video streaming. NKN will support IPv4 as well as IPv6 protocols. NKN is a IP-MPLS network that has already connected over 360 institutions (as on Sep 29, 2011). On completion, it will connect more than 1500 institutions. There are many criteria that must be fulfilled by organizations willing to join the NKN. These include compliance with policies for security and malware filtering among others.

3 Security Issues

One unfortunate aspect of the NKN design is that it depends on multiple bandwidth providers since no single provider has the geographical spread for creating a pan-India network. It should be emphasized that while the NKN will take care of the security of its core layer, it will not be able to address the security aspects of its numerous end nodes. The end nodes have to troubleshoot applications themselves. Since there are going to be over 1500 end nodes this only means that a large number of people specializing in information security are needed. They are currently unavailable and are unlikely to be available even after 2 or 3 years time. This only means that the potential users of the NKN must be provided information security education.

Various threats such as worms and viruses have shown that they can spread rapidly in networks and from one network to another network. Connecting networks benefits users, however, it also brings its own drawbacks such as the potential for the rapid spread of viruses, worms, spyware and malware. So the NKN must deal with all these threats. Since the NKN will be set up on commercial IP-MPLS networks and since there will be Virtual Private Networks (VPNs) based on these networks, the security aspects of such VPNs must be well studied. The NKN will be a massive network so it will be hard to say how secure it will be. Paraphrasing the well-known adage, we can say that the security of a network will only be as much as its weakest link. If a huge network such as the NKN is going to be designed using network components (such as routers and switches) not produced indigenously it will be hard to ensure its security as there could be Trojans, backdoors, spyware and malware in such network components. It must be ensured that at least core routers and switches are produced indigenously. But that is not going to be an easy task.

There is no doubt that the end nodes of the NKN must protect vital data using anti-virus and anti-malware packages, and by employing firewalls. The deployment of unified threat management systems for securing the NKN must be explored. Open source security software must be studied and developed for utilization by the NKN. It should be noted there is hardly any worthwhile open source anti-virus package. Such specialized software is produced by vendors with huge market presence. So issues such as licensing come into the picture. Updating anti-virus, anti-malware, anti-spyware packages is no easy task. Such updates are currently possible only by accessing the servers of some commercial vendors. We should also note that strict security policies (for say anti-virus, firewalls, anti-spyware, anti-malware) only retards the speed at which applications can be executed. We must also note that Network Address Translation has a similar effect on the performance of applications. However, we should also note that there can be no compromise on security at any point of time.

The NKN should have a dedicated Computer Emergency Response Team (CERT) (such as CERT-IN) on the lines of the emergency response teams of other RENs. The CERT must be responsible for security on a daily basis. Security policy for the NKN should be well-defined and those responsible for its compliance must be identified. Authentication, authorization and access control issues must be taken care of at all points in the network. Security features of the NKN must be clearly established. Security aspects of newer technologies and protocols such as MPLS and IPv6 must be well understood. Spam should be controlled so that it does not spread through the NKN. Denial-of-service attacks should be handled effectively. Hacking of core components on the NKN must be prevented. The principle of least privilege should be used when necessary. Special tools must be developed for checking the health of the NKN. Strong password policies must be used all through the NKN.

Packet filtering should be used wherever needed. Secure shell access must be restricted. Illicit traffic on the NKN must be handled effectively. Vulnerabilities of equipment to denial-of-service attacks should be monitored carefully. Core routers should be well protected from various types of attacks. Intrusion detection systems and intrusion prevention systems should be deployed. Attempted attacks on the NKN infrastructure must be spotted. Ways of protecting core equipment must be thoroughly studied. Anti-spoofing measures should be employed. Network performance must be monitored and poor performance detected and remedial measures should be taken. Packets exceeding rate-limiting thresholds must be observed. There should be notifications when such thresholds are exceeded. The security of roaming access services should be studied before they are deployed. Digital certificates issued by certification authorities must be used to guarantee secure communication between servers, between users, or between a server and a user.

Secure authentication procedures should be employed before allowing access to grid resources especially at sensitive locations (such as BARC). In the future, mobility of users will become paramount so the security of wireless local area networks will become an important concern. Computer security incidents require fast as well as effective response from the organizations concerned. Computer Security Incident Response Teams (CSIRTs) are responsible for responding to computer security incidents. International collaboration is essential to CSIRTs and much depends on their willingness to trust one another. The issue of privacy of users is often overlooked in huge networks. It must be ensured properly in the NKN. System administrators, site security teams and CERTs must receive adequate training and they should be familiar with the latest trends in the security arena. We should remember that security does not come gratis and also that it makes life more complex and difficult. Since RENs such as the NKN connect with other RENs located elsewhere this only implies that close co-operation between their respective CERTs will be required for successfully handling incidents.

4   Conclusion

We have seen that security is a complex subject and this is true for huge research and education networks such as the National Knowledge Network. The current shortage and possible future shortage of skilled information security professionals could be a major impediment for ensuring the security of the NKN. We have studied various ways of making the NKN a more secure and more profitable network.

Acknowledgements. The author is thankful to his institution as well as the Society for Electronic Transactions and Security (SETS).

References

1. National Knowledge Network, http://www.nkn.in
2. Nagaraj, S.V.: National Knowledge Network: Applications and Challenges. In: Proc. International Conference on Advances in Engineering and Technology (ICAET 2011). Coimbatore Institute of Information Technology, India (2011) ISBN-978-1- 4507-6433-9

Pattern Based IDS Using Supervised, Semi-supervised and Unsupervised Approaches

Vinod K. Pachghare, Vaibhav K. Khatavkar, and Parag Kulkarni

Dept. of Computer Engg. & IT,
College Of Engineering, Pune, MS, India
{vkp.comp,vkk.comp}@coep.ac.in, paragakulkarni@yahoo.com
http://www.coep.org.in/

Abstract. Intrusion detection aims at distinguishing the behavior of the network. Due to rapid development of attack pattern, it is necessary to develop a system which can upgrade itself according to new attacks. Also detection rate should be high since attack rate on the network is very high. In response to this problem, Pattern Based Algorithm is proposed which has high detection rate and low false alarm rate. The work is divided into three parts: supervised approach, semi-supervised and unsupervised approach. Besides supervised learning approach, semi-supervised learning has attracted much attention in pattern recognition and machine learning for intrusion detection. Most of the semi supervised algorithms used for intrusion detection are binary classifiers, but our approach is to classify the data into multiclass. Our experimental results on KDD cup data set shows that the performance of the proposed method is more effective.

Keywords: Intrusion Detection System, Pattern Based Algorithm, Security, supervised learning, semi-supervised learning, Machine Learning, Neural Networks.

1 Introduction

There are two main approaches to design IDS: misuse based IDS and anomaly based IDS [20]. Both misuse and anomaly detection approaches are typically presented in terms of distinct training and testing phases.

Modern IDS's are extremely diverse in the techniques they employ to gather and analyze data. Rule-based analysis depends on sets of predefined rules that are provided by an administrator. This design approach usually results in an inflexible detection system that is unable to detect an attack if the sequence of events is slightly different from the predefined profile [5, 14]. The principal constituents of soft computing techniques are Fuzzy Logic (FL), Artificial Neural Networks (ANNs), Probabilistic Reasoning (PR), and Genetic Algorithms (GAs) [2].

In this paper we propose three approaches: supervised , unsupervised and semi supervised approach for intrusion detection. In the supervised approach we use the labeled data for training and unlabeled data for testing. However,

N. Meghanathan et al. (Eds.): CCSIT 2012, Part I, LNICST 84, pp. 542–551, 2012.

supervised learning approach requires labeled ground truth data. With the immense amount of network and host data available, expert labeling of the data is very expensive and time consuming. The labeled data available is often from controlled environments. This proves to be a bottleneck in applying supervised learning methods to detect novel or unknown attacks. Relying only on supervised learning methods which require a large amount of labeled data is impractical for real network environment. This motivates a need for a new and more practical learning framework.

Semi-supervised learning approach can leverage unlabeled data in addition to labeled ones. They have received significant attention, and are more suitable for real network environment because they require a small quantity of labeled data while still taking advantage of the large quantities of unlabeled data.

Several algorithms have been proposed for semi-supervised learning which is naturally inductive. Usually, they are based on an assumption, called the cluster assumption [9]. It states that the data samples with high similarity between them, must share the same label. This may be equivalently expressed as a condition that the decision boundary between the classes must pass through low density regions. This assumption allows the unlabeled data to regularize the decision boundary, which in turn influences the choice of classification models.

Many successful semi-supervised algorithms like TSVM and Semi-supervised SVM [3] follow this approach. These algorithms assume a model for the decision boundary, resulting in an inductive classifier. Manifold regularization [16] is another inductive approach, which is built on the manifold assumption. It attempts to build a maximum-margin classifier on the data, while minimizing the corresponding inconsistency with the similarity matrix. This is achieved by adding a graph-based regularization term to an SVM based objective function. A related approach called LIAM [16] regularizes the SVM decision boundary using a priori metric information encoded into the Graph Laplacian, and has a fast optimization algorithm.

The proposed semi supervised learning approach can use small amount of labeled data and large amount of unlabeled data for learning, and gives performances similar to supervised learning approach which using much larger amounts of labeled data.

The rest of the paper is organized as follows. Section 2 describes the related work about intrusion detection system. Section 3 describes our proposed approach for all the three approaches. Section 4 describes experiments and results followed by a conclusion in Section 5.

2   Related Work

2.1   Supervised Learning Based Approaches

In recent years, methods from machine learning and pattern recognition have been utilized to detect intrusions. Both supervised learning and unsupervised learning are used. There are mainly supervised neural network (NN)-based approaches [15], [19], and support vector machine (SVM)-based approaches [12] are used in supervised learning for intrusion detection.

NN-based approaches: Many approaches have been proposed in neural network to distinguish between the behaviors of intrusions and normal. They unify the coding of categorical fields and the coding of character string fields in order to map the network data to the neural network. Some approaches propose hierarchical neural networks and evolutionary neural networks to detect intrusions.

SVM-based approaches: Mukkamala et al. [16] use SVMs to distinguish between normal and intrusions network behaviors and further identify important features for intrusion detection. The TreeSVM and ArraySVM have been proposed for solving the problem of inefficiency of the sequential minimal optimization algorithm for the large training data set in intrusion detection. Zhang and Shen [21] propose an approach for online training of SVMs for real-time intrusion detection based on an improved text categorization model. Also for intrusion detection, decision tree and discriminate analysis are applied. Comparisons between different classifiers and fusion of multiple classifiers for intrusion detection are studied in [18], [19], and [17].

2.2   Unsupervised Learning Based Approaches

Supervised learning methods for intrusion detection can only detect known intrusions. Unsupervised learning methods can detect the intrusions that have not been previously learned. K-means-based approaches and self-organizing feature map (SOM)-based approaches are the examples of unsupervised learning for intrusion detection [3].

K-means-based approaches: For intrusion detection, Guan et al. [22] propose a K-means-based clustering algorithm, which is named Y means. Xian et al. [23] combine the fuzzy K-means method and a clonal selection algorithm to detect intrusions. Jiang et al. [9] use the incremental clustering algorithm that is an extension of the K-means algorithm to detect intrusions.

SOM-based approaches: Pachghare et al. [3] gives various approaches of SOM like hierarchical SOM.

While these existing methods can obtain a high detection rate (DR), they often suffer from a relatively high false positive rate (FPR), which wastes a great deal of manpower. Meanwhile, their computational complexities are also oppressively high, which limits their applications in practice, because IDS would affect the regular tasks of the target systems if it employs too much resource. Adaboost is one of the most prevailing machine learning algorithms in recent years. Its computational complexity is generally lower than SOM, ANN and SVM in the case that the size of the data set is voluminous while the dimensionality is not too high. For this and other advantages, we employ Adaboost algorithm for our Pattern-based network security.

2.3 Semi-supervised Learning Based Approaches

Graph-based approaches represent both the labeled and the unlabeled examples by a connected graph, in which each example is represented by a vertex, and pairs of vertices are connected by an edge if the corresponding examples have large similarity. The well known approaches in this category include Harmonic Function based approach, Spectral Graph Transducer (SGT), Gaussian process based approach, Manifold Regularization and Label Propagation approach [11]. The optimal class labels for the unlabeled examples are found by minimizing their inconsistency with both the supervised class labels and the graph structure.

3 Proposed Algorithms

3.1 Supervised Algorithm

The framework of proposed algorithm is explained in our previous work [1].

Weak Classifier Design: A group of weak classifiers has to be prepared as inputs of Adaboost algorithm. They can be linear classifiers, ANNs or other common classifiers. In our algorithm, we select decision stumps as weak classifiers due to its simplicity. For every feature f, its value range could be divided into two non overlapping value subsets C_p^f and C_n^f, and the decision stump on f takes the form as follow:

$$h_f(x) = \begin{cases} +1 & x(f) \in C_p^f \\ -1 & x(f) \in C_n^f \end{cases}$$

where, $x(f)$ indicates the value of x on feature f.

Algorithm: In the AdaBoost algorithm, weak classifiers are selected iteratively from a number of candidate weak classifiers and are combined linearly to form a strong classifier for classifying the network data. In the AdaBoost algorithm,

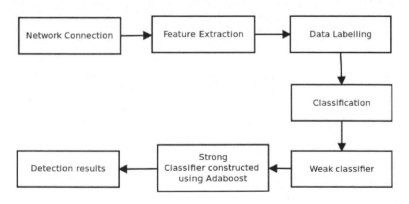

Fig. 1. Architecture for supervised IDS

weak classifiers are selected iteratively from a number of candidate weak classifiers and are combined linearly to form a strong classifier for classifying the network data.

Let $H = \left\{ \tilde{h}_f \right\}$ be the set of constructed weak classifiers. Let the set of training sample data be $\{(x_1, y_1), ..., (x_i, y_i), ..., (x_n, y_n)\}$, where x_i denotes the ith feature vector, $y_i \in \{+1, -1\}$ is the label of the ith feature vector, denoting whether the feature vector represents a normal behavior or not; and n is the size of the data set. Let $\{w_1, ..., w_i, ..., w_n\}$ be the sample weights that reflect the importance degrees of the samples and, in statistical terms, represents an estimation of the sample distribution. The AdaBoost-based algorithm for intrusion detection is described as follows:

1. Initialize Weights as:

$$w_i(1) \, (n = 1, 2, ..., n)$$
$$\text{satisfying } \sum_{i=1}^{n} w_i = 1$$

2. Observe the following for $(t = 1...T)$.
   (a) Let ϵ_j be the sum of the weighted classification errors for the weak classifier h_j

   $$\epsilon_j = \sum_{i=1}^{n} w_i(t) \, I \, [y_i \neq h_j(x_i)] \tag{1}$$

   where,

   $$I_{[\gamma]} = \begin{cases} 1 & \gamma = true \\ 0 & \gamma = false \end{cases} \tag{2}$$

   Choose, from constructed weak classifiers, the weak classifier $h(t)$ that minimizes the sum of the weighted classification errors

   $$h(t) = arg \; min_{h, j \in H} \; \epsilon_j \tag{3}$$

   (b) Calculate the sum of the weighted classification errors $\epsilon(t)$ for the chosen weak classifier $h(t)$.
   (c) Let
   $$\alpha(t) = 1/2 \log((1 - \epsilon(t))/\epsilon(t)) \tag{4}$$

   (d) Update the weights by
   $$w_i(t + 1) = \left(w_i(t) \exp(-\alpha(t) \, y_i h(t)(x_i)) / Z(t) \right) \tag{5}$$

   where,

   $$Z(t) = \sum_{k=i}^{n} \exp(-\alpha(t) \, y_i h(t)(x_k)) \tag{6}$$

3. The strong classifier is defined by

$$H(t) = sign \left(\sum_{t=1}^{T} \alpha(t) \, h(t)(x) \right) \tag{7}$$

We explain two points:

- By combining the decision stumps for both categorical and continuous features into a strong classifier, the relations between categorical and continuous features are handled naturally, without any forced conversions between continuous and categorical features.
- The decision stumps minimize the sum of the false-classification rates for normal and attack samples. It is guaranteed that the misclassification rates for the selected weak classifiers are lower than 50.

3.2   Semi-supervised Algorithm

The algorithm for Semi-supervised approach is given as:

1. Train the system with supervised approach using only label data from the mixed data.
2. Give unlabelled data from mixed data for testing.
3. If the confidence of data is above the threshold value then add data with label into the training data set.
4. Train the system with this new data.

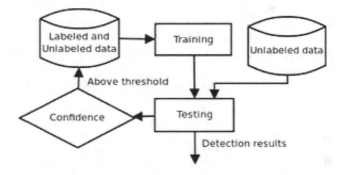

Fig. 2. Architecture for semi-supervised IDS

3.3   Unsupervised Algorithm

Heirarchical SOM have been proposed and implemented in our previous work [3].Specific attention is given to the hierarchical development of abstractions, which is sufficient to permit direct labeling of SOM nodes with connection type. Hierarchical SOM for intrusion detection use the classification capability of the SOM on selected dimensions of the data set to detect anomalies. Their results are among the best known for intrusion detection.

4   Results

We utilize the KDD CUP 1999 data set [17] for our experiments. There are four general types of attacks appeared in the data set: DOS (denial of service), U2R (user to root), R2L (remote to local) and PROBE. In each of the four, there are many low level types of attacks. Detailed descriptions about the four general types can be found in [31]. The number of samples of various types in the testing data set is listed in Table 1.

Table 1. Performance of supervised algorithm in Testing Data Set

	Normal	DOS	R2L	U2R	PROBE	%
Normal	97218	19	9	0	32	99.93
DOS	20	391413	3	4	18	99.98
R2L	15	0	1102	4	5	98.04
U2R	5	0	0	45	2	88.46
PROBE	40	11	9	0	4047	98.53

First, we run the classical Adaboost algorithm, whose result is shown in Table 2.

The data set for testing semi-supervised approach contains 11000 labeled data out of which 10000 are considered as unlabeled. Now, we run the semi-supervised algorithm on testing data set, whose result is shown in Table 5.

Table 6 gives the detection rate and false alarm rate for both the approaches.

Table 2. Performance of supervised algorithm in Testing Data Set

Normal	DOS	R2L	U2R	PROBE
97218	19	9	0	32
20	391413	3	4	18
15	0	1102	4	5
5	0	0	45	2
40	11	9	0	4047

Table 3. Testing Data Set for semi-supervised approach

Labeled data	Unlabeled data	Total data
1000	10000	11000

Table 4. Number of samples in testing data for semi-supervised

Normal	Attack				Total
	DOS	U2R	R2L	PROBE	
	7392	86	446	137	
1939	8061				10000

Table 5. Performance of Semi-supervised algorithm in Testing Data Set

	Normal	DOS	U2R	R2L	PROBE	%
Normal	1884	22	2	11	20	**97.16**
DOS	159	**7033**	45	106	49	**95.15**
U2R	7	24	**48**	2	5	**98.23**
R2L	28	353	23	**22**	20	**98.23**
PROBE	11	19	2	1	**104**	**97.07**

Table 6. Number of Samples in Data Set for Un-supervised approach

Normal	Attack				Total
	DOS	*U2R*	*R2L*	*PROBE*	
386	162	54	118	132	**852**
	466				

Table 7. Number of Samples in Performance of Un-supervised approach

	Normal	DOS	U2R	R2L	PROBE	%
Normal	380	3	1	0	2	**98.44**
DOS	1	159	0	0	1	**98.14**
U2R	3	2	0	48	1	**88.88**
R2L	2	1	114	0	0	**96.61**
PROBE	3	2	1	1	125	**94.69**

Table 8. Detection Results in Testing Data Set

Approach	Testing Set	
	FPR(%)	DR(%)
Supervised	0.06	**99.7**
Semi-supervised	0.028	**96.90**
Unsupervised	1.57	**95.35**

5   Conclusion

In the last twenty years, Intrusion Detection Systems have slowly evolved from host and operating system specific application to distributed systems that involve a wide array of operating system. The challenges that lie ahead for the next generation of Intrusion Detection Systems are many. Traditional Intrusion Systems have not adapted adequately to new networking paradigms like wireless and mobile networks. Factors like noise in the audit data, constantly changing traffic profiles and the large amount of network traffic make it difficult to build a normal traffic profile of a network for the purpose intrusion detection.

A perennial problem that prevents widespread deployment of IDS is their inability to suppress false alarms. Therefore, the primary and probably the most important challenge that needs to be met is the development of effective strategies to reduce the high rate of false alarms.

The experimental results show that the proposed algorithms have very low false alarm rate for training and testing. The semi-supervised algorithm shows better results for training and testing. The proposed algorithms have a competitive performance as compared with the published intrusion detection algorithms on the benchmark sample data.

References

1. Patole, V.A., Pachghare, V.K., Kulkarni, P.: AdaBoost Algorithm to Build Pattern Based Network Security. International Journal of Information Processing 5(1), 57–63 (2011)
2. Pachghare, V.K., Kulkarni, P.: Performance Analysis of Pattern Based Network Security. In: 2nd International Conference on Computer Technology and Development (ICCTD 2010), pp. 277–281. IEEE (2010)
3. Pachghare, V.K., Patole, V., Kulkarni, P.: Self Organizing Maps to Build Intrusion Detection System. International Journal of Computer Applications 1(8) (February 2010)
4. Song, E., Huang, D., Maa, G., Hung, C.-C.: Semi- supervised multi-class Adaboost by exploiting unlabeled data. Journal of Expert Systems with Applications (2010)
5. Pachghare, V.K., Kulkarni, P., Nikam, D.: Overview of Intrusion Detection Systems. International Journal of Computer Science and Engineering Systems 3(3), 265–268 (2009)
6. Wei, X., Huang, H., Tian, S.: Network Anomaly Detection Based on Semi-supervised Clustering. In: Proceedings of the 7th WSEAS International Conference on Simulation, Modelling and Optimization, Beijing, China, September 15-17 (2007)
7. Ermany, J., Mahantiy, A., Arlittyz, M., Cohenz, I., Williamsony, C.: Semi-Supervised Network Traffic Classification. In: SIGMETRICS 2007, San Diego, California, USA, June 12-16. ACM (2007)
8. Nigam, K., McCallum, A., Mitchell, T.: Semi-supervised Text Classification Using EM. In: In Chapelle, O., Zien, A., Cholkopf, B. (eds.) Semi-Supervised Learning. MIT Press, Boston (2006)
9. Jiang, S., Song, X., Wang, H., Han, J., Li, Q.: A clustering-based method for unsupervised intrusion detections. Pattern Recognit. Lett. 27(7), 802–810 (2006)
10. Mukkamala, S., Sung, A.H., Abraham, A.: Intrusion detection using an ensemble of intelligent paradigms. Network and Computer Applications 28(2), 167–182 (2005)
11. Zhu, X.: Semi-supervised Learning Literature Survey. Technical Report 1530, Department of Computer Sciences, University of Wisconsin, Madison (2005)
12. Hong, P., Zhang, D., Wu, T.: An intrusion detection method based on rough set and svm algorithm. In: Proceedings of International Conference on Communications, Circuits and Systems, vol. 2, pp. 1127–1130 (June 2004)
13. Rudin, C., Daubechies, I., Schapire, R.E.: The Dynamics of Adaboost: Cyclic Behavior and Convergence of Margins. Journal of Machine Learning (5), 1557–1595 (2004)

14. Mukkamala, S., Sung, A.H.: A comparative study of techniques for intrusion detection. In: Proc. Int. Conf. Tools Artif. Intell., pp. 570–577 (2003)
15. Liu, Y.H., Tian, D.X., Wang, A.M.: Annids: Intrusion Detection System Based on Artificial Neural Network. In: Proceedings of International Conference on Machine Learning and Cybernetics, vol. 3, pp. 1337–1342 (November 2003)
16. Mukkamala, S., Janoski, G., Sung, A.H.: Intrusion detection using neural networks and support vector machines. In: Proc. Int. Joint Conf. Neural Network, vol. 2, pp. 1702–1707 (2002)
17. Stolfo, S., et al.: The third international knowledge discovery and data mining tools competition (2002),
    http://kdd.ics.uci.eduidatabases/kddCup99/kddCup99.html
18. Bace, R., Mell, P.: NIST Special Publication on Intrusion Detection Systems, August 16 (2001)
19. Haykin, S.: Neural Networks: A Comprehensive Foundation, 2nd edn. Prentice Hall (1999)
20. Denning, D.: An Intrusion-Detection Model. IEEE Transactions on Software Engineering SE-13(2) (February 1987)
21. Zhang, Z., Shen, H.: Application of online- training SVMs for real-time intrusion detection with different considerations. Journal Computer Communications 28(12) (July 2005)
22. Guan, Y., Ghorbani, A.A., Belacel, N.: Y-Mean: A Clustering method For Intrusion Detection. In: ICCECE 2003, pp. 1–4.,
    www.jatit.org/volumes/researchpapers/Vol4No9/5Vol4No9.pdf
23. Guo, H.-X., Zhu, K.-J., Gao, S.-W., Liu, T.: An Improved Genetic k-means Algorithm for Optimal Clustering. In: Sixth IEEE International Conference on Data Mining Workshops, pp. 793–797 (2006)

A Secure Session Transfer Protocol for Downloading a Large File across a Cluster of Servers in the Presence of Network Congestion

Natarajan Meghanathan[1] and Bhadrachalam Chitturi[2]

[1] Jackson State University, Jackson, MS 39217, USA
nmeghanathan@jsums.edu
[2] Amrita Vishwavidyaapeetham University, Amritapuri Campus, Kerala, India
bhadrachalam@am.amrita.edu

Abstract. We propose the design of a Session Transfer Protocol (STP) that allows a client to download a large file replicated across several servers. STP runs at the session layer, on the top of the standard Transmission Control Protocol (TCP). A client can sequentially download the entire file from one or more servers, from one server at a time, with just one TCP session. A STP Server, currently sending the contents of a file to a client, can proactively detect congestion in the network and transfer a file download session to another peer STP Server that is located in a different network. At any stage (initial session establishment or session transfer), the STP Client chooses a particular server by executing certain selection tests among the servers in the list sent by the STP Gateway, which is the public face of the cluster of STP Servers in the Internet. Unlike the traditional File Transfer Protocol (FTP) that requires users to repeatedly initiate the entire download process upon the failure of each FTP connection, STP is seamless, incremental and provides improved Quality of Service while downloading a large file. The user working at the STP Client is unaware of the congestion and resulting session transfer to a different STP Server. STP is security-aware and has appropriate encryption, authentication and anti-spoofing features incorporated at different stages of its execution.

Keywords: Session Transfer Protocol, Sequential Download, Large File Download, Quality of Service, Secure Download.

1   Introduction

With the phenomenal growth in the Internet and the diversity of consumer applications, the size of the files being downloaded keep increasing from KB through MB to GB. The traditional File Transfer Protocol (FTP) with a single server that runs on the top of the connection-oriented Transmission Control Protocol (TCP) [10] is often considered unsuitable for downloading larger files over the Internet. A commonly employed strategy to counter the single server bottleneck problem is to employ multiple mirror servers and let the client choose one of these servers for download. Even in this scenario, once a server is chosen, the client has to stay with

N. Meghanathan et al. (Eds.): CCSIT 2012, Part I, LNICST 84, pp. 552–562, 2012.
© Institute for Computer Sciences, Social Informatics and Telecommunications Engineering 2012

that server for the entire download process. If a client starts experiencing more delay in the download process and wishes to download from another server, the client has no option other than completely disconnecting from the first server and opening a new TCP connection with the second server and starting the download all over again from the first byte of the file. For example, if a client is downloading a huge file (such as an .iso file for virtual machine operating systems) that is in the order of GB and if network congestion sets in after half of the file has been downloaded and the client apparently sees no appreciable progress in the download, it becomes quite exasperating for a client to start the process all over again with a new server. There is no guarantee that the client will not again experience the same problem with the new server after a while.

To counter the problem of relying on a single client - single server model, downloading in parallel has been considered as a viable alternative (e.g. [1][2]). Here, the distinct segments of a file are downloaded in parallel from multiple servers and the downloaded contents are merged at the client to reconstruct the original file. However, parallel downloading has several drawbacks. A critical drawback is the requirement to maintain multiple TCP connections at the client side, with each of the parallel servers from which the file is being downloaded. It becomes tedious for thin clients (client machines with very limited resources) to maintain multiple TCP connections and the associated memory buffers for a download session. The client is overloaded until the download is completed. In addition, proper security features need to be embedded in the parallel downloading schemes.

Another strategy that is gaining prominence in recent times is peer-to-peer file sharing with technologies such as the BitTorrent protocol [9]. Here, files are no longer hosted at a particular server or a mirror of servers. A file is broken into pieces and distributed among several machines across the Internet; the information about these machines is stored as part of a metadata for the file. An interested client wishing to download a file contacts the machines listed in the metadata of the file. As the different pieces of the file get downloaded, the client itself becomes a host from which other interested peer clients can download. Peer-to-peer file sharing again requires the client to re-order the downloaded pieces of the file before being delivered to the application and it is highly prone to out-of-order packet arrival. Hence, peer-to-peer file sharing systems are not typically suitable for streaming applications that require progressive or contiguous downloading.

We propose a novel Session Transfer Protocol (STP) for downloading a huge file over the Internet in a sequential fashion using just one TCP session at any given time (between the client and a chosen server) while providing improved Quality of Service (QoS) and a secure (reliable) download. The STP runs at the session layer, on top of TCP at the transport layer. Here, we conceptualize a cluster of cooperating file servers, each of which hosts the entire file. The cluster is publicly identified through a gateway, which is the initial point of contact for an interested client. The gateway, by itself, does not store any file – however, it maintains a database (STP database) that has information about the cooperating servers hosting each of the files. The gateway merely forwards this information to the requesting client in the form of a secure STP ticket, which has to be used by the client to initiate a download session with any of the cooperating servers of the file. During the download process, as the client sends out Acknowledgments for the last packet that has arrived in-order, the server evaluates the variance in the round-trip times (RTT) of the acknowledgment packets. If the RTT starts to increase beyond a threshold, the server considers this as a sign of impending congestion on the path to the client. As a proactive measure, the server decides that the client has to choose some other server to continue the session and hands-off by sending an encrypted 'Transfer Session' message that includes the session details (such as last byte acknowledged, window size, etc); the client selects the next suitable server from the list of cooperating servers for the file through a ping-request-reply cycle [10] and forwards the encrypted Transfer Session message and the STP ticket originally sent by the gateway. If the chosen server can accommodate the new session with the required QoS, it responds positively. Otherwise, it rejects the connection request.

The STP Client maintains a list of overloaded and unavailable servers and updates this list based on the recent STP sessions it has gone through. After a server positively responds to the session transfer, the STP Client continues to download the remainder of the file from that server. If the session has to be further transferred to another server, the above process is repeated. However, we anticipate that there will not be several session transfers as a STP Server accepts a connection request only if it is able to provide the required QoS in terms of maintaining the same sender window size, etc. The only unknown parameter here is the network bandwidth. The bandwidth on the path between the client and server may be sufficient at the beginning of the session transfer or session initiation. But, after a while, the intermediate networks and the routers on the path between the client and server may be overloaded with traffic, necessitating a session transfer for quick, real-time download. However, at any time, a client has to run only one TCP connection and has to deal with only one server. Hence, STP is perfectly suitable for thin clients. The File Transfer Protocol (FTP) that runs at the application layer, on the top of TCP, can be suitably modified to run STP at the Session layer. We will refer to the modified FTP as STP-aware FTP.

The rest of the paper is organized as follows: Section 2 analyzes related work on parallel downloads and motivates the need for a secure sequential download, especially for thin clients, and at the same time provides the required QoS. Section 3 presents a detailed design of the proposed Session Transfer Protocol (STP) and provides a qualitative comparison with that of the traditional FTP. Section 4 concludes the paper and discusses future work.

2   Related Work

In [1], the authors propose a Parallelized-File Transfer Protocol (P-FTP) that facilitates simultaneous downloads of disjoint file portions from multiple file servers distributed across the Internet. The selection of the set of parallel file servers is done by the P-FTP gateway when contacted by a P-FTP client. The number of bytes to be downloaded from each file server is decided based on the available bandwidth. We observe the following drawbacks with P-FTP: (1) The P-FTP client would be significantly overloaded in managing multiple TCP sessions, one with each of the parallel file servers. Thus, P-FTP cannot be run on thin clients that are limited in the available memory and resources to run concurrent TCP sessions for downloading a single file. (2) If the path to a particular file server gets congested, the P-FTP client is forced to wait for the congestion to be relieved and continue to download the remaining bytes of the portion of the file allocated for download from the particular file server. The QoS realized during the beginning of the download process may not be available till the end due to the dynamics of the Internet. (3) P-FTP has no security features embedded in it. Hence, it is open for spoofing-based attacks on the availability of the parallel file servers by unauthorized users/clients who simply launch several parallel download sessions that appear to originate from authentic users/IP addresses.

In [2], the authors propose a Dynamic Parallel Access (DPA) scheme that is also based on downloading a file in parallel from multiple servers, but different from P-FTP in the sense that the portion of the file and the number of bytes to be downloaded from a particular file server is not decided a priori; but done dynamically based on the response from the individual servers. In this scheme, the client chooses the set of parallel servers to request for the file. The download is to be done in blocks of equal size. Initially, the client requests one block of the file from every server. After a client has completely received one block from a server, the client requests the particular server for another block that has not yet been requested from any other server. Upon receiving all the blocks, the client reassembles them and reconstructs the whole file. Unlike P-FTP, DPA is less dependent on any particular mirror server as it requests only one block of the file from a server at a time and does not wait for several blocks of the file from any particular server. However, with DPA, the client cannot close its TCP connections with any of the mirror file servers until the entire file is downloaded. This is because, if a client fails to receive a block of the file from a particular mirror server and has waited for a long time, then the client has to request another peer mirror server for the missing block. In order to avoid opening and closing multiple TCP connections with a particular mirror server, the client has to maintain the TCP connection with each of the file servers until the entire download is completed. The client has to keep sending some dummy packets to persist with the TCP connections. On the other hand, a P-FTP client can close the TCP connection with a P-FTP server once the required portions of the file are downloaded as initially allocated from the particular mirror server. DPA also does not have any security features embedded in it.

Many other related works (e.g., [3][4][5]) on simultaneous partial download have also been proposed in the literature for better QoS. All of these schemes use parallel downloading to fasten the throughput and minimize the delay. But, this will be a significant overhead on the part of the client. Also, as mentioned above, the parallel download schemes rarely take into account incorporating modules that will address the security issues. In [6], the authors analyzed (through simulations) the impact of large-scale deployment of parallel downloading on the Internet as well for network dimensioning and content distribution service provisioning. They show that with proper admission control and dimensioning, single-server downloading can perform just as well as parallel downloading, without the complexity and overhead incurred by the latter. The above observation forms the motivation for our work in this paper. Ours is the first novel approach to expedite file download in a sequential fashion by incorporating the idea of a secure session transfer protocol that can be run on thin clients, with just one TCP connection for the entire download process, and is also adaptive to the congestion in the Internet.

3   Design of the Session Transfer Protocol

The Session Transfer Protocol (STP) will run at the session layer on the top of TCP. To use STP at the application layer, the traditional FTP Protocol has to be modified to run on the top of STP. The modified FTP can be referred to as the STP-aware FTP and it needs to run on a separate port number. In other words, the STP-aware FTP would be an alternate to the standard FTP. If a client does not want to go through the file transfer that could potentially involve more than one server, then the client can use the standard FTP; if the client wants to use STP in order to get better QoS and be able to successfully transfer the files even in the presence of network congestion, then the client can use the STP-aware FTP. Figure 1 illustrates the TCP/IP protocol stack for the standard FTP and the STP-aware FTP.

There are three entities involved in the STP protocol: (i) STP Server Cluster – A group of servers, each located in different networks, one or more of which are involved in the file download session with a client. Note that, only a subset of the cluster might carry a specific file and this information resides in the STP Gateway Server. (ii) STP Client – A client machine that runs the STP protocol and is involved in downloading a file from the STP Server Cluster. (iii) STP Gateway Server – The public face of the STP Cluster. The STP Client first contact the STP Gateway Server to initiate the file downloading process. The STP Server Cluster and STP Gateway Server are organization-specific. There could be multiple STP Server Clusters and an appropriate STP Gateway Server (one for each organization) running in the Internet.

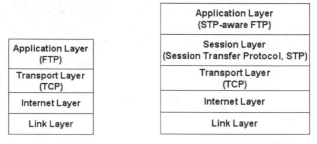

Application Layer (FTP)	Application Layer (STP-aware FTP)
Transport Layer (TCP)	Session Layer (Session Transfer Protocol, STP)
Internet Layer	Transport Layer (TCP)
Link Layer	Internet Layer
	Link Layer

Traditional FTP   STP-aware FTP

Fig. 1. TCP/IP Protocol Stack for the Traditional FTP and the STP-aware FTP

3.1   STP – Details

1. The STP Client initiates the download session by contacting the STP Gateway Server. The client passes the username and password to first get authenticated by the Gateway Server. Once authenticated, the client sends the path and the name of the file to download. We assume the file hierarchy for a particular user is maintained the same across all STP Servers. The Gateway server resolves the tuple <username, path> in its database and extracts the list of STP Servers that store the file. The STP Servers are ranked in the order of the number of hops from the client network.

2. The Gateway server creates a STP Ticket that contains the username, path of the file requested, filename, IP address of the client machine, the byte number in the file (set to 0) and the time of contact information. The time of contact information is included to avoid any replay attack. STP Tickets lose their validity beyond a certain time after their creation. All of the above information in the STP Ticket is encrypted using a secret key that is shared by all the STP Servers and the Gateway Server. Along with this information, the Gateway also includes the set of IP addresses of the STP Servers in the increasing order of the hop count from the client network. For security purposes, the IP address list of the candidate STP Servers is encrypted through a key that is derived (using a Key Derivation Function agreed upon by the user while creating an account at the Gateway Server) based on the user password. Figure 2 illustrates the contents of the STP Ticket along with the STP Server IP address list. We show only the payload portion of the Ticket message; we do not show the standard IP header (containing the STP Gateway IP address as the sender address and the STP Client address as the destination address) that is part of the message.

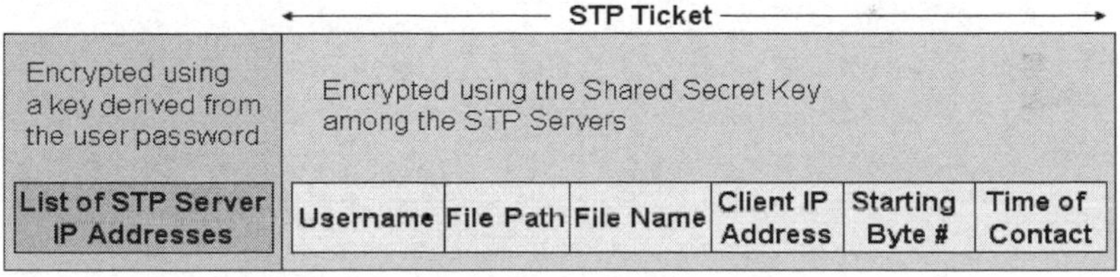

Fig. 2. Structure of STP Ticket along with the List of Server IP Addresses

3. The client decrypts STP Server List and pings the top three servers in the list by sending four short "Echo Request" messages to each of these servers. The client measures the Round Trip Time (RTT) of the "Echo Reply" ping messages. The STP Server that returns the Reply message at the earliest (i.e., incurred the lowest RTT) is selected. Ties are broken by the lowest hop count and other predefined criteria.

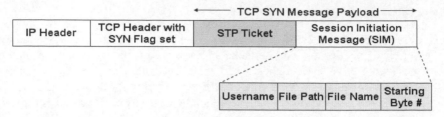

Fig. 3. TCP SYN Message with the Payload STP Ticket and SIM

4. The STP Client attempts to establish a TCP Session with the chosen STP Server and sends a TCP SYN message (structure shown in Figure 3) – the payload of which includes the STP Ticket and a Session Initiation Message (SIM) containing the username, path, filename and the byte number, starting from which the download is requested. The STP Server first decrypts the STP Ticket using the secret key shared among the servers in the STP Cluster as well as the Gateway Server. If the extracted contents of the Ticket matches with the username and file path (sent by the client) as well as the IP address of the client machine, then the STP Sever accepts the TCP connection request (sends a TCP SYN/ACK message) if it can allocate the required resources for the file download session. Otherwise, the STP Server sends a 'Connection Request Reject' message. Once the STP Server has accepted for the TCP session, the STP Client begins to download the contents of the requested file using TCP. In order to avoid any IP-spoofing triggered session transfers, we recommend the STP Client and STP Server to form an IPSec security association (SA) before establishing a TCP session. One of the pre-requisite steps for establishing an IPSec SA is to run an Internet Key protocol Exchange (IKE) session between the concerned Client and Server machines and exchange their public-key certificates. All subsequent communications, including the TCP session establishment messages, packets of the file being downloaded and the Transfer Session message – all of these could be encrypted at the sender using the public key of the receiver and decrypted at the receiver using its private key.

5. If the STP Server denies the TCP connection request, the STP Client includes the STP Server to the 'Overloaded List of STP Servers' and then tries to establish a TCP Session with the STP Server that responded with the next lowest RTT. If all the three first-choice STP Servers deny the connection request, the STP Client chooses the next three STP Servers in the list sent by the Gateway Server and pings them. This procedure is repeated until the STP Client manages to successfully find a STP Server; otherwise, the STP Client returns an error message to the user indicating that the file cannot be downloaded.

6. After receiving a packet in-order, the STP Client acknowledges for all the packets that have been received in-order and not acknowledged yet. The STP Server measures the RTT for the acknowledgment packets received from the STP Client. If the RTTs start increasing significantly for every acknowledgment received (the actual rate of increase of the RTT is an implementation issue), then the STP Server decides to handoff the session to another peer STP Server.

7. To handoff the session, the STP Server sends a 'Transfer Session' message to the STP Client and includes the sequence number of the last byte whose acknowledgment has been received by the Server and the position of this byte (i.e., the byte number) in the actual file being downloaded. The STP Server also updates the STP Ticket with the byte number that was last sent to the Client and acknowledged by the latter. The STP Server encrypts the updated STP Ticket using the secret key shared among all the servers in the STP cluster. The updated STP Ticket along with the Transfer Session message is sent to the STP Client.

8. After receiving the Transfer Session message, the STP Client confirms about the last byte number that was received in-order from the previous STP Server (which is now added to the Overloaded list). The STP Client now goes through the original Server List sent by the STP Gateway Server. Unlike the previous procedure adopted (i.e., to look for potential STP Servers in the increasing order of the number of hops), the STP Client randomly permutes the list and pings all the Servers in the Cluster, except those in the locally maintained Overloaded list.

Sequence # of the last byte for which ACK was received from the client before session transfer	Position of the byte Number in the file, corresponding to the last Sequence # acknowledged	STP Ticket with the Starting Byte field updated based on the next Byte to be downloaded

⟵ Encrypted and can be Decrypted only by the ⟶ STP Servers

Fig. 4. Contents of the Transfer Session Message Sent by an STP Server

9. The STP Server that responds back with an "Echo Reply" at the earliest is chosen as the next Server to transfer the session. The STP Client attempts to open a TCP session with the new chosen server by sending a TCP SYN message – the payload of which includes the STP Ticket received from the previous STP Server as well as a 'Transfer Request' message containing those forwarded to the first STP Server: username, path, filename and the byte number (one more than the previous value), starting from which the download is requested.

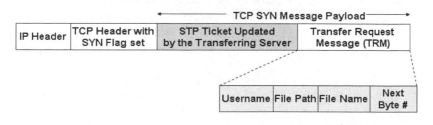

Fig. 5. TCP SYN Message with the Payload – Updated STP Ticket and Transfer Request Message

10. Once the newly chosen STP Server receives the STP Ticket along with the Transfer Request message, it decrypts the STP Ticket using the secret key for the STP Server cluster and compares the contents of the STP Ticket with those in the Transfer Request message. If everything matches and it is ready to allocate the required buffer space for this session and offer the requested window size, the new STP Server agrees to continue with the download session and sends a TCP SYN/ACK message; otherwise, it sends a Connection Request Reject message.

11. The STP Client adds the last chosen STP server that sent the Connection Request Reject message to the Overloaded list. Another STP Server that is not in the Overloaded list is contacted and this procedure is repeated until a new STP Server to transfer the session is found. If unsuccessful over the entire STP Server List, the STP Client quits and reports an error message to the user.

12. Once the new STP Server has accepted the TCP connection request and to continue with the transferred session, the STP Client begins to download the subsequent contents of the file. A secure-TCP session established on the top of IPSec is recommended.

13. After a while, if the new STP Server decides to handoff the file download session, then Steps 7 through 12 are again followed.

3.2   Qualitative Comparison with Standard FTP

FTP does not support session transfer during the middle of a file download. If a client or server experiences frequent timeouts and/or packet loss due to network congestion, the TCP session running as part of FTP has to be discontinued and a new TCP session has to be established. Nevertheless, we cannot be sure whether the new TCP session would be of any remedy to the network congestion problem as packets are more likely to be again routed through the same set of congested routers (and networks) as long as the server and client remain the same. STP handles the network congestion problem by initiating the transfer of a session to another server. This transfer is done in a secure fashion, through the encrypted session transfer ticket, in order to avoid the scenarios wherein an attacker initiates the transfer without the consent or knowledge of the actual server or the client. There could be some delay involved in transferring a session from one server to another server. However, the transfer delay is expected to be smaller enough to offset the delay incurred if the packets are continued to be sent on a congested route without any session transfer.

STP sincerely attempts to avoid session thrashing wherein a newly transferred session to a server I does not get immediately transferred to some other server J. Note that in Step 10, the STP Server receiving the Transfer Request message accepts the message only if it can allocate resources and offer the download service as requested. However, from a network congestion point of view, we cannot guarantee that session thrashing will be totally avoidable. As IP works on a per-packet basis, it is possible that after the session transfer is implemented, one or more networks on the route between the client and the server start to get congested and the session has to be again transferred to some other server within the set of clusters.

4   Conclusions and Future Work

The high-level contribution of this paper is the design of a secure Session Transfer Protocol (STP) that can be used even by thin clients to download a large file, distributed across several servers that constitute the STP Server Cluster. If there is an impending congestion on the path between a STP Client and the STP Server, the latter proactively initiates a session handoff by sending a Session Transfer message with the details on the last byte acknowledged and etc., updated in the STP Ticket. The STP Client contacts the other STP Servers in the list originally sent by the STP Gateway (during the authentication phase) and chooses the best alternate STP Server that agrees to continue with the download session. The user working at the STP Client is totally unaware of this session transfer process among the servers in the STP Cluster. The entire session transfer will occur in a secure manner with no scope for any denial of service or spoofing attacks, if the TCP session is run on the top of IPSec. Throughout the download session, an STP Client is required to maintain only one TCP connection – a feature that suits thin clients, unlike the protocols for parallel download that require a client to simultaneously run/maintain multiple TCP connections. Compared to the parallel and peer-to-peer download schemes, STP can be the preferred choice for streaming applications, of course with some jitter experienced during session transfer. Faster the session transfer, smaller is the delay. Our strategy to let the STP Client randomly choose STP Servers (from a list of putative servers) to contact for session transfer helps to minimize the session transfer delay. Also, because of sequential download, data packets of the file are highly likely to arrive in-order at the client. In the near future, we plan to implement STP, first as a prototype in a laboratory scale, simulating with client-server programs and then implement in a larger network with traffic actually sent over the Internet. Through simulations, we plan to compare the performance of STP with that of the P-FTP and DPA parallel download protocols as well as the BitTorrent peer-to-peer protocol.

Acknowledgments. The authors made equal contributions. The work of Natarajan Meghanathan leading to this paper has been partly funded through the U. S. National Science Foundation (NSF) CCLI/TUES grant (DUE-0941959) on "Incorporating Systems Security and Software Security in Senior Projects." The views and conclusions contained in this document are those of the authors and do not represent the official policies, either expressed or implied, of the funding agency.

References

1. Sohail, S., Jha, S.K., Kanhere, S.S.: QoS Driven Parallelization of Resources to Reduce File Download Delay. IEEE Transactions on Parallel and Distributed Systems 17(10), 1204–1215 (2006)
2. Rodriguez, P., Biersack, E.W.: Dynamic Parallel Access to Replicated Content in the Internet. IEEE Transactions on Networking 10(4), 455–465 (2002)

3. Karrer, R.P., Knightly, E.W.: TCP-PARIS: A Parallel Download Protocol for Replicas. In: The 10th International Workshop on Web Content Caching and Distribution, Sophia Antipolis, France, pp. 15–25 (2005)
4. Brock, M., Goscinski, A.: A Parallel Download Protocol for Internet-based Distributed Systems. In: International Conference on Internet Computing, Las Vegas, pp. 3–9 (2008)
5. Chang, R.-S., Guo, M.-H., Lin, H.-C.: A Multiple Parallel Download Scheme with Server Throughput and Client Bandwidth Considerations for Data Grids. Future Generation Computer Systems 24(8), 798–805 (2008)
6. Koo, S.G.M., Rosenberg, C., Xu, D.: Analysis of Parallel Downloading for Large File Distribution. In: The 9th Workshop on Future Trends of Distributed Computing. IEEE, San Juan (2003)
7. Neglia, G., Reina, G., Zhang, H., Towsley, D., Venkataramani, A., Danaher, J.: Availability in BitTorrent Systems. In: International Conference on Computer Communications, pp. 2216–2224. IEEE, Anchorage (2007)
8. Measche, D.S., Rocha, A.A.A., Li, B., Towsley, D., Venkataramani, A.: Content Availability and Bundling in Swarming Systems. In: The 5th International Conference on Emerging Networking Experiments and Technologies, pp. 121–132. ACM (2009)
9. BitTorrent,
   http://www.bittorrent.org/beps/bep_0003.html
   (last accessed: July 26, 2011)
10. Peterson, L.L., Davie, B.S.: Computer Networks: A Systems Approach, 5th edn. Morgan Kaufmann (2011)

An Improved Anti Spam Filter Based on Content, Low Level Features and Noise

Anand Gupta[1], Chhavi Singhal[2], and Somya Aggarwal[1]

[1] Department of Computer Engineering
[2] Department of Electronic and Communication Engineering,
Netaji Subhas Institute of Technology, New Delhi, India
{Omaranand,chhavisinghal28,somya3322}@gmail.com

Abstract. Spammers are constantly evolving new spam technologies, the latest of which is image spam. Till now research in spam image identification has been addressed by considering properties like colour, size, compressibility, entropy, content etc. However, we feel the methods of identification so evolved have certain limitations due to embedded obfuscation like complex backgrounds, compression artifacts and wide variety of fonts and formats .To overcome these limitations, we have proposed a 4-stage methodology which uses the information of low level features and content of the spam images. The method works on images with and without noise separately. Also colour properties of the images are altered so that OCR (Optical Character Recognition) can easily read the text embedded in the image. The proposed method is tested on a dataset of 1984 spam images and is found to be effective in identifying all types of spam images having (1) only text, (2) only images or (3) both text and images. The encouraging experimental results show that the technique achieves an accuracy of 92%.

Keywords: Low level feature, anti obfuscation technique, noise.

1 Introduction

Image spam is a kind of spam in e-mail where the message text of the spam is presented as an image file. Anti spam filters label an e-mail (with image attached) as spam if they find suspicious text embedded in that image. For that, the filters employ OCR that reads text embedded in images. It works by measuring the geometry in images, searching for shapes that match the shapes of letters, then translating a matched geometric shape into real text. To defeat OCR, spammers upset the geometry of letters enough—by altering colours, for example—so that OCR can't "see" a letter, even though the human eye easily recognize it. To overcome this falsity, low level features of images are extracted as they are effective against randomly added noises and simple translational shift of the images. We now review the prior significant work in the area of image spam identification.

N. Meghanathan et al. (Eds.): CCSIT 2012, Part I, LNICST 84, pp. 563–572, 2012.

2   Prior Work

Till now spam identification has been carried out by considering the following spam image properties.

1. Content (C) 2. Metadata features (M) 3. Low level features (L) 4. Text region (T)
The following matrix shows the properties as used in the previous works. Whereas the left most column shows the reference numbers, the top most row 1 shows the properties employed as given above. Numerals '1' and '0' mean that the given property is used and not used respectively.

$$
\begin{array}{c}
 & \text{C} & \text{M} & \text{L} & \text{T} \\
[1] & 1 & 0 & 0 & 0 \\
[2] & 1 & 0 & 0 & 0 \\
[3] & 0 & 1 & 0 & 0 \\
[4] & 0 & 0 & 1 & 0 \\
[5] & 0 & 1 & 1 & 0 \\
[6] & 1 & 1 & 1 & 0 \\
[7] & 0 & 0 & 0 & 1 \\
\end{array}
$$

In [1], a scheme is proposed which implements a spam filter based on both the text in the subject and body fields of e-mails, and the text embedded into attached images. The traditional document processing steps (tokenization, indexing and classification) are improved upon in [1] by employing text extraction using OCR from attached images. SpamAssassin (SA)[2] is a widely deployed filter program that uses OCR software to pull words out of images and then uses the traditional text based methods to filter spam. This happens to be an improvement of the earlier.

In the year 2008, a spam filtering technique has been proposed in [3] that uses image information (metadata features) such as file size, area, compressibility etc., and states a characteristics that appears for each information entity.

On the contrary, [4] identifies spam using a probabilistic boosting tree based on global image features (low level features), i.e. colour and gradient orientation histograms. In the year 2010, a feature extraction scheme that concentrates on both low-level and metadata features is proposed in [5].It does not rely on extracting the text.

In [6], a mechanism is proposed to ascertain spam embedded main body e-mail file, called as Partial Image Spam Inspector (PIMSI). The significant feature of this method is that it evaluates both low level features and metadata features to confirm whether a mail is spam or not. It analyses spam images by dividing it into 2 databases. Database of object image spam consists of images and its properties such as RGB colours, contrast, brightness. In the database of Vocal Spam, all keywords of the advertised spam images are recorded and are compared with the text extracted using OCR.

To overcome the shortcomings of the methods mentioned above, a spam identification model has been proposed in [7] which does not exploit low level features and OCR to extract text from images. Instead, it identifies spams by using the visual-BOW (VBOW) based duplicate image detection and statistical language model. Computation-efficient edge-detection method is used to locate possible text regions, and then text coverage rate in an image is calculated. Text region in a large majority of normal image is less than 15%, while text region in most spam is larger than such a threshold.

2.1   Motivation

The following drawbacks in prior related works have motivated us to develop a method that mitigates them.

Nowadays, spammers use different image processing technologies to vary the properties of individual messages e.g. by changing the foreground colours, backgrounds, font types or even rotating and adding artifacts to the images. Thus, they pose great challenges to conventional spam filters.

[4][6][5][8] use colour histograms to distinguish spam images from normal images. Colour histograms of natural images tend to be continuous, while the colour histograms of artificial spam images tend to have some isolated peaks. We point out however that the discriminating capability of the above feature is not likely to be satisfactory, since colour distribution is solely dependent on the format of the image. Figures 2 and 3 illustrate the difference between the colour histograms of a single image shown in Figure 1 but saved with different formats (gif and jpeg).

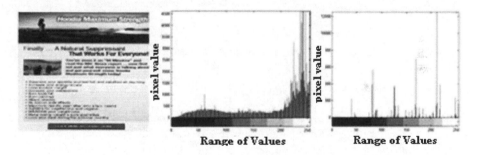

Fig. 1. Image   **Fig. 2.** Colour histogram in jpeg   **Fig. 3.** Colour histogram in gif

[3][5][6] use metadata features. Different images can have similar (even same) metadata features. This technology of image spam detection may be wrong and has low accuracy rate. After carrying out experiments we have found that 58.65% of spam images and 44.28% of normal images are smaller than 10KB. It implies that metadata features can be similar for both kind of images. Hence it is not a reliable method to distinguish between spam images from normal images.

The method mentioned in [7] has helped achieve significant results in identifying spam images which contain only text. However, few spam images contain both text and images. Figures 4 and 5 show that edge detection is not able to distinguish between text and images. Also edge detection will detect noise and treat it as text.

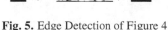

Fig. 4. Original Image   **Fig. 5.** Edge Detection of Figure 4

3   System Architecture

Figure 6 depicts the System Architecture of the proposed approach.

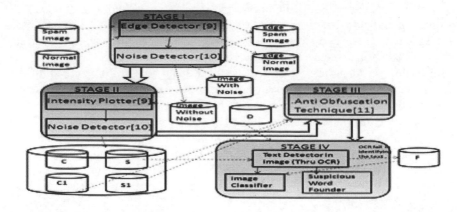

Fig. 6. System Architecture

3.1   Stage I (Identification of Noise)

Canny's edge detection [9] is used to identify noise in images. Images with noise are stored in set A and images without noise are stored in set B. Edge detection highlights even the slightest of noise added in an image. Images in Set A are more likely to be spam images. Set A is further classified into databases, namely -(A1) Dots & Dashes (A2) Lines. This classification is done on the basis of type of noise usually found in spam images. Figures 8 and 10 show a sample image for each kind of noise found in Figures 7 and 9 respectively. They also display the difficulty to identify noise without edge detection.

Fig. 7. Sample Image 1 **Fig. 8.** Image 1 noise **Fig. 9.** Sample Image 2 **Fig. 10.** Image 2 noise

3.2   Stage II (Extraction of Low Level Features)

In this stage, all the input images pass through Intensity Plotter [9], which plots the variation of intensity along a line segment or a multiline path of an image. Since spam images are artificially generated, we expect their low level features to be different from those of images typically included as attachments to personal e-mails. The plots thus obtained do not change on varying the format of the image (from gif to jpeg or vice versa). Stage II has two sub stages.

3.2.1 Sub-Stage II (a)

Images without noise are classified into two sets, S and C. The classification is based on the difference in the shape of the plots obtained. Figures 11 and 12 show the intensity plots of normal and spam images respectively. Herein X and Y are two element vectors specifying X and Y data of the image. Images common to both Set B and Set C are labelled as normal images and are not processed further. Images in set S are directly passed to stage IV.

3.3   Sub-Stage II (b)

Images with noise are classified (as mentioned above) on the basis of plots obtained in two sets, S1 and C1. Images in set S1 and C1 are passed to stage III.

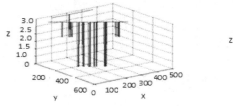 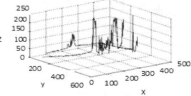

Fig. 11. Intensity plot for normal images   **Fig. 12.** Intensity plot for spam images

3.4   Stage III (Removal of Noise)

Spammers add noise in images so that it becomes difficult for OCR to read the embedded text. To overcome this difficulty, obfuscation techniques are applied. Therefore, only images with noise are passed through this stage. In this technique we alter the RGB properties of the images. Images thus obtained are stored in set D. Table 1 shows a comparison between the words identified by OCR before and after applying stage III on Figure 13.

Fig. 13. Original Image

Table 1. Comparison between the words identified by OCR before and after stage III

Text identified in Fig. 13 before applying anti obfuscation technique	Text identified in Figure 13 after applying anti-obfuscation technique
DEMDEAG ERANDE ING CITC:DMGB,PI(—~,I,._- Teda•,r's Breaking news sent shares up +122% in just a few minutes, revelutienaryr new pre-duet in eenstruetien. r___..F-——— u_\ Huge PR campaign is under wa•,r, eemhined with teda•,r's news there's ne telling where this stuck is geing te end up, ——	DEMOBAG BRANDS INC OTC:DMGB.PK Today's Breaking news sent shares up +122% in Just a few minutes, revolutionary new product in construction. Huge PR campaign is under way, combined with today's news there's no telling where this stock is going to end up,

3.5   Stage IV (Content Extraction Using OCR)

Input to this stage comprises of images in set S and D. Images are passed through OCR, which identifies embedded text and compares it with a list of keywords. If text identified matches with the list of spam words, then the image is labelled as spam image else it is a normal image. If OCR fails, then the graphs plotted in stage II are considered. Images in sets S1 and S are labelled as spam images. Images in set C1 are labelled as normal images.

4   Experiments and Results

We have collected two sets of images to test the filter: spam images and normal images. The dataset consist of spam images in gif and jpeg format. A set of 1984 images are taken out of which 802 are normal images and 1182 are spam images from [12]. Experiments are performed on a system with the following specifications: 32- bit operating system, 2.40 Ghz processor and 4 Gb RAM. Matlab version 7.7 is used. It employs image processing techniques like Canny's edge detection and intensity plotter. For applying anti obfuscation techniques, we make use of an online editor [11]. Free OCR V3 is used to extract the content of the spam image. The experiment has shown that our technique is effective in identifying spam images in any format. According to the experimental results, detection rate of the new system is 0.92, false positive rate is 0.0064 and false negative rate is 0.059 by calculation. The following are the results.

4.1   Result I

Figures 14 and 15 show the efficiency of spam and normal images which were correctly identified by using our methodology. We have tabulated the results by classifying hams and spam images into the following categories.

Spam Images: Advertisement, URL (Uniform Resource Locator), Pornography, Stock.

Normal Images: Only Text, Text and Images, Only Images.

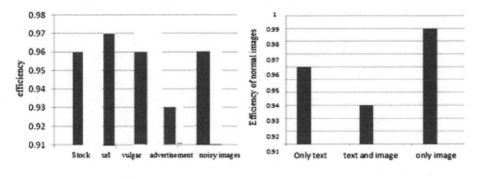

Fig. 14. Efficiency of spam images   **Fig. 15.** Efficiency of normal images

4.1.1 Discussion

Hams with only images are easiest to identify because the range of colour components used is quite vast. Their intensity plots are curved and continuous. Their plots are easily distinguishable from those of spam images. Hams with only text consist mostly of survey forms, documents and newspaper articles. Due to the use of limited colours (mostly black and white) intensity plots of these images may be similar to that of spam images. Hence their efficiency is less than that of hams with only images. However hams with only text have efficiency higher than that of hams with both text and images because the former can be easily read by OCR .The presence of colourful images in the background of the latter makes it difficult for OCR to read the embedded text. Spam images concerning Advertisements are made attractive by adding colourful images and text so that they look like real advertisements. Hence, they are often confused with hams with both text and images and are toughest to identify.

4.2   Result II

We have taken five samples of a single image and increased its brightness from 20% to 80%. Table 2 shows that OCR depends on the brightness of images. Tick (✓) shows images that OCR could read, cross (×) shows images that OCR could not read and P shows images that OCR could partially read.

Table 2. Effectiveness of OCR on varying brightness of images

Type of images	20%	35%	50%	65%	80%
URL Spam	×	✓	✓	✓	×
Stock Spam	×	✓	✓	P	×
Vulgar Spam	×	✓	✓	P	×
Advertisement Spam	×	✓	P	P	×
Noise Spam	×	✓	✓	✓	×

4.2.1 Discussion

OCR reads successfully the embedded text in an image if its brightness is confined to a particular range. However, it fails if brightness of an image deviates from a particular threshold having both upper and lower limit.

4.3   Result III

We have varied the background colour of an image keeping its font colour constant. We have set the font colour at [R:255 G:0 B:0] and decreased the background colour from [R:255 G:240 B:240] to [R:255 G:0 B:0] in sets of 30 keeping R constant. Figure 16 shows that the detection rate of OCR decreases as background colour approaches font colour. Black dots (•) show that OCR has failed. Red dots (◆) show that OCR has been successful. The largest circle is [R:255 G:0 B:0].

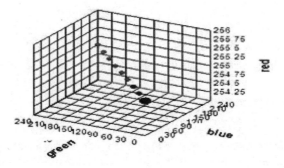

Fig. 16. Detection rate of OCR decreases as background colour approaches font colour

4.3.1 Discussion

OCR reads successfully the embedded text in an image if there exists a dissimilarity between font colour and background colour. As font colour approaches background colour it becomes difficult for OCR to read text.

4.4   Result IV

We have artificially added 'salt & pepper' noise in spam image, and have gradually increased the amount of noise added from 0.005 to 0.020. On increasing noise, distortion in the graphs obtained by intensity plotter also increases.

4.4.1. Discussion

Intensity plot of artificial spam images tends to be straight. Intensity plotter gives correct plot for spam images till a particular amount of added noise, above that it gives a distorted plot for spam images.

5   Conclusion and Future Work

In this paper we present a method for addressing image spam problems. It takes into account some of the recent evolutions of the spammers tricks in which obfuscation techniques are used to the extent that standard OCR tools become nearly ineffective. The paper proposes a method for identifying spam images by exploiting low level features and content of an image. Also anti-obfuscation techniques are applied to improve text filtering performance of the system.

According to the experimental results, we have concluded that the detection rate depends on the type of spam images, i.e. whether it contains only text, text and images or images only. Spammers add noise and changes brightness of an image till an extent only because then it hampers the clarity of the images and the user is unable to read the text.

Therefore, we aim to extend the proposed methodology by implementing a more efficient algorithm for Intensity Plotter so that it gives appropriate results for images with low signal to noise ratio.

References

1. Fumera, G., Pillai, I., Roli, F.: Spam Filtering Based On The Analysis Of Text Information Embedded Into Image. Journal of Machine Learning Research (JMLR) 7, 2699–2720 (2006)
2. Apache.org. The apache spamassassin project (2011),
   http://spamassassin.apache.org/index.html (last accessed May 3, 2011)
3. Uemura, M., Tabata, T.: Design and Evaluation of a Bayesian-filter-based Image Spam Filtering Method. In: Proceedings of the 2nd International Conference on Information Security and Assurance (ISA 2008), Busan, Korea, April 24-26, pp. 46–51 (2008)
4. Yan, G., Ming, Y., Xiaonan, Z., Pardo, B., Ying, W., Pappas, T.N., Choudhary, A.: Image Spam Hunter. In: Proceeding of the International Conference on Acoustics, Speech and Signal Processing (ICASSP 2008), Las Vegas, Nevada, USA, March 30-April 4, pp. 1765–1768 (2008)
5. Wang, C., Zhang, F., Li, F., Liu, Q.: Image Spam Classification based on Low Level Image Features. In: Proceeding of the 8th International Conference on Communications, Circuits and Systems (ICCCAS 2010), Chengdu China, July 28-30, pp. 290–293 (2010)
6. Klangpraphant, P., Bhattarakosol, P.: PIMSI: A Partial Image Spam Inspector. In: Proceeding of the 5th International Conference on Future Information Technology (Future-Tech), Busan, South Korea, May 21-23, pp. 1–6 (2010)
7. Hsia, J.H., Chen, M.S.: Language-Model-based Detection Cascade for Efficient Classification of Image-based Spam e-mail. In: Proceeding of the International Conference on Multimedia and Expo (ICME 2009), New York, USA, June 28-July 3, pp. 1182–1185 (2009)
8. Soranamageswari, M., Meena, C.: Statistical Feature Extraction for Classification of Image Spam Using Artificial Neural Networks. In: Proceeding of the 2nd International Conference on Machine Learning and Computing (ICMLC 2010), Bangalore, India, February 9-11, pp. 101–105 (2010)

9. Mathworks The Matlab image processing toolbox.M,
   http://www.mathworks.com/access/helpdesk/help/toolbox/images
   / (downloaded on July 10)
10. Bag of Visual words Model: Recognizing Object Categories,
    http://www.robots.ox.ac.uk/~az/icvss08_az_bow.pdf
11. Image editor, http://www.lunapic.com/editor/?action=contrast (down-
    loaded on July 10, 2011)
12. Image spam dataset,
    http://www.cs.jhu.edu/~mdredze/datasets/image_spam/
    (downloaded on June 3, 2011)

Diameter Single Sign On – Secure and Personalized Service Provision via Authentication and Authorization Mechanisms

Robayet Nasim

Faculty of Science, Engineering and Technology,
University of Science and Technology Chittagong, Chittagong
robayet@kth.se

Abstract. Network Services universally rely upon Authentication and Authorization mechanisms to ensure secure and personalized service provision. Protocols, such as Diameter provides a reliable framework for efficient access control to network services utilized by network devices. This framework can also encompass application level services e.g. web applications accessed via web browsers [1]. On the other hand, the prevalence of Internet based services and applications have brought about the burden of identity management among distributed security domains, an issue not specifically addressed by protocols such as Diameter. Efforts such as OpenID alleviate this difficulty by proposing an application level framework based on open standards to realize single sign on/off [2] semantics with regard to application level services. However, these technologies do not build upon existing security infrastructure, require significant investment in terms of technology adoption and have yet to receive industry wide acceptance and support. This paper presents Diameter Single Sign On – a framework that provides single sign on/off semantics in the context of network and application level services by harnessing the strengths of existing and proven authentication and authorization infrastructure. Because of combination of the Diameter protocol with Single Sign On and OpenID the proposed architecture overcomes the problem of identity management and also builds on existing security infrastructure.

Keywords: Diameter, OpenID, Authentication, Authorization, Single Sign On.

1 Introduction

As Internet becomes a popular medium of doing everyday works, ensuring security to the users to access a network or application level resources is a raising question in the modern world. Furthermore, providing privileges to the users for accessing resources as well as storing users history about their usage of the resources is also taken the concern. AAA (Authentication, Authorization, Accounting) security services provide the primary framework through which a network administrator or a service provider can set up access control on network points of entry or network access servers, or set up an access control on applications [10]. Authentication checks the identity of the

N. Meghanathan et al. (Eds.): CCSIT 2012, Part I, LNICST 84, pp. 573–581, 2012.
© Institute for Computer Sciences, Social Informatics and Telecommunications Engineering 2012

users, Authorization confirms the proper access control rights of the users, and Accounting declares the history of the users [11]. The core elements [11] of AAA are: *Clients* for authentication (itself or another user); *Policy Enforcement Point* (Authenticator), provides the constraints for a client access to the resources; *Policy Information Point* (PIP), stores information about devices or user access requests and helps to make the access decision; *Policy Decision Point* (AAA Server), takes final decision about a resource access and takes the access request from the clients through PEP and queries for relevant information to the PIPs for decision making; *Accounting and Reporting System,* records usage of the resources with details information, such as – who are using the resources now, from where the resources are accessed, who are granted to access the resources, etc.

In recent times each and every user has a large number of accounts for using different types of web applications or network resources. It is quite natural that a single user may not have the same user ID in all of these accounts and that's why, it is difficult for that user to manage all of his IDs (combination of both user name and password). To solve this identity management problem an open decentralized, true framework is introduced named OpenID, [12] which offers the way of authentication to a user for several services by providing his OpenID password only once.

Diameter [3] is a network protocol that provides AAA to the end users. Because of the flexibility of this protocol it can be used efficiently for the basic purpose of the AAA realm. Although this protocol has reliable framework, efficient access control and support for the application level services, it suffers from lack of identity management capabilities. However, Single sign On [6] with OpenID solve this problem of identity management by authenticate users by providing their passwords only once. But it does not build upon existing security infrastructure and requires significant investment in terms of technology adoption.

Motivated by identifying these problems I proposed a framework *Diameter Single Sign On* for secure and personalized service provision via authentication and authorization in this paper. It provides single sign on/off semantics in the context of network and application level services by harnessing the strengths of existing and proven authentication and authorization infrastructure.

The remainder of the paper is organized as follows: In Section 2, I present the related work. Section 3 represents the detailed description of my solution and Section 4 illustrates possible future research directions. Finally, section 5 presents the conclusions of this paper by including the achievements.

2   Related Work

2.1   Network Service Authentication and Authorization with Diameter (RADIUS X 2)

The Diameter [3] is a network protocol for centralized Authentication, Authorization and Accounting. It is an application layer protocol that handles the communication between clients and servers through reliable transport. It is an upgrade to the RADIUS [4] (Remote Authentication Dial in User Service) protocol that is in wide use for access control to various network services including local area networks, wireless networks and the Internet. Fig. 1 illustrates a typical Diameter deployment scenario.

In a typical Authorization and Authentication transaction [5], the following sequence of events takes place.

1. User via User Agent (UA) initiates authentication procedure with the Network Access Server (NAS) to access a network service.
2. NAS Diameter client forwards Access-Request with user credentials to the Diameter Server.
3. Diameter Server checks the authenticity of user credentials and responds with Accept or Reject.
4. Based on the type of response and associated attribute value pairs, the Diameter client provides appropriate services to the User.

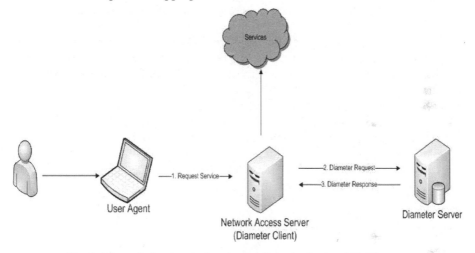

Fig. 1. Network Service Authentication & Authorization with Diameter

Although Diameter provides an efficient access control to network and application level services, the issue of identity management in Internet based applications is not addressed properly.

2.2   Single Sign On with Open ID

Single sign on [6] refers to the facility that allows a user to a number of application services by providing his/her credentials only once. OpenID realizes Single Sign On / Off [7] by allowing a user to authenticate with multiple security domains using a single identity such that the security domains trust certain authentication authority. Fig. 2 illustrates a higher level view of Single Sign On with OpenID.

After the user has established a trust relationship with an OpenID Identity Provider / Server (e.g.*provider.com* by registering an OpenID Identifier (an unique URL e.g. *bob.provider. com*), the following sequence of steps takes place while signing in.

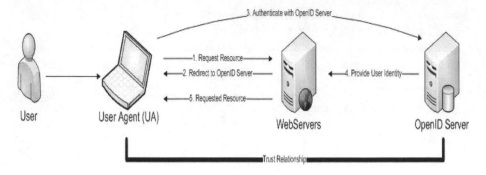

Fig. 2. Single Sign On with Open ID

1. UA requests a resource hosted by a relying party Web Server and presents an OpenID identifier.
2. The Web Server determines the OpenID Identity Provider from the presented Open ID Identifier and determines its Service URL. The Web Server and the Identity Provider establish a shared secret. The Web Server then redirects UA to the Identity Provider.
3. The User via UA provides authentication credentials to the Identity Provider.
4. Having successfully authenticated the user, the Identify Provider forwards users identity credentials to the Web Server with the user's consent.
5. The Web Server verifies the authenticity and integrity of received identity information using the shared secret established earlier. Upon successful verification, the requested resource is presented to the user.

However, Open ID does not build on existing security infrastructure and therefore, requires an industry wide accepted standard infrastructure.

3   Solution

Single Sign On Service that allows manageable and end user friendly access control for network and application level services can benefit from the reliability and mass deployment of Diameter / RADIUS infrastructure. In the proposed framework, end user security credentials and associated information including preferences as well as access rights are stored in a data store (LDAP, RDBMS) connected to the Diameter Server. Each user is uniquely identified by an identifier of the form *User@SecurityDomain*, where SecurityDomain represents the globally unique identifier (URI) of the Diameter Server and User represents a unique user name within the security domain. Thus, a trust relationship is established between the user and the Diameter Server. Fig. 3 depicts an envisioned deployment of my proposed architecture. Among other benefits, the proposed architecture provides a uniform mechanism for gaining access to both network and application level services. Below, I detail the flow of events associated with access control of network and application level resources.

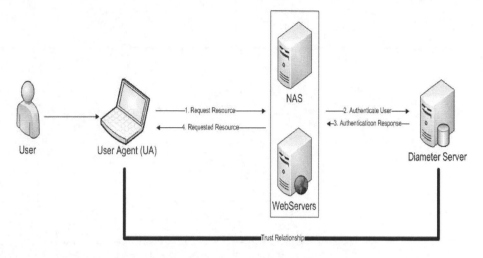

Fig. 3. Diameter Single Sign On

3.1   Network Service Single Sign on

1. User via UA communicates with the NAS to access a network service.
2. Diameter client on NAS initiates a Challenge Handshake Authentication protocol with the Diameter Server on behalf of UA.
3. Depending upon result of authentication process, the Diameter Server responds with Accept or Reject.
4. Based on the type of response and associated attribute value pairs, the Diameter client provides appropriate services to the User.

3.2   Application Service Single Sign On

1. User via UA requests a resource hosted by a Web Server and presents his/her unique identifier.
2. The Web Server determines the Diameter Server from the suffix of the presented Identifier and determines its Service URL and initiates a Challenge Handshake Authentication Protocol with the Diameter Server on behalf of UA.
3. Having successfully authenticated the user, the Diameter Server forwards user's identity credentials to the Web Server.
4. The Web Server presents the requested resource to the user.

Furthermore, I define two modes of Single Sign On for the Diameter Server i.e. Active and Passive. In active mode, the Diameter Server actively signs in the user to a set of previously specified services. In this case, the user may access all services from the set by only specifying user's unique identifier to the Service Provider. In passive mode, the Diameter Server provides the user's identity information to a Service provider only when the user chooses to request for the service. In both cases,

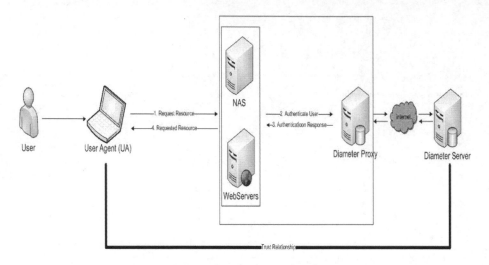

Fig. 4. Diameter Single Sign On Roaming

the Diameter Server and Service providers must ensure that only the authenticated user may access the available services by reliable and appropriate techniques such as checking for IP Address or Certificates.

3.3   Architecture

The Diameter provides a rich framework sufficient to implement my proposed architecture. Being a Peer-to-Peer architecture [8], a Diameter node can create, send, forward, modify and receive Diameter protocol messages. It is of interest for the purpose of this text to signify the following Diameter node / agent types and concepts.

- A *Relay Agent* forwards messages.
- A *Proxy Agent* forwards and optionally modifies messages.
- A *Redirect Agent* assists with routing messages.
- A *Peer Table* is kept at every Diameter node and lists particulars such as address and capabilities of all known Diameter nodes.
- A *Peer Routing Table* is kept at every Diameter node and specifies the correct processing for a received message, that is, forward, modify, redirect or process locally.

I illustrate, in Fig. 5, a basic yet comprehensive scenario that depicts the feasibility of the Diameter framework for implementing my proposed architecture. I aggregate the various possible User Agent entities into one entity specified as *User Agent* which could be software or a device. Similarly, various Diameter clients providing a variety of services have been collectively represented as *Client*. The scenario depicts the basic interaction between a User Agent and a Service Provider, whereby the User Agent is interested in a privileged resource available at the Service Provider. The Service Provider ensures authenticated and authorized access to the resource by taking on the role of a Diameter Client node as outlined below.

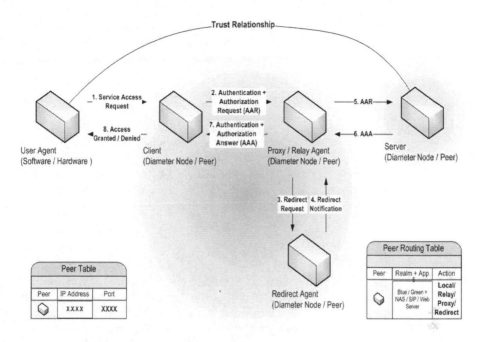

Fig. 5. Diameter Interaction Scenario

1. User Agent (UA) requests access to a service *S* along with its unique identifier UID (and security credentials encrypted with server's Public Key if PKI is used).
2. Client creates an Authentication and Authorization Request (AAR) on behalf of the UA and sends the AAR to the Diameter node indicated by the Peer Routing Table for the Realm and Application indicated by the requested service *S* and User Agent's *UID*.
3. The Next Hop of the AAR, in this case a Proxy / Relay Agent, might determine that the AAR is to be forwarded to another realm and that it requires routing information from a Redirect Agent to accurately forward the message.
4. The Redirect Agent would return redirection information sufficient for accurate routing of the AAR.
5. Having received the necessary routing information, the AAR would be relayed to the appropriate Diameter Server.
6. After having recognized that the message should be processed locally, the Server node would return the appropriate Authentication and Authorization Answer (AAA), based on the received AAR, to the Relay/ Proxy agent.
7. The Proxy / Relay Agent would then forward the AAR to the Client.
8. The Client would inspect the AAR and grant or deny access to service accordingly.

The sequence of steps outlined above presents a bare bones interaction among partici-pating entities and a number of interactions involving connection and session set-up, capabilities negotiations and session tear down have been omitted for sake of simplicity.

3.2   Security Considerations

Diameter Base Protocol [9] mandates support for TLS and IPsec at Diameter Serv-ers and IPsec at all Diameter nodes thereby ensuring ample on the wire security for Diameter protocol messages. Though the security mechanism (CHAP and PAP) pro-vided by Diameter Base Protocol for securing user credentials are sufficient, usage of Public Key Infrastructure is recommended in order to reduce the complexity of interactions among User Agent and various Diameter nodes.

4   Future Work

The framework presented in this paper is the first step to build an Authentication and Authorization framework to provide single Sign On/off for network and appli-cation level services. Therefore, as a future work, I plan to focus on a detailed eval-uation of the proposed architecture against different security threats to compare robustness of the architecture against contemporary schemes.

5   Conclusions

The demand for an Authentication and Authorization framework that leverages the capabilities of exiting AAA infrastructure to provide single sign on/off for network and application level services has been widely felt. The Diameter protocol provides ample support to serve as the foundation for a candidate architecture that meets these criteria. The proposed architecture benefits from the elements of the Diameter framework including Diameter Agents, Protocol Messages as well as Security Mechanisms.

References

1. Neumann, N., Fu, X.: Diameter WebAuth: An AAA-based Identity Management Frame-work for Web Applications. In: 51th Annual IEEE Global Telecommunications Confe-rence, Computer and Communications Network Security Symposium, New Orleans, LA, USA, pp. 86–88. IEEE Press, New York (2008)
2. Build and Implement a single sign-on solution,
   http://www.ibm.com/developerworks/web/library/wa-singlesign
3. Mehta, N.: Introduction to Diameter protocol,
   http://blogs.oracle.com/naman/entry/introduction_to_diameter_protocol
4. Remote Authentication Dial in User Services,
   http://tools.ietf.org/html/rfc2865

5. How Does RADIUS Work?,
   http://www.cisco.com/en/US/tech/tk59/technologies_tech_note0
   9186a00800945cc.shtml
6. Introduction to Single Sign-On,
   http://www.opengroup.org/security/sso/sso_intro.htm
7. Eldon, E.: Single sign-On service OpenID getting more usage,
   http://venturebeat.com/2009/04/14/single-sign-on-service-
   openid-getting-more-usage/
8. Liu, J., Jiang, S., Lin, H.: Introduction to Diameter,
   http://www.ibm.com/developerworks/wireless/library/wi-
   diameter/
9. Diameter Base Protocol, http://tools.ietf.org/html/rfc3588
10. Authentication, Authorization, and Accounting,
    http://www.cisco.com/warp/public/cc/pd/iosw/prodlit/
    aaans_ov.pdf
11. Network Authentication, Authorization, and Accounting: Part One-The internet Protocol
    Journal 10(1),
    http://www-fr.cisco.com/web/about/ac123/ac147/
    archived_issues/ipj_10-1/101_aaa-part1.html
12. What is OpenID?, http://openid.net/get-an-openid/what-is-openid

Application of Genetic Algorithms for Detecting Anomaly in Network Intrusion Detection Systems

K.G. Srinivasa

Machine Learning Applications Laboratory,
Department of Computer Science and Engineering,
M.S. Ramaiah Institute of Technology, Bangalore-560 054, India
kgsrinivas@msrit.edu

Abstract. Intrusion Detection System (IDS) can handle intrusions in computer environments by triggering alerts to help the analysts for taking actions to stop the possible attack or intrusion. But, the IDS make the job of analyst more difficult by triggering thousands of alerts for any suspicious activity. In this paper, an anomaly based network intrusion detection system using a genetic algorithm approach is adopted. The proposed method is efficient with respect to good detection rate with low false positives. The experimental results demonstrate the lower execution time of the proposed algorithm *GANIDS* (Genetic Algorithms based Network Intrusion Detection System) when compared with PAYL [1]. The proposed payload based IDS uses an adaptive genetic algorithm for both learning and detection. The proposed *GANIDS* is benchmarked with PAYL [1] using the 1999 DARPA IDS dataset.

Keywords: Intrusion Detection Systems, Genetic Algorithms, Anomaly Detection.

1 Introduction

An intrusion detection system is used to detect many types of malicious activities in network traffic and computer usage. Typically, the types of attacks include network attacks against vulnerable services, data driven attacks on applications, host based attacks such as privilege escalation, unauthorized logins and access to sensitive files. An IDS monitors network traffic and monitors for suspicious activity and alerts the system or network administrator. In some cases the IDS may also respond to anomalous or malicious traffic by taking action such as blocking the user or source IP address from accessing the network. IDS come in a variety of *flavors* and approach the goal of detecting suspicious traffic in different ways. There are IDS that detect based on looking for specific signatures of known threats similar to the way antivirus software typically detects and protects against malware; there exist IDS that detect based on comparing traffic patterns against a baseline and looking for anomalies [2-5].

NIDS: Network Intrusion Detection Systems are placed at a strategic point or points within the network to monitor traffic to and from all devices on the network. Ideally you would scan all inbound and outbound traffic; however doing so might create a bottleneck that would impair the overall speed of the network [9].

N. Meghanathan et al. (Eds.): CCSIT 2012, Part I, LNICST 84, pp. 582–591, 2012.
© Institute for Computer Sciences, Social Informatics and Telecommunications Engineering 2012

HIDS: Host IDS are run on individual hosts or devices on the network. A HIDS monitors the inbound and outbound packets from the device only and will alert the user or administrator of suspicious activity is detected. The other classifications of intrusion detection systems are signature based and anomaly based [13].

Signature based systems: A signature based IDS work with an intrusion database populated offline by knowing of the characteristics of the attack. Thus the IDS have to compare the input and classify it into normal and abnormal categories. A signature based IDS will monitor packets on the network and compare them against a database of signatures or attributes from known malicious threats. This is similar to the way most antivirus software detects malware. The problem is that there will be a lag between a new threat being discovered in the wild and the signature for detecting that threat being applied to the IDS under consideration. During that lag time the IDS would be unable to detect the new threat.

Anomaly Based Systems: An Intrusion Detection System (IDS) which is anomaly based will monitor network traffic and compare it against an established baseline. The baseline identifies normality for that network with respect to the sort of bandwidth to be generally used, the protocols to be used, the ports and devices to connect to each other, and finally alerts the administrator or user when the traffic is detected with anomaly, or significantly different than the baseline. Anomaly based systems have only the normal behaviors in their profiles and any deviation above a threshold is signaled as an anomaly. Unlike signature based systems which give low detection rates and low false positive rates anomaly based system suffer from high false-positive rates; however they have a good detection rate [14].

Signature based systems cannot detect new attacks until they are known and added to the database. This results in lower detection rates. Signature based systems are preferable to detect attacks on the operating systems. However, anomaly based systems have the ability to detect zero-day worms. And hence are preferable for network related attacks. Most of the systems used till now are predominantly signature based however a considerable amount of research is going on for reducing the false positive rates and increasing the detection rates in anomaly based systems. An anomaly based system can classify the input based on either the header information or the payload. In this paper we describe a payload based IDS with applied Genetic Algorithms.

Contribution: In this paper, a genetic algorithm based approach to network intrusion detection system is adopted. The literature demonstrates that the Genetic Algorithms provide better and faster classification than any neural network architectures, and also takes less time for training and gives detection rate. Since GANIDS is payload based, it uses only the destination address and the service port numbers for building profiles and all the other header information is ignored. Further, it uses a single tier architecture where a GA is used for both classification and detection. We have benchmarked our system with respect to PAYL using the 1999 DARPA IDS dataset. On this dataset the proposed system shows a reasonable detection rate with low false positives and a faster running time than PAYL.

2   Related Works

Genetic Algorithms belong to the evolutionary algorithms and is very efficient in machine learning. Genetic algorithms are search procedures often used for optimization problems. The genetic algorithm works by slowly evolving a population of chromosomes that represent better and better solutions to the problem. It has emerged to be a very effective tool in data mining applications. Since in an IDS the incoming packet needs to be classified into normal and abnormal categories a GA functions best in this job since it can classify with a higher accuracy than any other methods for example Neural Networks etc. The objective of using a GA is to obtain a better classification of the input data resulting in higher detection rates with lesser false positives, which is a major concern for an Anomaly Based IDS. In addition to that genetic algorithms are relatively faster than neural networks and requires less time for training and hence the performance of the system increases considerably [15]. Neural networks are trained to detect intrusion systems. An n-layer network is constructed and abstract commands are defined in terms of sequence of information units, the input to the neural in the training data. Each command is considered with pre-defined w commands together to predict the next coming command expected from the user. After training, the system will have the profile of the user. At the testing step, an anomaly is said to occur as the user deviates from the expected behavior [16]. Evolving fuzzy classifiers have been studied for possible application to the intrusion detection problem. System audit training data is used to extract rules for each normal and abnormal behavior by the genetic algorithm. Rules are represented as complete expression tree with identified operators, such as conjunction, disjunction and not [8].

An efficient and biologically inspired learning model for anomaly intrusion detection in the multi-agent IDS is designed for decentralized intrusion detection and prevention control in large switched networks. The proposed model called Ant Colony Clustering Model improves the existing ant-based clustering approach in searching for near-optimal clustering heuristic. The multiple agent technology and Genetic programming (GP) are used to detect network attempts. Each agent monitors one parameter of the network packet and GP is used to find the set of agents that collectively determine anomalous network behaviors. This method has the advantage of using many small autonomous agents, but the communication among them is still a problem. Also the training process can be time consuming if the agents are not appropriately initialized [7, 11]. Researchers in [6, 7, 8,9,10, 12] have proposed paradigm consist from; neuro-fuzzy network, fuzzy inferences, and GA to detect intrusion activities in networks. This method firstly used a set of parallel nero-fuzzy classifiers (five layers 4- for type of attack, and one for normal). Then fuzzy inference used the output from classifiers to take a decision whether the current action is normal or not. The role of GA was used to optimize the classifier engine to give the right decision. This Method also used the same data KDD CUP 99 for training and for testing the system.

3   Architecture

The architecture of GANIDS is as shown in the Figure 1. An initial population of chromosomes is generated randomly where each chromosome represents a possible solution to the problem (an set of parameters).The incoming traffic is first captured using a packet capture engine which is then used to extract the payload by removing all the header information present in the packet and the payload is given as input to the genetic algorithm which in the training phase uses it to build profiles.

Two Point Crossover: In our system we use a two point crossover scheme where the two parents crossover at two different points producing a total of eight off springs out of which two are replicas of the parents itself which are discarded. The remaining two are then tested for fitness. If they are fit enough then they are added to the population else they are not. Selection of the parents for crossover is done by finding the fittest chromosome from the existing population and the input data forms the other parent. Since the input data is used to construct profiles the network behavior will be mapped on to the profiles efficiently.

Replacement Strategy: There are mainly two types of replacement techniques that are widely used viz. *Complete Replacement* and *Partial Replacement*. Complete replacement though easy to implement lose some of the fittest members in the population. However it is desirable for some of the chromosomes that are fit to survive in the population, hence we use a partial replacement technique where only some of the members are replaced and the rest are retrieved as it is. In our system we use a *steady state replacement* technique which is a partial replacement technique where the off springs replace the parents in the population. Also in our system parents that are unable to produce an offspring that is fit enough to be added to the population will also be removed from the population.

Fig. 1. GANIDS Architecture

Mutation: Mutation is very necessary in a genetic algorithm because it enables the algorithm to explore the search space more effectively and hence produces better results. In our system we perform mutations based on a mutation probability which varies dynamically during the course of execution. The algorithm used in the proposed system is presented below.

Problem Definition: Let x_i be the input payload at time instance i, then the problem is to find the Chromosome c which yields the lowest value for the computation *manhattan_distance* $(c.weight[\ ]\ , x_i\ )$

Pseudo code: Here we give the pseudo code for crossover and mutation functions and finally the pseudo code for the genetic algorithm that we have used. If *pm* is the mutation probability and *G* the number of generations and nc_i the number of crossover points is two.

    The algorithm given below is used during the training phase i.e. the machine learning phase of the IDS. In the training phase, the input from the training data is used to build profiles. The machine learning phase functions as follows. First the input payload is used to find the fittest chromosome. Then the fittest chromosome and the payload itself are crossed to produce a total of eight offsprings out of which two of them are the replicas of the parents itself which are discarded. The remaining six children are checked for fitness and checked against a threshold value. Only children which are fit enough are added to the population and others are discarded. Also if none of the six children are fit enough to be added to the population then even the parents are also removed from the population.

CROSSOVER	MUTATION
Input:	Input:
x_i - payload at time i.	c – Chromosome
fittest – fittest chromosome	Output:
Output:	c^l – mutated chromosome
children created and added if fit.	begin
begin	*r=random()*
Children[6]=Cross(fittest,x_i)	*if r > pm then*
for all c ε Children	*mutate(c)*
find the fitness of *c*	end
if *fitness(c) > threshold*	
add_to_population(c)	
remove(fittest)	
end	

Genetic Algorithm:

```
Input:
        x_i – payload at time i
Output:
        fittest – the fittest chromosome
begin
  for i=0 to G do
                min_dist = INFINITY
                fittest = 0
                for every c ε Chromosome do
                        dist = manhattan_distance( c , x_i )
                        if dist ≤ min_dist then
                                fittest = i
                                min_dist = dist
                crossover( fittest , x_i )
                for every c ε  Chromosome
                        mutation(c)
end
```

Then mutation is applied in order to explore the search space better. Mutation is done as follows; a random number r is generated for every chromosome in the population. If the value of r is greater than the mutation probability then some random numbers of weights are changed to some random values. In the testing phase the fittest chromosome is found as in the algorithm but the crossover and mutation operations are not performed. Instead when the fittest chromosome is found, the minimum distance obtained is checked against a threshold and if it is higher than the threshold then it is flagged off as an anomaly.

4   Performance Analysis

The two architectures GANIDS and PAYL are benchmarked using the same data used by PAYL, the DARPA 1999 data set. This standard data set is used as reference by a number of researchers and offers the possibility of comparing the performance of various IDS. This data set has been criticized because of the environment in which data were collected, but it is possible to tune an IDS in such a way that it scores particularly well on this particular data set: some attributes – specifically: remote client address, TTL, TCP options and TCP window size – have a small range in the DARPA simulation, but have a large and growing range in real traffic. IDS which take into account the above-mentioned attributes are likely to score much better on the DARPA set than in real life. Since our system does not consider these attributes, we can legitimately expect that the system in real life performs as well as it does on the DARPA benchmark. The GANIDS is trained using internal network traffic of week 1 and week 3. Then, the same data is used to build PAYL models taking advantage of the classification given by the neural network. After this double training phase, it is possible to use the testing weeks (4 and 5) to benchmark the network intrusion detection algorithm. This data contains several attack instances (97 payload-based attacks are detectable applying the same traffic filter mentioned above), as well as legal traffic, directed against different hosts of the internal network: the attack source can be situated both inside and outside the network. Figure 2 shows the graph of percentage of false positive packets versus percentage of instances of detected attacks on FTP packets on port 21 of DARPA. The percentage of true negatives in case of GANIDS is almost 10% less on average when compared to PAYL. Similar graph in Figure 3 shows better performance of GANIDS when compared to PAYL when test on TELNET packets on Port 23. False Positive attack instances was found to be linearly increasing with increase in detected attack instances on the application on GANIDS which was an improvisation over the existing performance.

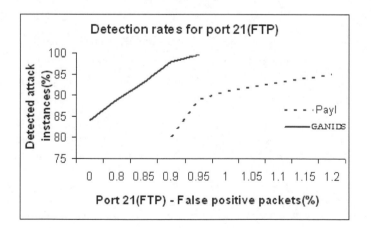

Fig. 2. A comparison of PAYL and GANIDS in terms of percentage of true negatives (reported on y axis) w.r.t the percentage false positives(x axis)

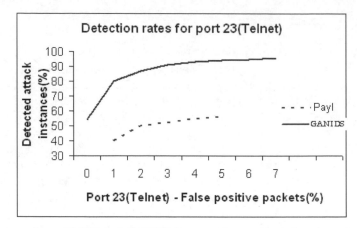

Fig. 3. A comparison of PAYL and GANIDS in terms of percentage of true negatives (reported on y axis) w.r.t the percentage false positives(x axis)

The experiments on SMTP and HTTP packets on Ports 25 and 80 also demonstrates better performance of GANIDS when compared to PAYL as shown in Figure 4 and Figure 5.

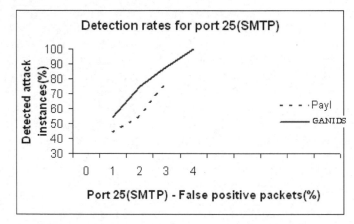

Fig. 4. A comparison of PAYL and GANIDS in terms of percentage of true negatives (reported on y axis) w.r.t the percentage false positives(x axis)

Table 1 reports a summary of these results: the first column reports PAYL's statistics and the second column reports the result of GANIDS. It is possible to observe that GANIDS overcomes PAYL on every benchmarked protocol: there is a remark about FTP protocol. During FTP protocol benchmarks we found a high rate of false positives both with PAYL and with GANIDS: all these packets are sent by the same source host, which is sending FTP commands in a way that is typical of the Telnet protocol (one character per packet, with the TCP flag PUSH set). These packets are marked as an attack because the training model does not contain this kind of traffic over the FTP control channel port, although it is normal traffic. During our experiments with PAYL we found the same behavior.

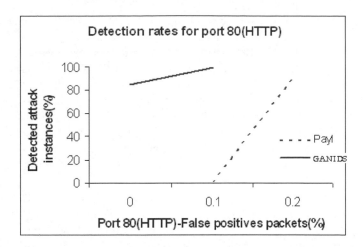

Fig. 5. A comparison of PAYL and GANIDS in terms of percentage of true negatives (reported on y axis) w.r.t the percentage false positives(x axis)

We trained our intrusion detection models, i.e., the base models and the meta-level classifier; using the 7 weeks of labeled data, and used them to make predictions on the 2 weeks of unlabeled test data (i.e. we were not told which connection is an attack). The test data contains a total of 38 attack types, with 14 types in test data only (i.e., our models were not trained with instances of these types). The reason for high false positive rate in *GANIDS* using was due to the obsolete nature of the DARPA 1999 dataset.

Table 1. Comparison between PAYL and GANIDS; DR stands for detection rate, while FP is the false positive rate

Architecture Used		PAYL	GANIDS
HTTP	DR	89.00%	95.00%
	FP	0.17%	0.01%
FTP	DR	95.50%	98.00%
	FP	1.23%	1.00%
Telnet	DR	54.17%	85.12%
	FP	4.71%	6.72%
SMTP	DR	73.34%	95.00%
	FP	3.08%	3.69%

5   Conclusions

It is often difficult to know which items from an audit trail will provide the most useful information for detecting intrusions. The process of determining which items are most useful is called feature selection in the machine learning literature. We have conducted a set of experiments in which we are using genetic algorithms both to select the measurements from the audit trail that are the best indicators for different classes of intrusions and to "tune" the membership functions for the fuzzy variables. *GANIDS* is a Genetic Algorithm based approach for anomaly based Network Intrusion Detection systems. The experiments on the DARPA set show that this approach reduces the number of profiles used by PAYL (payload length can vary between 0 and 1460 in a Local Area Network, while the proposed approach considers less than one hundred nodes). The experiments show that PAYL three times more the profiles as with the GANIDS. We benchmark *GANIDS* extensively against the PAYL algorithm and performance analysis shows a higher detection rate and lower false positives rate.

Acknowledgement. This project is partially funded by Research Grants of DRDO ER&IPR for the project titled *Machine Learning Techniques for Data Mining Based Intrusion Detection Systems,* to Dr. Srinivasa K G, Professor, Department of Computer Science and Engineering, M S Ramaiah Institute of Technology, Bangalore for the year 2010-12.

References

[1] Wang, K., Stolfo, S.J.: Anomalous Payload-Based Network Intrusion Detection. In: Jonsson, E., Valdes, A., Almgren, M. (eds.) RAID 2004. LNCS, vol. 3224, pp. 203–222. Springer, Heidelberg (2004)

[2] Bolzoni, D., Etalle, S., Hartel, P.: POSEIDON: a 2-tier anomaly-based network intrusion detection system. In: Fourth IEEE International Workshop on In Information Assurance, IWIA 2006 (2006)

[3] Zhang, L.-H., et al.: Intrusion detection using rough set classification. Journal of Zhejiang University Science 5(9), 1076–1086 (2004)

[4] Zhao, J.-L., Zhao, J.-F., Li, J.-J.: Intrusion Detection Based On Clustering Genetic Algorithm. In: Proceedings of the Fourth International Conference on Machine Learning and Cybernetics, Guangzhou, August 18-21 (2005)

[5] Lunt, T.: Detecting intruders in computer systems. In: Proceedings of Auditing and Computer Technology Conference, pp. 23–30 (1999)

[6] Ryan, J., Lin, M., Miikkulainen, R.: Intrusion detection with neural networks. In: Advances in Neural Information Processing Systems, vol. 10. MIT Press (1998)

[7] Crosbie, M.: Applying genetic programming to intrusion detection. In: Proceedings of AAAI Fall Symposium Series, pp. 45–52 (1995)

[8] Gomez, J., Dasgupta, D., Nasraoui, O.: Complete expression trees for evolving fuzzy classifiers systems with genetic algorithms and application to network intrusion detection. In: Proceedings of the NAFIPS-FLINT Joint Conference, pp. 469–474 (2002)

[9] Heady, R., Luger, G., Maccabe, A., Servilla, M.: The architecture of network level intrusion detection system, Technical Report, Department of Computer Science, University of New Mexico (1990)

[10] Ozyer, T., Alhaji, R., Barker, K.: Intrusion detection by integrating boosting genetic fuzzy classifier and data mining criteria for rule prescreening. Journal of Network and Computer Applications, 99–113 (2007)

[11] Crosbie, M., Spafford, E.: Applying genetic Programming to Intrusion Detection. In: Proceedings of the AAAI Fall Symposium (1995)

[12] Toosi, N., Kahani, M.: A new approach to intrusion detection based on an evolutionary soft computing model using neuro-fuzzy classifiers. Computer Communications 30, 2201–2212 (2007)

[13] Vokorokos, L., Balaz, A.: Host-based intrusion detection system, Technical University of Koaice, Department of Computers and Informatics, Slovak Republic (2010)

[14] Depren, O., Topallar, M., Anarim, E., Kemal Ciliz, M.: An intelligent intrusion detection system (IDS) for anomaly and misuse detection in computer networks. Bogazici University, Electrical and Electronics Engineering Department, Information and Communications Security (BUICS) Lab, Bebek, Istanbul, Turkey (2007)

[15] Li, W.: Using Genetic algorithms for Intrusion Detection System, Department of Computer Science and Engineering Mississippi State University, Mississippi State (2004)

[16] Ryan, J., Lin, M.-J., Miikkulainen, R.: Intrusion Detection with Neural networks. The University of Texas, Austin (1998)

A New Symmetric Key Cryptosystem Based on Feistel Network: Parallel Dependent Feistel Network (PDFN)

Indrajit Das[1] and R. Saravanan[2]

[1] SCSE, VIT University, Vellore-632014, India
[2] SITE, VIT University, Vellore 632014, India
indrajit.das23@gmail.com, rsaravanan@vit.ac.in

Abstract. In this paper a new Symmetric Key Cryptosystem, based on Feistel Networks has been proposed. The Cryptosystem demonstrates a few effective features like variable size key, variable size plain text encryption depending on data and key, padding by random variables etc. The cryptosystem is designed to be efficient on processors using simple operations.

Keywords: Symmetric Key Cryptography, Encryption, Decryption, Feistel Networks, Avalanche Effect.

1   Introduction

Secure communication and secure data storage is a necessary part of our everyday lives. A few examples are ecommerce, phone calls, transfer or storage of proprietary information, email, secure money transfers and military applications. It has all become possible because of the evolution of cryptography over the past couple of decades. Originally cryptography dealt with the science of secret writing, whence its name is derived. The first major step in the development of modern cryptography was Shannon's concept of perfect secrecy based upon an information theoretic model [1].

In this paper a new secret key cryptosystem is presented. The major points taken into consideration while designing the algorithm were

- It should guarantee substitution and permutation for all bits in each round.
- It should guarantee some randomness which will cause an unpredictable change on every encryption.
- It should be able to encrypt a block of variable plaintext. The size of the plain text to be encrypted should be determined on a dynamic basis.
- It should use a variable size key.
- It should be a word-oriented algorithm.
- It should use operations which are comparatively efficient on processors.

1.1   Symmetric Key Cryptography

Symmetric-key algorithms are a class of algorithms for cryptography that use identical cryptographic keys for both encryption and decryption and therefore

N. Meghanathan et al. (Eds.): CCSIT 2012, Part I, LNICST 84, pp. 592–601, 2012.

sometimes called *secret-key cryptography*. In contrast *public-key algorithms*, uses two keys - a public key to encrypt and a private key to decrypt messages. Symmetric Key Cryptosystems consists of the following five ingredients:

- *Plaintext*: This is the original intelligible message or data that is fed to the algorithm as input.
- *Secret Key*: The secret key is also input to the encryption algorithm. The exact substitutions and permutations performed depend on the key used, and the algorithm will produce a different output depending on the specific key being used at the time.
- *Encryption Algorithm*: The encryption algorithm performs various substitutions and permutations on the plaintext.

  - Input: (M, K)
  - $C \leftarrow Enc_K(M)$
  - Output: (C)

- *Cipher text*: This is the scrambled message produced as output. It depends on the plaintext and the key. The cipher text is an apparently random stream of data, as it stands, is unintelligible.
- *Decryption Algorithm*: This is essentially the encryption algorithm run in reverse. It takes the cipher text and the secret key and produces the original plaintext.

  - Input: (C, K)
  - $M \leftarrow Dec_K(C)$
  - Output: (M)

The main advantages of symmetric-key cryptography are

- High speed of data encryption.
- Shorter keys compared to public key algorithms.
- Symmetric-key ciphers can be used as primitives to construct various cryptographic mechanisms (i.e. pseudorandom number generators).
- Ciphers can be combined to produce stronger ciphers.
- Symmetric-key encryption is perceived to have an extensive history.

1.2   Feistel Network

A Feistel network is a general method of transforming any function into a permutation. It was invented by Horst Feistel and has been used in many block cipher designs [2, 3]. The most important part of a Feistel Network is a non-linear and irreversible function F. The function F of a general Feistel Network can be expressed as

$$F: \{0, 1\}^{n/2} * \{0, 1\}^{k} \to \{0, 1\}^{n/2}$$

Where n is the size of the block, F is the function taking n/2 bits and k bits of key of key as input and producing an output of length n/2 bits. One round of a general Feistel network can be described as

$$X_{i+1}= (F_{ki} (msb_{n/2}(X_i))\ XOR\ lsb_{n/2}(X_i))\ \|\ msb_{n/2}(X_i)$$

Here X_i is the input to the round and X_{i+1} is the output. K_i is the key, n is the block length, lsb_u and msb_u are the least and most significant u bits of the block X respectively, XOR indicates modulo 2 addition and $\|$ indicates concatenation.

Diagram of a general Feistel round in given in Figure 1. The working of a Feistel Network is given below:

- Split each block into halves
- Left half becomes new right half
- New left half is the final result when the right half is XORed with the result of applying F to the Left half and the key.

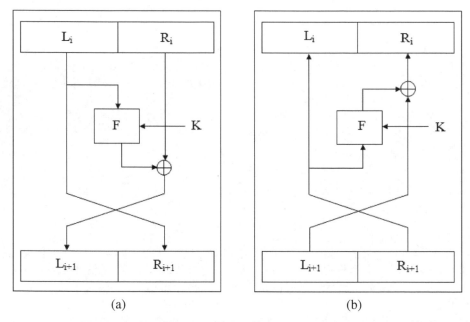

(a)   (b)

Fig. 1. a) Feistel Encryption Round b) Feistel Decryption Round

Let F be the round function and let k_0, k_1, k_2....k_n be the sub-keys for the rounds r_0, r_1, r_2 ... $r_n$respectively. Then the basic operation is as follows:

Split the plaintext block into two equal pieces (L, R)

For each round r_i where i= 0, 1, 2... n compute

$R_{i+1} = L_i$

$L_{i+1} = R_i\ XOR\ F\ (L_i, K_i)$

The cipher text is (L_{n+1}, R_{n+1}).

Decryption of a cipher text (L_{n+1}, R_{n+1}) is done by computing for round r_i where i=n, n-1, n-2,...0

$L_i = R_{i+1}$

$R_i = L_{i+1}$ XOR F (R_{i+1}, Ki)

Then (L_0, R_0) is the plaintext.

1.3   S-Box Design

The substitution layer in a Substitution-Permutation Network (SPN) is of critical importance to security since it is the primary source of nonlinearity in the algorithm (permutation is a linear mapping from input to output). S-Box substitutes the input with the output such that any change to the input results in a random-looking change to the output. Research into cipher design and analysis [4, 5, 6] suggests that s-boxes with specific properties are of great importance to avoid certain classes of attacks. However, it can be very difficult (and, in some cases, impossible) to satisfy some of these properties using "small" s-boxes.

Four general approaches can be made [12]

- **Choose Randomly.** It is clear that small random S-boxes are insecure, but large random S-Box may be good.
- **Choose and Test.** Some ciphers generate S-Boxes and then test them for the required properties.
- **Man Made.** This technique uses little mathematics: S-Boxes are generated using more intuitive techniques.
- **Math made.** Generate S-Boxes according to mathematical principles so that they have proven security against linear and differential cryptanalysis and good diffusive property.

2   Proposed Design: PDFN

The name "Parallel Dependent Feistel Network" is given to the algorithm since the algorithm can be viewed as two or three Feistel Networks working in parallel and are dependent on the each other. The proposed design PDFN encrypts variable size plain text and has variable length key and data dependent circular shift operation. The proposed design PDFN encrypts 128 bit block.

In the block size of 128 bits, the 96 higher order bits are plain text bits and the remaining 32 bits is a combination of plain text bits and random bits selected by the sender. This feature increases the security of the algorithm since the attacker, despite of the knowledge of the algorithm, is not able to predict the actual size of the plain text being encrypted. The size of the plain text is determined by the 96 higher order bits and the key. We calculate N where N= (96 plain text bits + Key) MOD 32. In the next 32 bits of the block, N bits are plaintext bits and rest 32 – N bits are random bits depending on the encoder. The same calculation is done by the decoder and the last 32-N bits are discarded after decryption.

It can be observed that during encryption, every time the algorithm encrypts a block of different size and the random bits used for padding results in a random change in the value of data in every round. When the algorithm is used in Cipher

Block Chaining mode (CBC) the Initialization Vector (IV) can be used to influence the value of N.

There are total 14rounds and each round uses 5 sub keys hence 70 sub keys each for both encryption and decryption. The large number of sub keys increases the security of the algorithm. The advised minimum length of key is 320 bits and the upper limit is 2240 bits which is very large making it unrealistic for a brute force attack.

The keys are calculated before encryption or decryption.

- Each Sub Keys is of 32 bit and are named as:
  SK0, SK1, SK2, SK3,……, SK69

- There are four 32-bit S-boxes with 256 entries each:
  $S_{1,0}, S_{1,1}, S_{1,2}, \ldots, S_{1,255}$
  $S_{2,0}, S_{2,1}, S_{2,2}, \ldots, S_{2,255}$
  $S_{3,0}, S_{3,1}, S_{3,2}, \ldots, S_{3,255}$
  $S_{4,0}, S_{4,1}, S_{4,2}, \ldots, S_{4,255}$

2.1   Encryption Process

For encryption there are 14 identical rounds. Each round divides the 128 bit block into four 32 bit words which are XORed with the corresponding sub key. Each of these words then undergoes a cyclic shift operation where the number of shifts is governed by the data and the sub key. The next part of the encryption process is a Feistel Network [2, 3]. The algorithm for encryption round is as follows

```
Encryption_PDFN (128 bit data block X)      /*Round i*/
{
128 bit data block B is divided into four 32 bit blocks: A, B, C and D
A = A XOR SK5i+0
B = B XOR SK5i+1                          // round i
C = C XOR SK5i+2
D = D XOR SK5i+3
A = A << (B XOR SK5i+4)                   //circular shift operations
B = B << (C XOR SK5i+4)
C = C << (D XOR SK5i+4)
D = D << (A XOR SK5i+4)
A = A XOR F (B)
B = B XOR F (C)
C= C XOR F (D)
TEMP = A
A = B
B = D
D = C
C = TEMP
Return X
}
```

The block diagram for encryption is given in figure 2.

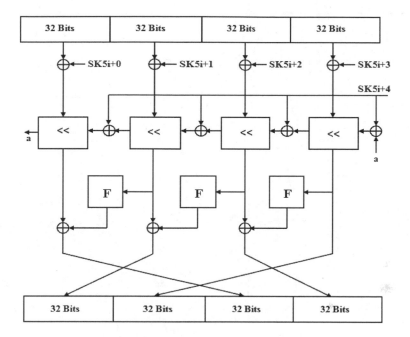

Fig. 2. Block diagram of PDFN Encryption

2.2 Decryption Process

For decryption there are 14 identical rounds. The algorithm for decryption round is as follows

Decryption_PDFN (128 bit data block X)   /*Round i*/
{
128 bit data block B is divided into four 32 bit blocks: A, B, C and D
TEMP=D
D=B
B=A
A=C
C=TEMP
C=C XOR F (D)
B=B XOR F (C)
A=A XOR F (B)
D = D >> (A XOR SK5i+4)
C = C >> (D XOR SK5i+4)
B = B >> (C XOR SK5i+4)
A = A >> (B XOR SK5i+4)
A = A XOR SK5i+0
B=B XOR SK5i+1

C=C XOR SK5i+2
D=D XOR SK5i+3
Return X
}

The block diagram for encryption is given in figure 3

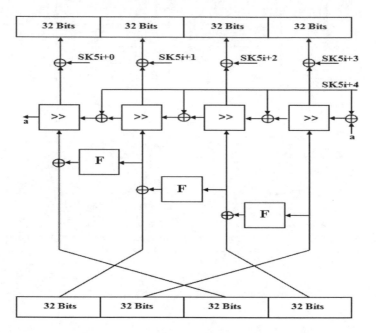

Fig. 3. Block diagram of PDFN Decryption

2.3   Function F

The most important part of a Feistel Cipher is the non-reversible function. This function uses simple operations like XOR and Modular Addition. The algorithm for function F is given below

Function_PDFN (32 bit block)
{
32 bit block is divided into four 8 bit blocks: A, B, C and D
Val_A= S_BOX_1 [A]
Val_B= S_BOX_2 [B]
Val_C= S_BOX_3[C]
Val_D= S_BOX_4 [D]
Val_AB= Val_A XOR Val_B
Val_CD= Val_C XOR Val_D
Val_F = (Val_AB+Val_CD) mod 32
Return Val_F
}

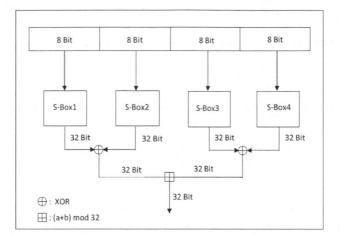

Fig. 4. Block diagram of PDFN function F

2.4   Sub Key and S-Box Generation

Sub Key and S-Box generation play a very important role providing high security to a symmetric key cryptosystem. The key schedule should satisfy completely or partially Strict Avalanche Criterion (SAC) [3, 6] and Bit Independence Criterion (BIC) [3, 6] in order to avoid certain key clustering attacks. Grossman and Tuckerman [7] showed that cryptosystems like the Data Encryption Standard (DES) where the key does not vary with successive rounds can be broken. It is therefore required that the primary key bits used to create sub key for a particular round i are different from those used in round i+1. PDFN uses 70 Sub Keys and four S-Boxes of dimension [1x256] of 32 bit each for encryption and decryption. The algorithm for Sub Key and S-box is as follows

SK_SBox_PDFN (variable size key)
{
Step1. Initialize each element of the four [1x256] S_Box, 70 Sub keys SK and 128 bit block B i.e. 4 words in order with decimal values of e^{π}.
Step2. Initialize array X of size 1098 words with decimal values of exponential e.
Step3. Initialize array Y of size 1098 words with decimal values of pi.
Step4. Initialize array SEQ of size 35136 bits or 1098 words by using key as a trajectory to select bits from X and Y. Repeat the key if necessary. Exp: If key bit is 0 select bit from X, if 1 select from Y. There are two approaches while selecting bits from X and Y which are described later.
Step5. XOR every element of S-Box, Sub key and B with SEQ.
Step6. XOR consecutive word (32 bits) of key with consecutive sub key i.e. XOR first 32 bits of key with the first sub key, second 32 bits of key with second sub key and so on. Repeat key if necessary.

Step7. Encrypt block B with same algorithm and sub keys to get 128 bit cipher text i.e. 4 words.XOR the 4 cipher text words with S-Box and repeat step 6 using 128 bit cipher text block B until   all the elements of S-Box and Sub-Key have been XORed.

}

Selection of bits from array X and Y as stated above, can be done in two ways which differ in speed and security of the algorithm.

- **FixedBitPosition:** In this approach, the ith bit of trajectory Key determines the selection between j^{th} bits of array X and Y where j= n *length (key) + i and n is the number of times the key is repeated. This selection process can be executed effectively using parallelism but has a weakness - if the bit is 0 or 1 in both X and Y then the value of bit in SEQ is predetermined.
- **NextBitPosition:** In this approach, the ith bit of the trajectory SEQ determines the selection between the $p+1^{th}$ and $q+1^{th}$ bits from array X and Y where p + q = i and p, q are the bit positions from where the last bit was selected from X and Y respectively. This selection process is sequential but distributes the entropy of the key throughout SEQ.

3   Analysis

- Parallel dependent Feistel network is designed in such a way that every higher order 32 bit gets affected by lower order 32 bits and the sub keys thus increasing the security of PDFN.
- The algorithm encrypts variable plain text size on every encryption even if the key is same because the size of plain text to be encrypted depends upon both key and plain text.
- Data and Key dependent cyclic shift operations makes the algorithm more secured.
- Function F is non-reversible in nature which gives PDFN quality avalanche effect.
- Use of four different S-boxes avoids symmetries when input bytes are equal.
- The key-dependent S-boxes protect against differential and linear cryptanalysis. The structure of the S-boxes is unknown to the attacker. Key-dependent S-boxes are easier to implement and can be created on demand, reducing the need for large data structures stored with the algorithm.
- The sub key generation process is designed in such a way that all the sub keys are affected by the key. One major advantage of the sub key generation algorithm is that parallel execution can be done for Step 4, Step 5 and Step6.
- If compared to Blowfish, PDFN uses key dependent string to encrypt and finalize the S-Boxes and sub key.
- Padding is done by random values known only to the sender which causes random change in the data which adds to the strength of the algorithm.

4   Future Work

- In proposed system the Key Generation algorithm can be modified for achieving more parallelism.
- The algorithm could be modified for variable number of rounds.
- The function F could be modified for better speed and security.

5   Conclusion

In this paper a new cryptosystem based on Feistel network has been proposed. The algorithm exploits Feistel structure to provide better security. Its variable size key makes the key space very large and hence brute force attack is not possible. Variable block size makes it difficult for the attacker to guess the size of the plaintext. Padding by random variables causes an undeterministic change in data in all rounds of encryption. Its testing against Differential and Linear attacks is yet to be done.

References

[1] Shannon, C.E.: Communication theory of secret systems. Bell Systems Technical Journal 28, 656–715 (1949)
[2] Feistel, H.: Cryptography and Computer Privacy. Scientific American 228(5), 15–23 (1973)
[3] Feistel, H., Notz, H.W., Lynn Smith, J.: Some cryptographic techniques for machine-to-machine data communications. IEEE Proceedings 63(11), 1545–1554 (1975)
[4] Webster, A.F., Tavares, S.: On the design of S-Boxes. In: Williams, H.C. (ed.) CRYPTO 1985. LNCS, vol. 218, pp. 523–534. Springer, Heidelberg (1986)
[5] Evertse, J.-H.: Linear Structures in Blockciphers. In: Price, W.L., Chaum, D. (eds.) EUROCRYPT 1987. LNCS, vol. 304, pp. 249–266. Springer, Heidelberg (1988)
[6] Youssef, A., Tavares, S., Mister, S., Adams, C.: Linear Approximation of Injective S-boxes. IEEE Electronics Letters 31(25), 2168–2169
[7] Grossman, E., Tuckerman, B.: Analysis of a Feistel-like cipher weakened by having no rotating key, Technical Report RC 6375, IBM (1977)
[8] Biham, E., Shamir, A.: Differential Cryptanalysis of DES-like Cryptosystems. In: Menezes, A., Vanstone, S.A. (eds.) CRYPTO 1990. LNCS, vol. 537, pp. 2–21. Springer, Heidelberg (1991)
[9] Matsui, M.: Linear Cryptanalysis Method for DES Cipher. In: Helleseth, T. (ed.) EUROCRYPT 1993. LNCS, vol. 765, pp. 386–397. Springer, Heidelberg (1994)
[10] Rivest, R.L.: The RC5 Encryption Algorithm
[11] Schneier, B.: Description of a New Variable-Length Key, 64-Bit Block Cipher (Blowfish)
[12] Schneier, B.: Applied Cryptography. John Wiley & Sons, New York (1994)

Survey of Shape Based Boundary Methods for Leaf Retrieval

Komal Asrani[1], Renu Jain[2], and Deepak Asrani[3]

[1] Department of Information Technology, B.B.D.N.I.T.M, Lucknow
komalasrani@rediff.com
[2] Department of Computer Science, U.I.E.T, Kanpur
jainrenu@gmail.com
[3] Department of Computer Application, I.I.S.E, Lucknow
deepakasrani_in@yahoo.com

Abstract. With explosive growth of plant species, it is becoming difficult for the botanists to manage the details of leaf. Moreover, extracting the specific leaf from the huge collection is a big job. Hence, an effort is done so as to help the botanists identify the specific leaf. The basic approach for leaf identification is based on textual information. But the effort involved in manual annotation is comparatively tedious and moreover it is impossible to represent the vast features of the image in limited keywords. Fundamentally, the identification of a plant is based on leaf. We present a summary of different boundary based methods for image retrieval of leaf. The methods have been explored for maple leaf and advantages and disadvantages have been highlighted.

Keywords: Image Retrieval, Image Processing, Leaf Identification, Boundary Based Identification, Shape Representation.

1 Introduction

With the emergence of multiple digital devices like cameras, mobiles etc, there have been a huge collection of digital images. However, this ever increasing digital collection has put forth a challenge for image retrieval. For image retrieval, textual annotation could be a possible option. But the issues like manual annotations and incomplete representation makes textual representation ineffective. Another option which defines retrieval based on image features is referred to as Content Based Image Retrieval (CBIR) CBIR provides retrieval based on image details like color, texture, color layout and shape. Considering human perspective, shape is a strong descriptor of image features.Shape is probably the most important property that is perceived about objects. Shape allows predicting more facts about an object than other features, e.g. colour. Thus, recognizing shape is crucial for object recognition. In some applications, it may be the only feature present which would help in recognising the shape e.g. logo recognition. Elaborate work has been proposed for many applications like face recognition, iris recognition, fingerprint recognition.

N. Meghanathan et al. (Eds.): CCSIT 2012, Part I, LNICST 84, pp. 602–610, 2012.
© Institute for Computer Sciences, Social Informatics and Telecommunications Engineering 2012

The main focus of this paper is on image retrieval based on shape for identification of leaves. Looking into the surroundings, there exist millions of varieties of plant species. Managing this huge information in digital format requires lot of efforts. However, it has been explored that identification of leaf is very helpful in recognizing the plant. But identification of leaf is not an easy task. The reason behind this is that the contour of a leaf remains the same for same species. So besides contour, it is important to get into the interior details of leaf for recognizing the leaf appropriately.

For efficient retrieval, it is important that shape representation should be invariant of basic transformations and should be able to deal with noise. The effectiveness of shape based image retrieval system depends on the features used for representing the shape, the type of queries and the effectiveness of shape matching strategies. The steps required for shape based image retrieval are:

a) Convert image into binary form.
b) Use suitable edge detectors to extract edges from binary image.
c) Represent edges as feature vectors.
d) Match feature vector of query to that of database images to generate similar set of images.

In above steps identified, third point defines shape representation and fourth point defines shape matching. An effective shape representation is helpful in visual image information representation.

2   Classification and Approaches of Shape Representation

Shape representation can be classified into: Boundary Based Image Representation and Region Based Image Representation. Boundary based approach helps in representing information of image only at boundaries whereas region based approach represents details of image, including the interiors of the contour.

Various papers have been referred in context to Shape Based Image Retrieval for different applications. The approaches have been analysed and implemented for identification of leaves.

2.1   Tangent Angle Approach

In this approach, the image is broken into line segments and the curvature of the line segments is measured at the boundary points[1]. The tangent angle function at any point $P(x_n, y_n)$ is defined by the tangential direction of the contour. The formula for tangent angle approach is as follows:

$$\theta_n = \frac{y(n) - y(n-w)}{x(n) - x(n-w)}$$

where w is the small window to calculate tangential angle θ_n accurately. The tangential representation can be done by generating a plot of the length of the segment along the x-axis and the curvature of the segment along the y-axis.[2]

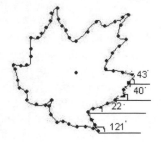

The image shows the boundary points highlighted. Thereby, at the boundary points, moving anticlockwise, tangential vectors are drawn and angles are measured. Also the distance between the consecutive points is measured.

Thus, the values are in the form of magnitude and angles, when started referring anticlockwise is as follows:

$$50 \angle 121°, 33 \angle 22°, 21 \angle 40°, 31 \angle 43°$$

This method is able to maintain the details of the shape boundary by accumulating the values of curvature and magnitude [3]. To make the approach rotation invariant, cumulative angular function is calculated as follows:

Cumulative Angular Function= θ(n)- θ(ref)

where θ(n) is the angle measured at the shape boundary and θ(ref) is the reference angle value. The additional advantage of this approach is that it is possible to regenerate the shape by reading the magnitude and angle values. The approach is scale, rotation and position invariant and the computational complexity is low.

2.2   Triangle Area Representation

In this method, the area is computed from the area of triangle formed by taking into consideration three consecutive boundary points [4]. The area is useful to calculate the curvature of the boundary shape.

Let the consecutive boundary points be $P_{n-ts}(x_{n-ts}, y_{n-ts})$, $P_n(x_n, y_n)$ and $P_{n+ts}(x_{n+ts}, y_{n+ts})$ where n belongs to [1,N] and t_s belongs to [1,N/2 -1] is even. Thus the area for these consecutive points would be given by:

$$TAR(n, t_s)= \frac{1}{2} \begin{vmatrix} x_{n-ts} & y_{n-ts} & 1 \\ x_n & y_n & 1 \\ x_{n+ts} & y_{n+ts} & 1 \end{vmatrix}$$

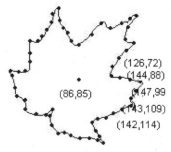

where the boundary points are traversed in clockwise direction and the values of TAR help to judge the contour. Positive TAR values refer for convex, negative TAR values refer for concave and zero values for straight line.

The array of the concave, convex and straight lines helps to understand the curvature of the boundary. A matrix is generated by taking 3 consecutive boundary points in anticlockwise direction and determinant value is calculated.

Mathematically,

$$TAR(, t_s)= \frac{1}{2} \begin{vmatrix} 142 & 114 & 1 \\ 143 & 109 & 1 \\ 147 & 99 & 1 \end{vmatrix}$$

= 142(109-99)-143(114-99)+147(114-109)
=142*10-143*15+147*5
=1420-2145+735=10(+ve value)

The value of the determinant helps to judge that the curve generated by the combination of 3 points(142,114) (143,109) and (147,99) is a convex curve. In this way, the complete shape is analyzed to be defined in the form of concave, convex or straight line and the output is an array of concave, convex and straight line representing the boundary. The method is scale, translation and rotation invariant [5].

2.3 Adaptive Grid Resolution (AGR)

In AGR, a square sufficient enough to cover the whole image is considered and overlaid upon the image [6]. The resolution of the grid cells varies from one portion to another according to the content of the portion of the shape. The interior dense portion of the image requires the higher resolution, thus smaller grids are required to represent the boundary whereas the areas of the image with coarser regions are represented with relatively big grids.

To represent the AGR image, quad tree is applied. Each node in the quad tree covers a square region of the bitmap. The level of the node in the quad tree determines the size of the square. The internal nodes represent 'partially covered' regions.

Minimum Bounding Box

Image 1

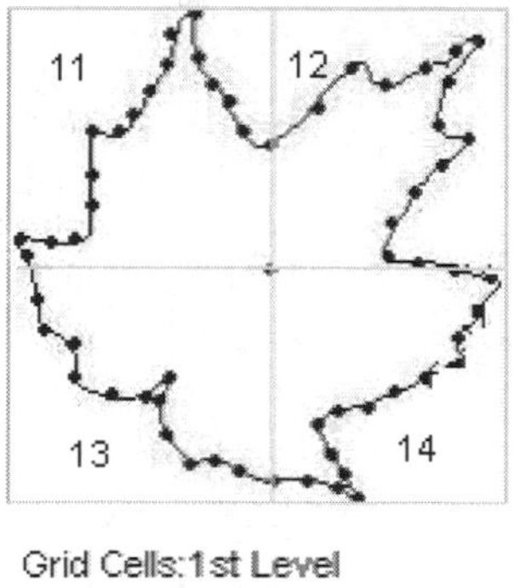

Grid Cells:1st Level

Image 2

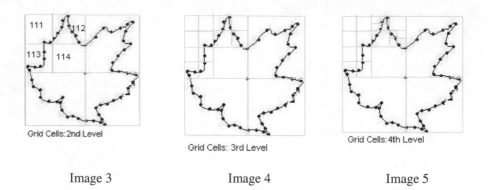

Image 3   Image 4   Image 5

As shown in the above sequence of the leaf images, the Image 1 depicts the image represented using minimum bounding box and a centroid at the centre. The Image 2 depicts the image represented as a grid of 4 cells. The centre of the bounding box is defined using centroid. The Image 3 depicts the grid cells further refined. Here grid 11 is segmented into four grids 111,112, 113 and 114. At the next level of defining grid cells, only those grid cells are sub-divided where the boundary pixels are prominent. The cell 114 need not to be divided as there are no pixels in the cell. In Image 4, the cell 111 is further divided into 1111, 1112, 1113 and 1114. Cell 112 is further into 1121, 1122, 1123 and 1124.The sub-division into further grid cells manages the accuracy of the depiction of data. Below a quad-tree has been generated using the grid based representation. Only those nodes are darkened where there is existence of pixels in the grids.

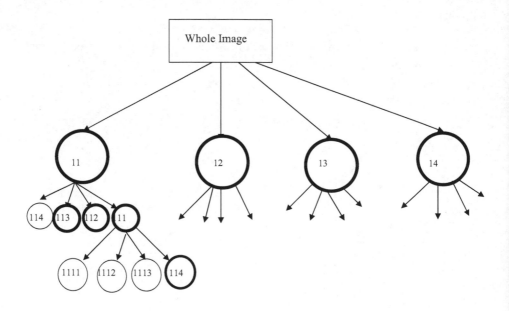

This approach is translation, scale and rotation invariant and the computational complexity is also low. This approach is important where the image boundaries are required to be explored in great details.

2.4   Bounding Box Approach

Bounding box approach computes homomorphism between 2D lattices and its shapes. To make bounding box, first the shape is normalized [7]. Then the image is broken into n columns, such that the dimensions of the columns overlap the image exactly, thus chopping the extra dimensions of the columns. The column segmented image is superimposed by m rows. The row dimensions are chopped which extend beyond the image. Then bounding box of each resulting pixel is calculated.

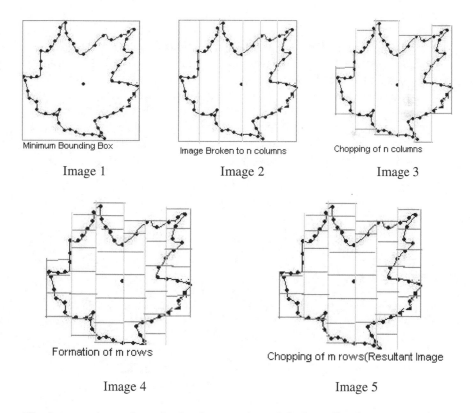

Image 1   Image 2   Image 3

Image 4   Image 5

The images above show the implementation of the bounding box method. Image 1 shows the bounding box for the image. The Image 2 is broken into n columns. The Image 3 shows the columns being chopped depending on the image boundaries. The Image 4 depicts the image segmented into m rows. Thus boundary box representation is a simple computational geometry approach to compute homomorphism between shapes and lattices. It is storage and time efficient. It is also invariant to rotation, scaling and translation invariant and has relatively higher computational complexity[11].

2.5   Directional Fragment Histogram (DFH)

A generic shape descriptor is computed using the outline of a region. The contour is defined to be formed of m elementary components. These elementary components are merged to form line segments having approximately same slope [8]. Thus the elementary components can be line segments or pixels. The computational details of the method are as given below:

Contour C= $ec_1, ec_2, ec_3, ec_4, ec_5$............ ec_n
where $ec_1, ec_2, ec_3, ec_4, ec_5$............ ec_n are elementary components.
Segment 1= ec_1, ec_2, ec_3
Segment 2= ec_4, ec_5, ec_6

....

Segment n= ec_7, ec_8............ ec_n.

Thus the contour is identified as combination of line segments which are represented as:
    Contour C= Segment 1 , Segment 2, Segment 3....... Segment n . Such groups are called directional fragments[10].
    Image 1 shows the elementary components. Image 2 represents the image as segments (red) and vertices (blue).The relative lengths of the individuals segments and their relative angles are calculated. The values can be tabulated as, magnitude of length of line segments along x-axis and angle between the line segments along y-axis where the angles are merged into 8 directions.

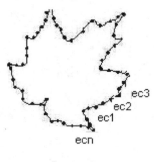

Image 1

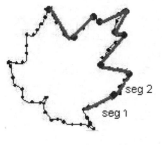

Image 2

Directional Fragment Histogram provides two kinds of information. At local level, it codes the relative length of elementary components within a given segment. At global level, DFH codes the elementary component's frequency distribution. The advantage of this method is that relative directions allow the representation to be rotation invariant by focusing on only directional changes.

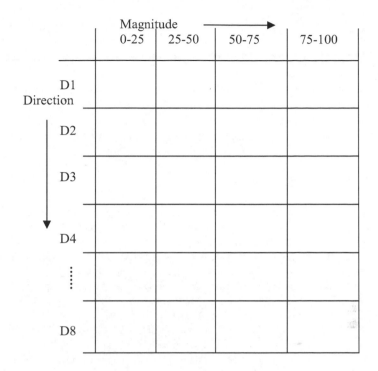

To make the approach scale invariant, the length of the segment should be represented as ratio of the length of the segment to the total length of the contour. The drawback of the approach is that it approximates the directional values and hence does not capture accurate information like Chain code.

3   Summary and Conclusion

Several image retrieval methods have been discussed and their advantages and disadvantages of each have been mentioned after analyzing the methods in detail. For any boundary based shape representation, it is important that the description should be translation, scale and rotation invariant and should handle noise effectively. Feature vectors extracted to represent the shape boundary should be stored in such a manner that it reduces space complexity but improves efficiency in image retrieval. We can say that it is a process of making a trade-off between space and effectiveness.

Summarizing the results, we come to the conclusion that the tangent angle approach is an accurate approach for representing information. But it is too tedious to calculate the angles at each pixel and would also increase the space complexity. The triangle area representation makes a good representation of boundary contours in the form of concave, convex and straight line and overcomes the drawback of tangent angle by reducing the space complexity though both the methods are affine invariant. Adaptive Grid Resolution method has the advantage of matching the shape contour iteratively, grid wise. Thus, it's possible to match the shape contour at each level depending on the level of the accuracy required. Boundary box approach segments the image contour into small cells and is highly space and time efficient. Directional Fragment Histogram approximates the direction and magnitude values representing the boundaries.

Among the approaches discussed above, it is impossible to identify a method which can be defined as perfect for boundary representation, as every method represents the processing of pixels coordinates in an exclusive way. Moreover, the effectiveness of any approach depends upon the complexity of the leaf image.

References

1. Zhang, D.S., Lu, G.: A comparative study on shape retrieval using Fourier descriptors with different shape signatures. In: Proc. International Conference on Intelligent Multimedia and Distance Education, ICIMADE 2001 (2001)
2. Zahn, C.T., Roskies, R.Z.: Fourier descriptors for plane closed curves. IEEE Trans. Computer c-21(3), 269–281 (1972)
3. Lu, K.-J., Kota, S.: Compliant mechanism synthesis for shape-change applications: Preliminary results. In: Proceedings of SPIE Modeling, Signal Processing, and Control Conference, vol. 4693, pp. 161–172 (March 2002)
4. Alajlan, N., Kamel, M.S., Freeman, G.: Multi-object image retrieval based on shape and topology. Signal Processing: Image Communication 21, 904–918 (2006)
5. Alajlan, N., Rube, I.E., Kamel, M.S., Freeman, G.: Shape retrieval using triangle-area representation and dynamic space warping. Pattern Recognition 40(7), 1911–1920 (2007)
6. Chakrabarti, K., Binderberger, M., Porkaew, K., Mehrotra, S.: Similar shape retrieval in mars. In: Proc. IEEE International Conference on Multimedia and Expo. (2000)
7. Bauckhage, C., Tsotsos, J.K.: Bounding box splitting for robust shape classification. In: Proc. IEEE International Conference on Image Processing, pp. 478–481 (2005)
8. Yahiaoui, I., Herve, N., Boujemaa, N.: Shape Based Image Retrieval in Botanical Collections
9. Ankerst, M., Kriegel, H.P., Seidl, T.: Multistep approach for shape similaritysearch in image databases. IEEE Trans. Knowledge Data Eng. 10(6), 996–1004 (1998)
10. Arkin, E.M., Chew, L.P., Huttenlocher, D.P., Kedem, K., Mitchell, J.S.B.: An efficiently-computable metric for comparing polygonal shapes. IEEE Trans. Knowledge Data Eng. 13(3), 209–216 (1997)
11. Flickner, M., Sawhney, H., Niblack, W., Ashley, J., Huang, Q., Dom, B., Gorkani, M., Hafner, J., Lee, D., Petkovic, D., Steele, D., Yanker, P.: QBIC: Queryby image and video content. IEEE Comput. 28(9), 23–32 (1995)

Modified Chain Code Histogram Feature for Handwritten Character Recognition

Jitendra Jain, Soyuj Kumar Sahoo,
S.R. Mahadeva Prasanna, and G. Siva Reddy

Electro Medical & Speech Tech. Lab., Indian Institute of Technology Guwahati,
Guwahati–781039, Assam, India
{j.jitendra,soyuj,prasanna,r.gangireddy}@iitg.ernet.in

Abstract. In this work, we have proposed modified chain code histogram (CCH) based feature extraction method for handwritten character recognition (HCR) applications. This modified approach explores the dynamic nature of directional information, available in character patterns, by introducing the Differential CCH which is termed as Delta (Δ) CCH. A comparable and higher recognition rate is reported which emphasizes that the dynamic nature of directional information captured by the ΔCCH is as important as that of CCH. All the experiments are conducted on MNIST handwritten numeral database. Finally, an improved recognition rate is observed at higher end by using combination of both the features which shows the effectiveness of dynamic directional feature in the classification of handwritten character patterns.

Keywords: Differential Chain Code Histogram, Handwritten Character Recognition, Misclassification Rate, Feature combination.

1 Introduction

Handwritten character recognition is an important application of human computer interface. The most significant part of any character recognition system is feature extraction which affects the recognition performance to an extent. The feature selection should be such that it holds all the variations of handwriting and hence makes it invariant with respect to shape variations caused by individuals. Chain code histogram (CCH) is one of the most successful feature extraction technique in character recognition task. The directional information captured by the CCH is the key method in identifying the exterior information of any shape or pattern. Hence, it has been widely used in Japanese, Devnagari, Oriya, Arabic handwritten character recognition applications with the higher recognition rate [1,2,3,4,5].

Dynamic information, i.e. the way feature vectors vary with respect to time, is also very much important in pattern classification as observed in automatic speech and speaker recognition tasks [6]. A very good performance is reported in all these tasks by using the dynamic information derived from the cepstral domain features like first and second derivative of mel-frequency cepstral coefficients [6,7,8]. Motivated by this approach, here we have proposed differential

N. Meghanathan et al. (Eds.): CCSIT 2012, Part I, LNICST 84, pp. 611–619, 2012.

CCH feature extraction method by taking the successive derivatives of CCH feature which captures the dynamic nature of directional information available in character patterns.

In this work, we have developed a handwritten character recognition system by using the modified CCH feature. Differential CCH feature is computed by block processing approach and performance of the proposed feature is evaluated on MNIST handwritten numeral database [9]. The different information contained in CCH and differential CCH features are further exploited to make the character recognition system more robust and accurate by using score level fusion. Here we have used the well known vector quantization (VQ) based nonparametric modeling and nearest neighbor classification technique for pattern matching [10].

The organization of the remaining work is as follows: Section 2 describes the modified directional feature extraction technique. Section 3 describes the different stages of handwritten character recognition system based on modified CCH feature. Experimental results and discussion are presented in Section 4 and finally summary and future work are provided in Section 5.

2   Modified Chain Code Histogram (CCH) Feature Extraction

CCH is an extensively used technique in character recognition tasks. Considering the importance of dynamic directional information, a modified technique is used for finding the differential characteristics of CCH feature. Both the methods are explained in the following sections.

2.1   CCH Feature

The CCH method utilizes the contour shape of character pattern for feature extraction. In this method, the directional information of all contour points are captured. The complete steps involved in CCH feature computation are described below.

1. **Step 1:** Find out the contour representation of character pattern.
2. **Step 2:** Divide the complete image into a particular number of blocks by using a fixed block size.
3. **Step 3:** Compute the directional information of each contour pixel by considering the 8-directions as shown in Fig. 1 by using top-to-bottom or left-to-right traversing approach.

Fig. 1. Chain code directions (adopted from [3])

4. **Step 4:** The above step is repeated for each block by using block processing approach.
5. **Step 5:** Hence we get 8-directional CCH feature vector for the complete character image.
6. **Step 6:** Finally assuming direction 1 and 5, 2 and 6, 3 and 7 and 4 and 8, as same, we get 4-directional CCH feature vector.

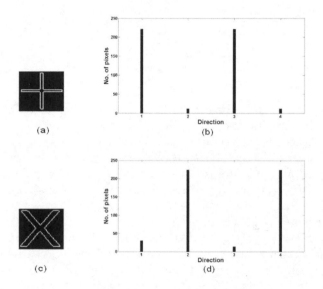

Fig. 2. (a) and (b) Contour and Chain code histogram representations for the symbol +, (c) and (d) Contour and Chain code histogram representations for the symbol ×

The CCH representations of the symbols + and × are shown in Fig. 2. As the major object part of the symbol image + is in the horizontal and vertical directions, so we find higher values at feature indices 1 and 3 i.e. more number of object pixels, in CCH representation of symbol + as shown in Fig. 2(b). On the other hand, we get more no. of object pixels at feature indices 2 and 4 in case of the symbol image × as the major object part is in slanted directions. As the object part is almost absent in horizontal and vertical directions so we get a few no. of object pixels at feature indices 1 and 3 for the same as shown in Fig. 2(d). This clearly illustrates the effectiveness of CCH in directional representation.

2.2 Differential CCH Feature

CCH feature provides the directional information of character patterns, but it does not convey any information about the variations available in the directional information with respect to spatial co-ordinates. This can give an additional level of information to discriminate any handwritten shape. To get this dynamic directional information, we have derived the differential CCH feature by taking the successive derivatives of the conventional CCH feature.

The differential CCH is computed from the 4-directional CCH feature vector by using the following polynomial approximations of the first and second derivatives [11].

$$\Delta \mathbf{c}(n) = \frac{\sum\limits_{i=-r}^{r} i.\mathbf{c}(n+i)}{\sum\limits_{i=-r}^{r} |i|} \qquad (1)$$

$$\Delta\Delta\mathbf{c}(n) = \frac{\sum\limits_{i=-r}^{r} i^2.\mathbf{c}(n+i)}{\sum\limits_{i=-r}^{r} i^2} \qquad (2)$$

where $\mathbf{c}(k)$ represents the 4-directional CCH feature vector of kth block, i shows the position of preceding and succeeding blocks, and r shows the total no. of preceding or succeeding blocks to be used in Δ and $\Delta\Delta$ computation.

The CCH and ΔCCH feature representations of numeral images 0 and 8 are shown in Fig. 3. As the patterns of these numerals are almost confusing so we get a look like CCH feature representations in this case as shown in Fig. 3(b) and (e). Again we can clearly observe that variations of CCH feature lies only in positive range where as ΔCCH contains variations in both positive and negative range as shown in Fig. 3(c) and (f). This shows the bipolar characteristic of ΔCCH in comparison of unipolar CCH. This makes the differential CCH robust for classification of degraded characters. For instance, if a character image is degraded with noise or blurred, it may add some extra undesirable directional

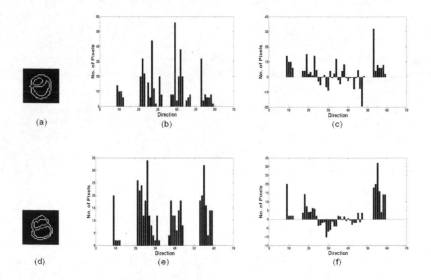

Fig. 3. CCH and ΔCCH feature representations for numerals 0 and 8; (a), (b), and (c) contour, CCH, and ΔCCH representations of numeral image 0, respectively; (d), (e), and (f) contour, CCH, and ΔCCH representations of numeral image 8, respectively.

information in case of CCH feature but this extra information is nullified in case of ΔCCH due to the differentiation operation.

3   Modified CCH Based Handwritten Character Recognition

The block diagram of modified CCH based handwritten character recognition system is shown in Fig. 4. The different stages used in this system are illustrated in the following sections.

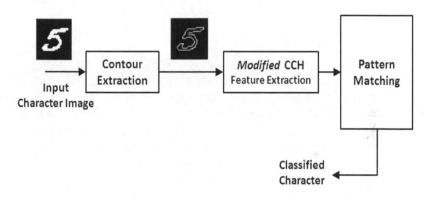

Fig. 4. Block diagram of the modified CCH based handwritten character recognition system

3.1   Contour Extraction

In this stage, the incoming gray scale images of characters are converted to binary images and resized to a default dimension. Here we take pixel value 1 as an object point and pixel value 0 as a background point. For contour extraction, consider a 3×3 window surrounded to every object point in the image. If any one of the four neighboring directions excluding corner directions has a background point then that object point is considered as a contour point. For instance, extracted contour of numeral image 5 is shown in Fig. 4.

3.2   Modified CCH Feature Extraction

In the feature extraction stage, modified CCH features are computed from the incoming contour image of the character. To capture the directional information of the contour, we have used the conventional CCH approach as described in Sec. 2.1. After getting the CCH features of the complete image, differential CCH features i.e. ΔCCH and $\Delta\Delta$CCH are computed by taking the first and second derivatives of the same as discussed in Sec. 2.2.

3.3   Pattern Matching

In the training phase, models are built for every individual class from their respective features. The extracted modified CCH features of each character class are fed to vector quantization (VQ) modeling stage. It builds a defined size of codebook for every character class by using binary split and k-mean clustering algorithm.

In testing stage, after finding the test feature set by using the same feature extraction technique, euclidean distances of this feature set is computed from all the code-vectors of the each character model. Then the test image is identified by using nearest neighbor classifier which works on minimum euclidean distance criterion.

4   Experiments and Outcomes

A robust character recognition system should be able to identify an unknown character image by classifying it to the correct character class. Generally performance of such a recognition system is measured in terms of recognition rate. Recognition rate is defined as the percentage of total number of samples of a class which are correctly classified. Again the percentage of total number of samples which are misclassified is termed as misclassification rate.

4.1   Experimental Details

For the present work, we have considered MNIST handwritten numeral database which includes $60,000$ training images and $10,000$ testing images. We have used 64×64 resized numeral images for our recognition task. For 4-dimensional CCH computation we have considered block size of 16×16 by taking the neighborhood object pixels in available directions as described in Sec. 2.1. Hence, we get total 16 no. of 4-dimensional feature set for CCH, 14 no. of 4-dimensional feature set for ΔCCH and 12 no. of 4-dimensional feature set for $\Delta\Delta$CCH in each image, respectively. In the VQ modeling stage, total 9 no. of 512-size codebooks are built for all numeral classes.

4.2   Experimental Results and Discussions

The performance of handwritten numeral recognition system for CCH, ΔCCH and $\Delta\Delta$CCH feature extraction techniques, in terms of recognition rate is given in Table 1. We can clearly see from the Tabel 1 that the performance of ΔCCH and $\Delta\Delta$CCH is almost comparable to that of CCH based recognition system. It is also observed from Table 1 that for some numerals like, 2, 6, and 9 the recognition rate is high in case of ΔCCH as compared to CCH, where as for remaining numerals we get better recognition accuracy in case of CCH feature. It shows that the dynamic information captured by the differential CCH is as significant as that of the directional information captured by CCH for the classification of handwritten numeral patterns.

Table 1. Individual recognition rate of handwritten numerals for CCH, ΔCCH and $\Delta\Delta$CCH features

Numeral	Recognition Rate (in %)		
Class	CCH feature	ΔCCH feature	$\Delta\Delta$CCH feature
0	98.50	98.20	98.00
1	98.94	98.76	98.76
2	92.80	93.60	93.70
3	94.09	93.31	90.79
4	95.20	94.70	94.30
5	96.52	95.71	95.02
6	98.32	98.72	97.73
7	93.74	93.08	93.08
8	93.75	92.27	88.98
9	90.49	90.80	90.70

Table 2. Misclassification rate of some misclassified numerals for CCH feature

Misclassified	Misclassification Rate (in %)									
Class	0	1	2	3	4	5	6	7	8	9
0	–	0.00	0.30	0.10	0.10	0.00	0.20	0.10	0.40	0.30
2	0.60	1.00	–	1.70	1.10	0.20	0.30	0.60	0.80	0.90
5	0.00	0.00	0.12	1.51	0.00	–	0.58	0.12	0.70	0.46
6	0.49	0.49	0.00	0.00	0.49	0.10	–	0.00	0.00	0.10
8	1.17	0.32	0.64	0.53	0.85	0.53	0.64	0.32	–	1.27
9	0.31	0.31	0.20	0.31	3.37	0.00	0.10	4.70	0.20	–

Misclassification rate of some numerals with each numeral class is given in Table 2 and 3 for CCH and ΔCCH features, respectively. It is observed that the misclassification rate of numeral 0 with that of numeral class 3, 5, 6, and 9 is less in case of CCH than ΔCCH. But, for the numeral classes 2 and 8, the misclassification rate of the numeral 0 is less in case of ΔCCH. It shows that both the features carry some different information. This type of dissimilarity in misclassification rate of CCH with that of ΔCCH feature is also observed for other numeral classes like, 2, 5, 6, 8, and 9, as shown in Table 2 and 3. These observations strongly validates the point that the dynamic feature carries some different information in comparison to that of directional feature. Hence, the combination of CCH and ΔCCH features may give a better improved performance in pattern classification task.

The average recognition rate of complete handwritten numeral set for different feature extraction techniques is given in Table 4. The recognition rates of ΔCCH and $\Delta\Delta$CCH features are nearly equal to that of CCH feature over the huge MNIST handwritten numeral database. This shows the effectiveness of dynamic directional information in feature representation of handwritten characters. As discussed earlier, the different information representation of all these features is

Table 3. Misclassification rate of some misclassified numerals for ΔCCH feature

Misclassified	Misclassification Rate (in %)									
Class	0	1	2	3	4	5	6	7	8	9
0	–	0.00	0.10	0.50	0.10	0.10	0.40	0.10	0.10	0.40
2	0.50	0.90	–	1.60	0.60	0.40	0.50	0.60	0.80	0.50
5	0.35	0.23	0.12	1.39	0.00	–	0.35	0.23	1.04	0.58
6	0.30	0.30	0.00	0.00	0.39	0.00	–	0.10	0.20	0.00
8	1.06	0.53	0.21	1.27	0.74	1.48	1.53	0.53	–	1.38
9	0.41	0.20	0.00	0.61	3.68	0.00	0.10	3.78	0.41	–

Table 4. Average recognition rate of handwritten numerals for different features

Feature Extraction Technique	Recognition Rate (in %)
CCH	95.24
ΔCCH	94.92
$\Delta\Delta$CCH	94.11
CCH+ΔCCH+$\Delta\Delta$CCH	96.09

exploited by using the score level fusion of CCH, ΔCCH and $\Delta\Delta$CCH. We have used the max normalization technique to compensate the different range of scores followed by the simple sum rule of fusion. Finally, an improved recognition rate of 96.09% is reported in case of feature combination which gives an improvement of nearly 1% over the classical CCH approach. It is also significant from the fact that the reported improvement of 1% in recognition rate is nearly equals to 100 handwritten numeral examples over the 10,000 numeral samples of MNIST testing set.

5 Summary and Conclusions

We have presented modified chain code histogram feature extraction technique for handwritten character recognition task. A handwritten numeral recognition system is developed by using conventional CCH and differential CCH features and a comparable recognition rate is reported. All the experimental results show the effectiveness of dynamic directional information available in character images captured by differential CCH features. The different information available in CCH and differential CCH feature extraction techniques are exploited by score level fusion of CCH, ΔCCH, and $\Delta\Delta$CCH features. The improved performance justifies the importance of the proposed features extraction techniques over the large MNIST handwritten numeral database.

In future we may try to make the character recognition system more robust and accurate by exploring different classification techniques. Future work may include to find a better feature representation of character images by using different level of fusion.

Acknowledgements. The authors would like to thank the Technology Development for Indian Languages (TDIL) Programme, Department of Information Technology, Ministry of Communication and Information Technology, Government of India for sponsoring this work.

References

1. Kimura, F., Wakabayashi, T., Tsuruoka, S., Miyake, Y.: Improvement of handwritten Japanese character recognition using weighted direction code histogram. Pattern Recognition 30(3), 1329–1337 (1997)
2. Pal, U., Sharma, N., Wakabayashi, T., Kimura, F.: Off-Line Handwritten Character Recognition of Devnagari Script. In: Proc. 9th Int. Conf. Document Analysis and Recognition (ICDAR), vol. 1, pp. 496–500 (2007)
3. Arora, S., Bhattacharjee, D., Nasipuri, M., Basu, D.K., Kundu, M.: Combining Multiple Feature Extraction Techniques for Handwritten Devnagari Character Recognition. In: Proc. IEEE Region 10 and the 3rd Int. Conf. Industrial and Information Systems (ICIIS), pp. 1–6 (2008)
4. Roy, K., Pal, T., Pal, U., Kimura, F.: Oriya Handwritten Numeral Recognition System. In: Proc. 8th Int. Conf. Document Analysis and Recognition (ICDAR), vol. 2, pp. 770–774 (2005)
5. Lawal, I.A., Abdel-Aal, R.E., Mahmoud, S.A.: Recognition of Handwritten Arabic (Indian) Numerals Using Freeman's Chain Codes and Abductive Network Classifiers. In: Proc. 20th Int. Conf. Pattern Recognition (ICPR), pp. 1884–1887 (2010)
6. Furui, S.: Comparison of speaker recognition methods using statistical features and dynamic features. IEEE Trans. Acoustics, Speech and Signal Processing 29(3), 342–350 (1981)
7. Furui, S.: Speaker-independent isolated word recognition using dynamic features of speech spectrum. IEEE Trans. Acoustics, Speech and Signal Processing 34(1), 52–59 (1986)
8. Furui, S.: A VQ-based preprocessor using cepstral dynamic features for speaker-independent large vocabulary word recognition. IEEE Trans. Acoustics, Speech and Signal Processing 36(7), 980–987 (1988)
9. Lecun, Y., Bottou, L., Bengio, Y., Haffner, P.: Gradient-based learning applied to document recognition. Proc. of the IEEE 86(11), 2278–2324 (1998)
10. Linde, Y., Buzo, A., Gray, R.M.: An algorithm for vector quantizer design. IEEE Trans. Communications COM-28, 84–95 (1980)
11. Bimbot, F., Bonastre, J.F., Fredouille, C., Gravier, G., Chagnolleau, M.I., Meignier, S., Merlin, T., García, O.J., Delacrétaz, P.D., Reynolds, D.A.: A tutorial on text-independent speaker verification. EURASIP J. Appl. Signal Process. 4, 430–451 (2004)

A Novel Image Edge Detection Method
Using Simplified Gabor Wavelet

C. Sujatha[1] and D. Selvathi[2]

[1] Department of ECE, Sethu Institute of Technology,
Kariapatti, Tamil Nadu, India
sssujathac@yahoo.co.in
[2] Department of ECE, Mepco Schlenk Engineering College, Sivakasi, Tamil Nadu, India
selvathi_d@yahoo.com

Abstract. The Edge Detection is used in wide range of applications in image processing such as object detection, recognition, automated inspection of machine assemblies, diagnosis in medical imaging and topographical recognition. An efficient algorithm for extracting the edge features of images using simplified version of Gabor Wavelet is proposed in this paper. Conventional Gabor Wavelet is widely used for edge detection applications. Due do the high computational complexity of conventional Gabor Wavelet, this may not be used for real time application. Simplified Gabor wavelet based approach is highly effective at detecting both the location and orientation of edges. In this approach, Simplified Gabor Wavelet features are employed for two different scales and four different orientations. The results proved that the performance of proposed Simplified version of Gabor wavelet is superior to conventional Gabor Wavelet and other edge detection algorithm. And also the required run time for proposed work is faster than all other edge detection methods.

Keywords: Gabor wavelet, Simplified Gabor wavelet, edge detection, Peak Signal to Noise ratio.

1   Introduction

Edges are predominant features in images and their analysis and detection are an essential goal in computer vision and image processing [1].Edge detection is one of the key stages of image processing and objects recognition [2]. An edge is defined by a discontinuity in gray level values. In other words, an edge is the boundary between an object and the background. The shape of edges in images depends on many parameters: geometrical and optical properties of the object, the illumination conditions, and the noise level in the images [3].

Research in automatic edge detection has been active because of this topic's wide range of applications in image processing, such as automated inspection of machine

N. Meghanathan et al. (Eds.): CCSIT 2012, Part I, LNICST 84, pp. 620–630, 2012.

assemblies, diagnosis in medical imaging, and topographical recognition [4]. Edge detection is a very difficult task. When viewing an image, humans can easily determine the boundaries within that image without needing to do so consciously. However, no single edge-detection algorithm, at present, has been devised which will successfully determine every different type of edges [5].Many edge detection algorithms have been proposed and implemented. These algorithms differ from each other in many aspects such as computational cost, performance and hardware implementation feasibility.

Simplified version of Gabor Wavelets (SGW) is proposed in this work, whose features can be computed efficiently and can achieve better performance for edge detection. Proposed SGWs can replace the GWs for real time applications.

1.1   State of the Art

An edge is in general a border which separates the adjacent zones of image having distinct brightness. The development of an edge detector is often based on a specific characteristic of the image [6].First generation of edge detection algorithms are represented by Gradient operators such as Sobel's, Robert's and Prewitt's operator[7].The drawbacks of these operators are their inability to detect weak edges and their inability to detect weak edges and their poor performance in the presence of noise. Compass operators are enhanced version of the gradient operators. More computations are required in the compass operators in order to detect more edges and produce better results [2].

Another well known operator, based on the occurrence of zero crossings after applying LOG filter is Marr's operator, known as Laplacian of Gaussian [7]. Since not all zero-crossings correspond to edges, some false edges may be introduced. Canny's operator [1] is one of the most widely-used edge detection algorithms in the computer vision community because of its performance. In this algorithm, edge pixels are detected based on first derivative of that pixel. In addition, two thresholds are applied to remove false edges. The problem with this operator is that these two thresholds are not easily determined and low threshold produces false edges, but a high threshold misses important edges.

Brannock and Weeks [3] have proposed an edge-detection method based on the discrete wavelet transform (DWT), which combines DWT with other methods to achieve an optimal solution to edge-detection algorithm. Y.P.Guan [8] has proposed a multiscale wavelet edge detection algorithm for lip segmentation. In noiseless images with high contrast, Canny's edge detection has proven to be very successful [1].But that algorithm is not efficient for noisy image. For noisy images, Lu and Zhang has proposed algorithm to detect diagonal edge information, based on the wavelet transform with shifted coefficients [3].

The section 2 describes conventional Gabor Wavelet and edge detection using Gabor wavelets. Section 3 describes about proposed methodology of this work. Section 4 discusses about the obtained results and conclusion the work.

2   Conventional Gabor Wavelet

Gabor Wavelets (GWs) [9] are commonly used for extracting local features for various applications such as object detection, recognition and tracking. The human visual system can be viewed as composed of a filter bank. The responses of the respective filters can be modeled by Gabor functions of different frequencies and orientations. The Gabor features have been found to be particularly appropriate for texture representation and discrimination and have been successfully applied to texture segmentation, face recognition, handwritten numerals recognition, and fingerprint recognition. In the spatial domain, a 2D Gabor filter is a Gaussian kernel function modulated by a sinusoidal plane wave as follows:

$$G(x,\ y) = \exp\left[-\frac{x^2 + y^2}{2\sigma^2}\right] \exp[j\omega(x\cos\theta + y\sin\theta)] \tag{1}$$

Where σ is the standard deviation of the Gaussian function in the x- and y-directions and ω denotes the spatial frequency. Family of Gabor kernels can be obtained from eqn.(1) by selecting different center frequencies and orientations. These kernels are used to extract features from an image.

2.1   Edge Detection Using Conventional Gabor Wavelet

Gabor wavelets can effectively abstract local and discrimination features. In textural analysis and image segmentation, GW features have achieved outstanding results, while in machine vision, they found to be effective in object detection, recognition and tracking. The most useful application of the Gabor Wavelets is for edge detection [10].For given an input image I(x, y), the Gabor Wavelet features are extracted by convolving I(x,y) with G(x,y) as in equation (2).

$$\Phi(x,\ y) = G(x,\ y) \otimes I(x,\ y) \tag{2}$$

Where $\otimes$ denotes the 2-D convolution operation [8]. The Gabor wavelets (GWs) respond strongly to edge if the edge direction is perpendicular to the wave vector ($\omega\cos\theta$, $\omega\sin\theta$). When hitting an edge, the real and imaginary parts of $\Phi(x, y)$ oscillate with the characteristic frequency in- stead of providing a smooth peak.

3   Proposed Work

The computation required for Gabor Wavelet based feature extraction is very intensive. This in turn creates a bottleneck problem for real time processing. Hence, an efficient method for extracting Gabor features is needed for many practical applications.

3.1   Simplified Gabor Wavelets

Wei Jiang.et.al.[9]have proposed that the imaginary part of a Gabor filter is an efficient and robust means for edge detection. The imaginary part of a GW is as in equation (3):

$$S(x, y) = \exp\left[-\frac{x^2 + y^2}{2\sigma^2}\right] \sin\left[\omega(x \cos \theta + y \sin \theta)\right] \tag{3}$$

Edges can be detected by using this simplified Gabor Wavelet. Set of Simplified Gabor kernels can be obtained from eqn. (3) by selecting different center frequencies and orientations. These kernels are used to extract features from an image. This method is known as Simplified Gabor wavelet.

3.2   Shape of an SGW

The equation for 1-D Gabor Wavelet is shown in equation (4).

$$s(x) = \frac{1}{2\Pi\sigma^2} \exp\left[-\frac{x^2}{2\sigma^2}\right] \sin(\omega x) \tag{4}$$

The values of imaginary part of 1-D GW are continues one. Its values are quantized to a certain number of levels. The same number of quantization levels is used for the positive and the negative values of the Gabor function because it is antisymmetrical [4]. For 2-D cases, the imaginary part of a 2-D GW, with the gray-level intensities representing the magnitudes of the Gabor function.

3.3   Determination of Quantization Levels

The determination of the quantization levels for an SGW is the same as that in [10]. One of the quantization levels of the SGW is set to zero. As the imaginary part of a Gabor function is antisymmetrical, the number of quantization levels for the positive and negative values are equal and are denoted as n_1. Then, the total number of quantization levels is $2n_1+1$. Suppose that the largest magnitude of the GW is A, the corresponding quantization levels for positive levels and negative levels are as in equation (5)

$$q_+(k) = \frac{A}{2n_1 + 1}.2k \quad . \quad q_-(k) = -\frac{A}{2n_1 + 1}.2k \tag{5}$$

where $k = 1 \ldots n_1$. These SGWs are then convolved with an image to extract the SGW features at different center frequencies and orientations to form a simplified Gabor jet.

3.4   Determination of the Parameters

The values of important parameters for the GWs or SGWs are determined for edge detection, which are the values of ω, σ, and θ. Edges of an image can be detected in different directions, by setting different values for θ [11]. Computational can be reduced by setting four values for θ.Hence, the number of orientations used in this proposed work is four,i.e.,$\theta_k = k\pi/4$ for k=0,1,2,3.As edges are very localized feature of an image, the value of ω should be small when compared to that for face recognition[4]. So, in this proposed work edges can be detected efficiently by setting ω = 0.3 π and 0.5π.

3.5   Efficient Edge Detection Using SGWs

Edge detection can be done efficiently by using SGWs of two different scales (ω) and four different orientations (θ). The convolution of an SGW of scale ω and orientation θ with the image I(x,y) generates the SGW features and is denoted as $\phi'_{\omega,\theta}(x_c, y_c)$.The resulting SGW feature $\phi''_{\omega,\theta}(x_c, y_c)$ at a pixel position (x_c, y_c) is equal to the absolute maximum of the eight $\phi'_{\omega,\theta}(x_c, y_c)$, i.e.,

$$\phi''_{\omega,\theta}(x_c, y_c) = \max\{\phi'_{\omega i,\theta j}(x_c, y_c), i = 0,1 and j = 0,...,3\} \tag{6}$$

where $\omega_0 = 0.3\ \pi$, $\omega_1 = 0.5\ \pi$, and $\theta_j = j\pi/4$, for j = 0, . . . , 3. The SGW feature $\phi'_{\omega,\theta}(x_c, y_c)$ is computed by convolving the image I(x, y) with the SGW whose patterns are dependent on the scale ω and the orientation θ. As edges are much localized in an image, so the window size of the patterns is either 3 × 3 or 5 × 5. The SGWs are formed using two levels of quantization for the positive and the negative magnitudes of the GWs.These two quantization levels are denoted as q1 and q2 with q2 > q1 for positive magnitudes and the corresponding quantization levels for the negative magnitude are −q1 and −q2, respectively. Two different scales and four different orientations are adopted for this proposed work. The required computation for a $\phi'_{\omega,\theta}(x_c, y_c)$ is not more than 2 multiplications and 22 additions. Hence the computational cost is very lower than conventional Gabor Wavelet [11].

4   Result and Discussion

The performance of the proposed SGW based approach with different scales and different orientations are evaluated. Then relative performance with the use of the GW features and the SGW features will be compared. Finally, performance of the Canny, Sobel, Robert, and Prewitts and conventional Gabor wavelet operators are compared with SGW based Edge Detection Algorithm.

4.1   Performance Analysis of SGWs with Different Quantization Levels for Edge Detection

The effect of the number of quantization levels on edge detection using Simplified Gabor Wavelet can be evaluated using three, five and seven quantization levels. In this analysis, the coins images and cameraman images are used as shown in Fig.1 and

Fig 2. The edge detection results based on SGW with ω=0.3π and three different quantization levels for coin image are shown in Fig.1(a) - 1(d).And for the same image, result for ω=0.5 π and three different quantization levels are shown in Fig.1(e) - 1(g). Fig.2(a)-2(g) shows the results for cameraman image for ω=0.3π and ω=0.5π with three different quantization levels.

From Fig.1 and Fig. 2, the performance of edge detection using SGWs of five and seven quantization levels are better than three quantization levels, while the performances of five and seven quantization levels are very similar. More computation can be required for higher number of quantization levels. Hence, five quantization levels are chosen in this proposed work.

4.2   Performance Analysis of SGWs with Different Scales for Edge Detection

The most promising performance in terms of accuracy and computation can be achieved by using SGWs with five quantization levels, which is proved in Sec 4.1. This section evaluates the effect of SGWs with five quantization levels and with different scales ω=0.125 π, ω=0.3 π, ω=0.5 π and ω=0.65 π. The edges of the cameraman image and coins image based on SGW features of the four different scales are shown in Fig 3 and Fig 4. The edge detection results   based on SGW with five quantization levels and four different scale ω=0.125π, ω=0.3π, ω=0.5π and ω=0.65π. of cameraman image are shown in Fig 3(a) - 3(e). And the Fig. 4(a)-4(e) shows the results of coin image for ω=0.125π, ω=0.3π, ω=0.5π and ω=0.65π with five different quantization levels. From this comparison, two scales ω=0.3π, ω=0.5π can be identified for better performance.

4.3   Comparing the Performance of SGWs with other Edge Detection Algorithms

The performance of SGWs based edge detection algorithm are compared with some conventional edge detection algorithms, such as Canny, Sobel, Prewitt, Robert and conventional Gabor Wavelet methods. In order to get best performance, the SGWs with two scales ω=0.3π, ω=0.5π, four orientation θ = {0, π/4, π/2, 3π/4}, and five quantization levels are used for this comparision.Fig.5 shows the results of various edge detection algorithm for cameraman image, coins image, Angiogram brain image and pears image. This result comparison proved that proposed Simplified Gabor Wavelet is an efficient algorithm for all type of images.

4.4   Comparison of Quantitative Analysis for SGWs with Other Edge Detection Algorithms

The performance comparison was discussed in last section. The Quantitative measures for all the edge detection algorithm is described in this section. For quantitative analysis of the proposed method performance measures for cameraman image such as average run time and PSNR are calculated and are tabulated in Table 1 and Table 2

Original images

Results for ω=0. 1"
and three quantization
levels.

Results for ω=0. 1"
and Five quantization
levels.

Results for ω=0. 1"
and Seven quantization
levels.

Results for ω=0.5 "
and Three quantization
levels.

Results for ω=0.5 "
and Five quantization
levels.

Results for ω=0.5 "
and Seven quantization
levels.

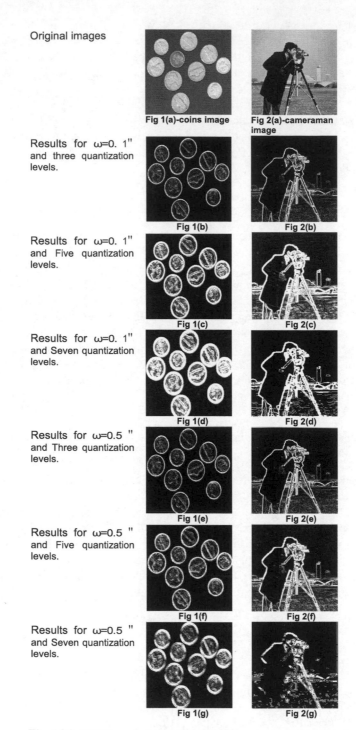

Fig 1(a)-coins image   Fig 2(a)-cameraman image

Fig 1(b)   Fig 2(b)

Fig 1(c)   Fig 2(c)

Fig 1(d)   Fig 2(d)

Fig 1(e)   Fig 2(e)

Fig 1(f)   Fig 2(f)

Fig 1(g)   Fig 2(g)

Fig. 1&2. SGW based edge results for different quantization levels

Original
images

ω=0.125 "

ω=0.3 ".

ω=0.5 π.

ω=0.625 "

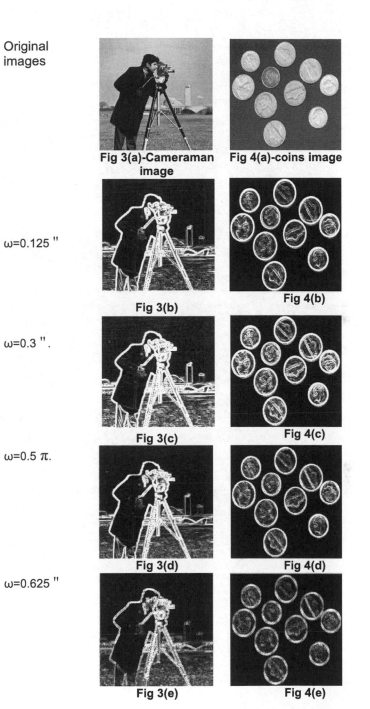

Fig 3(a)-Cameraman image   Fig 4(a)-coins image

Fig 3(b)   Fig 4(b)

Fig 3(c)   Fig 4(c)

Fig 3(d)   Fig 4(d)

Fig 3(e)   Fig 4(e)

Fig. 3&4 SGW based edge detection results for different values of ω

Original
image

Canny

Prewitt

Robert

Sobel output

Conventional
Gabor
output.

Proposed
Simplified
Gabor
Wavelets
output

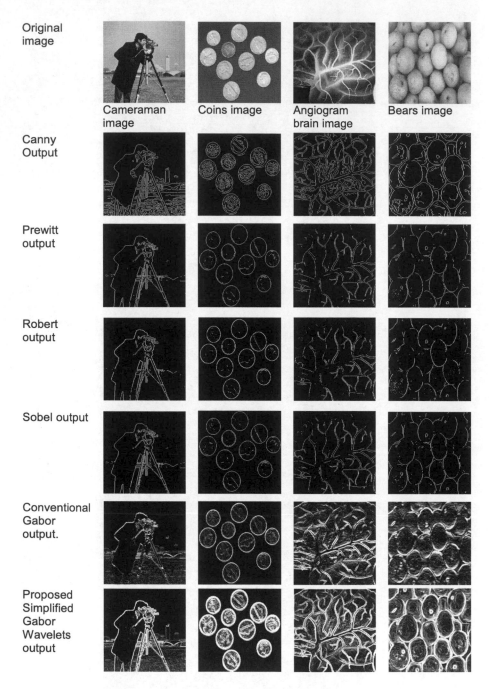

Fig. 5. Comparison of Simplified Gabor Wavelet results with different algorithms

for different edge detection algorithms respectively. The average runtime required by SGWs is compared with other conventional methods. This comparison is tabulated in Table1. The run time required by SGW based edge detection algorithm is smaller than that required by conventional Gabor Wavelet and Canny edge detection methods. The average run time is similar to that of Prewitt and Roberts's method, but compared with their performances the proposed Simplified Gabor Wavelet is superior to all other methods.

Table 1.

S.No	Algorithm	Run Time
1	Canny	76.5 ms
2	Prewitt	23.4 ms
3	Roberts	21.8 ms
4	Sobel	78 ms
5	Gabor Wavelet	47 ms
6	Simplified Gabor Wavelet	31 ms

Peak Signal to Noise Ratio is measured between edge images of original image and noisy image. In this PSNR measure, Gaussian noise is added to the original image and that is considered as noisy image. PSNR values for different algorithms are compared with proposed SGW based edge detection. Those measures are tabulated in Table.2.

Table 2.

S.No	Algorithm	PSNR in db
1	Canny	8.45
2	Prewitt	17.45
3	Roberts	16.61
4	Sobel	17.77
5	Gabor Wavelet	25.23
6	Simplified Gabor Wavelet	33.41

From this quantitative analysis the proposed Simplified Gabor Wavelet based edge detection provides better performance than other conventional methods. Fast run time of proposed work realize that it is most suited for real time application.

5   Conclusion

In this paper, an efficient algorithm for edge detection using simplified version of Gabor Wavelets is proposed. Proposed work is based on the conventional Gabor wavelet, but it can detect more edge pixels than the conventional one. The various experiments prove that   proposed algorithm clearly outperforms other edge detection methods. The proposed algorithm very effectively used for biomedical images also. The results prove that the edge features of angiographic brain images using proposed Simplified Gabor Wavelet are better than other conventional methods. The quantitative measures show that proposed SGW based edge detection is fast and better PSNR than other conventional methods. The performance comparisons and quantitative analysis proves that the proposed Simplified Gabor Wavelet based edge detection is very much suited for real time applications.

References

1. Canny, J.: A computational approach to edge detection. IEEE Trans. Pattern Anal. Mach. Intell. PAMI-8(6), 679–698 (1986)
2. Alzahrani, F.M., Chen, T.: A Real Time Edge Detector: Algorithm and VLSI Architecture. Real-Time Imaging 3, 363–378 (1997)
3. Brannock, E., Weeks, M.: A synopsis of recent work in edge detection using the DWT. In: Proc. IEEE Southeastcon, pp. 515–520 (2008)
4. Jiang, W., Lam, K.-M., Shen, T.-Z.: Efficient Edge Detection Using Simplified Gabor Wavelets. IEEE Transactions on Systems, Man and Cybernetics- Part B: Cybernetics, 1–11 (2009)
5. Hao, J.-J., Jiang, Q., Wei, J.-W., Mi, L.: Research of Edge Detection Based on Gabor Wavelet. IEEE International Conference on Measuring Technology and Mechatronics Automation 2, 1083–1086 (2010)
6. Bouda, B., Masmoudi, L., Aboutajdine, D.: A New Model for Edge Detection in Digital Images. GVIP Special issue on Edge Detection 7, 25–30 (2007)
7. Gonzalez, R., Woods, R.E.: Digital Image Processing. Addision- Wesley Publishing Co. Inc. (1992)
8. Guan, Y.P.: Automatic extraction of lips based on multi-scale wavelet edge detection. Computer Vision 2(1), 23–33 (2008)
9. Jiang, W., Shen, T.-Z., Zhang, J., Hu, Y., Wang, X.-Y.: Gabor Wavelets for Image Processing. In: IEEE International Colloquium on Computing, Communication, Control, and Management, CCCM, vol. 1, pp. 110–114 (August 2008)
10. Mehrotra, R., Namuduri, K., Ranganathan, N.: Gabor filter-based edge detection. Pattern Recognition 25(12), 1479–1494 (1992)
11. Choi, W.P., Tse, S.H., Wong, K.W., Lam, K.M.: Simplified Gabor wavelets for human face recognition. Pattern Recognit. 41(3), 1186–1199 (2008)

Low Power Spatial Modulation Scheme for Wide Band Multiple Input and Multiple Output Wireless Communication Systems

Dhirendra Kumar Tripathi, S. Saravanan, and HarNarayan Upadhyay

School of computing, SASTRA University Tirumalaisamudram,
613402 Thanajvur, Tamilnadu, India
dkt@core.sastra.com, saran@core.sastra.edu, hnu@ece.sastra.edu

Abstract. In this paper, we present design and FPGA implementation of a low power fractional bit encoded (FBE)–spatial modulation (SM) based transmitter for the multiple-input multiple output (MIMO) systems. This Modulation scheme includes the data dependency check before the spatial multiplexing. The proposed data dependency check allows efficient selection of antennas for parallel transmission of data. The Fractional bit encoding is modulus conversion scheme which convert the incoming bit stream to numbers in an arithmetic base, or modulus, that is not a power of 2 .When applied to SM, FBE results in a more versatile system design allowing transmitter to be equipped with an arbitrary number of antennas for a wider range of spectral efficiencies given restrictions on space and power consumption. The synthesis results of the implementation of transmitter on FPGA are included in the paper

Keywords: Low power, data dependency, Fractional Bit Encoding (FBE), Inter Channel Interference (ICI), Multiple input multiple output (MIMO) system, Spatial modulation (SM).

1   Introduction

Multiple Input Multiple Output (MIMO) transmission systems have been proposed to significantly increase the spectral efficiency of future wireless communications. A spectral efficiency of 20-40 bps/Hz can be achieved in the Vertical Bell Laboratory Layered Space Time (VBLAST) architecture when considering an indoor rich scattering propagation condition [1]. VBLAST is used in the multi user diversity scenario and various studies are reported in relation to it [2][3] . However, simultaneous transmission on the same frequency from multiple transmitting antennas causes high interchannel interference (ICI). This significantly increases system complexity as the number of transmitting antennas increases [2]. SM avoids ICI and the need of accurate time synchronization amongst antennas by making only one antenna active at any instant of time and employing the antenna index as additional source of information [4]. The use of transmit antenna number to convey information increases the spectral efficiency by a factor equals to $\log_2$ (the number of transmit antennas) [5]. In SM any group of information bits is mapped into two constellations; signal constellation based on the type of modulation and space constellation to encode

N. Meghanathan et al. (Eds.): CCSIT 2012, Part I, LNICST 84, pp. 631–639, 2012.

the transmit antenna number [4, 5]. At the receiver, maximum ratio combing is used. The detection process consists of two steps. The first one is the transmit antenna estimation while the second one is the transmit symbol estimation.

In SM, the number k of information bits that are encoded in the spatial domain is directly related to the number M of transmit antennas, in particular $M = 2^k$. This means that the number of transmit antennas must be a power of two. This paper implement a solution to this limitation in SM which increases the granularity of the data encoding process in the spatial domain by using fractional bit encoding; the method is called FBE–SM [8].These schemes do not consider the data dependency on the switching of antennas from the low power perspective. As shown in the present paper that by exploiting the data dependency with spatial multiplexing it is possible to achieve higher bit rate at low power consumption.

FPGA implementation of MIMO systems is reported in [9] while [10] reports FPGA based implementation of the VBLAST MIMO architecture. The aim of this paper is to implement and FPGA based FBE-SM transmitter which overcomes the limitation on the number of transmit antennas in SM and allow the transmitter to be equipped with an arbitrary number of antennas. In [11] a low power MIMO signal processor is designed however it was specific to the Ethernet application only. A layered based approach was suggested in [12]. The proposed approach divided the signal processing regions in the low power and high power however it do not discus about the data dependency on the power consumption. To the best of the authors knowledge this is the FPGA based implementation reported in literature.

The paper is organized as follows. In Section 2, the theory of fractional bit encoding is given. In Section 3, the FBE–SM scheme is introduced. In section 4 numerical results are shown to analyze the performance of FBE–SM, Section 5 gives the details of digital implementation of FBE-SM modulator and FPGA synthesis results and section 6 concludes the paper.

2   The Fractional Bit Encoding

Application of FBE to a pulse amplitude modulation (PAM) communication system is reported in [13]. It reports two ways of fractional bit encoding:

1)*Constellation switching*-It alternates between the transmission of D and D+1 bits per symbol to achieve the FBE. This approach suffers from the inherent bit shift that results from incorrectly decoded symbols making it prone to error propagation effects.

2)*Modulus conversion- This approach* minimize the error propagation effect that afflicts the performance of the constellation switching method [14]. In this paper the theory of modulus conversion is applied to SM.

Modulus conversion achieves fractional bit rates by converting the incoming bitstream to numbers in an arithmetic base, or modulus, that is not a power of 2. In particular, the modulus converter operates as follows: i) Extracting the blocks of PU bits from the incoming bitstream, where U is the desired fractional bit rate and P is a positive integer; ii) The extracted block is converted to P numbers of base R. The modulus is defined as the smallest integer number, R, such that $R \geq 2^k$.

Though the theory of modulus conversion can be used to achieve an arbitrary fractional bit rate, yet by choosing both R and P are positive integer numbers limits its application to only rational bit rates. However by using the inequality (1) it is possible to closely approximate U, with given as the ratio of two positive and relatively prime integers x and y.

$$0 \leq nU - \lfloor nU \rfloor \leq 1 \Rightarrow 0 \leq U - \lfloor nU \rfloor / n \leq 1/n \tag{1}$$

where $\lfloor . \rfloor$ denotes the floor function and n is an arbitrary and positive integer number. From (1), it follows that $PU \cong P\tilde{U} = P(\lfloor nU \rfloor / n)$, which, according to the theory of modulus conversion, must be a positive integer. It is worth mentioning that, in general, $P \neq n$. From (1) it can found that by selecting larger n is, the approximation error($U - \tilde{U}$) can be minimized. On the other hand larger P is, leads to greater error propagation within each block of bits[9].Accordingly, for any given U and provided that $P(\lfloor nU \rfloor / n)$ is a positive integer, n and P should be chosen as large and as small as possible, respectively.

3   The Fractional Bit-SM Scheme

As mentioned earlier FBE–SM scheme avoids fundamental constraints on the number of transmit antennas that can be used by classical SM systems. The fractional bit coding is done in the spatial domain, while the encoding process in the signal domain is left unchanged. Following guidelines can be used for designing a FBE-SM system [9]:

1) As per the system constraints(bit rate, cost, available space   etc.) chose the desired number of transmit antennas, M,
2) Set the modulus R equal to M..
3) Compute the maximum spatial multiplexing gain offered by the system as $U = \log_2(M)$.
4) Choose the pair (P,n) $P(\lfloor nU \rfloor / n)$ is a positive integer and following the design guidelines described in Section II, *i.e.*:

   (a) Optimize $\tilde{U} = (\lfloor nU \rfloor / n)$, such that it is as close as possible to U This allows the system to approach the spatial multiplexing gain offered by the M transmit antennas. This is achieved, in general, for larger values of n.
   (b) Optimize P such that it is as small as possible: this reduces the decoding delay and, more importantly, minimizes error propagation in the decoded bitstream.

5) Map each of the P base–M encoded numbers in the transmission block to a transmit antenna index in the range$[0, M-1]$.

Since at each time instant, only one transmit antenna of the set will be active. The other antennas will transmit zero power. Therefore, ICI at the receiver and the need to synchronize the transmit antennas are completely avoided. At the receiver, maximum receive ratio combining (MRRC) is used to estimate the transmit antenna number, after which the transmitted symbol is estimated. These two estimates are used by the spatial demodulator to retrieve the block of information bits. The spatial constellation points (the base-M encoded numbers) are grouped into blocks of P points each, and each block is converted to the equivalent base–2 bitstream of $P(\lfloor nU \rfloor /n)$ bits each.

Let us consider a simple example with $M=6$ .Thus, we have $U = 2.5850$ By choosing, e.g. $(P,n)=(4,4)$, we get $\tilde{U}=2.50$, which closely approaches U and is greater than the spatial multiplexing gain offered by a system with $M = 4$. If, for instance, the block of $P \ \tilde{U}$ bits is equal to $(1010111011)_2$, then the modulus converter will return an $(P \ \tilde{U})_M$ block equal to $(3123)_6$ where $(x)_b$ denotes the base- b representation of x Then, the output of the modulus converter is mapped to a spatial constellation point. First, the antenna with index 3 transmits an energy signal, then the antenna with index 1 transmits the same signal, etc.

The receiver will estimate each received antenna index by using MRRC. After decoding the antenna indexes, ideally with no errors, it will recover the original data stream as: $(3123)_6 = (1010111011)_2$.

At Fig.1 and Fig 2 shows FBE-SM Transceiver architecture. We use the following notations: bold and capital letters denote matrices, bold and small letters denote vectors, $(.)^H$ and $(.)^T$ denote Hermitian and transpose of a vector or matrix, respectively. The FBE block encode numbers in the transmission block to a transmit antenna index in the range$[0,M-1]$ while the signal domain encoding remain unchanged. . Then it maps the resultant symbols into a vector:$\mathbf{x}=[x1 \ x2 \ ....x_{Nt}]$, where it is assumed that $E_x[\mathbf{x}^H\mathbf{x}]=1$; i.e unity channel gain. Since only one antenna is active, only one of x_j is nonzero in the vector $\mathbf{x}$. For the jth active transmit antenna and the qth symbol from M-ary constellation, the output of the SM mapping can be written as : x $_{jq} =[0 \ 0 \ 0...x_q \ 0 \ 0 \ ..0]^T$[6]. This output of is fed to digital modulator to transmit the information to j^{th} subchannel. The signal is transmitted over a MIMO channel H=[h_1 h_2 .... h_{Nt}] and the corresponding Channel vector from the jth transmit antenna to all receive antennas is $\mathbf{h_j}=[h_{j, \ 1} \quad h_{\ 2, \ j}...h_{\ Nr,j}]^T$ Each channel in the system can be modeled as Rayleigh flat fading Channel. The received signal $\mathbf{y} =\mathbf{Hx} + \mathbf{n}$, where n is Nr dimension additive white Gaussian (AWGN) noise $\mathbf{n}= [n1,n2...n_{Nr}]^T$ The detection of information bits can be achieved by first estimate the antenna number then estimate the transmitted symbol according to the following rule [4, 6]:

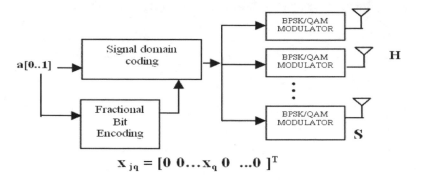

$$\mathbf{x}_{jq} = [0 \ 0...\mathbf{x_q} \ 0 \ ...0 \ ]^T$$

Fig. 1. FBE-SM Transmitter

$$\hat{j} = \arg_j \max |\mathbf{h}_j^H \mathbf{y}|$$ (2)

$$\hat{g} = \arg_q \max \text{Re}\{(\mathbf{h}_{j\,xq})^H \mathbf{y}\}$$ (3)

where ĵ and ĝ are the estimated Antenna number and transmitted symbol respectively.

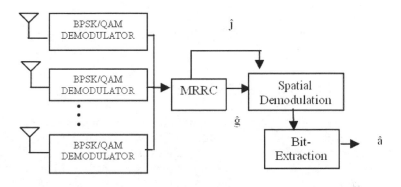

Fig. 2. FBE-SM Receiver

These two estimates are used by the spatial demodulator to retrieve the block of information bits. In the bit-extractor The spatial constellation points (the base-M encoded numbers) are grouped into blocks of P points each, and each block is converted to the equivalent base−2 bitstream of $P(\lfloor nU \rfloor / n)$ bits each.

4   Algorithm for the Data Dependent Antenna Selection

The proposed algorithm for data dependency check is given below. Input stream (I) is generated from LFSR. Total number of available antennas is known by its base value (B). Selection of antennas is also depends upon the input data stream as mentioned earlier . If the input is less than base value only one antenna is activated. For larger number base value several antennas will activate simultaneously. Thus checking the available free antenna can be utilized for next input stream of data. This can be done with parallel mode, so that the utilization of antennas will be more efficient than normal way of approach. This proposed algorithm is suitable for low power design approach of spatial modulation.

Algorithm DataDependencyCheck (I, B, A[], N, F[])

> ***Input:*** LFSR input stream (I), Base value (B)
> ***Output:*** Selection of antennas A[] with No. of Antennas N,
>   List of antennas F[] freely available for next Input Stream I_{NEXT}
>
> Find the decimal equivalent (D) of input stream (I)
> If D is less than or equal to B then

                       Assign D to A[0]

                       Count the number of antennas N as 1

      Else

                       Find Base B of D (D_B)

                       Store the digits of D_B in A[]

                       Store the number of digits of D_B in N

      End if

      Find the free Antennas F[] from A[]

      The Antennas in F[] can be used in next Input Stream I_{NEXT}

End

5   Performance Analysis of Scheme

The following system setup is considered: i) Each transmit antenna, when activated, transmits a 4–QAM (quadrature amplitude modulation) signal. ii) The channel is assumed to be Rayleigh distributed with uncorrelated fading among the wireless links. It is static and flat-fading for the duration of a transmission block. iii) The noise at the receiver input is assumed to be white complex Gaussian, with zero-mean and mutually independent samples. iv) The receiver is equipped with 6 antennas and uses a MRRC detector to jointly detecting spatial and signal constellation points.

    Two performance metrics will be investigated: 1) the symbol–error–ratio (SER), which is defined as the average probability of incorrectly detecting a constellation and signal point and 2) the bit–error–ratio (BER), which is defined as the average probability of incorrectly detecting a bit in the decoded bitstream In Figs. 3 and 4, we show the SER and BER of FBE–SM for various antennas at the transmitter, respectively. If $M = 2^j$, the system reduces to conventional SM. As expected Fig. 3 we notice that the SER gets monotonically worse for increasing values of M. However, this leads to an increase in the system bit rate When looking into Fig. 4 we observe that the BER does not get worse monotonically for increasing value of M. This is mainly due to the error propagation effect of the FBE process.

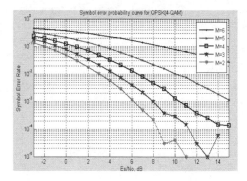

Fig. 3. SER of FBE–SM. for different values of transmit antennasM   Setup: i) P= 4, and ii) n= 4

6   FPGA Implementation of FBE-SM

The implementation of FBE-SM transmitter is done on Cyclone-II EP2C35F672C6 family of FPGAs . The modulus conversion module which is integral part of the Fractional Bit encoding is replaced by the look up table. The approach to implement modulus converter as suggested by [11] require embedded multiplier and dividers which not only consume more silicon area but also consumes more power.

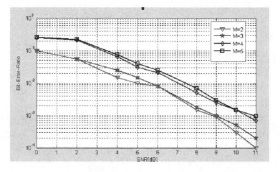
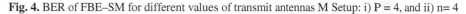

Fig. 4. BER of FBE–SM for different values of transmit antennas M Setup: i) P = 4, and ii) n= 4

Further more with the increase in the number of antennas, modulus converter size increases in turn it will require more number of multipliers and dividers and the highest speed to be achieved by the FBE-SM system will be limited by the size of modulus converter [8]. The look up table based approach is more area efficient and consumes less power. The reduction in power consumption is achieved by not using embedded multipliers and also with the help run time reconfiguration [13] design flow it is possible to update this look table for any arbitrary base at run time. A controller is designed to synchronize the operation of the FBE-SM transmitter module.The modulation scheme used is the 4-QAM (Quadrature amplitude

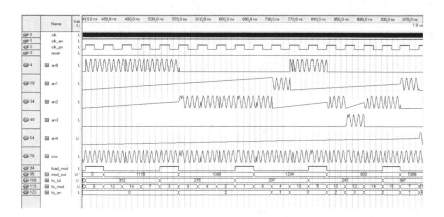

Fig. 5. Post Layout simulation Results for the Cyclone-II FPGA

Table 1. Resource Utilization Summary for Cyclone-II

SN.	Resource	Consumption
1	Logic Elements	546
2	Combinational Functions	497
3	Logic registers	280

modulation) or QPSK(Quadrature phase shift keying) .The modulator uses unrolled pipelined CORDIC structure which allows it to operate at the higher frequencies than the non pipelined CORDIC structure[14] . The intermediate operating frequency forthe transmitter is chosen to be 12.5 MHz. This can be up-converted to the desired frequency by using suitable RF front end. Table 1 shows the FPGA resources consumed by the FBE-SM transmitter. Fig. 5 shows the post layout simulation results of the FBE_SM implemented on the FPGA. The channel 5,6,7,8,9 are showing the output of FBE-SM transmitter for the antenna number one to five.

For the five antenna system the traditional FBE-SM transmitter consumes 6 mW dynamic power however the proposed solution consumes only 4mW dynamic power. Thus one third of dynamic power consumption can be reduced through this scheme.

7   Conclusion

In this paper we have implemented a more versatile low power SM scheme called FBE–SM on the FPGA. The method relies on the application of modulus conversion to achieve fractional bit rates, and allows any SM–MIMO wireless system to use an arbitrary number of antennas at the transmitter. By exploring the data dependency on antenna selection a higher data rate with low power consumption is achieved. MATLAB results for the SER and BER shows its viability for the design of compact mobile devices using SM. The proposed method offers the desired degrees of freedom for trading–off performance, low power consumption, highest achievable bit rates, and cost.

References

1. Wolniansky, P., Foschini, G., Golden, G., Valenzuela, R.: V-BLAST: an Architecture for Realizing very High Data Rates over the Rich-Scattering Wireless Channel. In: URSI International Symposium on Signals, Systems, and Electronics (ISSSE 1998), pp. 295–300 (1998)
2. Rashid, M.M., Hossain, E., Bhargava, V.K.: Cross-layer analysis of downlink V-BLAST MIMO transmission exploiting multiuser diversity Source. IEEE Transactions on Wireless Communications Archive 8, 4568–4579 (2009)
3. Bhagavatula, R., Forenza, A., Heath Jr., R.W.: Impact of antenna array configurations on adaptive switching in MIMO channels. In: Proc. of Int. Symp. on Wireless Pers. Multim. Comm. (2006)
4. Goldsmith, A., Jafar, S., Jindal, N., Vishwanath, S.: Capacity Limits of MIMO Channels. IEEE Journal on Selected Areas in Communication 21(5), 684–702 (2003)

5. Mesleh, R., Haas, H., Sinanovic, S., Ahn, C.W., Yun, S.: Spatial Modulation. IEEE Transactions on Vehicular Technology 57(4), 2228–2242 (2008)
6. Mesleh, R., Haas, H., Ahn, C.W., Yun, S.: Spatial Modulation - A New Low Complexity Spectral Efficiency Enhancing Technique. In: IEEE International Conference on Communication and Networking in China (CHINA- COM 2006), pp. 25–27 (2006)
7. Jeganathan, J., Ghrayeb, A., Szczecinski, L.: Spatial Modulation: Optimal Detection and Performance Analysis. IEEE Communications Letters 12(8) (2008)
8. Serafimovski, N., Di Renzo, M., Sinanović, S., Mesleh, R.Y., Haas, H.: Fractional Bit Encoded Spatial Modulation. IEEE Communications Letters 14(5) (2010)
9. Wang, H., Leray, P., Palicot, J.: Reconfigurable architecture for MIMO systems based on CORDIC operators. Comptes Rendus - Physique 7(7), 735–750 (2006)
10. McKeown, M.A., Lindsay, I.A.B., Cruickshank, D.G.M., Thompson, J.S., Farson, S.A., Hu, Y.: Re-scalable V-BLAST MIMO system for FPGA. IEE Proc., Vis. Image Process. 153(6), 747–753 (2006)
11. Wang, L., Shanbhag, N.R.: Low-power MIMO signal processing. IEEE Transactions on Very Large Scale Integration (VLSI) Systems 11(3), 434–445 (2003)
12. Lozano, A.: Per-Antenna Rate and Power Control for MIMO Layered Architectures in the Low- and High-Power Regimes. IEEE Transactions on Communications 58(2) (2010)
13. Betts, W.L., Ko, K.D.: Fractional bit rate encoding in a pulse amplitude modulation communication system: U.S. Patent 6 993 067 (2006)
14. Betts, W. L.: Modulous converter foir fractional rate encoding: U.S., Patent 5 103 227 (1992)
15. W.P 01055 ver 1.0 (Altera Corp): FPGA Run-Time Reconfiguration: Two Approaches (March 2008)
16. Volder, J.E.: The COR.DIC Trigonometric Computing Technique. IRE Transactions on Electronic Computers, 330–334 (1959)

Author Index